D1442665

THIRD EDITION

Research Methods

for Criminal Justice and Criminology

Dean John Champion

Texas A & M International University

Upper Saddle River, New Jersey 07458

A CIP catalog record for this book can be obtained from the Library of Congress.

Executive Editor: Frank Mortimer, Jr.
Associate Editor: Sarah Holle
Executive Marketing Manager: Tim Peyton
Editorial Assistant: Kelly Krug
Production Editor: Patty Donovan, Pine Tree Composition, Inc.
Production Liaison: Barbara Marttine Cappuccio
Director of Manufacturing and Production: Bruce Johnson
Managing Editor: Mary Carnis
Manufacturing Manager: Ilene Sanford
Manufacturing Buyer: Cathleen Petersen
Creative Director: Cheryl Asherman
Cover Design Coordinator: Miguel Ortiz
Cover Designer: Joseph DePinho
Cover Photo: Ken Usami/Getty Images
Formatting and Interior Design: Pine Tree Composition, Inc.
Printing and Binding: R.R. Donnelley & Sons

Copyright © 2006 by Pearson Education, Inc., Upper Saddle River, New Jersey 07458.
Pearson Prentice Hall. All rights reserved. Printed in the United States of America. This publication is
protected by Copyright and permission should be obtained from the publisher prior to any prohibited
reproduction, storage in a retrieval system, or transmission in any form or by any means, electronic,
mechanical, photocopying, recording, or likewise. For information regarding permission(s), write to:
Rights and Permissions Department.

Pearson Prentice Hall is a trademark of Pearson Education, Inc.
Pearson® is a registered trademark of Pearson plc
Prentice Hall® is a registered trademark of Pearson Education, Inc.

Pearson Education LTD
Pearson Education Singapore, Pte. Ltd.
Pearson Education, Canada, Ltd
Pearson Education—Japan
Pearson Education Australia PTY, Limited
Pearson Education North Asia Ltd
Pearson Educaçion de Mexico, S.A. De C.V.
Pearson Education Malaysia, Pte. Ltd.

10 9 8 7 6 5 4 3 2 1
ISBN 0-13-118928-X

CONTENTS

PREFACE

Research Methods for Criminal Justice and Criminology, Third Edition is about how to do research and investigate various types of research questions that arise in criminology and criminal justice. Why do police officers sometimes use excessive force when subduing criminal suspects who seemingly offer no resistance to arrest? Why do youths join gangs and commit violent acts? Why do some persons become career criminals? Which types of supervision work best for those on parole? What interventions seem to work best in preventing delinquency? Why do nonwhites seem to receive harsher sentences from judges compared with whites in many jurisdictions? Does the death penalty deter persons from committing murder? Why do public defenders appear less effective in defending their clients against criminal charges in court compared with privately appointed counsel? These are just some of the endless kinds of questions criminologists and criminal justice professionals examine when they conduct research.

In the social sciences, there is a broad range of research strategies, including a variety of data collection techniques and other analytical tools, that exist to serve the needs of most professionals who conduct different kinds of research investigations. While certain research procedures may be relevant for one type of investigation, these same procedures may not be equally suitable for other investigations. There are many research strategies that investigators may choose to collect information to answer any issues they may choose to investigate.

This book explores the entire research process from beginning to end. This exploration begins with an examination of theorizing about different kinds of research questions and why different kinds of events occur. Generally, theories are designed to offer explanations for why certain events occur and make predictions about them. There are different kinds of theory that can be used by investigators who want to explain why certain events happen. Because different kinds of theory exist, researchers have choices they can make in deciding which theories are best for assisting them in answering particular research questions. This book examines different types of theory and explains the weaknesses and strengths of these theories for particular research questions.

When a particular research question is raised, criminologists don't always agree on which answers to these questions seem most plausible. Every social scientist has a point of view or a frame of reference for viewing different kinds of issues or research questions. These frames of reference almost always influence one's approach taken in attempting to explain crime, delinquency, and other related events. Also, the way a problem or question is examined will suggest a particular theoretical approach. Thus, the relation between frames of reference and theories will be examined.

Most criminological investigations involve studying people under different types of circumstances: police officers, judges, inmates of prisons or jails, correctional officers, juveniles, defense counsels and prosecutors, probationers or parolees, probation officers or parole officers, community corrections personnel, including volunteers and paraprofessionals, jury members, those on pretrial diversion, and others. It is beyond the resources of most investigators to study all persons about which information is sought. Therefore, only some of these persons are selected for investigation. This is called sampling. There are many types of sampling, and again, researchers have choices about which types of sampling methods they will use in any given set of circumstances. This book examines sampling procedures in great detail, including a broad discussion of sampling issues.

Also, there are many ways information about research questions can be gathered. Information may be gathered by examining public documents in a library. Or persons may be interviewed or observed. Others may be given questionnaires, distributed to them personally or by mail. The fact is that there are numerous ways of collecting data. Most data collection techniques available to criminologists will be thoroughly examined, including their weaknesses and strengths for particular types of applications.

As criminal justicians and criminologists study different phenomena, it is inevitable that they must devise measures for whatever they study. Attitudes are most frequently investigated, since they are invariably linked with the behaviors criminologists are trying to explain. Therefore, an in-depth examination of measurement is provided. Measurement often results in the development of scales, often attitudinal scales, that yield approximations of how strongly persons possess views toward one or more important issues. Always raised in the process of measurement are whether the scales devised to measure different phenomena are valid and reliable. Validity refers to the accuracy of scales we create, and whether these scales measure the phenomenon we intend to measure. Reliability refers to the consistency of scales we create to yield consistent degrees of certain phenomena over time. Measurement, and its accompanying properties of validity and reliability, is extensively examined. Various issues related to measurement, validity, and reliability will be raised and analyzed.

Once information about a particular research question has been collected, it must be analyzed and interpreted to assess its significance and viability as a useful explanation. Several examples of data presentation, analysis, and interpretation are provided in order to illustrate what investigators do with their collected information. The ultimate aim of most researchers is to advance our knowledge about whatever it is we choose to study. This is consistent with the various goals of scientific inquiry, which are followed closely by criminal justice and criminology.

Researchers find it difficult, if not impossible, to separate their personal beliefs and attitudes about things from whatever it is they choose to study. Also, the frames of reference and theories chosen are often reflective of researchers' opinions and views formed by their social and personal experiences. Because one's values play an important part in the research process, and because different types of persons are studied under a wide variety of circumstances or conditions, it is important to raise and examine the matter of ethics in social research. Thus, several critical ethical issues in criminological research are given extensive coverage. Examples are provided of unethical research practices as well as some research that is questionably ethical. Several standards for evaluating appropriate ethical approaches in criminology and criminal justice have evolved over the years, largely through the efforts of professional organizations such as the American Society of Criminology, the Academy of Criminal Justice Sciences, the American Sociological Association, and the American Psychology Association. These and other organizations have established ethical codes of conduct for their membership, and they suggest proper ways for one's research to be conducted.

In order to assist students in their own investigations and attempts to answer different kinds of research questions, one section of this book is devoted to helping students write research papers. This involves suggestions on how and where to gather information about the topics they are investigating, how to organize the information they collect, and how such information may be concisely expressed in a paper they are preparing for a class or other presentation.

Level of Book

This text has been written with the beginning student in mind. Therefore, much of the technical language and symbolic notation used to describe methodological strategies has been simplified. At the same time, consideration has been given to those who may wish to use this book as a reference or guide in their future research work. Thus, several topics have been included that are often given extended coverage in more advanced texts. A useful feature that enhances student comprehension of more difficult material is the extensive use of examples drawn from the criminological and criminal justice literature. Students should find this book user-friendly and relate easily to new concepts and principles that are introduced in the context of criminological language and examples.

Organization

The book has been organized as follows. Chapter 1 explains what is meant by doing research and why it is conducted. This explanation discusses some of the kinds of research topics undertaken by professionals in criminology and criminal justice. An integral part of any research activity is the creation of a theoretical scheme or explanatory framework that accounts for relationships between things. The role of theory in the research process is described and discussed. Several different types of theory are presented and explained.

Since the research enterprise is a process, this process consists of several important parts. Each part will be given appropriate attention. In a sense, the research enterprise is like a chain with many links. In that respect, since a chain is no stronger than its weakest link, the research enterprise is no better than the weakest part or stage of that enterprise. And all stages or parts of this process are very important for affecting the quality of the final research product. An overview of these stages is provided.

Almost all research conducted by criminologists and criminal justicians is closely related to scientific inquiry. Science is a method of knowing, and criminal justice and criminology are deeply rooted in scientific principles. Science demands objectivity and systematization. Furthermore, science makes certain critical assumptions about the data we study. Several of these important assumptions will be discussed. Researchers usually establish plans for carrying out their scientific investigations. These investigations or plans often begin with a research proposal, including particular objectives or goals sought by the researcher. Several important functions of research are identified and described. These functions include exploration, description, experimentation, and decision making. Theory and research are closely intertwined. This complementarity will be examined. The chapter concludes with an examination of the value of theory and research.

Chapter 2 examines frames of reference and problem formulation. When investigators begin their research, they usually start with an idea about what they want to study and how they want to study it. Those who study juvenile delinquency, for instance, will approach this topic using one of several alternative explanations—perhaps the idea that delinquency is largely the result of family instability, or that delinquency is largely the result of the significant influence of one's delinquent peers, or that delinquency is largely the result of cultural deprivation. These are ways of looking at and accounting for any phenomenon we wish to study. These ways of looking at criminological phenomena are also frames of reference or simply our particular ways of viewing problems we wish to explain.

Closely associated with frames of reference are variables used by investigators to explain different phenomena. Variables are any quantity that can assume more than one value. Gender, race, age, year in school, political affiliation, socioeconomic status, and rural or urban background are just a few of the many variables that can be used by researchers in developing their theoretical schemes and planning their research. Depending on the nature of the research conducted, each variable operates in unique ways in relation to other variables. Some variables influence other variables to change in value, while other variables are influenced to change. Different uses of variables will be examined. Variables may also be distinguished according to whether they are discrete or continuous. Discrete variables have a limited number of subdivisions. For most purposes, gender is a discrete variable, because it only has two subclasses: male and female. The same is true about political affiliation. However, other variables, such as prejudice, job satisfaction, burnout, and professionalism, may have an infinite number of subclasses. In these instances, such variables are labeled as continuous, since they may be divided and graded into infinite subdivisions. But for all practical purposes, criminologists and other social scientists reduce all variables examined to a series of discrete subclasses, regardless of the particular variable's discrete or continuous qualities. Thus, different types of variables and their functions will be presented and explained, and their relation to frames of reference and problem formulation will be examined. The chapter concludes with a discussion of causal relations between variables. Most social scientists seek to identify what factors cause certain variables to change in value. What variables cause some juveniles to become delinquent? What variables cause police misconduct, improvements in professionalism, or labor turnover among correctional officers? Causation is difficult to establish. Causal relations between variables will be explored in some detail.

Chapter 3 discusses different types of research designs as well as the various kinds of objectives sought by investigators. Research designs refer to different ways of structuring one's research so as to achieve particular outcomes. Two useful categories of research designs are case studies and surveys. Some important advantages and disadvantages of case studies and surveys will be presented. All research designs are influenced by our research goals or objectives. These goals are usually exploratory, descriptive, or experimental. The most complicated types of research designs are experimental, and there are several different kinds of experimental designs that will be presented, discussed, and compared.

Experimental research designs often involve two or more groups of persons and comparisons between them on different variables. Whenever two or more groups of persons are compared for whatever reason, it is important to establish their equivalence to justify any subsequent differences they may exhibit. Several important methods for establishing equivalence between two or more groups will be presented and discussed. These include individual matching, persons used as their own controls in before–after experiments, group or frequency distribution control matching, and random assignment. Other experimental designs will be examined, including classical experimental design, quasi-experimental designs, time-series designs, and cost–benefit analyses.

Chapter 4 is a detailed examination of the sampling process. When populations of persons are investigated, it is extraordinary that all persons in these populations are studied. Most researchers investigate only a portion or sample of persons taken from the entire population of them. A discussion of the decision to sample will be provided. There are several types of sampling plans, therefore, including probability and nonprobability sampling plans. These will be distinguished. Several important criteria for identifying probability sampling plans, including randomness, will be described. The functions of sampling will also be presented.

The next part of Chapter 4 examines various probability and nonprobability sampling plans in some detail, featuring examples as well as the advantages, disadvantages, and applications of these plans for criminological research. Different sampling scenarios are also distinguished, such as when single samples of persons are studied, or whether two or more samples of persons are investigated. The independence or relatedness of different samples will also be discussed. The chapter concludes with a discussion of several important sampling considerations and issues.

Chapter 5 is the first of three chapters that examine different ways that information about people can be gathered. Each research plan includes provisions for collecting data or information about the problem studied. The substance of Chapter 5 is questionnaire construction and administration. Much of the time, information about people is gathered by criminologists through the administration of questionnaires. Questionnaires contain much information that may be quantified and used to verify one's theories and frames of reference. Questionnaires always contain information useful in the conceptualization of variables used to explain different social phenomena.

But not all questionnaires are alike. Different questionnaire formats are described, as well as their weaknesses and strengths for particular research applications. Questionnaires may be administered under a variety of different conditions. Questionnaires can be mailed, administered to persons face-to-face, or given to persons in groups. Questionnaires also vary in their construction. Some questionnaires are simple and short, while others are long and complex. Some items in questionnaires have fixed-response answers, while other items have an open-ended format. These different formats are described, and their weaknesses and strengths for different groups of persons are discussed. Several important issues about the use of questionnaires will be examined. Some of these issues include nonresponse and what to do about it. Not everyone returns their questionnaire. Not everyone receives questionnaires mailed to them. When persons do receive and complete questionnaires, we have no way of knowing whether they gave truthful or false information. Sometimes persons lie about how they feel, and this deception influences the credibility of questionnaire information. All of these issues and others will be examined in some detail.

Chapter 6 examines interviewing as a data-gathering technique. Like questionnaires, interviews may be administered different ways. Interviews may be conducted face-to-face, or they may be conducted over the telephone with different persons who are investigative targets. Usually interviews are more or less structured like questionnaires, in that previously prepared questions or items are formulated and particular kinds of information are solicited from selected persons. Interviewing is believed by some social scientists to be a skill that is learned over time and with experience. This chapter examines the qualities of interviewers, and some of the weaknesses and strengths of interviewing will be examined. Comparisons of interview information with information yielded from questionnaires will be made and evaluated. The chapter concludes with an examination of several important issues associated with the interviewing process.

Chapter 7 discusses observation as a data-gathering technique. Observation is defined, and different types of observation are described. Persons who observe others for the purpose of gathering information about them may be participants or nonparticipants. This means that they may or may not be members of the groups about which they seek information. Also, if persons know they are being observed, they may behave differently so that their true feelings or attitudes cannot be interpreted correctly. Therefore, the impact of the observer on the observed will be discussed. By the same token, behaviors of persons being observed can influence the behaviors and attitudes of those who observe. Both of these potentially problematic situations will be discussed.

This chapter also examines the use of secondary sources, such as public records, as a means of gathering information. Examinations of archival reports, biographies, autobiographies, organizational documents, and court records are considered secondary sources. Because most secondary source information was collected for purposes different from those of the researcher, some of the weaknesses and strengths of using secondary sources will be described. Secondary sources may also be examined for their content. Content analyses of secondary sources will be described. Some government and private agencies have compiled databases and records for general research applications. These data may be easily accessed and analyzed, although there are certain considerations that should be made for analyzing these data sets. Finally, some studies seek to examine numerous investigations of a single topic as an aggregate through meta-analysis. Meta-analysis will be described and explained.

Chapters 8 and 9 focus on the measurement of social and psychological variables in criminological research. Because much criminological research involves contacting others and soliciting information concerning their ideas and attitudes about things, attention is also given to the measures we use to quantify the information collected. In Chapter 8, the measurement of variables is closely examined as well as some general functions of measurement for social research. Attention is directed toward variables and how they are conceptualized numerically. Variables may be measured according to different levels of measurement, including the nominal, ordinal, interval, and ratio levels. Several popular scaling procedures, including Likert and Thurstone scaling, are examined and described in detail. These types of scales are geared toward attitude measurement. Their weaknesses, strengths, and general research applications are presented. Other types of scales are also presented, including the semantic differential, Guttman scaling, the Salient Factor Score Index, and Greenwood's Rand Seven-Factor Index. Several issues relating to measurement are presented to conclude this chapter.

Chapter 9 examines whether the scales we devise actually measure what they purport to measure and whether these scales have consistency in their application. Do our measures of things have validity; that is, do these measures actually measure what we say they measure? Are these measures reliable? Can we depend on them to give us consistent results over time? Validity and reliability are two critical scale properties and are given extensive treatment in this chapter. Several types of validity are described and explained. Accordingly, there are several types of reliability. These different types are also described. Because of the fact that we often measure attitudinal phenomena, there are numerous factors that may interfere with a scale's reliability and validity. These factors are presented and discussed in detail.

Chapter 10 is an examination of the coding process and the conversion of information we have obtained from questionnaires, interviews, and/or observation into numerical quantities for scientific purposes. Whatever we measure, whether it be crime rates or police professionalism, this information must be coded in some way. Coding is an integral feature of the scientific process and enables researchers to share their research with others in more meaningful ways. Also presented in this chapter are various methods for portraying or illustrating the information investigators have collected. Different types of graphs, charts, and/or tables are presented. Examples from current criminological literature are provided to show how data may be cross-tabulated and meaningfully interpreted. All of this data presentation is central to verifying the theories we have chosen to use and which guide our research enterprise. The decision-making process is discussed to illustrate the criteria we use to choose which forms of data presentation are best for our particular research.

Chapter 11 focuses on hypothesis formulation. Hypotheses are statements, usually derived from theory and consisting of one or more variables, which can be empirically tested. These statements are often depictions of different parts of one's theory in testable form. Several types of hypotheses are described, including research, null, and statistical hypotheses. In each case, ample illustrations are provided to show how these hypotheses are constructed and tested. Some hypotheses are relatively simple and are easily tested, while others are more complex. Hypotheses may contain one or more variables, and thus our research must be fashioned in ways that make it possible to conduct scientific tests of these hypotheses to verify the particular theory we use. Hypothesis testing is not a cut-and-dried process. Some investigators consider hypothesis testing to be an art form. Several important considerations must be made whenever interpreting the results of hypothesis tests. These considerations have to do with our theory, the sampling procedure we have used, the measures we have used, the data-collection methods we have employed, and the validity and reliability of our measures.

Chapter 12 examines several critical ethical issues that arise whenever social research is conducted. Virtually every professional organization, including the American Society of Criminology and the Academy of Criminal Justice Sciences, has established codes of ethics to guide their respective memberships in conducting ethical research. Invariably different ethical problems will arise and over which investigators may have little or no control. Some of these ethical problems will be described and discussed. Several ethical issues will be presented, as well as several solutions and proposals for minimizing unethical practices in social research.

Finally, an appendix has been provided to assist students in their individual research projects and assignments. It explores paper writing and offers considerable assistance in where to look for various types of information. Suggestions are given for different types of paper formats, including master's thesis and doctoral dissertation organization and preparation. A useful feature is a discussion of legal references and citation methods for those who seek information from legal publications.

Using This Book Most Effectively

Perhaps the best way to approach the material in this book is as a collection of strategies for problem solving. Each strategy that might be employed in the investigation of particular criminal justice–related or criminological problems has weaknesses and strengths, limitations and benefits. These features must be weighed carefully as they are considered for application in problem–solutions. The problems are research questions, questions about criminological and criminal justice-related phenomena about which we seek information and answers.

Because the research process is multidimensional and involves numerous phases or stages, each exhibiting technical and sometimes complicated procedures, it might be helpful to regard this collection of strategies from the standpoint of building blocks. Thinking of a pyramid, base blocks form the foundation, and blocks on higher levels can only be supported by the foundation we have provided. Thus, our knowledge of research methods proceeds accordingly, as we master knowledge of basics and proceed to more technical strategies in later chapters. And, like the pyramid that, once in place, is a beautiful, complete assemblage of blocks, the research process unfolds similarly to yield a distinctive whole that can best be appreciated when viewed as an interconnected constellation of numerous components.

The general intention is to improve our understanding of the events that occur around us. Perhaps our investigations will lead to certain practical policy decisions. However, our investigations may be unrelated to public policy or to anything of practical value other than a simple understanding and appreciation for why certain events occur. My position is that we should seek a healthy balance between our practical, substantive concerns and our theoretical ones. While some research may have direct relevance for a particular intervention program to be used for parolees in halfway houses to assist in their community reintegration, other research may not be adapted easily to any helping program. This state of affairs is perhaps as it should be, especially in view of the great diversity of interests among criminologists and criminal justice professionals, the problems they select for study, and the ways they choose to investigate these problems.

Special Features and Ancillaries

The book has several special features, which are as follows:

- All technical expressions involved in sampling, scaling, and attitudinal measurement have been simplified, with careful, step-by-step instructions about how to complete one's calculations.
- All methodological procedures are fully explained and their interpretation is simplified with examples from the criminological literature.
- Current illustrations have been extracted from the literature of criminology and criminal justice. Topics for illustrations were deliberately chosen because of their variety and because of their topical importance in view of their frequency of treatment in the professional literature. All methodological procedures covered in this book were found among these articles, and the ideas from these articles were the basis for most examples provided.

- Questions are provided at chapter ends for review. All key terms are included with definitions in the comprehensive glossary in the Appendix.
- An appendix describes how to write papers and scientific essays. Students will learn how to structure their term paper projects, and master's and doctoral students will glean an idea of how to construct theses and dissertations, which involve a variety of research questions.
- Instructional aids include an instructor's manual and a computerized test bank of 1,000 questions and are available for examination preparation. Versions of the computerized test bank are available on computer diskette and hard copy.

Acknowledgments

Many persons play important parts in the production of a textbook. I would like to acknowledge the generous support and assistance of my editor, Frank Mortimer, who provided encouragement and helpful criticisms at key points throughout project development. A special thanks is extended to Associate Editor Sarah Holle, who facilitated and supervised the production of the book through copy editing to page proofs. However, any possible errors of fact, if detected, are solely my responsibility and not the reviewers. And last but not least, I wish to thank the many contributors who sent me biographical information and photos for inclusion at critical points throughout the book. Many of these contributors are key leaders in criminology and criminal justice, persons who have strongly influenced the shape and nature of these fields. I think that a book's value is enhanced by true-to-life experiences of actual researchers who are constantly exploring answers to difficult research questions and can share their research experiences with students. I found these contributions to be most interesting and hope students will find them of interest also.

Dean John Champion

ABOUT THE AUTHOR

Dean John Champion is Professor of Criminal Justice, Texas A & M International University, Laredo, Texas. Dr. Champion has taught at the University of Tennessee–Knoxville, California State University–Long Beach, and Minot State University. He earned his Ph.D. from Purdue University and B.S. and M.A. degrees from Brigham Young University. He also completed several years of law school at the Nashville School of Law.

Dr. Champion has written over 35 texts and/or edited works and maintains memberships in eleven professional organizations. He is a lifetime member of the American Society of Criminology, Academy of Criminal Justice Sciences, and the American Sociological Association, and he actively participates in the American Correctional Association, American Probation and Parole Association, and American Jail Association. He is former editor of the ACJS/Anderson Series on *Issues in Crime and Justice* (1993–1996) and the *Journal of Crime and Justice* (1995–1998). He is a contributing author for the *Encarta Encyclopedia 2000* for Microsoft. He has been a Visiting Scholar for the National Center for Juvenile Justice and is a former president of the Midwestern Criminal Justice Association.

Among his published books for Prentice-Hall include *Basic Statistics for Social Research* (1970, 1981); *Research Methods for Criminal Justice and Criminology* (1993, 2000, 2006); *The Juvenile Justice System: Delinquency, Processing, and the Law* (1992, 1998, 2001, 2004, 2007 forthcoming); *Corrections in the United States: A Contemporary*

Perspective (1990, 1998, 2001, 2005); *Probation, Parole, and Community Corrections* (1990, 1996, 1999, 2002, 2005); *Policing in the Community* (w/George Rush) (1996); *Criminal Courts* (w/Gary A. Rabe) (2002, 2007 forthcoming), and *The Administration of Justice Systems* (2003). Several of Dr. Champion's books have been published in Russian, Portuguese, Chinese, and Spanish editions. Dr. Champion's specialty interests include juvenile justice, criminal justice administration, corrections, and statistics/methods.

CHAPTER

1

The Research Enterprise in Criminal Justice and Criminology

CHAPTER OUTLINE

CHAPTER OBJECTIVES

As the result of reading this chapter, the following objectives should be realized:

1. Understanding the general organization of the research process or enterprise and the interrelation of its various components.
2. Learning the difference between pure and applied research and their respective value as investigative tools.
3. Describing the sequential development of the research process, including problem formulation, research design, formulating explanations, study design, collecting and analyzing data, presenting and interpreting findings, and generating tentative conclusions.

1

4. Learning about several key assumptions made by investigators who study criminological phenomena, including underlying patterns of social behaviors and attitudes, variable interrelations, and causality.

5. Understanding why research is conducted and how probability and objectivity play important roles in the research enterprise.

6. Examining various functions of research, including exploratory, descriptive, and experimental functions.

7. Understanding the meaning and importance of evaluation research.

8. Learning about theory, its essential components, and the value of theory in explaining and predicting relations between two or more variables.

9. Distinguishing between different kinds of theory, including deductive, inductive, grounded, and axiomatic theory and how each functions to account for variable interrelations.

10. Learning to define variables and their roles in theoretical schemes, including independent, dependent, discrete, and continuous variables.

11. Understanding the complementarity of research and theory as well as atheoretical evaluations of social settings and the people in such settings.

Introduction

Here are some potential research questions for criminologists:

- Is home confinement an effective deterrent to crime?
- Should criminal court judges be elected or appointed?
- Is restorative justice a viable method for resolving conflicts between criminal perpetrators and their victims?
- Is the criminal justice system a racist system, or do different racial or ethnic minorities offend at disproportionate rates?
- Is there a rising crime wave among female offenders?
- Do female correctional officers perform their jobs with equal effectiveness commensurate with male correctional officers?
- Is electronic monitoring unconstitutional?
- Does the privatization of corrections result in unprecedented inmate population growth and result in larger numbers of offender incarcerations?
- To what extent do prosecutors engage in misconduct by encouraging their witnesses against criminal defendants to lie or distort the truth?
- Do criminal court judges discriminate between persons according to whether they are represented by private counsel or public defenders?
- Do white-collar offenders receive lighter sentences compared with offenders who commit street crimes?
- Are boot camps effective interventions at deterring youths from committing delinquency?
- Are youth courts or teen courts more effective than juvenile courts at holding juvenile offenders accountable for their offenses?
- Do parole boards discriminate in their early-release decision making according to one's socioeconomic status, race, or gender?

These questions are just a few of the thousands of research questions asked by criminologists and criminal justicians in their constant pursuit of knowledge about the people and situations they investigate. All areas of criminal justice are fair game for these social scientists and the questions they raise. Are there clear-cut answers to any of these and other questions these social scientists ask? No. But at least they continually explore possible explanations for whatever phenomena they choose to study.

This book is about how these researchers and other social scientists go about doing their research. The research process itself is an enterprise, literally a research enterprise, which is devoted to gaining knowledge about subjects of interest to all of us. We are always seeking more information about things. Whether we wish to know more about boot camps and their effectiveness for reducing delinquency, whether we want to know whether parole boards discriminate in their early-release decision making, whether there is a rising crime wave among females, whether there is racism throughout the criminal justice system, whether criminal violence is increasing, whether privatization in corrections and other areas is good or bad, whether women do as well as men performing corrections work, or whether home confinement/electronic monitoring are viable supervisory alternatives to offender management, our research investigations seek possible answers to these and other questions. As criminologists, we have inquiring minds. We want to know.

One important difference between ourselves as students of criminology and criminal justice and the person on the street with ideas about why people do different things, like commit crimes, is that we restrict our explanations for different events in more or less tangible ways. Through applying the scientific method to our research endeavors, we introduce a high degree of **objectivity** and systematization in our research work. We carefully construct our research projects and implement them according to a set of rigorous rules. We spend several years learning about research and its many facets. We learn that there are good ways to approach the subject matter of our inquiry, and we learn that there are also poor ways fraught with weaknesses and problems. We profit from what others have done, and we also learn from their mistakes. We learn that virtually every research project is flawed in one respect or another, and we seek to avoid as many flaws as possible. We soon realize that perfection in research implementation is probably an impossible dream, but we also learn that we should do our best to do our research and avoid as many hazards as possible. In the long-range view, we learn that all research is cumulative, and that ultimately, we will realize some benefits from our work as well as from the work of others.

We also learn that the research process is an interconnected chain of events, where each chain is an important piece of the puzzle we are attempting to solve. This book describes this chain of events, and the different chapters are each important links in the research chain. Since no chain is any stronger than its weakest link, we realize that all points in our research work are important and deserve serious consideration. This chapter starts us off on our quest to learn more about events of interest to us.

In the first part of this chapter, an overview of the research process is presented. The research enterprise begins with an event or problem in need of an answer. By posing a particular research question, which may be an event such as delinquency, high labor turnover among probation officers, low morale among correctional officers, variations in police professionalism among different police departments, or the incidence of racial profiling and the implications of such profiling for social policy, we are attracted to one or more explanations of these events or problems that seem to have explanatory value. These explanations are often influenced by our own reading or experiences, and thus there is always some subjectivity inherent in the explanations we choose to link with the problems for which we seek possible answers. Any research problem has numerous alternative explanations. Some explanations are better than others. Through our research efforts, we seek to discover which explanations are best.

We construct studies that will enable us to collect data relevant to the problems we wish to explain. We identify samples of persons who possess information about the questions we raise. We will use different data collection methods, such as questionnaires or observation, to glean important information from others. This acquired information will be analyzed and interpreted. Finally, we will conclude various things about our research findings. Our conclusions will always be tentative, and they may or may not have theoretical or practical value. Therefore, a distinction between pure and applied research is presented. It is not uncommon for researchers to be disappointed by their research findings, doing a lot of work only to find that their explanations for problems or events do not seem to be particularly effective or insightful. But at the same time, much research is rewarded by positive findings, where our research results seem to support our particular explanations of events. The interrelatedness of the research process and its various components is examined.

Engaging in social research involves making certain assumptions about the people and situations studied. The next section of this chapter examines several important assumptions that must be made in our quest for information. These assumptions include the fact that most behaviors we observe are patterned behaviors; these patterns can be depicted; there are persistent interrelationships between different variables such that cause–effect relations can be detected and forecasted; that the variables we examine can be measured or quantified in some way; and that inconsistencies will inevitably occur when findings from different studies are compared. We will also examine why research is conducted generally. Also examined are some of the important rules of scientific inquiry that social scientists observe.

The next section of this chapter describes several important functions of social research, including exploration, description, and experimentation. Each research enterprise emphasizes one or more of these general research objectives. Some research is conducted to determine the benefits of a particular intervention or experimental variable intended to bring about a desired result. This is known as evaluation research, and it is described.

Guiding almost all research is theory, an explanatory and predictive scheme we construct to show the interrelations between variables, such as the events we wish to explain and the explanations we use to account for these events. Theory itself consists of assumptions, propositions, and definitions of variables. Theory and its important components are described. There are several different kinds of theory as well. Theories may be deductive, inductive, grounded, or axiomatic. Each of these types of theory is defined and discussed. Occasionally some studies are conducted where no theory is evident. These studies are atheoretical. Despite the absence of a particular theory, such atheoretical studies have been important for criminology and criminal justice. This type of theory will be examined.

Because different variables, such as race/ethnicity, type of crime, judicial discretion, and income, are included in theories or theoretical schemes, variables themselves will be examined in some detail in terms of their different characteristics. Variables may be considered independent, dependent, discrete, or continuous, again depending on our theoretical schemes and how we choose to use certain variables in these schemes. These characteristics of variables will be described and discussed.

The chapter concludes with a brief discussion of the complementarity between research and theory, since both are mutually important to the success of the other. This discussion extends to the importance of both research and theory and to the respective roles each plays as we seek to discover more knowledge about what we study.

Overview of the Research Process

The Research Enterprise

The **research process** or research enterprise consists of all activities that pertain to problem formulation and definition. **Research** consists of all investigations, studies, or systematic efforts designed to increase our knowledge about events and their occurrence. Research includes developing a theoretical explanation for why problems exist; collecting information that will verify or refute the explanation of problems; analyzing, presenting, and interpreting this information; and drawing tentative conclusions that will either support or refute the theoretical explanation provided. You may become interested in certain events and why those events occur. You read about wrongful convictions, where innocent persons were convicted of crimes they did not commit, in the newspapers or hear about them on television. Why did these wrongful convictions occur? Were they the result of prosecutor misconduct or ineffective assistance of counsel? Was the judge biased in the case? You speculate about the causes of these events. One or more reasonable explanations for the event occur to you, but you are uncertain about these explanations. You select what you regard as the best explanation of the event and seek answers to your questions. You examine your evidence and evaluate whether the explanation of the event is acceptable or feasible. The strength of the evidence you have gathered may require that you collect additional evidence and retest the explanation elsewhere, in new social settings. You repeat this process until you achieve an acceptable level of certainty about why the event has occurred. Or you may reach a dead end, where the explanation you have chosen is not or does not appear to be sound. You select an alternative explanation for the event and conduct a new investigation. The research process continues, and your research work is never done to your complete satisfaction.

Steps to Conduct Research in Criminal Justice

There are many different kinds of research that may be conducted. Despite these differences in research, there are certain basic steps that are usually followed. There is no perfect research format, although most researchers follow a general organizational plan when conducting their investigations. Ordinary steps to be followed include (1) problem formulation, (2) research design, (3) data collection methods, (4) analysis of data, (5) presentation of findings, and (6) conclusions.

Problem Formulation

Problem formulation means to focus on a subject for study and define one or more specific research questions that need to be answered. Suppose we were interested in juveniles and the extent to which they are represented by attorneys in juvenile court. Given the greater rights extended to juvenile offenders during the last few decades and the increasing criminalization of the juvenile court itself, we might suspect that juveniles might have greater cause to use attorney services. Furthermore, we might want to know whether the use of attorneys by juveniles results in greater leniency from juvenile court judges compared with adjudications of juveniles who are not represented by counsel. Finally, we might want to know if attorney use varies according to juvenile offense seriousness, or whether there is greater attorney use by juveniles regardless of the nature of their offense.

This particular research problem is somewhat unique, since relatively little is known about attorney involvement in juvenile matters. Also, we have little direct evidence about the impact of attorneys on juvenile court outcomes and leniency. The problem we have selected is noteworthy, in part, because of increasing juvenile violence in recent years. Media attention has focused on juvenile courts in different states and how especially violent juveniles have been disposed by these courts.

Another problem we might select for study might focus on the factors affecting police officer decisions to engage in a code of silence and not report the misconduct of other officers. What factors cause police officers to look the other way whenever their fellow officers violate civilian rights when making arrests or obtaining evidence?

A third problem we could select for study might involve probationers and their response or reaction to electronic monitoring. Is electronic monitoring an effective offender management method? Does electronic monitoring reduce the likelihood of offender recidivism?

In each of the above problems, we will need to collect information from either juvenile courts, police officers, or probationers. We will need to identify potential sources of pertinent information and attempt to collect data that will enable us to answer our research questions.

Conceptualizing a **research problem** means to identify a general topic for study, specify a particular dimension of the topic for more intensive examination, and then pose several pointed questions that will guide the investigator's inquiry. Research problems are events in need of explanations. The questions posed at the beginning of this chapter are examples of research problems. Other types of research problems include the following questions:

1. Is intensive supervised probation more effective at reducing client recidivism compared with standard probation?
2. Is it feasible to allow death row inmates to mingle in the general prison population compared with isolating them in maximum-security death rows?
3. Are furloughs for prison inmates helpful in fostering their community reintegration and rehabilitation?
4. Do juvenile status offenders generally escalate to more serious delinquent offending over time?
5. What factors contribute to correctional officer turnover in jail and prison settings?

Each of the questions above directs our attention toward a researchable problem. From the above questions, we know that our investigations will target probationer recidivism; or death row inmate adaptability to mingling in the general prison population; or the use of furloughs for rehabilitative and reintegrative purposes; or a study of career escalation from status to delinquent offending; or factors causing correctional officers to quit their jobs.

Often the different social or employment experiences of particular researchers strongly influence them to explore certain topics. Some investigators have worked in law enforcement or corrections or with juveniles. Or perhaps these researchers have read interesting articles about the **subjects** they plan to study. Most of us who do research are going to investigate topics of interest to us. Some examples of the research of others and their particular backgrounds are shown below.

- Susan Bednar, a licensed clinical social worker and certified domestic violence counselor in Illinois, conducted a study of the relation between substance abuse and the abuse of women in domestic violence situations (Bednar, 2003). Her professional experiences and training no doubt influenced the nature of her investigation, as well as the theories she chose to analyze the co-occurrence of these phenomena.
- Stephen Metraux and Dennis Culhane, respectively affiliated with the University of Sciences in Philadelphia and the University of Pennsylvania, have studied the homeless, homelessness, and incarcerations/reincarcerations of the homeless (Metraux & Culhane, 2004). These investigators have backgrounds in health policy and social welfare policy, and their direct research interests include studying the relation between the homeless and health, mental health, the criminal justice system, risk factors for HIV/AIDS among indigent drug users, and property, neighborhood, and human services **policy analysis,** program planning, and evaluation. Their 2004 study examined a sample of parolees from New York State prisons, homeless shelter use, and subsequent reincarcerations, and the impact of shelter use on the risk of subsequent reincarcerations.
- Jeffrey S. Magers, a professor at Stephen F. Austin State University, has studied the Compstat model of policing, a results-driven strategy utilizing high-pressure tactics on police commanders to improve their crime reduction efforts. Compstat, a strategic management model or goal-oriented strategic management process employed by the New York City Police Department, seeks to identify crime and disorder problems and immediate solutions to those problems (Magers, 2004). Coincidentally, Magers is also a retired captain, a former administrator, with the Jefferson County Police Department in Louisville, Kentucky. What can you reasonably conclude from Magers's former police affiliation and his investigation of police management methods?
- Michael F. Higgins has described various vocational, educational, and counseling programs at the Alvin S. Glenn Detention Center, a South Carolina correctional facility (Higgins, 2002). Higgins has included in his description health education awareness courses, alcohol and drug abuse counseling opportunities, GED/Pre-GED programs, life skills and domestic violence courses, and an inmate library. Oh, by the way, Higgins started his career as a line officer in corrections, moving up the ranks to captain. Over time he has spent much of his work in prison security, working as a maintenance supervisor, a manager of inmate programs and community corrections, and is currently a division manager of a 24-bed juvenile facility. Prior to that experience, Higgins worked as a corrections officer for the South Carolina Department of Corrections.

• Dawna Komorowsky, a professor at Western New England College, has written extensively about incarcerated mothers and the importance of jail visitation of mothers with children. An advocate of visitation programs between inmate mothers and their children, Komorowsky has a master's degree in marriage and family therapy and has previously worked for several years with children and families in the foster care system.

When we identify a problem for investigation, we usually have a pretty good idea of which explanation we are going to use for why the problem exists. Our research will test whether our explanation is good or bad, productive or unproductive. For instance, we may think that one-parent families may have a greater incidence of delinquency than two-parent families. Our thinking may be that one-parent families are less stable than two-parent families, and that youths in one-parent family situations may be more inclined to commit delinquent acts. However, we may discover that at least for those families we have selected for study, there are *more* delinquents in two-parent families than in one-parent ones, at least among the families we study. This finding suggests that our idea about one-parent families and delinquency is questionable. More research about this potential relationship is needed before we may conclude anything definite about it.

It is conventional for researchers to suggest several plausible explanations for why particular events (e.g., delinquency, correctional officer turnover) occur. This activity shows that we have done some critical thinking about the problem we are investigating. We have explored various alternative **explanations** for why the problem exists, and we have chosen a particular explanation that fits the particular rationale we have created. Therefore, if we should find that our explanation is not particularly satisfactory, we can turn to other alternative explanations for further research. Or we may persist with our first explanation, but we will conduct one or more additional studies with different research subjects.

For instance, we might investigate sentencing disparity among judges. Sentencing disparity occurs whenever judges impose quite different sentence lengths or more or less severe sentences on several different offenders who have committed the same offense. A judge may impose a 10-year sentence for one burglar, while the same judge may impose a sentence of probation for another burglar. Why does one burglar get 10 years while another burglar gets probation? This is sentencing disparity and it needs to be explained.

Researchers may explain sentencing disparity according to several different explanations. One explanation may be that one's race or ethnicity leads to different sentences. Another explanation is that gender differences explain disparities in sentencing. Maybe one's age or socioeconomic status contributes to such disparities. Also, whether a defendant is represented by privately acquired counsel or a public defender may explain sentencing disparities. If it is believed that racial or ethnic differences among defendants lead to different sentencing outcomes, racial/ethnic factors are investigated. It may occur that the researcher is unable to show that sentencing disparities vary according to race or ethnicity. However, the investigation discloses that sentencing disparities seem to vary according to the type of legal representation. Those defendants represented by public defenders may tend to receive harsher sentences compared with those defendants represented by private counsels. While the researcher is disappointed that she didn't find sentencing disparities according to race or ethnicity, the public defender–private counsel finding suggests that further research might be conducted in other jurisdictions using this alternative explanation.

Research Design

Each of the problems formulated above require that we formulate a research plan. This plan is referred to as a **research design.** Research designs are blueprints for research activity. Common research designs include exploratory, descriptive, or experimental research objectives. How much do we know about the persons we wish to study? What do we know about the study settings, such as police departments, court systems, or correctional institutions? Sometimes we must do some exploratory research in order to determine what the people and settings are like before we leap into a research project. Or do we merely wish to collect information about our research problem and describe what we have found? Or do we want to conduct a more complex experiment to determine the effect of one variable on one or more other variables? The research design, therefore, is our plan of attack. It sets forth the steps we will follow to answer our research questions.

Data Collection Methods

Depending on the goals of our research, we will use one or more types of **data collection methods.** For a juvenile court study of attorney use, for instance, we might obtain information from the National Center for Juvenile Justice. This organization maintains computerized records of juvenile arrest and adjudication activity in every state. These records are kept for many years, according to when each state began automated compilations of juvenile justice information. We may wish to study juveniles in all states, or we may focus our attention on only a few states. We will probably want to narrow our time frame to a block of years, such as 2000–2005. This assists us in observing trends in attorney use by juveniles over time. We can also select certain variables for study, such as type of offense, type of attorney (e.g., private counsel or public defender), gender, age, prior adjudications, dispositions, and ethnicity/race.

If we were to wish to study police misconduct and the apparent code of silence that exists among many police officers, it is likely that there are no computerized records from which to glean relevant data. We will probably have to interview police officers directly. We might select a large police department for our research. Since it will be difficult to get reliable information from most police officers about their personal perceptions of misconduct by other officers, it may be necessary to work with some of our police officer friends, if we know any. Some of our work associates may know officers in various police departments. Working through these connections, we can establish a rapport with a few police officers. With assurances of anonymity, we might be able to obtain much valuable information about police officer misconduct, its nature and frequency.

For a study of probationers and how electronic monitoring might help to decrease their recidivism, we might wish to contact some probation officers. These probation officers may assist us in arranging visits and/or interviews on a voluntary basis with some of their probationer-clients who are on electronic monitoring. Perhaps the probation office maintains records of recidivism activity for offenders involved in their electronic monitoring program. However, we might wish to interview or send questionnaires to a **sample** of probationers for additional information. Personal interviews or questionnaires may sensitize us to how electronic monitoring influences probationer behaviors and how these probationers react to this offender management method.

Each research problem suggests one or more data collection methods. More than one data collection method might be used for the same study. Investigators must decide how best to collect information or **data** that will help them answer their research questions. The type of data collection method(s) chosen by researchers often depend on the type of research problem we have formulated and the nature of data required to provide answers to our research questions. Less obvious behaviors we might choose to study, such as swinging, police, prosecutorial, or judicial misconduct, probation officer attitudes toward their work and clients, or the reactions of victims to victimizations, might be studied by direct interviewing or observation, while general trends for different sorts of activities for criminal justice organizations may best be approached through surveys or longitudinal investigations. In many instances questionnaires may be mailed to those from whom we seek information. Or we may use multiple data collection techniques. This practice is known as **triangulation,** since it involves collecting information about the same phenomenon with two or more data collection methods. Some investigators believe that triangulation gives them a better "feel" for the subject matter and targets under research investigation.

Therefore, we can observe those about which we seek information. Or we can interview them. We can sometimes participate directly in their activities and learn about them from our own experiences. We can give them questionnaires to fill out, or we can ask them to write about their experiences. We can sometimes find information in the library that has been collected about them and their characteristics. We can also read the research of others in professional journals and other outlets, in an effort to learn more about those we wish to study.

Suppose we wish to know whether death row inmates can be blended into general inmate populations without incident. Answering this question requires that we find a prison where authorities are willing to release death row inmates into the general inmate population. Furthermore, we must be in a position to observe whether incidents between inmates occur during this blending process. Suppose we study the integration of death row inmates with the general inmate population for a year. Suppose that death row inmates behave in an orderly fashion, and that no serious incidents among inmates occur. At the end of a year, we report our findings that show that at least for this particular prison, death row inmates assimilate well into the general inmate population. Our data are our observations of inmate conduct and inmate incidents.

In another study, we may focus on Internet dating services. We might join clubs or affiliate ourselves with Internet sites with explicit chat rooms in order to become acquainted with certain people who might provide us with valuable information we seek about Internet dating. Much information about people and their dating habits and behaviors can be gleaned from these anonymous experiences. If our interest pertains to deviant conduct, especially sexually deviant conduct, the Internet has an abundant number of sources through which valuable research data about these phenomena can be obtained. Sometimes researchers may join groups and pretend to be interested and active members in order to glean data about those groups they wish to study. In at least one instance, a male and female graduate student at the University of California–Riverside actually joined a swinger's group to describe group sex and sex norms among such persons at member homes in the San Gabriel, California valley. Was safe sex practiced? Was consensual sex between different partners conducted behind closed bedroom doors or in the open with other couples? What were the dos and don'ts of these groups of swingers? In this research, the students were willing to place

BOX 1.1   PERSONALITY HIGHLIGHT

MARJORIE S. ZATZ
Arizona State University

Statistics: B.A. (sociology, Latin American studies), University of Massachusetts–Amherst; M.A. (sociology), Indiana University; Ph.D. (sociology, Latin American studies), Indiana University.

BACKGROUND AND INTERESTS

My research focuses on racial, ethnic, and gender-based discrimination in juvenile and criminal court processing and sanctioning. As spin-offs from this primary emphasis, I have also conducted considerable research on Chicano and Chicana gangs and the larger communities in which they form a part, gender and the legal profession, and social and legal change in Cuba, and to a lesser extent, Nicaragua.

For as long as I can remember, I have been active in struggles against inequality. I grew up in the midst of the civil rights movement and came of age at the height of the feminist and antiwar movements. When I was in the third grade, I canvassed my neighborhood for signatures on what became the Civil Rights Act of 1964. Beginning at an even earlier age, I accompanied my mother on weekly trips to a local "reformatory" (a nice name for a women's prison) to pick up and drop off the women she had hired to help clean our house. I kept up incessant conversations with the women while they worked, trying to understand why they were incarcerated, what they were going to do with the rest of their lives, and the effects of their incarceration on their families. It seemed odd to me, even then, that children were sent to live with grandparents and other relatives while their mothers were incarcerated for seemingly minor crimes, most of which had to do with drug and alcohol addictions. I also couldn't figure out how cleaning houses provided tools and training that might improve their lives.

Sociology was the natural field for me, and I delved into my college courses with a passion. There was no such thing as women's studies at the time, but I focused my studies on issues of gender, race, ethnicity, and class. My interests in Latin America grew during this time, culminating in a senior-level capstone course on the Cuban Revolution. I completed my bachelor's degree in 3½ years and spent the semester before graduate school traversing much of Latin America with another young woman. This trip remains one of the highlights of my life, and one of the most transformative events for me. Never before have I been exposed to such stark contrasts between utter poverty and excessive wealth. I was struck by the extent to which class, gender, race, ethnicity, and culture were intertwined and how these social relations jointly shaped and constrained peoples' options. I returned to the United States and to graduate school deter-

BOX 1.1   CONTINUED

mined to better understand the patterns I had seen, and to use that knowledge to help eradicate inequality and institutionalized forms of discrimination.

RESEARCH INVESTIGATIONS

My research since that time has focused largely on identifying overt and subtle forms of racial and gender discrimination in the legal arena. I have studied the ways in which race and gender directly and indirectly (through their effects on other factors) impact criminal and juvenile court processing and sanctioning decisions. I have also looked at U.S. immigration policies and state and local gang policies as examples of racialized policies, and I have explored the multifaceted ways in which racialized and gendered images of criminals and victims influence both policymaking and our societal responses to crime and injustice. Finally, I was intrigued for many years by the example of the Cuban Revolution as an effort to take a fresh look at the relationship between social and legal change in the context of a new legal order. I returned to Latin America frequently, gaining better understandings of the culture and contacts within the sociological and legal communities. In 1989 I was afforded the opportunity to spend a sabbatical year in Cuba as a researcher affiliated with the University of Havana Law School.

These varied projects have required me to merge strands from several distinct theoretical frames, and to employ different types of research methods in my work, including quantitative event history and regression analyses of criminal court cases and qualitative interview and ethnographic data analytic techniques. I enjoy writing alone and with coauthors, and I find that a balance between these two works best for me. My books include *Images of Color, Images of Crime,* coedited with Coramae Richey Mann (Roxbury, 1st ed. 1998; 2nd ed. 2002); *Producing Legality: Law and Socialism in Cuba* (Routledge, 1994); and *Making Law: The State, the Law, and Structural Contradictions,* coedited with William Chambliss (Indiana University, 1993). I have been honored to receive several awards for my scholarship, including the 2002 Distinguished Scholar award from the Division on Women and Crime of the American Society of Criminology, the 2000 W.E.B. DuBois Award for Significant Research on Race and Ethnicity in the Administration of Justice from the Western Society of Criminology, and the 1997 Herbert Block Award for Outstanding Service to the Society and the Profession from the American Society of Criminology.

ADVICE TO STUDENTS

Follow your passion and your heart. Find an issue that matters to you, and delve into it. As you are learning new theories and research methodologies, think about how these conceptual frameworks and tools can help you to more fully address the issue. Finally, stay open to new questions and new approaches, and never give up because something seems too hard, or because you think the question has already been answered adequately.

themselves in sexually unsafe circumstances and participate in the group's sexual activities. The results of their participant observation became the essential research data for their doctoral dissertations. Researching this phenomenon under different circumstances, other investigators may have chosen less direct methods to obtain data, such as interviewing group sex participants and not becoming involved in their activities.

Analysis of Data

Data analysis involves tabulating our information and arranging it into a form that can be interpreted. If we interview probationer-clients, we will need to translate our interview information into useable data. If some probationer-clients have negative reactions to electronic monitoring, we might wish to quote some of their answers to our questions as a way of highlighting these negative reactions. We might also codify the different answers they give to certain questions. Codification means to create categories into which different responses can be placed. Codifying data greatly simplifies our ability to make sense out of whatever we have found.

Suppose we wished to learn more about the amount of attorney involvement in juvenile court cases. Tables and charts can be used to track the percentage of attorney use in juvenile cases over time. We can distinguish between public and private counsel as well. This information can be cross-tabulated with the types of dispositions juveniles receive. Dispositions are tantamount to adult criminal sentences, including probation or jail/prison time. Tabular information can disclose whether leniency toward juvenile offenders varies according to the type of counsel used. We can also examine attorney use trends over time to determine whether the extent of attorney use has actually increased.

Presentation of Findings

Presenting our findings includes tables, **graphs,** figures, and other forms of graphic presentation, including pie charts and bar graphs. These visual effects are supplemented with a more or less extensive discussion of the study highlights. If we have found considerable evidence of a code of silence among police officers, for instance, we can describe it. We can also enrich our discussion with quotations from officers who explain why it is condoned.

If our study was of probationers and the effectiveness of electronic monitoring, we can describe how electronic monitoring is used and whether it is effective, at least for the sample of probationers we have examined. For a juvenile justice study and attorney involvement in juvenile cases, we can describe attorney use trends for various jurisdictions. We can describe which offenses seem more associated with attorney use than others. We can illustrate differential adjudication and disposition decisions, and this information can be compared with attorney involvement or noninvolvement.

The presentation of findings should be a concise portrayal of what the researcher has found. It should be directly relevant to one's original research questions. Readers should be able to examine the presentation of findings and acquire an understanding about what has been found and how it is interpreted. Tentative answers to one's research questions are provided in this section of one's research report.

Conclusions

The final section of any research report consists of one's tentative conclusions. These conclusions are based on one's findings and tabulated results. Conclusions as tentative, subject to further research on the subject. This is because no single study of anything is considered as the final authority on the subject. Because of the cumulative nature of scientific inquiry, investigators will view their own work as simply one additional bit of information that contributes to the growing knowledge about the subject investigated. The study conclusions themselves summarize the major highlights.

Investigators frequently include suggestions for future research that readers of their work can use in their own studies. These suggestions are often the result of unanticipated problems or emerging new questions. No investigator can anticipate every conceivable contingency when a research project is implemented. Every investigation involves the possible omission of certain critical questions from interviews or questionnaires. Perhaps an interviewee says something unusual or unexpected that suggests a new line of inquiry. Since one's questionnaire or **interview guide** cannot usually be revised in the middle of one's study, more research on the topic is often required. Researchers may say to themselves, "I wish I had included that question," or "I wish I had added this or that variable to my questionnaire." These afterthoughts are useful as a source of new ideas for novice researchers. Many graduate students have obtained ideas for their master's theses or doctoral dissertations from these suggestions for future research in various research articles.

Almost every empirical investigation where data are collected and analyzed contains a section where an **interpretation** is made of the research findings. Interpretations of findings are both objective and subjective. Reporting actual factual information and details is an objective disclosure of what the researcher has found. Suppose an investigator has studied the influence of furlough programs on inmate reintegration into the community and has found that 70 percent of all furloughees did not commit any program violations as inmates, and that they remained law-abiding once released into their communities. This means that 30 percent of the furloughees either had program violations or did not remain law-abiding while free in their communities.

The fact of a 70 percent success rate is impressive. Over two-thirds of these offenders were successful. But some investigators consider the 30 percent recidivism or failure rate among furloughees as unimpressive. Thus, researchers who report this information may want to explain why this failure rate occurred and how it can be decreased in the future with different furlough programming. Investigators can speculate about their findings and draw various conclusions. These discussions of findings and the different kinds of interpretations made are often interesting and insightful for readers.

Finally, the conclusions section might contain various implications of a substantive or theoretical nature. **Substantive implications** refer to how the information yielded by the study might be used in some practical way to solve contemporary problems. Perhaps probation departments can modify the use of electronic monitoring and supplement it with house arrest and intensive face-to-face visits by probation officers as a means of reducing client recidivism. Police misconduct might be minimized by different field supervisory practices or modifications in police officer training programs.

Theoretical implications pertain to using study findings for theory-building or devising an alternative approach in studying criminological problems. Perhaps the study of police officers and the code of silence might enhance the sociological phenomena of primary groups and group solidarity. Theoretical implications of one's research are not concerned with practical applications of one's research findings. Rather, theoretical implications either reinforce existing theoretical schemes or explanations of social events or fail to reinforce them. Can these findings be generalized to a theory of decision making in police organizations? Ultimately, however, theorizing about decision making or primary groups or group solidarity will be grounded in actual research settings. One or more solutions to practical problems in different organizations might be suggested from theories generated from and modified by criminological research. Thus, there is some amount of complementarity between theory and research.

The final report is a brief summarization of the study highlights and major findings. The investigator often recapitulates the study objectives, how the study was conducted, and what were the final results and their significance. The final report may contain several theoretical and substantive implications for further research. Theoretical implications of the research have to do with how the research illustrates and/or tests existing theory about the subject matter. Substantive implications relate to the practical applications of the research for practitioners.

For instance, Robert J. Beck (1997) investigated teen courts or peer courts used in different jurisdictions to hear and decide minor juvenile cases. Peer courts consist of juries of one's peers or school mates who hear cases against the accused juvenile, decide guilt or innocence, and recommend punishments. Beck believed that peer courts would be powerful sanctioning bodies against first-offender juveniles who would know that a jury of their peers disapproved of their offending. Thus, there was a good chance that teen courts would exert a deterrent effect on future delinquent behavior. This was the substantive or applied research component of Beck's study. The theoretical component involved a test of ecological development theory. This theory suggests that youths who undergo severe, traumatic, or stressful transition in their lives (e.g., becoming "offenders") actually undergo a change of role. In this transitional mode, many juvenile offenders are highly susceptible to change toward law-abiding behavior, especially when punishment is imposed by one's peers. In the actual study, Beck found modest support for teen courts as sanctioning mechanisms and delinquency deterrence. His findings relative to the ecological development theory were inconclusive. In a final section entitled "Implications of the Research," Beck encouraged further investigation to determine which of several teen court program components were most effective and predictive of nonrecidivism. Those interested in pursuing this research further will find this section of particular interest.

Mark Jones's Study of Boot Camp Graduates.   Mark Jones, a professor at East Carolina University, investigated whether boot camps are instrumental in fostering greater compliance with juvenile probation program requirements (Jones, 1996). Jones was interested in youthful offenders and factors influencing their recidivism rates while on probation. He focused on the boot camp as a promising intervention for youthful offenders in need of discipline and self-control. Boot camps are short-term (6-month) interventions involving military drill and ceremony, physical training, physical discipline, hard physical labor, and education. Boot camps are aimed at youthful offenders. Specifically, Jones wanted to know whether juveniles who were exposed to boot camp training would have better success rates in their subsequent probation programs compared with juvenile probationers who did not have boot camp training.

Jones began his study by reviewing the literature about boot camps. He discussed various studies of boot camps, the types of youthful clientele involved in boot camp training, and the different success rates as measured by various types of recidivism. Jones raised two pointed questions: (1) How do boot camp graduates perform compared with other juvenile offenders, when both types of offenders are placed in the same aftercare programs for approximately the same time periods? and (2) What variables correlate with success or failure among boot camp graduates and their non–boot camp counterparts in those aftercare programs?

Jones studied 307 juvenile delinquents in the Harris County, Texas Court Regimented Intensive Probation Program (CRIPP). Fifty-six of these delinquents were placed in the Harris County boot camp program. The remainder of the juveniles were placed in CRIPP. When the boot camp clients graduated, they were placed in CRIPP as well and their progress was charted and compared with the non–boot camp CRIPP clients. Jones's expectation was that the boot camp participants and graduates would have significantly lower recidivism rates at the end of the CRIPP compared with those juveniles not exposed to the boot camp program.

Jones's results were disappointing. First, Jones reported that only 59 percent of the original boot camp participants actually graduated from the boot camp. Of those that graduated, there was a recidivism rate of 59 percent when these graduates were combined with the other delinquents in CRIPP. The recidivism rate for non–boot camp participants was also high, about 60 percent. Therefore, the boot camp program did not have the desired effect of substantially reducing recidivism among the targeted juveniles.

Jones explored alternative explanations for what he found. First, the sample size of boot camp participants in his study, 56, was not particularly large. Furthermore, when he separated the boot camp graduates from nongraduates, the sample dropped to 33 participants. We can only speculate what Jones would have found if a larger sample of juveniles had been used. What if he had observed the influence of the boot camp on 500 juveniles instead of 33? We won't know the answer to this question unless and until another study is conducted of boot camp effectiveness on juvenile delinquent recidivism. The next study may or may not be conducted by Jones.

When Jones wrote the "Implications" section of his article, he said that while boot camps are not necessarily effective as deterrents to further juvenile recidivism, they are considered as a significant punishment. Thus, boot camps may be perceived by the general public as a suitable punishment for youthful offenders, despite the lack of promise shown for deterring delinquency, at least in the sample Jones studied. Finally, Jones noted that boot camps in other jurisdictions may be more effective as deterrents to delinquency. Some boot camps are operated for longer periods than the Harris County program. Perhaps the length of program is a crucial factor in promoting change among youthful offenders. Such speculation is both normal and essential in any research report. Some readers may be stimulated by the "what if's" of such speculation and conduct investigations of their own to answer specific **research questions.**

What if Jones had found that his boot camp **respondents** had a recidivism rate of only 10 percent? This would have met a success rate of 90 percent. What could Jones have concluded with that finding? Relatively little. First, we must return to the matter of the sample size Jones used. Thirty-three juveniles participating in a boot camp program is considered a small sample. Further studies are needed, with both larger and more diverse samples in other jurisdictions, before we can make sweeping conclusions about boot camps generally. In the present case, Jones would have been limited to stating that at least in his study, boot camp participants seemed responsive to the boot camp intervention or that the boot camp seemed to decrease recidivism among juvenile probationers.

Depending on the subject matter of one's study and the extensiveness of it, the research enterprise is a more or less elaborate plan we use for answering questions of interest to us. This plan will vary in complexity and sophistication. For instance, if Jones had studied 20 boot camps in various states over a 2-year interval, his sample size would be much larger than 33. His findings would have more general appeal, since greater numbers of boot camp participants would be involved. However, we should not be swayed by large numbers alone. It is entirely possible that a more large-scale study of boot camp effectiveness on juvenile recidivism rates would yield findings similar to those in Jones' original study.

In Jones's study, he studied these juveniles directly and tracked them over time. In other research, investigators may mail questionnaires to study participants with requests to answer questions and mail questionnaires back to the researchers. These **mailed questionnaires** enable researchers to accumulate a large amount of information about persons rather quickly. For some types of research, we may need to participate in the activities of those we observe. Some research may involve an **interview,** where respondents are contacted directly by researchers and asked questions through a **face-to-face questionnaire administration.** Some problems studied by researchers may not be easily investigated by mailing questionnaires or conducting interviews. If we want to know whether the **crime rate** is increasing faster than the rate of normal population growth in the United States, then an analysis of public documents compiled by the FBI, U.S. Department of Justice, and U.S. Bureau of the Census may be necessary. In such investigations, it is unlikely that others will have to be contacted directly for information about these research questions.

Some investigators spend several decades compiling information about problems they have selected for study in **longitudinal research.** For instance, Wolfgang (Wolfgang, Figlio, & Sellin, 1972) studied a large Philadelphia **birth cohort,** nearly 10,000 boys born in Philadelphia in 1945, and tracked them through official records until 1963. Among other things, Wolfgang wanted to describe the characteristics and behavioral patterns of chronic recidivists, or persistent juvenile offenders. In 1975, he conducted a further analysis of a sample of these persons at age 30 to see how many committed crimes as adults and became career criminals (Wolfgang, 1983). For comparative purposes, Wolfgang selected a much larger birth **cohort** of over 28,000 boys and girls born in 1958 and tracked them through official records for a similar 18-year period.

Wolfgang's research, regarded as classics by many criminologists, revealed that (1) a small core of offenders, approximately 6 or 7 percent, accounted for over 60 percent of all crimes committed by the 1945 cohort, and (2) the 1958 cohort had a violent offense rate almost three times as large as the 1945 cohort. Wolfgang speculated that successive generations of juveniles were committing increasingly violent offenses compared with earlier generations. Despite the magnitude of Wolfgang's analysis and the large samples studied, these investigators never regarded their findings as conclusive about chronic offender behavior patterns and characteristics. Nevertheless, it is noteworthy that Wolfgang spent over 30 years patiently investigating this phenomenon. This type of study, longitudinal research, is very laborious, because it spans a fairly lengthy time period and involves tracking the same sample at different time intervals.

Beginning students should recognize that generally, the pace of research is slow. Some topics, such as job burnout among probation and parole officers, are not investigated frequently, while other topics, such as the causes of delinquency, are investigated often. Therefore, research information in different topic areas accumulates at an uneven rate.

Pure and Applied Research

Research may also be pure, applied, or both. **Pure research** is often more difficult for students to understand and appreciate, because it may have intuitive relevance only for those investigators who do such research. It doesn't excite everyone to know that reported crime in the United States increased at a higher rate during the 1990s compared with general population growth. But for radical, critical, or Marxist criminologists, crime rate fluctuations may enable them to draw parallels between crime and changing political, economic, and social conditions. It doesn't always matter that the terms used to describe crime in relation to politics, social, and economic conditions are diffuse or intangible. Consider the following:

> "Capitalist interests have perpetuated an exploitative system wherein the rich dominate the poor. Laws are the manipulative tools of the capitalist class, and state repression of working class interests is evident in the differential punishments society imposes for street crimes compared with antitrust or white-collar crime."

It would be difficult to know where to begin in order to test these statements. Who comprises the capitalist class or the working class? What are capitalist interests? The intent here is not to malign pure research or radical criminology, but rather, to illustrate its diffuseness compared with applied research. Pure research is undertaken often simply for the sake of knowing. "Knowledge for the sake of knowledge" underscores what motivates many pure researchers. When you ask such persons what can be done of a practical nature with the research they have conducted, they may or may not be able to tell you. Questions about the practical aspects of what they do are often considered irrelevant.

Applied research or **basic research** is research undertaken mostly for practical reasons. Mark Jones's study of boot camp effectiveness had an applied aspect. One practical outcome was knowing whether boot camps were effective as interventions in reducing juvenile recidivism and improving program success among juvenile probationers. If Jones's results had been more impressive, then perhaps public policy could be affected in terms of allocations of funds to various jurisdictions to reduce delinquency and probationer recidivism. If the cost of boot camp operation and delinquency deterrence were effective, then boot camps would be used on a large-scale basis in many jurisdictions as a means of preventing future criminality.

Pure and applied research can also be distinguished by the influence of such research on various community programs and public policies. Investigations of probation officer job burnout and dissatisfaction may change how administrators in probation agencies supervise their officers and assign them duties. Studies of peer group influence on juvenile delinquency may help to establish intervention programs where delinquent peers are used to "un-do" delinquent behaviors through self-study and individual counseling (Empey & Erickson, 1972).

Research may be both pure and applied simultaneously. Studies of judicial discretion in sentencing offenders may show sentencing disparities that are explained by race, ethnicity, gender, or socioeconomic status. Radical or critical criminologists may investigate sentencing patterns in different jurisdictions and find these disparities. Their work may show support for the influence of social class on the criminal justice system (a pure research objective), but it may also lead to sentencing reforms to remedy sentencing disparities because of race, gender, or social class, such as a shift from indeterminate to presumptive sentencing (an applied research objective).

Some Basic Assumptions about Criminal Justice and Criminology

All scientific inquiry is based upon several important assumptions. These assumptions relate to **prediction,** to the predictability and regularity of any relation between two or more variables. A high degree of predictability and regularity among variables exists in the field of chemistry, for instance. Particular combinations of certain chemicals have regular, recurring, and predictable outcomes or reactions that can be forecast accurately in advance of their combination. Such predictability and regularity are more apparent among variables associated with the hard sciences (chemistry, biology, physics, engineering), where the controlled variables are tangible (e.g., temperature, dimensions, mass, energy). Their interrelations with other variables, as well as environment factors, are heavily controlled. Interactions of measured amounts of different chemicals under certain temperatures for designated time periods reflect the high degree of variable control achieved by chemistry, for example. But people are not chemicals and cannot be studied under such controlled conditions.

In criminology and criminal justice, for example, many of the variables studied, such as attitudes, ideas, and opinions, are less tangible than chemicals. Therefore, the presence or absence of these social and psychological variables must be inferred largely from other, usually indirect indicators. Attitudinal phenomena are not immediately apparent through observation, although the influence of attitudes or an assessment of their existence can be made by constructing various attitudinal scaling devices.

But because certain social and/or psychological variables are more difficult to study than chemical variables, this does not automatically exclude them from scientific investigation. Rather, it means that social scientists must make extraordinary efforts to measure these more elusive phenomena as behavioral predictors. Criminologists must devise indirect indicators of attitudinal variables in order to assess their effects on behaviors. Attitudes cannot be seen, but their presence may be inferred from how persons behave or respond to questions about their feelings and thoughts. Thus, attitudinal measures require a high degree of empirical proof of their accuracy and consistency. This is a major reason why we spend so much time studying the validity (accuracy) and reliability (consistency) of our measures of phenomena, which are more difficult to observe.

Research in criminal justice and criminology involves the use of **science** and attempts to explain and predict relations between variables. What is the influence of diet on crimi-

BOX 1.2   PERSONALITY HIGHLIGHT

FREDA ADLER
Rutgers University

Statistics: B.A. (sociology), University of Pennsylvania; M.A. (criminology), University of Pennsylvania; Ph.D. (sociology), University of Pennsylvania.

BACKGROUND AND INTERESTS

There are two ways of dealing with an agenda: you write it, or you follow it. In my four decades as a criminologist, I have done both (but you will soon learn which I prefer). When I entered the field of criminology, I found a ready-made agenda. It centered on the development of theories of criminal behavior. A number of theories had been well developed. Few had been tested and validated. Looking deeper into the field, I was also astounded by the number of criminological areas that had not been subjected to scientific inquiry. Consequently, the next question was "Why?" And that led to the question of who had developed the theory—and who had been excluded from the development? It turned out that crime victims had not participated in theory development. Nor had perpetrators. Nor had those without an academic degree. Nor had women.

Agenda Item 1: Women? Let us return to my first sentence. There are two ways of dealing with an agenda: you write it, or you follow it. Women were precisely those people who were not allowed to write the agenda—they were to follow it, with a few exceptions to the contrary notwithstanding: historically, Cleopatra, Eleanor of Aquitaine (Queen of England and Queen of France), Mme. Curie, and, more recently, our own scientist, Eleanor Glueck.

A young criminologist, as I was in the 1960s, has to choose: follow the traditional agenda, or write a new one. Of course, it is presumptuous for a freshly minted PhD to attempt to turn the established agenda upside down. But it did not seem presumptuous to me to search for the lacunae in the existence of the prevailing agenda. (It was, after all, the 1960s, when women began to think about assertion of equal rights in all fields, including academia.)

And thus began my quest. My first research focus was on women offenders. *Sisters in Crime,* a book arising out of my PhD dissertation, "discovered" that half (or more) of the human population had been ignored in criminology theory-building and empirical research (with the exception of the early work of Lombroso and Pollack). As those in our discipline know, the book stirred controversies far beyond expectation. Inasmuch as I saw a relation between the role of women in contemporary life and their participation in criminal activity, my adversaries charged me with wanting to confine women to the kitchen, the church, and to child-rearing. Nothing was further from my mind. My hypothesis simply amounted to saying that as

BOX 1.2   CONTINUED

social and economic roles of women changed in the legitimate world, their participation in crime would also change. Equalization of roles would lead to similar behavior patterns, both legal and illegal, on the part of both men and women. In other words, why not test opportunity theory on males *and* females?

Agenda Item 2: Theories of criminality, as well as ways of dealing with various forms of criminality, had developed over the years, and they have been developing at increasing rates. What I did not see in the existing guide was a reasonable scientific effort to determine whether criminological theories and the criminal justice system responses thereto were related. An opportunity to do such research arose when I became a member of a team that was evaluating drug treatment programs in an effort to determine whether the millions of dollars spent on treatment programs were having a beneficial effect or, to put it scientifically, whether theories on which the programs were designed were scientifically sound. In the 1970s, comparing programs with outcome data (e.g., length of time addicts remained drug-free upon release) was a novel approach. Research methods for evaluation research have since become more sophisticated and in most cases have to be built into newly funded programs.

Agenda Item 3: the next major lacuna in criminological research and theory that virtually leaped out at me was the fact that almost all criminological problems studied empirically and theoretically were confined to the United States—as if our own experience, that of 5 percent of the world's population, could determine answers to crime problems worldwide. My association with the United Nations was instrumental in pushing me to look beyond our borders for both questions and answers related to criminological problems. In a report for the United Nations Congress on the Role of Women, I could demonstrate that in the United States and among other countries, women were underutilized in efforts to deal with the crime problem, very much to the detriment of those countries. My next major assignment for the United Nations was to identify the countries in the world with the lowest crime rates and to find out why they had lower crime rates than other nations within their own region, including their immediate neighbors.

This was a methodologically demanding assignment. Comparisons using 47 socioeconomic and demographic indicators (predictor variables) such as gross national product, infant mortality, income, number of telephones, and density of population could not be done. It became clear that, given the serious flaws and gaps in the data sets, we could not design our study using available statistical data. We went back to the drawing board and designed a qualitative case study approach. A small team went to the 10 subject countries (including Saudi Arabia, Costa Rica, Bulgaria, Japan, Peru, Nepal, the Republic of Ireland, Switzerland, the former East Germany, and Algeria) where we lived with local people in their homes, farms, desert tents, and skyscrapers; worked with functionaries in their criminal justice systems, and met in their places of assembly, factories, and schools. While these 10 countries ranged from monarchies to republics, from dictatorships to democracies, from rural to urban, from wealthy to poor, they all had one thing in common: each had developed its own system of sharing and perpetuating norms. I called this phenomenon "synnomie" (a word that I created to designate the opposite of Emile Durkheim's *anomie*). My book, *Nations Not Obsessed with Crime*, details this project.

BOX 1.2   CONTINUED

Agenda Item 4: While there are many criminological theories in existence, there are too few scientists in our discipline examining the relationship among theories. To make a 10-year saga short, after much reading, contemplation, and analyzing of the study of the low-crime countries, it appears to me that each of these theories explains crime causation, but only at a given point in social evolution. Hence, I have developed my synnomie-to-anomie paradigm, which integrates extant criminological theories to explain rising crime and its relationship to social development—a good place to begin cross-cultural research.

Agenda Item 5: If you think about it, what is criminology all about? It is concerned with the crimes on only 29 percent of the earth's surface. No wonder, then, that I would next turn to criminality on the high seas, as reflected in the book *Outlaws of the Ocean* (coauthored with G.O.W. Mueller).

Agenda Item 6: Close to 10 percent of the world's land mass is represented by the Antarctic continent. There are no permanent residents there. And so does this mean that there is no crime? We decided to find out! And guess what? Antarctica is of immense criminological significance—for the survival of humankind. The study is in progress.

ADVICE TO STUDENTS

The author of your text has asked me to conclude with a bit of advice to students of criminology and criminal justice. But then, I think my advice lies within the narrative just presented. In sum: Do not take anyone else's agenda as definitive and given. Look for the gaps. Develop your own agenda. There is no such thing as criminology without frontiers—frontiers yet to be discovered, yet to be traversed. Enjoy it!

---

nality? Do convicted black offenders receive harsher sentences compared with convicted white offenders? What barriers slow the influx of women into correctional officer and probation/parole officer work roles? How do our perceptions of powerlessness influence our adaptability to our jobs? What factors reduce stress and burnout? Is there a rise in female delinquency, and if so, why? Are successive generations of delinquents more violent than previous generations of delinquents? Can criminals be rehabilitated? If so, what intervention strategies seem to work best for purposes of rehabilitation? These questions require considerable research in order for conclusive answers to be provided. Before undertaking any investigation of relations between these and other variables, several assumptions are made by criminologists and criminal justice professionals. These assumptions are not unique to criminology or criminal justice. Rather, they extend to all types of **scientific inquiry.** Some of these assumptions are as follows:

1. A pattern exists among certain variables of interest to criminologists. This assumption is generally accepted by those conducting criminological research. If we do not believe that there is a pattern associated with certain variable interrelationships, then prediction, forecasting, and regularity cannot be assumed. This means that relations between sentence length and socioeconomic status, between probation officer turnover and burnout and stress, between police cynicism and effectiveness of community-oriented policing, between family stability and delinquency, and between police use of force and public perceptions of police effectiveness are random. Few of us believe that these and similar variable interrelations are purely random.

2. Patterns of variable interrelationships can be described and used as the bases for hypothesis tests. This assumption stems from the first. It coincides with the empirical nature of criminological phenomena. It means that we can use the identifiable patterns of interrelationships between variables for the purpose of testing our theories about these variables.

3. A **causal relation** exists between certain criminological variables. While we are interested in establishing **causality** or cause–effect relations among the variables we study, it is also true that causal relations between phenomena are difficult to establish. Nevertheless, a major aim of criminologists is to determine which variables cause other variables to occur and to describe these causal relationships. For example, if we believe that judges discriminate in the sentences they impose on convicted offenders according to their race or ethnicity, and if minority offenders draw longer and harsher sentences compared with nonminority offenders where both have been convicted of essentially the same crimes, then these sentencing disparities can be minimized or eliminated entirely by restricting judicial sentencing discretion. Restricting judicial sentencing discretion may be accomplished by modifying existing sentencing structures to a guidelines-based scheme, where judges must impose sentences within certain ranges for different crimes if offenders are convicted of these crimes. While other variables may be manipulated to invoke the desired response or outcome, such as greater fairness in sentencing, the fact is that we can sometimes effect changes in one variable by manipulating other variables that are causally related to it.

4. Relevant variables for criminal justice professionals and criminologists are **empirical** and amenable to measurement. Empirical means to be amenable to our senses in some way. Some social and psychological variables are more easily measured than others. For instance, if we study the influence of peer groups on delinquency, for example, this means that we must devise a measure of peer group influence. **Definitions** of delinquency are already standardized among jurisdictions to a high degree. Thus, delinquency is easily conceptualized (e.g., delinquent or nondelinquent), although peer group influence is more difficult to quantify.

5. Inconsistencies inevitably exist among studies of the same phenomena, although these inconsistencies do not mean necessarily that no association between these phenomena exists. Fictitious researchers Peterson and Phillips might find, for instance, that criminal behavior tends to decline with advanced age in their study of inmates. However, fictitious investigators O'Rourke and Finnegan may find that the incidence of crime among the elderly in Florida is increasing annually. How should we regard the relation between age and criminal behavior? Apparent contradictory findings such as these reported by our researchers, Peterson and Phillips and O'Rourke and Finnegan, should not discourage us from pursuing our own similar research interests enthusiastically. After all, there are different jurisdictions involved, different samples of criminals investigated, different types of crime examined, and a myriad of other factors that can explain away these inconsistencies. Thus, research is cumulative, and through repetition, **replication,** and **replication research,** our knowledge about variable interrelations is greatly enhanced. Eventually, we discover general, consistent patterns of relations between variables, although these patterns may exhibit occasional inconsistencies.

These are just a handful of the many **assumptions** made about our fields of inquiry. Criminology and criminal justice offer a wealth of interesting information for research. Investigators are limited only by their imaginations about what can be studied and how. Subsequently, we will examine more closely the notions of theory, frames of reference, variables, and hypotheses, and how each of these relates to the research process.

Why do Research?

Some of the major reasons for conducting criminological research include: (1) acquiring knowledge for the sake of knowledge; (2) determining answers to practical questions; (3) adding to the growing body of knowledge in the profession; and (4) acquiring useful knowledge and skills to transmit this information to others and direct their investigations.

1. Some people are interested in simply knowing about things. The "knowledge for the sake of knowledge" approach is typical of pure research. The objective is to acquire more knowledge about the complexities of interrelations between variables, not to solve current social problems.

2. Many practitioners seek answers to practical questions. Regardless of their rightness or wrongness, decisions are made about public policy or program components. For example, research investigations of judicial sentencing patterns in certain jurisdictions have disclosed evidence of sentencing disparities. While these disparities may not be overt, it is strongly implied by researchers that subtle, yet significant disparities exist. Thus, state legislatures may seek to correct these disparities by modifying their state sentencing systems. This is not intended to mean that all judges are biased or deliberately sentence offenders of different genders or races to different incarcerative terms, despite their offense similarities. Rather, legislatures may wish to take preventive action to eliminate possible allegations or the appearance of judicial favoritism or wrongdoing.

3. Many researchers want to add to the growing body of knowledge in each criminological or criminal justice topic area. Whether we are interested in the relation between age and crime or offense escalation among juveniles arrested for status offenses, our knowledge of these and other topics is enhanced through objective research that is conducted. Any profession is noted for a body of grounded literature pertaining to specific subject areas. More research conducted on specific topics can do much to enhance the body of literature about the topic so that other researchers may benefit from it.

4. Researchers wish to understand the work reported by other investigators and how such work relates to their professional interests. Students entering criminology or criminal justice will carve out an interest area or area of specialization. They will read research reported in various professional journals and trade publications, and it is in their best interests to acquire extensive knowledge of the work of others. If they should eventually teach subjects reflecting their areas of specialization, their previously acquired information will be an invaluable resource from which to draw examples and illustrations. They will be more capable of directing the research of students to seek to conduct their own investigations of topics of interest to them.

The Emergence of Science and Criminal Justice

Criminology and criminal justice are social sciences. Criminology is the study of crime, the science of crime and criminal behavior, the forms of criminal behavior, the causes of crime, the definition of criminality, and the societal reaction to crime. It is an empirical social-behavioral science that investigates crime and criminals. Criminal justice is an interdisciplinary social science studying the nature and operations of organizations providing justice services to society. As academic disciplines, they are considered products of sociology, a key social science. Sociology is a relatively young discipline, where the first national organization, the American Sociological Association, was founded in the 1890s. Prior to such formal organization, independent researchers, both sociologists and criminologists, worked to explain various forms of criminality and deviance. August Comte (France), Herbert Spencer (England), Cesare Lombroso (Italy), Cesare Beccaria (Italy), Emile Durkheim (France), and many of their contemporaries were prolific writers and analysts during the 1800s. Much of their writing formed the foundations of social science and criminology as we know these fields today.

Criminal justice was spawned by criminologists and sociologists in the 1960s. The Law Enforcement Assistance Administration (LEAA) was created by the President's Crime Commission in 1968. The LEAA was designed to provide resources, leadership, and coordination to state and local law enforcement agencies to prevent and/or reduce adult crime and juvenile delinquency. Millions of dollars were allocated to researchers and police departments over the next decade for various purposes. Departments of Criminal Justice were established in hundreds of colleges and universities during this same period. In 2005 there were over 30 Departments of Criminal Justice offering PhD degrees, and over 150 departments offering master's degrees. The major national organization for criminal justice, the Academy of Criminal Justice Sciences (ACJS), was founded in 1963. The American Society of Criminology (ASC), the primary national organization for criminologists, was founded in 1948. Most persons interested in crime and delinquency belong to both organizations, where their respective membership lists correlate at least 75 percent.

Members of both the ASC and ACJS consider themselves to be scientists. Science is a way of knowing about things, and it articulates strict guidelines for its users to follow. Science as a method of knowing about things embraces four fundamental elements:

1. Science is **empirical.** As criminologists, we study what is amenable to our senses or whatever is tangible. If we study attitudes or psychological factors that are not directly observable, these phenomena are eventually made observable through the construction of various indirect measures. Questionnaires and observation are indirect ways of investigating phenomena that are not directly observable, such as peer group influence, burnout, stress, or police cynicism. Observable phenomena, such as criminal activity, delinquency, race/ethnicity, age, gender, and socioeconomic status, easily fall within the scope of criminologists and criminal justicians.

2. Science is cumulative. This means that the information about any given phenomenon we study accumulates over time. The research conducted by different investigators is cumulative, in that it builds until there are obvious trends and characteristics that can be described. Journal articles contain research about a wide variety of topics. Reviews of the literature are indicative of the cumulative nature of criminology and criminal justice as scientific disciplines.

3. Science is nonethical. Whenever criminological investigations are undertaken, researchers are supposed to be neutral in their inquiry. They may observe findings that are different from or in conflict with what they expected to find. Because they are using science, they are encouraged to set aside their values and personal beliefs to the extent that they can objectively assess whatever is yielded from their scientific inquiry.

4. Science is theoretical. There is a pervasive theoretical basis underlying all social scientific research. Theory explains and predicts relations between different phenomena studied. Theory ties together different ideas and enables investigators to generalize their findings to larger populations and settings.

The Probability Nature of Science

The general public has a limited understanding of what science is. Scientific facts are presented daily about diverse subjects. Scientific factual information is often accepted as true in an absolute sense, without question. However, scientists themselves in every field admonish everyone to consider their information as tentative, subject to further evidence and confirmation. As we will soon see, tentativeness is a key word in any type of scientific investigation or inquiry.

In the 1960s the Surgeon General of the United States produced a document indicating that cigarette smoking was hazardous to one's health. A link between various forms of cancer and cigarette smoking was implied. An analysis of hundreds of studies of smoking and health was conducted. An impressive panel of statisticians and health experts reviewed past research and reanalyzed investigations. The Surgeon General's report was based on the tentative conclusions from these reports. The tobacco companies and most smokers took issue with the Surgeon General and countered with their own evidence showing cigarette smoking to be safe and not a cause of cancer.

Seven years would lapse before cigarette companies would be forced to place warnings on cigarette products and packages. The first warning read, "Cigarette smoking *may be* hazardous to your health" (italics mine). Several years later, other warnings would include the word *is*. "Cigarette smoking *is* hazardous to your health" (italics mine). Of course, by 2005, tobacco companies had already settled multibillion-dollar lawsuits with most states and private citizens, where tobacco has been causally linked with cancer and millions of deaths have resulted because of cigarette smoking. All public buildings in the United

States are smoke-free, and increasing numbers of private establishments are prohibiting smoking because of the high risk of cancer from secondhand smoke. Who would have predicted this outcome?

The point is that scientists originally studied cigarette smoking and its association with cancer. Early research was tentative. Later research was tentative. At least 70 years of research eventually led to a general policy change regarding tobacco consumption and the enactment of laws and legislation prohibiting smoking in public buildings and conveyances, such as buses, airplanes, and trains. In retrospect, we can say that the process of changing public attitudes about smoking was clearly sluggish. Like a movie in slow motion, we can review the pace of change in smoking policy over time. More than a few citizens today say, "Why did it take so long? Why didn't lawmakers and the public accept the scientific findings that were presented as facts and make policy changes in the 1960s? Wouldn't these changes have saved hundreds of thousands of lives?" Unfortunately, we cannot predict the future with certainty. We can only look back at historical events that have already transpired. Armed with this information, it is easy for us to say what should have been done earlier.

If it took so long for policy changes to occur with such heavily researched subjects as cigarette smoking and cancer, we can better understand why less heavily researched subjects, such as juvenile delinquency intervention programs, community policing programs, diversion programs, intensive supervised probation programs, electronic monitoring and home confinement programs, and victim–offender reconciliation programs are not easily sold to the public and adopted on large-scale bases. It takes considerable time and experimentation before we accept a particular explanation for or solution to a problem.

When any scientific project is undertaken and scientific findings are presented, these findings are *always* presented in a tentative context. Scientists do not say with certainty, "We have proved this or that." Rather, scientists say, "We have provided support for this or that idea or solution." This tentativeness and caution is very much justified. This is because all scientific inquiry is couched in the context of **probability.**

Every study of any phenomenon where science is used is considered a single incident or test or **experiment.** It takes numerous studies by many investigators to establish the sort of consistency we require to believe that a cause–effect relation exists between variables. The tobacco–cancer relation is a lesson for all of us. What about Mark Jones's study of boot camps and the overall effectiveness of boot camps for reducing juvenile probationer recidivism mentioned earlier? Jones's study was only one study. If we examine the literature and count the number of articles about boot camps generally, in 2004 there were 180 studies of boot camps reported by the popular abstracting service, *Criminal Justice Abstracts.* This compares with 125 studies of boot camps that were found in the abstracts in 1999. The research on boot camps is growing. There were 58 studies of boot camps where juveniles were studied. This is twice the number of juvenile boot camp studies found in the abstracts in 1999. Again, the literature in this area is growing steadily. How many more studies ought to be conducted before we can acquire a high level of certainty about boot camps and juvenile probationer recidivism as we have with tobacco and cancer? How long do you think it would take for these studies to be conducted, summarized, and reported? No one is willing to step forward and say "100 studies is sufficient" or "200 studies is sufficient." This is because absolute certainty about variable interrelationships is likely an unattainable goal. However, our knowledge about particular subjects increases steadily. Our predictive power improves with each study conducted as well, although perfection in social and psycholog-ical prediction is beyond our immediate grasp.

Science also uses **probability theory** when evaluating research findings. Whenever scientific findings are reported, there is usually a probability accompanying these reports of findings. For instance, "Smith and Anderson found a strong likelihood that an association exists between job stress and probation officer turnover in an Illinois probation agency." Virtually *every* scientific finding has a probability attached. It is not an absolute certainty that job stress and probation officer turnover are always related in every probation agency in the United States. The reported scientific finding pertained only to the Illinois agency and the sample of probation officers who were studied. Other contrary findings may be gen-erated if we were to study probation officer labor turnover and job stress in several other ju-risdictions, such as California or Michigan.

Returning to our original elements of scientific inquiry, science is empirical. Science is theoretical. Science is nonethical. And to the extent that research must be replicated and repeated numerous times before we can achieve certainty about events and associations be-tween variables, science is also cumulative. Previous knowledge or information about vari-ables and subjects is cumulative and builds upon itself. A virtual mountain of evidence, or scientific findings, is necessary to establish causality between variables. This is the proba-bility nature of science.

Objectivity in Scientific Research

Here is what I believe, what I *strongly* believe, about plea bargaining. I believe that plea bar-gaining gets criminals greater sentencing leniency than if they were to go to trial and get con-victed and sentenced for the same crime. I really believe this. For example, I believe that if you are a criminal, Joe Jones, charged with armed robbery and the police have a great deal of evidence against you, you should have your lawyer, Mike Smith, work with the prose-cutor, Phil Anderson, to cut a deal or plea bargain where you enter a guilty plea to the armed robbery charge and accept whatever Phil suggests as a punishment. Because I believe that if Joe is stubborn and insists on his legal right to a trial by jury, he will be found guilty and the judge will sock it to him and impose a very hefty prison term. Suppose Phil says, "Lis-ten, Mike, we have a clear-cut case against your client, Joe. He was caught in the act of rob-bing a bank. We've got bank videotapes showing Joe holding a weapon, taking the money, menacing customers. If Joe will plead guilty to armed robbery, I'll recommend a sentence of 5 years. If Joe fights this in court, he'll be convicted and the judge will probably slap him with 20 years in prison, minimum, maybe even 40 years! Take it or leave it." Mike discusses the plea with Joe, and while Joe doesn't want to go to prison, he would rather do 5 years than 20–40 years. Joe accepts the plea bargain, the judge approves, and Joe gets 5 years. This is what I believe. A criminal defendant will do much better and receive greater leniency through plea bargaining compared with going to trial and taking his or her chances with the judge.

Now, suppose I study thousands of cases in Wisconsin and New York and find that there are only slight differences in outcomes where criminals plead guilty to various crimes and the sentences they receive through plea bargaining or trial. This evidence I have found is defi-nitely contrary to what I would expect to find and what I personally believe to be true. I have a dilemma of sorts. I have just written a nice introduction to a research article where I have argued persuasively that plea bargaining results in greater leniency for criminals compared with punishments resulting from jury trial convictions. I have quoted from various articles that support what I believe to be true, that plea bargaining results in greater leniency for criminals than jury trial outcomes. But my research findings say otherwise. How should I resolve my dilemma?

As a scientist, no matter what I believe otherwise, I must report what I have found. In this instance, at least, I found that there is no difference in sentencing between those who plead guilty through plea bargaining and those who are found guilty and are sentenced as the result of jury trials. This is the objectivity required of me as a social scientist when I conduct research. I conduct my research not especially to advance my own agenda about what I believe to be true, but rather to investigate and report my findings.

The more sensitive the topic, the more important it is to be objective about what one finds. Suppose you are against the privatization of prisons. Some reasons for this are that you think it is morally wrong to profit from private prison inmate incarcerations. You think that privatization might eventually lead to a proliferation of prisons to the extent that anyone who commits a crime may be locked up, whether they should be incarcerated. On a moral level, at least, you oppose prison privatization. You probably conduct correctional privatization opinion research. You collect survey information from thousands of citizens and ask them whether they are for or against prison privatization. Seventy-five percent of them report that they are for privatization. This disappoints you because you are against privatization. But you are also a social scientist. You report what you have found.

Scientific inquiry isn't about what we like and dislike or the views about events that we oppose or favor. Science demands that we use objectivity at every stage of our investigation. Further study is needed before we can make conclusions about events with certainty. We must maintain a posture of scientific neutrality, at least in our **data collection,** analysis, interpretation, results, and implications of the research we conduct.

Returning to my beliefs about plea bargaining and sentencing, I can present my findings and then speculate at length in the "Implications" or "Discussion" section of my research report. I might point out that Wisconsin and New York may not be typical of other states. I might say that the sample of cases I chose to analyze may not be typical of the average case in other criminal jurisdictions. I might conjecture at length and speculate about a dozen problems with my study that may have led to my findings. All of this might make me feel better about why I didn't find what I expected to find. But I did my duty as a scientist and reported the findings as they occurred, despite the fact that they didn't agree with my personal feelings. This is as it should be.

Functions of Research

Research methods and statistics as applied to criminal justice and criminology fulfill several important functions. These functions are (1) exploratory, (2) descriptive, and (3) experimental.

Exploratory Functions

In some areas of criminology and criminal justice, little is known about observed events. Why do serial murderers kill? Why do spouses abuse each other and their children? What types of policing are best for particular neighborhoods or communities? What influence does the gender of criminal defendants have on juries comprised of the opposite gender? Are older judges more lenient in sentencing older offenders compared with younger judges? While some research exists to provide partial answers to these and other questions, few answers are presently available that adequately account for them.

For instance, a correctional innovation introduced on a limited scale in recent years is global satellite tracking of the movements of probationers and parolees in jurisdictions such as Florida (Mercer, Brooks, & Bryant, 2000). Many legal, moral, and ethical questions have arisen about the use of satellite tracking of offenders and its subsequent application for managing larger offender populations. While preliminary reports have been completed about the cost of using these systems in various jurisdictions, there are still unanswered questions about the technological implications of satellite tracking of offenders and the logistical problems to be solved if such equipment is to be used on a large scale. Therefore, exploratory studies are being undertaken to answer some of these questions.

Exploratory research identifies factors that seem to have more relevance than others for explaining things. Exploratory studies narrow our investigations to explanations of events that are more promising than others. For instance, satellite tracking of offenders has raised certain constitutional questions, such as the right to privacy. The U.S. Supreme Court had not ruled decisively on the constitutionality of satellite tracking in supervised release programs, and no jurisdictions have statutes prohibiting its use. An exploratory study might disclose little about the constitutionality of satellite tracking of probationers and parolees, and therefore, we might be better off studying the cost and logistical implementation of such satellite supervision in particular cities or states.

Descriptive Functions

Descriptive research is more focused compared with exploratory research. A descriptive study of marijuana growers was conducted by Sandra Hafley and Richard Tewksbury (1996). Hafley and Tewksbury wanted to describe the community culture within which marijuana growing thrives. They selected a Kentucky county known for its illegal marijuana production and on the basis of interviews with several community residents, they were able to characterize the culture of marijuana growing and distribution in great detail. Using the pseudonym, "Bluegrass County," Hafley and Tewksbury learned about different roles performed by largely male members of the community. Some of the roles performed were communal grower, hustler, pragmatist, young punk, and entrepreneur. Women in Bluegrass County were also described as performing several support roles, including decent women, strumpets, and women-in-between.

Penetrating the marijuana culture of any Kentucky county is difficult. However, one of the researchers was in fact a lifelong resident of rural Kentucky. Personal contacts and kinship network introductions were crucial in gaining access to the closed marijuana culture. Assurances of anonymity were mandatory before citizens agreed to share information with these researchers. Once trust had been established, Hafley and Tewksbury gathered extensive information about the Kentucky marijuana business. Communal growers, for instance, were those who believed that growing marijuana made a social statement to those opposed to marijuana use. Hustlers were those who have both used and sold marijuana. Pragmatists were those who grew marijuana because of economic hardship. They knew it was wrong, but they needed the money. Young punks were marijuana-grower wannabes. Women's roles included strumpets, or women of loose morals who provided sexual companionship and support for male marijuana growers. Decent women were highly respected and never placed in jeopardy by their men. These women are married or are related to male marijuana growers and are indirectly supportive of their activities, even though they are illegal. Women-in-between is a new category comprised of women who are neither decent nor strumpets. They are relatively new to the community and sometimes replace males who have been arrested in such activities as transporting marijuana or selling it to others. They are in transitional roles, where community residents have yet to categorize them one way or another for acceptance purposes.

Hafley and Tewksbury enriched their research with actual remarks from those interviewed. One entrepreneur said, "You don't know what it's like to work in that factory. I been shut up in that place for 10 years, day after day. I ain't making no money. Hell, when I retire, I won't draw nothin'. I spend my life in that box and will be ready to die when I leave it. Why shouldn't I grow a [marijuana] crop? So what if the law don't like it? A crop or two and I'll be set. At least I'll have something to put by" (Hafley & Tewksbury, 1996, p. 82). These remarks were made by a community member who was disgusted with his factory job and wanted to earn more money by entering the marijuana-growing business. These and other remarks are very helpful in providing explanations for why community residents might engage in deviant or criminal behavior. Descriptive research sets the stage for more controlled experimentation, where certain variables may be manipulated and controlled observations may be made.

Another example of a descriptive study is the work of Weitzer and Tuch (2004). These researchers studied racial differences among persons concerning their treatment by police agencies and officers. Specifically, these researchers wished to describe the attitudes of persons of different races relating to policing policies and reforms. Using national survey data, these investigators correlated racial and ethnic variables and support for police agency reforms with police misconduct, corruption, unwarranted vehicle stops, and reported verbal and physical abuse from police officers against citizens. They found that race and ethnicity are strong predictors of police agency reform. These researchers acknowledged that they made no deliberate effort to discover the determinants of attitudes of reform among minorities. Nevertheless, their descriptive research has enabled others to structure subsequent studies of an experimental nature to answer such questions in a more direct, cause–effect context.

Experimental Functions

Experimental research or **experimental social research** pertains to the amount of control researchers exercise over the variables (factors) or subjects (persons) they study. Experimental research is designed to see which factors make a difference in modifying a particular outcome. A standard type of experimental research is called the **before–after method** or **before–after design.** Ordinarily, the behaviors or attitudes of experimental subjects (persons who are being studied) are examined in one time period, a **stimulus** (a **treatment variable** or **causal variable**) is administered to these subjects, and then these subjects are examined again in a second time period, perhaps 4–6 weeks later. Comparing their behaviors or attitudes in the first time period (**time 1**) with their behaviors or attitudes in the second time period (**time 2**) supposedly indicates the impact of the treatment variable or causal variable on their behaviors or attitudes.

An example of an experimental study is a study of pregnant, substance-abusing probationers conducted by Vicki Markey, Sunny Areissohn, and Margaret Mudd (1997). Markey and her associates were interested in the growing problem of pregnant drug-abusing offenders and the subsequent births of infants with defects and deformities attributable to the mothers' drug use. The San Diego County Probation Department began a program in 1992 designed to decrease or eliminate birth defects among newborn infants by controlling the social environments of pregnant female probationers. The program was known as WATCh, or Women And Their Children. In 1992, for instance, there were 607,000 births in California, with 69,000 (11 percent) born to mothers who used alcohol and/or drugs prior to their deliveries. About 4,000 infants are born each year in San Diego County with drugs and/or alcohol in their systems. Costs to taxpayers for each of these infants are as much as $400,000, including medical care, foster care, and special education costs.

Markey and colleagues (1997) observed that prior to the implementation of the WATCh program, pregnant probationers were supervised by probation officers without any specialized training. Caseloads of officers ranged from 200 to 2,000 probationers. Many pregnant offenders continued to use drugs and alcohol, although they were expected to participate in a community recovery program. The primary focus was on the comfort of the pregnant offender rather than on the health and welfare of the developing fetus.

When the WATCh program was commenced, probation officer caseloads were drastically reduced to 35 per officer. The WATCh model provided for no tolerance for illicit drug use or alcohol consumption. Specialized probation officers were used to test pregnant women frequently for drug or alcohol use, and to ensure their immediate treatment and custody in the event that they tested positive for drugs and/or alcohol. All probation officers supervising pregnant probationers underwent special training and were made aware of several helpful emergency prenatal community-based organizations. At least two urine tests were administered per week. Judicial support was obtained for the no-tolerance policy. Under the WATCh program through 1994, there were 90 births among 84 probationer-mothers. Only 7 infants (8 percent) tested positive for drugs or alcohol, while 83 (92 percent) were drug/alcohol free. It was estimated that the program resulted in savings of $33.2 million.

Markey and colleagues (1997) concluded that their experiment was significant and showed low program costs of only $2,500 per probationer per year. Subsequently, the WATCh program was applied to pregnant teenagers who were in trouble with the law. By the end of January 1995, 124 adult women and 15 teenagers have delivered drug- and alcohol-free babies while in the WATCh program. This result was a 92 percent success rate for the WATCh program.

The experiment these researchers conducted was a comparison between standard probation officer–client supervision and the more intensive supervision according to WATCh program guidelines. A much larger percentage of babies with alcohol or drugs in their systems were associated with women under standard probation supervision compared with those delivering babies under the WATCh program. These researchers rightly concluded that "while the demonstration sample is too small to make sweeping statements, the outcomes are supportive of an optimistic view. Intensive probation does work to . . . bring about the birth of healthy, drug and alcohol-free babies" (Markey et al., 1997, p. 23).

One convenient way of distinguishing between these different studies and the functions they serve is to envision a continuum of uncertainty and certainty such as the one shown below.

As we move from the extreme left (uncertainty), our studies change in quality from exploratory, to descriptive, to experimental. Thus, experimental studies are those characterized by a high degree of certainty. What this means is that our knowledge about which factors are important has increased to the point that we can conduct specific tests and exert some degree of control over various factors. No studies reach absolute certainty about any topic studied. Some studies are closer to the certainty end of the continuum than other studies. Those closer to the uncertainty end of the continuum are most likely exploratory or descriptive studies rather than experimental ones. Those toward the certainty end of the continuum are often experimental studies.

Evaluation Research

Evaluation research consists of any study designed to assess the outcome of a particular program, intervention, or experiment, and whether the program or intervention goals have been achieved. Program evaluation is the process of assessing any law enforcement, corrections intervention, or other program for the purpose of determining its effectiveness in achieving manifest goals. Program evaluation investigates the nature of organizational intervention strategies or **interventions,** counseling, interpersonal interactions, staff quality, expertise, education, and the success or failure experiences of clients served by any program. Several examples below illustrate what is meant by program evaluation.

• *Sex offender probationers who participate in a special program of intensive probation supervision will have lower recidivism rates compared with sex offenders who participate in traditional probation supervision.* Whether we agree or disagree with this statement is irrelevant. The fact is, some researchers believe this. In fact, Michael J. Jenuwine, Ronald Simmons, and Edward Swies (2003) conducted an experiment to determine whether sex offenders who participated in an intensive supervision program known as the Cook County (Illinois) Adult Sex Offender Program (ASOP) had lower recidivism rates compared with a sample of standard probationers supervised by traditional probation methods. Their study involved 2,500 adults on probation in Cooke County, Illinois. The ASOP program consisted of extensive collaboration between probation officers, sex therapists, and other community treatment providers who worked closely with sex offenders under intensive supervision conditions. The program evaluation consisted of comparing recidivism rates of ASOP adult sex offenders before and after the intervention (collaboration between sex therapists, community services, and community treatment providers) with traditionally supervised sex offenders who did not participate in ASOP. Recidivism rates were lower among the ASOP sample compared with the traditionally supervised sample. At least in this instance, ASOP was considered to be a successful intervention.

• *Violent offenders who participate in a cognitive self-change program (SCG) will exhibit greater rehabilitation and less recidivism compared with violent offenders who do not participate in the SCG program.* Whatever we believe about violent offenders, their treatment, and recidivism potential is irrelevant. An investigation of the use of cognitive self-change was conducted by Thomas Powell, Jack Bush, and Brian Bilodeau (2001) on a sample of Vermont inmates convicted of violent crimes over 15 years. The SCG program was based on a psychiatric technique involving three steps: (1) offenders learn to be objective observers of their internal thoughts, attitudes, and feelings; (2) offenders learn to recognize how their thinking generates their violent behaviors; and (3) offenders practice new thinking techniques that lead them away from violence by learning coping strategies that enable them to change their violent conduct. Violent inmates selected for inclusion in the program were involved in a structured group format lasting from 6 months to 2 years, depending on inmate sentence lengths. Both institutional and community programs were delivered to inmate groups of eight by two trained staff members. These groups met 2–3 times per week. Typical groups included "cognitive check-in reports" and "thinking reports." These reports were brief reports by each group member about a description of a recent situation in the offender's life, his or her thoughts or feelings about that situation, and an explanation of how that thinking possibly could have led toward violent conduct or hurtful behavior. Suggested change strategies were introduced by the staff members or facilitators over time, and each inmate practiced new thinking skills relevant for their particular situation. The program evaluation consisted of contrasting the recidivism rates of these inmates following their involvement in SCG with non-SCG inmates. Powell and colleagues found that the SCG participants had 20 percent less recidivism compared with a sample of non-SCG violent inmates. The Vermont SCG program was declared successful as a result of this study.

• *Federal supervised releasees who use drugs while being supervised will be more overwhelmed with stress compared with non-drug users.* Whether we believe this is irrelevant. John D. Gurley and Jamie F. Satcher (2003) conducted an evaluation study to determine whether stress was greater among drug users under federal supervision compared with non-drug users. These investigators believed that preventing drug use among releasees would ultimately positively impact their quality of life and improve their chances of a successful probation experience. They obtained a sample of federal releasees from among 900 releasees supervised through the Northern District of Alabama. About 375 of these releasees were subject to drug checks at random times. Releasees not testing positive for drugs for 6 months or more were considered non-drug users, while those testing positive for drugs in the last 6 months were considered drug users. Data were gathered from all offenders by administering the 25-item Stress in My Life survey, which emphasized family, finances, employment, peer pressure, and social stress. The evaluation consisted of a comparison of scores between non-drug users and drug users on the Stress in My Life survey on the various dimensions. Actual findings were that drug users compared with non-drug users experienced higher levels of family stress, greater financial stress, more employment-related stress, more peer-related stress, and greater social stress. The study suggested alternative strategies federal probation officers might use to enable certain supervised releasees with

BOX 1.3   PERSONALITY HIGHLIGHT

D. WAYNE OSGOOD
Pennsylvania State University, University Park

Statistics: B.A. (psychology), University of California at Los Angeles; M.A., Ph.D. (social psychology), University of Colorado at Boulder.

BACKGROUND AND INTERESTS

My graduate training was not in criminology, but rather in the area of social psychology known as social cognition. By the time I finished graduate school, I could no longer remember why I had once found social cognition so interesting, and I was eager to take up something new. Fortunately, my skills in research methods helped open some doors, and I landed a job working on a national evaluation of juvenile diversion programs. By the time we finished that work, I was also hooked on the challenge of studying crime and delinquency.

RESEARCH INVESTIGATIONS

An ongoing aspect of my career has been research on programs in juvenile justice. I have contributed to evaluation studies intended to determine the effectiveness of prevention programs (e.g., Gang Resistance Education and Training, Communities that Care), diversion programs, and residential programs (e.g., Boys and Girls Town). My largest project in this area was a study of peer influence at four correctional institutions in Michigan.

I have also studied a variety of topics about the nature and causes of crime, delinquency, and other deviant behaviors of adolescents and young adults. I have investigated the generality of deviance (such as the tendency of youth who are involved in crime to also engage in activities such as substance abuse and dangerous driving), age trends in crime, criminal careers, community effects on offense rates, and biology and crime.

My biggest interest in recent years has been the connection between time use and individual offending. I was inspired by Cohen's and Felson's routine activity theory, which argues that important changes over time in rates of crime can result from alterations in the nature of ordinary, everyday life that inadvertently create (or eliminate) opportunities for crime. For instance, reliance on automobiles for transportation cuts down opportunities for muggings at bus and subway stops, but it also increases the chances for car theft. I have applied this to individual offending in terms of a general type of activity that turns out to be closely related to indi-

BOX 1.3   CONTINUED

viduals' level of offending: unstructured socializing with peers away from authority figures. The lack of structure leaves time available for deviance; peers can be an appreciative audience that makes deviance rewarding; and the absence of authority figures makes deviance far less risky. What I find most interesting about this perspective is its potential to explain (at least partially) the reason that many other factors are related to offending, such as age, gender, class, marriage, and community.

I make use of a variety of methodological techniques in my work, and I often write about methodological issues. Random assignment experiments are critical for the evaluation of justice programs, and I have been fortunate to work on several of these. Though random assignment is often hard to arrange, there is no substitute that can provide such strong evidence about the impact of a program. My colleagues and I have sometimes been able to conduct natural experiments by capitalizing on random processes in existing situations, such as assigning youth in correctional institutions to the living unit with the next opening or delivering a prevention program to whichever health class meets when the service provider is available.

When random assignment is not possible, such as when studying the effects of marriage on offending, the next best choice is often a longitudinal study following people over time. Careful use of this type of data lets us eliminate a broad range of alternative explanations by comparing people with themselves over time. If we find that offending is related to a factor like age, marriage, or time use, then we can be sure that the association is not due to any stable individual characteristics, such as gender, race, or stable personality traits.

ADVICE TO STUDENTS

A career in research on crime and justice can be very rewarding, and I encourage you to consider it. We address topics of great importance to society, and previous theory and research lay out many promising ideas that need to be tested and puzzles that need to be solved. Although this path requires several years of graduate school, you can usually expect to have your way paid if you are admitted to a strong program, and the job market has been very good for teaching and research in criminology and criminal justice for a long time. If you enjoy studying, thinking, and writing about crime and justice, it could be the right field for you. If you decide to pursue this career, my advice is to work hard at developing strong skills in research methods. Methodological skills can also bring you added opportunities. Colleagues are eager to collaborate with someone who can help them with research methods, but proficiency in this area will qualify you for many types of jobs at universities, research institutes, government agencies, and businesses. My final advice is to do the best work you can. It takes a long time and a lot of hard work to complete a well-planned, carefully executed study on an important topic and to effectively present it in an interesting and clearly written research article. Yet that study will be worth a lot more to the world (and to that researcher's career) than a huge stack of unconvincing studies built on shortcuts.

drug-related problems to cope more effectively with stress and prevent their own dependence on drugs.

• *Reparative justice as a form of community justice restores citizen confidence in community rehabilitation programs and significantly addresses the needs of crime victims.* Again, whether we agree with this statement is irrelevant. David R. Karp (2003) studied the Vermont Department of Corrections Reparative Probation Program, which commenced in 1995 and continues to receive support from various sources, including the federal government. Reparative probation involves a sentenced offender to appear before a local reparative board, consisting of trained citizen volunteers, where a workable solution to the problem created by the offense is attempted. Victims and other affected persons are invited to attend these reparative board meetings and actively participate in them. Board meeting length is from 30–45 minutes. The outcome is a negotiated agreement, specifying a set of tasks to be completed by the offender during a 90-day probationary period. Offenders are evaluated periodically during this period, and subsequently, if all program requirements are fulfilled, these persons are discharged from the program. Failure to comply with one or more program conditions is a probation program violation and results in a return to court for a new and harsher sentence. Karp found that during 2000, for instance, there were 320 volunteers who served on 49 boards serving all Vermont communities. Less than half of all cases presented to these boards involved victims. However, only 9 percent of all victims subsequently appeared at these board meetings and participated. An additional 11 percent of all victims gave written statements to be read at the board meeting in lieu of their appearance. The program evaluation consisted of (1) measuring the overall victim satisfaction with board meeting outcomes and (2) offender recidivism following a favorable board meeting resolution of problems and successful completion of the probation program requirements.

Karp found that 82 percent of all victims were satisfied with these reparative board outcomes and offender behaviors. Apology letters were sent to victims by offenders, and restitution to victims was ordered in 67 percent of all cases. About 87 percent of all victims reported satisfaction with the reparative contract as well as feeling better about the crime. The offender successful program completion rate was 81 percent. Those who did not complete the program violated one or more probation program rules and had their programs terminated. Of those offenders who successfully completed the program, 31 percent were rearrested within one year of their program completion; however, only 1.5 percent of these were rearrested for violent offenses. Karp concluded that the Vermont reparative justice program was "generally successful" (2003, p. 36).

Most of the experimental studies conducted in criminology are evaluative in nature, although their immediate study goals may not be articulated as such. Usually, an experiment is conducted involving one or more interventions with a sample of subjects whose behaviors are studied over time. The study results are usually the results of some experimental variable or intervention, and they may or may not lead to repeated investigations of the same phenomenon by the same or other researchers later. It is not always the case that the results of such investigations are overwhelmingly positive. Also, researchers often have more than their fair share of outcome "failures," where their findings are not as remarkable as they had originally anticipated, or where their findings do not appear to be significant either theoretically or substantively. Such is the nature of social research.

Theory Defined

Theory has many definitions, depending on the source. Some theorists consider theory to be a collection of **concepts.** Others say theory is an interconnected set of hypotheses. Yet others say theory is a set of concepts plus the interrelationships that are assumed to exist among those concepts (Selltiz, Cook, & Wrightsman, 1976). Another way of viewing theory is as a system of explanation. This definition tells us something about what theories do. Some professionals regard theory as a conceptual scheme, a **frame of reference,** or a set of **propositions** and **conclusions.** If we consult a dictionary, one of the worst places to look for a clear definition of theory, theory is a mental viewing, a contemplation, conjecture, a systematic statement of principles, or a formulation of apparent relationships or underlying principles of certain observed phenomena that has been verified to some degree (Guralnik, 1972).

All of these definitions of theory are legitimate, honest definitions. But are they *good* definitions? Are they *useful* definitions for criminologists and other social scientists? Probably not. No single definition above pulls together all of theory's essential elements. Theory is a conceptual scheme, a set of propositions and/or concepts, a contemplation, a conjecture, a statement of principles, and a formulation of relationships of observed phenomena. Perhaps one of the clearer and more comprehensive definitions of theory may be gleaned from a synthesis of two definitions provided by Robert Merton (1957, pp. 96–99) and the late theorist Arnold Rose (1965, pp. 9–12). According to these social scientists, theory is an integrated body of **assumptions,** propositions, and **definitions** that are related in such a way so as to explain and predict relationships between two or more variables.

Assumptions, Propositions, and Definitions

Assumptions are similar to **empirical generalizations** or observable regularities in human behavior (Merton, 1957). For our purposes, assumptions are statements that have a high degree of certainty. These are statements that require little, if any, confirmation in the real world. Examples of assumptions might be, "All societies have laws," or "The greater the deviant conduct, the greater the group pressure on the deviant to conform to group norms." Other assumption statements might be, "Prison inmates devise hierarchies of authority highly dependent upon one's physical strength and abilities," or "Most types of delinquency are group-shared phenomena," or "Most delinquents commit delinquent acts in the company of other delinquents." While some of us may take issue with these statements, there is little need to verify each of them. Social scientists and criminologists have found extensive support for each. We assume that these statements are basically true.

In contrast, propositions are also statements about the real world, but they lack the high degree of certainty associated with assumptions. Examples of propositions might be, "Burnout among probation officers may be mitigated or lessened through job enlargement and giving officers greater input in organizational decision making," or "Two-officer patrol units are less susceptible to misconduct and corruption than one-officer patrol units." Other propositions might be, "Reducing prison overcrowding will result in a proportionate decrease in inmate violence and prison condition-related court litigation." Each researcher has more or less strongly held beliefs about the truth or certainty of these statements. Sometimes, the same statement may be labeled as a "proposition" by one researcher and an "assumption" by another researcher. Depending on one's experience with the subject matter being investigated, varying degrees of certainty are associated with different statements made about the real world.

Theories consist of both assumptions and propositions. At any given point, researchers will construct theories that contain assumptions and propositions, although over time, these various statements change in the degree of certainty we associate with them. Accruing research about a given subject will eventually transform propositional statements into assumptions. Many of our assumptions have evolved from the proposition statements of earlier times. As more research is conducted and information is compiled, we gradually improve our understanding of why certain events occur. In effect, we become more certain about things.

Other components of theories are definitions. Definitions of terms we use or definitions of the variables we consider significant in influencing various events assist us in constructing a logical explanatory framework or theory. A common problem is that often, the same terms are assigned different definitions by different investigators. If we use the term *peer influence* in a statement about delinquents and their delinquent conduct, how should peer influence be defined? How should *stress* be defined if we are investigating the relation between stress and probation officer power within a probation agency? How should power be defined? As we will see later, there is a conceptual "Tower of Babel" phenomenon in most sciences, as different investigators assign different meanings to the same terms. Differences in definitions assigned common terms sometimes explain inconsistencies in research findings.

When different definitions are given to a common term, it is likely that researchers will arrive at different conclusions about variable interrelationships in independent investigations. For instance, Researcher Smith might study Probation Agency A. If Smith defines stress as physical fatigue and exhaustion, this may characterize how probation officers in Probation Agency A feel while performing their jobs. However, if Researcher Jones studies Probation Agency B and defines stress as an increasing inability to perform a variety of tasks involving conflicting expectations and the psychological frustration resulting from such role performances, it is likely that Jones will find that the probation officers studied in Agency B may not exhibit stress in the same way as officers exhibit it in Agency A. This is one of the many explanations we have for contrary or inconsistent findings when the same variables are researched by different investigators. Researchers Smith and Jones are using the same terms, but their different definitions of those terms may yield different kinds of associations with other important variables.

In criminology and criminal justice, theory is utilized frequently to account for most phenomena. In most criminology and criminal justice books, for example, theories of deviant conduct and crime are presented that link these phenomena with glandular malfunctions, early childhood socialization, unusual chromosomatic patterns such as the "*XYY* syndrome," body types, peer group associations and influences, criminal and delinquent subcultures, feeblemindedness and/or mental impairment, differential association, broken homes, cultural deprivation, anomie, social bonding, opportunity, hedonism, class conflict, unequal access to success goals, labeling, learning, cognitive developmentalism, behaviorism, gender, race, age, ethnicity, and social power differentials. For each of these linkages, such as the link between crime and labeling, for instance, an explanatory scheme is advanced that accounts for how labeling is related to criminal behavior.

Labeling theory, for example, explains deviant and criminal conduct by focusing on social definitions of acts of crime and deviance rather than on the acts themselves. Some of the assumptions underlying labeling theory are that (1) no act is inherently criminal, that

(2) persons become criminals through social definition of their conduct, that (3) all persons at one time or another conform to or deviate from the law, that (4) "getting caught" begins the labeling process, that (5) persons defined as criminal will, in turn, cultivate criminal self-definitions, and that (6) they will eventually seek out and associate with others who are similarly defined and develop a criminal subculture (Lemert, 1951).

The impact of social influence is strong in labeling theory. Accepting the definitions of others and acquiring self-definitions of criminality seems to lead to further criminal behavior. While the empirical evidence to support labeling theory as a good explanation for criminal conduct is inconsistent and sketchy, it is nevertheless an explanation accepted by more than a few criminologists. Some professionals might regard labeling theory as grounded conjecture, where occasional instances of support for the labeling perspective have been observed.

Another theory of criminality is the *XYY* syndrome. Sociobiologists and geneticists have studied the chromosomatic patterns of many criminals in an attempt to link these patterns with different types of criminal conduct. *X* and *Y* are sex chromosomes persons inherit from their parents. Male infants are typified with an *XY* chromosomatic pattern, while females are typified by an *XX* pattern. Y chromosomes are considered aggressive, while X chromosomes are considered passive.

Spectacular news events such as mass or serial murders stimulate interest in criminological theories. When Richard Speck murdered eight student nurses in Chicago during the 1960s, he was eventually studied by sociobiologists. They found that Speck had an unusual *XYY* chromosomatic pattern, with an extra *Y* chromosome. This aggressive chromosome provided at least one instance of support for the idea that crime and chromosomatic patterns are related. In Speck's case, his mass murders of nurses were thought attributable, in part, to his highly aggressive genetic structure. However, subsequent tests of chromosomatic patterns among incarcerated criminals, even violent offenders, have failed to disclose any systematic relation between chromosomes and particular criminal behaviors (Mednick & Volavka, 1980; Shah & Roth, 1974). In fact, Shah and Roth (1974) found that only 5 percent of a large sample of criminals had the *XYY* pattern. Although this percentage is slightly higher than that estimated for the general U.S. population, it is not significant as a consistent predictor of criminal behavior.

In both the labeling and *XYY* syndrome theories, various phenomena, social definitions, self-definitions of certain behaviors, and chromosomatic patterns are highlighted and featured as primary causes of other phenomena such as criminal behaviors. Those who use these explanations for criminal conduct write elaborate arguments to provide logical and plausible support for their beliefs. Eventually, research is conducted that may provide support for these assertions and explanations. If researchers look hard enough, they can find support for their theorizing somewhere. Richard Speck's case was considered proof of the plausibility of the *XYY* syndrome, although this proof was insufficient to justify incarcerating all persons with an *XYY* chromosomatic pattern because of some suspected association of this pattern with mass murder. These examples illustrate two important functions of theory: explanation and prediction.

Explanation and Prediction

Explanations of events are often given higher priority compared with predictions of events. There is not much difference between explanation and speculation. Brainstorming and thinking up ideas about which factors seem to create probation officer burnout, delinquency, or rising crime rates usually involves much speculation, often mislabeled as theorizing. When criminologists say, "My theory about why this or that occurs is . . .", what they usually mean is that their belief is that a particular variable seems a likely cause of some event. Seldom do they sit down and patiently and painstakingly develop a systematic explanatory scheme linking certain events with their believed causes of those events. True theorists among criminologists and criminal justice professionals are relatively few.

Theories can be rank-ordered according to their ability to predict events or occurrences. Theories with the greatest predictive utility are used most often, while those lacking predictive utility are discarded. Anyone can explain anything, but that doesn't mean that the explanations advanced are good ones. Often, the critical test is whether theories can predict events accurately.

For instance, judges and parole boards are in the business of predicting or anticipating a convicted offender's behavior. Judges must make decisions about whether to place convicted offenders on probation or to incarcerate them. Parole boards must decide whether certain prisoners should be released from prison short of serving their full sentences. Different sentencing and early-release criteria are applied by judges and parole boards in their decision-making activity. In most instances, their decisions are influenced, in part, by rational, nonrational, and/or irrational criteria, such as race, ethnicity, age, gender, socioeconomic status, prior record, drug or alcohol dependency, presence or absence of a family support system, nature of the conviction offense, compliance or noncompliance with prison rules and regulations, acceptance of responsibility for their criminal actions, and the prestige of their defense attorneys. These decisions may also be guided by theories of criminality, partial theories, or syntheses of several different theories of crime and criminal conduct.

Decisions made by judges and parole boards are flawed in various ways. Up to 70 percent of those placed on probation or parole eventually recidivate and commit new crimes. The criminal justice system considers these cases as failures. These failures are empirical evidence of poor judicial and parole board judgment to forecast the future behaviors of probationers and parolees.

Consistent with the idea that theories may be evaluated as either good or bad on the basis of their degree of predictive utility, sometimes theories may be considered more or less important according to the types of policy decisions that are influenced by them. In the early 1900s, for example, when criminologists believed that heredity was an important factor in causing criminality, prisoners in various states such as Oklahoma and Virginia were sterilized so that they would be incapable of fathering children. At the time, sterilization seemed to be a sound and logical policy to adopt so that future criminals could be prevented from being born.

During the rehabilitation era of 1940–1970, for example, many prisons offered educational and vocational-technical training, as well as counseling programs for inmates. These programs were believed to be remedies for various inmate deficiencies, since many prisoners lacked formal education, vocational skills, and a basic understanding of the etiology of their criminal conduct. However, sterilization (subsequently declared unconstitutional in *Skinner v. Oklahoma,* 1942) and many rehabilitative programs for inmates have failed to reduce criminality. In recent years, while most prisons have continued to offer a broad range of inmate programs, the emphasis in corrections has shifted from rehabilitation to crime control. This is evidenced by the great increase in probation and parole programs in recent years that stress close or intensive offender monitoring or greater probation/parole officer–offender/client contact.

Furthermore, increasing numbers of prisons are merely incarcerating or warehousing offenders rather than attempting to rehabilitate them. This fact has caused more than a few critics of prisons to accuse corrections of warehousing violence. The public expects to be protected from criminals, at least for the period of their sentence lengths. Whether rehabilitation occurs is unimportant to many citizens. They simply want offenders punished and out of public view for as long as possible. Thus, the warehousing violence charge against corrections is probably accurate.

Types of Theory

Although there are many kinds of theorizing, this discussion will focus on four types: (1) deductive theory, (2) inductive theory, (3) grounded theory, and (4) axiomatic theory.

Deductive Theory

Deductive theory is more common in social science today than inductive theory. It is based on deductive reasoning suggested by the early Greek philosopher, Aristotle (384–322 B.C.). Logical statements are deduced or derived from other statements. Typically, assumptions are made and conclusions are drawn that appear to be logically connected with these assumptions. A common example is, "All men are mortal. Aristotle is a man. Therefore, Aristotle is mortal." Another way of expressing this reasoning is, "All A's are B's; C is a B, therefore, C is also an A."

In research, any event that needs an explanation provides a foundation for deductive theory-building. Some examples of problems or unanswered questions or occurrences may be sentencing disparities among judges; juvenile delinquency; child sexual abuse or spousal abuse; crime among the elderly; the prisonization process; probation/parole officer burnout and stress; prosecutorial discretion; and social class variations in crime rates. Researchers will choose certain problems of interest to them, and then they will devise an explanation for their problems. They will include in their explanation various assumptions, propositions, and definitions of terms. The interrelatedness of these linkages among assumptions and propositions is a logical formulation. From this logical formulation, a **deduction** may be made. Deductions are always considered to be tentative deductions. They must be tested by gathering data. Through data gathering and analysis, researchers learn whether their deductions are valid. If the data suggest that these deductions should be questioned, further testing is done in other settings. Even if findings support certain deductions, further tests are ordinarily conducted, since these investigators want to be certain of their conclusions.

One example of deductive theorizing is Johnson's (1986) study of family structure and delinquency. Johnson reexamined the "broken home–delinquency" relation by using self-reports from 700 high school sophomores. Because of space limitations in professional journals, researchers are not always able to elaborate their theories for readers. Rather, they provide a sketchy view of their assumptions and propositions and how they are interconnected. Johnson's reported research is no exception. Johnson acknowledges initially that broken homes have, for many years, been thought to be a major factor in the cause of juvenile delinquency (p. 65). Also, he acknowledges that there is general, although inconsistent, support for this view in the professional literature.

A careful reading of his introduction and the discussion of what he found when the responses of 700 youths were examined permits us to identify several of his theoretical premises. For instance, Johnson (1986) observes that the process whereby delinquency and broken homes become related begins by a family breakup. The family breakup reduces the quality of parent–child relationships, possibly through the physical and/or psychological separation inherent in the breakup. The breakup, like ripples in a pond, influences different dimensions of a youth's life. Problems of familial breakups may lead to school difficulties, where the child has difficulty concentrating on schoolwork. Furthermore, Johnson notes that often, official agencies respond to children from broken homes in different ways compared with their responses to children where the children's homes are intact. Johnson's crucial question is, "Is there in fact an association between family structure and delinquency?" (p. 66). His data disclosed support, although moderate, for the claim that family structure is related to delinquency. Considerable statistical evidence is presented to support his tentative conclusions.

Although Johnson prepared a more elaborate version of these events and the interrelatedness of his basic assumptions and propositions, the skeletal aspects of his theorizing are there. Several traumatic events in a child's life trigger assorted problems of adjustment to other life events. We glean from his analysis that there are psychological rewards that youths obtain from intact familial experiences, and that physical separation minimizes or frustrates the youth's fulfillment of these rewarding experiences. School difficulties, one possible product of such frustration at home, generate further adjustment problems for affected youths. One product of such frustration is the commission of delinquent acts. Johnson doesn't claim that all youths from broken homes will become delinquent. Rather, he indicates that disruptive homes contribute with other factors in youths' lives to elicit delinquent behaviors. His discussion of these other factors (e.g., gender, age, and race of juveniles, mother–stepfather/father–stepmother situations, and official reports from police vs. self-reports from delinquents themselves) are excellent suggestions for follow-up research projects to be pursued by other interested investigators.

Johnson's study is largely deductive, where various assumptions and propositional statements have been made about the association between familial stability and propensity of juveniles toward delinquent conduct. A more comprehensive or sophisticated analysis of the problem would encompass an explanation or delineation of the nature of psychological rewards stemming from intact families, the reasons for mother–stepfather/father–stepmother differences in the incidence of delinquent behaviors among their respective children, and a detailed outline of why various "agents of society" would be inclined to respond differently toward children from intact homes compared with children from family breakups. Specific agencies of society could be identified, and a rationale could be given in each instance for why these agencies would respond in peculiar or unique ways to youths from broken homes. All of this would be encompassed within a more comprehensive and sophisticated theoretical framework. Space limitations for journal articles do not permit more extensive discussions of theory, however.

Johnson started by making a theoretical sketch of the relation between broken homes and delinquent behavior, and he found a setting where his theorizing could be tested. His data analysis led him to some of the conclusions noted above. He logically deduced an explanation for delinquent behavior and sought empirical confirmation or refutation of his explanation. All of this was accomplished through deduction.

Inductive Theory

Induction or **inductive logic** is a process whereby a specific event is examined and described, and where generalizations are made to a larger class of similar events. Suppose we wanted to devise an explanation for why offenders become recidivists and commit new crimes. Through induction, we could examine a sample of known recidivists from Connecticut prisons, or inmates who have a history of prior convictions. As the result of our observations and analyses of the Connecticut inmate sample, we might conclude that our recidivists are younger, black males who have alcohol/drug dependencies, who are in the lower socioeconomic strata, were unemployed or underemployed when originally arrested and convicted, and have less than a high school education. From these observations, we might make several generalizations about the broader class of recidivists nationally.

Or perhaps we are interested in learning about those persons most likely to recidivate while participating in their probation or parole programs. Again, judges and parole boards wish to know which criteria seem most relevant in forecasting the successfulness of prospective probationers and/or parolees. Observing samples of New York probationers and parolees who have been incarcerated or reincarcerated for violating one or more program conditions will enable us to identify some of their social, demographic, and psychological characteristics and backgrounds of these failures. From our descriptions of New York probationers and parolees who have recidivated while on probation or parole, we might generalize to the broader class of probationers and parolees throughout the United States.

Now, let's back up a moment and see what has been done in each of the instances mentioned above. In both cases, samples have been obtained and described. Then, these descriptions have been generalized to the broader class of persons represented by the samples. Are these generalizations we have made in each instance good generalizations? Should we deny parole or probation to all young, black, male offenders with drug or alcohol dependencies, who were unemployed or underemployed when they were initially arrested and convicted, and who lack a high school education? This general policy would be very controversial.

In both instances, we have examined the "events" (i.e., the samples of Connecticut inmates and New York probationers and parolees who have failed) and described various characteristics of these events. Then, we have attempted to generalize to the broader class of similar events. Clearly, our research goals include both explanation and prediction. We will tentatively explain recidivism and probation/parole program failures by using the characteristics of samples of inmates and program failures as predictors. But now we must see whether these predictors or characteristics will permit us to forecast recidivism and program failures in advance of their potential recidivism and program failure.

Using **deduction,** we abstract by generalizing. Using **inductive theory,** we generalize by abstracting. Although both deduction and induction help us achieve common research objectives, including data gathering and theory verification, they lead us to these objectives through different paths. In a deductive context, we state what we believe is a rational theory to explain some event such as delinquency. Then, we will obtain samples of delinquent and nondelinquent youths to test the adequacy of our theory. However, using induction, we may examine a few delinquents and nondelinquents, describe their similarities and differences, and attempt to generalize the characteristics uniquely possessed by these delinquents to a larger class of delinquents nationally. But again, we must follow up our induction with an empirical test situation and determine whether the characteristics we have identified on a smaller scale help us to predict delinquent behavior on a larger scale.

The distinction between deduction and induction can also be made according to whether we construct a logical explanatory and predictive scheme and observe facts consistent with that scheme, or whether we observe certain facts and generalize from the facts observed. It has been noted that "there are those who feel that the entire research process is initiated with theories. Deduction occurs when we . . .gather facts to confirm or disprove hypothesized relationships between variables [derived from theory]. Whether there were facts that precipitated the [theory] does not really matter. What matters is that research is essentially a hypothesis-testing venture in which the hypotheses rest on logically (if not factually) deduced relational statements" (Black & Champion, 1976, p. 65). Thus, deduction and induction are simply alternative ways for constructing theory.

Grounded Theory

Barney Glaser and Anselm Strauss (1967) have described another type of theorizing known as grounded theory. **Grounded theory** is the view that investigators enter research settings without preconceived theories and hypotheses about what they will find. Essentially, investigators will immerse themselves into the research setting and describe what they have found. On the basis of observations, interviews, and other data-gathering methods, investigators will generate explanations about various phenomena that are developed directly from what they see and understand. Thus, their theories about events are grounded in the empirical reality of their study settings. As researchers continue to discover more facts about the settings they observe, their theorizing will be modified and undergo a metamorphosis of sorts, as new information suggests changes in their theoretical explanations.

Grounded theory is distinguished from deductive theory, where a theoretical explanation of an event is developed in advance of the actual study. Subsequently, the theory is tested by examining a research setting and discovering whether what one has hypothesized is true or untrue. Grounded theory is probably closer to induction than deduction. But the appeal of grounded theory is that any theoretical explanation devised is rooted in observed behaviors and social exchanges. Glaser and Strauss believe that grounded theorizing is more realistic than other types of theorizing, and that more valid hypotheses will emerge from empirical data.

Karen Rosen (1992) used grounded theory in her study of how young women cope with dating violence. She selected a sample of 10 women from a college campus. These women had previously been identified as victims of dating violence. Rosen conducted in-depth interviews with these women to determine which interpersonal, intrapersonal, and contextual factors seemed relevant in enabling these women to cope with their victimization. Major constructs that were disclosed through interviews included women's vulnerabilities, couple imbalances, seductive processes, and disentanglement processes. Rosen found that vulnerable young women who formed fused, imbalanced relationships with vul-

BOX 1.4   PERSONALITY HIGHLIGHT

GORDON BAZEMORE
Florida Atlantic University

Statistics: B.A., M.S. (sociology), Memphis State University; Ph.D. (sociology), University of Oregon.

BACKGROUND AND INTERESTS

My interests include juvenile justice, community and restorative justice, community policing, crime victims, and victimology. On the first night in one of the first criminal justice graduate classes I taught, a student made an interesting comment that has stuck with me. After introducing myself and telling the class members about some of the research areas of most interest to me— juvenile justice reform and detention alternatives, community-oriented policing, victim involvement and assistance, youth development, and restorative and community justice—this student, a relatively high-ranking local police officer, commented: "Oh, it sounds like you're mostly focused on a bunch of hopeless causes." Caught off guard, I had to respond by saying, "Yeah, that sounds about right."

At that moment, this student crystallized what I now realize has been a unifying theme in much of my academic work, criminal justice reform. More broadly, I am also interested in social reforms that might help to bring about a better quality of justice and quality of life in communities. Thinking back, this interest in value-based, somewhat radical, and often very difficult to implement reforms seemed to describe, in part, what it was that attracted me to this field. This was first a sense that the part of the system I knew most about as a young person, and then as a sociology student and professional, the juvenile justice system, was not working very well. In addition, the interest and curiosity that led me to criminology and social deviance courses was in part a very personal reflection on how I and some of my adolescent friends managed to grow up to be more or less law-abiding, while other peers doing pretty much the same things we did became increasingly caught up in the juvenile justice and criminal justice systems and more involved in crime. I sensed then that what happened to most of us had a lot to do with *not getting caught,* and/or not being brought into those systems when we were caught, and something to do with remaining connected to school, work and having other kinds of what sociologists call "commitments to conforming behavior."

This sense of a need for major reform in juvenile justice and curiosity about those "other things" unrelated to any formal system response that help young people "grow out of" whatever trouble they might get involved in led me also to a more general interest in intervention.

BOX 1.4   CONTINUED

While training as a sociologist in the doctoral program at the University of Oregon had created a deep appreciation for theory and some interest in longitudinal research that could follow co-horts of young people in trouble as adolescents into their adult years and thereby help to explain why some kids stopped their delinquency and others did not (my dissertation topic), I knew early on that I was not simply interested in such knowledge for its own sake. Rather, it was first the implications of theory and basic research for better program and policies, and second, for better evaluation of criminal justice interventions.

These days I think a lot about how the major criminological theories that have guided the best research could, but generally haven't, guided intervention programs and policy. In particular, I think that the best of the theoretical perspectives in the social disorganization tradition and related social capital theories, new symbolic interaction theories that address how long-time offenders reconstruct their identities, and the best and most holistic control theories and organizational perspectives could be used to inform intervention related to some of the aforementioned "hopeless causes" criminal justice reforms. The field of criminal justice intervention is in a sense wide open to this kind of application precisely because it has been so atheoretical. In my view, especially problematic are intervention programs that tend to individualize what are in fact collective problems and issues (e.g., how offenders can be reintegrated, how the needs of victims can be met, how to prevent crime). Once we have begun to make this theory/practice connection, the real excitement for researchers and scholars should be to develop and test intervention theories.

RESEARCH INVESTIGATIONS

Based on this commitment to a theory-building and testing agenda, I have since graduate school tried to become methodologically eclectic. I believe that research questions need to drive the research design and data collection methods rather than the reverse. I have dabbled in survey research, experimental and quasi-experimental evaluation, and both quantitative and qualitative case studies. In recent years, I have come back to qualitative, or mixed-method, research designs a lot because of what appears to be a clear need to develop better understandings of the logic of interventions, and to develop theories about these practices. For example, much of the work my colleagues and I have done in the past few years has been focused on trying to build grounded theory around restorative justice processes.

My connection with what is now called "restorative justice" began as a graduate student in the early 1980s when I had a unique opportunity to become involved as a research associate in an experimental evaluation of a national juvenile restitution program initiative (funded by the Office of Juvenile Justice and Delinquency Prevention). The evaluation of the initiative found positive impact of restitution and community service (with victim offender mediation in a couple of trials) on several outcomes, including recidivism. Equally important, the initiative itself laid important groundwork for a new way of thinking about accountability as making amends for the harm caused by one's crime, rather than simply submitting to punishment in-

BOX 1.4   CONTINUED

flicted by the state. This way of thinking later became one cornerstone of what is today the restorative justice paradigm.

In recent years, I have found restorative and community justice reforms challenging (and therefore interesting) in part because they pose such a broad and deep critique of current criminal justice responses. Restorative justice reforms seek to change outcomes from those offender-focused objectives based on punishment and rehabilitation to those focused on the goal of repairing harm to multiple stakeholders. As they also offer a new way of thinking about notions of public safety and reintegration, these approaches challenge the system to engage victims, offenders, and communities actively in the justice decision-making process. In doing so, they push practitioners toward interesting varieties of systemic and organizational reform, while focusing intervention on efforts to build community capacity to prevent and control crime. As a criminologist, what is especially interesting to me about all of this are issues about how restorative justice "conferencing" processes operationalize theories of social exchange, procedural justice, and reintegrative shaming. In addition, the potential of these processes to strengthen informal social control and even build social capital at a micro level is especially intriguing.

With regard to methodology, gaining an understanding of the meaning, implementation, and impact of these restorative community justice reforms creates a need for a continuing eclecticism. There are currently important experimental and quasi-experimental tests of restorative conferencing programs underway or recently completed, led by Larry Sherman, John Braithwaite, Kathy Daly, and others (my colleagues and I are at the front-end of our own impact study of school-based restorative justice as a preventative alternative to zero-tolerance policies in an urban school district). I have become convinced in the past few years of the need for continuing application of qualitative approaches—even when used within experimental designs—in order to discover what these processes really look like, to learn whether or to what degree restorative justice principles are actually being implemented, and to discover the underlying theories of intervention. It seems important in a new intervention reform to understand how practitioners and participants in restorative processes conceptualize the linkage between these interventions, intermediate outcomes (like victim satisfaction and offender empathy), and long-term outcomes such as recidivism reduction and healing. Limits of impact designs *alone* it seems are that, while they may indeed tell us that a particular program model "worked" in one experimental trial in one jurisdiction, they generally fail to tell us much about *why* the intervention worked. We may therefore be unable to say what underlying theory of change was responsible for the success, or failure, of the intervention to achieve its desired outcomes, and therefore be unable to generalize from the experiment to a broader theory of offender change, for example. From a policy and practice perspective, the lack of understanding about why a program worked or didn't work may mean that we may also be unable to replicate the intervention in alternative contexts because we must rely only on programmatic guidelines rather than a clear understanding of underlying principles that can be applied in multiple and diverse contexts. We may even be unsure, if we do not pay close attention to whether the intervention that brought about the positive or negative results was truly restorative justice, or some other approach.

BOX 1.4   CONTINUED

ADVICE TO STUDENTS

My advice to students these days is to develop a strong theoretical grounding for their work, and to try in writing about even the smallest studies to think about how this research fits into a bigger conceptual picture. One of the greatest weaknesses I see in reviewing manuscripts (aside from poor writing and disorganization) is a failure to link one's research, policy, or theoretical position to a larger theoretical, policy, or research issue. The significance of important research can be lost for lack of consideration in the narrative about how one's study fits into a body of research or a larger policy debate; on the other hand, even small and apparently insignificant studies that explore some underinvestigated phenomenon in context—when presented as "case studies" in the theoretical sense—can make important contributions to criminology and criminal justice.

One key to convincing readers that one's study or theoretical or policy position is important in a universal sense is to present it *in context.* In other words, there may be a reason why an examination of an issue in South Florida detention centers, for example, is essential to make one's case. If so, then tell us why your study or issue is important in this time and place. But, in any case, *don't be afraid to publish your work.* The greatest difficulty in my early years after finishing graduate school, while working for private nonprofit research organizations such as NCCD and the Pacific Institute for Research and Evaluation, was gaining confidence that my research or my theoretical and policy observations had anything to offer. I believed more or less that if my data, or theory, or both were flawed in some way, my findings were not worthy of publication. Critical reading of published articles in a variety of journals (don't limit yourself to *Criminology* or *American Sociological Review*) should convince students that no research is perfect, and there are many methodological and/or theoretical problems in much published work. Get into the mindset that you should write up your findings and send them out, but work hardest on writing clearly and organizing your work.

While I continue to encourage methodological eclecticism, and think we need more and more in-depth, qualitative studies, I advise students to get as much training in quantitative methods as possible. In particular, a strong sense of quantitative research *design* is essential even for those who end up doing mostly qualitative work. As I get older and busier, I find it is very difficult to invest the time needed for good ethnographic work, but I encourage students and junior faculty to try to build in qualitative components to even the most quantitative studies. Others are better role models for how to do this in a rigorous way, but I have found at least that my own comfort level with a quantitative study increases to the extent that I have spent some time "on the scene." Michael Patton's books on qualitative evaluation provide the ultimate practical guide to students who want to build in qualitative methods into what are mostly quantitative studies. Robert Yin's work on the logic and importance of "case studies," for me, breaks down barriers between qualitative and quantitative and gets to the logic of how we use findings from any study to generalize to theory—or, more broadly, to build knowledge.

BOX 1.4   CONTINUED

Finally, because research and writing, and academic life generally, can become a grind that makes one lose focus and commitment, it is important to find a way to remain inspired. Constantly thinking about the interplay between theory and practice keeps me interested in both, and thinking too much about one or the other in isolation can get pretty boring. Intervention practice gets reduced to program manuals, and theoretical discussions in the abstract do not seem relevant. The people in the field who I find most interesting seem to move rather easily between the two and are able to think in big and bold, and sometimes outrageous, ways about policy as well as research. Ultimately, these writers keep us interested in the prospects for better justice and energize us for a commitment to study, and at times be activists in, "hopeless causes."

nerable men tended to use system-maintaining coping strategies to deal with the violence and were subject to powerful seductive processes until they began to disentangle themselves from their relationships. Rosen eventually generated a contextual stress and coping theoretical framework, which had been grounded with in-depth interviews and observations.

Another study using grounded theory was conducted by Tony Ward and colleagues (1995). They studied 26 incarcerated child molesters, who were interviewed and asked to describe their most recent or typical offense. Their descriptions of events, including the contributing factors, cognitive and behavioral components, led Ward and colleagues to develop a theoretical **model** of an offense chain, incorporating the possible interactions among various stages and factors. Subsequently, the authors applied the developed model to an independent sample of 12 other child molesters to see whether the model had predictive value.

Yet another study using grounded theory was conducted by Irene Carvalho and Dan A. Lewis (2003). These researchers investigated a theory of the fear of crime among a sample of welfare recipients in run-down and crime-ridden neighborhoods in Chicago. According to past research, the literature about fear of crime in neighborhoods suggested that most residents became isolated from others, and that they tended to let their fear of crime control their daily lives and social interactions with others. However, Carvalho and Lewis discovered quite different reactions among those they studied. They found that rather than fear, which a few persons exhibited, other reactions emerged, such as anger and safety. Most persons they investigated were either angry with crime in their neighborhoods or viewed their neighborhoods as safe havens for normal activity, since they regarded certain youth gangs, who controlled these neighborhoods, as more protective of neighborhood residents rather than threatening. These investigators developed alternative explanations for what they found that countered the "fear of crime" view. They noted, for example, that crime and incivilities do not always raise fear, even in inner-city, high-disorder communities. Fear is not always of crime. In their study, a sense of safety, not fear, was the prevalent reaction to neighborhood disorder/crime. With this sense of safety, crime/incivilities or the dangers they pose are not central to individual life, but rather they are peripheral (Carvalho & Lewis, 2003). Thus, these researchers provided a viable foundation for subsequent research, seeking to show alternative patterns of reactions to crime among residents in other cities and neighborhoods.

In each of the three studies above, investigators evolved theoretical schemes to account for what they observed. Their explanations of events were grounded in empirical facts disclosed through interviews and observation. Each of the investigators would presumably use their developed models in other settings to test their validity and predictive utility. Consistent with grounded theory, as these researchers would conduct further investigations, new and different factual information might mean that they would refine or refocus their initial theories, shaping them in accordance with additional empirical evidence gathered from new subjects.

One criticism of grounded theory is that it is self-serving and might lead to researcher bias. Thus, theories derived from empirical observations of research settings will be couched in the interpretations of events by investigators. These interpretations of observed events are flawed because of the researcher's own input into what is observed and what it means. Subsequent observations of similar settings with new research subjects will no doubt be influenced by a researcher's previous interpretations of similar events. This argument is weak, however, since grounded theory is self-correcting. The very nature of grounded theory is continual refinement and development, as new factual information is disclosed about new research settings. However, it is difficult to imagine how one's own feelings, sentiments, and biases would intrude in this process, since the discovery of new information would be the basis for changes in one's theorizing.

Axiomatic Theory

Unlike grounded theory, which is somewhat similar to inductive theory, axiomatic theory is closely associated with deductive theory. **Axiomatic theory** uses **axioms,** or truisms, as building blocks from which testable hypotheses can be derived and tested. Axioms are the equivalent of statements about reality, which are accepted as true. Sufficient numbers of these assertions that are believed to be true will enable theorists and researchers to derive tentative statements, hypotheses, that can be tested through subsequent social research.

Norman Denzin (1989, pp. 60–61) says that the ordering of propositions into a theoretical scheme is conventionally seen as the logical outcome of concept formulation, construction of definitions, and the collection of data. Denzin notes that in axiomatic theorizing, certain propositions are treated as axioms; furthermore, lower-level predictions or theorems are derived. From this strategic blend of axioms and theorems, hypotheses are logically deduced and subjected to empirical testing.

For example, French sociologist Emile Durkheim wrote about suicide and the reasons why it is committed. Durkheim analyzed a vast **data set** in France in the late 1800s relating to suicides investigated by police. He was able to develop various propositions and axioms from which statements about the causes of suicide could be deduced. The following statements are some of the types of axioms Durkheim may have used in his theory of suicide.

1. Persons are gregarious and desire close social bonds with others.
2. Close social bonds provide persons with security and comfort.
3. Disruptions in one's life that alter social bonds are traumatic and generate social and psychological stress.
4. Persons with greater attachments and bonds to others are less stressed compared with persons who have few or no attachments or bonds to others.

5. Suicide is more prevalent among persons who suffer greater stress compared with those who suffer no or little stress.

Are these true or generally accepted statements? Should we tend to agree with them? Let's engage in a little "if-then" reasoning. This is the type of reasoning that says, "*If* statement A is true, and *if* statement B is true, and *if* statement C is true, *then* we can generate one or more other statements that should logically follow." Let's assume for the sake of illustrating axiomatic theory that the above statements are true. Furthermore, let's assume that Durkheim developed these statements and accepted them as true.

Durkheim devised additional, more specific statements, possibly theorems, that were used to enhance other, more general statements. For instance, Durkheim observed that some religions, such as Protestantism, emphasized individual means of achieving a spiritual salvation. Thus, Protestants might be more inclined to rely on their own individual efforts and work as a means of becoming "saved" than persons of other religious faiths where individuality was not considered a prominent factor. Catholicism and Judaism were examined by Durkheim. Based on his understanding of the different basic belief systems in each religious faith, he speculated that compared with Protestantism, persons with Catholic beliefs would be more inclined to be less individualistic in their thoughts about their own salvation. Persons of the Jewish faith might be even more disinclined toward individuality in their worship and salvation. Thus, Durkheim argued, we might find the closest social bonds among those of the Jewish faith, followed by Catholics, followed by Protestants. Protestants, according to Durkheim, would emphasize individuality and thus play down the significance of social bonds. Using the axioms and theorems about persons developed above, persons with greater social bonds would be less inclined to suicide, while those persons with fewer social bonds would be more inclined to suicide. This thinking led Durkheim to examine suicide rates among Catholics, Protestants, and Jews and compare them. He found that Jews had the lowest suicide rates, while Protestants had the highest suicide rates. In this respect, his theorizing about suicide and its relation to social bonds was supported by the evidence he disclosed about religious affiliation and suicide rates.

Durkheim didn't complete his research with these religious comparisons. He also investigated other scenarios where social bonds varied. He noted that as persons age, they have fewer social bonds compared with younger persons. This is because of the greater likelihood of natural death occurring among one's peers through the aging process. Those with the greatest likelihood of having the fewest social bonds were older men. Through his analysis of French suicide records, Durkheim discovered that suicide rates were highest among elderly men.

Durkheim's research about suicide rates and social bonds directly illustrates how we can use axioms and theorems to derive testable hypotheses. In Durkheim's case, he had access to national data about suicides and the circumstances under which they occurred. It was relatively easy for him to see whether suicide rates varied according to various specific social or individual variables such as religion or age. Thus, axiomatic theory might be used to construct various criminological theories about events. However, a search of the *Criminal Justice Abstracts* in 2004 showed that only six abstracted articles referred to axiomatic theory, suggesting the theory's waning popularity.

Variables and Theory

Variables refer to any phenomena that can assume more than one value. Again, there are several alternative definitions of variables. Two such definitions are that variables are categories that may be divided into two or more subcategories (Fitzgerald & Cox, 1987) and concepts that have been operationalized or concepts that can vary or take on different values of a quantitative nature (Fitzgerald & Cox, 1987). Both of these definitions of variables are accurate. However, the first definition is preferred because it avoids the usage of terms such as "operationalization" and "concepts." These terms have specific and separate meanings in this book.

What are phenomena that can assume more than one value? First, any attitudinal phenomenon we can name (e.g., prejudice, achievement motivation, burnout, work satisfaction, alienation, positive feelings toward police officers) are variables. We can have large or small amounts of burnout, work satisfaction, positive feelings toward police officers, alienation, and achievement motivation. The actual amounts of these phenomena possessed by different persons depend on how these variables are measured. Other phenomena that can assume more than one value are:

> gender
> social class
> race
> ethnicity
> political affiliation
> religious affiliation
> urban–rural background
> age
> income
> types of crime
> crime rates, delinquency
> city size and population
> judicial, prosecutorial, and parole board discretion
> police–community relations
> employment discrimination

For instance, gender assumes more than one value. The values are subclasses on the gender variable, or **variable subclasses,** including "male" and "female." A single **subclass** is "male." Another subclass is "female." Different values on the "type of crime" variable might be "violent offenses" and "property offenses." Different values on the political or religious affiliation variables might be "Democrat," "Republican," "American Independent," "Catholic," "Protestant," and "Jewish." These are more like designations than values in a numerical sense. It is helpful to think of these variables as consisting simply of two or more different subclasses. And we determine which subclasses will be used in our research for any variable.

Any research problem we choose to investigate is also a variable. We use other variables to explain the variable we are investigating. We illustrate the interconnectedness of these variables (the variable to be explained and the explanatory variables) in our theory. Thus, our definition of theory makes more sense now as "an integrated body of assumptions, propositions, and definitions that explain and predict the relationship between two or more variables." One of these variables is the problem we wish to explain, while one or more other variables are used to explain or account for the existence of the problem (i.e., the variable to be explained). In Emile Durkheim's suicide research, suicide was the problem or phenomenon Durkheim wished to explain. Social bonds were used as the explanatory variable. Durkheim found different situations where differences in social bonds occurred. Where variation in the degree of social bonds was observed, Durkheim reasoned, then variation in suicide rates would also be observed. This reasoning led him to theorize about different religious faiths and persons of different ages, and whether suicide rates fluctuated in predictable ways according to one's religious faith or age.

Variables, essential to all theories, perform different functions. In order to best portray these functions, some distinctions between variables can be made. These include considerations of variables as (1) independent, (2) dependent, (3) discrete, and (4) continuous.

Independent Variables

Independence and dependence mean that some variables cause changes in other variables, while some variables are influenced by other variables. An **independent variable** is one that elicits changes in other variables. For instance, some researchers wish to explain why certain offenders persist in committing new crimes and seem to rationalize their previous criminal conduct. Courts desire that criminals accept responsibility for their actions, although it is difficult for some offenders to accept responsibility. Shadd Maruna (2004) sought to explain the persistence of criminal conduct by examining the explanations various criminals provided for engaging in criminal behavior. Persistent offenders tended to blame society or fate for their criminality (e.g., "That's just the type of person I am"; "Born to lose"; "Bad breaks"). Maruna referred to these characterizations of one's offending persistence as externality. Thus, these criminals' rationalizations of their criminal conduct contributed significantly to the conduct's persistence or repetitiveness. Externality, therefore, would be regarded as an independent variable that accounts for or explains persistent criminal conduct.

In another investigation, Ronald Weitzer and Steven A Tuch (2004) investigated reforming police departments and racial differences. Among other things, these researchers found that racial differences among those surveyed helped to explain whether certain groups more or less strongly supported police reforms as well as perceptions of police misconduct. The race variable, a composite of race/ethnicity, was used by these researchers as an independent one, and upon which the nature and degree of police reform, including heightening police accountability and minimizing police misconduct, depended.

Dependent Variables

A **dependent variable** is one whose value is affected by one or more independent variables. Dependent variables are those phenomena that derive their values largely from the influences or actions of other variables. In the Weitzer and Tuch (2004) study, accountability and police misconduct were identified as key dependent variables whose change was partially explained by changes in the race/ethnicity variable. In the Maruna (2004) study, repetitive criminal conduct or criminal persistence was the dependent variable explained by criminals' rationalizations.

A study by John Wooldredge and Amy Thistlewaite (2004) examined court dispositions relative to spousal assaults. These researchers wanted to know whether the socioeconomic status (SES) of neighborhoods where spousal abuse cases were reported and prosecuted contributed to extralegal disparities in judicial sentencing patterns. Actually, Wooldredge and Thistlewaite found that persons of lower SES were less likely to be charged with spousal assault in domestic violence cases compared with persons in the upper SES, although persons of lower SES who were convicted were more likely to receive jail sentences compared with those in the upper SES who were convicted. Thus, charging decisions and sentences to jail, two dependent variables, were significantly influenced by whether persons were of lower or upper SES.

In criminology and criminal justice, dependent variables are easy to identify. Often, they are "standardized" as dependent variables. That is, their use as either independent or dependent variables is fairly consistent from study to study. A silly but informative illustration is the gender–delinquency relation. Which variable, gender or delinquency, would be the more likely choice as the independent variable in relation to the other? Obviously, differences in gender are far more likely to produce changes in delinquent behavior rather than delinquent behavior producing changes in gender. Dependent variables from various components of the criminal justice system might be:

> probation officer burnout and stress
> crime rates
> prisonization
> prosecutorial, judicial, and parole board discretion
> police officer discretion to use deadly force in apprehending fleeing offenders
> police professionalism
> police misconduct
> inmate suicides
> inmate rioting frequency
> inmate rehabilitation
> parolee and probationer success in conditional intermediate punishment programs
> turnover among correctional personnel
> sentencing disparities

Most variables are not fixed as either independent or dependent ones. Race, SES, and gender are exceptions. Many variables perform both independent and dependent variable functions depending on the nature of one's study. Furthermore, there are occasions when more complex combinations of variables are articulated. The use of more than two variables in some type of explanatory sequence means that certain variables may function as both independent and dependent at the same time.

For instance, suppose we wish to study the relation between type of correctional officer supervision, correctional officer stress, and correctional officer turnover. We may read research reports indicating that if correctional officer supervisors were to involve their cor-

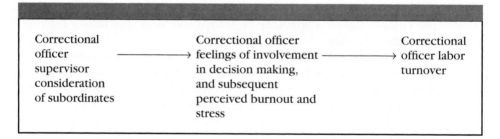

FIGURE 1.1   Hypothesized relation between correctional officer supervisor consideration of subordinates, correctional officer self-perceptions of involvement in decision making, and correctional officer labor turnover.

rectional officer subordinates in decision-making power more often, they might reduce the amount of burnout or stress experienced by correctional officers. Also, burnout reductions may incline correctional officers to consider remaining for longer employment periods with their prisons or jails. We have just linked three variables together. We will need to explain how each relates to the other, but this will be done in our theoretical scheme. The three-variable linkage we have formulated might look something like Figure 1.1.

Notice in Figure 1.1 that correctional officer self-perceptions of involvement in decision making and subsequent perceived burnout and stress are considered influenced by behaviors of correctional officer supervisors, such as their consideration of subordinates in decision-making matters. Notice also that these correctional officer feelings of burnout and stress are linked in an implied causal fashion with labor turnover. Therefore, if you're the boss and don't give your workers power in decisions affecting their work, they may stress out, burn out, and possibly quit their jobs.

In the variable scenario in Figure 1.1, correctional officer burnout and stress is functioning in a dual capacity—it is a dependent variable in relation to correctional officer supervisor consideration, and it is an independent variable in relation to officer labor turnover. Labor turnover is the main dependent variable in this example. Usually, when researchers formulate theories to explain things, they specify which variables will be considered relevant and how they will be used—as independent, as dependent, or as both independent and dependent under certain circumstances.

Discrete Variables

Discrete variables are phenomena that have a limited number of exclusive subclasses. For all practical purposes, gender is a discrete variable You are either a male or a female. You cannot be in the two variable subclasses at the same time. Type of crime is also a discrete variable. Divisions or subclasses on this variable include violent and property crime, misdemeanor and felony, or some other discrete designation. There are exceptions, of course. In biology, varying the amount of estrogen, androgen, or testosterone in the bodies of males and females may make them more or less male or female. In fact, biologists may be able to make a convincing case for "degrees of maleness or femaleness." Also, criminals may commit several types of crime during a crime spree. They may steal a car, burglarize a dwelling, rob a bank, kill a teller, and kidnap the bank president. Later, they may assault a police officer, resist arrest, and commit perjury on the witness stand later at their trial. For convenience, however, criminologists will likely place them in one criminal category or another, depending on the type of research conducted. They will either be classed as "violent offenders" (most likely), or possibly "property offenders" (least likely).

Continuous Variables

Continuous variables are phenomena that can be infinitely divided into a variety of subclasses. All attitudinal variables are continuous variables. Income is a continuous variable. The crime rate is a continuous variable. Each of these phenomena may assume an infinite or nearly infinite number of values. In actual practice, however, and largely for the convenience of researchers and readers, almost all continuous variables are reduced more or less arbitrarily to a limited number of discrete categories. For instance, we could report incomes of 50,000 city residents to the penny. Frank Smith earns $30,267.83 per year, and John Jones earns $16,271.26 per year. But more often than not, income is reported in a series of discrete categories, such as "High Income," "Moderately High Income," "Moderately Low Income," and "Low Income." Dollar amounts can be assigned each of these categories, so that we will know where to place Frank Smith and John Jones. Zero dollars to $5,000 will define the "Low Income" category, while $5,001–$10,000 will define the "Moderately Low Income" category. The "High Income" category may be $30,000 or over, depending on the community we study and how we have chosen to define our categories.

Again, there is a strong subjective element here. We define how many categories or subclasses will comprise given variables, and we usually make up our own definitions or criteria for those categories or variable subclasses. These are often arbitrary decisions. Eventually, we shall see that certain guidelines, **conventions**, or standards may be invoked in the construction of our variable subclasses.

Causal Relations Between Variables

One aim of theoretical schemes is to identify causal relationships between variables. Logically, if we know what variable or variables cause another variable to occur or change in value, we might be able to exert some control and produce expected and desirable outcomes. When elementary school teachers hear about some of their former third- or fourth-graders who are now teenagers and who have committed serious offenses, they might say, "I just knew so-and-so was going to turn out that way—you just 'know' about certain children like that! Something could have been done earlier to prevent that!," what they are alluding may be an intervention program of some sort that may have "caused" the child to grow up differently and not become delinquent. While it is often difficult for teachers to define the specific nature and properties of an effective intervention program that might deter children from becoming delinquents, it is significant that they believe that "something" could and should have been done (as an intervention) for certain "problem children," whomever they are, and that that "something" could have "caused" a different outcome.

Most of the research in the professional literature avoids using "cause–effect" phrase-ology. Rather, more conservative tones are ordinarily adopted. Statements such as, "There is an apparent association between X and Y," or "There may be a connection between X and Y," or "Evidence suggests that X may contribute to Y" are typical of the conclusions drawn by most researchers. And this is precisely how it ought to be. We may be in the business of at-tempting to establish cause–effect relationships between variables, but we also understand that it is very difficult to establish cause–effect relations between variables in any absolute sense.

The Complementarity of Theory and Research

There is considerable interplay between theory and research. Much of the time, theory is a guide for our research investigations. Theory focuses our research in particular directions, and it directs us to examine certain variables and ignore the influence of other variables. Thus, theory is like blinders on horses: Horses see directly ahead and are less disturbed or distracted by events not directly in their field of vision. Theory is also value-laden, because it is formulated in the context of our beliefs about what causes certain events. If we believe that criminal behavior is a function of glandular malfunction, we probably won't focus our attention on delinquent subcultures or the socialization process of differential association. However, we will pay attention to potential relations between different types of crime and glandular irregularities or problems among criminals. However, if we adopt labeling theory as our preferred explanation for criminal behavior, we will be concerned with public reac-tions to and definitions of crime and the criminal's response to such reactions. We will not conduct biochemical analyses of criminals to determine the possible presence of glandular irregularities.

Research allows us to test our theories empirically. We can evaluate whether our the-ories are adequate in accounting for the events we try to explain. Our predictions of events either will be supported or refuted, depending on what we observe from our collected data. We may discover facts about our data that were unknown or less apparent to us when we started our investigation. Upon further analysis, however, it seems that certain variables have become more important to us because of their association with the event we are ex-plaining. This is sometimes called **serendipity,** where we discover several important things about the people we study that we weren't looking for initially. When serendipity occurs, we might reformulate our original theoretical schemes and include these previously un-known or less important variables. Thus, research we conduct may suggest theories, the ap-plication of different strategies to collect and analyze data, or the modification of existing theories according to newly discovered criteria.

Hypotheses and Theory: A Preliminary View

Research is the means whereby theories are tested. We must collect and examine relevant data in order to show whether any theory is supported or refuted. Conventionally, investi-gators will focus on a research problem, select or devise a theoretical scheme to explain the problem, and then generate specific hypotheses to test. These hypotheses are directly deduced from theories. In Durkheim's study of suicide, he theorized that social bonds among groups were crucial in accounting for or explaining suicide. He hypothesized about different scenarios where variations in social bonds would occur. Durkheim didn't know what he would eventually find, nor did he know whether his findings would support or refute his theory of suicide and social bonds. Therefore, he hypothesized about different situations. Based on French suicide records and descriptive information of suicide victims, some of Durkheim's hypotheses were:

1. Protestants will have higher suicide rates compared with Catholics.
2. Catholics will have higher suicide rates compared with Jews.
3. Elderly persons will have higher suicide rates compared with younger persons.
4. Men will have higher suicide rates compared with women.
5. Single persons will have higher suicide rates compared with married persons.
6. Married persons with no children will have higher suicide rates compared with married persons with children.

All of these statements are **hypotheses** that can be tested. Durkheim had access to this French data; his father was a French government official with political connections. Durkheim analyzed suicide data for a period of years and found that each and every one of his hypothesis statements was supported. He based his tentative conclusions on empirical data.

In another example, Wang (1996) was interested in Asian gang affiliations, and whether Asian gang affiliation patterns were different from other types of gang affiliation patterns, including white, black, or Hispanic gangs. Wang noted that some gang investigators studied Asian gangs and found essentially no differences between these and other types of racial/ethnic gangs according to how they are formed and perpetuated. Yet Wang described the research of others who believed that Asian gangs are influenced more by their traditional belief systems and unique culture, as well as by ethnocentric identity crises. Wang decided to use the social developmental model, a blend of social control theory and social learning theory. These theories stress factors such as attachment, commitment, involvement, belief, peer influence, and the impact of school and neighborhood environment. He applied the statistical method of multiple regression analysis to isolate variables relevant to gang affiliation patterns. Wang collected data from 358 Asian American high school students from 20 cities in five regions of the country. Wang believed that on the basis of the theory he used, he would *not* find significant differences separating Asian gang affiliation patterns from other racial or ethnic gang affiliation patterns previously described by other researchers. Thus, he set forth an hypothesis where he predicted no differences between gang affiliation patterns according to race/ethnicity. His results supported his hypothesis. The support of this hypothesis was also support for the social developmental theory he tested.

Generally, criminologists and criminal justicians proceed in this fashion. They identify a problem for study. They devise a theoretical explanation for the problem. They fashion various hypotheses to test from their theory. They collect data relevant to their hypothesis tests and generate findings that either support or refute these hypotheses. Supporting or refuting hypotheses derived from theory is the equivalent of supporting or refuting the theory itself. However, a single study, such as Wang's gang affiliation investigation, does not by itself prove or disprove a theory. Many subsequent studies must be conducted before we can cautiously conclude a theory has been proved or disproved. In the meantime, we use careful language to guard against rushing to judgment about a given theory. Thus, we "find support for a theory," or we "fail to find support for a theory," or "tentative support for theory X has been found," or "on the basis of these findings, we cannot support Theory X."

The Value of Theory

Often, distinctions among social scientific fields have been made according to their theoretical sophistication. Some evidence exists that criminal justice has not advanced theoretically to the same degree as criminology (Willis, 1983). Despite this evidence or its validity, there is a strong trend within criminal justice departments in the United States to improve the current state of theory throughout the discipline.

Theoretical sophistication has also been equated with the degree of professionalization in any academic discipline (Dingwall & Lewis, 1983). One reason for the perceived absence of theory in criminal justice has been its historical emphasis on process and application within the criminal justice system. In contrast, criminology has historically emphasized crime causation (Henderson & Boostrom, 1989). Whatever the merits of these arguments, the fact is that theory is receiving greater attention from both criminologists and criminal justice professionals alike. Theory is increasingly perceived as the integrating medium through which the administration of justice, the criminal justice system, and explanations of crime can be productively blended.

Intermediate punishment programs such as intensive supervised probation, furloughs, work/study release, and home incarceration/electronic monitoring must increasingly respond to questions about those inmates and criminal candidates most likely to benefit from these supervisory services. In turn, these services may be treated by criminologists as intervening factors in theoretical schemes, where these factors may change criminal behaviors and reduce recidivism in different ways. Theory not only functions to explain and predict events, but it acts as a general policy guide for how offenders are or should be processed throughout the criminal justice system. The observed factual information—crime rates, recidivism rates, crime escalation, effects of decriminalization, plea bargaining, shock probation, short- or long-term incarceration—all conspire to tell us something about the validity of theories we have formulated.

Atheoretical Evaluations

Not every study is based on or grounded in a theory. Conventionally, criminologists and criminal justicians perhaps prefer that criminological investigations are theoretically based in some way, because theory enables researchers to generalize their findings to wider varieties of settings. However, some research is undertaken simply to answer direct questions unrelated to theory of any kind. In these cases, the investigators who conduct such research have inquiring minds and simply want to know. These are known as **atheoretical evaluations.**

One example of an atheoretical evaluation is a study by Magnus Seng (1996), who described campus thefts at the main and downtown campuses of Loyola University in Chicago. Seng depicted studies of theft as not especially newsworthy or popular. But he described campus thefts, at least on these two campuses. He didn't know much if anything about campus thefts, since studies of this phenomenon were practically nonexistent. Seng simply wanted to study campus theft to "increase our knowledge of college-campus theft . . . and to relate

. . . findings to [theft] prevention strategies" (p. 34). After much description, data analysis, and comparisons, Seng concluded that at least for the two campuses he studied, no differences in theft patterns existed. There were no differences in items stolen, type of victim, or gender of victim. However, Seng found that thefts were more likely to occur in libraries or in faculty offices on both campuses. He speculated about different crime prevention measures that might reduce thefts on campuses generally, and what faculty and students could do to reduce thefts from libraries and campus offices.

Because Seng didn't know much about campus thefts and because little or no research literature existed on the subject, this piece of research may also be considered exploratory and descriptive. Seng never advanced a particular theory of campus theft. Thus, his research was atheoretical.

Atheoretical research is extensively conducted and reported in conventional journal outlets. The fact that theory is not used does not mean that the research itself is somehow unscientific or that it is less scientific compared with other, more conventional investigations. Seng was very conscientious in using sound scientific principles while conducting his investigation. A great deal of evaluation research is atheoretical. In evaluation research, investigators want to know whether programs work, what their level of effectiveness is, and what can be done to make programs work better.

The Value of Research

Research provides support for or refutes our theories. Generally, research advances our knowledge about things, raising our level of certainty about why events that are of interest to us occur in ways that they do. Much of the research used in examples throughout this chapter will benefit greatly from additional research. We may eventually be able to describe fully the process whereby police officers acquire professional attitudes about themselves and how the types of uniforms they wear influence this process. We might eventually learn the true relation between delinquency and homes that are or are not intact. Furthermore, some day we may be able to predict with amazing accuracy those settings where inmate suicides will be highest, and we may be able to structure things or juggle inmate environments in ways that curb inmate suicidal propensities.

Research is not limited exclusively to testing theories, however. As we have seen, some research is evaluative, where we seek to discover the efficacy of a particular intervention strategy or the influence of certain factors on others. Of course, we can carry our research findings into the classroom to enhance our lectures on specific subjects. Student interest in course content is frequently stimulated by presenting some of the findings from new research on selected subjects. Research uncovers topic areas that need further study. Research suggests ideas that might be useful in modifying older theories or developing new ones.

SUMMARY

The research enterprise is a scientific process seeking answers to an infinite number of questions relevant to those in criminal justice, criminology, other social sciences, and throughout the entire academic community. Research consists of investigations and studies that are systematically designed to increase our knowledge of events and the variables that initiate their occurrence. This enterprise consists of several important components. A problem is formulated and an explanation for it is suggested. A research design is constructed for the purpose of gathering relevant information about the designated problem. Theory, or an integrated body of assumptions, propositions, and variables, guides our efforts to discover why the problem or event occurs by articulating interrelationships between variables. Theory explains and predicts the linkages between events and the explanations we suggest for their occurrence. Different types of data collection methods are used, and collected data are tabulated and systematically analyzed to reveal both substantive and theoretical information about events. When more than one data collection method is used to gather information, this is known as triangulation, and the information from different sources is used to cross-validate collected data. Tentative conclusions are drawn that either support or fail to support the theory used to explain the event.

Research investigations may be either pure or applied, or a combination of both. Pure research merely seeks more information about events and why they occur. Clear-cut applications of pure research findings are difficult to determine or identify. Knowledge for the sake of knowledge is often the guiding principle of such research efforts. In contrast, applied or basic or substantive research is implemented to achieve practical ends, such as discovering the worth of particular interventions in bringing about or preventing different kinds of behavior, such as crime or delinquency.

Research conducted in the social sciences, particularly in criminology and criminal justice, is undertaken within the context of certain basic assumptions about the situations, settings, and persons to be studied. It is believed that there is a pattern to social and psychological behaviors and attitudes, and also that these patterns are discoverable. Once such patterns have been identified, it is assumed further that the variables under investigation can be measured so that their impact on the event we wish to explain can be determined. This is the empirical nature of the investigated information sought. Causal relations between events and explanations of them are difficult to demonstrate, at least in the short term. Nevertheless, it is believed that such cause–effect relationships do exist and that eventually, such relationships will emerge with a high degree of regularity and certainty of occurrence.

Social scientists conduct research for a variety of reasons. Persons simply want to know more about the events occurring around them. Practitioners want to know what solutions to their particular problems have the greatest usefulness or predictive utility. Many investigators wish to accumulate more knowledge about events, believing eventually that sufficient information will be compiled to enhance our ability to understand and predict the events we seek to explain. Science, or a way of knowing or discovering, is used by social scientists to provide guidelines in the collection and analysis of data. Elements of science present in all social sciences, including criminal justice and criminology, include the fact that the phenomena studied are empirical; that information is cumulative; that our orientation toward such data collection and analysis is nonethical or ethically neutral; and that fundamental theoretical principles guide all of our research work.

Criminal justice was spawned largely as the result of significant funding from the Law Enforcement Assistance Administration during the late 1960s, and sociology was the discipline where this interest area was often headquartered. Today, criminal justice and criminology are pervasive throughout the United States and the world. The scientific method is embraced by all criminologists and criminal justicians. Explicit and consistent with scientific inquiry are the facts that information generated must be interpreted in a probabilistic context, where no single research study is absolute proof that a solution to a problem has been devised. Also, objectivity is an essential scientific component of our research. Through the exercise of objectivity, all scientific principles may be incorporated into our investigations and elevate the quality of information yielded by the social research enterprise.

Research has several important functions. These functions include exploration, especially in those instances where little is known about the subject investigated. Another function is description, where key variables relevant to events we wish to explain are identified and described in meticulous detail. Another research function is experimentation where one or more effects of certain variables are observed as they impact on the events to be explained. Slowly and gradually, improvements in our knowledge about events and their occurrence increases, and our certainty about things is raised. Much research is evaluation research, as social scientists test various interventions or experiment with different suggested solutions for events. Evaluation research is an applied type of research where various solutions to common research problems or events are tested and evaluated, both in terms of costs of implementation and the heuristic value such solutions yield.

At the forefront of our research is theory, which is a complex tool designed to predict and explain variable interrelationships in systematic ways. Unlimited numbers of hypotheses can be derived from theories and subjected to empirical tests. Different types of theory include deductive theory, inductive theory, axiomatic theory, and grounded theory. Some research investigations are atheoretical in the sense that no specific theory is associated with them.

Integral features of theories are variables. Variables are quantities that can assume more than one value and can be measured in a quantitative sense. Variables may be independent, where their influence upon other variables is profound. Or variables may be dependent and influenced by other variables. Variables are also distinguished according to whether they are discrete or divisible into finite subparts, or continuous, where their subdivisions are infinite. For most research applications, although most variables studied by criminologists, such as attitudes, are continuous, they are almost always reduced to a limited number of finite or discrete subcategories.

Finally, there is a close complementarity between research and theory. Research is the mechanism by which the efficacy of theories is usually tested. And theory almost always provides guidance for research and how it is implemented. Thus there is a true symbiotic relation between research and theory, and it is difficult to separate them in any practical sense.

QUESTIONS FOR REVIEW

1. What is meant by the research enterprise? What are some important components of it? In what ways are these components interconnected?

2. How is problem formulation subjective? How do we influence the explanations we use to explain the events or problems we seek to explain? How do we balance the subjectivity inherent in our choice of explanations and the objectivity demanded of us by scientific inquiry?

3. What are some important differences between theoretical and substantive implications of the studies we conduct? How do each of these implications relate to pure and applied research?

4. Why are our conclusions from research considered tentative? What is the continuing problem we face when attempting to show causal relations between events and explanations of them? Why is it difficult to establish cause–effect relations between variables?

5. What was the significance of the study by Mark Jones? Should we be discouraged from conducting further research when our findings turn out not to be as we expected? Why or why not?

6. What are four critical assumptions about criminal justice and criminology we make in order to study social phenomena?

7. What are some important reasons for doing research? How are probability theory and objectivity related to the research we conduct?

8. What are three important functions of social research? What are some major differences between these different functions?

9. What is meant by evaluation research? Why is evaluation research important? Is evaluation research more pure or more applied? Why?

10. What is a theory? What are some important components of theory? What are some differences between assumptions and propositions? What are two vital functions of theory? Which function is more important? Why?

11. What are four different kinds of theory? What are some key differences between the types you have identified? Is any one type of theory better than the others? Why or why not?

12. What are variables and why are they important components of our theoretical schemes? How can variables be conceptualized? What are four different ways that variables can be defined? What are the major differences between them?

13. How are theory and research complementary? How does research contribute to theory? How does theory contribute to research?

2

Frames of Reference and Problem Formulation

CHAPTER OUTLINE

CHAPTER OBJECTIVES

As the result of reading this chapter, the following objectives will be realized:

1. Understanding the meaning of frames of reference for viewing different types of research problems or events.
2. Describing the influence of our value systems upon the choices of frames of reference used to account for different events or problems.
3. Examining the close relationship between frames of reference and the theoretical schemes we develop in our research investigations.
4. Understanding the process of acquiring information about the subjects we choose to study, including the literature we review to learn what is known about the problem investigated.
5. Describing some of the sources for seeking information about research problems or events.
6. Discovering the difference between "hands-on" research, where investigators collect their own data firsthand, and drawing from information provided by others in their research reports or data sets they have collected.
7. Delineating and describing some of the issues involved in formulating research problems, such as nonresponse and reactivity.

Introduction

Whenever we undertake a research investigation, we focus on an event or occurrence that is of interest to us. The event may be serial murder. Why do some people become serial murderers? The event may be labor turnover in a correctional institution. Why do some correctional officers quit after being on the job a year or less? The event or occurrence may be the use of home incarceration or electronic monitoring for supervising offenders. What is the effectiveness of home confinement and electronic monitoring in the supervision of dangerous probationers and parolees? Does the public feel safe with convicted felons roaming about in their neighborhoods under little or no supervision? The event may be capital punishment and whether murderers should be executed for their crimes. Does capital punishment deter others from committing murder? What are the public's attitudes about capital punishment? All of these and other questions arise in the course of criminological research.

All of us have our own ideas about these and other events or occurrences. We think we know why these events occur, or we think we know what prevailing public opinion is about these events. Regardless of whatever we believe or what we think others believe, we realize that we must subject our explanations and opinions to some sort of test in order to determine whether these explanations are good or not so good. We get our ideas and explanations of events or problems from our own experiences or from the experiences of others. We read articles in the research literature that shape our opinions about particular issues or events. We listen to papers presented at professional conferences and are persuaded in one direction or another by the convincing arguments advanced by our colleagues or those whose research we read about. If we are students working for professors in their own research projects, often our ideas about things are predetermined by the professor's interests and opinions. We may not have choices in this regard. Whatever the source, all of us acquire opinions and develop explanations for why certain events occur.

This chapter is about the ways we choose to look at research problems. The approaches we take in the events or problems we investigate are frames of reference. Each event has numerous frames of reference that may be used by individual investigators to guide their research work. One's choice of a frame of reference is largely subjective, although it is conceded that many chosen frames of reference have been chosen simply because other former researchers have used them in their own work. Thus, we are influenced by existing research and the promising nature of frames of reference used by others. At the same time, our own value systems influence our frame-of-reference choices. We choose one frame of reference over other alternatives because our frame of reference toward a particular problem or event is more feasible than others. The power of values in problem formulation and selecting frames of reference is examined.

When it is decided what we will study and which approach or frame of reference we will choose, we must review existing literature about the event to see what others have found out about it. The literature review process is examined. Various sources for literature reviews are presented and described. Journals and books are common sources of information about the topics we have chosen to investigate. Increasingly, databases of abstracts from a wide variety of journals and books are made available to libraries and individual subscribers, who are often researchers. These databases of information are quite useful in compiling informative data about our research problems. Other sources for data include the *Uniform*

Crime Reports, National Crime Victimization Survey, and *The Sourcebook of Criminal Justice Statistics.* But the information yielded from literature reviews and examinations of existing data sets and information compendiums suggests some amount of inconsistency. This inconsistency does not mean that no consistent information about our investigative topic exists. Rather, it is suggestive of a variety of approaches or frames of reference used by different researchers over time, and the fact that these different approaches as well as different data collection methods will tend to generate inconsistent study findings. Also, the samples selected for data collection are varied. Thus, some inconsistency throughout the research literature is anticipated by seasoned researchers. Some of the problems of conducting literature reviews and discovering existing findings from books, journals, and research papers are presented.

Next, "hands-on" research and investigations from a distance are delineated. Some researchers choose to collect data for their research directly, while others use data collected by others. Collecting one's own data is usually time-consuming and costly, whereas using data collected by others is a relatively inexpensive way of conducting research. Some of the problems associated with each type of investigation are described.

The chapter concludes with an examination of selected issues associated with formulating research problems and selecting frames of reference to approach these problems. These problems include keeping one's research enterprise within manageable limits; whether permission is required to study persons who have the needed information about studied events; the incidence of nonresponse, where some persons refuse to answer one's questions or return questions that have been mailed to them; instrumentation defects, such as inappropriately worded questionnaires or socially insensitive questions posed to prospective respondents; whether the data-gathering methods are valid and/or reliable, and measure what we believe they should measure and in a consistent fashion; whether persons respond to our questions truthfully or give socially desirable responses that may not be true reflections of how they really feel; and whether respondents feel coerced to participate, which may lead to deception and dishonest responses. All of these problems are discussed.

What are Frames of Reference?

Frames of reference are the ways investigators view the research problems they study. It is the approach they choose for problem-solving situations. Several examples from criminology literature will be helpful here. Suppose we are investigating sources of stress among correctional officers who work in prisons and jails. Several different sources of stress for corrections officers have been identified. Variables such as gender, rank, job assignment, ethnicity, competition with peers for attractive work assignments, and a lack of support from coworkers and supervisors have been linked with correctional officer stress.

Shannon Black (2001) investigated stress among a sample of 201 male and 71 female correctional officers from seven maximum-security prisons in the Midwest. Black categorized stress into seven categories, including inmate-related matters, administrative issues, supervisor issues, policy procedures, work in corrections, and crisis/emergency situations. While inmate-related matters and work in corrections emerged as the most frequently occurring categories, Black's study also disclosed a certain amount of employee discontentment with their lack of involvement in decisions affecting their work. Also, the officers reported that their job definitions and responsibilities were quite limited and inflexible. This made it difficult for them to act independently whenever staff–inmate problems arose. Black believed that these stress sources could be alleviated by allowing correctional officers greater input in the development of prison policies and procedures that impact daily institutional functions. Furthermore, Black believed that officer stress could be alleviated by permitting them greater flexibility and variety in the job responsibilities. At least this is what was gleaned when correctional officers were interviewed in the settings Black studied. Black suggested that future research about correctional officer stress should address these issues and explore the implications of permitting officers greater input into institutional policy decision making and making provisions for greater flexibility in their job definitions and responsibilities.

A subsequent study of stress was conducted by Luis Garcia, Dale K. Nesbary, and Joann Gu (2004). These investigators examined the stress associated with police work. Like Shannon Black, these researchers noted that there was considerable literature on the subject of stress, particularly among police officers. The continuing hazards of law enforcement and the exposure of officers to life-threatening situations, much like correctional officers in prisons that house hard-core and dangerous offenders, create stressful conditions. These investigators chose a sample of Boston Police Department officers and studied 1,383 of them by means of a survey. In this study, stress emanated from different sources compared with the Black study. These investigators found that public criticisms of police officers and working late-night shifts generated more stress, especially for those officers with more than 5 years of policing experience. Stress was also associated with worries about fellow officer safety when performing dangerous work assignments. Changes in counseling techniques were suggested by these researchers, and it was implied that varying one's work shift (i.e., giving officers greater work shift variety, including daytime assignments) might enable officers to cope more effectively with these sources of stress.

For comparison purposes, another study of stress was conducted by Jimmie L. Marston (2003). Like Black and Garcia, Nesbary, and Gu, Marston reviewed the stress literature and identified various stress sources, such as marital problems, career concerns, critical incident traumas, difficulties with coworkers, supervisor–subordinate difficulties, and retirement concerns. He studied a sample of personnel at the Jefferson County, Colorado, Sheriff's Office and was particularly interested in the referral program the Sheriff's Office established, which is essentially a peer-support program. The peer-support program is an alternative to psychological counseling techniques and relies upon voluntary support services from other employees in the Sheriff's Office. Stress training sessions were designed to provide interested employees with identifying various sources of stress and how to cope with stress-creating situations. One outcome of Marston's study was that stress levels among employees decreased as they discussed their problems more openly with their peers. The peer-support program was influential in stress reduction.

If we consider each of these studies of stress on their own merits, what can we learn about frames of reference? First, there are many sources of stress. Second, stress occurs in a variety of work environments. No particular working environment is necessarily free of stress. There are some common sources of stress as well as some unique sources of stress, depending on the research setting studied. Different explanations of stress may be used to account for it. These explanations reflect the beliefs of these researchers and suggest particular ways of viewing stress-related problems or frames of reference. Below is a simplified summary of the above studies discussed according to researcher(s), setting, type of stress, and frame of reference.

Investigator(s)	Setting	Type of Stress	Frame of Reference
Black	Seven prisons	Inmate-related, lack of work flexibility	Participation in decision making, job enlargement, enrichment
Garcia, Nesbary, and Gu	Police department	Personal and fellow officer safety, late-shift work dangers	Changing counseling techniques, varying shift responsibilities
Marston	Sheriff's office	Difficulties with other employees, supervisor–subordinate problems	Peer-counseling program and training to cope with stress

Choosing a Frame of Reference

Choosing a frame of reference depends on several factors. First, when a review of recent literature is conducted, investigators learn which frames of reference seem most popular. Although the popularity of certain frames of reference compared with others may be indicative of their success in explaining some phenomenon, they may not be the best frames of reference to use. However, new investigators are drawn toward more popular frames of reference used more frequently by other researchers, particularly if they are new to the discipline and are hesitant to risk selecting less popular frames of reference for their investigations. Another reason why certain frames of reference are chosen over others is that the researcher may be more familiar with it and believes it is the best one to use, unless a better alternative exists. Other researchers may select particular frames of reference that reflect their earlier coursework and experience.

Values and Frames of Reference

Values and frames of reference are closely connected. Values are standards of acceptability we acquire from our peers or from society in general. These values cause us to prioritize, or to allocate greater importance to some things and less importance to others. Thus, each of us learns to value things differently, and these differences explain, in part, the diversity of approaches to various subjects or the different frames of reference chosen to account for or explain events.

There is much subjectivity associated with our values. It follows, therefore, that the research we conduct is largely subjective. With the exception of externally funded research sponsored by national or private agencies, we choose the research topics we will investigate. We study certain problems and issues because of our interest in them. We also select particular frames of reference over others, often because we find them more interesting or important. Our choice of **methodology** and how we will collect data and analyze it also reveals our priorities and interests, although sometimes we may be unaware of alternative research strategies. All of these choices are value-laden choices.

Apart from the requirements of degree programs and the personal preferences of the professors who guide us in our graduate research, the decisions we make often reflect our own value system. The fact that our decisions are closely linked with our values is not necessarily bad. But we need to recognize the influence of values in our research choices at the outset, lest we label someone else's research choices and approaches as poor or irrelevant. The state of the art today in criminology and criminal justice is such that no single frame of reference in any topic area is considered the best one. Differences of opinion abound about how events ought to be explained. And one will always have a chance to link his or her frame of reference to the event they want to explain through theory.

Are Frames of Reference Used in All Research?

It may seem from this discussion that frames of reference will be found in all reported research in the literature. This is not always the case. Simple descriptions of work settings, atheoretical investigations, and cost–benefit analyses of different programs may not reflect any particular frame of reference. Evaluation research may not use particular frames of reference, since the point of such research is to assess the impact of some variable upon another.

For instance, Alexander J. Cowell, Nahama Broner, and Randolph Dupont (2004) studied the cost-effectiveness of jail diversion programs used especially for persons with serious mental illnesses and with the co-occurring condition of substance abuse. (Cost–benefit analyses will be presented at length in Chapter 3.) The potential advantages of such programs to participants include improved mental health functioning, reduced substance use and abuse, and reduced recidivism. Community benefits might include reducing caseloads in overburdened courts and crowded jails and prisons. These investigators compared jail diversion program costs with the costs of imprisonment, court processing, and other factors associated with traditional offender processing. The outcome of their research showed great promise for jail diversion programs, as these programs reported lower rates of recidivism and greater rates of success among divertees with mental illness and substance abuse problems. The essence of this investigation was comparing the various costs associated with treating criminals with mental illness and substance abuse problems through different forms of processing (e.g., the courts, incarceration in jail or prison, and jail diversion).

Another almost purely descriptive study was conducted by Megan C. Kurlychek and Brian D. Johnson (2004). These researchers studied sentencing outcomes of young adults in criminal courts. Some of these young adults were transferred from juvenile court, while other young adults were processed initially as adult offenders. Initially believing that those youthful criminals who were transferred from juvenile courts would receive greater sentencing leniency compared with young adults originally processed by the criminal justice system, a sentencing outcome comparison was made between both types of offenders during a 3-year period (1997–1999) in Pennsylvania. The findings were surprising. Those juveniles who were transferred to criminal court for processing and who were convicted were given significantly more severe sentences than their youthful adult counterparts. These researchers offered a variety of reasons to explain these findings, although their primary research purpose was to find out whether there were any sentencing outcome differences. No particular frame of reference was used in this research project. It involved statistical comparisons of two offender groups over a 3-year period and disclosed significant differences in sentencing outcomes. Perhaps another investigator will develop an explanation for why such sentencing outcome differences occurred. This subsequent explanation will reflect the investigator's frame of reference and will result in a different type of study than that conducted by Kurlychek and Johnson.

Frames of Reference and Theory

A frame of reference suggests a particular explanation for why a research problem exists. We attempt to unravel the complexities of certain criminological problems, and so we begin by developing a view of the problem we have selected for study. The frame of reference we choose is quite important, since it is the foundation of our explanation for why certain problems exist or events occur. The next step in the research process is to articulate how our explanation of the event or problem relates to the problem in some logical fashion.

Thus, frames of reference and theory are inevitably linked together. Our theory consists of numerous statements reflecting linkages between variables. If we are studying crime deterrence, for example, and we decide to use a demographic approach, our theory becomes the explanatory and predictive tool we will use to show how it came to be so that crime deterrence and demographics are related. If we choose to view crime deterrence largely as a function of police aggressiveness or family instability, we must demonstrate the possible causal relation between crime deterrence and police aggressiveness or between crime deterrence and family instability in our theory or theoretical scheme. If we study spousal abuse and wish to explain it or account for it by using underemployment or alcoholism as predictor variables, then our theoretical scheme should lay out our reasoning for why spousal abuse and underemployment or why spousal abuse and alcoholism are related.

Some researchers specialize in theory construction, and they heavily stress the importance of different theoretical components such as axioms, propositions, assumptions, and postulates. In a logical fashion, they weave an explanatory and predictive web that yields certain tentative conclusions or hypotheses that may be tested empirically. For instance, it is insufficient to say simply that because someone is unemployed or underemployed, he will feel bad and beat his wife. It is insufficient also to say simply that if one consumes considerable alcohol, he will become drunk and physically abuse his spouse. We want to know why these events are related or interconnected. Why should underemployment or unemployment contribute to or cause spousal abuse? Why should family instability raise crime rates? Why should large alcohol consumption precipitate family violence?

As we attempt to explain the "whys" involved, we continue asking why, until we have exhausted this explanation or have given a reasonably full account of how these events are related. What is reasonable? Again, value judgments enter the picture, and we must rely on our own standards and assessments about how much completeness in our explanations of phenomena is an adequate amount of completeness. No one agrees on how complete our theoretical explanations must be. In fact, theory is perhaps the weakest link in the chain of events known as the research process. This is because it is difficult to develop theory or construct theory or create theory.

At least the frame of reference we use in relation to any given problem or event focuses our attention on a limited number of explanatory options. But remember that whenever we choose one frame of reference over other ways of viewing the problem, we are temporarily preventing ourselves from considering other explanatory options. Our choices may not be the best ones, and our results may be inconclusive as good explanations for and predictors of the problems we investigate. This is one reason why so much replication and reinvestigation occurs in any kind of social research, criminological or otherwise. And perhaps this is as it should be, considering how science operates and affects what we do. We acquire knowledge and certainty about things slowly, and we continually subject our views and explanations for things to experimentation and empirical testing. Gradually, some explanations of things emerge as better predictors than other explanations. Over time, we develop a stronger sense of what fits and what doesn't fit, of what seems to work and what doesn't seem to work.

Deciding What to Study: Topics of Investigation for Criminal Justice and Criminology

Choosing a topic for investigation in criminology and criminal justice is often associated with one's interests and previous experience. Persons who have worked in law enforcement and have been police officers or correctional officers or probation/parole officers may seek out and research topics involving these areas. It is not unusual to find that researchers who study police officers have previously been police officers themselves. Many investigators find it comfortable to study topics in areas where they have some intimate familiarity. Some former corrections officers may study prison settings and prisoners, or they may study the lives of corrections officers. For other researchers, their research topics may be chosen for them.

For instance, if you are in a graduate department or working toward a graduate degree, or if you are working as a graduate research assistant on a grant supervised by one of your professors, deciding what topics to study may not be one of your options. In short, you may already be locked into a particular topic and expected to investigate a particular aspect or dimension of it. However, in most graduate departments, there is considerable latitude extended to researchers concerning what they study and how they choose to study it.

It is unnecessary to list each and every interest area in criminology and criminal justice where research may be conducted. At professional meetings, such as the annual meeting of the American Society of Criminology, criminologists convene and present papers or give reports about research they have conducted. These papers reflect the diverse interests among these professionals. An examination of the program for the annual meeting of the Academy of Criminal Justice Sciences, which was held in Las Vegas, Nevada, in March 2004, disclosed that over 500 panels, workshops, and roundtables were offered, with an average of three or four papers per session. These panels included topics such as the impact of AIDS in law enforcement, psychosocial aspects of criminal behavior, police officer safety, a historical perspective of women in criminology, crime control trends, the sexual integration of prison and jail guard forces, community corrections models, victimization, crime prevention strategies, police education, electronic monitoring and house arrest, sentencing policies, elderly abuse, prisoner rights, juvenile gang patterns and trends, and corrections institutional management.

The subject matter of criminal justice and criminology is boundless. While there are some standard topic areas related to different components of the criminal justice system (e.g., law enforcement, courts, corrections), there are an infinite number of subtopics that may be investigated. In the area of prosecution and the courts, for example, plea bargaining has been a popular topic for investigation. What factors influence prosecutorial discretion? How do race, ethnicity, gender, and socioeconomic status influence the plea bargaining decision and the contents of a plea bargain agreement? What are the implications of different types of sentencing schemes for various types of offenders? Are defendants more likely to receive greater leniency from judges at the time of sentencing if they pleaded guilty through plea bargaining or if the guilty verdict was rendered against them by a jury through a jury trial?

Regarding jury trials, many researchers have investigated the jury deliberation process. What are the dynamics of jury deliberations? Does racial and/or gender composition of juries make a difference and influence these deliberations, depending on the race or gender of defendants? Can jury verdicts be predicted with any degree of accuracy? Are smaller juries more likely to reach consensus compared with larger juries? Is there an optimum jury size? What can prosecutors and defense attorneys do to influence juries one way or another, unfavorably or favorably, toward defendants? These are just a few of the many questions researchers raise when investigating juries, jury deliberations, and other jury-related factors.

When police officers are investigated, some researchers focus on factors that influence the exercise of police discretion in effecting arrests of suspects. Does a more educated police officer relate to the community better than a less educated officer? What types of training should police officers receive in order to prepare them for the realities of police work? Is there a distinctive police personality? How much stress do police officers experience while on the job? What coping mechanisms are put into play as a means of handling such job stress? How do stress and burnout affect job performance? Are one- or two-officer patrol units more effective in combating crime? Again, there is a virtually limitless range of topics within the component of law enforcement that may be selected for scientific study.

Before we make a final decision about what to study, however, we should assess our abilities, our personal strengths and weaknesses, and our interests. Sometimes, inexperienced researchers will identify grandiose research problems that are well beyond their means, both personally and financially. The topics selected are noteworthy, but often, the study objectives are unobtainable, simply because they are beyond the investigator's financial means. We might wish to conduct a study of a large sample of all officers of the Los Angeles Police Department. But we quickly find that the cost of such a study would be prohibitive. This is one reason why professors, researchers, and others apply for grants from different funding agencies, both public and private, in order to secure appropriate funding for their investigations. Perhaps we want to study a sample of district attorneys in various cities in several states. Maybe we don't at first consider the travel time involved, the appointments we would have to make, and other logistical factors that would make it possible for our study to materialize.

If we plan to study others in public organizations or agencies, one of the first things we do is assess our connections. Do we know anyone who can help us get our "foot in the

BOX 2.1   PERSONALITY HIGHLIGHT

MARTHA A. MYERS
University of Georgia

Statistics: B.A. (history) University of Michigan; M.A. (sociology) University of Massachusetts-Amherst; Ph.D. (sociology), Indiana University.

BACKGROUND AND INTERESTS

For as long as I can remember, I was intellectually drawn to just two subjects: history and anthropology. Each, in its own way, was exotic and escapist. History transported me to other times, anthropology to other places. In college, I enrolled in as many Russian literature and history courses as I could; cultural anthropology and archeology classes followed closely behind. I have absolutely no memory of my first [and probably only] sociology undergraduate course. So, you may ask, how did I come to spend the next nearly 30 years of my life teaching courses in crime and deviance and researching criminal justice responses to crime?

The answer appears clearer today than it probably was when I spent a year after college weighing my future. To pursue my interest in Russian history would require an advanced degree. An advanced degree would require fluency in Russian. Since fluency in German, even after an intensive 6 weeks in Salzburg, had eluded me, I suspected Russian would pose an insurmountable challenge. So, with that choice foreclosed, enter my best friend at the time: a graduate student in the sociology program at the University of Michigan. In idle conversation, she encouraged me to read some of her course material ("Try it, you might like it!"). I did. A little later, I took the GRE in both history and sociology. My fate was sealed as soon as the results arrived in the mail: I had scored higher in sociology than in history!

Once accepted into graduate school, I knew my major field of interest immediately: deviance in general and crime in particular. Again, these topics seemed so exotic and escapist—from this conformist's point of view. The 1970s and early 1980s were the heyday of the labeling or societal reaction perspective on deviance, and my research life reflects this milieu. Researchers had begun to raise serious questions about the accuracy of official records of criminality. They developed and administered self-report questionnaires in an effort to arrive at less biased estimates of race, class, and gender differences in crime. For my master's thesis, I too developed a questionnaire on crime, mailed it to a random sample of students at the University of Massachusetts and several private colleges in the area, and explored gender differences in self-reported crime.

The fellowship I received at Indiana University allowed me to pursue my interests in official reactions to crime. What I most appreciated about its program was its insistence upon a broad

BOX 2.1   CONTINUED

theoretical and methodological foundation in sociology. I took courses in qualitative and quantitative methodology and, much to my surprise, liked them equally well. A dissertation topic, however, had failed to present itself, and time appeared to be getting short. Enter, again, a fellow student who, in idle conversation, mentioned that no one had really explored the role that the victim plays during the prosecution process. In short order, I had a topic and subsequently received funding to collect data—enough data, in fact, to generate research for the next 5 years!

RESEARCH INVESTIGATIONS

Since my degree, I have continued to conduct research that seeks to identify, in a systematic fashion, the factors that prosecutors, judges, and juries rely on when making their decisions. In one way or another, I've been asking the same question. Which matters more: who you are [e.g., your race, age, gender], what you did, or where you did it? Most of this research has been heavily quantitative, relying only lightly on interviews and conversations with those actually involved in decision making. Sustained use of quantitative methods has made me often painfully aware of their strengths as well as their weaknesses: We know with some precision what has an impact on decisions but, in the absence of qualitative data, we often can only speculate on the how and the why of that impact.

Colleagues at the University of Georgia unwittingly brought me full circle back to my first intellectual love—history. In the course of working on a lynching project, they drew my attention to the existence of data on incarceration in the state of Georgia after the Civil War. Again, idle conversations proved to be instrumental to my career. In this case, they launched a project that was to span 10 years. I learned a new method, time series analysis, about which I knew absolutely nothing. I learned also about a period of our own history about which I knew little. I was able, for the first time, to blend both quantitative and qualitative [historical] analytic techniques, and have the best of both worlds. More so than in earlier projects, I was able to demonstrate the complicated ways in which decisions within the criminal justice system are shaped not only by who the offender is and what he or she purportedly did. Decisions also take place within and are shaped by contexts that extend well beyond the courthouse and reach into the community—its inequality, racial diversity, and level of urbanization.

ADVICE TO STUDENTS

Too often, we think of conducting research as a solitary endeavor. But the theme that runs through my sociological biography is that sociology is a social process. Studying together and talking with fellow students about what you and they have been reading and thinking about have the power to stimulate your interests and, so, to take your intellectual journey in unanticipated directions. If you are open to those directions, despite the challenges they may present, your sociological life will never be dull.

BOX 2.1   CONTINUED

One of the most challenging directions your research interests may take you lies in the realm of data collection. Preexisting data sets abound. Many include finely crafted, pretested questions. Often, the samples are large and representative. Nevertheless, you may find that there is an imperfect fit between the question that *truly* interests you and the data sets that have asked a similar question. To thine own research interests be true! Collecting your own data is often time-consuming and sometimes tedious. Yet, it is the most rewarding of endeavors. Armed with a theoretical perspective and a clear understanding of the literature, you can design and execute projects that allow you to pursue your own research agenda and, in so doing, to make a contribution to the discipline that is unique.

door"? Are we personally employed at an agency that would allow us to study it? In short, we identify who we know relative to the problem we intend to study, or we assess the connections of friendly others who may be in a position to help us in our research endeavors. If our choice is to do library research and rely exclusively on the contents of documents and other library materials for information, it is unnecessary to obtain permission from anyone or go through the often difficult and tedious process of gaining access to organizations and agencies. But even if "quiet" research is done in our own library settings, there are still practical concerns that must be addressed beyond our immediate research interests. We must pay attention to some of the dilemmas that often arise between what ideally should be done and what, in reality, can be done. This is the ideal–real scenario that is common to all researchers in all subject areas.

Reviewing the Literature

Getting started in any research project requires that investigators should become very familiar with existing literature about the problem to be studied. It is conventional in all social and criminological research to conduct a **literature review** or a review of the existing literature. What is known about the problem to be studied? What have other researchers written about it? What other research has been done and what has been found?

One important purpose for a literature review is to determine whether your ideas are current and relevant to others. Some novice researchers think that they have a highly interesting research problem or a novel way of studying it. But when they seek out articles and information about the research problem, they discover that many other researchers have investigated the topic in the past and do not consider it important any longer. Furthermore, the "novel" approach used to study the research problem may turn out to be an old approach and no longer used by contemporary investigators. Thus, the literature review is a learning experience in several respects. We learn about what information exists about the problem we are studying. We glean ideas about studying the problem from what other researchers have done. We become aware of possible controversies and issues surrounding the problem.

BOX 2.2   PERSONALITY HIGHLIGHT

SUSAN R. TAKATA
University of Wisconsin, Parkside

Statistics: B.A. (sociology), California State College, Dominguez Hills; M.A., Ph.D. (sociology), University of California, Berkeley.

BACKGROUND AND INTERESTS

Difference has always fascinated me. It's all about perception and perspective. When I was an undergraduate student, I wondered, how and why does one become labeled? Which labels stick and why others do not? I am first-generation college in my family. I know the struggles of balancing between family obligations while writing term papers and cramming for exams during the various holidays. My mother received her high school diploma in "camp" while my father dropped out. During World War II, my parents, grandparents, aunts, uncles, and cousins were incarcerated in internment camps. I am third-generation Japanese American (although I've been mistaken for Chinese, Korean, Filipina, and even Mexican American). Early on, my interest in race and ethnic relations focused on stereotyping, perceptions, societal reactions, and unstated assumptions (back then, they didn't call it "racial profiling").

While at Dominguez Hills, I had several classes with Professor Jeanne Curran. She was different from the rest of the faculty. She made learning fun. Jeanne created an undergraduate student-operated research center. Undergraduates usually don't do "real" research, write research grant proposals, or present papers at professional meetings, but we did. By the time my cohort graduated, there were too many probation officers, but we applied anyhow. That's what I was supposed to be. As a "backup" plan, I applied to graduate schools. Wasn't exactly sure what it was all about but because I did so well in school, I figured more school couldn't hurt. Jeanne took the time to explain what graduate school was about. Little did I realize that this was the beginning of a lifelong "teaching/learning" friendship. We have coauthored articles, textbooks, and we even team-teach long-distance between California and Wisconsin.

When I was accepted into the PhD program in sociology at Berkeley, I was interested in the radical school of criminology but it was closed when I got there (what luck!). By the way, a year after I moved to Berkeley, the Los Angeles County Probation Department sent a letter offering me a position (am I lucky or what?).

BOX 2.2   CONTINUED

RESEARCH INVESTIGATIONS

Sometimes being first-generation college leads to doing things differently, meaning going against the norms because one doesn't know not to. I did a number of things that way. For example, I drafted a $50,000 federal research grant proposal, which was eventually funded (it took a year of groundwork and was very "risky," especially if it didn't work out). I evaluated alternatives to jail incarceration (an offshoot of my dissertation research). At first, UC Berkeley didn't know what to do with me. Graduate students don't usually write research grant proposals, and get funded! Fortunately, there were a few supportive faculty members who understood—Herb Blumer, Bob Blauner, Troy Duster, and David Matza.

My dissertation focused on discretionary justice within two local correctional systems in California. Theoretically, it was a synthesis of symbolic interactionism (labeling theory), and phenomenology (the social construction of reality). My dissertation was about the different perceptions of the formal and informal structures inside the county jails. I utilized a multi-methodological research design (i.e., surveying jail inmates, interviewing parolees and parole board members, observing parole board hearings, reviewing parole board minutes and parolee records). Triangulation provides a methodological "checks and balance." I have always thought that no one methodology can tell us everything. The social world is far too complex. But, multiple methodological strategies and approaches can provide a variety of dimensions to a research problem.

Since 1984, I have been at the University of Wisconsin, Parkside, moving up the ranks from assistant professor to full professor. During my second year at UWP, I was approached by the Racine Mayor's Task Force Commission on Gangs and Juvenile Delinquency to study whether or not the city had a gang problem. I immediately replicated the student-operated research center at UWP. This project was theirs, not mine. The students divided into subgroups to: (1) survey middle school and high school students, (2) survey the community, (3) interview gang members, (4) interview task force members and other community leaders, (5) observe task force meetings, and (6) analyze local media coverage. When I told Jeanne what I had done, her reaction was "You did what!?!" I did not realize how "risky" this could be for an untenured assistant professor. But my students were so successful with their initial research project that three more projects followed supported by a private foundation as well as local and state funding.

When students have a real research problem to tackle, it has meaning—"it's really real!" The research experience is unpredictable, political, and the students are confronted with real dilemmas and decisions. To illustrate, I was recently appointed to the Racine County Citizens Task Force on Criminal Justice to examine the jail overcrowding problem. Three students researched alternatives to incarceration (i.e., drug courts, sobering stations). They presented their findings before the commission and at the Midwest Criminal Justice Association meetings. Students have attended and participated in professional meetings at the state, regional, and national levels. Because many students at UWP are first-generation college, this kind of professional socialization is critical, which goes back to my own undergraduate research experience with Jeanne.

BOX 2.2   CONTINUED

For over 30 years, Jeanne and I have been conducting a longitudinal research experiment on innovative approaches to teaching and learning. In other words, we keep asking ourselves, "What motivates a student to learn? How can we create an environment to nurture that learning? What works? What doesn't and why?" My teaching is my research and my research is my teaching. I have always looked at teaching, research, and service as interdependently linked; in particular, connecting the university to its surrounding communities. More recently, Jeanne and I have been team-teaching and conducting research long-distance through our website, *Dear Habermas* (*http://www.csudh.edu/dearhabermas*). This website is a journal of postmodern and critical thought devoted to academic discourse on peace and justice. Our class assignments, texts, resources, and even textbooks are online free and open to all. We got tired of the more traditional, mainstream publication process (i.e., the long review process, the "old boys" network, the inability to find a "place" for our research, the delays and lags in publishing, not to mention the exorbitant costs of textbooks to our students). Our website is eclectic and very interdisciplinary. Beyond sociology and criminology, we cover just about everything—politics, philosophy, science, humanities, business, and even art! *Dear Habermas* is an academic forum, for dialog with our students at two state universities, and with the community at large. All are welcome to our site, for inclusion is one of the paths to participation and legitimacy for all.

In 1997, I spearheaded the creation of the Criminal Justice Department on campus, and in 1999, I moved from Sociology/Anthropology to the new Criminal Justice Department. Today, we have over 200 criminal justice majors, and have graduated as many. I am currently a Professor of Criminal Justice and the department chair (again). In addition to criminology and corrections, I teach "Race, Crime, and the Law," "Media, Crime, and Criminal Justice," "Law and Social Change," and "Law and Society." My classes are heavily theoretical, as I introduce students to cutting-edge theories (i.e., critical race theory, chaos theory, feminist criminology, queer theory). For me, theory construction is an offshoot of grounded theory, a "bottom-up" approach connecting the academy with the community. By listening to their voices and stories, this leads to critical discussions on the interrelationship between theory, policy, and practice, both inside and outside of the classroom. Sometimes we go from practice to policy and try to trace the underlying theory and other times, we begin with policy. It is very important to understand this interrelationship between theory, policy, and practice in order to critically analyze what works and what doesn't work, especially in the field of criminal justice. For example, a new program might make good sense in theory but turns out to be a disaster in practice. Why is that? Or, in practice, a program has become a huge success after much "trial and error," and then to trace its underlying theory.

ADVICE TO STUDENTS

It's all about perceptions and perspectives. "If men define situations as real, they are real in their consequences" (W.I. Thomas). This quote fits with all my research whether I'm focusing on gangs, jail overcrowding, or student motivation to learn. Listen in good faith to the perspective

BOX 2.2   CONTINUED

of the other. By listening very carefully to the stories and lived experiences, especially from those who have been silenced (i.e., jail inmates, parolees, gang members, students), we can better understand what is going on and why.

And finally, if someone tells you, "You can't do this," "You aren't suppose to do that," or "That's not the way we usually do things around here," there is always "the road not taken." It's exhilarating. And yes, it is sometimes extremely frustrating and even scary. But it's intense excitement! Making a difference in your own way. Be the difference in creatively making this world a better place. "Two roads diverged in a wood, and I—I took the one less traveled by, And that has made all the difference!" (from my favorite poem by Robert Frost).

The most logical place to begin a literature review is the library. A college or university library will contain much informative information about just about any research topic. Libraries maintain more or less extensive collections of journals and periodicals. Journals publish research findings by criminologists and others. Articles cover an array of subjects and may be essays or analyses of data. If you are studying correctional officer labor turnover and why it occurs, there are specialized journals that cater to studies about institutional corrections and corrections officers. *The Prison Journal, Corrections Today,* and *American Jails* each publish such articles. If you are studying probation officer burnout and stress, the Administrative Office of the U.S. Courts publishes *Federal Probation,* a journal that includes numerous articles about probation work. The American Probation and Parole Association publishes *APPA Perspectives,* which includes useful articles about different aspects of probation and parole. Libraries also have sourcebooks that list all journals and periodicals they collect. It is fairly easy to scan this list and determine which journals might contain information you are seeking.

There are also technical reports and books about the subjects you study. Suppose you are interested in international terrorism. Library personnel are available to assist you in locating several of these sources. And once you have located certain areas where these books about terrorism are found, you will see other books about terrorism on the same library shelf. Whether you examine books or articles or both, you will glean much informative material from your examination of the literature. What you learn from published reports and research will often cause you to rethink your original research problem or modify your frame of reference.

Sources for Literature Reviews

Besides the library, there are other sources for conducting literature reviews. For example, since 1968 Willow Tree Press in Monsey, New York, has published a quarterly periodical of abstracts from articles and books. Called *Criminal Justice Abstracts,* this publication has been used by thousands of researchers who investigate criminological problems. Abstracts are abbreviated summaries of research articles or book contents. An abstract of a research article might include the focus of the study, the sample selected and methods used for data analysis, a synopsis of findings, and some statement about the significance of the article. Abstracts are usually one- or two-paragraph summarizations on what was studied and what was found. These abstracts are very informative for researchers.

Since the early 1990s, Willow Tree Press has made available these abstracts on CD-ROM. Thus there are annual updates of abstract information available on CD, such as 1968–1998, 1968–2004, and so on. Each year a new CD is issued. These CDs contain over 140,000 abstracts of articles and books. With the proper CD-ROM and a computer, researchers can conduct data searches on these CDs using key words. If a researcher wanted to find out information about probation officers and firearms, deadly force, police cynicism, correctional officer professionalism, judicial sentencing disparity, or virtually any other valid criminal justice topic, simply entering key words and pressing a computer button will yield several hundred abstracts on a particular subject. These abstracts can be downloaded onto a computer diskette and translated into some software format, like MS Word for Windows, WordPerfect, or some other software program. From there, a document can be printed that contains all of the downloaded abstracts. These abstracts can be scanned to determine what is known about a given subject. Interestingly, when you scan 25 or more abstracts on a given subject, you begin to acquire a sense of what is known about the subject and how investigators have studied it. Since abstracts report research findings, you can easily spot articles that seem to contradict other articles with contrary findings.

Contrary findings in any given subject area are common and should not be interpreted that the field is in disarray or that researchers haven't developed any consistent information about a topic. For instance, suppose we are studying judicial sentencing disparity. Disparities in sentencing occur when convicted offenders with similar criminal histories and conviction offenses are given widely different sentences. Disparities are attributable to any of several factors, including race/ethnicity, socioeconomic status, use of private counsel or public defender, gender, or age. An examination of abstracts of articles studying sentencing disparities may disclose seemingly inconsistent findings. One abstract, a hypothetical article by Smith and Jones, may show that a study of 35 judges in Pennsylvania revealed that in 550 sentences imposed for offenders convicted of the same felonies, 56 percent of the white convicted offenders were placed on probation, while 38 percent of the nonwhite convicted offenders received probation. However, in another hypothetical study, Peters and Johnson found that of 728 same-felony sentences in Georgia, 64 percent of the white convicted offenders received probation, while 65 percent of the nonwhite convicted offenders received probation. Thus, it would seem that sentencing disparity was found in the Smith and Jones study but not in the Peters and Johnson study.

If we were to look more closely at these studies, however, we may find that actual sentence lengths were quite different, depending on whether the offenders were white or nonwhite. We might find that for *both* the Smith and Jones and the Peters and Johnson studies, white offenders spent an average of 4 years in prison, while the nonwhite offenders spent an average of 6 years in prison. While these figures do not prove that judges or parole boards discriminate against nonwhite offenders, the differences in time served raise serious questions about the equity of the sentences imposed and time served.

In order for us to make a serious case showing sentencing disparities, we must examine the findings of many studies. Surveying the abstracts on sentencing disparities will give us a very good idea about how much disparity exists and which variables seem to explain sentencing disparities in different jurisdictions.

There are many other sources for literature reviews. Besides the *Criminal Justice Abstracts* on CD, the *National Criminal Justice Reference Service Document Data Base* is available annually on CD. This database is funded by the U.S. Department of Justice National Institute of Justice. This database contains over 140,000 abstracts of articles, books, and government publications. One significant difference between this resource and *Criminal Justice Abstracts* is that it contains a much larger variety of government document abstracts. There is also some duplication as the result of abstracting many of the same articles and books. This resource is used in the same way the *Criminal Justice Abstracts* CD is used, with word searches. Abstracts on selected subjects can be downloaded to a computer diskette and subsequently formatted and printed, using some type of word processing program. Various other abstracting services relevant for specific fields, such as sociology and psychology, are available. Many of these sources are available to students in their university libraries. Table 2.1 shows various journals and abstract databases that might be used to locate relevant articles and other types of publications.

Depending on the magnitude of the research project, whether it is a class or term paper or the beginning of a full-fledged research study, the literature review will be a fairly

TABLE 2.1   Journals and Abstract Compilations

Journals

American Jails	*Journal of Contemporary Law*
American Journal of Criminal Justice	*Journal of Crime and Justice*
American Journal of Police	*Journal of Criminal Justice*
American Journal of Sociology	*Journal of Criminal Law and Criminology*
American Sociological Review	*Journal of Legal Studies*
APPA Perspectives	*Journal of Offender Counseling, Services*
Corrections Compendium	*and Rehabilitation*
Corrections Today	*Journal of Offender Rehabilitation*
Crime and Delinquency	*Journal of Quantitative Criminology*
Criminal Behavior and Mental Health	*Journal of Research in Crime and Delinquency*
Criminal Justice and Behavior	*Judicature*
Criminal Justice Ethics	*Justice Professional*
Criminal Justice Policy Review	*Justice Quarterly*
Criminal Justice Review	*Law and Society Review*
Criminology	*Police Chief*
FBI Law Enforcement Bulletin	*Police Studies*
Federal Probation	*Prison Journal*
Journal of Child Sexual Abuse	*Social Problems*
Journal of Contemporary Criminal Justice	

Abstracts

Abstracts on Police Science	*Police Science Abstracts*
Criminal Justice Abstracts	*Psychological Abstracts*
Criminal Justice Periodical Index	*Social Science Index*
Criminology and Penology Abstracts	*Sociological Abstracts*
National Criminal Justice Reference	
Service Document Data Base	

thorough coverage of existing literature on the subject. Literature reviews are not meant to be exhaustive. That is, you don't have to summarize 650 articles that may be available. Many of the sources you cite will be somewhat repetitive. Thus, if 40 articles report similar findings regarding a given subject, then it is only necessary to reference 10–12 articles and briefly summarize what they have concluded. If there are different findings reported in other articles, you can easily document these differences in findings. Often, these study differences heighten reader interest. Why are there discrepancies in the research literature? What factors might account for these discrepancies in findings? A part of your job might be to offer one or more explanations for these contrary study findings. Indeed, your major task might be to explain them. Your paper might be dedicated to that sole objective.

Literature reviews vary in their complexity and extensiveness, depending on the particular paper or research project. Term papers written to satisfy the requirements of an undergraduate course may contain 15–20 references. If the research is a master's thesis or doctoral dissertation, the writer may include 100 or more references in the literature review. The Appendix of this book contains a detailed discussion about writing papers and research reports. Different types of reports and papers are described and distinguished. Generally, the literature review is geared to acquaint readers with what is known about the subject studied.

A warning is in order for students and others who turn to textbooks for literature review summaries. While it is true that most textbooks summarize some of the literature in selected areas, it is also true that textbooks are somewhat limited in what is reviewed. Textbooks must cover a lot of material within relatively short page limits. This means that most often, articles are discussed as "one-liners," where the author merely asserts a specific study finding. For example, "Rogers found that correctional officers who worked on death row at Suburban Penitentiary had significantly greater stress and burnout levels compared with correctional officers who worked in the general inmate population." Or, "Smith showed that a sample of police officers in Detroit, Michigan, admitted to accepting illegal gratuities from businesses while on foot patrols." These observations are interesting and probably help to illustrate certain topics in textbooks. But they are of little value in literature reviews. Furthermore, by the time a textbook is published, the printed material is already dated by one or more years. This is because it takes about a year to publish a book once the final manuscript has been submitted to the publisher. Thus, textbooks generally are not good current resources to consult for generating up-to-date or timely literature reviews. Textbooks *do* provide interesting ideas for potential research topics, however. And examining the bibliographies of textbooks can identify classic works on a wide variety of topics.

"Hands-On" Research and Investigations from a Distance

"Hands-On" Research

Anyone doing research has several choices. By far the more difficult choice is actually collecting original data and conducting **hands-on research.** This means that a **target population** must be identified, such as all police officers or probation officers in a community, county, or state. Then, a sample of these persons will need to be contacted in some way. Commonly used methods for contacts include personal visits and interviews, telephone calls, or mailed questionnaires. Prior to making these contacts, questions will have to be formulated

BOX 2.3   PERSONALITY HIGHLIGHT

VALERIE JENNESS
Professor and Chair Department of Criminology, Law and Society University of California, Irvine

Statistics: B.S. (sociology), Central Washington University; M.A. (sociology), University of California, Santa Barbara; Ph.D. (sociology), University of California, Santa Barbara.

BACKGROUND AND INTERESTS

When I was a young girl growing up in Washington State, I often heard my mother say "Damn it, there ought to be a law against that!" She said this when something occurred that outraged or disappointed her. When she barked these words in response to both trivial and consequential events, it was clear to me that she was annoyed with her inability to invoke the authorities on her behalf to respond to an "infraction" of some sort. On each occasion in which I heard her say these words, I was made aware that somehow the law was a valuable resource when it comes to defining wrongdoing and remedying wrongs. Also during my growing-up years, I often heard my mother respond with "Damn it, Valerie, don't make a federal case out of everything!" She said this when *I* expressed outrage or disappointment after observing an infraction of some sort. When she barked these words, it was clear to me that she expected me to solve my own problems and not call on authorities, including her (the most looming authority figure), to intervene on my behalf. On each occasion in which I heard her say these words, I knew that somehow the law was not to be resorted to in all instances of wrongdoing. Although the logic of my mother's quips—that the law should serve her interests but not mine—was not lost on me, it came to pass that I grew up confused about the role of law (and all that surrounds it) in my life.

I also became interested in and suspicious of the complicated nature of rules, especially the epitome of rules—namely, law. In particular, I wondered, "When and how does the law enable one to invoke the authorities (and all the resources connected to them) on their own behalf?" I recall wondering on many occasions, "Who makes the rules?" (i.e., "Who says?"); "When do the rules get invoked to resolve wrongdoing?" (i.e., "Why should there be a law against some things, but no federal case made against other things?"); "How is such an invocation and its consequences contingent upon who one is and where one is located in society?" (i.e., "Why do my mom's concerns matter, but mine don't?"); and most importantly, "Why are the rules used to serve some and not others?" (i.e., "Why my mom, but not me?").

BOX 2.3   CONTINUED

These questions continue to loom large in my professional life as a sociologist, criminologist, and sociolegal scholar.

RESEARCH INVESTIGATIONS

Unlike many criminologists who study "Who breaks the law and why?" and many other criminologists who study how the criminal justice system processes criminal law breakers (as well as those, we often find out later, who did not break the law), I have spent the majority of my professional life researching and teaching about the formation of criminal law itself. As most introductory criminology textbooks make clear, it is only through the formation of criminal law—a process called "criminalization"—that some conduct is rendered criminal (rather than, say, immoral, bad, or sinful). In simple terms, criminalization is best treated as one of several regulatory approaches and practices authorized by the State that, to quote Neal Shover, is "an approach to crime control that leans heavily on threatened criminal penalties, criminal prosecution, and punishment." In contrast, it is only through decriminalization that select features of social life escape the domain of crime.

I have studied the twin processes of rule-making (criminalization) and unmaking (decriminalization) for almost two decades (for a recent installment along these lines, see Jenness, 2004). In my earlier work I focused on the decriminalization of vice-crime. In particular, I analyzed contemporary efforts to decriminalize prostitution in the United States and abroad (see, e.g., *Making it Work: The Prostitutes' Rights Movement in Perspective* [1993]). In my more recent work, I have examined the ways in which various forms of bias-motivated violence—violence against racial and ethnic minorities, violence against Jews, violence against immigrants, violence against gays and lesbians, violence against girls and women, and violence against people with disabilities—increasingly have become criminalized in the United States and abroad. As a result, in the latter part of the 20th century a new type of criminal activity, so-called hate- or bias-crime, was recognized, named, given meaning, and responded to by citizens, social movements, policymakers, and, most importantly, for the purposes of this volume, the criminal justice system (see, e.g., *Hate Crimes: New Social Movements and the Politics of Violence* [1997] and *Hate Crime: From Social Movement to Law Enforcement* [2001]). As the titles of my books suggest, in my work, I am keenly interested in the ways in which organized social movements in particular play a key role in determining public policy, including the contours of criminal law. When successful, they translate movement goals into law and thereby ensure that the law is on the side of some people and not others.

Ultimately, however, "Whose side is the law on?" is a tough question to answer. I would not be the first scholar, practitioner, citizen, victim, or perpetrator to respond to this question with "it depends"—clearly, this is a less-than-satisfying answer. For me, an academic housed

BOX 2.3   CONTINUED

in a research university, determining "Whose side is the law on and why?" is the fun of social science research. It requires rejecting my mother's heartfelt proclamations and, instead, systematically examining the roles a plethora of factors play in the constitution of law, including the presence and social location of individual moral entrepreneurs and experts, triggering events, interest groups and interest group politics, organized social movements, the shape of political opportunities, diverse structural conditions, and, increasingly, globalization. This is a lot to consider and a lot to disentangle. It is even more daunting when gathering empirical data, and making good use of social science theory is a "must" in solving this puzzle.

Indeed, what separates the social scientist from others interested in answering this question is, I hope, a commitment to data collection and systematic theory-building. The former enables us to understand what "is" the case; the latter enables us to understand why "what is" is the case. From my point of view, relying on one without the other is a less-than-acceptable way to reach conclusions. One without the other is too easy.

This reminds me of a joke. A philosopher and an empiricist are driving down a country road when the philosopher observes some sheep in a field on the side of the road. Upon observing the sheep, the philosopher declares to her companion, "Those sheep have recently been shorn." Her companion, an empiricist, responds by saying, "Well, at least on one side." My mother, whom I love dearly, operates more like the philosopher. I operate more like the empiricist, albeit hopefully with less rigidity. Indeed, although my mother can easily get away with offering authoritative statements about the nature of criminal law without collecting data or developing theory, I can't. And that is perhaps as it should be. After all, she speaks as a mom and I speak as a social scientist. The game rules for each are different. Of course, it is fair to ask the question, "Who made those rules?"

ADVICE TO STUDENTS

Anyone who wants to do social science research on crime and criminal justice issues needs to first master the basic tools of social science: data collection and analysis and theory testing and building. And then they should ask the related questions: Who makes the rules?" and "With what consequences?" By "rules" I mean the rules of social science research as well as the rules of social-legal life. Both are worthy of understanding. And, regardless, it's a lot of fun.

References: Jenness, Valerie. (1993). *Making It Work: The Prostitutes' Rights Movement in Perspective.* New York: Aldine de Gruyter; Jenness, Valerie, and Kendal Broad. (1997). *Hate Crimes: New Social Movements and the Politics of Violence.* New York: Aldine de Gruyter; Jenness, Valerie, and Ryken Grattet. (2001). *Making Hate a Crime: From Social Movement to Law Enforcement.* New York: Russell Sage Foundation; Jenness, Valerie. (2004). "Explaining Criminalization: From Demography and Status Politics to Globalization and Modernization." *Annual Review of Sociology* 30:147–171; Shover, Neal. (2003). Corporate Crime, Law, and Social Control. *Contemporary Sociology* 32:500–501.

that reflect the investigator's research goals and objectives. Much preliminary work is involved before the research project is launched.

Data collection may not be easy. Persons refuse to be interviewed. Some persons are simply inaccessible. Organizations may have policies that bar researchers from contacting their employees. Even if data are eventually collected, analyses of data will have to be made. A knowledge of statistics and analysis techniques is imperative. Once data have been tabulated and interpreted, a summary of major findings and implications of the research will have to be prepared. Thus, considerable work goes into carrying out an actual research project involving direct contact with samples of persons to be studied.

Investigations from a Distance

The line of least resistance and choice offering the least trouble is an investigation from a distance. This means that a researcher can study data already collected by others. It is possible for a researcher to spend his or her professional lifetime examining data collected and reported by others. One of the largest data sources is state and federal governments. Both state and federal governments publish statistical and descriptive information about every criminal justice topic. An annual compilation of general criminal justice statistical information is the *Sourcebook of Criminal Justice Statistics.* Not only is a hard copy of this *Sourcebook* published annually, but it is also available on CD. Thus, for $15–20, any person may obtain a CD version of the *Sourcebook* for recent years.

A growing number of agencies are producing data sets available in a variety of formats. One of the most popular formats is a computer diskette. The National Center for Juvenile Justice (NCJJ), headquartered in Pittsburgh, Pennsylvania, distributes diskettes of juvenile justice data. These diskettes are distributed for free to professionals at annual conferences of the Academy of Criminal Justice Sciences and American Society of Criminology. Interested persons can write the NCJJ for these diskettes as well. Other diskettes are produced by the National Judicial Reporting Program for various years. With their home computers, investigators can perform simple cross-tabulation functions with these diskettes and analyze these large data sets rather easily. The National Institute of Justice publishes lists of existing data sets annually, and this information is available to interested consumers for a nominal charge.

The *Uniform Crime Reports* and *National Crime Victimization Survey*

Other data sources include the ***Uniform Crime Reports (UCR),*** compiled by the Federal Bureau of Investigation. This publication includes statistics about the number and kinds of crimes reported in the United States annually by over 15,000 law enforcement agencies. The *UCR* is the major sourcebook of crime statistics in the United States. The *UCR* is compiled by gathering information on 29 types of crime from participating law enforcement agencies. Crime information is requested from all rural and urban law enforcement agencies. However, not all agencies report their crime information on a regular basis to the FBI. Others don't report at all, while still others report their information inconsistently (e.g., the same offense may be reported differently to the FBI by New Mexico authorities compared with how it is reported by California authorities).

The FBI has established a crime classification index. Index offenses include eight serious types of crime used by the FBI to measure crime trends. Information is also compiled about 21 less serious offenses ranging from forgery and counterfeiting to curfew violations and runaways. Index offense information is presented in the *UCR* for each state, city, county, and township that has submitted crime information during the most recent year. The eight index offenses and their definitions according to the Uniform Crime Reporting Program are shown below:

1. Murder and Nonnegligent Manslaughter: the willful (non-negligent) killing of one human being by another.
2. Forcible Rape: the carnal knowledge of a female forcibly and against her will; assaults or attempts to commit rape by force or threat of force are also included.
3. Robbery: the taking or attempt to take anything of value from the care, custody, or control of a person or persons by force or threat of force or violence and/or by putting the victim in fear.
4. Aggravated Assault: an unlawful attack by one person on another for the purpose of inflicting severe or aggravated bodily injury.
5. Burglary: the unlawful entry of a structure to commit a felony or theft.
6. Larceny-Theft: the unlawful taking, carrying, leading, or riding away of property from the possession or constructive possession of another; includes shoplifting, pocket-picking, purse-snatching, thefts from motor vehicles, and thefts of motor vehicle parts or accessories.
7. Motor Vehicle Theft: theft or attempted theft of a motor vehicle including automobiles, trucks, buses, motorcycles, motorscooters, and snowmobiles.
8. Arson: any willful or malicious burning or attempt to burn, with or without intent to defraud, a dwelling house, public building, motor vehicle, or aircraft, and the personal property of another.

The *National Crime Victimization Survey (NCVS)* is another source of information. The *NCVS* is a compendium of crimes reported by crime victims from an annual survey. The *NCVS* was implemented in 1972 and known originally as the *National Crime Survey*. In 1991 it was changed to the *NCVS*. It consists of an annual national survey of 50,000 households involving over 100,000 persons. These households are subdivided into subsets of 10,000 households each, where each subset is interviewed each month. Every 6 months one subset of 10,000 households is dropped from the survey and replaced by a fresh subset of 10,000 households. This feature ensures household diversity and incorporates transitional elements that keep the *NCVS* up-to-date. This material is usually referred to as victimization data. The *NCVS* distinguishes between victimizations and incidents. A victimization is the basic measure of the occurrence of a crime and is a specific criminal act that affects a single victim. An incident is a specific criminal act involving one or more victims.

Criticisms of the *UCR* and *NCVS*.   Even though the *UCR* publishes the most current crime figures from reporting law enforcement agencies, it is inaccurate in several respects. First, when criminals have been questioned about other crimes they have committed, the results show discrepancies between *UCR* figures and "self-report" information. In short, criminals escape detection or capture for many crimes they commit. Thus, it is generally accepted that there is more crime committed each year than official estimates such as the *UCR* disclose. Second, not all law enforcement agencies report crimes in a uniform manner. Many jurisdictions define the same crimes differently. Errors also occur in tabulating arrest statistics by clerks in local police departments (e.g., a clerk may classify a robbery as a burglary). Thus, the *UCR* may be more a reflection of police arrest practices rather than a true measure of the amount of crime that really occurs.

Third, in some jurisdictions, police crackdowns will lead to numerous arrests, but there will be few convictions. The implication is that arrest statistics are more a measure of police activity rather than criminal activity. A fourth criticism is that not all law enforcement agencies report their crime figures on a consistent basis. Sloppy record-keeping and lax record-keeping policies contribute to faulty reporting. Also, many crimes are committed that are never reported to the police. Fifth, when a crime *is* reported and a report is submitted to the *UCR,* only the most serious offense is often reported. For example, a burglary suspect is arrested at a crime scene in possession of burglary tools—a law violation—stolen goods—another law violation—and a concealed weapon—another law violation. However, law enforcement officials may report a single crime, burglary. This practice (i.e., reporting the most serious offense where more than two offenses have been committed by a single suspect), together with the fact that many crimes remain undetected or are not reported, causes some experts to charge that the *UCR* underestimates the actual amount of crime committed in the United States. The result of comparing *NCVS* (victimization) information with *UCR* (officially reported) data is that the amount of crime reported by the *NCVS* is from two to three times greater than the amount of crime reported by the *UCR.*

There are several criticisms of the *NCVS.* Some crime victims cannot remember when or where the offense occurred. Other victims are reluctant to report a rape, particularly if the rapist is known, such as a family member or close friend. Nonreporting is also related to victim fear, feelings of helplessness or apathy, the perceived powerlessness of police, and fear of the authorities themselves. The poor are especially reluctant to report crime because they fear reprisals from the criminals who are often known to them. Additionally, both the *UCR* and *NCVS* overemphasize street crimes and deemphasize corporate crimes.

Issues in Formulating Research Problems

It is difficult to refrain from structuring ideal research scenarios for yourself as you prepare to examine one topic or another. One major reason is that most of your academic work in preparation for research, your statistics and methods courses, has presented you with the ideal way of proceeding under maximally ideal conditions. Many of the articles you have read describing the research of others may have given you the impression that everything proceeded smoothly, without complications of any kind. Few research reports contain detailed descriptions of data gathering, of the actual interviews conducted, of the reactions of others to being observed by the researcher and the researchers' assistants. We seldom hear about having doors slammed in the researchers' faces, of investigators being told off by various irate respondents who have been sent questionnaires by anonymous persons and agencies for the past 10 years or longer.

BOX 2.4   PERSONALITY HIGHLIGHT

CHRISTY A. VISHER
The Urban Institute, Washington, D.C.

Statistics: B.A. (sociology), Trinity University; M.A., Ph.D. (sociology), Indiana University, Bloomington.

BACKGROUND AND INTERESTS

My research interests include criminal careers, substance use and abuse, communities and crime, and the evaluation of strategies for crime prevention and control. I have published widely on crime and justice topics, including the arrest process, jurors' responses to sexual assault trials, youthful offending, incapacitation, crime prevention, and drug testing in the criminal justice system. Presently, I am conducting research and evaluation on prisoner reentry and reintegration and coordinated community and criminal justice responses to domestic violence.

My career has had many nontraditional elements. While in graduate school, I realized that I was not eager for an academic career and was interested in exploring other options. Although the senior professor on my dissertation committee felt that a nonacademic career would be "a waste of my degree," it was fortunate that the chair of my committee was not so discouraging. In fact, during the year I was completing my dissertation, she was in Washington, D.C., managing a review of research and policy on sex segregation in the workplace for the National Academy of Sciences. She learned of a postdoctoral position with the Committee on Law and Justice (see *www7.nationalacademies.org/claj/*) and recommended that I apply for it. I was chosen to be a postdoctoral fellow and moved to the Washington, D.C., area.

RESEARCH INVESTIGATIONS

The National Academy of Sciences was a wonderful opportunity for me. My work there really initiated my lifelong interest in the policy implications of criminology and criminal justice. Because criminology has such important ramifications for everyday life, I believe it is vital that criminologists provide information that will address the problems of crime and delinquency and contribute to effective community responses.

The Committee was just beginning a review of research on criminal careers, and that effort was chaired by Alfred Blumstein. I summarized the findings from studies of the prevalence of delinquency and crime, reanalyzed the Rand Inmate Survey, and was the fourth editor of *Criminal*

BOX 2.4 CONTINUED

Careers and "Career Criminals." In the process, I worked with many of the leaders in academic criminology and criminal justice practice, and developed valuable professional relationships.

I further expanded my interest and appreciation for crime and justice policy research at the National Institute of Justice (NIJ), the research arm of the U.S. Department of Justice. At NIJ, I conducted research, developed solicitations, provided advice on proposals and final reports, and managed research projects. I was also heavily involved in the research publication process, and helped to develop procedures for ensuring that research results were accessible to a broad audience.

Early in my career I developed an appreciation of and expertise in research synthesis (including meta-analysis) and secondary data analysis. Both techniques are low-cost ways of conducting research and for me, these techniques led to several journal articles that I published during graduate school and shortly thereafter. Secondary data analysis involves a combination of creativity and analytical skill that is just as challenging and rewarding as collecting original data.

For the last 4 years, I have been at the Urban Institute, a nonprofit research organization in Washington, D.C., devoted to research and evaluation on social and economic policy issues that affect individuals in everyday life (*www.urban.org*). I am located in the Justice Policy Center, a unit of over 40 staff that carries out research and evaluation on a variety of crime and justice issues. Our work is frequently cited in the media and we receive lots of requests for information from criminal justice practitioners across the nation. Our primary funders are the federal government (Justice, Health and Human Services, Education) and private national and local foundations. My work is stimulating, fast-paced, and very rewarding.

ADVICE TO STUDENTS

My advice to students who are interested in a research career, especially one involving policy-related research and evaluation, is to gain broad experience as a student in different types of research, both in terms of research methodologies and substantive areas. This experience might be from a class assignment (honor's project or thesis), as a student working with a professor or graduate student on a specific research project, or as a summer intern or assistant working in a research environment. At the Urban Institute, we hire most frequently at the B.A. or M.A. level. Strong candidates have a 3.5 GPA or better, solid training in quantitative methods, hands-on experience with qualitative and quantitative research techniques, strong writing skills, and enthusiasm for the research process. To gain valuable experience, students should approach professors who are doing research that interests them and offer to help with their research project, even on an unpaid basis.

I would also strongly encourage criminology students to attend the annual meeting of the American Society of Criminology as often as possible. Those meetings are useful for learning about different kinds of research and substantive areas, gaining experience in making research presentations, and networking with other students and researchers (academic and nonacademic).

This doesn't mean that making ideal plans for investigating certain research problems is necessarily bad or should be discouraged. What it does mean, however, is that often, our ideal plans about how to proceed may be fraught with problems, hurdles, and all manner of obstacles from the outset. And that even if everything seemingly were to go smoothly and perfectly as we initially planned, other obstacles of a theoretical or philosophical nature might intervene and affect adversely the interpretations we have made of our findings. It is good to devise our research plans in ways that adhere to the ideal formulations and conceptions we have learned. But at the same time, we must recognize that in all likelihood, those ideal scenarios we have structured will not be realized fully, and that we will fall to some extent short of them. This is the "gap" between the ideal and real worlds. The standards to guide us are in place at all stages of the research enterprise.

The reality is that some departure from these standards is inevitable, and it is the price paid for engaging in research of any kind. Therefore, we must prepare ourselves for these "less than perfect" experiences and what we will say about our work when it is completed. The researcher decides almost everything about the implementation of a research project and oversees it through its completion. But dealing with people poses various risks and certain problems that widen the ideal–real gap. Even in those research situations where secondary sources are exclusively relied upon for research information in libraries, certain problems exist such that we must readjust our original objectives and procedures at various research stages.

It is important that some consideration be given to both ideal and real situations that may be confronted as the investigation progresses. Below are several pitfalls that may or may not occur in the research we conduct. We cannot forecast their occurrence, but we should be made aware that certain of these pitfalls may be encountered along the way, and that it might be wise to store up various strategies or Plan Bs in such cases. When things don't go the way we want, when we rely on someone to provide us with certain important information and they let us down and fail to provide it, when the findings, for some reason, turn out precisely opposite from the ways we originally predicted, when we are promised access to an organization and that access is later denied, these are some of the real experiences that frustrate our investigative efforts and contribute to the ideal–real gap. The list below is by no means exhaustive, but it does provide you with an indication of the sorts of things to be aware of, to possibly anticipate, as the research investigation proceeds.

1. A common pitfall is not containing one's research objectives within manageable limits. When a topic is selected, there is a frequent tendency to be too ambitious and extend the problem boundaries beyond your personal means. Researchers must carve out investigations that can be completed within reasonable time frames. It would be foolish and most likely impossible for graduate students to design a longitudinal study over a 10-year period (e.g., observing a cohort of youths from age 11 until they reach age 21 for purposes of determining factors that may influence some of them to adopt delinquent behaviors), for example, since the graduate schools of their universities limit the time students have to complete their degree work to 7 or fewer years. In many cases, students must finish their research work (e.g., their dissertations and theses) within a 6- to 9-year period, after they have completed their coursework. These are maximums, and few students ever stay that long in any given graduate department. Thus, much of the research conducted by graduate students is of short duration. Also, it is common to define a topic in such a diffuse way that there are many loose ends. The researcher will never be able to connect these loose ends within a reasonable time frame.

2. If permission is required to study certain **elements** (persons in this case), it may not be granted. Some investigators may wish to study a sample of juveniles at a secure detention facility or inmates in a prison or jail. They may do all of their preliminary work, prepare their research design, write their study objectives, define their population to be studied, and construct measuring instruments and questionnaires. Then, when they approach the target institution with their study proposal, permission to interview, observe, or in other ways examine the detained delinquent youths is denied by institution authorities. Even when permission to study a particular setting is granted in advance, that permission may be withdrawn later with little or no notice.

3. When samples of persons are designated for study, some of those persons selected may refuse to participate. If you mail questionnaires to certain respondents, they may trash your questionnaires. If you visit certain people with the idea of interviewing them, they may refuse to be interviewed. This is **nonresponse.** No matter how well you plan ahead and identify certain persons for investigation, little, if anything, can be done to force them to comply with your requests. Even when your research doesn't involve people directly and your research efforts are exclusively library-related, it is not always the case that the materials you examine will be directly relevant for your specific research interests. Anytime data have been collected by others, their personal objectives may not directly coincide with yours. Therefore, if you design a research project involving the **analysis of secondary sources** in the library, that material may not exist, or it may not exist in the form that would best fit your own objectives. Thus, researchers often adjust their original investigative sights to fit the data available.

4. The instruments designated for studying various samples may be deemed unsuitable, because they may elicit actions on the part of participants that may be detrimental to the goals of the organization. If the proposed research is threatening in any way to the participants or those in charge of specific settings, they may refuse cooperation. Asking prisoners whether their grievance procedures are adequate, for instance, may evoke negative, and unwarranted, responses. It may even provoke lawsuits filed by inmates against corrections officials, if the inmates believe they should be entitled to a grievance procedure they don't already have. Questionnaires are not only a source of information for the investigator, but they can also educate respondents about things that are not always favorable for the organization. For instance, considering the example above, asking penitentiary inmates whether they have inmate grievance committees or various privileges may precipitate minor rioting if they have no such committees or lack certain privileges. Thus, seemingly innocent-appearing questionnaires can be a key source of future respondent discontent.

5. The measures selected for use in the research project may lack **validity** and **reliability.** This means that despite everything else going well for the researcher, there is always a problem relating to the adequacy of measures measuring what they are supposed to measure, and also the extent to which these measures are measured consistently. Measuring social phenomena accurately is a complex task. At the outset, it is important to recognize that our measures of social and psychological variables are flawed in various respects. Besides these instrument flaws, some persons who know they are being studied may act in ways that are different from the way they might behave if they were not being observed. This is **reactivity** and can adversely affect one's findings.

6. The problem selected for investigation has been heavily researched in the past. Regardless of how recent one is to a field of study, there is the matter of selecting a researchable problem and a solution that have already been implemented and found to be unproductive. This means that recent familiarity with the topic area may not disclose previous approaches that are not considered noteworthy. The researcher needs to experiment with different research methods, and also with different frames of reference, before actually implementing a research project. It is confusing, and especially frustrating, for a researcher to investigate a problem in a certain way that may have been researched earlier using the same approach, the same explanation, and the same investigatory techniques.

7. The data collection methods selected for use may not be the best for the problem under investigation. Sometimes, researchers will select problems for investigation that lend themselves to specific kinds of data collection techniques. Some techniques may be more appropriate for certain kinds of research compared with others. Again considering the example of inmates above, it would be unreasonable, for instance, to expect researchers to investigate inmate grievance procedures in prisons through the use of surveys (e.g., questionnaire administration). The superficial nature of responses to questionnaires would not provide researchers with a complete picture of the grievance process used by inmates. There might be some hesitancy on the part of correctional officials to disclose their own procedures for processing grievances, and inmates may not be entirely truthful about the administrative and internal grievance mechanisms that are currently in place for the resolution of interpersonal or legal problems, especially when they are required to do so in writing. If correctional officers or administrators see the written responses of prisoners, some inmates may be subject to reprisals later or have their privileges withdrawn. Personal interviews and observations of the grievance process in action would be better depictions of what is going on and why.

8. Depending on the data collection method used, respondents may say things that they believe the researchers want to hear, but that are not necessarily true. Investigators have termed these kinds of responses **social desirability.** Social desirability is the propensity of respondents to place themselves in a favorable light when being interviewed or questioned. Black interviewers, for instance, may not obtain truthful answers from white respondents if the subject area has racial overtones. Topics such as race prejudice or the death penalty issue are touchy subjects for many persons, and often there is an element of cat-and-mouse interplay between an interviewer and an interviewee. Once interviewees sense that the interviewer has a particular attitudinal disposition or mindset, they may say and do things that they believe the interviewer wants to hear or see. Regardless of whether they are wrong in their beliefs, their statements of opinion and belief are nevertheless distorted to conform to an acceptable social image.

9. The samples selected may not be representative of the population from which they have been drawn. Those persons who are subsequently studied may not necessarily be typical of the population-at-large. If investigators study police officers in Omaha, Nebraska, for example, how do we know that Omaha police officers are typical of police officers in other jurisdictions such as Los Angeles, Chicago, or New York? We don't know how typical they are. Thus, some caution should be exercised in generalizing our findings to settings beyond those immediately studied. There is little researchers can do to influence the representativeness of the samples they obtain for research investigation. There are absolutely no guarantees that certain samples are better than others.

10. If subject participation is coerced, responses may not be an accurate portrayal of their real world. Studies of detained juveniles, jail or prison inmates, or probationers and parolees are basically studies involving a degree of coercion. If permission is granted to study persons with any of these or similar characteristics, such research may be tainted by respondent retaliation because of the coercive nature of their involvement. These are captive audiences. Inmates of prisons and jails may deliberately lie to researchers. Detained juveniles may overdramatize their involvement in delinquent activities and admit to juvenile acts they never committed or contemplated committing. Probationers and parolees studied by investigators may feel compelled to participate in research projects because of their belief that failure to comply might dispose their probation/parole officers to file negative reports about them. Again, the coercive nature of their involvement raises the serious question of the meaningfulness of their responses. It is not so much that they will say what they think we want to hear, but rather, they may say what they want us to hear. We have no direct ways of controlling for the influence of coercion on participant responses. We can recognize some of the elements of coercion in the research we conduct and act accordingly and cautiously when interpreting our data.

As noted above, this is not a comprehensive listing of all of the ideal–real problems that can influence the research enterprise. However, the listing does bring to our attention the idea that many factors can operate in a variety of ways to complicate or frustrate our research efforts and shake the investigation's ideal foundations. Throughout the book, you will detect a strong element of conservatism. This is not political conservatism, but rather a conservatism that urges us to be cautious when collecting data, analyzing it, and drawing conclusions about it. There are simply too many weak points in the research process where things can go wrong. Murphy's Law may apply here. If something can go wrong, it probably will go wrong. Although investigators should be prepared to accept some failure in their work, they should also recognize that research has many rewarding features.

SUMMARY

Social researchers study a myriad of events of interest to them. These events may be labor turnover among correctional officers; get-tough policies and their implications for juvenile justice and the treatment of juvenile offenders; police professionalism and public reaction to community policing; the efficacy of home confinement and electronic monitoring for supervising offenders; the type of discretion exercised by police officers in responding to incidents of domestic violence; public views toward the death penalty and the implications of wrongful convictions of some of those condemned to death; judicial and prosecutorial misconduct and how it is sanctioned; and alternative ways of administering different criminal justice agencies.

From the outset and preceding the investigation of particular events or research problems, investigators deliberately select a certain problem for research. Furthermore, they approach this problem from a particular point of view, which is a frame of reference or way of looking at the problem. Usually frames of reference are influenced by many factors, including one's own belief system, values, and the opinions and research work of others who have investigated similar phenomena. There is considerable subjectivity inherent in selecting particular problems for study, as well as choosing certain frames of reference to study such problems or events. The influence of values on this process is pervasive, and this influence extends to certain data collection methods that are believed to yield information necessary to answer one's research questions. Sometimes research is conducted without any apparent frame of reference. Much descriptive research occurs without clearly articulated frames of reference. However, descriptions of settings, people, and situations are helpful to other researchers in that they suggest particular ways problems may be approached and investigated subsequently.

Once chosen, frames of reference influence one's theoretical choices. Theories are constructed so as to explain and predict interrelationships between variables. Any frame of reference is focused on a limited number of variables, and other alternative variables that may be used to explain events are automatically excluded from consideration. This is because multiple explanations of events, although more realistic, are also more difficult to implement and test empirically whenever the research enterprise is undertaken. Thus, some amount of simplification occurs as our research is clearly defined and a particular approach is identified.

When a particular topic is chosen for investigation and a frame of reference is selected, social researchers examine existing literature to find out what is known about the event to be explained. Some topics or events are more heavily researched than others, and thus the amount of existing literature on certain subjects more or less varies. Literature reviews involve studying research findings discussed in journal articles or in books. Because different settings and persons are studied, and because different frames of reference and data collection strategies have been used, not all information yielded in these literature reviews is totally consistent. Researchers have learned to expect some amount of inconsistency in the literature. However, they are not terribly concerned about such inconsistencies, because they are often explained away by the fact that different approaches were taken, or different samples were studied, or different data collection methods were used in the data-gathering process. Also, instruments, such as questionnaires, may contain a wide variety of scales and measures of essentially the same phenomena. This fact alone is destined to yield inconsistent study findings. Social scientists persevere in their data collection efforts, despite interstudy inconsistencies, because they wish to learn more about their research problems or events.

When data are gathered, researchers may choose to gather information directly or they may choose to analyze data collected by others. Some conventional data sources are the *Uniform Crime Reports,* a compilation of crime information by the Federal Bureau of Investigation. Another source is the *National Crime Victimization Survey,* which is an annual accounting of the amount of crime committed against crime victims. A third source of valuable information is *The Sourcebook of Criminal Justice Statistics,* which is compiled by researchers under the sponsorship of the Hindelang Center at SUNY–Albany and the Bureau of Justice Statistics of the U.S. Department of Justice.

When investigators choose to collect their own data, this is often an expensive and time-consuming undertaking. "Hands-on" research means to collect original data relevant to one's research purposes. Investigations from a distance portray the use of information gathered by others, such as research institutes, government agencies, or private foundations. Increasingly, data sets are being provided to social researchers to encourage them to study the collected information to learn more about it. Much of this research is subsequently analyzed and reported in one of hundreds of criminal justice or criminology journal outlets.

When problems are formulated and frames of reference are suggested to approach these problems, there are various issues to be considered. One issue concerns the magnitude of one's research objectives. Novice researchers often want to enlarge the scope of their research to the extent that it would be impossible to implement with their existing financial and person-power resources. Thus it is important to keep one's research objectives within manageable limits. Another problem may arise if permission is required to study certain persons who possess needed information relevant to the problem studied. If juvenile records are sought, for example, these records are often privileged and unavailable to most citizens, including social investigators. Many levels of approval may be required before access to such records is approved. And in many cases, approval for access to certain information may simply be denied. Thus, no matter how worthy one's research enterprise, it may not occur if access to necessary information cannot be obtained.

Other common problems include nonresponse, where some persons do not respond to an investigator's request for information. If questionnaires are mailed to large numbers of persons, some persons may not return their questionnaires. Nonresponse rates are as high as 70 percent in many criminological studies. There is little researchers can do to make someone respond to their questions, no matter how much researchers endeavor to increase their **response rate.** Therefore, some investigators may have to rely instead on analyses of existing collected data that are marginally relevant to their study problem or event. Also, data-gathering instruments themselves may omit important questions, or the questions themselves may be poorly worded or phrased. Some information sought may be sensitive and potentially embarrassing for respondents. These factors may increase nonresponse as well. Some items or scales used in connection with various data-gathering tools such as questionnaires or interviews may lack validity and/or reliability. We may not be measuring what we think we are measuring, or whatever we are measuring may not be measured consistently. When such problems arise, there are certain steps investigators must follow in order to verify their research results and resolve these issues.

Some problems and frames of reference selected may be previously heavily researched. The solutions or frames of reference used in this previous research may not be particularly productive or useful. Again, novice researchers may not be familiar enough with available literature to know whether their event and frame of reference is unique and productive or outdated and not useful. Sometimes mismatches occur between problems investigated and certain data collection methods chosen. Quite simply, some data collection methods work better for certain types of research problems than others.

Another common problem is that respondents may give answers to researchers' questions that are socially desirable, and that respondents believe investigators want to hear.

This social desirability problem arises and increases in importance as the sensitivity of information to be gathered increases. Thus, questions having to do with one's income, sexual habits, prior delinquent conduct, criminal record, or personal beliefs may cause some respondents to say things they believe researchers want to hear. But this information may not be true of these respondents. One's research findings are tainted as a result.

Finally, when certain samples are chosen for investigation, it may be that these samples are not typical of the populations about which researchers seek information. It is uncertain whether particular types of persons, such as police officers in Los Angeles, are typical of police officers in other jurisdictions, such as New York, Chicago, or Miami. Therefore, generalizing from any particular sample may not be warranted or it may be misleading. Sample representativeness in any research investigation is something a researcher can never guarantee. Also, if some persons are coerced into participating in one's study, such as prison inmates, confined delinquents, or persons on probation or parole, they may engage in deliberate deception and give less than truthful answers to questions asked of them by researchers.

QUESTIONS FOR REVIEW

1. What are frames of reference? How are frames of reference chosen in relation to particular research problems or events investigated?

2. Can different frames of reference be used to study the same phenomenon? Why or why not?

3. Are frames of reference used in all research investigations? Under what circumstances might frames of reference not be used?

4. How do values influence one's choice of a frame of reference?

5. What is the relationship between theory and frames of reference?

6. How are different topics chosen for investigation? What factors tend to influence one's choice of topic for study?

7. What is a literature review? What do literature reviews disclose about one's research problem and chosen frame of reference?

8. What are inconsistencies in study findings and how do such inconsistencies occur? Should researchers be unduly concerned with inconsistencies in study findings? Why or why not?

9. What are three important sources researchers may use to gather criminological and criminal justice information? How useful and reliable are these sources?

10. What are some important differences between "hands-on" research and investigations from a distance?

11. What are some problems associated with the *Uniform Crime Reports* and *National Crime Victimization Survey?*

12. What are five important issues in formulating research problems? Why are each of these issues important to investigators?

3 Research Designs

CHAPTER OUTLINE

CHAPTER OBJECTIVES

As the result of reading this chapter, the following objectives will be realized:

1. Distinguishing between qualitative and quantitative research and the characteristics of each.
2. Learning the differences between explorative, descriptive, and experimental research designs, including their objectives and potential research applications.
3. Understanding what it means to control for different variables in the research enterprise.
4. Examining survey research, its useful applications, and some of its important advantages and disadvantages.
5. Contrasting and understanding case studies in relation to surveys, including what is meant by case studies, some general applications, and their weaknesses and strengths.
6. Describing the differences between experimental and control groups and how these distinctions are useful in hypothesis tests.
7. Discovering the importance of establishing equivalence between groups through individual matching, using the same groups as their own controls in before–after experiments, frequency distribution control matching, and random assignment.
8. Learning the difference between pretests and posttests and how they influence experimental designs.

9. Describing the classical experiment and several different variations of it, including the after-only design, the before–after design, and their respective applications, advantages, and disadvantages.

10. Distinguishing between true and quasi-experiments and how such experiments are useful in hypothesis tests.

11. Learning about time-series and multiple time-series designs, their uses, weaknesses, and strengths.

12. Describing cost–benefit analyses, their utility for social researchers, their potential research applications, and their advantages and disadvantages.

13. Learning about internal and external validity and the factors that influence these study characteristics.

Introduction

This chapter is about research designs, or plans investigators use to implement their studies of events or occurrences they wish to explain. We have already examined various types of research in terms of exploration, description, and experimentation. This chapter parallels these research types by describing their objectives and characteristics. The chapter opens with a description of the distinction between qualitative and quantitative research. Qualitative research is often associated with exploration and description, and with data collection techniques closely aligned with observation and interviewing. Some examples of qualitative research will be provided. Quantitative research emphasizes statistical applications, usually where large amounts of data are assembled and subjected to statistical analysis and testing. Again, examples will be provided to describe such research. Today, much of the research conducted in criminal justice and criminology is heavily quantitative, although qualitative research is slowly increasing in popularity as researchers learn more about its usefulness for explaining events and characterizing them.

The chapter examines exploratory research designs first, by describing several classic studies of settings where little was known about such settings at the time this type of research was conducted. This is typical of exploratory research. It is often associated with discovering more about settings and topics about which little information has been generated. The more we learn about the settings we study, the more sophisticated we can be about describing those settings. Thus, a second type of research design, the descriptive design, is depicted in some detail. Descriptive research designs are the most common designs found in the research literature. The literature is rich with descriptions of all types of settings throughout the criminal justice system. Elaborate descriptions of research settings eventually lead to more sophisticated types of research where experimentation may be conducted.

Experimental research designs are intended to assess the impact of one variable, usually known as an **intervening variable,** upon other variables. Sometimes these variables are discussed as independent and dependent, and theoretical schemes may be examined in order to determine how these variables function relative to one another. Experimentation also involves controlling certain variables, where some variables are isolated and held **constant** to ascertain their influence on events we attempt to explain. Thus, in experimental research, some variables are controlled while others are free to vary. Experimental research is designed to produce cause–effect relations between variables, although researchers who engage in experimental research encourage their readers to interpret their findings cautiously. It is quite difficult to establish cause–effect relations between events and explanations of those events. This research design is described in some detail and various examples are provided.

Some conventional research designs are surveys and case studies. Survey research is a common way of collecting large amounts of information. Surveys may occur at a single point in time, or they may be extended to examinations of large groups of persons known as panels over several different time periods of one or more years. This type of research usually involves information gathered by administering questionnaires. The advantages and disadvantages of surveys will be described, and several research applications will be presented.

Case studies are intensive examinations of specific social settings or places or groups of persons. Exhaustive examinations of these settings are conducted, usually by using interviewing and/or observation. Case studies are intentionally limited to smaller groups of persons rather than large assemblages of them. Often, dialogue between persons is transcribed and used to depict events and why these events occur. Much can be learned about prominent actors in these research settings, and thus, case studies offer an in-depth examination of a setting that surveys cannot possibly assess. The advantages and disadvantages of case studies will be discussed. Case studies and surveys are also contrasted in retrospect.

Next, different types of experimental designs are described. The classical experimental design is presented where experimental and control groups are described. Variables are selected and used for experimental purposes to determine their influence or effect on other variables. Treatment or experimental variables will be described, as well as the meaning of control groups. When conducting experimental research, investigators often seek to equate different groups so that the influence of treatment variables can be clearly ascertained without the possible contamination of individual differences and personality or social variations. Thus, some attempt is made to establish equivalence between groups for experimentation purposes. Establishing equivalence may be accomplished several different ways. Each method of establishing equivalence has particular advantages and disadvantages or weaknesses and strengths. These will be explained.

Four methods are described for establishing equivalence between groups. One method is individual matching, which involves using different persons in experimental and control groups that share many of the same personal characteristics. Another method is to use persons as their own controls in before–after experiments. This method uses the same group of persons over time and charts particular changes in their behaviors in relation to introductions of one or more experimental variables at different points. A third method is to match experimental and control groups according to group-shared characteristics, such as the average age, gender breakdown, or on-the-job experience of persons. Where two groups share many of the same characteristics as aggregates, this is known as group or frequency distribution control matching. Finally, groups may sometimes be equated through random assignment, where randomness is used to place persons from a larger aggregate of them into one group or another, each respectfully designated as the experimental and control group. Each of these methods for establishing equivalency between groups are discussed in detail and different priorities are assigned to those that seem to work best for experimental purposes.

Experimental groups consist of persons who are exposed to the treatment or experimental variable, while this variable is withheld from the control group. Ideally, behavioral reactions exhibited by the experimental group are compared with those same behaviors of the control group, and any differences in exhibited behaviors are generally attributable to the experimental variable. This type of experimentation utilizes pretests and posttests, where both the experimental and control group are measured according to particular variables before the experiment is conducted and then again once the experiment has occurred. The effects of the experimental variable can often be determined through comparisons between these groups.

Different types of experimental designs include the classical experimental design, which includes two variations: the after-only design and the before–after design. The after-only design involves comparing experimental with control groups after an experimental variable has been introduced to an experimental group. Thus, there is no pretest in such a circumstance. Under the before–after experimental scenario, a pretest is conducted as well as a posttest, and any differences between the two groups in the posttest period are highlighted as significant. These types of variations in the classical experimental design will be examined and discussed. The advantages and disadvantages of these types of research designs will be described.

Subsequently, true experiments and quasi-experiments are distinguished. True experiments involve random assignment, which is not the most effective way of equating groups for experimental purposes. Quasi-experiments typically involve individual matching or persons used as their own controls in before–after experimentation. The weaknesses and strengths and advantages and disadvantages of true experiments and quasi-experiments will be discussed.

The chapter concludes with a discussion of time-series designs, multiple time-series designs, and cost–benefit analyses. Time-series designs involve multiple time periods over which different behaviors or events are described. At some point during this process, an intervening variable is introduced, and the originally observed behaviors or events continue to be tracked following the introduction of this intervening variable. Multiple time-series designs track behaviors or events similar to time-series designs, although more than one experimental variable is introduced at different points over time. Again, continued tracking of the event or behavior discloses the impact, if any, of one or more experimental variables. Cost–benefit analyses attempt to assess the cost of different kinds of interventions intended to influence particular behaviors or situations. Some proposed interventions are more costly to implement than others. The overall results disclose whether certain interventions are most cost-effective than others. Social policies are influenced as a result. For each of these types of designs, various advantages and disadvantages will be described and explained.

Qualitative and Quantitative Research

Qualitative Research

There are many different kinds of research conducted by criminologists and criminal justicians. Often, two broad categories are used to distinguish between different types of research. These categories are qualitative and quantitative. **Qualitative research** is the application of observational techniques and/or the analysis of documents as the primary means of learning about persons or groups and their characteristics. Sometimes qualitative research is called fieldwork, referring to the immersion of researchers into the lives and worlds of those studied. Investigators may observe persons or groups from afar, or they may join groups and describe their experiences and interactions with group members. Qualitative research is intended to enrich our descriptions of social settings and persons participating in them. Such research offers a level of detail that is generally missing from a self-administered questionnaire or interview situation.

One example of qualitative research is a study referenced earlier by Shadd Maruna (2004). Among other things, Maruna was interested in a criminal's explanatory style, which is the person's tendency to offer different sorts of explanations or attributions for significant and unexpected life events, such as becoming involved in a life of crime. Maruna believed that reformed former offenders would tend to focus on positive events in their lives, describing their changed behaviors as the product of more internal, stable, and global causes (i.e., "Because I am a good person deep down"), while active offenders might focus on external, unstable, and negative events when explaining their persistence in offending (i.e., "I'm bad to the bone" or "Others get the lucky breaks, not me" or "That's just the type of person I am"). Maruna studied 100 British citizens who once spent time in prison. These persons were a part of the Liverpool Desistance Study (LDS) and involved life story interviews with all 100 persons. Of the 100 persons, 55 were considered "desisters" who refrained from further criminal activity, while 34 were considered as persisting or active in their criminal careers. Maruna conducted an in-depth analysis of their life stories, seeking information that would enable him to typify each person's explanatory style. Maruna found evidence to support the explanatory styles used by desisters and persistent offenders. It was a qualitative study to the extent that Maruna relied upon statements these persons had made in providing others with accounts of their lives.

Another type of qualitative study was conducted by Richard R. Johnson (2001). Johnson, who is a domestic violence investigator for Kane County, Illinois, was interested in the impact of an intensive supervision program for a select sample of persons convicted of domestic violence. The intensive supervision program for higher-risk, domestic-violence offenders was implemented in November 1998 by the Kane County Court Services. Participants were screened for the 26-week domestic-violence counseling program according to various criteria. Johnson tracked offender progress over time, and he also determined the amount of victim involvement or participation in counseling and therapy during the same time interval. Interviews with probationers throughout the 26-week program were conducted regularly by supervising probation officers. Recidivism rates (rearrests for new violent offenses) were used to measure program success. Although participants in the domestic violence program had relatively high recidivism rates (52 percent), these rates were not as high as for those not participating in the program (78 percent). The qualitative nature of the study included in-depth interviews with participants and their own impressions of the impact of the counseling program on their violent behaviors.

Quantitative Research

Quantitative research is the application of statistical procedures and techniques to data collected through surveys, including interviews and questionnaire administration. Quantitative researchers are known as numbers-crunchers, since a wide variety of sophisticated statistical techniques exists to describe what they have found. By far the lion's share of articles in contemporary journals are quantitative. Elaborate tables, charts, and graphs are constructed to portray numerical data. An advanced knowledge of statistics is often required to understand what researchers have done and to interpret their findings. Quantitative research is most often associated with different types of experimentation.

A survey of parole officers was conducted by Richard P. Seiter (2002). Seiter wanted to know what parole officers did while supervising offenders on parole and assisting them in becoming reintegrated into their communities. He decided to send questionnaires to all probation and parole officers in the Eastern Probation and Parole Region of Missouri. He received 114 questionnaires back from these officers, or a response rate of 46 percent. He gleaned considerable information about these officers and their duties based on the 114 respondents studied. Actually, Seiter decided to conduct personal interviews with some of these respondents and asked them on the questionnaires they returned to indicate if they would permit him to interview them. Most agreed to an interview, but he subsequently selected a small sample of respondents to contact and interview personally. This portion of his study was qualitative in that interviews were recorded and documented. It is seldom the case that any particular research project is purely quantitative or purely qualitative. Elements of both types of research are commonly found in criminological investigations.

Another largely quantitative study was conducted by Rudy Haapanen and Lee Britton (2002). These investigators studied the influence of the **frequency** of drug testing on a sample of 1,958 juvenile parolees. These parolees were divided randomly into five groups, where the groups ranged from "no drug testing" to weekly or biweekly drug testing. It was believed by Haapanen and Britton that more frequent drug testing would contribute to greater law-abiding behaviors among parolees and less recidivism over periods ranging from 24 months to 42 months. These researchers conducted extensive statistical analyses of the data they compiled and reached the conclusion that more extensive drug testing seemed to have little or no effect on parolee recidivism. However, they did find that those parolees who tested positive for drugs during the early stages of their parole programs were more inclined to recidivate than those who did not test positive for drugs. There were also qualitative and descriptive dimensions of this study, as Haapanen and Britton described the background characteristics of the five groups of participants. Furthermore, these investigators interviewed various parole officers to determine the nature of their supervision of juvenile parolees during the study period.

More than a few studies combine aspects of both qualitative and quantitative research. For instance, Alexander Weiss and Steven Chermak (1998) investigated the news value of African American victims and the media's presentation of homicides. They collected all articles covering homicides in Indianapolis, Indiana, during 1995. They examined each of these articles and determined the number of victims, and gender and racial/ethnic information. These investigators created various categories of media coverage based on their impressions of the articles they read. This was a heavily qualitative dimension. They also counted words in each article, as well as the numbers of articles published about each murder incident. Subsequently, they applied several statistical techniques to this information in an effort to discover any **correlation** or statistical observation that might be significant and interesting.

Research Objectives and Designs

The goals of researchers are grouped according to (1) exploration, (2) description, and (3) experimentation. No single research design is universally applicable for all investigators at any particular time. Each of these research designs functions to allow researchers to conduct their social inquiries in different ways and at different levels of sophistication. Selecting the appropriate research design, therefore, is dependent, in part, upon the kinds of questions researchers attempt to answer. Often, several different research objectives may be combined in the same research project to answer specific research questions. However, most research projects will usually emphasize one research design over the others. Decisions about selecting the best designs must be made by considering the weaknesses and strengths of each design relative to the others. There are no restrictions preventing researchers from customizing their investigations with characteristics of several different kinds of research designs.

Exploration and Exploratory Objectives

Research designs may have exploratory objectives. An **exploratory design** is characterized by several features. First, it is assumed that investigators have little or no knowledge about the research problem under study. A general unfamiliarity with a particular group of people does not provide investigators with much opportunity to focus on specific aspects of the social situation. One of the strengths of exploratory research is that potentially significant factors may be discovered, assessed, and described in greater detail with a more sophisticated type of research design developed later.

For instance, if researchers wanted to study social interaction patterns among inmates in prison systems but knew little or nothing about the structure and functioning of penal institutions, an exploratory research project would be in order. Such was the case in the early 1930s when Joseph Fishman described inmate subculture and sexual aggression. Little was known about prisoners and prison life, and even less was known about their sexual aggressiveness and patterns of sexual assault. Fishman was a federal prison inspector who became interested in depicting various dimensions of prisoners' lives. In 1934 Fishman's work, *Sex in Prison,* was published. Although this classic work described the prevalence and nature of inmate homosexuality behind prison walls, it also acquainted the outside world with several new concepts and inmate jargon that suggested to other researchers a new and rich source in need of greater social description. Fishman used the term "subculture" to describe unique social arrangements among the separate, smaller social system of prisoners behind prison walls but within the greater societal culture.

Fishman's work stimulated other investigators to describe similar prison environments and inmate culture. Donald Clemmer wrote *The Prison Community* in 1940, which described inmate subculture in a Menard, Illinois, penitentiary. Clemmer was a correctional officer who spent nearly 3 years observing inmate life and interviewing various prisoners. Especially noteworthy was his description of how new inmates were introduced to prison life. He described new inmates using inmate jargon. Thus, new inmates or "fish" would undergo a certain amount of "prisonization" (a term equivalent with the sociological concept of socialization, or learning through contact with others), where older inmates would take them aside and tell them about the do's and don't's of prison life at Menard. Prisonization was the descriptive term that portrayed inmate customs and who controlled the flow of scarce prisoner goods and contraband as well as certain inmate privileges.

The works of Fishman and Clemmer stimulated other social scientists to provide more detailed descriptions of prison life in later years. For example, a classic study of prison life is *The Society of Captives* (1958) written by Gresham Sykes. Sykes acknowledged the impact of both Fishman and Clemmer upon his own research and writing when describing inmate culture at the New Jersey State Maximum Security Prison at Trenton. His analysis of prisoner culture introduced terms such as "rat" (an inmate who informs or squeals on other inmates), "merchant" (an inmate who barters scare goods in exchange for favors), and "real man" (an inmate who is loyal and generous, but tough in his or her relations with other inmates). Sykes extended his analysis of prisoners to include an elaborate description of the inmate code and pecking order.

The distinguishing feature of exploratory studies is that relatively little is known about one's research target. Thus, investigators who wanted to study delinquent gangs in the 1940s and 1950s had to become acquainted with youth gang norms and patterns of formation and persistence before they could conduct more sophisticated descriptive investigations. Today, many metropolitan police departments have special gang divisions or gang units and specialty teams of officers whose exclusive function is to monitor gang movements and activities in their jurisdictions. For novice observers several decades ago, the significance of different types and colors of wearing apparel among juvenile gang members would be largely unknown and possibly considered irrelevant. Today, much descriptive information is available about gang members, their colors and signs, and the meaning of certain types of graffiti in their "turfs" or neighborhood territories. Thus, in many schools throughout the United States today, both teachers and non-gang-affiliated students refrain from wearing certain-colored clothing for fear of being victimized by juvenile gangs. It has been found, for instance, that random, drive-by shootings of innocent bystanders are perpetrated by juvenile gang members, in part, because of the color of clothing worn by innocent pedestrians and passersby. Wearing a blue shirt in a neighborhood controlled by a notorious gang, the Bloods, whose gang color is red, is an invitation to become a target of drive-by shooters. By the same token, wearing red articles of clothing (e.g., hat or coat or pants) in a "blue" neighborhood controlled by a rival gang, the Crips, whose distinguishing color is blue, is also an invitation to become a target of drive-by shooters.

Exploratory studies, therefore, serve primarily to acquaint researchers with the characteristics of research targets that should be described or examined more extensively. Another example of early exploratory research would be the initial investigations conducted by researchers into our drug culture of the 1920s and 1930s. At one time in our history, marijuana was believed to cause irreversible insanity and cause persons to murder others. Gradually, we have learned much about marijuana and other drugs, and under certain medical conditions, different types of drugs have potential therapeutic value for such disorders as glaucoma. Thus, over a 70-year period, we have gradually moved our level of inquiry about the social, biological, and psychological influence of different drugs from exploration to description, and from description to experimentation.

Description and Descriptive Objectives

Description is the most common design objective in criminology and criminal justice. Almost every study conducted by social scientists and where human subjects are involved has some descriptive characteristics. Before we can discover patterns for various phenomena, such as sentencing disparities, prison violence and rioting, civil disorder, probation and parole officer burnout and stress, law enforcement officer misconduct or use of excessive force, or any other event we wish to explain, we must first obtain some amount of descriptive information about these phenomena.

A **descriptive design** means depicting the characteristics of whatever we observe. We select settings for investigation, we target particular features of those settings for special attention, and we describe in various ways whatever we find. Different data collection strategies can be used for this purpose. All of the information derived from various data collection strategies provides rich descriptions that often have explanatory value for researchers. It should be noted, however, that description, true scientific description, is considerably more structured than casual descriptions of social settings. Researchers know in advance what they wish to describe, and their accumulated data reflect a focus on specific social and psychological dimensions of persons and their environments.

The works of Fishman and Clemmer described above have inspired more than a few researchers to investigate new inmate populations and describe existing inmate codes. The work of Paula and William Faulkner (1997) is an in-depth description of the inmate code of conduct at a maximum-security state penitentiary in the Midwest. When the Faulkners conducted their study, there were 550 inmates housed in the facility. They obtained a random sample of 67 inmates, with subsequent participation by 33 inmates. The Faulkners wished to describe the existing inmate code, as well as status relations among inmates. Extended interviews with inmates yielded much descriptive information. The inmates said that primary inmate code characteristics were (1) loyalty ("don't be a snitch"); (2) "doing your own time"; (3) "standing up" for one's self; and (4) "smartness." The type of conviction offense had a significant impact on one's status among other inmates. The Faulkners concluded that the inmate code in the prison they studied was virtually identical to the inmate codes described by previous researchers, including Fishman and Clemmer. Thus, it is significant that inmate culture of the 1990s is not particularly different from inmate culture of the 1940s. The Faulkners also discussed certain historical changes in the structure and organization of penitentiaries in their analysis and the relevance of their findings for sociological theory and prison policy.

Descriptive research is also illustrated in the work of Mark Umbreit, Robert B. Coates, and Betty Vos (2002), who have described restorative justice programs in various communities. Restorative justice is not especially new historically, but its application as an alternative to criminal prosecution is considered to be a recent innovation and intervention in correctional programming for low-risk offenders. These investigators used a qualitative approach to describe the use of restorative justice in South St. Paul, Minnesota. Restorative justice involves establishing peacemaking circles, which involve circles of understanding, healing circles for offenders and their families, for victims and their families, and for the general community. The process is a preprosecution initiative where victims and offenders are brought together in face-to-face interaction similar to victim–offender mediation. Long a practice among Native Americans, restorative justice often targets youthful offenders in a milieu involving emotional and spiritual elements. Participants or those who choose to participate express their feelings about the incident, their desire for the offender to accept responsibility in the incident, and express their concern about their future relationship with the offender. Mediators, also known as circle keepers, are encouraged to be focused, organized, nonjudgmental, good listeners, compassionate, respectful, patient, and clear regarding the ground rules and understanding. They believe that everyone is human and can make mistakes; circles have a chance to fix those mistakes in a good way.

The St. Paul restorative justice process involved 28 cases where participants met for 2-hour sessions from January 1997 through June 30, 2000. The number of circles per case averaged from 4 to 16 during this time interval. One sister of an offender said, "You can't turn and run." A mother of a victim said, "I was able to let [the perpetrator] know the impact of what he did; the continued fear of invasion of what was going to happen next." A second-grader who had been bullied on the playground said that the bully apologized and that there were no more school fights. The most important outcomes were that offenders had the opportunity to be held accountable and accept responsibility, as well as to become aware of the support from the community. Participants especially liked the connection with people in the circle, changing attitudes and behaviors, and telling one's story and listening to others. The rich description of restorative justice circles presented by the investigators permitted those less familiar or unfamiliar with restorative justice to see what it was like in action and grasp the potential impact of this process as a viable alternative to criminal prosecution.

Contrasted with exploratory studies, descriptive designs are more specific in that they direct our attention to particular aspects or dimensions of the research target. The heuristic value of descriptive studies must be considered a major contribution as well. Descriptive studies may reveal potential relationships between variables, thus setting the stage for more elaborate investigations later. Subsequently, in view of the St. Paul restorative justice example, it is likely that other investigators will explore the impact of restorative justice as an intervention capable of reducing recidivism among certain types of both juvenile and adult offenders. More sophisticated research designs may be formulated, and hypotheses about restorative justice can be generated and tested in experimental settings.

Experimentation and Experimental Objectives

Designs with the objective of experimentation implicitly include the **control of variables.** Researchers experiment by observing the effects of one or more variables on others, under controlled conditions. The use of the term **control** in criminological investigations has several connotations. First, control means to hold constant one or more factors while others are free to vary. For instance, if the variable, gender, were believed to be a crucial factor in an experimental situation, then gender is controlled by observing the different reactions of males and females to some specific stimulus or an experimental variable. An experimental variable might be a sound, an electrical shock administered to the skin, a drug dosage, a changed social situation, such as replacing a lenient supervisor with a strict supervisor, or any other external condition to which the sample of males and females is exposed. If we control for the variable, age, then this variable is said to be held constant or controlled. In other words, how do all individuals between the ages 16 to 19 behave compared with individuals in the age category 20 to 23 when exposed to a common stimulus?

An illustration of how variables are controlled is shown below and is based on a research idea by Kowalski, Shields, and Wilson (1985). These researchers conducted a descriptive study of female murderers in Alabama during the years 1929–1971. Among other things, they wanted to know about the contributory effects of alcohol and other possibly precipitating events, as well as whether there has been increased use of firearms among female offenders. Among the descriptive information they compiled were questions about race, age, the nature of the victim–offender relationship, and the type of weapon used. Table 3.1 shows an hypothetical **distribution** of race and the method whereby victims were murdered.

**TABLE 3.1   Hypothetical Relation between Race and Method Used
by Female Offenders to Commit Homicide**

	Race of Offender	
Method of Murder	**Black** $N_1 = 125$	**White** $N_2 = 140$
Shooting	36%	64%
Stabbing	55%	10%
Beating	3%	18%
Other	6%	8%
Totals	100%	100%

In Table 3.1, the variable, race, has been controlled and divided into two categories, "Black" and "White." An inspection of this cross-tabulation (i.e., the method of murder has been cross-tabulated with the race of offenders) shows that the majority of black murderesses stabbed their victims, while a majority of white murderesses used a firearm. A substantial number of white offenders murdered their victims by beatings, while beatings accounted for very few murders by black offenders. Had we wished to "experiment" with the variable, race, and determine its relation with the method whereby these murders had been committed, then Table 3.1 would have given us the relevant information we would need.

More elaborate tables can be constructed, and several variables may be controlled simultaneously. Suppose we wished to determine whether one's race has any bearing on the original charges filed and the final charges associated with the murder conviction. Some hypothetical information is shown in Table 3.2.

In Table 3.2, it would appear that 60 percent of the black offenders were charged with first-degree murder initially and that that charge was the subsequent conviction offense. This figure is contrasted with only 20 percent of the white offenders who were originally charged

**TABLE 3.2   Hypothetical Cross-tabulation of Original Charges Filed
and Eventual Conviction Offense, by Race.**

	ORIGINAL CHARGE					
	First-Degree Murder		**Second-Degree Murder**		**Manslaughter**	
	(Race)					
FINAL CHARGE	*Black* *N = 50*	*White* *N = 55*	*Black* *N = 20*	*White* *N = 60*	*Black* *N = 55*	*White* *N = 25*
First-Degree Murder	60%	20%	23%	10%	5%	0%
Second-Degree Murder	30%	50%	70%	30%	35%	15%
Manslaughter	10%	30%	7%	60%	60%	85%
Totals	100%	100%	100%	100%	100%	100%

with first-degree murder and eventually convicted of it. It would also appear that a substantial portion of white offenders had the charges against them reduced to less serious charges compared with black offenders. For instance, about 7 percent of the black offenders had their second-degree murder charges reduced to manslaughter, whereas 60 percent of the white offenders had their second-degree murder charges reduced to manslaughter. Although these findings are hypothetical, they demonstrate certain possibilities that tentative conclusions about variable interrelationships may be drawn from cross-tabulations such as these.

Another meaning of the word *control* is a reference to groups or individuals who are not exposed to experimental variables, whatever they might be. For instance, if we were to administer a particular drug to persons in one group and withhold the drug from persons in another group, the group receiving the drug would be called the **experimental group,** while the group not receiving the drug would be called the **control group.** Ordinarily, the reactions of the experimental group and the control group are observed and compared. Differences between the two groups are attributed largely to the effects of the **experimental stimulus,** in this case, a drug.

In such experimental situations, it is assumed that the two (or more) groups are equated or equivalent in some way when the experiment is commenced. Persons or groups are matched in some respect, or persons are used as their own "controls" in a before–after experiment. That is, persons are measured according to some characteristic in an initial time period before an experiment begins, and then the same persons are measured later according to that same characteristic in a later time period. During these time periods, researchers introduce an experimental variable that is designed to change behaviors in predictable ways. In the general case, it would be predicted that the dependent variable measured in the first time period would change between the first and second time periods. The experimental variable, an independent variable, would be regarded as responsible for any score changes observed between the two time periods, since its introduction was the only new event to influence dependent variable values. Experimental studies may be more or less elaborate or sophisticated in terms of the number of variables used and controlled.

Some experiments are conducted in less formal ways. For example, Robin Campbell and Robert Victor Wolf (2002) were interested in reducing recidivism among youthful probationers. Boston is one of many cities plagued with gang problems. Juvenile probation officers in Boston must acquaint themselves with gangs, their symbols, terminology, and other dimensions of gang culture in order to be more effective in dealing with some of their gang-affiliated probationers. In May 1992, for instance, during the funeral of a gang member, gunfire erupted and someone was stabbed when rival gang members interrupted the ceremony. The incident triggered retaliation by the rival gang, and more gang violence occurred. Boston Anti-Gang Units in the police department met with probation department officials and officers and established Operation Night Light, a cooperative initiative (and an experiment) where probation officers would ride along with police officers during their night patrols. Participating in ride-alongs with police officers was a new experience for probation officers, who often worked during daytime hours only and had minimal contact with their probationers. On one of these occasions, a probation officer discovered one of his youthful probationers out on the streets after his court-imposed curfew. Caught violating curfew and facing the possibility of having his probation program revoked, the probationer said, "That's not fair. Probation don't ride in no police car!" Over time, the probation officers learned much about the real lifestyles of their active probationers. This police officer–probation officer partnership, Operation Night Light, did much to reduce recidivism among youthful probationers over the next few years. This experiment seemed to accomplish what the police and probation officers had intended—to reduce client recidivism and decrease street violence among gang members.

Some Conventional Research Designs

In this section we will examine several conventional research designs used by criminologists and others to answer various kinds of questions. These are (1) surveys, (2) case studies, and (3) the classical experimental design.

Surveys

Survey research is the gathering of information about a large number of people by interviewing a few of them (Backstrom & Hursh, 1963). Hyman (1955) differentiates between exploratory and descriptive surveys, and although no formal definition of **survey design** is apparent in his classic work, the meaning of survey research implicit in his writing is very similar to that described by Backstrom and Hursh (1963). Generally, survey designs are specifications of procedures for gathering information about a large number of people by collecting information from a smaller proportion of them.

Survey researchers apply at least three standards in their research work that center around the quality of data collected. The quality of surveys depends, in part, on (1) the number of people obtained for the study, (2) the typicalness of persons sampled in relation to the populations from which they are drawn, and (3) the reliability of data collected from them.

One example of survey research is the work of Evelyn H. Wei, Rolf Loeber, and Helene Raskin White (2004). This study explored the longitudinal associations of alcohol and marijuana use and violence, how they covaried both concurrently and over time, and whether frequent substance abuse led to violence. These researchers wanted to know whether alcohol and substance abuse among youths was strongly associated with violence. They used survey information derived from the Pennsylvania Youth Study (PYS), a longitudinal investigation of the development of delinquency, substance use, and mental health problems among inner-city adolescent males. Over 5,000 youths between the ages of 11 and 20 were surveyed by the PYS. These investigators found that nearly 90 percent of all youths had engaged in some alcohol use by age 20, although only less than a third of these youths engaged in violent acts. Between 50–60 percent of all youths had used marijuana or some other illegal substance between the ages of 11 and 20, although a low correlation existed between marijuana use and violence.

Another example of survey research is the work of G. David Curry (2000). Curry studied the relation between youth gang involvement and self-reported delinquency in Chicago. He examined existing literature, which tended to show a strong correlation between gang affiliation and the incidence of delinquency among those declaring themselves to be gang members. Self-reports involve disclosures by juveniles (or adults) about the delinquent acts they have actually committed, whether or not the police have discovered their involvement

BOX 3.1   PERSONALITY HIGHLIGHT

CASSIA SPOHN
University of Nebraska at Omaha

Statistics: B.A. (journalism and political science), University of Nebraska–Lincoln; M.A. and Ph.D. (political science), University of Nebraska–Lincoln.

BACKGROUND AND INTERESTS

Although my research interests are diverse, they generally revolve around issues related to criminal case processing decisions, especially judges' sentencing decisions. Much of my research focuses on the effect of the offender's race, ethnicity, gender, and age on sentencing outcomes. Also, I have conducted research on prosecutors' charging decisions in sexual assault cases and the impact of rape law reform on the outcome of sexual assault cases. Early in my career, I dabbled in research related more closely to my background in political science. I published a number of articles examining adolescents' attitudes toward women in politics and the role of advisory boards in the policy process.

I followed a rather circuitous route to criminal justice. Throughout high school and college, I had my heart set on a career in journalism. At the University of Nebraska–Lincoln, I majored in journalism and political science, envisioning myself a political reporter for the *Washington Post,* the *Chicago Tribune,* or *Time* magazine. When I graduated in 1973, Watergate and the role played by "all the President's men" dominated the news. Like many other fledgling journalists, I wanted to follow in the footsteps of Carl Bernstein and Bob Woodward, the investigative reporters for the *Washington Post* who, with the help of the mysterious "Deep Throat," fit the pieces of the puzzle together and wrote a series of stories that won the *Washington Post* a Pulitizer Prize. Instead, I found myself writing about engagements and weddings, symphony debutantes, and "the volunteer of the week" for the *Lincoln Journal.* As the summer of 1973 wore on and my dreams of investigative journalism faded, I began to consider other options.

During my senior year in college, one of my political science professors had urged me to apply to graduate school. I made an appointment to see him and found out that there was still time to apply for the fall semester. My fate was sealed when he offered me a graduate assistantship, which, although it paid very little, would enable me to leave the society desk behind and prepare myself for a career in teaching and research. My goal now was a teaching position in a political science department at a university located in a state other than Nebraska, where I had lived since I was 11 years old. However, this was not to be. When I received my Ph.D. in

BOX 3.1   CONTINUED

1978, I decided, for personal reasons, to accept a position at the University of Nebraska at Omaha (UNO), which was only 60 miles—a manageable commute—from Lincoln. I started out with a joint appointment in political science and the Goodrich Scholarship Program, an academic program for bright but economically disadvantaged students. During this time, my research interests shifted from politics and public policy to prosecutorial and judicial decision making. Vince Webb, who was the chair of UNO's criminal justice department, asked me if I would like to teach a course in criminal justice. Gradually, I began teaching more courses in criminal justice than in political science and in 1986, I joined the criminal justice department full time.

RESEARCH INVESTIGATIONS

If there is one theme or issue that has motivated my research over the past 25 years, it is the issue of equity and justice in the criminal justice system. This issue, which continues to ignite controversy and spark debate, has led me down three distinct but interrelated research avenues. The first, and I think the most important, concerns the effects of race and ethnicity on sentencing decisions. One of the first articles I published after leaving graduate school was titled "The Effect of Race on Sentencing: A Re-Examination of an Unsettled Question." Although I continue to examine this important issue, the questions I'm asking now are somewhat different from those I was asking in 1980. Like other researchers in this field, I've moved beyond simply asking *whether* race and ethnicity make a difference in attempting to identify the *contexts* in which and the *circumstances* under which blacks and Hispanics are sentenced more harshly than whites. As my colleagues and I suggest in our book, *The Color of Justice: Race, Ethnicity, and Crime in America,* the criminal justice system in the United States is characterized by contextual, rather than systematic, racial discrimination.

The second and clearly related research avenue I've taken concerns the effect of victim characteristics on processing decisions in sexual assault cases. The research that I've done in this area responds both to feminists' allegations that only "real rapes" with "genuine victims" are taken seriously and also to assertions that intraracial and interracial sexual assaults are treated very differently. I've conducted research designed to determine whether rape victims who engage in risk-taking behavior (such as hitchhiking or going to a bar alone) or whose moral character is called into question by allegations of sexual promiscuity or drug use are treated differently—that is, more punitively, than other racial dyads. Consistent with my belief that the criminal justice system reflects contextual racial discrimination, I've also engaged in research designed to determine whether the treatment of black men accused of sexually assaulting white women depends on such things as the relationship between the victim and the offender or the behavior of the victim at the time of the assault.

My third avenue of research concerns the impact of rape law reform on the processing of rape cases. My former colleague, Julie Horney, and I spent several years addressing this question. We collected data on every sexual assault case bound over for trial in six cities—At-

BOX 3.1   CONTINUED

lanta, Chicago, Detroit, Houston, Philadelphia, and Washington, D.C.—from 1970 to 1985. The research that we published in this area focused on evaluating the impact of legal changes designed to eliminate statutory and evidentiary impediments to the successful prosecution of rape cases. For example, we wanted to find out whether the passage of rape shield laws restricting the introduction of evidence concerning the victim's prior sexual behavior reduced the number of complaints that were unfounded by the police, the number of charges that were rejected by the prosecutor, or the number of cases that resulted in an acquittal. The findings of our study are detailed in our coauthored book, *Rape Law Reform: A Grassroots Movement and Its Impact.*

My circuitous route to criminal justice notwithstanding, the research that I have conducted over the past 25 years has been firmly grounded in issues of justice and fairness in the criminal justice system. I would like to think that my research has added to what we know about the treatment of those who either find themselves in the arms of the law or are victimized by a violent crime like sexual assault. I hope that over time, my work will influence criminal justice policy and practice.

ADVICE TO STUDENTS

Although the availability of electronic databases has made it easier to "do research," good research is guided by theory, and not by the availability of data. It is more satisfying, although certainly more costly and time-consuming, to design a research project to test a theory and then to collect the data needed for that project yourself than to download a data set from a website and hope that it will suffice for the project at hand. Good research also requires more than a mastery of statistics and **quantitative analysis;** it requires the ability to effectively communicate your findings and conclusions to students, colleagues, and policymakers. Knowing the difference between "affect" and "effect" is just as important as understanding the assumptions of regression analysis.

in such activities. Curry studied 662 incident reports for 1992 involving 429 youths from two different Chicago schools. Of these, 192 youths were gang-affiliated. Subsequently, Curry found that gang-affiliated students were over twice as likely to be involved in delinquency compared with non-gang-affiliated students. In this instance, Curry found support for the idea that delinquency and gang affiliation are correlated. It is interesting to note that for both the Curry study and the study by Wei and colleagues (2004), survey data collected by others were studied by these researchers. Thus, it is not necessary when conducting survey research to actively collect new information from new samples of persons each time an investigation is conducted. These researchers were able to take advantage of existing data sets collected in surveys by others for the information used in their own research.

BOX 3.2   PERSONALITY HIGHLIGHT

JAMES D. ORCUTT
Florida State University

Statistics: B.A. (sociology and psychology), M.A. (sociology), University of Iowa; Ph.D. (sociology), University of Minnesota.

BACKGROUND AND INTERESTS

Most of my research deals with drug and alcohol problems. This area is rich with opportunities to examine general theories of deviance and social control, and I have explored a number of those theoretical leads over the years. Like a lot of sociologists who were in graduate school during the 1960s and 1970s, much of my initial research was inspired by work in the interactionist tradition, especially Howard Becker's influential studies of marijuana use and reactions to deviance. However, unlike many of my interactionist colleagues, I preferred to use survey methods and quantitative analysis rather than qualitative methods in my early research. For instance, I conducted surveys of students, community members, and law-enforcement officers to examine how ideological and situational factors influence social definitions of deviant drinking and drug use. I also focused on the implications of differential association and social learning theories for understanding how social relationships influence marijuana and alcohol use, again using survey data. More recently, my interests have shifted toward macro-level problems, such as the epidemiology of deviant drinking and archival research on the social construction of "drug crises" by politicians and the news media.

My long-standing interest in drug- and alcohol-related deviance probably has something to do with my experiences and observations as a member of a rock band during high school and college. On a number of occasions, I was struck by the inane and destructive things that intelligent, sociable people would do while "under the influence" of alcohol at parties or dances. I also noticed that, under certain circumstances, musicians and other people who were "high" on marijuana acted pretty much the same as those who were drunk on alcohol. Even then, I wondered whether these displays of intoxication were shaped more by the peculiar social scene at parties than by the drugs themselves. My curiosity about the social foundations of marijuana and alcohol effects turned into an idea for a dissertation several years later, when I read Becker's interactionist rendition of the process of "becoming a marijuana user" and Craig MacAndrew and Robert Edgerton's anthropological account of cultural influences on "drunken comportment." My dissertation on the "social determinants of recreational drug effects," which began

BOX 3.2   CONTINUED

with some casual observations at high school dances, became the basis for approximately eight articles and a career of research on deviant and nondeviant patterns of drug and alcohol use.

While I was pursuing my interests in the social definition of drug use and effects, some talented teachers in my undergraduate and graduate programs got me hooked on deviance theory. At the University of Iowa, I took courses in criminology with John Stratton as well as courses in the sociology of mental health with Steven Spitzer—both of whom helped me see the common theoretical ground between these two branches of deviance inquiry. Spitzer eventually supervised my dissertation at Minnesota, where I was also fortunate to work with Harold Finestone, an ethnographer whose research on heroin users deepened my appreciation for qualitative methods. As a participant in the NIMH Training Program in Deviance at Minnesota, I got to meet some of the leading theorists and researchers in the field who were brought in as guest lecturers and mentors. These teachers and mentors showed me how the study of deviance could contribute to our understanding of social reality and social order. Through their example, they also helped me become a better teacher.

ADVICE TO STUDENTS

Never underestimate the importance of informed and constructive criticism as a scholarly activity. I tell my own students that critical analysis ranks with empirical research and theory as an essential tool of social scientific inquiry. My first publication was a critical review of research on juvenile delinquency and the self-concept. Since that time, I have written a number of critiques of theoretical and empirical work, and I took on the role of constructive critic as editor of a professional journal, *Social Problems.* In all of this critical work, my aim was to advance knowledge by pointing out limitations, problems, unresolved issues, and possible solutions in the research and writing of professional colleagues. In return, my own work has benefited from the thoughtful and detailed criticism of others. So, if you've heard that "it's not nice to be a critic," forget it. You can provide a most valuable service for your colleagues if you read and reflect on their work carefully, try to understand it as they see it, and, then, offer constructive comments, suggestions, and critical guidance for improving their research and writing.

Another example of a survey design is the **National Youth Survey (NYS),** an ongoing longitudinal (over time) study of delinquent behavior and alcohol and drug use among the American youth population. The NYS uses a fairly typical sample of youth ranging in age from 11 to 17. Self-report questionnaires are administered, where youths disclose whether they have committed any status or criminal offenses and whether they have been apprehended for any of these offenses. The NYS utilizes this sample of youth over successive time periods as a **panel.** A panel is some designated sample that is studied repeatedly over time, and comparisons are made between "panels" or the responses given by these youths within each time frame. Krisberg and colleagues (1987) used the NYS to investigate the differential rates of incarceration of minority youth. Key research findings from this **panel study** were that minority youth were being incarcerated at a rate three to four times that of white youths, and that over time, minority youth incarcerations are increasing proportionately. Self-reports of delinquent conduct among both whites and minorities disclosed similar patterns, and thus, one's minority status is seen as a primary predictor of subsequent incarceration or involvement with police compared with being white.

　　All of these studies involve somewhat superficial examinations of data. However, this is not an unfavorable observation. By their very nature, survey designs are superficial. In each case, limited numbers of social and personal characteristics are solicited from respondents. These characteristics are tabulated and analyzed statistically. They yield broad conclusions about large aggregates of persons. No attempt is made to conduct in-depth investigations of family systems, personality systems, or any other intimate details of participants' lives. Details such as these are disclosed by means of an alternative design known as the case study. Case studies are examined in the next section.

Advantages and Disadvantages of Surveys.　　The major advantages of survey designs are the following:

1. Surveys can provide information about a large number of persons at relatively low cost.
2. **Generalizability** to larger populations of elements is enhanced because of the larger numbers of persons who are included in survey designs.
3. Surveys are flexible enough to permit the use of a variety of data collection techniques.
4. Surveys sensitize researchers to potential problems that were originally unanticipated or unknown.
5. Surveys are useful tools that enable investigators to verify theories.

Some of the disadvantages of survey designs are:

1. Surveys are superficial reflections of population sentiments.
2. Surveys, particularly political surveys, are unstable reflections of population characteristics.
3. Researchers have little or no control over individual responses in surveys.
4. Statements about populations from which samples are drawn are tentative.

Case Studies

Although some investigators might claim that a **case study** is not a design in a technical sense, a **case study design** is one of the most popular types of research designs used by criminologists and other social scientists today. Case studies are relatively thorough examinations of specific social settings or particular aspects of social settings, including detailed psychological and behavioral descriptions of persons in those settings. Words such as "intense" and "in-depth" characterize the type of information yielded by case studies, whereas survey designs yield data of a superficial nature, as we have seen. An example of a case study is the work of Michael T. Charles (1989).

Charles investigated the social and psychological impact and effects of electronic monitoring on six juvenile delinquents. He conducted in-depth interviews with probation officers, parents/guardians of the juveniles, the juveniles themselves, and probation department administrators. His close contact with juveniles themselves disclosed details about wearing electronic wristlets associated with electronic monitoring programs that he otherwise wouldn't have known had he not conducted the case study. For example, one activity, "hanging out," frequently led to delinquent acts, since youths who "hung out" were bored, with little or nothing to do. Charles found that youths could avoid trouble in their schools by using their wristlets as a "crutch" to withstand peer pressure and refuse invitations to "mess around," "hang out," and commit delinquent acts (1989, p. 168). The wristlet worn by these participating youths also reminded others of their probationary status. Thus, Charles was able to penetrate the social worlds and minds of these boys to a limited degree and to understand their motives and rationales for different behaviors.

One interesting characteristic of case studies is that much rich information about social settings is disclosed. Another example of such research is an ambitious case study undertaken by Charles E. Frazier and Donna M. Bishop (1990). In 1987, these researchers sent observers and interviewers to Florida's 67 county jails to investigate booking and inmate processing. They were particularly interested in the extent to which Florida jails were in compliance with a general mandate to remove juvenile offenders from adult jails and lock-ups. Jail personnel were interviewed, and the ways and places in which juveniles were processed and detained were observed. Approximately 13 percent of all juvenile jail admissions were considered out of compliance with the Juvenile Justice and Delinquency Prevention mandate.

Through conversations with jail officials and other personnel, Frazier and Bishop (1990) found that both law enforcement officers and jail officials held basic misconceptions about detaining status offenders. Although holding status offenders in adult jails is a violation of Florida law, 237 cases in 1985 and 219 cases in 1986 were reported where status offenders were held for various periods in these county jails. Some officials believed that status offenders could be held in adult jails, as long as sight and sound separation was provided, or as long as they were placed in general holding areas and not in individual cells. Interviews and casual conversations also disclosed that many jail officials were resistant to unwanted reform and had complacent attitudes about jailing juvenile offenders of any kind.

This quality of information could not have been obtained through more superficial survey instruments. It took an intensive investigation and description of these settings, together with detailed interviews with jail officials and examinations of jail records, in order to generate such information. After all, not many jail officials are going to admit to violating any Florida statute on an anonymous questionnaire mailed or distributed to them. Furthermore, they are probably not going to say that they have complacent attitudes about whether juveniles are jailed in their facilities, or that they are stubborn or resistant to juvenile jailing reforms. Case studies, therefore, provide us with an in-depth grasp of social environments. However, because they consume so much time and energy of researchers, they are not conducted on the same broad magnitudes as surveys. This is one reason why both types of designs have offsetting weaknesses and strengths.

BOX 3.3   PERSONALITY HIGHLIGHT

ROBERT J. BURSIK, JR.
University of Missouri–St. Louis

Statistics: B.A. (sociology), Rutgers University; M.A. (sociology), University of Chicago; Ph.D. (sociology), University of Chicago.

BACKGROUND AND INTERESTS

I have been a Professor of Criminology and Criminal Justice at the University of Missouri–St. Louis (UMSL) since 1996. Prior to my current affiliation, I was a Research Scientist at the Institute for Juvenile Research in Chicago (1978–1983) and then came through the professorial ranks in the Department of Sociology at the University of Oklahoma (1983–1996). I am a Fellow of the American Society of Criminology (ASC), a former Vice President of the ASC, and a former editor of *Criminology* (1998–2003).

Although I have conducted research in a variety of criminological areas, my favorite endeavors by far have focused on the structure and dynamics of urban neighborhoods and the degree to which they affect local community rates of crime and delinquency. Most recently I have begun to explore the applicability of urban models to rural patterns of crime.

One of the key events in my education was being assigned to Donald Bogue as a graduate research assistant. My senior thesis at Rutgers University entailed several months of living and socializing with Skid Row alcoholics in New York City's Bowery district, and Don had conducted some of the most influential Skid Row research in the United States. I applied to the University of Chicago specifically to study with him. One hallmark of his work was an explicit emphasis on the neighborhood, and it was not long before I shared his "Chicago School" perspective. My fascination with this framework was fostered further in classes I took from Morris Janowitz and Gerald Suttles.

When it came time for me to put together a dissertation proposal, Don told me that he thought it would seriously damage my chances on the job market if I did not broaden the scope of the project beyond the narrow Skid Row–related topic that I had in mind. He recommended instead that I take advantage of a different kind of a deviance research opportunity that was available at the Cook County Juvenile Court, and use it as the basis for my dissertation. I did, and my primary academic interest eventually shifted from the sociology of deviance in general to the sociology of crime in particular as I used court and police records to study individual trajectories of delinquency during adolescence.

BOX 3.3   CONTINUED

My dual interest in neighborhoods and crime was not reflected in my research until I took a position at the Institute for Juvenile Research (IJR), where Clifford Shaw and Henry McKay had conducted the community studies that culminated in their classic *Juvenile Delinquency and Urban Areas.* The specific turning point in this regard was a case of pure luck. My colleague, Jim Webb, and I were looking for something in the basement storage area when we literally bumped into an old file cabinet filled with thousands of 3 × 5 index cards. To our astonishment, we realized that we had found the raw Shaw and McKay delinquency data. We spent many months reconstructing the series, updated them through 1970 (and eventually 1980), integrated the Chicago **census** materials for the corresponding time periods, and published our first neighborhood paper in 1982.

Unfortunately and shortly thereafter, the State of Illinois experienced one of its periodic economic crises and, as a state agency, the future of the IJR was in jeopardy. As a result, when the University of Oklahoma advertised for a criminologist, I applied for and was offered the job, and I accepted the appointment.

At Oklahoma, I continued pursuing the neighborhoods and crime question with the Chicago data. It was an exciting period because, after a long hiatus, the neighborhood question was capturing the imaginations of such rising stars as Steve Messner, Rob Sampson, and Ralph Taylor. My Oklahoma experience peaked with the publication of *Neighborhoods and Crime: The Dimensions of Effective Community Control* (with Harold Grasmick, 1993). Yet, once again the vagaries of state funding began to take their toll as our department experienced a series of substantial budgetary cuts that devastated faculty and staff morale. Just as the situation seemed its bleakest, the Criminology and Criminal Justice Department at the University of Missouri–St. Louis contacted me to see if I might be interested in a position. I had been aware of this department for many years and had watched in admiration as it steadily built itself from almost nothing into one of the top criminology departments in the country. I jumped at the opportunity and have never regretted the decision.

ADVICE TO STUDENTS

One of the trends I witnessed during my tenure as editor of *Criminology* was a growing tendency of authors to rely strictly on the work of other criminologists when crafting their arguments, thereby failing to capitalize on the rich, relevant insights generated by studies that do not focus on crime *per se*. For example, the concepts of systemic network structures, social capital, and collective efficacy originated in sociology, political science, and social psychology, yet they have had a major effect on contemporary neighborhood studies. Likewise, the consequential notion of "doing gender" was adapted from the interpersonal communication work of two sociologists (Candace West and Don Zimmerman) who, to the best of my knowledge, have never studied crime. Similar examples can be identified in virtually every topical area. Nevertheless, while the very best research continues to incorporate the implications of work conducted outside of criminology, there definitely has been a growth in theoretical insularity. One of the greatest challenges facing subsequent generations of criminologists will be to recapture the fertile eclecticism upon which our discipline was built.

Advantages and Disadvantages of Case Studies.   Some of the advantages of case studies are:

1. Case studies are flexible in that they enable researchers to use multiple data-gathering techniques, such as interviewing, observation, questionnaires, and examinations of records and statistical data.

2. Case studies may be conducted in almost any type of social environment.

3. Case studies are specific instances of tests of theories. If researchers have adequately prepared a theoretical framework within which to cast the research activity, then case studies provide them with an opportunity to test theories. Thus, case studies may be viewed as a test of a more general theory to the same degree that survey designs are able to achieve this objective. Surveys make possible certain generalizations to the extent that the elements surveyed are representative of the population from which they are drawn.

4. The flexibility of case studies may be extended to virtually any dimension of the topic(s) studied.

5. Case studies may be inexpensive, depending on the extent of inquiry involved and the type of data collection techniques used. A researcher's costs may be kept to a minimum if data can be collected firsthand. It is not unusual to find researchers conducting case studies of social settings of which they are a part.

Some disadvantages of case studies are:

1. Case studies have limited generalizability. Although they are geared to provide detailed information about social units, they are often criticized for being quite limited in scope and insufficient for meaningful generalizations to be made to larger social aggregates. Representativeness, however, is a key concern in the assessment of the quality of survey information as well.

2. Findings from case studies may or may not support theories. Researchers do not regard case study findings as conclusive proof of anything. Neither do survey researchers. Only through the accumulation of information from many case studies and many surveys investigating similar phenomena can we begin to generate statements about the social world that have little or no exception.

Comparison of Surveys and Case Studies

It is clear that both types of research designs discussed above may be used for hypothesis testing. In fact, in some instances, both types of study designs may be used to test the same hypotheses. Case studies appear to have greater utility for hypothesis tests about certain structural and procedural characteristics (e.g., mobility patterns, status relations, interpersonal characteristics) of specific social units (e.g., organizations, small groups, cliques, communities). In addition to their descriptive value, surveys are of great utility for testing

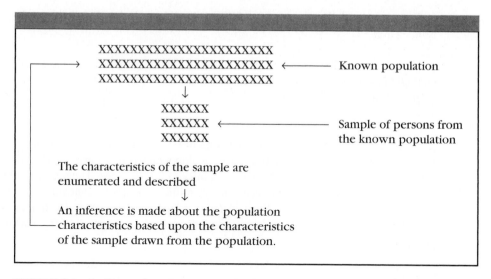

FIGURE 3.1   An illustration of the generalizability of samples studied with survey designs.

hypotheses about large social aggregates (e.g., female criminals between the ages of 20 and 25, background differences of convicted felons, sentencing disparities among judges that pertain to racial or ethnic factors, or describing the social and demographic characteristics of juvenile delinquents).

Figures 3.1 and 3.2 illustrate more clearly how each type of research design treats the social aggregates studied and their generalizability to larger populations. Figure 3.1 shows that a survey derives elements from the total population, which is generally known. Characteristics of a sample of elements are generalized tentatively to the entire population of elements. Figure 3.2 depicts case studies in relation to some unknown population. The typicality or representativeness of the case under investigation is unknown and is all but impossible to assess. However, because social situations are usually involved, certain theoretical propositions and hypotheses can be put to the test, again on a tentative basis.

Classic Experimental Design

Experimental research designs are those that control the conditions under which persons are observed and analyzed. The nature and types of experimental designs range from simple to complex and are quite varied. Any conventional or **classic experimental design** contains three important elements: (1) experimental and control groups, (2) equivalent groups, and (3) pretests and posttests.

Experimental and Control Groups

In any discussion of experimental designs, two types of groups must be distinguished: experimental groups and control groups. Experimental groups consist of persons who are exposed to

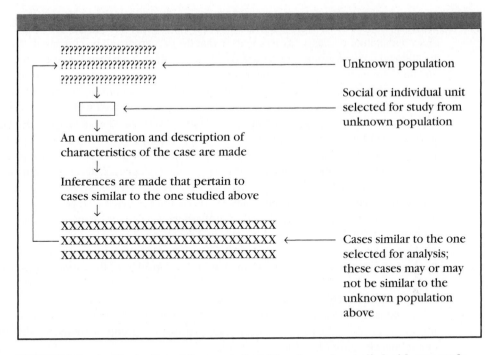

FIGURE 3.2   An illustration of the generalizability of samples studied with case study designs.

experimental variables or treatment variables. Treatment variables or **experimental variables** might be a new type of group or individual counseling method; a different method of supervision; increased pay or job benefits; larger or smaller client caseloads for probation or parole officers; longer or shorter working hours for correctional officers; or the creation of inmate grievance councils in prisons. We might want to know if a new type of group or individual therapy is effective in treating sex offenders. Or we might want to know if changing the method of supervision or pay or job benefits has any effect on the morale of police officers in a police department. Or we might want to know if changes in working hours change the job satisfaction levels of corrections officers. Or we might want to know if decreasing client caseloads for probation officers makes the officers more effective in their supervision of offenders. Or we might want to know if creating inmate grievance councils in prisons decreases inmate violence. All of these variables we intend to manipulate or change are possible experimental variables.

Control groups consist of those persons not exposed to experimental or treatment variables. A comparison of the attitudes and behaviors of the experimental and control group should tell us whether the experimental or treatment variable had any effect on those attitudes or behaviors. Effects of treatment or experimental variables are detected whenever there is a change in behaviors or attitudes of the experimental group but the attitudes or behaviors of the control group remain unchanged.

Equivalent Groups and Establishing Equivalence

A second feature of classic experiments is that the two groups to be compared, the experimental and control group, are assumed to be equivalent. This means that the two groups should share many of the same characteristics. If we compared two groups, one consisting entirely of females and one consisting entirely of males, we would not consider these groups equivalent. Likewise, a group of 80-year-olds would not equate well with a group of 16-year-olds. Generally, any two-group comparison should be conducted where it can reasonably be assumed that for all practical purposes, the two groups are very similar in several of their primary characteristics. Therefore, researchers attempt to equate control and experimental groups on as many salient characteristics as possible (e.g., gender, age, rural or urban background, socioeconomic status, prior record, years of experience, years of education, and certain personality factors). Then, when theorized and predicted changes occur within the experimental group but not within the control group, investigators may infer a cause–effect relation between the experimental variable and the changed behavior, whatever it might be. In short, behavioral changes are more likely attributable to the experimental variable than to obvious differences in the sociodemographic composition of the experimental and control groups.

In order to achieve equivalence between two or more groups designated for experimentation, social scientists select one of the following four methods: (1) individual matching; (2) persons as their own experimental controls; (3) group or frequency distribution control matching; or (4) random assignment.

Individual Matching.   **Individual matching,** or simply **matching,** is the most difficult method of equating two or more groups. If researchers wanted to match 25 persons in an experimental group with 25 other persons according to several important characteristics, it is often necessary that a large population base must exist in order to find sufficient numbers of persons who will match up with those in the experimental group. Usually, experimenters will want to match persons according to their gender, age, years of education, socioeconomic status, occupation, race or ethnicity, and perhaps some additional personality factors. The addition of each new matching characteristic greatly limits the available pool of persons from which matching individuals may be drawn. And assuming "matches" can be made, there are no guarantees that those who are found to match others will participate in one's research as a part of the control group. Even if persons participate later who have been matched with others on certain characteristics, there is a definite likelihood that the two groups will remain unmatched on numerous other important characteristics. Thus, if differences are later observed between the two groups on some dependent variable, then it will be unknown whether the experimental variable caused changes in variable values or if unknown differences between the two groups were responsible for these discrepancies. Figure 3.3 illustrates individual matching.

Using Persons as Their Own Experimental Controls.   One way of overcoming the matching problem and equating persons more directly is **persons used as their own controls** in an experimental situation. Therefore, a target sample of persons is identified, measures on some dependent variable are taken, the group is exposed to some experimental variable, and then measures are again taken on the dependent variable. Score changes ob-

EXPERIMENTAL GROUP		CONTROL GROUP
Individual:	MATCHED WITH:	Individual:
1⟨ ---		⟩7
2⟨ ---		⟩8
3⟨ ---		⟩9
4⟨ ---		⟩10
5⟨ ---		⟩11
6⟨ ---		⟩12

FIGURE 3.3   A hypothetical illustration of individual matching.

served under this circumstance cannot be attributed to differences between individuals, since the same persons who were tested in the first time period were also tested in the second time period. An example of persons used as their own controls is illustrated in Figure 3.4.

In Figure 3.4, the same persons are measured on some dependent variable in two or more time periods. Perhaps a new program is being implemented in a parole agency to bolster morale and work attitudes, or to improve interpersonal relations. The new program is the experimental variable. Perhaps the researcher has a Quality of Life **scale** that measures contentment with the working environment and one's work associates. Scale scores in time 2 are compared with these same scale scores in time 1, and differences observed are attributed more to the new program rather than to "individual differences" between the two groups in the two time periods, since it is the same group in both time periods.

Group or Frequency Distribution Control Matching.   **Group distribution matching** or **frequency distribution control matching** means to equate two groups on the basis of their aggregate similarities. Suppose we identified two groups of 250 prison inmates, each distributed as follows on the following characteristics, and also illustrated with a similar example in Figure 3.5.

TIME 1	EXPERIMENTAL VARIABLE INTRODUCED	TIME 2
Individual:	E	Individual:
1⟨ -----------------------------		----------------------- ⟩1
2⟨ -----------------------------		----------------------- ⟩2
3⟨ -----------------------------		----------------------- ⟩3
4⟨ -----------------------------		----------------------- ⟩4

FIGURE 3.4   A hypothetical illustration of persons used as their own controls in a before–after experiment.

EXPERIMENTAL GROUP $N = 100$	CHARACTERISTICS USED FOR MATCHING PURPOSES	CONTROL GROUP $N = 100$
34.1 ⟨ --------------- 1.	Average age -------------------⟩	34.2
14.9 ⟨ --------------- 2.	Average years of education --------⟩	15.3
35/65 ⟨ --------------- 3.	Male-female composition ---------⟩	33/67
83.9% ⟨ --------------- 4.	Percentage favorable -------------⟩ toward issue X	81.8%
etc. ⟨ ---------------------- etc. ----------------------⟩		etc.

FIGURE 3.5   A hypothetical example of group matching or frequency distribution control matching.

Characteristic	Group 1	Group 2
Average age	34.2	33.9
Gender	40% female	42% female
Prior record	3.2 felonies	3.3 felonies
Prior delinquency	39% prior delinquency	40% prior delinquency
Race	40% black, 60% white	38% black, 62% white
Urban background	72%	75%
Average level of custody	94% medium-security	95% medium-security

On the basis of group or aggregate characteristics, these two groups are very similar. On the average, they are approximately 34 years old; 40 percent female; have 3+ felonies as prior records; are 40 percent black; 72 percent are from urban backgrounds; and 94 percent are in medium-security custody. These two groups may also have other characteristics in common. They may have similar attitudes about prison life; similar write-ups or incidents of misconduct; similar good-time credit earned; and similar sentence lengths to serve. We justify their equivalence on the basis of how many characteristics they share. The more characteristics the two groups share, the more they are considered equivalent for experimental purposes.

Random Assignment.   The fourth method for equating groups is to select them from an overall sample by means of **random assignment.** Thus, we might draw a sample from some population, such as a sample of students from a large introductory criminal justice course. Suppose we drew a sample of 20 students from a large class. Using random assignment, we would place 10 students in the experimental group and 10 students in the control group. Figure 3.6 shows how random assignment would divide these persons. In Figure 3.6, 20 students have been numbered from 1 to 20. Using a random procedure, each of the 20 students is placed in either the experimental group or the control group.

Random —————————⟶
Assignment   ⟶   ORIGINAL GROUP   Random
EXPERIMENTAL GROUP ⟵   N = 20   Assignment
                                          ⟶ CONTROL GROUP

Individual #:	Individual #:
20	1
2	5
19	16
3	18
11	13
12	15
7	9
10	8
6	4
17	14

FIGURE 3.6   **A hypothetical illustration of random assignment.**

An example from the research literature is provided in a study of drunk drivers conducted by Dean G. Rojek, James E. Coverdill, and Stuart W. Fors (2003). These researchers wanted to know the effect of deterring drunk drivers that a victim impact panel (VIP) would have for a sample of persons convicted of drunk driving (driving under the influence, or DUI) in a Georgia county. A VIP program was established in Clarke County, Georgia, in 1994. At that time, those convicted of DUI were obligated by the court to attend VIPs, which consisted of four or five victims of drunk driving, each of whom offered a short description of how a drunk driver impacted their lives as well as the lives of family members. Exposure to the VIP was regarded as the experimental variable, and it was anticipated that attending these VIPs would cause those convicted of DUI to abide by the law in future years and not drive drunk. Since judges began requiring all of those convicted of DUI to attend these VIPs in 1994, it was not possible to obtain a control group for comparison purposes that same year. Therefore, the researchers decided to select a sample of convicted DUI offenders from 1993, one year prior to the mandatory VIP attendance. Offenders in both the control and experimental groups were residents of Clarke County, Georgia. The duration of the experiment was 5 years. Those convicted of DUI during the first 6 months of 1993, 430 DUI offenders, were compared with 404 Clarke County residents convicted during the first 6 months of 1994. Both groups differed on several salient variables, such as gender, age, race, and prior DUI convictions. Nevertheless, the differences on these different dimensions were not substantial. Both groups were tracked for the next 5 years to determine whether they engaged in further DUI offending. Interestingly, during the 5-year follow-up period, 33.5 percent of the control group who did not participate in the VIPs were rearrested for DUI compared with only 15.8 percent of the VIP group. Cautiously interpreted, these findings suggest that the VIP was effective in reducing DUI recidivism among the VIP participants. As these investigators noted, further research in this important area would be needed in order to establish greater certainty about the true impact of VIPs on those convicted of DUI.

Pretests and Posttests

The third integral feature of **experimental designs** is the inclusion of pretests and posttests. What are the characteristics of the experimental and control groups before any experimentation has been conducted? Have certain characteristics of the experimental and control groups changed after the experiment has occurred?

Assuming that we have two **equivalent groups** for purposes of carrying out an experiment, we need to know whether the two groups being compared are similar in their attitudes and behaviors before the experiment occurs. Thus, we observe and measure certain important characteristics of both the experimental and control groups before the experimental variable is introduced. This activity is known as a **pretest.** Thus, we pretest the experimental and control groups and record their present behaviors and attitudes. Ideally, both the experimental and control groups will be sufficiently similar according to the characteristics we have chosen to measure. If these two groups differ substantially on the characteristics we have chosen, our subsequent results following experimentation will be contaminated and unreliable.

Following the administration of an experimental or treatment variable, we will perform a **posttest.** This means that we will measure our experimental and control groups according to their behaviors and attitudes following the experiment. Ideally, we expect that a comparison of pretest and posttest results for the control group will indicate that the control group has not changed, at least in terms of the characteristics we have measured. Since the control group was not exposed to the experimental variable, it was not expected to change anyway. Our expectation is that when the experimental group pretest and posttest results are subsequently compared, we expect that the experimental group has changed in some important way. After all, the experimental variable was intended to cause a behavioral or attitudinal change in the experimental group.

Suppose we have two groups of 25 parole officers in two different parole agencies, Agency A and Agency B. We determine that the two groups are generally equivalent for experimental purposes. The parole officers in both agencies have average caseloads of 75 parolees each. Designating Agency A parole officers as the experimental group and Agency B parole officers as the control group, we obtain measures of their morale and job interest in a pretest. Later, we reduce the caseloads of parole officers in Agency A to 25 client/parolees each, while we leave alone the caseloads of those parole officers in Agency B. We think that reducing one's client/parolee workload will improve morale and raise job interest because of the more personalized attention officers can direct to fewer numbers of clients. After an interval of 3 months, we subject both groups of parole officers to a posttest, again assessing their work morale and job interest. We find that morale and job interest has increased appreciably for the parole officers in Agency A, while the morale and job interest levels of parole officers in Agency B remained the same over time. This finding supports our idea that lowering caseloads of parole officers will heighten their morale and job interest. We might also conjecture that the client/parolees themselves will benefit as well from the improved morale and job interest of their parole officer/supervisors.

In the above example, we carried out a classic experiment. We had an experimental group and a control group. We had equivalent groups. And we had a pretest and a posttest. When an experimental variable was introduced, we determined that it had a predictable effect on the behaviors or attitudes of the parole officers in the experimental group. Our evidence showed this. Furthermore, our evidence showed that no change occurred in the parole officer sample where the experimental variable did not occur. With these concepts in mind, we can now look at a typical experimental scenario where an experimental and a control group are used. Figure 3.7 shows a hypothetical experimental situation involving one experimental group and one control group.

The classic experimental design is easily illustrated by an example provided by Goode and Hatt (1952, pp. 76–78): ". . . in its simple statement, it can be formulated in this fashion: If there are two or more cases, and in one of them observation Z can be made, while in the other it cannot; and if factor C occurs when observation Z is made, and does not occur when observation Z is not made; then it can be asserted that there is a causal relationship between C and Z." Figure 3.8 illustrates the classic experimental design defined by Goode and Hatt.

Another illustration is helpful here. Suppose we were to observe two random samples of parolees over a 2-year time period. Both samples of parolees have similar prior records, and all parolees were earlier convicted of robbery. Further suppose that previous information about these parolees indicates that one sample has a history of drug/alcohol abuse, while the other sample of parolees does not show any drug or alcohol use or dependencies. From the literature we know that if recidivism is going to occur, it usually occurs within a 2-year time interval from the time inmates are paroled from prison. If we observe these two samples of parolees over the next 2 years, we might find that no parolees within the group with no drug or alcohol abuse history have recidivated, while all parolees in the group with a history of drug/alcohol abuse have recidivated and have been returned to prison. This hypothetical example would suggest that a history of drug or alcohol dependency or abuse would be a strong predictor of subsequent recidivism among parolees. Unfortunately, our findings about parolees and other groups throughout the criminal justice system are not that clear-cut. We usually find perhaps higher rates of recidivism within one group compared with

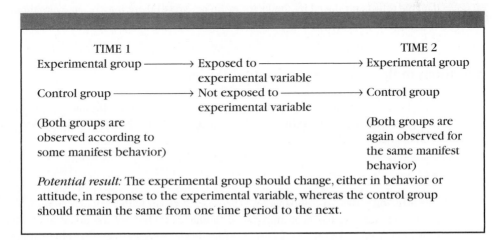

FIGURE 3.7   A hypothetical illustration of an experiment with an experimental group and a control group.

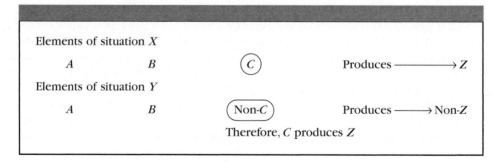

FIGURE 3.8   The classic experimental design.

another, or we might find higher levels of work satisfaction among one group of parole officers compared with another. Seldom, if ever, do we find "all" or "none" differences that might be suggested under a pure or perfect classic experimental design format.

The idea of "all" or "none" is important, however. Thus, if the presence of certain factors triggers certain events or behaviors, even a greater frequency of those events, and the absence of those same factors does not elicit the same events or behaviors, or if the same events or behaviors are not elicited as frequently, we might view these factors and events/behaviors as causally related.

Criticisms of the Classic Experimental Design.   Goode and Hatt (1952, pp. 78–81) caution, however, that when it comes to "proof" of the effectiveness or impact of an experiment, the classic experimental design has certain weaknesses. Some of these weaknesses are that (1) researchers are unable to control all relevant variables in the research project; (2) there is a lack of clarity in the causal relation between the two variables; (3) there are unpredictable effects produced by the factor of time; and (4) there may be an oversimplification of cause–effect relations between the different variables.

Variations in the Classic Experimental Design

The classic experimental design has been refashioned several different ways in the criminological literature. Variations of this design include the after-only design and the before–after design.

The After-Only Design

The **after-only design** compares an experimental group with a control group after an experimental variable has been introduced to one group but not the other. Sometimes, the terms experimental group and control group are loosely defined. In some studies, these terms may refer to similar neighborhoods or similar cities. For instance, police departments throughout the United States have experimented with various police patrol methods either to prevent crime or decrease it. An example is the Tampa, Florida Police Department.

Believing that a "back-to-the-people" program might be helpful in reducing crime in Tampa, the Tampa Police Department inaugurated sector patrolling, where police officers would be assigned particular city sectors. Offices were established in each sector and manned 18 hours a day. Police officers were assigned to patrol specific neighborhoods and became familiar with residents and merchants. Supposedly, reported crime in those areas of the city receiving sector patrolling, compared with other city areas, decreased "significantly" during the first 6 months of the program and greater police–citizen cooperation occurred (Smith & Taylor, 1985). In this case, the "experimental group" was comprised of those city sectors receiving sector patrolling, while the "control group" consisted of those city areas not receiving sector patrolling.

On a more conventional and smaller scale, suppose a state were to change the type of administrative leadership in several of its probation offices in various cities. State officials might believe that different, more authoritative leadership might improve officer accountability and responsibility. Assuming we had measures of officer accountability and responsibility, those offices undergoing this administrative change (the experimental group, in this case) could be contrasted with those offices with no administrative changes (the control group, in this case). Subsequently, the two sets of offices would be compared in an after-only contrast, and any differences in officer accountability and responsibility would be noted. Theoretically, those offices that underwent administrative changes would subsequently have greater officer accountability, as indicated by the appropriate instruments.

Criticisms of the After-Only Design.   Unfortunately, the after-only design fails to identify the respective conditions of the experimental and control groups before changes have occurred. Thus, it is difficult to make conclusive statements about any observed differences between the experimental and control groups that might be more attributable to general differences within the groups themselves rather than to the experimental variable. One weakness of the after-only design is that unless some method has been used to establish the equivalency of the experimental and control groups, it is impossible to assess the impact of the experimental variable with certainty.

The Before–After Design

An improvement over the after-only design, the before–after design consists of obtaining measures on some dependent variable for two groups that are presumed equivalent for experimental purposes, introducing an experimental variable to one group and withholding it from the other, and comparing the two groups after the experiment has been completed. An example of the before–after experiment, again using police patrol styles as the theme, is the work of Kelling et al. (1974).

Kelling et al. (1974) conducted what became known as the classic Kansas City Preventive Patrol Experiments between June 1972 and September 1973. Funded by a grant from the Police Foundation, the Kansas City Police Department varied the numbers of routine preventive patrols within 15 of Kansas City's beats. The beats were divided into three groups of five each. In the "control" beat grouping, patrols were continued according to previously "normal" patterns. In the two "experimental" beat groupings, routine patrols were both increased and eliminated. In one experimental beat grouping, known as the "proactive" beats, the "normal" one-car patrols were increased to three-car patrols. In the other experimental beat grouping, the "reactive" beats, all one-car patrols were removed, and police officers serviced those areas strictly on the basis of calls from residents who reported crimes as they occurred.

It was expected, and predicted, that crime would increase in the reactive beats, decrease in the proactive beats, and remain about the same in the "control" beats. The experiment failed to produce these results. Crime remained about the same or occurred with about the same frequency in all beats, regardless of the patrol style used. These results generated much controversy, since police agency funding is based, in part, on the argument that more police presence tends to deter crime. Clearly, this was not the case, at least in those experimental and control beats studied. In fact, since crime did not increase in those areas where police patrols were withdrawn, some citizens questioned the value of police patrols in any city sector. In all fairness to the Kansas City Police Department, some experts surmised that criminals "thought" that police patrols were continuing as usual. After all, how were criminals supposed to know that the city was experimenting with varying police patrol styles? Thus, a "phantom effect" was described to account for the lack of increased crime in those areas not patrolled by police.

Criticisms of the Before–After Experimental Design.   The principal advantage of the before–after experimental design is the ability of the researcher to evaluate experimental and control group subjects both before and after experimentation, and to isolate and eliminate (or take into account, take into consideration) extraneous factors that might otherwise obscure the true effect(s) of the experimental variable. In the Kansas City study, for instance, crime rates in various beats were known before the experiment was conducted. Thus, comparisons were easily made among beats after the experiment ended to determine the experimental effects on crime rates of varying the intensity of police patrols. Again, reference may be made to Figure 3.7 where the before–after experimental design is illustrated.

True Experiments and Quasi-Experiments

Depending on the method researchers use to establish equivalence between experimental and control groups, they may conduct either true experiments or quasi-experiments. True experiments involve comparisons of two groups where random assignment has been used to establish their equivalence. The classical experimental design described earlier is an example of a **true experiment.**

Frequently, researchers conduct experiments where random assignment has not been used to establish equivalent experimental and control groups. Under these circumstances, such experiments are known as **quasi-experiments.** Quasi-experiments utilize matching, frequency distribution control matching, or persons used as their own control in before–after experiments.

A good example of a quasi-experimental research investigation is a study by Suman Kakar (1998). Kakar studied families with children who had been involved in delinquent gangs or were children at risk of becoming gang members. She compared these families with a sample of other families where the children were not at risk or involved in any gang activity. According to Kakar, "The sample consisted of 114 families. Half of these families, the experimental group, had children identified either as gang members or at risk of being gang members. These families participated in the Gang Reduction and Sports Program (GRASP), where the child is officially identified as a gang member or is officially identified as at risk of being a gang member. . . . The other half of the families, the control group, were participating in the Police Athletic League (PAL), located in Miami, Florida. . . . The only condition for enrollment in the [PAL] program is that the child is not officially identified as delinquent or as a gang member."

Kakar's (1998) research goals were to contrast these families according to their different levels of satisfaction and subjective well-being and to investigate the effect of the number of children in gangs on parental well-being. She matched the two sets of families according to (1) responding parent's age, (2) the number of children in the family, (3) ages of children, (4) child's grade in school, (5) family's socioeconomic status measured by annual income, (6) family structure, (7) church attendance, and (8) gender of the child in the program. Her findings showed that parents with children in gangs report significantly lower scores on subjective well-being than parents without children in gangs. Also, having more than one child from the same family involved in gangs lowered parental subjective well-being.

Another quasi-experimental type of study was conducted by Kevin Knight and Matthew Hiller (1997). These researchers studied 492 probationer/clients who became involved in a Texas substance abuse program during a 1-year period from 1993–1994. Knight and Hiller determined that of the original 492 participants, 100 were expelled because of program violations and other reasons, and 41 clients were transferred out of the program elsewhere. The 351 graduates were compared with the 141 expelled/transferred clients according to their recidivism. The graduates were considered as the experimental group, while the expelled/transferred clients were considered the control group. Subsequent comparison for recidivism revealed that the expelled/transferred clients had rearrest/recidivism rates twice as high as the graduate (experimental) group.

In Knight and Hiller's study, the expelled/transferred clients became the control group, inasmuch as they no longer were participating in the experiment designed to bring about change among drug users. The substance abuse program was the experimental variable. As a result of this experimental variable, according to Knight and Hiller, graduates should recidivate at a lower rate compared with those who were not exposed to the drug abuse program. The findings were supportive of this position. But Knight and Hiller rightly noted in a conclusion that ". . . however, this study did not include random assignment, and causal attribution cannot be determined" (1997, p. 67). In research-ese, this means that the study was not absolute proof of a cause–effect relation between the drug abuse program and lower recidivism rates. But they also said that "[the study demonstrated that] probationers who receive treatment for their substance abuse problems are less likely to recidivate than are those who do not receive treatment [at least as shown in this study]" (1997, p. 67).

Other types of research involving quasi-experimental designs might include comparisons of different inmate populations and inmate subcultures, where several salient inmate characteristics have been controlled; comparisons of different samples of correctional officers according to officer–inmate ratios; or comparisons of different groups of citizens according to their attitudes toward capital punishment or plea bargaining. Also, the study reported earlier about drunk drivers conducted by Rojek and colleagues was considered a quasi-experimental one.

Criticisms of Quasi-Experimental Designs.   The major advantage of quasi-experimental research is that so many natural situations exist for such experimentation. There are first-offenders and offenders with prior records. There are black and white or male and female corrections officers. There are drug abusers and non-drug abusers or alcoholics and nonalcoholics. There are program participants and non-program participants. There are parolees in halfway houses and parolees not in halfway houses. There are plea-bargained cases and cases concluded by trials. The list of such different segments of society is endless. From a purely functional point of view, it is the easiest of experimental research strategies to use without a great deal of design complexity. Quasi-experimental research is simple, and natural situations where it can be applied are abundant.

A disadvantage is that quasi-experimental research lacks the equivalence between experimental and control groups that random assignment would provide. Therefore, conclusions drawn from such research are more tentative. But scientific research in general is tentative anyway. We are trained not to draw absolute conclusions on the basis of a single study, regardless of its magnitude or complexity. Research about different topics accumulates gradually, and over time, we develop sound explanations for why certain events occur. Quasi-experimental research is a sound tool for contributing a growing amount of evidence to explanations of criminological problems.

Time-Series and Multiple Time-Series Designs

Time-Series Designs.   More than a few experiments occur over long periods of time, such as 10, 15, or 20 years. Investigators may examine phenomena such as the murder rate over time. For instance, we might chart the murder rate for the United States, beginning in 1960, and track the murder rate through 1990. At certain points in this yearly murder rate tracking, we might note significant U.S. Supreme Court decisions about how murderers are punished, such as the use of capital punishment or its nonuse.

It has been argued, for example, that the application of the death penalty is not a significant deterrent for prospective murderers. Other investigators say that the death penalty *is* a deterrent to murder. In 1972 the U.S. Supreme Court ruled against the death penalty according to how it was being applied in a racially discriminatory manner in Georgia in the case of *Furman v. Georgia* (1972). Georgia and other states using the death penalty temporarily suspended its application. This suspension lasted 4 years, until the U.S. Supreme Court ruled again in *Gregg v. Georgia* (1976) that the application of the death penalty in Georgia was no longer discriminatory and therefore constitutional. Thus, researchers were presented with an ideal situation for examining murder rates in the United States under conditions where the death penalty was allowed or disallowed.

Contrary to the beliefs of persons supporting the death penalty, the murder rate in the United States did not escalate appreciably when the death penalty was suspended for 4 years. Neither did the murder rate decline when the death penalty was reinstated in 1976.

The significance of this example is that it illustrates a **time-series design.** Time-series designs include numerous observations of a variable (e.g., the murder rate) over time. During these observations, another variable, an intervening variable, occurs (e.g., suspension of the death penalty). Observations of the original variable (murder rate) continue to be made. Eventually, investigators can draw tentative conclusions about the impact of the intervening or treatment variable (suspension of the death penalty) on the original variable (murder rate).

Symbolically, the time-series design involves numerous observations (O) with an experimental variable (E) introduced at some point among these observations. Changes likely attributable to the experimental variable can then be charted (e.g., the pre-experimental variable period and the post-experimental variable period). A conventional time-series design also known as an **interrupted time-series design** because of the introduction of the experimental variable, E, is:

Time 1	Time 2	Time 3	Time 4	Time 5	E	Time 6	Time 7	Time 8	Time 9	Time 10
O	*O*	*O*	*O*	*O*	↓	*O*	*O*	*O*	*O*	*O*

Another example is an examination of attorney involvement in juvenile court cases over time. In the 1950s and 1960s, attorney involvement in juvenile court cases was minimal. However, the U.S. Supreme Court ruled in several cases that led to greater constitutional rights and protections for juveniles during the 1966–1976 period. Since greater constitutional rights for juveniles might also mean greater responsibility and accountability on their part, it has been suspected by many researchers that the juvenile court has become increasingly criminalized. Thus, greater attorney involvement in juvenile cases will probably occur, largely as the result of a greater need for attorneys in defense of juveniles.

The National Center for Juvenile Justice in Pittsburgh, Pennsylvania, compiles information about juvenile court cases in most states. This information has been collected for many years. If we were to examine juvenile cases across many years in different states, we could see whether attorney involvement in juvenile cases increased or remained the same. Several studies of attorney involvement in juvenile court cases have indicated greater attorney involvement over the years. In states such as California, attorney involvement has increased over the years from 40 percent of the cases in 1960 to over 90 percent in 1994.

The experimental or treatment variable in this case might be a U.S. Supreme Court decision about particular juvenile rights. We might also use an event such as the get-tough movement toward crime and delinquency, which seems to have gained considerable momentum in the mid-1980s. The get-tough movement promotes tougher sanctions or penalties, sentences, or dispositions for both adult and juvenile offenders. Tracking attorney involvement during the 1980s during a time when the get-tough movement evolved, we might see a dramatic upsurge of attorney involvement in juvenile cases seemingly coinciding with the get-tough movement.

Another application of the time-series design might be a study of the impact of divestiture of certain juvenile court cases in a city such as Yakima, Washington. In the 1980s the juvenile court in Yakima divested itself of jurisdiction over status offenders (e.g., runaways, truants, curfew violators). This meant that juvenile court judges would no longer hear cases involving status offenders. Rather, the juvenile court would concentrate solely on more serious delinquent offenders (theft, robbery, rape, murder). It was predicted that divestiture would be followed by a reduction in the sheer numbers of cases to be processed by the juvenile court. Using the number of juvenile court cases processed by the Yakima juvenile courts on a monthly basis, a time-series design would track these cases over several years. Following divestiture of jurisdiction over status offenders, it was found that actual numbers of juvenile court cases increased appreciably. This didn't make any sense to investigators. However, researchers learned later that the divestiture action was not received well by Yakima police officers, who perceived divestiture as a challenge to their decision-making authority when confronting juveniles on city streets. In fact, Yakima police were "redefining" juvenile status offenses as delinquent acts and arresting more youths in the postdivestiture period than in the predivestiture period. Many of the arrested youths in the postdivestiture period would have received only verbal warnings in the predivestiture period. A time-series design was useful in detecting this unusual police activity and response to divestiture.

Multiple Time-Series Designs.   A **multiple time-series design** is similar to conventional time-series designs, with the exception that an additional comparison group or population is examined. For instance, in our previous discussion of time-series design used to track murder rates in the United States and the application of the death penalty, the entire U.S. murder rate was examined. Suppose we wanted to compare the murder rates of two states over time, where one state used the death penalty and the other state did not use it. For example, Texas uses the death penalty for capital offenses. In recent decades, Texas suspended its application of the death penalty only as the result of *Furman v. Georgia* (1972). Texas reinstated the death penalty in 1976 when *Gregg v. Georgia* (1976) was decided. Suppose we were to track the murder rate in Texas over time, encompassing the 1972–1976 period when the death penalty was temporarily suspended. Further suppose that we were to track the murder rate of another state where the death penalty is not used, such as Michigan. We might suspect that suspending the death penalty in Texas might cause changes in the Texas murder rate, whereas for the same period of time, the Michigan murder rate might not fluctuate. This multiple time-series design might be illustrated as follows across the years 1968–1979:

Murder Rate by Year

	1968	1969	1970	1971	1972	E	1973	1974	1975	1976	E	1977	1978	1979
						↓					↓			
Texas	O	O	O	O	O	E	O	O	O	O	E	O	O	O
Michigan	O	O	O	O	O	E	O	O	O	O	E	O	O	O

The above example actually shows two *E*'s, the first being the *Furman v. Georgia* (1972) decision. The second *E* is the *Gregg v. Georgia* (1976) decision. We might expect that the murder rate in Texas would increase following the 1972 decision, since capital punishment was suspended for murder. However, when capital punishment is reintroduced in 1977 following the *Gregg v. Georgia* (1976) decision, we might expect the murder rate in Texas to decline. But in Michigan, we would expect little or no change in the murder rate across these same years, since Michigan has no death penalty and made no changes relative to it. All of these expectations are premised on the idea that the death penalty per se is a profound deterrent to murder. Indeed, if we saw the murder rate significantly rise in Texas for the years 1973–1976, and then if the murder rate were to decline substantially in 1977, 1978, and 1979, we might conclude that the death penalty deters persons from committing murder.

Criticisms of Time-Series and Multiple Time-Series Designs.   A compelling strength of a time-series research design is the fact that changes in our observation of a single variable over time may be indicative of the influence or impact of a treatment or experimental variable. If appreciable changes occur in the variable under observation, and if these changes occur contemporaneously with the new event or intervening, treatment, or experimental variable, then a potential cause–effect relation may be established. For instance, if several new juvenile rights are conveyed by the U.S. Supreme Court in 1966 and we are tracking the percentage of attorney use in juvenile cases, we might infer that these rights changes cause increased attorney involvement in juvenile court cases if we observe something like the following:

Percent of Attorney Involvement in Juvenile Court Cases

E

1960	61	62	63	64	65	66	67	68	69	70	71	72	73	74	75	76
40%	40%	40%	40%	40%	40%	40%	55%	60%	70%	80%	81%	82%	85%	85%	86%	90%

where E = more rights for juveniles because of U.S. Supreme Court decisions

Our analysis of this trend in attorney use by juveniles in juvenile court cases would certainly arouse our suspicions that U.S. Supreme Court decisions conveying more rights to juveniles seemed to prompt greater attorney involvement in juvenile cases.

One drawback of time-series designs is that we don't know for sure if a variable such as the murder rate for any given state would have changed anyway or remained the same, regardless of events or U.S. Supreme Court decisions. For instance, attorney use may have escalated in juvenile court cases because of new state legislature provisions mandating attorneys for juveniles in all serious cases. The fact that juveniles have more rights in the post-1966 period than they did in the pre-1966 period may be irrelevant.

Even where multiple time-series designs are used, there are problems regarding whether two samples or populations being compared are equivalent. Murder rate comparisons between Texas and Michigan may be influenced by factors other than whether these states use or don't use the death penalty. The U.S. economy fluctuates. Persons may engage in more violent crime when unemployment is high. The death penalty may be an irrelevant consideration. Thus, the presence and potential influence of one or more factors unknown to us may actually cause changes or not cause changes in the variables we examine. This is one important reason why researchers conduct investigations of the same events and variables again and again. After considerable investigation, we are able to discern patterns in our findings that give us more confidence in our explanations of events.

Cost–Benefit Analyses

Another type of research design is **cost–benefit analysis (CBA).** The focus of CBA is on the useful and practical results of an intervention or experimental variable and the cost of these results compared with alternative interventions. Two examples from the research literature illustrate CBA.

• *Drug Courts versus Traditional Court Processing of Drug Offenders.* Increasingly popular in dealing with drug offenders are drug courts, which utilize and network with a variety of community resources to provide more effective and long-term treatment milieus for those convicted of drug offenses. Traditional court responses to those convicted of drug offenses are often no treatment. Rather, those with drug convictions are jailed for particular periods and subsequently serve their time and are released back into their communities without receiving any meaningful drug treatment. Advocates of drug courts say that these types of specialized courts are more cost-effective compared with traditional court processing of drug offenders. How do we know whether or not drug courts are more cost-effective compared with traditional courts? Do drug courts save more taxpayer dollars compared with traditional court processing?

Shannon M. Carey and Michael W. Finnegan (2004) wanted to find out, and so they conducted a study of a comparison of drug courts established in Multnomah County, Oregon, with traditional criminal courts. Drug offenders in both types of courts were investigated and contrasted. Subsequently, these researchers obtained aggregate matched samples totalling 1,167 persons, consisting of 594 drug court participant members, referred to as the intensive group, and 573 non-drug court participants, simply referred to as the comparison group. Costs of processing both the intensive and comparison group were calculated on the basis of budgets and other financial information from 2000, 2001, and 2002. These researchers eventually determined that the drug court was more cost-effective in processing and treating the intensive group in relation to the comparison group. The ultimate savings for the intensive group amounted to over $1 million a year contrasted with the comparison group. The researchers concluded that overall, the results of this study demonstrate that drug courts can be a cost-effective use of the criminal justice system and taxpayer resources. Demonstrable per-client savings for drug court participants averaged $4,788, or about $478,000 per 100 participants. Attaching dollar values to program costs are always critical in establishing the cost-effectiveness of different types of offender treatment. From a criminal justice policy perspective, these researchers have provided support for greater use of drug courts when drug offenders are processed. Drug courts may not be a panacea for all drug offenders in every jurisdiction, but at least in Multnomah County, Oregon, the cost-effectiveness of drug courts was clearly demonstrated.

• *The Cost-Effectiveness of Pretrial Services in Los Angeles County.* It is expensive to house arrestees in jails and prisons. Jails are particularly vulnerable to large influxes of persons who are often accommodated for short terms to await a later trial. Many of these persons are not dangerous and would not flee the jurisdiction if freed temporarily. They take up valuable space that otherwise might be occupied by more dangerous offenders. In order to save the Los Angeles County Jail money, various programs have been established to permit various offenders release from custody on their own recognizance, or OR. Two programs established during the 1980s under the umbrella of pretrial services were the Bail Deviation Program (BD) and the Own Recognizance Program (OR). A researcher, David Grkinich (2001), decided to investigate the cost-effectiveness of pretrial services programs such as these. An examination of inmates processed by the Los Angeles County Jail was conducted for the fiscal year, 1999–2000. Grkinich found that the BD program processed 25,981 applications for release, where background checks and prior records are examined, and every applicant's suitability for BD is assessed with a point scale measuring various factors, such as family ties, employment history, and history of failure to appear (FTA). A total of 1,627 defendants were released under BD during this period with a resulting savings to Los

Angeles County Jail of $5,729,460. Also during the fiscal year, 1999–2000, the OR program received 33,051 applications for temporary release, of which 2,515 were approved. The cost savings to Los Angeles County Jail was $9,759,636. The FTA rates for the BDs and ORs were 3.66 percent and 7.48 percent, respectively. Because of the great savings accruing to Los Angeles County, the various pretrial service programs such as BD and OR will continue, and considerable savings associated with these programs will be realized. These programs are particularly important in jurisdictions where funds and space are scarce for accommodating different types of jail inmates.

Criticisms of Cost–Benefit Analysis.   When investigators seek to determine the effectiveness of an intervention, program, therapy, drug, or other experimental variable, they may have a vested interest in the outcome. If their research is sponsored by a private organization, their vested interest in the outcome may be heightened. Also, cost–benefit analyses are often subjective. Researchers are trained to be objective, although some investigators may be tempted to focus only on the most positive aspects of study outcomes.

Depending on the variables examined, cost–benefit analysis may be a simple and direct way of determining which of several interventions is best at bringing about desired results at the least cost. However, demonstrating the effectiveness of an intervention may take considerable time. Longitudinal studies, or studies that span one or more years, may be inconclusive, where study findings are diffuse. It may be difficult to distinguish between several competing strategies according to mixed results. Increasingly, the National Institute of Justice and other funding organizations are obligating researcher/grantees to limit the time frames of their investigations, so that research results are reported more quickly. The shorter-term nature of research projects might reflect greater impatience of organizations and agencies for study results that can be used to support changing policies and procedures.

Internal and External Validity

Depending on the research design used for one's investigations, questions often arise about the quality or structural integrity of the study itself. Also, questions arise concerning how generalizable the findings of one study are to other similar studies. These questions refer to a study's internal validity and external validity.

Internal Validity and Threats

Internal validity is the theoretical and methodological integrity of the study itself (Farrington, 2003). Internal validity assesses the study design and construction of instruments. Theoretical adequacy and the soundness of derived hypotheses are integral parts of a study's internal validity. Any criticism of one's research plan and its implementation is a criticism of the internal validity of a study (Esbensen, 1999).

It is desirable for investigators to conduct studies that heighten internal validity. However, no study is perfect. Investigators can enhance the likelihood of a study's internal validity by following conventional research strategies and avoiding situations that might undermine the integrity of the research plan (Minor, Hatmann, & Davis, 1990; Thompson, 1990).

Several threats to a study's internal validity have been identified (Campbell & Stanley, 1963; Cook & Campbell, 1979). The following factors influence the internal validity of any study, particularly experimental ones that are conducted over two or more points in time.

History.   What are the specific events that occur between the first and second measures taken and where an experimental variable has been introduced? Sometimes during an experiment over the course of a few weeks or months, events may occur to cause changes in one's behavior or attitudes that are totally unrelated to the experimental variable or stimulus. Some persons may experience tragedies in their lives. Some persons may get promotions in their work, while others may lose their jobs. Several persons may get divorced. The list of possible events than can occur in one's life is virtually endless and is known as the **history** of occurrences during an experiment that may affect it. The point is that things may happen between the first and second time periods during which changes are anticipated because of the introduction of a stimulus or experimental variable. Any behavioral changes noted may not be due to the experimental variable, but rather to the events in one's life that we know little or nothing about. There is little we can do to know for sure whether our experimental subjects experience attitude-changing experiences apart from our experimental conditions.

Maturation.   Some persons mature at faster rates than others. If one's experiment is conducted over an extended time interval, there is a likelihood that some amount of **maturation** will occur. If investigators are looking at the effects of some experimental variable upon one's mechanical aptitude, verbal facility, or some other performance-related variable, maturation itself may induce improvements in one's performance apart from any changes elicited by the experimental variable.

Testing Effect.   When subjects are given a measuring instrument in an earlier time period and then given the same measuring instrument in a later time period, the second measured results may be affected by the results of the first administration of the instrument. This is known as the **testing effect.** In effect, people may remember how they responded at an earlier point in time and attempt to conform their later answers to match those they gave earlier, even though they may feel differently later and have different attitudes. This situation occurs as the result of repeated testing.

Instrumentation.   Sometimes when persons are investigated over time, different observers may be used in a later time period than were used in an earlier time period. Also, the instrument itself may be modified in different ways, with subtle word changes made or other items introduced. Such changes in instrumentation, observers, or even the scoring process may jeopardize a study's internal validity. Problems with measures and their contents are sometimes called **mechanical factors.**

Statistical Regression.   It is possible that during the selection process where experimental subjects are selected, some of the lowest performers may be selected. Or those with the lowest attitudinal scores on some variable may be included for an experiment. Suppose investigators introduce an experimental variable that is designed to improve their performance on some other variable. Low performers in almost any area we examine will probably show some improvement over time, simply because they have learned a little more as the result of the experiment. Such a threat to internal validity occurs whenever the lowest performers or those with extremely low scores on some critical dimension are selected for analysis and experimentation. This is known as statistical **regression.**

Selection of Subjects.   Sometimes bias may occur as the result of selecting certain types of subjects for experimentation. For some reason unknown to outside observers, experimenters may select certain subjects for participation in their research on the basis of their appearance, age, or some other variable or characteristic. Thus, the subjects themselves are not especially ideal for before–after types of experimentation. In some instances, the subjects may be volunteers. In other cases, there may be a self-selection process that leads to the inclusion of persons that are not especially representative or typical of others investigators want to study. Their inclusion may bias study results. One way of defeating this type of internal validity problem is to randomly select subjects to form experimental and control groups.

Experimental Mortality.   It is common that during the course of an experiment, especially an experiment that extends over several months or years, some original participants may drop out, die, or otherwise become unavailable for further experimentation. This is **experimental mortality.** If an investigator wishes to learn about whether Web-based online coursework is effective at improving one's performance in learning a particular subject, the course may extend over several months and several hundred students may be involved. By the time the Web-based course ends, several students may have dropped out or withdrawn from the course. Job transfers, unexpected call-ups for military service, pregnancy, or some other unanticipated event may reduce the original number of persons participating in the online study experiment. This is experimental mortality.

Selection–Maturation Interaction.   Sometimes during an experiment, control group members may share their experiences with certain experimental group members. This is **selection–maturation interaction.** They may compare their experiences and figure out what the experimenter is attempting to accomplish. Simply knowing a researcher's objectives may decrease the study integrity and lower the study's internal validity.

The John Henry Effect.   Historically, John Henry was a worker who outperformed a machine under an experimental setting, because he was aware that his performance was being compared with that of a machine. In various work settings, if persons are fearful that a machine or some technological innovation may replace them as workers, they may work much harder than usual in order to show that they are indispensable to an organization. If the organization is studying them and their behaviors, the wrong kinds of conclusions may be drawn from whatever is observed. A study's internal validity will be jeopardized as a result by the **John Henry effect.**

External Validity and Threats

External validity is the generalizability of study findings to other studies and research settings (Eck, 2002). The major question raised by external validity is how representative or typical the sample is that was used in the study (Moran, 2002). Investigators want to know how the sample was selected, how large the sample was, and what evidence exists that reflects favorably on **sample representativeness.** Generally, we know that a probability sample is more often more representative of the populations from which it was drawn compared with a nonprobability sample. But then we also know that certain nonprobability samples, such as saturation or dense samples, contain such a large proportion of the population, as much as 50 percent or more, that they are somewhat representative as well.

The fact is that we never know how representative any sample is unless the entire population is studied (Moran, 2002). And this event, studying entire populations, defeats the economizing purpose of sampling (Farrington, 2003). Such analytical methods as meta-analysis can enhance a study's external validity to the extent that it seems consistent with the findings of similar studies.

Several conditions have been identified that affect a study's external validity. Threats to a study's external validity include the following factors.

Reactive or Interaction Effect of Testing.   Sometimes one's exposure to a pretest may increase or decrease that subject's sensitivity to the experimental variable, which is introduced later. The is known as the **reactive effect.** Pretesting may be harmful and jeopardize a study's subsequent generalizability to other research settings and subjects.

Interaction Effects of Selection Biases and the Experimental Variable.   The experimental variable may have little or no effect on persons who have been included because of certain characteristics favored by experimenters or investigators. Their own personal characteristics may make them immune to the experimental variable and the changes in their behaviors the variable was intended to make. This **selection bias** and subsequent **interaction effects** may interfere with assessing the true experimental results.

Reactive Effects of Experimental Arrangements.   Because of the very nature of experimental research and the fact that some of it is contrived, it may be difficult to generalize from such settings to other nonexperimental settings, which are more natural and less contrived. If persons know they are being observed or tested, for instance, they may behave differently under these experimental conditions than under conditions where they know they are not being observed.

Multiple Treatment Interference.   When persons in an experiment are subjected to repeated experimental variables, such as different drugs and dosages, it is possible, indeed likely, that the effects of prior experimentation may carry over and interfere with subsequent experimental effects.

Generally, both internal and external validity are important factors in assessing the integrity and generalizability of different studies. Internal validity is controlled more easily, in that experimenters or investigators can control study conditions and other factors related to study implementation and design more directly. It is more difficult to control those conditions that affect a study's generalizability, such as the persons selected for study participation and their typicality or representativeness of the population about which the researcher seeks information. It is well known that any threat to a study's internal validity is also an indirect threat to a study's external validity (Campbell & Stanley, 1963).

SUMMARY

Research designs are research plans used for the purpose of gaining information about events we are attempting to explain. The particular type of research design researchers select depends a great deal on the problem or event they wish to explain and the frame of reference they have chosen to explain it. There are many types of research designs.

Research is often dichotomized according to whether it is qualitative or quantitative. Qualitative research, less frequently used compared with quantitative research, is largely nonstatistical and utilizes softer data collection methods, such as interviewing and observation, for small groups of persons. Quantitative research is more often associated with large-scale administration of questionnaires to large numbers of persons. It also involves the application of various more or less complex statistical procedures that involve intricate data analyses. Both types of research yield different characteristics and information about persons studied. Usually qualitative research consists of extensive descriptive embellishments of study settings, descriptions of verbal exchanges between principal actors in these settings, and detailed observational descriptions of persons and events. Quantitative studies are inherently more superficial compared with qualitative research, in that in-depth information is usually not solicited because of the nature of data-gathering that occurs. Sometimes elements of both quantification and qualitative research may be incorporated into a single study to yield a fuller elaboration or description of the setting and persons in it.

There are several different kinds of research objectives. These parallel the types of research examined earlier and include exploration, description, and experimentation. Exploration and exploratory objectives involve studies of settings about which little or nothing is known by researchers conducting the investigation. Donald Clemmer's investigation of prison settings in 1940 was considered precedent-setting and exploratory, because few persons had studied these settings previously. In the 1980s exploratory research was conducted about electronic monitoring and its feasibility as a method of supervising dangerous offenders on probation or parole. Little or nothing was known about electronic monitoring at the time. Subsequently, the exploratory nature of such investigations has progressed to the levels of description and even experimentation. Thus, exploratory research serves primarily to acquaint researchers with certain characteristics of research targets that seem relevant and should be described in greater detail later.

Description and descriptive objectives are intended to disclose much rich detail about study settings and the people in those settings. Important characteristics of study settings and persons are identified, and later, investigators may conduct experimental research where one or more of the described variables may be controlled and assessed. Descriptive designs are the most common in criminological research. Virtually every agency and component of the criminal justice system has been described in great detail. As investigators learn more about the settings they study, the sophistication of their research grows proportionately. Eventually, experimental research is conducted.

Experimentation and experimental objectives are geared to demonstrate cause–effect relations between variables, although investigators caution their readers to be wary of jumping to conclusions about cause–effect variable interrelationships. This is because cause–effect relationships between variables take a great deal of time and repeated research efforts to establish. Key elements in experimental designs are experimental and control groups. Experimental groups are those persons who receive the experimental or treatment variable, an intervening factor intended to cause one or more changes in their behaviors or the event under investigation. Control groups are those closely equated in some way with the experimental group, but from which the treatment or experimental variable is withheld. Usually a subsequent comparison between the experimental and control groups according to certain variables will show the influence, if any, of the experimental or treatment variable on the experimental group. Our understanding of how these variables operate on or influence one another is thereby enhanced. Some variables are controlled, meaning that we simply take them into account and hold them constant during the course of an experiment.

Some conventional research designs include surveys and case studies. Surveys are large-scale assessments of larger numbers of persons and are closely associated with quantitative research. Survey research is usually associated with gathering information from large numbers of persons, often distributed in diverse locations, through the use of questionnaires. Various methods are used to randomize the selection of persons who receive questionnaires, and it is believed that they are representative of the population at large and about which the researcher seeks information. But no researcher can guarantee the typicality or generalizability of any sample in relation to the population from which it was drawn. Furthermore, there is considerable superficiality associated with survey research, where in-depth information is not yielded. Nevertheless, much information from surveys is useful for describing particular populations of persons. Sometimes, surveys are conducted on the same aggregate of persons over time, and these aggregates of persons are known as panels.

Because of the relative magnitude of surveys, they can often provide information about many persons at lower cost compared with other research designs. Also, generalizability to larger populations may be enhanced because of the sheer magnitude of persons included in one's survey. Various data collection techniques may also be used in surveys, including questionnaires, interviewing, and the analysis of written policies and other information. But surveys are also superficial. Researchers also have little or no control over who responds to their surveys. Thus, the intended persons for questionnaires may not be those who complete and return them. This circumstance may undermine the credibility of such investigations. But surveys can contribute much information to the theory verification process, although sample results are regarded as highly tentative.

Case studies are in-depth examinations of social settings. Usually they are associated with observation and interviewing. Because more intensive analyses of social settings are conducted, the sample sizes associated with case studies are smaller compared with survey information. Interviewing and observation consume large amounts of time. However, much rich information about particular settings may provide valuable insights into why certain people behave in different ways and why events occur. Virtually every social environment is amenable to a case study. Furthermore, multiple data collection strategies may be employed. Researchers may use interviews, questionnaires, observation, and the analysis of secondary sources such as letters and documents to portray the characteristics of the sample selected for study. Case studies may be relatively inexpensive, especially where observation and interviewing are used. Investigators may probe respondents to determine the meaning of certain things disclosed or said, or they may ask for interpretations of observed events. Case studies have limited generalizability, however. Nevertheless, they may be conceptualized as specific instances of theoretical tests that have some heuristic value. Comparing surveys with case studies suggests that the amount of detail furnished by each varies greatly. An examination of the research literature in criminology and criminal justice suggests that surveys are used overwhelmingly compared with case studies. Thus it would seem that researchers favor larger data sets and more data superficiality compared with smaller samples and more in-depth information. The information from both types of research is of value in theoretical tests, however.

A popular type of research design is the classic research design. Two alternatives of this design are the after-only and before–after design. The after-only design seeks to determine the influence of a treatment or experimental variable only after the experimental variable has been introduced. An experimental and control group are compared after the treatment variable has been introduced. In the before–after variation of this design, measures are obtained before the treatment variable has been introduced, and then measures are obtained later, following the introduction of the treatment or experimental variable. This method involves pretests and posttests. Pretests are measures taken before the treatment variable is introduced. The posttest occurs following the introduction of the treatment or experimental variable. The before–after version of the classic experimental design is considerably more popular in its usage among criminologists.

When comparisons are made between experimental and control groups, it is assumed that both groups are similar in various ways or share many of the same characteristics. At least four different methods have been identified and used to equate groups for experimental purposes. One method used involves individual matching, where persons in an experimental group are closely matched on selected variables with persons in a control group. This individual matching is very difficult to accomplish, and thus it is the least frequently used method for establishing equivalence between groups. The second method is to use persons as their own controls in before–after experiments. This means that the same persons are used over time, and they function as their own controls as an experimental or treatment variable is introduced. If their behaviors or attitudes change over time, it is assumed that the treatment variable caused the behavioral or attitudinal change. Researchers do not have to spend a lot of time matching persons on selected personal and social characteristics, because the same persons are used in before–after experimentation. Unfortunately, persons used as their own controls can recall how they responded earlier, and such recollections may influence their subsequent responses. It may be difficult for researchers to determine the true effects of the treatment variable upon these persons under such circumstances.

A third way of equating groups is to match the experimental and control groups according to aggregate criteria, such as their average ages, similarity in gender distributions, or any other relevant factor. This is much easier to accomplish compared with individual matching. A fourth method for equating groups is random assignment. The poorest method of equating groups, random assignment involves the assignment of a large group of persons either to the experimental or control groups randomly. Unfortunately, individual differences between persons randomly placed in both groups cannot be taken into account.

And when the groups are subsequently compared after a treatment variable has been introduced, the results may be misleading.

Additional types of experimentation include true experiments and quasi-experiments. True experiments are so-named because random assignment is used as the means for assigning persons to the experimental and control groups. Quasi-experiments involve alternative methods for establishing equivalence, such as individual matching or using persons as their own controls in before–after experiments. Considering the weaknesses of random assignment, it is doubtful that true experiments are appropriately named.

Other experimental designs are time-series and multiple time-series designs and cost–benefit analyses. Time-series designs involve tracking a particular event or behavior over time. One example is an examination of the murder rate in the United States and the use of the death penalty. Murder rates have been tracked across years, from the 1950s through the 1980s or longer. In 1972 a U.S. Supreme Court case declared the way the death penalty was decided in Georgia courts was unconstitutional. The death penalty was suspended during the period, 1972–1976, when the U.S. Supreme Court eventually sanctioned an alternative way in Georgia for arriving at a decision by juries to recommend death penalties. Annual observations in the murder rate before, during, and after the suspension of the death penalty enabled researchers to see whether or not the death penalty actually deterred persons from committing murder. A time-series design was helpful in disclosing important trend information, the murder rate, in relation to temporarily suspending the death penalty, the treatment or intervening or experimental variable, and whether the murder rate changed to any significant degree during the years when the death penalty was not imposed. The multiple time-series design involves several intervening or treatment variables that are introduced over time. Thus, there may be several points over time where different treatment variables are introduced. Specific events or behaviors may be tracked, and changes in these behaviors can be tracked in relation to introducing different experimental variables across different time periods.

Cost–benefit analyses seek to determine the cost-effectiveness of certain types of interventions or treatment variables. For instance, some investigators may believe that boot camps reduce delinquency. Other investigators may believe that locking up juvenile offenders for short periods of time will have a greater deterrent effect. In order to determine the cost-effectiveness of boot camps versus incarcerating youthful offenders, cost–benefit studies are conducted. These studies assess the dollar value of different types of interventions (e.g., boot camps, incarceration) in relation to reducing certain events (e.g., delinquency). Those interventions that cost less but yield greater reductions in the delinquent behavior may be increasingly used as their cost-effectiveness is more economically sound. Very often, these studies reflect the relative costs associated with different interventions or treatment variables, and evaluations are made in terms of dollars and cents. Policy changes are made accordingly in terms of which delinquency control methods (or other types of behaviors or events) work best at the least cost.

Internal validity encompasses the adequacy of one's theoretical scheme; the hypotheses derived for test; the sample and how it was obtained; the appropriateness of the data-gathering methods; the actual validity and reliability associated with the attitudinal measures used or scales designed to assess the existence of other variables; the type of data analysis used by the investigator; and the nature of conclusions drawn about the substantive and theoretical implications of one's research. External validity pertains to the degree to which one's study findings or results can be generalizable to other settings similar to the one being studied. If a study of California probation officers is conducted, the research findings have a high degree of external validity to the extent that generalizations can be made to groups of probation officers in other jurisdictions, such as Tennessee, Colorado, or New York. Therefore, internal validity refers to study integrity and implementation.

QUESTIONS FOR REVIEW

1. What is qualitative research? What are some important characteristics of it?

2. What is meant by quantitative research? What are some important characteristics of it? What are some general contrasts between qualitative and quantitative research and the type of information yielded by each?

3. What is a research design? What are three types of research designs and what are their respective objectives?

4. What are some general differences between exploratory and descriptive research designs? What are some of the criteria used to determine whether exploratory or descriptive research designs will be used?

5. What is meant by experimentation? What is an experimental research design? What are its general objectives?

6. What is meant by variable control? What are some differences between experimental groups and control groups?

7. What is an experimental or treatment variable? What are the uses of experimental or treatment variables in experimental research designs?

8. What is a survey design? What are some of its primary characteristics? What are some applications of survey designs? What are some weaknesses and strengths of survey designs?

9. What are case studies? What are some of their important applications? What are some limitations associated with case studies?

10. How do survey designs compare and contrast with case study designs in terms of the information each yields?

11. What is meant by the classic experimental design? What are two variations of the classic experimental design? What are some important differences between each of these two variations?

12. What are four ways of establishing equivalence between groups for experimentation purposes? Which method is used most frequently and why? Which method is the most difficult to use and why?

13. Why is random assignment considered an inferior method of establishing equivalence between groups compared with individual matching, using persons as their own controls in before–after experiments, and group distribution matching?

14. What are some important differences between true experiments and quasi-experiments?

15. What are meant by pretests and posttests? How are these used in experimental research?

16. What is a time-series design? How does it differ from a multiple time-series design?

17. What is cost–benefit analysis? What are some general aims of cost–benefit analysis?

CHAPTER OUTLINE

CHAPTER OBJECTIVES

As the result of reading this chapter, the following objectives will be realized:

1. Distinguishing between populations, parameters, samples, and statistics.
2. Learning how different types of sampling plans can influence the generalizability of one's findings.
3. Understanding the decision to sample and how large the sample size should be relative to the size of the population.
4. Describing the criteria influential to the sampling process, including the convenience and accessibility of sampling elements and the cost of obtaining sample elements.

5. Understanding the functions of sampling, including economizing resources, manageability, meeting assumptions of statistical tests, and meeting the requirements of experiments.

6. Learning about sampling fractions and the principles of randomness, including equality and independence of draws of elements from designated populations.

7. Describing different types of probability sampling plans, including simple random sampling, proportionate and disproportionate stratified random sampling, and cluster, area, or multistage sampling, and their weaknesses, strengths, and applications.

8. Describing different types of nonprobability sampling plans, including accidental or convenience sampling, systematic sampling, judgmental or purposive sampling, quota sampling, dense sampling, and saturation sampling, including each plan's weaknesses, strengths, and potential research applications.

9. Knowing how to use a table of random numbers for sampling purposes.

10. Differentiating between single sample, two samples, and k samples and the conditions under which these different kinds of samples are used.

11. Learning the difference between independent and related samples and the conditions and applications underlying these types of samples.

12. Describing certain sampling problems, including determining sample size, what to do about nonresponse, sample representativeness, sampling and statistical analyses, ideal and real sampling considerations, and the sampling of potentates.

Introduction

An essential component in a majority of research projects is sampling. Sampling involves targeting populations and selecting some of them for subsequent investigation. For instance, researchers may wish to study correctional officers from jails and prisons in order to compare their degrees of professionalism. Or researchers may want to know opinions of professionals in community-based probation agencies about agency volunteers and how the effectiveness of these volunteers is determined. Other investigators may want to see whether shock probationers make better adjustments in their communities compared with those offenders who do not participate in shock probation. Some researchers may want to profile the characteristics of convicted female murderers currently serving time in penitentiaries.

Each of these topics raises several common questions. These are (1) "Where can relevant data be obtained?" and (2) "How will this information be obtained?" Many researchers know in advance where their data can be found. Also, they have a general idea about how they will get the data needed to answer their research questions. Perhaps they have important contacts within various institutions and agencies. Some researchers may be employees of organizations they wish to study. Using one's organizational contacts or the contacts of others is a good means of initially getting one's "foot in the door" to conduct research.

A third question is suggested by each of these topics. "What sampling method should be used to obtain persons from the larger aggregate of those we wish to study?" Because there are so many different topics, so many target audiences available for study, and so many different conditions that might exist whenever studies are conducted, no single sampling method has universal application. Over the years, many sampling techniques have evolved for use in different types of social research. Each technique has different strengths and weaknesses, depending on the unique circumstances of its application.

The organization of this chapter is as follows. First, several conventional terms of sampling methods will be identified and described. Sampling fulfills several important functions. These functions will be outlined. Questions about why we sample will be answered. All of the major sampling plans discussed here have been grouped into probability sampling plans and nonprobability sampling plans. Respectively, these plans either permit or do not permit generalizations to populations we have selected for study. Several types of probability and nonprobability sampling plans have been devised to meet investigator needs under different kinds of research conditions. Each of these types of sampling plans will be illustrated, and the weaknesses and strengths of each will be discussed. Suggested applications will be made for each type of plan in relation to problems that may be investigated in criminal justice or criminology.

Finally, several important sampling issues will be examined. Investigators may want to know whether their samples are representative or typical of the general class of persons they are studying. What factors intervene to affect the representativeness of samples adversely or favorably? What should researchers do if some persons they want to study refuse to participate or fail to return their mailed questionnaires? What should be the appropriate sample size? Some samples are difficult to access, since permission may be required to study them. Prisoners and juveniles are examples of persons requiring permission from others before researchers can contact them. Some persons may not require the permission of others before they can be studied. But they may be nearly inaccessible as well. Judges and prosecutors are often insulated from researchers by a protective group of assistants and a loyal secretarial pool. Thus, a broad class of potentates will be examined as a sampling problem and consideration. These and other issues will be presented and discussed.

What is Sampling?

Statisticians refer to the units they study as **elements.** Elements refer either to things or people. Thus, we may study light bulbs, shoes, telephones, or people, and in the general case, our references to them will be "elements." In the social sciences, "a study of 100 elements" means that researchers are studying 100 persons. Usually, these persons have characteristics of interest to the researcher. These characteristics may be male juvenile delinquents, female murderers, probation officers, defense attorneys, juvenile court judges, intake officers, jail or prison inmates, correctional officers, wardens or superintendents, or volunteers in a community-based correctional agency. They comprise the **sampling frame.** Because of our research interests, we seek information about these persons. **Sampling** means to take a proportion of persons from the whole class of persons about which we seek information.

Populations and Parameters

A **population** comprises the entire class or aggregate of elements about which one seeks information. For example, we may seek information about the inmates in the Alabama State Penitentiary. We may want to study Illinois probation officers. Or we may seek information about juvenile delinquents in Las Vegas, Nevada. Therefore, the three populations about which we seek information are all inmates at the Alabama State Penitentiary, all probation officers in the State of Illinois, and all juvenile delinquents in Las Vegas, Nevada. In each of these cases, the characteristics of these populations of elements are designated as parameters. Thus, the average age of all Alabama State Penitentiary inmates is a **parameter.** The average caseload of all Illinois probation officers is a parameter. And the average height of juvenile delinquents in Las Vegas, Nevada, is also a parameter or population characteristic. We want to know about these and other characteristics or parameters of these populations.

But because of the sheer magnitude of these populations, it is frequently difficult for researchers to study all of the population elements. We can appreciate this difficulty more easily by imagining what our task would involve if we wanted to study all probation officers or juvenile delinquents or inmates in the entire United States! Imagine the time, money, and person power it would require to complete this task. However, our task of studying these populations is greatly simplified if we are less ambitious and choose to study only samples of elements taken from these populations.

Samples and Statistics

Samples are proportions or smaller collections of elements taken from the larger population of them. Using the population examples above, samples of them would be (1) a sample of all Alabama State Penitentiary inmates, (2) a sample of all Illinois probation officers, and (3) a sample of all Las Vegas, Nevada, juvenile delinquents. If the Alabama State Penitentiary inmate population consists of 1,200 inmates, we might study 200 of these inmates as our sample of elements. The characteristics of our inmate sample would be designated as **statistics.** Statistics are characteristics of samples of elements taken from a population of them. Some sample statistics might be the average age of a sample of Las Vegas, Nevada, juvenile delinquents or the average caseload of a sample of Illinois probation officers. Table 4.1 illustrates the population–sample relation.

Generalizability and Representativeness

A prevalent concern of researchers who study samples of elements rather than entire populations of them is whether their samples are representative of those populations. Can investigators make generalizations about populations of elements by only studying samples of them? How do we know if our samples are representative of the populations from which they were taken? As long as we study samples of elements rather than entire populations, we will never know if our samples are representative of those populations.

Generally, sample **representativeness** is assumed or implied, depending on how the sample is selected and its size in relation to the population. If we must choose between two samples of different sizes that have both been selected using the same sampling procedure, the larger sample would be assumed to be more representative of the population than the smaller sample. If different types of sampling procedures were used, however, we could not make this statement about the two samples, regardless of their different sizes.

Thus, **sample size** alone does not make a sample representative of its population. For instance, if we wanted to generalize about all incarcerated adult offenders in the United

TABLE 4.1   **The Distinction between a Population and a Sample**

Population (100%)	Sample (20%)
(1) All Alabama State Penitentiary inmates	(1) Some Alabama State Penitentiary inmates
(2) All Illinois probation officers	(2) Some Illinois probation officers
(3) All Las Vegas, Nevada, juvenile delinquents	(3) Some Las Vegas, Nevada, juvenile delinquents
Some Characteristics of Elements	
(1) The average age of all inmates in the Alabama State Penitentiary	(1) The average age of the sample of inmates in the Alabama State Penitentiary
(2) The average caseload of all Illinois probation officers	(2) The average caseload of the sample of Illinois probation officers
(3) The male/female proportion of all Las Vegas, Nevada, juvenile delinquents	(3) The male/female proportion of the sample of Las Vegas, Nevada, juvenile delinquents

States, but if we select a sample of 20,000 offenders from half of all U.S. maximum-security penitentiaries only, we would have no inmate representation from jails (facilities that house short-term or less serious offenders) or other, less secure incarcerative facilities. Although quite large, our sample of prison inmates would not be representative of all adult inmates, since only the most serious and long-term offenders would be included in our sample, and all short-termers in jails or less serious offenders housed in medium- or minimum-security facilities would be excluded.

In another hypothetical research situation, suppose that investigators may have responses from 350 out of 375 inmates of a particular prison. If the investigators want to generalize only to the inmates of that prison, then the sample size of 350 is considered quite large for such generalizing purposes. Over 90 percent of all inmates have been obtained. However, what if the researcher wants to use the sample of 350 inmates and generalize to all inmates of all U.S. prisons? Because of the dramatic shift from the population of a single prison to the population of all U.S. prisons, the sample of 350 inmates cannot be used as the basis for generalizations about all U.S. prison inmates.

In a study of a day reporting center, Martin and colleagues (2003) wanted to assess the impact of a day reporting center in Cook County, Illinois, on clients for a given year, and whether the day reporting center experiences and treatments received by clients would cause their recidivism to decline. These researchers selected 1995 as the target year to enable them to track or follow up on clients to see whether they recidivated after participating in the day reporting experience. They started out with the entire 1,391 clients who were assigned to the day reporting center and attempted to track them for the next several years. Over time, some clients moved away from that jurisdiction, some died, others absconded. Ultimately these researchers had a large portion of the original 1,391 clients, but they did not have all of them. Once they analyzed the data collected, they could generalize about the effects on day reporting center clients for 1995, but they had no way of determining whether these effects were consistent for subsequent or prior years. Their generalizations were limited to those clients from the 1995 aggregate. And since not all of these clients were included in their final tabulations, their generalizations were affected accordingly. Their research was important nevertheless, because it provided us with one snapshot of the influence of a single day reporting center on a fairly large number of clients. Together with other studies of day reporting center clients from other jurisdictions, this information would be valuable in formulating opinions about day reporting centers in general, and whether such services were worthwhile in rehabilitating offenders.

Therefore, answers to questions about the representativeness and generalizability of one's sample on the basis of its size are relative. Much depends on what the researcher wants to do with the results and how large the sample is in relation to the population from which it was drawn. Sometimes samples are narrowly defined and encompass only a small fraction of the persons about which one seeks information. We must learn to identify the limitations of various sampling plans and adjust our generalizations about populations of elements accordingly. No sample, regardless of its size, is considered ideal for our generalizations in any absolute sense.

The Decision to Sample

When the research design has been formulated, decisions have usually been made whether or not to include elements. An analysis of the current literature in criminal justice and criminology shows that much of it describes data collected from samples. The decision to sample is made according to at least three criteria: (1) the size of the target population, (2) the cost of obtaining the elements, and (3) the convenience and accessibility of the elements.

Size of the Target Population

How large is the target population? The target population is the one about which researchers seek information. If researchers want to study the effectiveness of defense counsels in criminal cases, for instance, their target population might be all licensed criminal lawyers in the United States or all criminal defense counsel who are members of the American Bar Association. Perhaps the investigator wishes to study how AIDS inmates are segregated and treated in prisons and jails. Maybe the project is focused on the amount of knowledge correctional officers have about their legal liabilities in their interactions with inmates. These are fairly large populations, and it would be a demanding task to study all of these elements, even if they could be identified and contacted. Bureaus of social research, survey research centers, and most other large-scale public or private research organizations have the resources to conduct research projects on a grandiose scale. Nevertheless, even these large bureaus with extensive resources limit the scope of their inquiry to samples of elements rather than entire populations. However, most independent researchers must engage in small-scale studies with limited funds, unless one's project is funded by the Department of Justice, Bureau of Justice Statistics, or some other public or private funding agency.

Cost of Obtaining the Elements

How much money is available for the study? The cheapest ways of collecting data include observing others or going to libraries and analyzing information from surveys and reports. These are considered secondary sources. The *Uniform Crime Reports, National Crime Victimization Survey,* or the *Sourcebook of Criminal Justice Statistics* contain much information about crime and criminals. Another excellent source of data relevant to crime and the criminal justice system is the National Archive of Criminal Justice Data, which is funded by the Bureau of Justice Statistics, U.S. Department of Justice and operated by the Inter-University Consortium for Political and Social Research headquartered in Ann Arbor, Michigan. Working through universities and colleges, professors, students, and others may access all types of information, including data sets, surveys, and statistical compilations about runaways, truants, prison and jail inmates, judicial decision guidelines, career offender characteristics, national crime figures, and correctional facility censuses. Nominal fees are charged for such services, which have been converted into computer-readable formats.

Convenience and Accessibility of the Elements

Consideration must be given to the convenience and accessibility of elements to be studied. Students are frequently used for research purposes, primarily because researchers are often professors who teach large university classes. It is easy to distribute questionnaires to large numbers of students and ask them their opinions about diverse issues. Thus, student samples enable investigators to collect large amounts of information from captive audiences seated in one place at a given time. But student audiences are not typical of the general population in many respects. Their educational level sets them apart from the general population. Also, they come from diverse places. Investigators may have a great deal of information about students, but what generalizations can be made from such information? What population is described based on large numbers of student responses?

If someone wishes to interview HIV-positive inmates in prisons and how they are treated, permission must first be obtained from the wardens or superintendents of those facilities. Then, the consent of HIV-infected inmates is also required. Wardens and superintendents of prisons may not grant researchers permission to carry out their study. Even if they did, there are no guarantees that HIV-infected inmates would consent to being studied. The best research plans may be devised, but they may never be implemented, simply because of the inaccessibility of the target population.

Therefore, decisions to sample are based, in part, on the size of the population, the anticipated cost of the study in relation to the budget of the researcher, and the convenience and accessibility associated with obtaining the elements. Other factors are involved in this decision as well. Some of these factors are in a latter portion of the chapter.

Some Functions of Sampling

The functions of sampling include: (1) economizing resources, (2) manageability, (3) meeting assumptions of statistical tests, and (4) meeting the requirements of experiments.

Economizing Resources

Sampling saves researchers time, money, and person power. Fewer elements are selected, less expense is incurred as the result of sending fewer questionnaires to respondents or interviewing fewer of them, and fewer assistants are necessary to help perform these necessary chores.

Manageability

Sampling helps to make data tabulation and analysis more manageable. It is easier to tabulate information from smaller numbers of elements. Also, many statistics programs for personal computers have data limitations, where the number of variables is restricted and smaller sample sizes are recommended. But small numbers of variables and sample sizes are not necessarily small. One computer program may prescribe, "This program may only be used for data sets with 40 or fewer variables and sample sizes of 1,200 or less." This statement covers 99 percent of all research projects conducted by criminologists and criminal justice professionals. Much of the time, samples analyzed in the current literature (e.g., articles, reports) contain 500 or fewer elements.

Meeting Assumptions of Statistical Tests

Certain assumptions associated with statistical test applications must be satisfied. **Probability sampling** is a requirement of all statistical procedures involved in statistical inference and decision making. Other assumptions must be satisfied as well, besides the probability sampling requirement. The importance of meeting the assumptions is that meaningful and valid interpretations of test results can be made only if these assumptions are fulfilled.

Also, each statistical test and measure of association has a "recommended sample size range" where optimum sample sizes are specified. Some procedures are designed for small samples, where "small" means 12 persons or less. Other procedures prescribe a range from 25 to 250 persons for optimum application. Applying these statistical tests outside of these sample ranges may be done, but the reliability and dependability of these tests is adversely affected. We cannot be sure of what the numerical test results mean under these less-than-optimum conditions. While this book is not going to explore statistical tests and their application, it is important to understand that one's sampling plan influences one's statistical test choices, and in several very important ways. The statistical results one achieves may be meaningless if the proper type of sampling plan is not used initially, or if the sample sizes obtained do not fit the requirements of certain statistical procedures.

Meeting the Requirements of Experiments

Certain types of research experimentation require that the samples obtained must be of specified sizes. In some experimental situations, several samples of elements must be obtained. A requirement of an experiment might be that the samples should be of equal size and that they share other characteristics or similarities. For instance, these sample similarities may be equivalent proportions of males and females, equivalent proportions of different offense categories, or equivalent proportions of years on the job, depending on the target population being investigated. Specialized statistical procedures have been devised to analyze these unusual experimental situations as well.

Probability Sampling Plans

Probability sampling plans are those that specify the probability or likelihood of inclusion of each element drawn from a designated population. Technically, the following facts need to be known by the researcher in advance of selecting the sample:

1. The size of the target population or universe from which the sample will be obtained must be known. (The term *universe* is used interchangeably with population, since it refers to all persons about which one seeks information.)
2. The desired sample size must be specified.
3. Each element in the population or universe of elements must have an equal and an independent chance of being drawn and included in the sample.

Symbolically, when comparisons of population and sample sizes are made, *N* is the actual population size, while *n* is the desired sample size. A **sampling fraction** can be determined by *n/N*. If the sample size is 10 and the population size is 100, the sampling fraction is 1/10th or .10. A sample that makes up 10 percent of its population is generally considered ideal. Under many conditions, these ideal criteria can be invoked. However, much smaller sampling fractions may be used if the population of elements about which one seeks information is quite large. A population of 100,000 would ideally require a sample size of 10,000. However, it may be impractical, too costly, and cumbersome to obtain 10,000 elements. Thus, a sample of 500 may be used instead. This means that the sampling fraction will be 500/100,000 or .005, far from ideal. But a sample size of 500 may be adequate for the researcher's purposes. And it is affordable.

An example illustrating different sampling fractions for several different samples of elements from the research literature is the work of Robert A. Shearer (2003) who wanted to measure the special needs of female inmates. Many female inmates have substance abuse problems, dependent children, poor parenting skills, low self-esteem, and other problems. Shearer wanted to devise a measure of female inmate needs in order to determine special programming requirements for different inmates. He created the Female Offender Critical Intervention Inventory (FOCII) and sought to empirically test it with several samples of female inmates. Shearer decided to obtain four groups of female inmates from four different prison or jail units in a southwestern state. His four groups of female inmates consisted of 52 female offenders taken from a state jail, which contained 900 offenders. His second sample consisted of 52 females from a substance abuse felony facility that housed 270 female offenders. His third group consisted of 52 females from a 460-woman therapeutic community facility. And his fourth group consisted of 32 female offenders from a prison unit containing 2,144 inmates. Thus, his sampling fractions were 52/900 = .06, 52/270 = .19, 52/460 = .11, and 32/2,144 = .01. With the exception of the second and third samples, his sampling fractions were well below the ideal recommended sampling fraction of .10. Nevertheless, his samples of 52, 52, 52, and 32 were compared according to their scores on the FOCII.

All participants were selected by directors of the substance programs based on their avail-ability at the time of his testing. One result of his research was the potential utility of using his FOCII for determining female offender needs. From this determination, client-specific programming could be done in order to meet female inmate needs more effectively.

It is instructive to know what Shearer said about his own findings and their general application to other populations of female inmates. Shearer said that his FOCII "appears to be a reliable and valid instrument that can be used for assessing the critical needs of female offenders. Although the results are not definitive, the instrument (FOCII) has shown initial promise as a psychometric tool" (2003, p. 49). Thus, Shearer used very conservative lan-guage when citing the benefits of his research and the applicability of the FOCII for other female inmate populations. This caution is commendable and strongly recommended in any criminological research. At no time did Shearer say, for instance, that "My study has proved the worth of the FOCII for measuring female inmate needs," or "I have conclusively demon-strated the reliability and validity of the FOCII for needs assessments." These statements would have been unwarranted. One statement he made is worth repeating: "The results are not definitive." No study results of any research project are ever definitive. This is an im-portant caveat to remember when engaging in sampling of any kind.

Some populations of elements are more elusive and cannot be enumerated easily, if at all. Studies of the parental characteristics of abused children are difficult to conduct, since child abuse is infrequently reported. Even if it is reported, many cases are not handled by courts, but rather by referrals to social welfare agencies. Prostitution and illegal gambling are other phenomena that are difficult to study, since the incidence or extent of these activ-ities is largely hidden or unknown. Even if we know about the target population and where it can be located, there may be serious logistical problems encountered when attempting to sample from it. Knowing about the population of all jail inmates in the United States is the-oretically possible, but our attempt to enumerate them would be frustrated by the fact that this population changes daily through admissions and releases.

A practical approach is best for dealing with large populations of elements. We will scale down our target population to a more manageable level. If we wish to study inmates, correctional officers, or juvenile delinquents, we can limit the scope of our investigation to a particular jurisdiction, such as a state, county, city, or suburb. Even if these smaller populations of elements do not include everyone, we can nevertheless conduct meaning-ful research and suggest to others that our findings are potentially generalizable to other settings. Researchers will often make qualifying remarks or statements in their work that highlight deficiencies in the target population or problems that occurred in the selection of sample elements.

Natural conditions may exist that limit the population's magnitude. For example, Meadows and Trostle (1988) studied police misconduct in the Los Angeles (CA) Police De-partment for the years 1974–1986. They wanted to describe the nature of the misconduct al-leged as well as the legal outcome. The city attorney's office permitted them to examine 79 closed cases during that time interval. From their research report, it is unknown whether these 79 cases represented a small or large proportion of the total number of police mis-conduct cases handled by the city attorney's office between 1974 and 1986. Under these cir-cumstances, the researchers had no alternative but to label their sample "nonprobability," since it was not possible to enumerate all cases from which their sample was obtained.

BOX 4.1 PERSONALITY HIGHLIGHT

PAMELA TONTODONATO
Kent State University

Statistics: B.A. (sociology and criminology),
University of Maryland; M.A., Ph.D. (criminology),
University of Pennsylvania.

BACKGROUND AND INTERESTS

My interests are juvenile delinquency, research methods and statistics, and victimology. I started out at the University of Maryland (College Park) majoring in sociology. I enjoyed it but found the lack of focus in the curriculum somewhat troubling. I knew a little bit about different parts of the field, but not a lot about any one area. I wanted to learn more in-depth about certain issues, like crime and deviance. I picked up a psychology minor and a second major in criminology. I knew that I had made the right decision as I enjoyed the courses and did well in them. As I got close to graduating, I thought about what I wanted to do for a living. I had no thought or idea until then of ever going to graduate school or even being a college professor! I considered my options using the process of elimination and decided to try to get my master's degree. I went to my professors and the graduate students I had as instructors for advice. They recommended some programs to me. I earned good grades and had my pick of graduate programs. I chose the University of Pennsylvania in Philadelphia.

During my studies in graduate school, I had the privilege of studying with Marvin E. Wolfgang. I developed interests in criminological theory, quantitative methods, and juvenile delinquency. As a graduate student I participated in the day-to-day activities involved in doing research—collecting records, coding data, and computer programming/data analysis. The actual process of doing research was very interesting, and much less dry than learning about methods and statistics from a book. I saw the relevance of what I was learning in the classroom and understood that this knowledge is a tool to help us to study crime, criminals, and the justice system in a scientific way.

RESEARCH INVESTIGATIONS

My research interests lie in the areas of juvenile delinquency, quantitative methods, program evaluation, and victimology. I have published works on event history analysis, crime victims and their experiences with the justice system, and sexual harassment in the criminal justice system,

BOX 4.1 CONTINUED

just to name a few. I hope to continue to work in these areas in the future. I also have coauthored a reader on research methods in criminal justice. Currently, I am focusing on individual predictors of crime and violence using longitudinal data. I have been active recently in some university-related research involving our criminal justice students. I also work with a local corrections agency to help them with research issues and serve in the same capacity for several state agencies.

The good points of researching in criminal justice include the many opportunities in the field to do research, to study unexplored and underexplored topics. There is a need for good researchers to collect and analyze data. Most people in the field are helpful and cooperative, and the issues involved are very important. On the downside, there is still the problem of establishing good relationships with practitioners and the need to improve the quality of the data available. We have many good ideas about what to study and how to study it, but sometimes the information is not collected or easy to measure. We need more planning and foresight in setting up programs in part to facilitate useful information in the evaluation stage. Researchers need to demonstrate the utility of their work to policymakers and practitioners.

ADVICE TO STUDENTS

Although every student's situation is different, I would suggest trying to get good grades, especially in classes like methods and statistics. You may never think you will want to go to graduate school, or do research, but I see many cases where due to lack of foresight, those options are excluded. There are many students who want to return to school to pursue advanced study, but who can't because of weak undergraduate performance. Furthermore, you may think you will never "use this stuff," but you may be surprised. Some of what you learn in these types of classes is very helpful when you work in the field. I would suggest getting involved in a research project with one of your professors. The research "bug" may bite you. In terms of issues involved in doing research in the field, I would note that training and expertise aren't everything. You need good people skills and the ability to make connections with criminal justice groups and agencies. If you work at an agency rather than in an academic setting, there are many opportunities for collaboration with university researchers.

In another study, Walters (1988) wanted to examine correctional officers' perceptions of powerlessness in their work. Powerlessness was defined as the probability that individuals could not determine the occurrences or outcomes they seek. Walters wanted to know if powerlessness was perceived by correctional officers, and whether powerlessness was the result of specific environmental factors and self-concepts. Walters identified a large prison in the "Intermountain West." The facility housed 750 inmates and employed 193 correctional officers. Walters sent questionnaires to all 193 officers, but only 126 completed questionnaires were returned for a 65 percent response rate. In this study, no attempt was made to enumerate all of the officers. Rather, the entire population of 193 was targeted, although only two-thirds responded. Two-thirds of the population of officers is a rather large proportion under these circumstances. Despite this large proportion of responses, the sample cannot be considered as a **probability sample.** The reasons for officer nonresponse are unknown, but Walters's results may have been quite different had some or all of these nonrespondents actually responded and returned their completed questionnaires.

Some studies are conducted where it is impossible to identify the target population. In these cases, researchers must settle for a microcosm of the population, and there may even be additional limitations. For instance, Charisse Coston and Lee Ross (1996) studied a sample of female prostitutes and streetwalkers who had been arrested for soliciting in a large city in the East. These investigators wanted to know about the nature and extent of victimization occurring among these women who were considered high risks as crime victims. Coston and Ross identified 77 women who had been arrested and attempted to interview all of them. Eighteen women refused to be interviewed, leaving the authors with only 59 women. Thus, 59 30-minute interviews were conducted with a sample of their original sample of 77 prostitutes. Compared with the study by Walters where the entire population of prison correctional officers was known, Coston and Ross were dealing with only a small number of prostitutes in a single city. Their sample was not random, and the authors could not say with certainty what population these prostitutes were from. These limitations did not detract from the fact that Coston and Ross were able to generate much informative data about prostitute victimization.

Finally, a study by Jacqueline Helfgott (1997) of ex-offender needs versus community opportunity was conducted in Seattle, Washington. Helfgott wanted to know about ex-offender needs in Seattle, what employment and service opportunities existed for them, and what could be done locally to maximize their opportunities. Ex-offender needs included food, clothing, housing, transportation, mental health counseling, medical and dental care, legal assistance, employment, and social relationships. Her research targeted 326 community transition agencies, 500 employers, 500 property managers, 22 educational institutions, and 1,440 community residents drawn from a Seattle telephone directory.

All of these agencies and persons were drawn at random from various directories and listings. Helfgott didn't obtain the cooperation of everyone she contacted. Her sample results were as follows: 56 out of 326 community transition agencies (17 percent); 156 out of 500 employers (31.2 percent); 196 out of 500 property managers (39.2 percent); 22 out of 22 educational institutions (100 percent); and 306 out of 1,440 community residents (21.2 percent). She also obtained the cooperation and involvement of 20 out of 40 ex-offenders, a 50 percent response. Thus, in just about every category she targeted, Helfgott only obtained a portion of those she sought to include. While her subsequent investigation of the participants yielded much valuable information about how the community could assist ex-offenders in meeting their diverse needs, it was virtually impossible for Helfgott to say with certainty that her findings typified any particular population. This says much about the difficulty of acquiring a probability sampling plan despite our best efforts to do so.

Randomness

The crucial features of probability sampling plans have to do with the **equality of draw** and **independence of draw** or selecting elements for inclusion in our samples. Actually, equality and independence are essential defining characteristics of randomness, which is the process of selecting elements such that each element has an equal and independent chance of being included. **Randomness** is the primary control governing all **probability sampling plans.** Equality of draw refers to giving all population elements an equal chance of being included in the sample. Independence means that the draw or selection of one element will not affect the chances of the remaining elements of being drawn later.

Equality of Draw.   Equality of draw is simply illustrated by the following hypothetical example. Suppose we were studying defense attorneys in Detroit, Michigan. Our records might show that there are 2,000 defense attorneys in Detroit. We will use a sampling method that will give each of these 2,000 attorneys 1/2,000th of a chance of being included in our sample *n*. If our population $N = 50,000$, then everyone should have 1/50,000th of a chance of being included. If our population N were 100, then everyone would have 1/100th of a chance of being included. This is what is meant by giving everyone in the population an equal chance of being included.

Independence of the Draw.   Independence of draw means that the draw of any particular element will not influence the chances of other population elements of being included in the sample. An example known as the **fishbowl draw** will be used to illustrate what is meant by independence. First, all elements in the population are enumerated from 1 to N. Second, their numbers are placed on identical slips of paper. Next, these slips are placed in a fishbowl. Next, someone who is blindfolded reaches into the bowl and selects slips of paper, one at a time. Then the numbers are recorded, and those persons matching the numbers become a part of our sample.

Suppose our target population consists of 100 elements. We number each person from 1 to 100, write these numbers on slips of paper, and place them all in a fishbowl. After mixing the slips of paper in the bowl, we reach in, blindfolded, and select the first slip of paper. Our first selection is a random one, since all element numbers were in the bowl and each had 1/100th of a chance of being included on the first draw. However, we have withdrawn one slip of paper. That leaves 99 pieces of paper in the bowl. The next time we dip into the bowl to retrieve a slip of paper, the remaining elements will have 1/99th of a chance of being included in our sample. Thus, continuous draws of slips of paper from the bowl will slightly increase the chances of the remaining elements of being included (e.g., 1/98th, 1/97th, 1/96th, and so on). These are not independent draws, since the chances of the remaining elements of being included in our sample are increased each time a slip of paper is removed from the bowl. Therefore, we will not have a **random sample** using this method.

What if we replace the slips of paper once we have drawn them? This way, there would always be 100 slips of paper in the bowl, and each person would have 1/100th of a chance of being drawn each time. Actually, this is an appropriate strategy for ensuring both independence and equality of draw, and it has been given a name by statisticians: **sampling with replacement.** The earlier method of withholding slips of paper from the bowl, once we have selected and recorded them, also has a name: **sampling without replacement.** In the social sciences, all probability sampling plans as well as all of the statistical tests used that require probability samples as one of their requisite assumptions assume that sampling with replacement has been used.

However, when sampling with replacement is used, some of us are going to worry about drawing slips of paper from the bowl that have been drawn before. Under these circumstances, the best procedure is to continue drawing slips of paper from the bowl, with replacement, until *n* desired elements are obtained. Simply skip or ignore those numbers that have already been drawn, replace them in the fishbowl, and continue to draw slips until you have selected *n* different numbers. Better procedures are available for selecting random samples of elements other than the fishbowl draw. We can obtain randomness by using either a table of **random numbers** or a computer-determined draw.

Simple Random Sampling and Random Numbers Tables

A **table of random numbers** is almost exactly the way it sounds. It is a table of digits randomly derived, where no digit occurs in any particular sequence and no digit occurs any more frequently than any other digit. Table 4.2 is a table of random numbers.

Examine Table 4.2 and observe that digits have been bunched up into groups of five rows and five columns, with spaces above and below, as well as on either side of, these bunches. There is no significance attached to these particular groupings. The blank spaces between the bunches of digits are simply for reading ease. Imagine what this table would look like if all of these bunches of digits were pushed together toward the centers of the pages. Below is a reproduced segment of the first page of Table 4.2, specifically the two bunches of digit groupings in the upper left-hand corner on page 163.

10097   32533
37542   04805
08422   68953
99019   02529
12807   99970

We use this table as follows. First, we identify our target population. Suppose it is an inmate population at the Colorado State Penitentiary. Suppose the population of inmates is $N = 850$. Suppose we wish to draw a sample *n* of 50 from this population of 850. We will first assign these inmates numbers from 001 to 850, and then we will select 50 different random numbers from Table 3.2. We begin this task by counting the number of digits in our population N, or three digits: 8, 5, and 0. We will move through this table in a systematic fashion, examining groupings of three digits each. Let's decide to start our selection of sample elements with the first three digits shown in the upper left-hand corner of page 163. These are the digit groupings reproduced above for your convenience. Let's record the first three digits, 1, 0, and 0. For our purposes, this is inmate #100. Moving directly downward in the table, we pick up the next three digits immediately below 100, or 375. This is inmate #375. Continuing to move downward toward the bottom of the table, we select 084 or inmate #84, then 990, the 990th inmate, and 128, the 128th inmate. Did you just sense something wrong? Yes. The "990th inmate" doesn't exist, since our population size extends only to 850 inmates. Therefore, we skip or ignore all inmate numbers that don't fit the limits of our population.

When we reach the bottom of page 163, our last three-digit grouping is 186 or inmate #186. Where do we go from here? We go back to the top of the page, almost where we started initially. But now, we will move over to the right precisely one digit, and then pick up the next

TABLE 4.2   Random Numbers

10097	32533	76520	13586	34673	54876	80959	09117	39292	74945
37542	04805	64894	74296	24805	24037	20636	10402	00822	91665
08422	68953	19645	09303	23209	02560	15953	34764	35080	33606
99019	02529	09376	70715	38311	31165	88676	74397	04436	27659
12807	99970	80157	36147	64032	36653	98951	16877	12171	76833
66065	74717	34072	76850	36697	36170	65813	39885	11199	29170
31060	10805	45571	82406	35303	42614	86799	07439	23403	09732
85269	77602	02051	65692	68665	74818	73053	85247	18623	88579
63573	32135	05325	47048	90553	57548	28468	28709	83491	25624
73796	45753	03529	64778	35808	34282	60935	20344	35273	88435
98520	17767	14905	68607	22109	40558	60970	93433	50500	73998
11805	05431	39808	27732	50725	68248	29405	24201	52775	67851
83452	99634	06288	98083	13746	70078	18475	40610	68711	77817
88685	40200	86507	58401	36766	67951	90364	76493	29609	11062
99594	67348	87517	64969	91826	08928	93785	61368	23478	34113
65481	17674	17468	50950	58047	76974	73039	57186	40218	16544
80124	35635	17727	08015	45318	22374	21115	78253	14385	53763
74350	99817	77402	77214	43236	00210	45521	64237	96286	02655
69916	26803	66252	29148	36936	87203	76621	13990	94400	56418
09893	20505	14225	68514	46427	56788	96297	78822	54382	14598
91499	14523	68479	27686	46162	83554	94750	89923	37089	20048
80336	94598	26940	36858	70297	34135	53140	33340	42050	82341
44104	81949	85157	47954	32979	26575	57600	40881	22222	06413
12550	73742	11100	02040	12860	74697	96644	89439	28707	25815
63606	49329	16505	34484	40219	52563	43651	77082	07207	31790
61196	90446	26457	47774	51924	33729	65394	59593	42582	60527
15474	45266	95270	79953	59367	83848	82396	10118	33211	59466
94557	28573	67897	54387	54622	44431	91190	42592	92927	45973
42481	16213	97344	08721	16868	48767	03071	12059	25701	46670
23523	78317	73208	89837	68935	91416	26252	29663	05522	82562
04493	52494	75246	33824	45862	51025	61962	79335	65337	12472
00549	97654	64051	88159	96119	63896	54692	82391	23287	29529
35963	15307	26898	09354	33351	35462	77974	50024	90103	39333
59808	08391	45427	26842	83609	49700	13021	24892	78565	20106
46058	85236	01390	92286	77281	44077	93910	83647	70617	42941
32179	00597	87379	25241	05567	07007	86743	17157	85394	11838
69234	61406	20117	45204	15956	60000	18743	92423	97118	96338
19565	41430	01758	75379	40419	21585	66674	36806	84962	85207
45155	14938	19476	07246	43667	94543	59047	90033	20826	69541
94864	31994	36168	10851	34888	81553	01540	35456	05014	51176
98086	24826	45240	28404	44999	08896	39094	73407	35441	31880
33185	16232	41941	50949	89435	48581	88695	41994	37548	73043
80951	00406	96382	70774	20151	23387	25016	25298	94624	61171
79752	49140	71961	28296	69861	02591	74852	20539	00387	59579
18633	32537	98145	06571	31010	24674	05455	61427	77938	91936

TABLE 4.2 Random Numbers (*continued*)

74029	43902	77557	32270	97790	17119	52527	58021	80814	51748
54178	45611	80993	37143	05335	12969	56127	19255	36040	90324
11664	49883	52079	84827	59381	71539	09973	33440	88461	23356
48324	77928	31249	64710	02295	36870	32307	57546	15020	09994
69074	94138	87637	91976	35584	04401	10518	21615	01848	76938
09188	20097	32825	39527	04220	86304	83389	87374	64278	58044
90045	85497	51981	50654	94938	81997	91870	76150	68476	64659
73189	50207	47677	26269	62290	64464	27124	67018	41361	82760
75768	76490	20971	87749	90429	12272	95375	05871	93823	43178
54016	44056	66281	31003	00682	27398	20714	53295	07706	17813
08358	69910	78542	42785	13661	58873	04618	97553	31223	08420
28306	03264	81333	10591	40510	07893	32604	60475	94119	01840
53840	86233	81594	13628	51215	90290	28466	68795	77762	20791
91757	53741	61613	62269	50263	90212	55781	76514	83483	47055
89415	92694	00397	58391	12607	17646	48949	72306	94541	37408
77513	03820	86864	29901	68414	82774	51908	13980	72893	55507
19502	37174	69979	20288	55210	29773	74287	75251	65344	67415
21818	59313	93278	81757	05686	73156	07082	85046	31853	38452
51474	66499	68107	23621	94049	91345	42836	09191	08007	45449
99559	68331	62535	24170	69777	12830	74819	78142	43860	72834
33713	48007	93584	72869	51926	64721	58303	29822	93174	93972
85274	86893	11303	22970	28834	34137	73515	90400	71148	43643
84133	89640	44035	52166	73852	70091	61222	60561	62327	18423
56732	16234	17395	96131	10123	91622	85496	57560	81604	18880
65138	56806	87648	85261	34313	65861	45875	21069	85644	47277
38001	02176	81719	11711	71602	92937	74219	64049	65584	49698
37402	96397	01304	77586	56271	10086	47324	62605	40030	37438
97125	40348	87083	31417	21815	39250	75237	62047	15501	29578
21826	41134	47143	34072	64638	85902	49139	06441	03856	54552
73135	42742	95719	09035	85794	74296	08789	88156	64691	19202
07638	77929	03061	18072	96207	44156	23821	99538	04713	66994
60528	83441	07954	19814	59175	20695	05533	52139	61212	06455
83596	35655	06958	92983	05128	09719	77433	53783	92301	50498
10850	62746	99599	10507	13499	06319	53075	71839	06410	19362
39820	98952	43622	63147	64421	80814	43800	09351	31024	73167
59580	06478	75569	78800	88835	54486	23768	06156	04111	08408
38508	07341	23793	48763	90822	97022	17719	04207	95954	49953
30692	70668	94688	16127	56196	80091	82067	63400	05462	69200
65443	95659	18288	27437	49632	24041	08337	65676	96299	90836
27267	50264	13192	72294	07477	44606	17985	48911	97341	30358
91307	06991	19072	24210	36699	53728	28825	35793	28976	66252
68434	94688	84473	13622	62126	98408	12843	82590	09815	93146
48908	15877	54745	24591	35700	04754	83824	52692	54130	55160
06913	45197	42672	78601	11883	09528	63011	98901	14974	40344
10455	16019	14210	33712	91342	37821	88325	80851	43667	70883

TABLE 4.2   Random Numbers   (*continued*)

12883	97343	65027	61184	04285	01392	17974	15077	90712	26769
21778	30976	38807	36961	31649	42096	63281	02023	08816	47449
19523	59515	65122	59659	86283	68258	69572	13798	16435	91529
67245	52670	35583	16563	79246	86686	76463	34222	26655	90802
60584	47377	07500	37992	45134	26529	26760	83637	41326	44344
53853	41377	36066	94850	58838	73859	49364	73331	96240	43642
24637	38736	74384	89342	52623	07992	12369	18601	03742	83873
83080	12451	38992	22815	07759	51777	97377	27585	51972	37867
16444	24334	36151	99073	27493	70939	85130	32552	54846	54759
60790	18157	57178	65762	11161	78576	45819	52979	65130	04860
03991	10461	93716	16894	66083	24653	84609	58232	88618	19161
38555	95554	32886	59780	08355	60860	29735	47762	71299	23853
17546	73704	92052	46215	55121	29281	59076	07936	27954	58909
32643	52861	95819	06831	00911	98936	76355	93779	80863	00514
69572	68777	39510	35905	14060	40619	29549	69616	33564	60780
24122	66591	27699	06494	14845	46672	61958	77100	90899	75754
61196	30231	92962	61773	41839	55382	17267	70943	78038	70267
30532	21704	10274	12202	39685	23309	10061	68829	55986	66485
03788	97599	75867	20717	74416	53166	35208	33374	87539	08823
48228	63379	85783	47619	53152	67433	35663	52972	16818	60311
60365	94653	35075	33949	42614	29297	01918	28316	98953	73231
83799	42402	56623	34442	34994	41374	70071	14736	09958	18065
32960	07405	36409	83232	99385	41600	11133	07586	15917	06253
19322	53845	57620	52606	66497	68646	78138	66559	19640	99413
11220	94747	07399	37408	48509	23929	27482	45476	85244	35159
31751	57260	68980	05339	15470	48355	88651	22596	03152	19121
88492	99382	14454	04504	20094	98977	74843	93413	22109	78508
30934	47744	07481	83828	73788	06533	28597	20405	94205	20380
22888	48893	27499	98748	60530	45128	74022	84617	82037	10268
78212	16993	35902	91386	44372	15486	65741	14014	87481	37220
41849	84547	46850	52326	34677	58300	74910	64345	19325	81549
46352	33049	69248	93460	45305	07521	61318	31855	14413	70951
11087	96294	14013	31792	59747	67277	76503	34513	39663	77544
52701	08337	56303	87315	16520	69676	11654	99893	02181	68161
57275	36898	81304	48585	68652	27376	92852	55866	88448	03584
20857	73156	70284	24326	79375	95220	01159	63267	10622	48391
15633	84924	90415	93614	33521	26665	55823	47641	86225	31704
92694	48297	39904	02115	59589	49067	66821	41575	49767	04037
77613	19019	88152	00080	20554	91409	96277	48257	50816	97616
38688	32486	45134	63545	59404	72059	43947	51680	43852	59693
25163	01889	70014	15021	41290	67312	71857	15957	68971	11403
65251	07629	37239	33295	05870	01119	92784	26340	18477	65622
36815	43625	18637	37509	82444	99005	04921	73701	14707	93997
64397	11692	05327	82162	20247	81759	45197	25332	83745	22567
04515	25624	95096	67946	48460	85558	15191	18782	16930	33361

TABLE 4.2   Random Numbers   (*continued*)

83761	60873	43253	84145	60833	25983	01291	41349	20368	07126
14387	06345	80854	09279	43529	06318	38384	74761	41196	37480
51321	92246	80088	77074	88722	56736	66164	49431	66919	31678
72472	00008	80890	18002	94813	31900	54155	83436	35352	54131
05466	55306	93128	18464	74457	90561	72848	11834	79982	68416
39528	72484	82474	25593	48545	35247	18619	13674	18611	19241
81616	18711	53342	44276	75122	11724	74627	73707	58319	15997
07586	16120	82641	22820	92904	13141	32392	19763	61199	67940
90767	04235	13574	17200	69902	63742	78464	22501	18627	90872
40188	28193	29593	88627	94972	11598	62095	36787	00441	58997
34414	82157	86887	55087	19152	00023	12302	80783	32624	68691
63439	75363	44989	16822	36024	00867	76378	41605	65961	73488
67049	09070	93399	45547	94458	74284	05041	49807	20288	34060
79495	04146	52162	90286	54158	34243	46978	35482	59362	95938
91704	30552	04737	21031	75051	93029	47665	64382	99782	93478

Source: The Rand Corporation, *A Million Random Digits* (New York: The Free Press, 1955). By permission of the publishers.

three-digit sequence. In this case, it will be 009, or the 9th inmate. The next, moving downward directly, is 754, or inmate #754, 842 or the 842nd inmate, 901 (skip it), 280 or the 280th inmate, and so on, until we reach the bottom of the page again. We repeat this process by moving to the top of the page, moving over precisely one digit, selecting the next three-digit sequence, which is 097 (inmate #97), and move downward again, making our selections. The next time we go back to the top of the page, we will move over to the right again one digit, and pick up the next three digits. In this case, we will pick up 973. The next three-digit groupings below this one in the example above are 420, 226, 190, and 079, respectively. The spacing between groups of digits means nothing, and it is intended only for ease of readability. We continue our selection process until we have identified 50 different random numbers for our desired sample size. By definition, this is a random sample of 50 elements from our population of 850.

Researchers often have access to computer systems with programs capable of generating *n* random numbers from a population of *N* elements through a **computer-determined draw.** This is a computer-determined random sample. In fact, this is precisely how Table 3.2 was generated by the Rand Corporation—by computer. Thus, the computer-determined draw and a draw of elements from a table of random numbers are synonymous.

Simple random samples are samples of size *n* taken from a population size of *N*. An example of simple random sampling is provided in a study by Crouch and Marquart (1990). These researchers were interested in the effects of prison reforms introduced by the Texas Department of Corrections (TDC) during a period of massive court-ordered reforms, 1978–1981. They wanted to know whether significant changes occurred in prison conditions, violence levels, and perceptions of safety among prisoners before, during, and after court-decreed reform implementation. Using TDC-assigned six-digit numbers that identified each inmate, Crouch and Marquart obtained simple random samples of inmates from different prison units, eventually drawing 614 numbers, or about 5 percent of the inmate population. However, 123 inmates were not available when these researchers collected their data. Some were ill, others were on furloughs, and others were in solitary confinement. Thirty of the available inmates refused to participate. Therefore, what started out as an ideally selected random sample of TDC prison inmates eventually dwindled to 461 inmates.

What should we call this sample of a simple random sample? First, the sample is no longer a random sample. Of the 614 inmates originally selected as the simple random sample, 153 inmates were either unavailable or refused to participate (Crouch & Marquart, 1990). This nonresponse represents nearly 25 percent of the original sample of 614 inmates. Who knows what effect this substantial number of inmates would have made had their responses been included in the data analysis.

What happened in Crouch and Marquart's study is what happens in almost any investigation where sampling is involved. These investigators obtained only a portion of the original number of elements they wanted to include. The ideal–real gap between following the ideal rules of sample selection and our resulting sample is most noticeable. In defense of their sample of a random sample, Crouch and Marquart said, "These refusals showed no pattern that would bias the sample" (1990, p. 107). It is assumed from this statement that Crouch and Marquart knew more about those who refused to participate than most researchers often know about nonrespondents. Usually, unless we know what the responses of refusals would have been to our questions, we really have no way of assessing their impact on the final study outcome. The refusals or nonrespondents refused to participate for various reasons, usually unknown to us. This certainly makes them different compared with those who did participate. For all we know, they may have been the hardcore leadership of the Mexican Mafia or Aryan Brotherhood, and their responses to questions about prison violence and inmate safety would have been most enlightening. When confronted with substantial nonresponse or refusals, therefore, it is probably best simply to acknowledge it and not comment about its significance, nonsignificance, or biasing effects. Nonresponse is merely one of several research shortcomings.

Advantages and Disadvantages of Simple Random Sampling Plans.   Simple random sampling plans have the following advantages:

1. All elements in the population are selected randomly, each having an equal and an independent chance of being included. Theoretically, at least, the sample obtained will have a good chance of being representative of the population.

2. This plan is used in conjunction with all other probability sampling plans. It serves as the foundation upon which all types of random samples are based.

3. It is easiest to apply of all probability sampling plans.

4. The true composition of the population does not need to be known in advance. Simple random samples theoretically reflect all important segments of the target population to one degree or another.

5. The amount of **sampling error** can be computed easily. While a more extensive discussion of sampling error will be presented later in this chapter, sampling error is the degree of departure of various sample statistics from their respective population parameters. Ordinarily, larger samples have less sampling error than smaller samples.

The disadvantages of simple random sampling plans are:

1. These plans may not exploit fully the knowledge researchers may have of the target population studied. Sometimes, researchers may know more about certain characteristics of the population that would enable them to draw more representative samples using some alternative probability sampling plan such as a stratified random sample. Simple random sampling ignores these valuable characteristics. For instance, in sampling from a prison inmate population using simple random sampling, suppose there are 20 inmates out of 800 who have AIDS. Unless something is done to provide for the inclusion of AIDS inmates, it is likely that because of their few numbers, they will not be included in the subsequent sample. Again, a stratified random sample would overcome this limitation.
2. Compared with stratified random samples of the same size, there is usually more sampling error in simple random samples. This is because stratified random samples use more information about the population to enhance representativeness, whereas such information is not ordinarily considered under the simple random sampling format.

Stratified Random Sampling

Stratified random sampling plans take into account one or more population characteristics. **Stratification** means to control for one or more variables and ensure their subsequent inclusion in a sample. If we study probation officers and determine from the population of them that 30 percent are nonwhite and 70 percent are white, we can "stratify" on race/ethnicity and ensure that both whites and nonwhites will be included. Furthermore, suppose that 10 percent of the population consists of females. We can stratify on gender as well, and we can ensure that some of the female probation officers will be included in our sample. Thus, **stratifying** means to take one or more variables into account in our sample selections and ensure their inclusion. Two types of stratified random sampling plans are presented here: disproportionate stratified random sampling and proportionate stratified random sampling.

Disproportionate Stratified Random Sampling.   When investigators possess some knowledge concerning the target population, such as its offense characteristics, race, gender, or some other variable, they may select their samples in such a way so that one or more of these characteristics are represented. These types of sampling plans are improvements over simple random sampling, since it is entirely possible when selecting a simple random sample that some of these relevant characteristics will not be included. In order to use **disproportionate stratified random sampling,** researchers divide their population into categories on those variables considered important. Then they select their sample from each of these subcategories.

For example, McShane (1987) studied prison inmates in the Texas Department of Corrections (TDC). She wanted to know whether inmates who are illegal aliens receive differential punishment and more severe punishment compared with nonalien inmates. At the time of her study, McShane found that the TDC had 27 prison units housing 36,653 inmates. About 1,500 of these were alien inmates. Because she wanted a substantial number of alien inmates to compare with nonalien inmates, it would be unlikely using a simple random sampling plan that she would randomly include many alien inmates. She decided to divide the entire inmate population into subpopulations of alien and nonalien. Next, she drew two separate simple random samples, **subsamples,** one from the alien inmate population and one from the nonalien inmate population.

McShane's alien inmate subsample consisted of 590 prisoners, while her nonalien subsample consisted of 603 prisoners. These different subsamples, roughly equivalent in size, were subsequently examined. If McShane had combined these subsamples into one large sample, her overall sample, randomly selected, would be disproportionate in relation to the general inmate population on the alien/nonalien variable. About 1.6 percent of the TDC inmate population consisted of alien inmates. However, her sample was made up of about 50 percent alien inmates. Therefore, these inmates were disproportionately represented or over-represented in her sample. Accordingly, nonalien inmates were underrepresented in the sample, since they made up nearly 99 percent of the TDC inmate population.

While McShane made direct comparisons of the two subsamples of inmates according to various factors such as sentence lengths, good time credit, and status level, she had other investigative options. She could have combined the two subsamples into one large sample of 1,193 (590 + 603 = 1,193) and made other analyses of her data. She would have referred to the combined subsamples as a "disproportionate stratified random sample, stratified according to alien/nonalien inmate status." Using some general figures that roughly parallel those reported by McShane (1987), Table 4.3 illustrates disproportionate stratified random sampling for the TDC inmate population.

Advantages and Disadvantages of Disproportionate Stratified Random Sampling.   The major advantage of disproportionate stratified random sampling is that it enables researchers to guarantee that specific characteristics or important variables that exist in the population will also be represented in their samples. The disadvantages are:

1. This sampling method does not give each of the subpopulations (total alien and total nonalien inmates in the TED population in this case) weight in the sample in accordance with their proportionate weight in the population. In this respect, the resulting sample is less representative of the population. However, an overriding consideration is the guaranteed inclusion of small numbers of elements that possess desired traits or characteristics, so that meaningful comparisons may be made between subsamples.

2. This method requires some in-depth knowledge about the target population in advance. This information is not always available, depending on the target population investigated. In McShane's case, TDC files helped her to determine those belonging in one subpopulation or another so that she could draw simple random samples from them.

TABLE 4.3   **Disproportionate Stratified Random Sampling Illustrated for 36,000 Texas Department of Corrections Inmates, Controlling for Alien/Nonalien Status**

Population (Stratified by Alien/Nonalien Status)		Sampling Method	Sample
Alien inmates	2000 (1.6%)	Simple Random ⟶	600 (50%)
Nonalien inmates	34,000 (98.4%)	Simple Random ⟶	600 (50%)
Totals	36,000(100.0%)		1,200 (100%)

3. Whenever samples are stratified on any variable, there is the possibility that classification errors may arise. In studies of the influence of socioeconomic status (SES) on delinquency, for instance, one's SES and the type of delinquency may be defined according to several broad categorizations. Subpopulations of persons on the SES variable will be identified, as well as subpopulations of juveniles on the delinquency variable. Some of these elements may be improperly assigned to certain categories. A nonviolent property juvenile offender might be misclassified as a violent offender, or persons classified as upper class may really be middle class. Using simple random sampling, however, will minimize errors that may result from misclassifications of elements.

Proportionate Stratified Random Sampling.   The major difference between disproportionate and **proportionate stratified random sampling** plans is that in proportionate plans, stratified characteristics exist in samples in the same proportionate distribution as they exist in the population. In McShane's study of TDC inmates, for example, it would have been easy to sample these inmates proportionately instead of disproportionately. She would have proceeded to identify the two **subpopulations** the same as before, but in the present instance, her interest would be in carrying over the proportionate distribution of alien/nonalien status into her resulting sample. For example, if she knew that 1.6 percent of the 36,000 TDC inmate population were aliens and 98.4 percent were nonaliens, then her sample would be made up of 1.6 percent aliens and 98.4 percent nonaliens. For comparative purposes, let's assume she wanted a large sample of 1,200.

Wishing to preserve the proportionate distribution of alien/nonalien status, she would ensure that 1.6 percent of 1,200 (.016 × 1,200 = 19) or 19 aliens would be included, and 1,181 nonaliens would be included. This would make her resulting sample a "proportionate stratified random sample, controlling for alien/nonalien status." Table 4.4 illustrates this procedure. In each case, McShane would simply calculate how much of her sample should consist of persons exhibiting certain characteristics. Since alien inmates made up 1.6 percent of the population, then her sample of 1,200 should have this proportion included, or (.016)(1,200) = 19. Nineteen of these 1,200 sample elements should be alien inmates, provided that she wanted to have a proportionate stratified random sample, stratified according to alien/nonalien inmate status.

Advantages and Disadvantages of Proportionate Stratified Random Sampling.   The advantages of this sampling method are:

TABLE 4.4   Proportionate Stratified Random Sampling Illustrated for 36,000 Texas Department of Corrections Inmates, Controlling for Alien/Nonalien Status

Population (Stratified) by Alien/Nonalien Status)		Sampling Method	Sample
Alien inmates	2,000	Simple Random ⟶	19 (1.6%)
Nonalien inmates	34,000	Simple Random ⟶	1,181 (98.4%)
Totals	36,000 (100%)		1,200 (100%)

1. Proportionately stratifying a sample on one or more important characteristics enhances the representativeness of the sample in relation to the population.

2. The resulting sample is superior to a simple random sample of the same size as the basis for estimates about population parameters or characteristics.

3. The amount of sampling error in proportionate stratified random samples is generally less compared with that found in simple random samples of the same size. This is because there are more similarities between the sample and the population that have been controlled.

The disadvantages of this sampling method are:

1. The researcher needs to know something in advance about the composition of the population in order to ensure proportionality on one or more characteristics. Like disproportionate stratified random sampling, this information is not always readily available.

2. Compared with simple random sampling, this method is more time-consuming, since subpopulations of elements with certain characteristics must be identified first before random samples can be taken from them.

3. Similar to disproportionate stratified random sampling, stratifying always creates the possibility that misclassifications may occur regarding population element placements in one sample or another. Simple random sampling overcomes misclassification problems.

Area, Cluster, or Multistage Sampling

If we consider that simple, disproportionate, and proportionate stratified random sampling are three different types of probability sampling plans, then **area sampling,** also known as **cluster sampling** or **multistage sampling,** is a fourth type. Area (sometimes areal) sampling is used primarily for the purpose of surveying public opinion about issues within a vast geographical territory, such as a country, state, or city.

Area sampling has its origin in agriculture. Farming experiments were often conducted to determine the effects of various types of fertilizers and soil nutrients as well as various planting methods on crop yield. A map of some specified acreage would be identified, and vertical and horizontal grids would be drawn for the entire area, creating numerous smaller squares or land plots. These squares would be enumerated, and a simple random sample of squares would be obtained by using the table of random numbers. Once the sample of land squares was obtained, the researcher could combine them into one large sample of land squares, calculate crop yield for the aggregate of squares, and compare the yield with the yield of some other aggregate of squares taken from land treated by different nutrients or fertilizers.

Social science applications of this method have been closely connected with public opinion polling and survey designs in field research. Thus, geographical divisions and horizontal and vertical grid lines are designated on a map of some previously identified territory, community, or neighborhood. Squares of smaller portions of territory are formed by the intersecting grid lines. These squares are numbered, and a simple random sample of squares is obtained. These individually selected squares are again criss-crossed with horizontal and vertical grid lines, the resulting squares are numbered, and a simple random sample of territorial squares is again taken from each of the previously drawn squares. This process involves different sampling stages, hence the term *multistage sampling.* This probability sampling method is illustrated in Figure 4.1.

Suppose the geographical territory was a part of the United States as pictured in Figure 4.1. Note that vertical and horizontal grids have been drawn and squares numbered. A simple random sample of these squares is obtained using the table of random numbers that we have already discussed. These squares comprising our initial sample are known as first-stage units. We will subdivide each of these first-stage units or territorial squares as shown, using similar horizontal and vertical grid lines. We will number these resulting squares and take simple random samples of them. We continue this procedure, possibly through a second stage to third-stage units as shown. We then combine all of the third-stage units into one large sample. This becomes our probability sample for a large geographical territory. From here, we identify persons who dwell within the territories of the squares we selected. Perhaps one of our third-stage units is a 6-square-mile area in Kansas.

Five farms are located within this area, as is shown in Figure 6.1. We might send an interviewer to the area to interview the heads of all families living in this cluster of farms, hence the name *cluster sampling.* This saves a lot of interviewer travel time, since interviewers only have to go to a few localities and interview all or most of those who live there.

Numerically, we might begin area sampling by selecting 10 squares from the original grid. Once these 10 squares (first-stage units) have been identified, each is vertically and horizontally criss-crossed again to yield numerous squares, which are numbered. Suppose we take 10 squares at random from each of the first 10. This will give us 100 squares (second-stage units). We can grid these squares with vertical and horizontal lines, thus creating numerous other squares. Of course, these squares are becoming smaller and smaller geographical areas. Taking 10 squares from each of these 100 squares will give us 1,000 squares (third-stage units as shown in Figure 4.1). Then, clusters of elements living in those third-stage units are interviewed or surveyed.

If it occurs that one of these squares is a city block of large apartment buildings in Los Angeles, it might be cost-prohibitive to canvass all persons living in that block of apartments. Perhaps we will interview every 10th family throughout all of these apartment buildings in the block. Actually, this is using systematic sampling (discussed below as a nonprobability sampling plan) with a probability sampling plan, but it does save us some time, particularly if we are conducting interviews.

While area or cluster or multistage sampling is primarily conducted by demographers and pollsters, criminologists and others might be interested in soliciting opinions about different controversial issues, such as abortion or the constitutionality of the death penalty. On the basis of survey data, researchers may eventually influence public policy relating to these issues.

An example of the use of cluster sampling to obtain a cross-section of police officers is a study by William McCamey and Gayle Carper (1998). McCamey and Carper were interested in learning about the level of social skills police officers acquired as the result of attending mandatory training classes in a large Midwestern state. A cluster sampling technique was used to select several subpopulations of 200 police officers from various locations throughout the state where these mandatory training classes were being conducted. This sampling technique yielded a probability sample and permitted the authors to use certain statistical techniques in their analysis, where probability sampling was assumed. These investigators learned much about what police officers learned from their mandatory training, and although

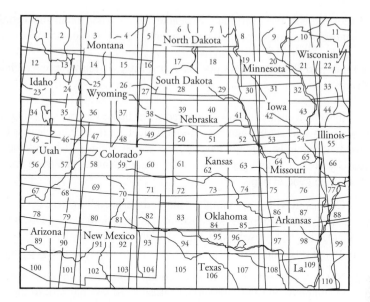

A hypothetical unit taken randomly from Figure 6.1.

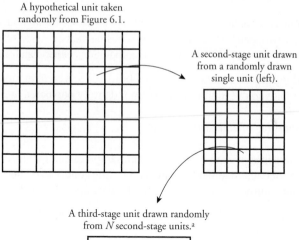

A second-stage unit drawn from a randomly drawn single unit (left).

A third-stage unit drawn randomly from N second-stage units.[a]

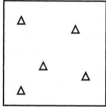

[a]Δ = a farm home or other dwelling unit within a third-stage unit.

FIGURE 4.1   Illustration of area sampling.

further research was recommended, McCamey and Carper found supporting evidence for the popularity of community-based policing and the importance of police social skills.

Advantages and Disadvantages of Area Sampling.   Area sampling includes the following advantages:

1. It is much easier to apply compared with simple random sampling, whenever large populations are studied or when large geographical areas must be canvassed. It is easier in the sense that researchers do not have to have predetermined lists of elements who inhabit the areas selected. Random geographical areas are included, and these are believed representative of the general population.

2. Compared with other sampling methods, especially where large geographical territory is involved, area sampling is less expensive. Interviewers may concentrate their efforts in specific regions, and consequently they save time and money by not having to travel great distances to interview different people living at random points in a geographical area.

3. Not everyone may respond when contacted by the researcher. Since clusters of elements are sampled, however, individual refusals are less harmful to the sample's representativeness compared with a simple random sample of elements from the entire territory.

4. If field research crews or work units are dispersed throughout a state or territory, cluster sampling saves them time and money by focusing their efforts in selected areas. This advantage is especially relevant for large research corporations rather than for individual investigators.

5. This sampling method offers flexibility, since a combination of sampling strategies might be employed to sample elements from densely populated areas.

The disadvantages of area sampling are:

1. There is no way to ensure that each sampling unit included (second- or third-stage units) will be of equal size. The researcher has little control over the size of each cluster sampled. This may introduce some bias in the final sample obtained.

2. Area samples have a greater amount of sampling error compared with simple random samples of the same size.

3. It is difficult to ensure that all elements surveyed in all clusters are independent of one another. For instance, someone interviewed in one cluster area may be visiting relatives. That person may travel to another area and be interviewed by other researchers involved in the same research project. Thus, the same person's opinion would be counted at least twice. The chances of this event occurring are remote, however.

Nonprobability Sampling Plans

Many types of research designs do not require that random samples be obtained. Rather, investigators may only be interested in obtaining sufficient numbers of elements to satisfy limited research objectives. Perhaps the investigator is testing certain research instruments or the readability of questionnaires. Only a sufficient number of warm bodies would be required to assist the researcher in pretesting these instruments. It is often unimportant if these persons have characteristics that are similar to those in the intended target population.

Some types of research are such that it is impossible to enumerate population elements in advance to draw random samples from them. For instance, if we were interested in describing the behaviors of looters who steal from others in the aftermath of natural disasters, such as earthquakes or floods, these types of events cannot be forecast with any accuracy. Also, some types of behaviors we might want to examine pertain to satanic cults and nefarious rituals carried out in secret away from the prying eyes of others. If researchers should gain access to such groups, the formality of obtaining random samples of elements would have to be abandoned.

The main distinction between probability and **nonprobability sampling plans** is that probability samples use randomness as the primary control feature and nonprobability sampling plans do not. Randomness permits inferences to be made about population characteristics based on observed sample characteristics. Random samples of elements are commonly considered generalizable to larger populations from which they are drawn, within a probability context. In the case of nonprobability samples, we cannot make inferential statements of any value about population parameters. We don't know what populations our nonprobability samples represent or typify. But this limitation does not mean that such samples are without merit. On the contrary, much of what we do in criminal justice and criminology is based on descriptions of nonprobability samples.

Another compelling argument suggesting that nonprobability samples have heuristic value is that often, researchers begin their investigations ideally seeking random samples to study. As so often happens, however, these researchers frequently fail to obtain all persons they originally included in their sampling plan. Relatively few research projects report that all of those originally selected for inclusion in the sample are subsequently included and studied.

MacKenzie and Shaw (1990) were fortunate in this respect in their investigation of inmate adjustment to shock incarceration. Shock incarceration involved placing convicted offenders in a jail for a period of up to 6 months. These persons were then brought back into court, and, provided that they behaved well while in jail, were paroled under intensive supervision. The shock of confinement does much to induce conformity to societal rules and parole program conditions. MacKenzie and Shaw studied inmates who participated in a Louisiana Department of Public Safety program known as IMPACT, or the Intensive Motivational Program of Alternative Correctional Treatment. They wanted to know whether the shock incarceration program was more effective at changing offender attitudes and behaviors than plain "flat time" or incarceration. They asked all 90 offenders who were entering the IMPACT program during a specified time interval if they would like to participate in their research. All offenders agreed to participate. This 100 percent response is rare in any social scientific project.

Nonprobability samples are categorically easier to obtain compared with probability samples. In this section, seven nonprobability sampling plans are presented. These include (1) accidental sampling, (2) systematic sampling, (3) purposive or judgmental sampling, (4) quota sampling, (5) snowball sampling, (6) dense sampling, and (7) saturation sampling.

Accidental Sampling

Accidental sampling, sometimes known as **convenience sampling,** is exactly what it sounds like. Researchers make virtually no effort to identify target populations in advance and ensure all elements an equal and an independent chance of being included. Rather, they attempt to obtain as many persons as they believe will make it possible for them to test their theories and the hypotheses derived from them. The roving reporter interviewing passersby on the street is obtaining an accidental sample of respondents. Persons who call others at random by telephone and solicit their opinions about different controversial issues are obtaining accidental samples. The professor who distributes questionnaires to large sections of criminal justice or criminology courses and surveys students has acquired an accidental sample.

An example of obtaining an accidental sample is a study of the effect of victim–offender relationship on the sentence lengths of violent offenders by Leonore Simon (1996). Simon wanted to know if the sentence lengths of offenders differed according to whether they were strangers or nonstrangers in relation to those they victimized. Previous research shows that stranger-offenders are usually sentenced to longer prison terms compared with nonstranger offenders, where they knew their victims. Simon went to a penitentiary in Arizona and with prison permission, she approached 341 inmates for possible interviews. These were all of the inmates identified by prison records as having been convicted of assault, homicide, kidnapping, sexual assault, and robbery. Subsequently, 273 consented to be interviewed, a response rate of 80 percent. Although Simon had narrowed her search of offenders only to those who had committed violent crimes, her sample was still an accidental one. She had no way of knowing which of the inmates she contacted would ultimately volunteer to be interviewed. Interestingly, about half of those she interviewed knew their victims, while the others did not. Simon had no way of knowing that her accidental sample would divide on this dimension so evenly. Simon found that at least for the sample of inmates she studied, sentence lengths were unaffected by whether the offenders knew or did not know their victims.

Advantages and Disadvantages of Accidental Sampling.   The primary advantages of accidental sampling are convenience and economy. The disadvantages include limited generalizability, considerable bias, and no evidence of a probability sample. Regarding bias, researchers often select elements because of their particular location in relation to the researcher. The major drawback of accidental sampling is that researchers have little or no idea about what population the sample is supposed to represent. This fact explains the limited generalizability, the bias, and the nonprobabilistic nature of such samples.

Systematic Sampling

Systematic sampling is a popular technique for selecting elements from alphabetized listings or other compilations of elements. Basically, it involves selecting every *n*th person from a list, whether the list is a telephone directory, inmate listing, or the membership list of a national or local professional association. In some instances, lists may not be involved. If investigators wish to canvass a particular geographical territory, such as a city block or small community, they can anticipate in advance how many persons or households exist. Then, they can select every *n*th household in the neighborhood or community for inclusion in their systematic sample.

This technique has some probability sampling aspects, although it is questioned as a probability sampling plan. When investigators determine the size of the target population, they calculate how many persons they want to include in their sample. Then they divide the population by their desired sample size and derive their value of *n*. For instance, if a listing of persons contained 5,000 names, and if researchers desired a sample size of 200 elements, they would need to select every *n*th person, where $n = N/n$ or $5,000/200 = 25$. Thus, every 25th person on the list or every 25th household in the neighborhood or community would be contacted. Automatically excluded from the sample are the persons between each 25th person. For some researchers, at least, these exclusions are troublesome. This is because one's placement on a list determines whether he or she will be included in the sample.

An illustration of the application of systematic sampling is found in the work of Kenney (1986). Kenney wanted to investigate the influence and effectiveness of various citizen groups that are created to combat street crime. In this particular study, Kenney focused on the group known as Guardian Angels. The Guardian Angels formed in 1979 and originally patrolled subways in New York City in an effort to minimize muggings and other subway crimes. One aspect of his investigation involved direct interviews with subway passengers about their perceptions of the effectiveness of the Guardian Angels. Therefore, a systematic sampling of subway passengers was obtained, consisting of passengers who were contacted while exiting subways as well as those waiting on subway platforms. Kenney notes that "individual passengers were then chosen in a systematic manner until the assigned number of interviews was completed" (1986, p. 484). About 79 percent of all passengers contacted by Kenney and his assistants responded to face-to-face interviews. We are not informed by Kenney's report as to the magnitude of *n* in "every *n*th person being selected," although Kenney's resulting sample was substantial, consisting of 2,693 passengers.

Advantages and Disadvantages of Systematic Sampling.   The primary advantages of systematic sampling are:

1. This method is easy to use, especially contrasted with having to use a table of random numbers in the identification of elements.

2. Because it is a nonprobability sampling form, mistakes in drawing certain elements are relatively unimportant. Mistakes might occur if one miscounts on the listing of elements and draws the 51st person instead of the 50th person, for example. This mistake is trivial.

3. If checks are employed to verify the accuracy of sample selection, systematic sampling makes it easier to spot mistakes that might have been made in counting. However, questions about the accuracy of systematic sampling are relatively unimportant, again because of the nonprobability nature of the method.

4. Systematic sampling is a fast method for obtaining a sample. If researchers are in a hurry to make their sample selections, systematic sampling would be much faster than any of the probability sampling methods discussed earlier.

The major disadvantages of systematic sampling are:

1. Systematic sampling systematically excludes persons from being included in the selected sample. Thus, it is sometimes questioned as a probability sampling method. Representativeness and generalizability are affected adversely as a result.

2. If the listing of elements is alphabetically arranged, some degree of ethnic bias will enter the picture. Sampling error will be increased accordingly, as some groups with minority/ethnic surnames, Oriental or otherwise, are selected less frequently compared with selections of names beginning with "Mc," "Smith," "Jones," "Anderson," or "Johnson." This bias will affect the generalizability of findings accordingly.

3. If the listing of elements is arranged according to some other characteristic, such as "severity of offense," "educational level attained," "age," or some other similar ordered characteristic, some bias will be introduced. Those characteristics most frequently listed will be overrepresented, while less frequently listed characteristics will be underrepresented.

Purposive or Judgmental Sampling

Purposive sampling or **judgmental sampling** involves hand picking elements from some target population. The researcher's intent is to ensure that certain elements will be included in the resulting sample. Because some or most elements will be included in the sample deliberately and others will be excluded deliberately, purposive sampling is a nonprobability sampling form. Why would researchers want to sample in this fashion? One explanation is that the investigators might have extensive familiarity with the population to the extent that they know those elements who would be most representative of it. Because of their knowledge about the population, the researchers may, in fact, be able to obtain a sample that would be better (i.e., more representative) than any probability sampling plan would yield.

Purposive or judgmental sampling has been used in the social sciences, particularly where studies of small communities are involved. Someone who is well known in the community and is familiar with most residents is asked to hand pick representative numbers of elements who typify the range of community sentiment on some issue. Thus, if a researcher wanted to know community sentiment about abortion, or civil rights issues, or capital punishment, the hand-picked sample, the judgmental sample, would be a good indication about what the community-at-large thought about the issue.

An example of a purposive sample drawn from the criminological literature is found in the work of Martin and colleagues (2003). They studied day reporting centers, which are designed for both probationers and parolees. Clients assigned to day reporting centers live in their communities but they must report to these centers on a regular basis where they can be monitored or supervised and receive relevant services depending on their unique needs and circumstances. Martin and colleagues studied the Cook County, Illinois, Day Reporting Center. She and her associates were interested in whether or not the day reporting center was instrumental in reducing recidivism rates among clients in contrast with clients who were assigned to more traditional probation or parole and who did not have to report to day reporting centers. Martin and colleagues selected the year, 1995, because it would enable them to conduct follow-up investigations of day reporting center clients over several years. An original population of 1,391 clients was identified, although a portion of these persons were no longer in the Illinois jurisdiction and could not be located. The average number of days spent in the day reporting center program by the remaining sample of participants was 49, with about half of the participants involved in the program for 20 days or fewer. Martin and colleagues divided the remaining sample, whose precise number was not reported, into two groups: those who stayed in the program for at least 70 days or longer, and those who left the program after 10 or fewer days. It was presumed by the authors that those who were in the program longer received more services and needed treatments than those who were hardly involved in it. Although recidivism rates among all known participants averaged 65 percent in a 1-year follow-up, those who had participated in the day reporting center program longer had lower rates of recidivism compared with those who had spent 10 days or fewer in the program. Thus, Martin and colleagues found some support for the idea that day reporting center participation tends to reduce recidivism rates.

Advantages and Disadvantages of Purposive Sampling.　The major advantage of judgmental samples is that certain elements will definitely be included in the resulting sample. If researchers know a great deal about the populations of elements they are studying in advance, this hand-picked sample could be a better representation of the population compared with any probability sampling method. Additional advantages are that this method is less cumbersome compared with probability sampling plans. The elements selected are likely more accessible to the researcher and relate most directly to one's study objectives. On the negative side, no amount of judging can forecast accurately that the sample will be a truly representative one. Unknown biases may enter into the selection process and make the sample quite atypical. There are generalization problems as well, since these samples do not conform to the requirements of probability sampling. Tests of **statistical significance** and inference would be inappropriate here and their use undermined by the nonprobability nature of sample selection.

　　Finally, an extensive amount of information about the population is required in advance of such element selections. This is seldom the case when researchers approach the target population for the first time. Thus, judgmental or purposive sampling plans are only infrequently applied in criminology or criminal justice research projects, although some investigators regard their representativeness as superior to all probability sampling plans.

　　Four other nonprobability sampling plans are discussed below. These include quota sampling, snowball sampling, dense sampling, and saturation sampling.

Quota Sampling

Compared with snowball sampling, dense sampling, and saturation sampling, quota sampling is most popular, largely on the basis of its more frequent use in criminology and criminal justice research. **Quota sampling** is obtaining a desired number of elements from the population by selecting those that are most accessible and have certain characteristics of interest to the researcher. The selection of elements is comparable to proportionate stratified random sampling, without randomness as the primary control. These characteristics might be age, gender, race/ethnicity, type of offense, profession, or any other factor that might be measured. Investigators want to obtain persons that possess certain characteristics that typify some population, and they want to obtain similar proportions of these characteristics in their samples. Thus, if a population is known to consist of 80 percent whites and 20 percent blacks, efforts will be made to secure a sample consisting of 80 percent white and 20 percent black participants. Quota sampling has been called "the poor man's proportionate **stratified sample.**"

　　An example of quota sampling from the criminological literature is found in the work of Stephen W. Baron (2004). Baron was interested in testing general strain theory, especially that portion of the theory having to do with how strain is conditioned by one's deviant peers, deviant attitudes, and external attributions. In order to test the theory, Baron decided to focus on a sample of homeless youth in the Vancouver, Canada, area. Because homeless youth comprise a very fluid, ever-changing population in any city, it was impossible for Baron to obtain any type of meaningful probability sample of them. However, he sought to include those homeless youth who had particular characteristics of interest to him, and that would enable him to test general strain theory. Thus, he used the following criteria: homeless must be 24 years of age or younger; they must be currently unemployed; they must have left (or finished) school; and they should have spent time without any sort of permanent address or shelter during the most recent 12 months. Armed with these criteria, Baron and his interviewers roamed the downtown portion of Vancouver seeking homeless youths who fit the characteristics he had identified. Subsequently, he identified 400 respondents (265 males and 135 females) who were used as his sample for the purposes of testing strain theory. There were many homeless youths who were contacted by Baron and his assistants, but for one or more reasons, they were not included in his research. In some respects, Baron's sample approached what has been described as an accidental or convenience sample. In fact, there were some elements of judgmental or purposive sampling evident in the procedure used by Baron in his sample selection. Because of the nonprobabilistic nature of his sample, Baron advised readers to use caution in interpreting his findings. This admonition should be made in any study where samples are studied, regardless of the sophisticated nature of the sampling plan one uses.

Advantages and Disadvantages of Quota Sampling.   The advantages of quota sampling are best appreciated when contrasting this sampling method with probability sampling plans. Quota sampling is considerably less costly than the probability sampling method. Furthermore, if quick, crude results are desired that will satisfy certain short-range research objectives, quota sampling is useful. Finally, use of quota sampling ensures the inclusion of certain types of elements, whereas simple random sampling might not. The major disadvantages of quota sampling are that while the most accessible elements are included that fit the desired characteristics of the researcher, these elements may not be typical of the rest of the population. There is limited generalizability, since this sampling method is a nonprobability one. Some bias may enter his selection procedure as the result of misclassifying elements. Of course, this may happen in any stratified sampling plan when we control for the inclusion of specific variables. Finally, although certain variables can be controlled for and their inclusion assured by quota sampling, other relevant variables perhaps unknown to the investigator might be better to use and have greater theoretical significance compared with the **control variable** he has chosen.

Snowball Sampling and the Use of Informants

For special sampling situations, Coleman, Katz, and Menzel (1957) have suggested **snowball sampling** as a type of relational analysis. These researchers were interested in studying the diffusion of medical information among physicians. Snowball sampling, named as such because of the "snowball effect" achieved by the method itself, relies on the use of initial element contacts to furnish researchers with additional element contacts, and so on, until some constellation or social network is outlined. These researchers asked several physicians to name those other physicians with whom they shared information about new pharmaceuticals or drugs. Those physicians named were contacted by researchers and asked the same question: "With whom do you share information about new drugs or pharmaceuticals?" These physician-respondents would supply additional names of other physicians, these would be contacted and asked the same question, until eventually, Coleman and his associates observed various group patterns.

Another application of snowball sampling in criminal justice is to use **key informants.** If investigators wish to study the drug subculture in a given community and how drugs are disseminated, they might begin by using an **informant.** An informant is someone who knows others who are involved in various types of activities. Police officers use informants to gather incriminating information about criminals. In much the same way, researchers can use informants, such as known drug users, to find out about the drug community.

Informants can introduce researchers to other drug users and dealers. It is imperative that a degree of trust is established between the researchers and those they wish to study, especially if the activity is illegal. One introduction leads to other introductions, and eventually, researchers are able to describe drug dissemination patterns.

It may be recalled from an earlier chapter that Sandra Hafley and Richard Tewksbury (1996) studied the marijuana-growing business in "Bluegrass County" Kentucky. They relied heavily on informants to introduce them to community residents who were involved in growing and distributing marijuana illegally. These researchers used a form of snowball sampling in their data-gathering process.

The use of informants is not limited to criminals and descriptions of illegal activities. Perhaps investigators are interested in studying police officer or correctional officer culture. Accessing police or correctional officers may be difficult, since few officers wish to disclose the nature of their work to others. However, if researchers know one or more police officers or corrections officers, their work is made easier to the extent that these officers can arrange introductions with other officers. Once a relationship has been established between researchers and the officers involved, other introductions can be arranged. In time, researchers can describe police and correctional officer interaction patterns and such phenomena as the police personality or correctional officer–inmate relations.

Advantages and Disadvantages of Snowball Sampling.   Some possible applications of snowball sampling in criminology and criminal justice might be discovering inmate communication and goods distribution networks in prisons and jails. Snowball sampling could be used to discover drug-distribution patterns in cities or the recreational patterns and interpersonal relationships among undercover law enforcement officers who work irregular hours and shifts. The major advantage of this technique is that it permits researchers to chart social relationships that are difficult to detect using conventional sampling strategies. But statistical procedures might have limited application in these situations, since randomness is not assured. Furthermore, if the population is large, the number of social networks detected might become unwieldy.

Dense and Saturation Sampling

Both **dense sampling** and **saturation sampling** are intended to overcome the deficiencies of a lack of randomness and small sample size that may hinder generalizability. Coleman (1959) suggested these sampling methods as they might be applied to the study of large-scale organizations. However, his work has been extended by others to applications in a variety of fields.

The theory behind dense and saturation sampling is fairly simple. If your sample size is substantial enough in relation to the population from which it was drawn, it won't make much difference whether randomness was used in the draw of sample elements. Coleman (1959) said that "dense sampling is sampling densely." Coleman elaborated further. He indicated that dense samples would involve the use of at least 50 percent of all population elements. Thus, if the population consisted of 500 juvenile delinquents, the dense sample would be any 250 delinquents, or about 50 percent of them. The overwhelming numbers of such a sample, even obtained accidentally, would be sufficient to warrant some amount of generalizing to and inferences about populations.

Saturation sampling, according to Coleman (1959), is almost like not sampling at all, since almost everyone in the population is subsequently included in the sample. When criminal justice professionals and criminologists send out questionnaires to all target population elements or seek to interview most if not all of them, saturation sampling is likely the method employed. Crank and colleagues (1986) used saturation sampling in their study of police chief cynicism among all Illinois police chiefs. They sent questionnaires to all 771 police chiefs in all jurisdictions, although the return rate was about 67 percent (519 chiefs responded). This large return was boosted, in part, by several follow-up letters to those chiefs who did not initially respond. According to Coleman's guidelines, their sample would be somewhere between a dense sample and a saturation sample. Nevertheless, the sheer numbers of police chiefs involved in their research seem convincingly representative of most police chiefs in Illinois. Of course, about a third of these chiefs did not respond, and again, we have no way of evaluating the influence of their impact on the final results had their responses been included and reported.

Another application of dense or saturation sampling is found in the work of Magnus J. Seng, Loretta J. Stalans, and Michelle Repp (2004). These researchers wanted to know whether there were any differences between violent and nonviolent probationers according to several salient socioeconomic and other variables. Because these investigators are affiliated with Illinois universities and have good working relationships with the Illinois Probation Division of the Administrative Office of the Illinois Courts, they decided to obtain probationer information directly from that office. They learned that the number of probationers in Illinois is quite large. In order to obtain a manageable sample, they elected to study probationers who had completed their probationary terms during a 4-week period between November and December 1997. The total number of probationers completing their programs was 3,364 during this particular period. They contacted the probation officers who had supervised all of these probationers and requested that they complete a questionnaire about each client, including their conviction offenses as well as their prior criminal records. Those with current or prior records of violent felony convictions were classified as violent offenders, while the rest were classified as nonviolent offenders. The resulting samples were 1,385 violent and 1,948 nonviolent offenders, or a total of 3,333 offenders.

This slightly smaller sample size from the original 3,364 persons was not explained, but it is likely that some probationers had missing record information or were otherwise unknown to their supervising POs.

Bear in mind that these researchers had discharged probationers only for one month from 1997. Imagine how cumbersome it would have been to obtain all of the probationers for the 1997 year? These researchers took these large samples and contrasted them according to age, race, marital status, number of children parented, employment status, educational status, illicit drug use, alcohol use/abuse, prior psychiatric treatment, total prior arrests, prior drug arrests, prior property arrests, prior adult probation sentences, and a host of other variables. These researchers were able to find significant differences between the violent and nonviolent felony probationers they studied. While their study involved a large number of Illinois probationers, their generalizations were limited. Generalizations of the study findings to the samples themselves were in order, but it was not possible to generalize to all Illinois probationers, even for the 1997 year. These researchers made no attempt to do that. But because of the large number of ex-probationers studied, they were able to glean much important information about violent and nonviolent probationer differences, which might be important for those in the future who attempted similar research. Although the sample they obtained was a nonprobability sample, it did yield useful information and suggest several policy changes for Illinois officials. By implication, probation officials in other jurisdictions might be interested in their findings as well.

Advantages and Disadvantages of Dense and Saturation Sampling.   Virtually any occasion when researchers seek to include all respondents suggests that a saturation sample has been obtained. An example of saturation sampling is a study of truancy and deterrence/intervention strategies by Gordon Bazemore, Jeanne B. Stinchcomb, and Leslie A. Leip (2004). These researchers collected data from the population of 12,330 youths stopped by police in a Southeastern urban jurisdiction during the 1999–2000 school year. A majority of youths stopped by police were subsequently processed through a government-funded truancy intake unit, simply called the Truancy Unit. Eligibility requirements included youths from ages 6–17 who were enrolled in public or private schools, not enrolled in either a GED or court-ordered program, not in a home study or work study program, not runaways, and not currently suspended or expelled from school. The truancy intervention was simple, in that it consisted of no longer than a 6-hour stay in the truancy unit. Truants were subject to a basic assessment, interview, enforced silence, and informal counseling by unit staff. After their short stay at the unit, youths were released to the custody of their parents or guardians. These researchers delineated two groups of students: those who were actually processed by the unit (7,395), and those who were released after preliminary questioning (4,935). Subsequently, the investigators sought random samples of 500 each from both student groups. However, nonresponse or unavailability of certain selected students (for a variety of reasons) led to resulting samples consisting of 350 in their "processed sample" and 200 in their "nonprocessed sample." Although these investigators eventually studied a much smaller portion of the original 12,330 youths, they had sufficient descriptive sociodemographic information to depict the entire aggregate and compare them with the same information obtained from their smaller samples.

Another example of saturation sampling is a study of domestic violence cases from a California county jurisdiction by Rodney F. Kingsnorth and Randall C. Macintosh (2004).

These researchers analyzed all cases (5,272) of domestic violence for Sacramento County between July 1, 1999, and December 31, 2000. Of these cases, 4,299 were selected for criminal prosecution. Subsequently studied were 3,120 cases, about 72 percent of those prosecuted. Descriptive information was provided for these cases as well as case outcomes. The nonrandom nature of these case selections is apparent. The investigators focused on a particular county for a particular time period and studied as many cases as they could reasonably obtain, where detailed case information was available. The discrepancy between the 4,299 charged cases and the 3,120 studied cases suggests that about 28 percent of these cases lacked important information for research purposes or were otherwise dropped for other reasons. The subsequent sample of 3,120 was a saturation sample.

If the population is fairly small, and if the instrumentation selected is not time-consuming, dense and saturation sampling plans might be useful, since they do not require time-consuming randomness procedures. The results of any research are almost certainly applicable to the general population, since so much of it is included in the samples obtained. The size of the target population is relative. Generally, any population of 1,000 or more would be considered a large population. If interviewing were proposed for such an investigation, the costs of interviewing using a dense or saturation sampling format would be prohibitive. Distributions of questionnaires to these elements for data collection purposes would be another matter altogether. In cases where survey instruments are used, such as questionnaires, dense or saturation samples would be extremely valuable in terms of their generalizability. Nevertheless, the technical requirements of probability sampling plans would not be fulfilled, and therefore, statistical applications would have to be viewed with caution.

Types of Sampling Situations

The types of sample situations presented here include a study of **single samples** of elements (sometimes called **one-shot case study**), studies of two samples, and studies of k samples. A further distinction is whether the two- or k-sample situations involve independent or related samples.[1] These terms will be defined below.

Single-Sample Situations

The most common research scenarios are studies of **single samples** at one point in time. A professor may administer a questionnaire to several classes of criminology students and combine these questionnaires to form a large sample. An investigator may study decision making of the Idaho Parole Board. Another may describe jail inmate characteristics in a particular county jail. Another researcher may study a sample of Miami delinquents. All of these studies have in common the fact that a particular population has been targeted and a sample has been drawn from it. It makes no difference whether these elements have been

---

[1] k technically means "two or more." Applied to samples, k would mean "two or more samples." However, statistical tests of significance of difference are conventionally categorized as "two-sample" and "k-sample" tests, where k is understood to apply to situations involving more than two samples.

randomly selected or chosen as the result of saturation or dense sampling. A single sample is described, interviewed, questioned, and/or observed. Statistical tests applied to such sample situations are referred to simply as "single-sample **tests of significance.**"

It is a common misconception that single samples of elements must be taken from a specific location. For instance, a study of Michigan forensics experts taken from numerous Ohio counties is simply a single sample of Michigan forensic experts. It is not a study of numerous samples of forensic experts taken from assorted Michigan counties. An investigation of Tennessee circuit court judges will likely involve responses from judges in many county jurisdictions throughout the state. The resulting sample will be referred to simply as "a single sample of Tennessee circuit court judges."

Two and *k*- Sample Situations

Many investigators study two or more samples of elements in their research. If researchers study two samples of elements, these studies are usually intended to compare the samples on one or more salient dimensions. If more than two samples of elements are studied, then three or more samples are involved. These situations involving three or more samples are conventionally known as *k*-sample studies. It is important to recognize the sampling plans used by different investigators. Different sampling plan variations tell us much about one's research objectives. Furthermore, statistical tests have been formulated to fit **two- and *k*-sample situations.** Two-sample **tests of significance of difference** determine whether two samples of elements differ significantly on some characteristic.

Researchers may wish to investigate two or more samples for comparative purposes. For example, Cindy J. Smith and Kimberly S. Craig (2004) studied two samples of youths who had been transferred to criminal court from the Maryland juvenile justice system during 1998. Approximately 250 youths were transferred to criminal court from juvenile court that year. Smith and Craig focused on a sample of 118 male juveniles taken from all youths transferred. They divided these into two groups. Group 1 consisted of youths who had a prior history of prior intakes and were younger than 13 at their first intake, suggesting that these were consistent with a general definition of chronic offenders. The second sample, Group 2, consisted of youths who were 14 or older at their first intake and had little or no previous intake experience. The two samples, 56 and 62 juveniles respectively, were compared on a number of salient dimensions, such as amenability to treatment, delinquency seriousness, drug and/or alcohol involvement, histories of court involvement, and the number of prior contacts with the juvenile justice system. Subsequently, these investigators were able to identify and recommend different treatment strategies or interventions for the two samples of juveniles on the basis of differences in characteristics they were able to identify.

It is important to note that Smith and Craig did not have to first seek out transferred youths age 13 or younger with long prior juvenile records, and then seek out another sample of transferred youths age 14 or older with little or no prior juvenile court contact. They were able to draw a single sample and subsequently subdivide it, thus creating two separate samples for comparison. This method of creating two samples from a larger single sample is quite common in social research.

K-sample situations are simply extensions of the two-sample case. For instance, Byron R. Johnson studied the Prisoner Fellowship (PF) program, a nonprofit religious ministry for prisoners. Johnson selected 201 former prisoners from four different New York State prisons where Prisoner Fellowship programs were offered. Johnson deliberately focused on former inmates who had participated several years earlier in PF programs offered in these prisons. As he indicated, he made no effort to randomly select these prisoners for inclusion in his study. His sample of former prisoners consisted of inmates who had participated in bible studies, in-prison religious seminars, and life-plan seminars. Johnson was interested in tracking these offenders over time, primarily according to their recidivism rates. If Johnson had desired, he could have contrasted those former inmates according to their former affiliation with bible-study programs, in-prison religious seminars, and life-plan seminars that they had taken. This scenario would give him an opportunity to compare recidivism rates of former inmates for the three programs. In this instance, he would have k-samples, where $k = 3$.

Another example might involve an investigation of three samples of inmates under minimum-, medium-, or maximum-security confinement conditions. Additionally, an investigator might describe five different types of administrative styles in five different police departments. Samples of police officers from each of these departments could be collected and studied according to whether they differ on self-perceptions of professionalism. Thus, this would be a k-sample situation or a five-sample study of police officers.

Independent Samples

For the two- and k-sample cases or situations, specific statistical tests have been devised for application according to whether the samples are independent or related. **Independent samples** are those that contain elements that are **mutually exclusive** of one another. The study by Smith and Craig (2004) described above involved two independent samples of juvenile delinquents. The hypothetical five-sample study of police officers would be a five-independent-sample situation or a k-independent-sample case. Elements in one sample are mutually exclusive of those in the other sample or samples. In these situations, the samples were drawn separately, each from a particular population of elements. Independent samples may be established by other means, however.

Suppose a researcher has obtained a large sample of 400 prison inmates. If the researcher desired, the entire sample of 400 inmates could be described, and hypotheses relevant to that sample could be tested. Single-sample statistical tests would be applied for more extensive data analyses. But the original sample of 400 could also be broken down or stratified according to type of conviction offense. This would be equivalent to treating various subsamples of elements as separate samples under either proportionate or disproportionate stratified random sampling discussed earlier in this chapter. Perhaps the researcher wanted to divide inmates according to whether they were violent or property offenders. A division of inmates according to this **dichotomy,** violent and property offenders, might yield 200 violent offenders and 200 property offenders. This would be a two-independent-sample scenario. This scenario has been created artificially by dividing the original sample according to criteria deemed important by the investigator.

It is apparent that similar breakdowns could be completed according to age, race, ethnicity, security level, years of confinement, inmate gang membership, or any other relevant variable. If these 400 inmates belonged to five different gangs and the researcher separated them according to their particular gang affiliation, the result would be a five-independent-sample case. Membership in one gang would rule out membership in the other gangs. The different gang subdivisions would be mutually exclusive of one another. Therefore, it is not necessary to visit five different prison sites to obtain five different samples of offenders. All of this can be accomplished by drawing one large sample of inmates initially and subdividing them later on selected variables.

Related Samples

Two or more related samples involve two- or k-sample cases, where the samples are not mutually exclusive of one another. **Related samples** are useful whenever researchers conduct experiments and wish to know whether the experimental variable induces changes on some behavioral or attitudinal **dimension.** If the samples are related, they are treated as though they are equivalent. Thus, any differences observed between the related samples on some measured characteristic are believed attributable to the experimental variable rather than to other extraneous factors, such as individual differences among sample elements. There are three ways of obtaining related samples. These include (1) using persons as their own controls in before–after experiments, (2) matching elements among samples, and (3) group or frequency distribution control matching. These alternative types of samples were described in detail in Chapter 3 in relation to experimentation.

For instance, in the study of Prison Fellowship (PF) programs conducted by Johnson (2004) and described earlier in this chapter, Johnson's sample of 201 former inmates from different New York prisons was matched with 455 former inmates who had not participated in PF programming. Johnson matched these non-PF participants with the PF participants according to seven different variables: age, race, religious denomination, county of residence, military discharge, minimum sentence, and initial security classification. As the result of such matching, Johnson was able to draw tentative inferences about the effectiveness of PF on recidivism rates of former inmates who had participated in PF programming compared with those who had not participated. Although the generalizability of his findings was limited because of the nonrandom nature of his selected samples, Johnson nevertheless found support for the idea that participating in PF programming decreased one's propensity to recidivate over time, compared with non-PF former prisoners.

Some Selected Sampling Problems

In this section, several important sampling issues are discussed that often arise in the course of one's research. No explicit rules exist as standards against which our own research can be assessed. The fact that gaps frequently exist between what ideally ought to be done to obtain samples and what actually occurs when selecting our samples generates several questions that have no universal answers. To a degree, we might rely on conventions followed by different disciplines. In criminology and criminal justice, there are conventional guidelines we may use for decision making, but individual research circumstances and limitations frequently require departures from these guidelines. Issues selected for discussion include (1) determining the sample size; (2) the problem of nonresponse; (3) evaluating the representativeness of samples; (4) the relation of sampling techniques and statistical analyses; (5) the ideal–real gap in sampling procedures; and (6) the inaccessibility of potentates and special populations.

Determining Sample Size

How large should our samples be in relation to the populations from which they are drawn? For purposes of generalization and statistical inference, a conventional rule of thumb is that the sample size, n, should be 1/10th of the population size, N, or $n/N = 1/10$th. This is called the sampling fraction. Applying this rule of thumb, if the population size is 500, the sample size should be 50. If the population size is 20 million, the sample size should be 2 million. However, this particular rule of thumb leads to unwieldy sample sizes whenever larger populations of elements are involved. Few researchers have the resources to obtain samples of 2 million elements. Do we necessarily need 2 million elements to make inferences about 20 million elements? No. Fortunately, the 1/10th rule of thumb becomes less important and may even be ignored whenever one's target population reaches or exceeds 2,500 elements. While this "2,500" figure is somewhat arbitrary, note that the 1/10th rule would yield a sample size of 250 in this instance. Larger populations would yield sample sizes larger than 250.

There are several logical reasons for limiting our sample sizes and violating the 1/10th rule of thumb by drawing samples that account for less than 10 percent of their respective population sizes. First, we can manage smaller samples more easily than larger ones. Sample sizes of 150 to 250 are more manageable than sample sizes of 1,000 or more. Second, samples that are extremely large are not proportionately more informative than smaller samples. A "diminishing returns" effect occurs as we increase our sample sizes substantially. In short, we do not double the accuracy of our sample statistics as estimates of population parameters if, for example, we were to double our sample sizes from 250 to 500. As more persons are added to our samples, many of these additional elements have characteristics similar to those elements we have already obtained. Thus, our larger samples are more costly than smaller samples, but they are not substantially more descriptive about the populations from which they were drawn. Provided that a probability sampling plan is used for one's sample selection, generally larger samples are more accurate than smaller samples for describing populations and their characteristics. But this improvement in population description is only marginally improved. The greater cost of obtaining larger numbers of elements often fails to yield an equivalent increase in descriptive information.

Nonresponse and What to Do about It

Nonresponse is the proportion of the original sample that is not included in the final sample studied by the investigator. For instance, if researchers have used a table of random numbers to identify 100 sample elements from their target population of 1,000 elements, nonresponse occurs when one or more of these sample elements is not included in the final sample studied. For example, if self-administered questionnaires are mailed to 5,000 persons and 2,000 of them do not return their completed questionnaires, this is a nonresponse or **nonresponse rate** of 2,000/5,000, or 40 percent. Nonresponse is not limited to questionnaire administration. Interviewers may attempt to interview certain persons, only to be refused. Often, those selected for interviews may not be at home or they may fail to keep their appointments with interviewers. Some persons are simply unavailable for interviewing for a variety of reasons, often unknown.

Almost all studies that describe and analyze samples drawn from larger populations have some degree of nonresponse. The amount of nonresponse varies among studies and no standards exist that define normal nonresponse rates. Different textbooks report "average"

BOX 4.2   PERSONALITY HIGHLIGHT

JODY L. SUNDT
Indiana University

Statistics: B.A. (English), Indiana University; M.S., Ph.D. (criminal justice), University of Cincinnati.

BACKGROUND AND INTERESTS

I became interested in criminal justice and research in a round-about way and would never have guessed when I was a student that one day I would be a social scientist. I began my college studies as an English major, with a vague idea of becoming a lawyer some day. I was first introduced to criminology in an introductory class that I took to meet a social science requirement. At the time, crime was the top national concern and the "get-tough" movement and the "war on drugs" had recently been launched. The class fascinated me and I began to take criminal justice classes whenever I had elective hours to fill. I also began to apply my new interests in crime to my study of literature and wrote an honor's thesis on, among other things, the fictional representation of violence in novels written during the Industrial Revolution. After this I was hooked.

When I graduated from college in 1991 there was a recession and no one seemed interested in hiring new graduates. Law school no longer appealed to me, but I was certain that I wanted to learn more about crime and criminal justice. I began volunteering in a probation department and was eventually hired as a probation officer aide. My job was to help supervise caseloads of offenders when officers were out sick, on a leave of absence, or just needed some extra help. This was a great experience because I worked with every type of offender and spent time in each of the courts. I also assisted the director and assistant directors occasionally and gained a comprehensive view of probation as a result.

BOX 4.2   CONTINUED

I went to graduate school with the intention of gaining the credentials needed to work in criminal justice administration. I thought I might become a director of a probation department one day. Really, this was only part of my motivation. My initial studies and experiences working with offenders had inspired my interest, compassion, and sense of social responsibility, but there was also an unsatisfied desire to know more about criminal offending and how best to respond to crime.

Social research, especially research methods and statistics, was something I was initially resistant to. I went to graduate school expecting to learn, but not to conduct original research. It was intimidating and sounded, frankly, boring. What I found, however, was that I really enjoyed my classes on research methods, and even statistics. I realized too that conducting research is a wonderful, challenging journey. I learned a new way of thinking about problems. I liked the order and logic of the scientific method, but what changed my career path was the excitement and satisfaction of discovery. For me this is the best thing about conducting research.

RESEARCH EXPERIENCES

My research interests center around punishment and corrections. I have conducted studies on the effect of supermax prisons on prison violence, public attitudes about punishment and correctional policies, the effectiveness of drug courts, the work experiences of correctional officers, the role of prison chaplains, and white-collar crime. Currently, I am working on a research study that examines whether individuals' religious beliefs affect how they think about punishment and the causes of crime.

Most of the research that I have done uses survey methods, which are excellent for accurately describing things like public attitudes. Surveys are also a good way to examine the relationships between complex beliefs, attitudes, and behaviors, like the relationship between fear of workplace victimization, work stress, and job performance. I have also used official data collected by correctional agencies and courts to examine the effect of programs. The study I conducted on the effectiveness of drug courts, for example, used data from criminal arrest records, court records, probation records, and drug treatment records. Existing data such as these are important sources of information about how the criminal justice system works.

ADVICE TO STUDENTS

Question everything and remain open to all answers, this is my advice. At the core of research methods is the process of asking and seeking answers to questions. Encourage yourself to do this: look for patterns; notice more; reject simplistic explanations and rigid dichotomies; dwell on details; observe before you judge; and be willing to reconsider your first impression. Training yourself to be an analytical thinker, to "think like a scientist," opens up the possibility for new insights. If you do this, you will be amazed what you will discover. It might even inspire you.

nonresponse rates from 20 percent to 70 percent, although these estimates are subjective. An analysis of social science literature suggests that average response rates to mailed questionnaires are about 30 percent. On the average, the response rate for direct interviewing is much higher, since this data collection method involves face-to-face contact between the interviewer and interviewee.

Professors and other researchers who administer questionnaires to students in large classrooms frequently report response rates of 100 percent. High response rates in these "captive audience" situations are commonplace, since classrooms are implicitly coercive settings. Sometimes teachers will require student compliance in completing administered questionnaires as one of several course requirements, or additional points will be awarded to those students who respond. Thus, many students participate to avoid being penalized.

The primary problem with nonresponse is that it affects adversely the typicality or representativeness of one's sample in relation to the population from which it was drawn. If ideal criteria are applied in one's initial sample selection, nonresponse detracts from these ideal sampling objectives. There is little or nothing that we can do about it. We can encourage those who did not respond to reconsider. This is often done through follow-up letters to nonrespondents, if mailed questionnaires are used. These follow-ups require that we somehow keep track of and identify those who do and do not respond. But anonymity cannot be assured under this circumstance. And we often offer anonymity to potential respondents as a means of encouraging them to return completed questionnaires that contain personal and/or confidential data. But even follow-up letters usually result in small increases in the final response rate. Among other strategies that have been used to prompt larger response rates are (1) using hand-stamped postage (compared with metered postage) on return envelopes to personalize them; (2) using **altruistic appeals** with cover letters that appeal to one's altruistic spirit; (3) using **egoistic appeals** with letters offering goods or money for responding; (4) offering prizes based on lottery selections from among those who respond; (5) using special delivery follow-up letters to nonrespondents, (6) making telephone calls to nonrespondents; and/or (7) making home visits to nonrespondents.

Sometimes for experimental purposes, researchers will deliberately **oversample** in order to obtain a desirable sample size. For example, if investigators want to obtain 200 elements in their final sample, and if they are using mailed questionnaires, they may send questionnaires to 600 elements, anticipating that their nonresponse will be about 65 percent. Unfortunately, the original 600 elements selected may have comprised an ideal random sample drawn from a table of random numbers. Excluding 400 of these elements through nonresponse from the resulting data analysis means that the sample is not a random one, despite the fact that the final sample consists of 200 elements, a desirable sample size. Therefore, oversampling is recommended only when investigators require minimum sample sizes for anticipated experimental research and certain research designs.

Oversampling may also occur if there is a good chance that certain persons in the population may not be included in sufficient numbers in the resulting sample. For example, if there are few women or Hispanics in a given population, researchers may wish to deliberately oversample to include more women or Hispanics so that they will have sufficient numbers of them for comparison with other sample elements. An example of oversampling is found in the work of Christopher Schreck, Bonnie Fisher, and Mitchell Miller (2004), who studied the social context of violent victimization among juvenile delinquents. Because the race of juveniles was regarded as an important independent variable, and because black youths made up about 10 percent of all youths in grades 7–12 who could be surveyed, black youths were oversampled to ensure that there would be sufficient numbers of black delinquents to compare with nonblack delinquents. The resulting sample would be disproportionate relating to race, but the disproportionality would be justified because of the need of researchers to include sufficient numbers of minority youths for legitimate comparisons on different variables.

Is the Sample Representative? Uncertainty about Representativeness

How do we know if a sample is representative of the population from which it was drawn? Never. Assessing sample representativeness accurately requires considerable knowledge about the population and its characteristics. If such knowledge about the population were possessed, it is unlikely that we would need to draw samples from it. Of course, we may select sample elements according to their known distribution in the population. We may know the different types of offenders in a state prison or local jail. Or we may know the gender and educational distribution of law enforcement officers in a large city. Or we may know some of the superficial characteristics of state correctional officers from personnel files or state records. These information sources may enable us to judge whether our samples exhibit certain population characteristics. Thus, we may say that our samples appear typical according to gender distribution, age distribution, educational level, type of offense, length of confinement, prior record, and any other recorded population information.

But thousands of other variables, attitudinal and otherwise, characterize the populations we study. Controlling our sample selections according to those criteria we know about will make those samples representative of their parent populations only for those criteria. Remaining uncontrolled are thousands of other individual, social, and psychological **attributes** and characteristics that may render our samples atypical or unrepresentative. We cannot possibly know when our samples are truly representative or unrepresentative of their parent populations in all respects, however. Thus, there is almost always considerable uncertainty about the representativeness of our samples. Investigators do not quit doing research because they are uncertain about the representativeness of their samples, however. There is much to be learned from the samples they obtain, regardless of their representativeness or lack of it. After all, the samples do come from target populations of elements. Some information is better than no information.

Sampling and Statistical Analysis

Ordinarily, investigators know in advance of conducting their **statistical analysis** which statistical techniques they intend to apply. Their familiarity with these statistical techniques will often indicate the sample sizes required for those intended statistical applications. Furthermore, any inferential tasks to be performed require the use of a probability sampling plan when a sample is selected. Randomness is an assumption underlying all statistical inference and decision making. Therefore, if we wish to generalize about population characteristics based on sample characteristics, our sample should be a random one. However, when the samples we obtain are not random or when there is some nonresponse, the typicality and representativeness of our samples are impaired, and any generalizations and inferences about population characteristics made from observed sample characteristics are similarly affected.

Ideal and Real Sampling Considerations

The quest to obtain ideal samples that meet ideal criteria is a noble one. But it is unrealistic to expect that perfection in our sampling will ever be realized. Whether we use the 1/10th rule of thumb or some exotic procedure for determining the desired sample size, Murphy's Law is likely to affect our work. Murphy's Law says that "whatever can go wrong will go wrong." Nonresponse is one of these problems. Additionally, we will see that many other events and factors may contaminate our research efforts. Our choice of sampling plan is only one of the many links in the chain of events that we know as the research enterprise. We must be prepared to deal with whatever elements we eventually obtain, regardless of our original ideal considerations. Eventually we do the best we can with what we have, and we encourage others who read our work to assess its importance in view of existing research limitations.

Potentates: Juveniles, Prisoners, and Permission to Sample Special Populations of Subjects

Potentates are those who require special permission to study them. Criminologists and others who study the criminal justice system often find that gaining access to specific populations targeted for study is difficult. It is not particularly easy for researchers to obtain samples of prison or jail inmates, or to gather large samples of delinquent offenders in various detention facilities. Studying probation officers, criminal court judges, law enforcement officers, federal judges, correctional officers, and district attorneys are not easy tasks. These persons are usually insulated from the general public by secretarial hierarchies, locked gates, and a general aversion to being studied by anyone.

Studies of juvenile delinquents are sometimes difficult to conduct because of the confidential nature of record-keeping relating to them. Not all juvenile courtrooms are open to the public, and court dispositions and adjudications relating to juvenile offenders are considered restricted material. Even if investigators wish to examine juveniles in school settings and obtain self-report information about delinquent conduct, permission must first be obtained from principals and teachers. There is often resistance to such investigations for a variety of reasons. School board and parental opposition to having their children involved in any type of research asking them to disclose personal details of their lives are barriers to certain kinds of research. Questionnaires are sometimes perceived as threatening or informative. Checklists of infractions and law violations may be interpreted by some juveniles as expected behaviors. In a sense, questions dealing with prohibited behaviors may prompt some youths to engage in those behaviors or at least be more susceptible to involvement in delinquent conduct.

Studying lawyers and district attorneys may be difficult, since their time is often limited by large numbers of clients and high caseloads. The sponsorship of research by a major college or university might help researchers gain access to some of these persons. Snowball sampling might be used as a means of obtaining an introduction to different attorneys, especially if some of their attorney-friends have referred interviewers to them.

BOX 4.3   PERSONALITY HIGHLIGHT

JOANNE BELKNAP
University of Colorado–Boulder

Statistics: B.A. (political science), University of Colorado–Boulder; M.S. (criminology and criminal justice), Michigan State University; Ph.D. (criminology and criminal justice), Michigan State University.

BACKGROUND AND INTERESTS

Most of my research is in the area of feminist criminology and social justice. I am invested in shedding light on girls' and womens' experiences as victims and offenders, and examining how sexism intersects with other forms of oppression, particularly racism, classism, and sexuality. My goal is to do this not only in terms of their experiences with the criminal processing system, but how girls and women experience victimization and offending in their lives outside of the formal system. I am also committed to a better understanding of the *link* between girls' and womens' victimization and offending. More specifically, how does their victimization place them at risk of becoming offenders, and how is offending related to subsequent victimization risks?

My interests include putting my research into practice by serving communities outside the university. Thus, in addition to my book, *The Invisible Woman: Gender, Crime, and Justice* (I'm currently working on the third edition) and many other publications, I spend a fair amount of time trying to find out from various communities (e.g., victim advocates and offender advocates) what type of research needs to be done and attempting to format my findings in a manner that can result in policy changes.

In the eighth grade I decided I wanted to be a physical therapist. I volunteered and worked a great deal with disabled people of all ages from that time through most of college. I was devastated when I found out at the end of my sophomore year in college at the University of Colorado (CU) that I was not even considered for an interview in the medical school (for physical therapy) due to my score on the MMPI (Minnesota Multiphasic Personality Inventory). I worked that summer as a horse wrangler and camp counselor for Easter Seals in Grand Mesa, Colorado. The nurse that worked there was from Wisconsin and talked me into dropping out of school (while I decided what to do about my major) and moving to Madison, Wisconsin, with her. Well, we were supposed to meet there in September, but she never showed up. I spent that year working at various minimum-wage jobs, and living, working, and volunteering with people who were disabled. I was very much impacted by a young woman with advanced multiple sclerosis for whom I was a roommate and live-in aide. Shortly after I lived and worked with her, she suffered a severe stroke after being raped by an acquaintance of her previous roommate/aide.

BOX 4.3   CONTINUED

In 1979 I returned to college and decided to major in political science with the idea of going into law school. At that time I was busy protesting Rocky Flats, a nuclear bomb site near CU, and learning about alternative energy sources, particularly solar power. My last semester at CU I took a course from a wonderful professor I'm still in contact with, Dennis Eckhart, on urban public policy. We spent one week studying prisons, and it literally changed my life. I became obsessed with the injustices of prisons in the United States and all of the channels of racism and poverty in the processing of people who end up in prisons. Somehow, I never thought about this pattern in imprisonment in terms of sexism.

My last summer at CU I was sexually assaulted by a stranger in the middle of campus in broad daylight when no one else was around. This was another life-changing event. My frustration with the criminal processing system and even some members of my own family resulted in an anger about sexism I'd never experienced so intensely. Meanwhile, some of my college friends had started law school and felt disillusioned with it, and I started believing that I would have that same experience. And so I went back to my favorite professor and mentor, Dennis Eckhart, and asked him what I should do with my interest in prisons. He suggested getting a master's degree in criminal justice.

In 1981 I headed to Michigan State University to start what I thought would be a one-year stint in the master's program. I had the empowering experience of working with Merry Morash, a new assistant professor in that program, and she encouraged me to go on for a Ph.D. I enjoyed economics as an undergraduate, and so I chose my dissertation topic to examine how poverty, unemployment, and income inequality affect the crime rate and how the crime rate, in turn, affected these economic rates.

RESEARCH INVESTIGATIONS

In 1986 I began my first faculty job as an assistant professor at the University of Cincinnati (UC). My first month there, I wrote the proposal for my textbook, *The Invisible Woman,* which took me 10 years to write. I basically fell into my first empirical research project at UC. I was asked to be on the board for the local battered women's shelter and to volunteer on the police-liaison subcommittee. Within a few months on that subcommittee, I developed a 10-page survey for police on how they handled and perceived domestic violence cases. This experience showed me the profound advantages of having research designs heavily informed and influenced by practitioners. The victim advocates, shelter workers, and police on the subcommittee thought of important survey items I never would have thought to include. This study resulted in many publications and the beginning of establishing myself as an expert in intimate partner violence.

After being on the short-lived Ohio Governor's Task Force for Incarcerated Women in the late 1980s, my long-standing interests and concerns about prison exploded; only this time, I was focused on women. I found, similar to many before me, how difficult it is to access women prisoners when conducting research. One male colleague was astounded when research similar to what he'd conducted in men's prisons was approved by the Ohio Department of

BOX 4.3   CONTINUED

Rehabilitation and Corrections, but denied by the warden of the women's prison. The practices in women's compared to men's prisons, particularly regarding significantly inferior medical care, higher levels of sexual abuse by guards, and more substandard legal libraries, make it far more difficult to do research on female (compared with male) prisoners, unless one is solely researching their experiences outside of prison. Although that study was thwarted, I was able to do a study of women jail guards, through a former student and the contacts I had made on the police liaison committee for the battered women's shelter.

In 1995 through a former undergraduate student, I was placed on a statewide committee to examine programming for delinquent girls. Along with my graduate student at the time, Kristi Holsinger, she and I worked with the group to design a focus group study with girls and practitioners. This was my first time using focus groups, and I remain convinced that it is an excellent way to start research in exploratory topics. I was profoundly struck with the frequency and severity of traumatic experiences these girls reported preceding their forays into crime. These traumas included witnessing a father's murder and a mother choosing to have the state send her daughter to foster care rather than agreeing to stop living with the boyfriend who had raped her daughter. Kristi and I turned the focus group study into a quantitative study of incarcerated boys and girls to examine the role of traumas in their lives. We found that while abuse and traumas were often gendered (i.e., the girls reporting significantly more of most abuse and traumas), the boys still reported epidemic levels of childhood traumas (including sexual abuse), leading us to conclude that childhood traumas are significant risk factors for subsequent delinquency.

During the data collection for the focus group and the survey studies, various folks working in the system started telling me about the new policy of waiving youth to adult court, and if convicted, housing them in adult inmate populations. I spent a couple of years trying to gain access to an adult prison where girls were incarcerated. Eventually, I found one that allowed our study, and Emily Gaarder (a graduate student) and I conducted intensive one-on-one interviews with 22 of these young women. It was the most difficult research I've done to date in terms of what I felt emotionally when I left the prison after the long days of interviewing. None of the girls were the "hardened criminals" we'd expected; indeed, most had no or very light criminal histories. Again, the traumatic experiences of their childhoods were shocking, particularly given how little intervention, if any, had occurred when they were victims; yet as offenders, they were tried at the deepest end of the system.

In 1998 I accepted a position in the Sociology and Women's Studies Departments at my alma mater, the University of Colorado. I always say, "I would have been voted least likely to be a professor here" had we taken such a poll among my friends in my dorm my first year. It never occurred to me that I'd ever be a professor as an undergraduate, and it was very exciting to come home. Since being in Colorado again, I've continued my research on delinquent girls and battered women. I work with practitioners in both of the areas and redid the focus group study of delinquent girls and practitioners (with some new twists suggested by the practitioners in Colorado). With a friend since graduate school, Cris Sullivan, we conducted a longitudinal study of battered women whose cases had reached the courts. I have been fortunate to have

BOX 4.3 CONTINUED

much of my research funded by the National Institute of Justice, although a lot of it has also been funded by my checking account.

ADVICE TO STUDENTS

I think that it is important to view research as a way to potentially make your mark on the world. When you identify a problem that concerns you, pursue a research design that is most appropriate to document the problem, and ideally suggest solutions and policy changes. I am also a huge advocate for practitioner-informed research. It is important as we design our studies, and even as we interpret our findings, to have a panel of nonresearch experts to guide us. I have used many research designs (qualitative and quantitative) and am a firm believer that the research question and the state of existing research should influence the approach the researcher takes.

Sometimes there are organizational constraints that restrict access to particular populations. If an investigator wished to study FBI agents, for example, local FBI offices do not disclose information to the public about their present roster of agents, where they live, or how they may be contacted. FBI agents usually have unlisted telephone numbers, live quietly and anonymously in neighborhoods for many years, and are advised by their superiors to refrain from divulging any information about their jobs. If you meet an FBI agent at a social gathering, chances are that he or she will reply, "I work for the government" when you ask him or her about his or her occupation or profession. This high level of secrecy about one's affairs is primarily a function of the organization itself, in much the same way that the Central Intelligence Agency would regulate the behaviors of its operatives.

In sum, any research plan must realistically evaluate the accessibility of target populations. It is one thing to write a research plan. It is quite a different thing to implement it. When researchers apply for research funds from public agencies or private foundations, it is customary for them to include supporting documentation and letters from those they intend to contact. This information lets the funding agency know that the researchers have anticipated certain data collection problems and have engaged in preliminary efforts to ensure that the data can be obtained if the study is funded.

SUMMARY

Most of the research conducted in criminal justice and criminology involves obtain samples of elements from diverse populations throughout the criminal justice system, including law enforcement, prosecution and the courts, and corrections at both the adult and juvenile levels. Sampling means to take a proportion of persons from the larger population of them.

Usually a sampling frame is designated that is a population about which we seek information. This sampling frame may be all parole officers in Alaska, all delinquent boys in North Dakota, all female inmates in Indiana, or all female victims of domestic violence for the years 2003–2004 in Iowa. These aggregates of persons are also known as populations. The characteristics of populations are known as parameters. When we draw a few persons from the population and describe them, these persons become our sample and their characteristics are called statistics. Our sample statistics are used, therefore, to make estimates about population parameters. The samples drawn from populations are considered more or less representative of the populations from which they have been drawn, depending on the selection process used.

Generalizations about populations are heavily dependent upon the typicality of the samples we obtain. Usually larger samples are more representative of populations from which they were drawn than smaller samples, although there are more than a few exceptions. Significantly influencing the sampling process and how many persons we should obtain for our sample is the original population size. Also, we must consider the cost of obtaining the elements we want from the sample. Elements may be selected because of their convenience and accessibility, and some elements may be obtained less expensively than other elements. These sampling decisions depend on our personal resources and study objectives.

Sampling performs several important functions. Sampling enables us to economize our resources. It is simply not practical to study all population elements, especially if the population is extremely large. Also, samples are more manageable than studying entire populations. Another consideration is whether we intend to use one or more statistical tests in the analysis of our collected data from the sample we draw. Certain statistical procedures require that we have certain numbers of elements, and thus our sample size becomes critical if we choose to use certain statistical methods. Furthermore, some experiments we choose to conduct require samples of specified sizes.

Ideally, we seek to obtain samples of elements that are typical or representative of the populations from which they are drawn. Randomness is used under ideal conditions, since it provides that we will include persons from the population where each person to be drawn has an equal and independent chance of being included in our resulting sample. Equality of draw means that each person has the same chance of being included. Independence of draw means that the draw of one or more elements for inclusion in our sample will not influence or change the chances of the remaining elements from being included. Sampling with replacement is used to ensure equality and independence of draw. It is assumed that random samples have been drawn using the principle of sampling with replacement. This means that persons once drawn for inclusion in our sample have an equal chance of being drawn again. This seldom happens in social research, however, and there are guidelines or rules of thumb to follow whenever the same persons are drawn two or more times in sample selection. Sampling without replacement means that persons once drawn cannot be drawn again. But eliminating them from the population means that the remaining elements have an increasingly greater chance of being included, and thus randomness is defeated by this less desirable selection method. Samples drawn in accordance with randomness principles are called probability samples, and statements can be made about population parameters based on sample statistics with a probability attached.

Random samples are typically drawn by using a table of random numbers or having a computer-determined draw to select elements for us. A single sample drawn from a table of random numbers is considered a simple random sample. Simple random samples are the easiest to use among probability sampling plans. Samples of specified sizes may be obtained, and the generalizability of such samples to populations from which they were drawn is often assumed. However, because not all persons in the population have been included in a sample, some amount of sampling error exists. The amount of sampling error varies according to sample size. Usually the larger the random sample, the smaller the sampling error.

If greater detail is desired in a probability sample, a sample may be obtained where certain variables, such as age, gender, or some other characteristic, can be controlled. Thus, if there are few females in a given population but researchers want to include a certain number of females, specific numbers of females may be drawn randomly from the subpopulation of females so that there are sufficient numbers of them in the resulting sample. The same is true about any other characteristic of persons that may occur infrequently in the population. When greater or lesser numbers of certain types of persons (e.g., male–female; freshmen, sophomores, juniors, seniors; persons over 21 and those 20 or younger) are intentionally included in samples, the random samples are stratified. These samples may be either proportionate stratified random samples or disproportionate stratified random samples. Proportionate stratified random samples are those where the distribution of certain sample characteristics exists to the same degree as the characteristics exist in the population. For instance, if the population consists of 40 percent male, then a proportionate stratified random sample would consist of 40 percent male, where the researcher has controlled for gender. If only 10 percent of the population consists of females, however, and researchers want to get even numbers of females and males for their sample, where 50 percent are male and 50 percent are female, then disproportionate stratified random sampling would be used. In these instances, both males and females are included randomly, but their numbers in the sample are carefully regulated by the researcher to reflect particular research purposes or objectives. Proportionate and disproportionate stratified random samples are useful for experimental purposes. Also, they may depict to a greater degree the typicality of the sample in relation to the populations from which they were drawn.

Some random samples are obtained from large geographical areas. Since it is often not feasible to send interviewers all over the United States to interview random numbers of persons, sometimes the United States is divided into horizontal and vertical grids, and further subdivisions of these grids yield clusters of persons in specific areas. An interviewer can travel to Iowa, therefore, and interview five or six families living in close proximity to one another as a "cluster" of families. Random samples drawn in this fashion are known as cluster or area(l) sampling, or multistage sampling, referring to the subsequent subdivisions of geographical areas into smaller subdivisions from which clusters of persons may be obtained. Cluster sampling is used infrequently, although it has considerable value if generalizing to large geographical populations is desired.

Another class of sampling plans are called nonprobability sampling plans. These plans do not use randomness in the selection of elements. Accordingly, the generalizability of nonprobability sampling plans is extremely limited. The most common nonprobability sampling plan is convenience or accidental sampling. Approaching persons on the street and asking them their opinions about events, or obtaining large samples of students from university classes, are examples of accidental or convenience samples. Their generalizability is limited or unknown, because the population from which they were selected is unknown. Another type of nonprobability sampling plan is systematic sampling. Systematic sampling occurs most frequently when researchers use alphabetized listings of persons and select every 10th or 50th person from the list. This guarantees the inclusion of every 10th or 50th person, but it also guarantees the exclusion of all persons in between. Thus, equality of draw, a critical element of randomness, is simply not present in systematic sampling. But it is easy to use, as are almost all other nonprobability sampling methods.

Another nonprobability sampling plan is purposive or judgmental sampling, which involves hand picking elements from a given population. If someone doing the hand picking knows the population very well, such as a small community, then the resulting sample may actually be more typical of the community than any random sample that could be drawn. But this type of sampling plan again fails to ensure equality of draw because elements are hand picked. Some persons are intentionally included, while others are intentionally excluded. Quota sampling is another nonprobability sampling method. Quota sampling seeks to include persons with specific characteristics or qualities of interest to the researcher. Persons are sought who have these characteristics, while those who do not possess these characteristics are excluded.

Snowball sampling is another nonprobability sampling method that is often used to chart interactions among persons who share different kinds of information. One person is asked who he or she interacts or communicates with, and these other persons are contacted. In turn, they are asked the same question, until the researcher has a good idea of the range of persons among which particular information is shared. Persons are interviewed and the result is a growing aggregate of persons such as a snowball gathering more snow as it rolls down a hill. Such a sampling method is nonrandom. Two additional sampling plans are considered nonprobability plans. These are dense and saturation sampling. Dense sampling means to sample densely, indicative of where researchers obtain about 50 percent of the population elements in nonrandom ways. Saturation sampling involves getting 90 percent or more of the population, again in a nonrandom way. The idea is that there are so many elements involved in the sample that they must be typical of the population from which they were drawn. Technically, however, such samples fail the randomness test and thus their generalizability to the larger population of elements is seriously impaired.

Because of certain types of experimentation, researchers may investigate either a single sample, two samples, or more than two samples, represented by k-samples. Whenever two or more samples are examined, questions arise as to whether they are independent or related with one another. Independent samples, whether there are two or more, consist of persons who do not belong to two or more samples at once. Related samples are samples that have been matched in certain ways, or are samples in before–after experiments where the same persons have been used as their own controls. When matched persons have been used, or when the same persons have been used in before–after experiments, they are considered related. Certain research objectives are designed for either independent or related samples, and also certain statistical tests may require that two or more samples be either independent or related.

Various sampling problems and issues often arise in the sampling process. How large should the sample be in relation to the population? A good rule of thumb is that the sample size should comprise about 10 percent of the population from which it was drawn. However, extremely large populations of 20 million or more make it unlikely that researchers will be able to sample 2 million people with their limited resources. Large samples in criminal justice and criminology are relative, depending on the researcher, but usually samples of 500 or more are considered large. Another issue or problem is nonresponse. Almost every study conducted has some nonresponse. In the social sciences, typical response to a mailed questionnaire falls in the 30–50 percent range, meaning nonresponse of from 50 to 70 percent. What do investigators call random samples that they have drawn but where nonresponse is 70 percent? With any type of nonresponse, it is not realistic to label the resulting sample of your random sample as a random sample. Where any nonresponse exists, randomness is not achieved. Nevertheless, researchers persist in their research projects and do the best they can with what they have. Little or nothing can be done to prevent or overcome nonresponse. Thus, randomness is seldom achieved in any social science research enterprise.

Sample representativeness is also problematic. How do we know that any given sample is representative or typical of the population from which it was drawn? We don't. Provided that we have complied with all random sampling provisions, there is good reason to believe that our samples are random and thus representative of certain populations, but in social research, this outcome can never be guaranteed. Also, there are gaps between ideal samples desired and real samples obtained. This is related in part to the nonresponse issue. But it suggests that we may have to settle for smaller samples of elements because of budgetary constraints. Thus, our ideals may be too lofty and our funds too limited to get the kinds of samples we would like to have. Finally, some persons are simply not available for study. If we seek to examine juvenile records, for instance, and attempt to determine whether certain delinquents are gang members and whether gang influence is growing or declining in a given geographical area, such as a state or city, we may draft a perfect research design. But when we attempt to gather information about juveniles, state or city officials may deny us access to this information because of confidentiality laws. Therefore, our research project is terminated early, simply because we can't gain access to the data we need.

QUESTIONS FOR REVIEW

1. Differentiate between probability and nonprobability sampling plans. Review briefly their general functions and limitations.

2. What are some major considerations in deciding to sample? Discuss these considerations briefly.

3. Discuss some of the problems researchers might have when studying potentates.

4. Sometimes systematic sampling is considered a probability sampling plan. What is the basis for this thinking? What can be said of systematic samples that might disqualify them as probability sampling plans?

5. What are some general rules that apply to determining one's sample size? Are extremely large samples necessarily better than smaller sample sizes? What factors should be considered when determining one's sample size?

6. What are some of the primary advantages of judgmental or purposive sampling plans? In what sense might some researchers consider them to be superior to probability sampling plans?

7. What is the primary control factor in probability sampling plans? Why is it important? How can this factor be achieved when samples are selected from target populations?

8. Distinguish between independence and equality of drawing sample elements.

9. Differentiate between independent and related samples. What are at least three ways that related samples may be obtained?

10. What is meant by sample representativeness? Can we ever guarantee that a sample of elements will be representative of the population from which it is drawn? Why or why not?

11. What is an accidental sample? Under what circumstances might accidental samples be the only samples available for study?

12. Define and differentiate between population parameters and sample statistics.

13. What is nonresponse in sampling and how can it be affected?

14. Why is there often a gap between ideal sampling plans and real samples of elements obtained by the researcher?

15. When would area or cluster sampling be appropriate to apply? Identify at least three different situations where such a technique would be useful.

5

Data Collection Strategies II: Questionnaires

CHAPTER OUTLINE

CHAPTER OBJECTIVES

As the result of reading this chapter, the following objectives will be realized:

1. Describing the general use of questionnaires as important data-gathering tools in the research enterprise.

2. Learning the functions of questionnaires for social research purposes, including description and measurement.

3. Understanding the different types of questionnaires, including fixed-response and open-ended item questionnaires, their weaknesses, strengths, and applications.

4. Describing different forms of questionnaire administration and their applications, including mailed questionnaires and face-to-face questionnaire administration, the research applications of each, and their respective advantages and disadvantages.

5. Studying the mechanics of questionnaire construction, including questionnaire length, wording, item selection, item order, the use of contingency questions, and question response patterns.

6. Examining questionnaire content and wording, and learning how to maximize response to questionnaire administration.

7. Learning about response and nonresponse and how to deal with nonresponse problems.

8. Understanding pilot studies and pretesting questionnaires.

9. Describing the importance of avoiding double-barreled questions and increasing the anonymity of response.

10. Understanding the value of self-reports and the information such self-reports disclose.

11. Learning about when respondents tell the truth or are deceptive in their responses.

12. Understanding the connection between respondents' cultural values and questionnaire wording.

Introduction

The most popular data-gathering tool used in criminological research is the questionnaire. Questionnaires are self-administered inventories that seek descriptive information about people and their opinions about things. From our earliest years in school, we are accustomed to completing questionnaires. Schools solicit information from us about our personal backgrounds, our previous educational experience, including high schools and elementary schools attended, where we live, the occupations or professions of our parents, and our immediate and long-range interests, including our declared academic majors and professional ambitions. Perhaps you have been in a class where your instructor has distributed questionnaires in connection with a research project being conducted, or maybe the instructor has distributed questionnaires to you and your classmates on behalf of someone else conducting research.

This chapter opens with a description of questionnaires and their functions. These functions include description and measurement. Almost always when questionnaires are administered to persons, various scales or inventories are included on these questionnaires to assess or measure certain qualities or properties these people are believed to possess. The descriptive nature of questionnaires will be explained and illustrated. Also, the measurement dimension of questionnaires will be examined.

Questionnaires are differentiated according to whether they are fixed-response or open-ended, which refers to the nature of the questions asked. Fixed-response questionnaires are used in order to make it easier for respondents to check the responses that best fit them. Little or no writing is required. Therefore, it is expected that the ease with which persons can respond to fixed-response questions will improve the chances of having them complete their questionnaires and return them. Other questionnaires contain open-ended items. These items require respondents to write more or less lengthy responses to questions and describe themselves or settings different ways. These types of questions are more difficult to answer for those with less education and who have a general inability to express themselves in writing. Some questionnaires consist of both types of questions, fixed-response and open-ended. Depending on the investigator's interests, the research design selected, the target audience, and whether questionnaires will be used as a major data-gathering tool, different types of items will be included. Most questionnaires used in criminology and criminal justice are fixed-response, because they are simply easier to score and tabulate. The advantages, disadvantages, and research applications of these types of questionnaires will be described and discussed.

The chapter next describes various ways questionnaires can be administered. A common way of administering questionnaires is through the mail. But questionnaires can also be delivered to respondents in person. The advantages, disadvantages, and research applications of mailed questionnaires will be presented in contrast with face-to-face questionnaire administration.

Questionnaires are relatively easy to construct, although there are several important guidelines to follow when developing questions as well as alternative responses for them. Thus, attention will be given to questionnaire construction and format as well as to some of the guidelines associated with the proper administration of questionnaires to others. This section of the chapter examines questionnaire length and describes details such as question selection, ordering of items, the use of contingency questions, questionnaire length, the general questionnaire contents and wording, including potential bias sources, double-barreled questions, the use of certain key words, and assurances of anonymity.

Also examined is the use of questionnaires for self-reports. Often persons are given questionnaires to determine whether they have engaged in particular behaviors that may or may not be legal or moral. Self-reports disclose important differences between official data sources compiled by government agencies and what people actually do or think.

Another consideration is whether persons tell the truth when they respond to questionnaires. How do we know whether persons are telling the truth about the statements they make or agree with? Sometimes questionnaires include items that are intended to function as lie indicators, in an effort to see whether or not someone is probably being truthful. Some of these items will be examined. Also influential is the cultural wording and dating of the questionnaire. If questionnaires are used that have been constructed by others, are they older questionnaires with much irrelevant or meaningless jargon that may have been used 20 or 30 years ago? Unfortunately, some researchers automatically use questionnaires others have prepared many years ago without first checking to see if they contain outdated or antiquated questions. Finally, there will always be some nonresponse to questionnaires. How do investigators deal with nonresponse when it occurs? What if one or more pages in a questionnaire are left blank? How do we deal with this situation? This and other problems are described and discussed.

Questionnaires in Criminal Justice Research

Each of the data-gathering tools discussed in this and the next few chapters should not be viewed in isolation. That is, we must consider questionnaires as one of several data-gathering strategies we might employ to gather information about people and their characteristics. It is not unusual for researchers to use several different types of data-gathering tools in the same research project. For example, if we were to study law enforcement officers in a particular city, we might obtain information from them through questionnaires. Furthermore, we might observe several officers as they conduct their patrol activities. Also, we might interview them at different times to determine why particular actions were undertaken. We might even supplement all of this information with reports about the police department generally, its organization and operation, and its change over time. Whenever two or more data-gathering tools or strategies are used by researchers for investigating the same social aggregate (e.g., a police department, community corrections agency, probation office, jail inmates, or juvenile delinquents), this practice is known as triangulation. Therefore, we would practice triangulation if we used both questionnaires and interviews, and possibly observation, in our investigations of law enforcement officers and their patrol activities.

The majority of criminal justice professionals and criminologists probably use two or more data-gathering techniques in their investigations of social phenomena. Different kinds of information are yielded about the people studied, depending on the data-gathering procedures used. For instance, Thomas Whetstone (2001) surveyed police officers from a Midwestern jurisdiction in order to find out why many of these officers decline to participate in the promotion process for the position of sergeant. He distributed questionnaires to 326 police officers who were eligible to participate in the process by sending them a packet containing a questionnaire, self-addressed stamped envelope, and other materials. The response rate was 46 percent, with 149 questionnaires returned. Whetstone selected 40 officers from these respondents and divided them into four **focus groups** of 10 each, where discussions and interviews were conducted in order to provide further insight into the officers' rationales for declining promotional opportunities. Not only did the questionnaire information reveal much about why these officers declined to participate in the promotional process, but the focus group interview information permitted Whetstone to learn more important details as well.

In order to describe fully the research contributions and limitations of these different data-gathering tools, specific chapters highlight each technique and illustrate its application. It will become more apparent that certain deficiencies inherent in one type of data-gathering tool will likely be compensated for or overcome by simultaneously using alternative data-gathering tools.

Throughout the criminal justice system, there are numerous aggregates about which we seek information. We have mentioned law enforcement officers as one important aggregate. Others include prosecutors, judges, court officials, defense attorneys, correctional officers, community corrections workers and ancillary personnel, and, of course, clients. Clients may be defendants, convicted misdemeanants or felons, probationers, jail or prison inmates, or parolees. These clients may further be distinguished according to whether they are divertees, halfway house members, work or study releasees, furloughees, shock probationers, or those participating in home confinement or electronic monitoring programs.

The literature in criminal justice and criminology is abundant with studies where questionnaires have been used as the principal data-gathering tool. Questionnaires are almost always equated with survey research. For instance, Frances Reddington and Betsy Kreisel (2003) studied fundamental skills training programs among the states relating to juvenile probation officers. They sent questionnaires to key persons in all state juvenile probation departments in an effort to solicit information pertaining to the nature of their course curricula for probation officer skills training. A cover letter included with the questionnaire asked these persons to send Reddington and Kreisel a copy of the course curriculum and other training materials. The questionnaire asked about training funding as well as opinions of these persons about nationally set training standards for various training topics. Responses were obtained from 35 states for a response rate of about 70 percent. Of these respondents, six states reported that their jurisdictions do not provide fundamental skills training for their probation officers. Thus, Reddington and Kreisel subsequently analyzed the responses received from the remaining 29 states. Much was learned about the amount of training hours required by different state programs, curriculum contents, and areas of competence stressed.

In another study, Eric Lambert, Nancy Hogan, and Shannon Barton (2002) studied the phenomenon of organizational commitment among correctional staff at a high-security Midwestern state correctional facility. They prepared and mailed questionnaires to 420 correctional staff members, subsequently obtaining 270 returned and usable questionnaires for a response rate of 64 percent. In this questionnaire administration, these researchers prepared items to measure one's commitment to the job according to different criteria, such as chances of promotion, recognition associated with work performed, and the amount of information received about one's work performance. These researchers also questioned respondents about their age, years of experience in correctional work, educational attainment, gender, type of work assignment, race/ethnicity, and a variety of other sociodemographic variables. Their results, when analyzed, provided much valuable information about the importance of different factors as they impact or influence one's level of organizational commitment.

Researchers often construct questionnaires that contain original questions and one or more scales that others have created in previous studies. This practice is quite common, since there are many existing scales that measure important social and attitudinal variables that are theoretically intertwined with criminal justice and criminological questions. Using existing scales exposes these instruments to further empirical testing, experimentation, and verification, while those using such scales benefit because they do not have to create their own measures. However, regardless of the popularity of certain existing scales, not everyone finds them suitable for their individual research applications. One or more questionnaire items may not fit the intended audience. Therefore, some customizing is necessary to produce questionnaires that are directly relevant for certain samples of elements. For instance, in the study by Lambert and colleagues (2002) mentioned earlier, these researchers included several items from a previously developed **scale** known as the Social Climate Survey, which had been created by W. Saylor and K. Wright (1992).

Functions of Questionnaires

Two basic functions of questionnaires are description and measurement.

Description

Information acquired through questionnaire administration may provide a **description** of individual and/or group characteristics such as gender, age, years of education, occupation, income, political and religious affiliation, civic group or fraternal order membership, urban or rural background, and job status.

Describing elements serves several useful purposes. For instance, a knowledge of the age distribution of a sample of law enforcement officers may provide researchers with plausible explanations for certain group phenomena that occur on the job, including clique formations, liberal or conservative positions on social issues, intra-officer esprit de corps, and

BOX 5.1   PERSONALITY HIGHLIGHT

RICHARD R. BENNETT
American University

Statistics: B.A., Randolph-Macon College; M.A., Florida State University; Ph.D., Washington State University

BACKGROUND AND INTERESTS

All good research is essentially comparative. We wonder why men commit more crimes than women, why violent crimes occur more often in poorer neighborhoods than in middle-class neighborhoods, why some police forces use lethal force more often than others, and why some states impose capital punishment and others don't use this punishment method. It is only relatively recently that criminology and criminal justice scholars have looked beyond their national borders to find answers to their research questions. The benefits of conducting cross-national comparative research are tremendous because nations show greater variation on many variables of interest to criminology and criminal justice researchers (such as the type of judicial system, approach to corrections, and level of economic development) than do states in the U.S. or regions in the United Kingdom. The research literature in our field doesn't contain many comparative crime and criminal justice research studies, however. My presidential address for the Academy of Criminal Justice Sciences (published in *Justice Quarterly,* Vol. 21, 2004) lists a number of obstacles comparative researchers have faced and solutions we can implement in the future.

Prior to and shortly after completing my doctorate, my scholarly interest and research endeavors focused on policing, especially police socialization and behavior. I became interested in the comparative aspect of policing in the 1970s after meeting a police scholar teaching and researching in the Netherlands. Although I had been trained as a quantitative researcher and my early publications were heavily data-driven, my first comparative publication was theoretical and argued the benefit of using a comparative approach to constructing and evaluating theories (see *Criminology,* Vol. 18, 1980). Surprisingly, this conceptual work moved me away from policing to an interest in the etiology of crime. I began building a large cross-national data archive that I call the Correlates of Crime data set using statistics from the United Nations and other international organizations. (The data set is available to all researchers through the Inter-University Consortium for Political and Social Research at the University of Michigan.) It contains data on crimes, offenders, social institutions, and political and economic variables for 52 nations over the 25-year period of 1960–1984. I've published numerous articles using this data

BOX 5.1 CONTINUED

set on issues such as the effect of development on crime, the cross-national determinants of juvenile delinquency, and the relevance of U.S.-based theories of crime (like routine activities theory) in explaining crime cross-nationally.

RESEARCH EXPERIENCES

While using the archival data, I became very aware of the pitfalls of relying solely on them (the pitfalls are detailed below). I then shifted to survey research and conducted a victim survey in Belize, Central America. One of the publications from that study used a comparative framework and contrasted Belize findings with those from a similar victim survey in Newark, New Jersey.

In the early 1990s I returned to my roots and began researching police issues but using a comparative approach. My positive experience in Belize led me to apply for a Fulbright Senior Research Grant to study policing in the English-speaking Caribbean. This time I decided to triangulate on the issues of interest and used three data collection methodologies. I drew on my experience with survey research to field an extensive survey of constables and officers in the police forces of Barbados, Jamaica, Trinidad, and Tobago. I collected archival data on crime and calls for service from each nation. I also employed observational techniques and spent approximately 250 hours observing the constables and their supervisors in each of the three police agencies. The resulting data set has served as the basis for numerous journal articles, which have appeared in *Justice Quarterly, Policing: An International Journal of Police Strategies and Management,* and *Police Practice and Research: An International Journal.*

My current research interests remain in the comparative field. I am designing a research project to field in Africa that will be methodologically similar to the one I undertook in the Caribbean and with the same focus: the effect of cultural variations on the delivery of police services and the relationships between the police and the policed. In addition, I am currently updating the Correlates of Crime archive to extend its coverage to 2002 so it will hold 43 years of data.

ADVICE TO STUDENTS

Here's my advice to students who wish to conduct comparative research:

1. Do it! Not only will you have the thrill of intellectual discovery, but you will also get to travel to new and wonderful places, meet interesting people, and learn about cultures that are vastly different from your own.

2. Let your theory direct your research design. Don't be a one-method researcher seeking a suitable topic. Theory will direct you to the appropriate concepts and variables and will guide you on how to operationalize them. Theory will also suggest analysis strategies and interpretations of results.

3. Begin your comparative career by reading all you can about crime and justice around the world. Fortunately for those who can read only English, many of the classic works by non-English writers have been translated into the English language.

BOX 5.1 CONTINUED

4. Be flexible and informed when deciding on a research design and data collection methodology, especially if you are interested in developing countries. If you decide that the best design for your study involves archival data, be sure that you understand their pitfalls such as differences in cultural and operational definitions of crime, variations in citizen and police reporting of crime, and differences in the way criminal incidents are recorded. Also, learn about the culture of the countries, especially their criminal justice systems (see my article in *Criminology,* Vol. 28 [with James Lynch], for a detailed analysis of errors in archival crime data). If you decide to conduct a survey, learn about the culture of the nation (or nations) so that you can design an appropriate questionnaire and administer it without the fear of committing fatal fielding errors. I've found defining a population and drawing a sample, using suitable idioms in question wording and ensuring quality control during questionnaire administration were the most daunting tasks in my survey experiences in developing nations.

If you wish to conduct an observational study, be aware of your perspective and try to leave your cultural biases home when you go into the field. Again, do your homework well and learn about the history, culture, traditions, and people of the nation or nations where you'll work. Also be aware of the formal and informal conventions that operate within these nations' criminal justice systems. Personally I find this methodology the most rewarding. Being there and experiencing it all firsthand adds a dimension to the inquiry that cannot be replicated by reading books or interviewing ex-patriots. Regardless of the data collection method or methods you choose, drawing cross-national comparisons will reveal more insights than any other approach I know.

5. Attend international scholarly conferences and learn about comparative work that is in process or recently concluded. If international conferences are too costly, attend the annual meeting of the Academy of Criminal Justice Sciences and the American Society of Criminology, which are held at different locations across the United States (one of them is probably close by this year or the next). Although most of the attendees and research are American-based, there are growing numbers of foreign attendees and sessions devoted to comparative research. These conferences will give you an entree into a network of researchers with firsthand knowledge of the dos and don'ts of comparative research who will perhaps serve as mentors or even co-investigators, and who may help you gain access to the organizations or archived data you want.

6. Regardless of whether or not you aspire to a career in comparative research, do yourself a favor and read some comparative literature. You will be surprised how much you can learn about the American system of justice and the etiology of crime by understanding how other systems are structured and how societal-level factors influence criminality.

7. Above all, enjoy your pursuit of knowledge.

the type and amount of possible officer misconduct. Are younger officers more inclined to use excessive force when taking suspects into custody? The educational characteristics of particular employees may help to account for different assessments of job content, supervision, job satisfaction, and work quality. Are more educated police officers more effective at resolving domestic disputes or quelling civil disorders? What factors seem most important for improving police–community relations? Accurate descriptions of elements in any social setting can benefit researchers in many ways. Insight, explanation, and prediction are but a few of the many contributions questionnaires make to social inquiry.

Measurement

A primary function of almost every questionnaire is the **measurement** of individual and/or group variables, particularly attitudinal phenomena. Questionnaires may contain single items or multiple items (i.e., questions about issues or simple statements) used in combination that are designed to measure various attitudinal phenomena, such as group cohesiveness, peer group influence, burnout and stress, alienation, professionalism, job security, role clarity, anxiety, or sexual permissiveness. The list of attitudinal dimensions that may potentially be tapped by questionnaires is endless. Annually, improvements are made on existing questionnaire measures, and new questionnaire instruments are continually being constructed as well.

Types of Questionnaires

Questionnaires are often classified according to whether they include fixed-response or open-ended items. Sometimes, questionnaires contain both fixed-response and open-ended items.

Fixed-Response Questionnaires

Fixed-response questionnaires consist of items (questions or statements) that have a finite list of alternative responses. Respondents are asked to select from among a number of fixed choices and check the responses that best fit them. Informational items with fixed choices include the following:

1. My age is: (CHECK ONE)

   _____ below 18

   _____ 18–21

   _____ 22–25

   _____ 26–29

   _____ 30 or over

2. My political affiliation is: (CHECK ONE)

   _____ Republican

   _____ Democrat

   _____ American Independent

3. The amount of formal education I have completed is: (CHECK ONE)

   _____ Less than eighth grade

   _____ Completed elementary school, some high school

   _____ High school graduate, no college

   _____ High school graduate, some college, did not graduate

   _____ College graduate, no advanced graduate work

   _____ College graduate, some graduate work completed

   _____ Completed a graduate degree (master's, doctorate, etc.)

Besides informational items, that may also include questions about race, ethnicity, income, occupation/profession, or rural–urban background, several items may be combined to form a scale. Below are three partial sets of items that form scales that purportedly measure group cohesiveness, desire for changing work tasks, and work alienation.

Partial Set of Items #1:

Group Cohesiveness Scale (Partial List of Items)

Below are various statements about your work group. Check the response that best fits you.

1. "Do you feel that other members of your work group give you ample consideration whenever issues concerning job matters are discussed?" (CHECK ONE)

    _____ My opinion is considered very important by other group members

    _____ Group members are fairly interested in my opinion

    _____ Group members are somewhat disinterested in my opinion

    _____ Group members ignore my opinion when job matters are discussed.

2. "To what extent do you and/or other members of your work group refer to your group as 'we' or 'us'?"

    _____ To a great extent (very frequently)

    _____ To some extent (fairly frequently)

    _____ To a small extent (fairly infrequently)

    _____ To no extent at all (seldom, if ever).

3. "How would you characterize the way the members of your work group get along?"

    _____ We get along better than most groups

    _____ We get along about the same as other groups

    _____ We get along less than other groups

    _____ We seldom, if ever, get along well.

4. "To what extent do you feel other members of your work group would come to your aid if you were in trouble involving your work tasks?"

    _____ My work group members would come to my aid without question

    _____ My work group members would be fairly indifferent about my problems

    _____ I feel that I am on my own and cannot depend on other work group members for assistance if I get into trouble on my job.

Partial Set of Items #2:

Desire for Changing Work Tasks (Partial List of Items)

Each statement below is followed by the responses (not reprinted here): "Strongly Agree," "Agree," "Undecided, Probably Agree," "Undecided, Probably Disagree," "Disagree," and "Strongly Disagree." Please check the response for each item that best fits you.

1. On my job it is important to me that I do new things frequently.
2. Changing my job to meet changing technology in the workplace would be very disturbing to me.
3. I like a job where I can perform the same tasks routinely every day.
4. Assembly-line type work appeals to me.
5. I dislike frequent disruptions of my work routine.
6. I like my present job and would feel bad about having to perform some other different tasks.
7. Doing a variety of things on the job each day helps make me feel that time goes by more quickly.
8. I would tend to feel comfortable performing most any job at my place of work, should higher-ups decide to switch me around from one job to another frequently.

Partial Set of Items #3:

Work Alienation (Partial List of Items)

Each of the statements below is followed by the responses (not reprinted here): "Strongly Agree," "Agree," "Undecided, Probably Agree," "Undecided, Probably Disagree," "Disagree," and "Strongly Disagree." Select the response for each item that best fits you.

1. On my job it is possible to make errors without too much disruption.
2. The way I do my work is important to my fellow employees.
3. Many times they think getting the job done is more important than the people who do the job.
4. If I ever stay home from work, this department would be in a real bind.
5. A person who likes to do work that requires thinking would like to perform my job.
6. Things are really regimented around here.
7. When I come to work each day, I look forward to a new and challenging experience.
8. Sometimes I wonder just how important I really am around here.
9. I think my job is too mechanical and repetitive.

These different kinds of fixed-response items contain certain implicit assumptions about the target audience. First, an assumption is made that the target sample has meaningful knowledge about the subject matter of the questionnaire. Second, it is assumed that the researcher knows enough about the sample under investigation to be able to anticipate the kinds of responses that would likely be expected and given. A third assumption is that most, if not all, relevant questions have been asked that relate to the basic research questions, depending on the manifest goals of the researcher. A fourth assumption is that the responses people give are truthful reflections about them and how they feel. This latter assumption focuses on the accuracy of questionnaires and whether they provide reliable information about the target sample.

Fixed-response items may be constructed to fit an infinite number of response patterns. In the above examples, a format was used employing "Strongly Agree" and "Strongly Disagree" options. Other possible formats may include arrays of options according to "Favorable–Unfavorable," "Most Intense–Least Intense," "Strong–Weak," "All–None," "Everybody–Nobody," and "Positive–Negative." Your choices of response options are limited only by your own imagination. There are no "standard" or "conventional" response options that are universally used or accepted by all researchers.

Open-Ended Questionnaires

Open-ended questionnaires consist of questions that require short or lengthy written replies by respondents. Below are some examples of open-ended items.

1. What is the title of your present position with this probation agency?

   _____

2. What are your primary responsibilities or duties? Please specify: _____

   _____

   _____

   _____

3. What are the chances for your advancement to a higher position in this agency in the future? Please explain:

   _____

   _____

   _____

4. What are your recommendations for an "ideal" work setting?

   _____

   _____

   _____

5. Do you feel that the present method of evaluating work quality is fair?

   Yes_____   No_____   Uncertain_____   (CHECK ONE)

6. Why do you feel this is so? Please explain: _____

_____

_____

_____

In these instances, rather than anticipate particular responses from the target sample through fixed-choice items, investigators instead simply provide several pages of open-ended items that request respondents to indicate their opinions and elaborate about them in some detail. Primarily, exploratory and descriptive research designs might be more likely to include open-ended items if questionnaires are used for survey and investigative purposes.

Combinations of Fixed-Response and Open-Ended Items

Many questionnaires consist of questions that are both **fixed-response items** and **open-ended items.** If there is the likelihood that not all alternative categories for particular questions can be anticipated in advance, an "other" category is often included along with the other fixed choices. For instance, if we were to distribute questionnaires to a sample of residents in ethnically heterogeneous communities, such as Los Angeles, New York, Miami, or Chicago, and if we were to include an item about one's religious affiliation, it would be awkward to attempt a complete listing of all possible religious affiliations for these respondents. In Los Angeles, for example, there are large numbers of Cambodians, Laotians, Vietnamese, Chinese, Japanese, Indians, and numerous persons from the Middle East. Therefore, an item might be constructed as follows:

My religious affiliation is: (CHECK ONE OR DESIGNATE YOUR FAITH IN THE SPACE PROVIDED BELOW)

_____ Catholic

_____ Protestant

_____ Jewish

_____ Other. If "none," write "none." Please specify: _____

There may or may not be sufficient numbers of "other" responses to justify creating additional categories when we commence our data analysis. Perhaps 85 percent of our sample of city residents are primarily Catholic, Protestant, and Jewish, but 10 percent are Buddhist (a major religion of India and China) and 4 percent are Shintoist (the major religion of Japan). One percent might consist of 30 other religious faiths, with two or three respondents associated with each. Assuming that religious affiliation is an important variable in our theory, we would probably want to use the five religious categories where sizable numbers of respondents are found. For this particular part of our data analysis, we might omit those in the "other" category, since statistical manipulations of such small numbers of respondents would be meaningless.

Comparison of Fixed-Response and Open-Ended Items

It is apparent that certain variables are more easily and directly taken into account by using fixed-response items. For example, gender, years of education, race, and political affiliation almost always are confined to a limited number of fixed-answer alternatives. For some variables, such as religious affiliation, "other" categories may be created and used together with a fixed-response format.

BOX 5.2   PERSONALITY HIGHLIGHT

VERNETTA D. YOUNG
Howard University

Statistics: B.A. (sociology and criminology), University of Maryland–College Park; graduate study, Florida State University; Ph.D. (criminal justice), State University of New York–Albany.

BACKGROUND AND INTERESTS

My interests include race and gender as they relate to patterns of crime and victimization, women and race in the criminal and juvenile justice systems, and the history and development of criminology and criminal justice.

Thinking back on it, criminology was the third of a succession of majors in my undergraduate career. I entered the University of Maryland as an aspiring mathematics major and then moved into psychology. My hopes of being a clinical psychologist were short-lived when my advisor informed me that I would have to be in school for at least 12 years.

My interest in crime and justice was piqued in an Introduction to Criminology class. The instructor presented a lecture on crime and criminals that seemed to suggest that there was some relationship between being black, the nomenclature of the time, and being a criminal. I was born in Washington, D.C., and raised in Southern Maryland and I had never associated blacks with crime, and so the veiled connection puzzled and angered me. I decided that I wanted and needed to know more about why some people thought that there was some sort of symbiosis with race, meaning being black, and crime.

The second major event occurred in graduate school. Literature on female offenders presented at the time portrayed what I thought was a very negative and stereotypical picture of blacks, especially black females who were involved in criminal behavior. Being both black and a female, I felt compelled to set the record straight. This moved me toward an interest in examining the involvement of black and white females in crime and to focus on the differen-

BOX 5.2   CONTINUED

tial response of the criminal justice system to women by race. The intersectionality of gender and race became my mantra.

By now I was well into my 10th year in college and although I had no misgivings about not pursuing clinical psychology, I was still overwhelmed by the time it had taken me to complete my educational sojourn. I received my Ph.D. 13 years after beginning my undergraduate education. Since then I have taught at American University and then back to the University of Maryland, my alma mater, before coming to Howard University.

RESEARCH INVESTIGATIONS

It was during my early years at Howard University, a historically black university, that I became consciously aware of the absence of views of African American scholars in textbooks on crime and delinquency. This led to a realization that there was a void in the field and that literacy in the field was weakened by the failure to recognize the contributions of these scholars. This led me to wonder about the role of race in the history of the development of criminal and juvenile justice institutions. I have discovered that a number of African American women were involved in the movement to remove black children from adult prisons. The history of the development of juvenile correctional institutions has failed to mention these women.

This interest in history presented me with a real dilemma. I had always hated history and now it seemed that it would be history that would give me the information I needed. Rummaging through the papers of the Federation of Colored Women's Clubs and collecting Maryland Penitentiary records was "grueling," although these data sources have proved invaluable. My appreciation for history and historians has increased immeasurably.

Finally, I have battled with the role of the concept of disproportionality for many years. The disproportionate involvement of African Americans in the criminal justice system seems to take over discussions on crime. While I can appreciate the importance of looking at the involvement of African Americans in crime relative to their contribution to the total population, I am also interested in looking at who is contributing the most to reports of crime, both unofficial and official. For me, what I perceive as an overemphasis on disproportionality contributes to the view that there is some symbiotic relationship between blacks and crime. It also takes attention away from some other areas of concern. For example, if we are totally focused on black youth and violence, we are apt to overlook the multiple occurrences of gun violence in schools that are predominantly white by offenders who are predominantly white. Recently, my interest in crime and delinquency has focused on looking at the involvement of those who are other than black. Are the patterns similar or different? Are the causes similar or different? There are many questions that we have yet to answer.

ADVICE TO STUDENTS

My advice to students is to find something that you are passionate about and pursue it as your career path. However, as you move along your journey toward a career, be open to changes in direction. It is also important to prepare yourself for change by taking advantage of opportunities.

Most attitudinal measures in questionnaires use fixed-response formats. These fixed-response formats enable researchers to score responses easily, sum individual item values, and determine overall **raw scores** for particular variables. Comparisons may be made directly between people or groups who possess certain raw scores or who fall within certain score ranges.

Survey research and the use of questionnaires are virtually inseparable, since it is almost always the researcher's intention to canvass large numbers of respondents who may be dispersed over large geographical areas. Questionnaires, particularly mailed questionnaires, enable researchers to acquire large amounts of data from large numbers of persons at minimal cost. Depending on what is known about the intended targets of questionnaires, these instruments will vary in their sophistication and format. Before we examine the task of constructing questionnaires, it is helpful to highlight some of the major weaknesses and strengths of fixed-response and open-ended questionnaire formats for particular research purposes.

Advantages and Disadvantages of Fixed-Response Items.   Among the major advantages of fixed-response questionnaires are the following:

1. Fixed-response items are easy to score and code. **Coding** is a procedure whereby researchers assign numbers to particular types of responses—for example, Democrat = 1, Republican = 2, American Independent = 3, and so on—in order to distinguish responses from one another in subsequent data analyses. Researchers can more easily transfer the data from questionnaires containing fixed-response items to computers where data may be stored for subsequent statistical treatment and analysis.

2. No writing is required of respondents. Respondents merely check the responses that best typify them. In cases where respondents cannot adequately express themselves verbally, the fixed-response item is definitely an advantage.

3. Fixed-response items facilitate completion of questionnaires. Lengthy questionnaires with fixed-response items are completed more rapidly compared with those containing large numbers of open-ended items.

4. If questionnaires are mailed to designated respondents, there is greater likelihood that respondents will complete and return questionnaires more frequently if little or no writing is involved in their completion.

Some of the disadvantages of fixed-response questionnaire items include the following:

1. Researchers may not be able to anticipate or think of all relevant response alternatives. Fixed-response items, as noted previously, require some familiarity with the population under investigation. If respondents are forced to make choices between several alternatives that do not fit them, researchers may obtain erroneous or misleading information.

2. Fixed-response items, especially those used in attitudinal scales (i.e., with "Strongly Agree" and "Strongly Disagree" response patterns), may lead respondents to lapse into a **response set** or **set response.** A response set is a particular response pattern that has nothing to do with question or statement content, but rather, is designed almost exclusively to complete the questionnaire rapidly or "get it over with quickly." Some respondents have been known to check the first responses for all statements or question items, regardless of whether such responses are true of them. For example, someone might check the "Strongly Agree" response to the statement, "I like my job." Later, in the same set of items, they will also check "Strongly Agree" in response to the statement, "I hate my job." It is apparent that they don't read the statements or questions asked. They are either bored with the questionnaire or consider the researcher's intrusion into their time as offensive. Thus, sometimes researchers build in **lie factors** or **lie scales** that seek to detect set responses whenever it is suspected they are being given. Lie factors are nothing more than including several statements that are directly contradictory. Either agreements with both statements or disagreements with them mean inconsistency, a contradiction in response, and a possible set response.

Advantages and Disadvantages of Open-Ended Items.   Some of the major advantages of open-ended questionnaires are as follows:

1. Open-ended items are particularly useful when researchers have little or no information available about the samples studied. Respondents are least restricted in terms of their possible answer choices that they can provide in response to specific questions.

2. In certain instances, open-ended items are helpful to researchers because they provide insights into one's thoughts and behaviors. There is always the possibility that researchers can anticipate many responses respondents might give, but often, the flexibility of open-ended items will elicit unanticipated and insightful replies from respondents. These responses will enhance the investigator's understanding of what is going on and why.

Some of the disadvantages of open-ended questionnaires are the following:

1. For open-ended items, written answers from respondents may be so diverse that researchers may find them difficult to code or classify into convenient categories. Also, different respondents may appear to provide similar responses to the same item on a questionnaire, when in fact, the meaning and importance each respondent attaches to the particular reply may be considerably different. Thus, although several respondents might be placed in common categories for purposes of classifying them on some measured characteristic, the results of such classifications may be erroneous or misleading.

2. A **bias** exists in open-ended questionnaires that stems from several sources. Some persons who cannot express themselves adequately on paper (and also orally) will be combined unfairly with more fluent persons. Therefore, an educational bias exists, particularly if the target population from which the sample is drawn is quite heterogeneous in this respect. By the same token, questionnaires in the general case (i.e., those containing both open-ended and fixed-response items) are subject to a similar type of educational bias. Not every respondent is equally adept in the art of self-expression.

The socioeconomic factor may yield misleading results and incorrect interpretations of findings as well. Persons of different socioeconomic backgrounds or professions and occupations may not view issues the same way, nor will they necessarily use the same vocabulary to describe their feelings or attitudes. The wording of questionnaires at the outset has certain built-in biases that must be considered in assessing the quality and meaning of information obtained.

3. A third disadvantage of open-ended items is that they are time-consuming to complete. If researchers mail questionnaires to respondents, response rates will likely be lower where open-ended items are used compared with those situations where exclusively fixed-response items are used. Many persons feel that they do not have the time or interest to sit down and write out lengthy replies to questions. Face-to-face interviews appear to be more successful with better response compared with open-ended questionnaires that are self-administered.

4. Applicable to both open-ended questionnaires and fixed-response questionnaires is the possibility that significant portions of heterogeneous urban populations may not understand English. Large numbers of immigrants from Asian, Middle Eastern, and European countries in the last several decades have created ethnic enclaves in many cities throughout the United States. Thus, when heads of households are surveyed by using mailed questionnaires, it is very possible that some language other than English may be native to these heads of households. If English cannot be read or understood, certain respondents may simply discard the questionnaires they receive. Furthermore, a significant minority of citizens is illiterate, despite the fact that their native language is English.

Questionnaire Administration

Basically, there are two methods for administering questionnaires to target samples of elements. These are the mailed questionnaire and face-to-face questionnaire administration.

Mailed Questionnaires

Survey researchers utilize the mailed questionnaire extensively in canvassing large numbers of subjects located over broad geographical territories. This method consists simply of mailing questionnaires of variable lengths to previously designated subjects. Instructions for completing the questionnaire and returning it are usually enclosed and a stamped, return envelope is provided. Researchers want to maximize the rate of return whenever questionnaires are mailed. They may enclose cover letters designed to familiarize respondents with their study and the reasons it is being conducted.

After questionnaires have been mailed initially, a waiting period of about 2 weeks passes, while researchers collect questionnaires from early respondents. If some attempt has been made to identify respondents within the questionnaires themselves, then researchers can determine from master lists of respondents which ones have returned their questionnaires and which ones have not returned them. Those who haven't, as yet, returned their questionnaires may be sent follow-up letters with additional questionnaires included. A statement might be included, such as "We recently sent you a questionnaire concerning [some topic] and we have not, as yet, heard from you. Your responses are important to us. Because of the possibility that you may not have received the questionnaire we recently sent you, we are sending you another for your convenience, together with a stamped, preaddressed envelope so that you may complete and return the questionnaire easily. We hope to hear from you soon. Thank you in advance for your important participation in our research project."

BOX 5.3   PERSONALITY HIGHLIGHT

DONNA BISHOP
Northeastern University

Statistics: B.A. (sociology), Wheaton College (Massachusetts); M.A. (sociology), The College of William and Mary; Ph.D. (criminal justice), State University of New York–Albany.

BACKGROUND AND INTERESTS

I have been interested in delinquency, crime, and justice for just about as long as I can remember. I recall a juvenile delinquency course that I took as a college sophomore. We read several books, but I was especially moved by *The Loneliness of the Long Distance Runner,* a story about a boy who grows up in an impoverished environment, steals, and is sentenced to a juvenile reformatory. He takes up long-distance running as an escape both from his past and from the dismal environment of the institution. It is a powerful account of a human spirit that will not be broken. It also says a lot about the link between structural inequality and delinquency and about the oppression of institutional life. It opened my eyes to worlds that I knew nothing about. I identified with the boy, felt compassion and anger, and was inspired to learn more.

After taking that course, I was determined to find out more about delinquent kids and institutional life. In the summer, and on evenings and weekends, I volunteered at a reception center for delinquent girls who had been committed by the courts and who were awaiting placement in long-term institutions. Most of the girls were runaways or had been referred to the court by their parents for being incorrigible and sexually active. At the center, they slept on cement beds in windowless cement cells with heavy steel doors, the stuff you would expect to find in a maximum-security prison. All the girls, even the very young ones, were forced to have gynecological exams to determine if they had been sexually active. I can only imagine how terrified they must have been to undergo that procedure. I thought it curious that the girls called all the staff members Auntie. They seemed so eager for relationships, even with people who treated them cruelly. I wondered if that was the way it had been all of their lives. Many, I would later learn from my studies, had been sexually or physically abused. Several of them told us they had been abused, but their accounts were dismissed as lies. This was the 1960s and sexual abuse, especially incest, was almost unheard of.

Most staff members viewed the girls as dangerous, though I did not understand why. I was disturbed by the physical conditions in the institution and by the institutional culture that endorsed ideas about delinquent girls that were so much at odds with my experience of them. All of the girls were sent to training schools. Each girl was supposed to be sent to the institution that best suited her needs. However, there were few options and staff were obliged to keep

BOX 5.3   CONTINUED

the beds filled at a Catholic institution with which the state had a contract. Where a girl ended up had a lot more to do with organizational needs than the girl's. I've subsequently learned that organizational needs frequently take precedence over the needs of clientele. I don't suppose that in this case it mattered much: One institution wasn't much different from another. I heard from some of the girls over the next couple of years. They related accounts of stern staff, strict rules, and harsh punishments. They received education, but some of it struck me as rather odd. For example, they learned table-setting dinner etiquette, menu planning, and how to serve tea. I believe the goal was to train them to be polite young ladies and good upper-middle-class wives. It seemed absurd, given the reality of their lives and the circumstances they would face when they returned home. When I graduated from college, I was very idealistic. I wanted to help females in trouble, and I wanted to change the way that institutions were run. I completed a master's degree in sociology and took a job as a counselor in a women's prison. The prison was in the south and it was segregated. I was from the north and I hadn't had much contact with minorities. The segregation bothered me a lot. So did the fact that the staff were all white. A lot of other things troubled me about the prison. Most of the inmates were mothers, and they missed their children terribly, but children weren't permitted to visit. Most of the women were very traditional. They defined themselves with references to husbands and boyfriends on whom they were emotionally and financially dependent. Sadly, many were imprisoned as accomplices in crimes planned and committed by their men. A great many had also been abused by their men. We didn't know much about domestic violence in those days. Nor did we see the connection between female homicide and the stress of living in long-term abusive relationships. I remember one inmate who had received a life sentence for killing her husband. The prison doctor discovered a bullet in her back. She had been shot by her husband previously and had treated her wounds at home. She was too afraid of her husband to call the police. Many women in prison formed pseudo-families and they referred to each other as "aunt," "uncle," "daughter," or "wife," even though they were unrelated, perhaps to compensate for the loss of their families on the outside. Many became involved in lesbian relationships with other women, although they had never done so before. I observed how important close relationships were to them and how difficult it was for them to do time. But institutional policy didn't condone close relationships. If a girl (as even elderly women were called) was suspected of having a close relationship with another woman, both were placed in solitary confinement for lengthy periods of time. Incarcerated women need job skills if they are to be freed from financial (and emotional) dependency. The institution wasn't very helpful in that regard. There were two typewriters for the 200 or so women who wanted to learn secretarial skills. Most inmates worked the vegetable farm, the chicken farm, or the laundry. The laundry equipment was old and was no longer used in commercial laundries on the outside. There surely wasn't much need in the city (and almost all the women came from cities) for vegetable or chicken farmers. The prison had cosmetology classes, which were popular with the inmates, but state law prohibited felons from becoming licensed cosmetologists. The inmates were all felons. I left that institution out of frustration and became a juvenile probationer officer. I thought I could do more good trying to help youth and their families in the community. I found a great deal that was positive in community corrections. For the most part, staff really cared about kids. (Institutions, on the other

BOX 5.3   CONTINUED

hand, have a way of hardening staff.) We worked collaboratively with mental health clinics, social service agencies, teachers, and private practitioners to provide services to youths and their families. Our caseloads were too large (a problem that continues today) and some youth and parents did not respond to our efforts. But many made progress. The work was meaningful and rewarding.

Two years later I was promoted to supervisor, which meant I supervised other probation officers and didn't have a caseload of my own. I missed working with kids. Shortly thereafter, I was offered and took a position with a federally funded agency that was doing juvenile corrections research. Here I got my first real exposure to research. I studied conditions in correctional institutions and made recommendations for change. I visited model juvenile corrections programs around the country, then assisted officials who wanted to replicate them in the communities where I worked. I learned that research could really make a difference: Local officials were quite receptive to our research and technical assistance.

Four years later I decided to obtain a Ph.D. in criminal justice. I wanted to learn more about crime and criminal justice and to become more proficient as a researcher and as an agent of change. I received my degree in 1982, and have been researching, writing about, and advocating for justice reform ever since. I have received many grants to support my research and have worked with wonderful colleagues. My research has focused especially on evaluation of juvenile justice programs; on gender and racial inequities in the justice system; on the operation of courts and correctional agencies; and on trends in youth policy. For the last several years, my research and writing have focused on recent get- tough juvenile justice reforms, especially the policy of transferring greater numbers of juvenile offenders to criminal courts to be prosecuted and punished as adults. My colleagues and I have researched the origins and implementation of these reforms, as well as their consequences for juvenile offenders, for the justice system, and for public safety. Our research in this area has included quantitative methods (analyzing automated state records data, manually coding and analyzing information from police and court records, conducting surveys and a variety of qualitative methods [e.g., observation, telephone, and face-to-face interviews with justice officials and young offenders]). I view both types of methods as important and complimentary. Qualitative methods have been especially useful in giving direction and focus to our large-scale quantitative research. Qualitative methods have also been critical to the interpretation of our quantitative research findings. My colleagues and I have published numerous articles and delivered many presentations about our research, not only to our colleagues at professional meetings but also to federal commissions, state legislators, and state and local prosecutors, defense attorneys, and judges. I hope and believe that our research has had and continues to have an influence on policy.

What has motivated me throughout my career is a desire to learn why people offend, to understand how our justice systems operate, and to promote the development of more humane and effective policies that are responsive to offender needs. I am delighted that, in my lifetime, there have been major advances in criminological theory and research, which have in turn influenced justice policies. For example, largely as a result of labeling theory and research, we have made good progress in removing runaways and incorrigibles from secure juvenile institutions. Research has taught us a great deal about the connection between childhood physical

BOX 5.3 CONTINUED

and sexual abuse and female delinquency, and we have begun to develop programming that is responsive to the special needs of girls. Research has shed light on gender and race inequities in the justice system, and both state and federal governments have made the reduction of these inequities program priorities. We have learned about causes and dynamics of domestic violence and how to respond to it more effectively (e.g., through mandatory arrest policies, batterer treatment programs, and a vast array of support systems for victims). We have learned that get-tough policies for juvenile offenders are largely ineffective, and that policies and programs that address underlying risk factors and needs of youth are far more effective as strategies of crime prevention and control. Still, there is much more to be learned, much educating to be done, and much change yet to be accomplished in justice policy and programming.

ADVICE TO STUDENTS

Find your passion and pursue it. It may take you in many directions but, if you remain faithful to it, you are likely to have a fulfilling and meaningful career. Don't be afraid to take risks. As you gather more life and career experience, be open to change. There are many careers open to students with degrees in criminal justice. Most of you will not become professors or professional researchers. But whatever you become, a police officer, a corrections officer, a prosecutor, whatever, continue to be a social scientist. Observe (i.e., gather data) and think critically. Reflect on the policies that the agencies in which you work have adopted and the theories on which they are based. (Remember that all policies are based on theory, though the theory is often not made explicit.) Reflect on and question agency views about offenders and victims and test them against your own observations. Continue to read research articles and books that apply to your field, and think about how the findings might be applied. Many of you will eventually be in administrative and managerial positions where you are able to influence research that is conducted within your agency. Many of you will be in positions to effect organizational change. I urge you to strive to make the criminal justice system more humane, just, and effective, using research to guide the policy and programmatic decisions that you make.

Response to mailed questionnaires varies among survey research projects. No one knows what a normal response rate is for any target respondent audience. Estimates of what is "normal" range from 30 percent to 75 percent. In the social sciences, return rates to mailed questionnaires are usually expected to be about a third. Thus, if we were to mail 1,000 questionnaires to a random sample of city residents, we might expect about 330 to be returned. Naturally, if we receive larger numbers of completed questionnaires, this will enhance the representativeness of our respondents relative to the overall questionnaire mailing, which is usually based on some type of random sampling plan. Subsequently, we will examine the issue of nonresponse, or those instances where persons receive our questionnaires but for various reasons elect not to return them. The rate of return for any mailed questionnaire depends on many factors.

Face-to-Face Questionnaire Administration

Another common method of distributing questionnaires is face-to-face questionnaire administration. Researchers may distribute questionnaires directly to target audiences. Many students have been a part of a target audience in the classroom, where investigators might pass out questionnaires to them during class time. Students are frequent target audiences of researchers because they are easily accessible and investigators can obtain direct responses to their questionnaires from large numbers of students in a matter of minutes.

Unfortunately, frequently selecting students in the classroom for questionnaire administration has led some professionals to allege that over the years, we have learned a great deal about students and their attitudes about things. But students are atypical from the population at large in several respects. Their general educational level is somewhat higher than the average community resident. Furthermore, many students in colleges and universities may be from elsewhere geographically. Thus, if students at some university are used for a professor's attitudinal research, and if that research is connected with one or more community issues, student responses may be interesting but irrelevant in relation to those issues.

Besides administering questionnaires to students in classrooms, investigators can visit work settings and distribute questionnaires directly to employees. Prisons may permit researchers to canvass prisoners about various matters through self-administered questionnaires distributed to various inmates by correctional officers. One advantage of such direct distributions of these questionnaires is that students or prisoners or employees may ask researchers for clarification about any statement or question that may be ambiguous or confusing to readers. Another advantage is that a large proportion of those who receive questionnaires will likely complete and return them. Thus, a high return rate is virtually guaranteed. Such guarantees cannot be made regarding mailed questionnaires.

Comparison of Mailed Questionnaires with Face-to-Face Questionnaire Administration

It should be apparent that the major benefit of mailed questionnaires is economy. Mailed questionnaires, therefore, are an inexpensive means of obtaining information about particular target samples. Some of the drawbacks to mailed questionnaires include the fact that you never are sure who completes and returns the questionnaires you have distributed. If researchers send questionnaires to organizational leaders in community corrections agencies, a secretary or volunteer worker in the agency may actually complete the questionnaire and return it. However, it is assumed by the researcher that directors or agency heads were the ones who responded to the questions. Another drawback is that researchers have no way of ensuring that people will return the questionnaires they have been sent. Thus, in most research projects involving mailed questionnaires, nonresponse is significant and limits the generalizability of subsequent research findings.

Another drawback of mailed questionnaires is that respondents may misinterpret certain statements or misread questions and provide answers that are unrelated to the intended statement meanings. Without the presence of the researcher as a resource, respondents must determine for themselves what the statements mean or how questions should be interpreted. Some inaccurate information is therefore expected among the returned questionnaires.

Favorably, mailed questionnaires allow respondents the option of completing the instrument in the privacy of their own homes or work settings, with a high degree of privacy and anonymity. If sensitive issues are being probed, or if personal behaviors or attitudes are being solicited, such as indicating one's participation in illicit drug use or sexual experiences, heightening respondent anonymity will improve the odds of greater return rates. Respondents might be more inclined to return questionnaires that contain sensitive materials if they believe their responses will be treated confidentially and anonymously. In such situations, however, follow-up letters that contain extra questionnaires might serve notice to potential respondents that the researchers know who they are and that they did not respond initially. Relatively little research has been conducted about the distinction between those topics considered sensitive and those labeled as innocuous. What is considered as sensitive by one person may not be considered as sensitive by another.

The major advantages of face-to-face questionnaire administration are that (1) researchers know who completes the questionnaires; (2) a high rate of questionnaire completion and return is expected; and (3) investigators are present to clarify any statements or questions that might otherwise be misinterpreted by respondents. A disadvantage is the fact that researchers must be present during the questionnaire administration, and that this presence might involve extensive travel to diverse locations. Thus, this type of questionnaire administration is very time-consuming.

Questionnaire Construction

For most persons, questionnaires are likely to be viewed as simple devices that anyone can create or throw together, given the time and/or interest. For serious social scientists who do research, however, questionnaires and questionnaire construction is both serious business and a complex task. In many instances, before the final questionnaire is determined for general distribution to some target sample, researchers will probably revise it several times. These revisions include modifications of question or statement wording, and actual questionnaire content and length. Most researchers would probably agree that constructing an appropriate questionnaire for any target audience is a tedious and arduous task. However, despite their best efforts, researchers have never devised the perfect questionnaire. Every questionnaire suffers at least a few imperfections that neither the researchers nor their assistants detected during its preparation.

This section will examine some of the major factors that researchers must take into account when constructing questionnaires for selected target samples. Let's begin by considering some of the questions that arise in the initial stages of questionnaire preparation:

1. What is the definition of the population about which we seek information?
2. What is the socioeconomic and/or educational level of people who will receive and complete our questionnaires?
3. What kinds of facts do we want to know about them?
4. How accessible are these people for research purposes?
5. How will we administer the questionnaire?
6. What kinds of response patterns will we use in our questionnaire construction?

7. How long should we make the questionnaire?

8. How much control will we be able to exert over ensuring their responses to our questionnaire?

Ideally, every element in the population to be studied should be identified and given an opportunity to be included in the research project. The socioeconomic level or educational background (if known) of the intended target population will enable the researcher to design questions or formulate statements at a particular level of readability commensurate with that of the respondents. If there is a strong likelihood that the population contains a substantial number of persons who might have difficulty with the English language for one reason or another, then interviewing might be a better strategy, although it will be considerably more expensive in time and money.

The kinds of things we want to learn about the sample will directly determine the content of our questionnaires. Some of the standard social and demographic items are age, gender, occupation/profession, years of education, and race/ethnicity. Other items are included as needed. For example, if we are studying probation officer burnout, we would want to include a scale that measures burnout. If we wish to assess job performance and cross-tabulate it with other variables, including burnout, we would need to include various measures that would enable us to evaluate one's job performance or effectiveness. We can use existing measures devised by other researchers or we can create our own measures.

Questionnaire length is a matter that is both controversial and unresolved. Some investigators have argued that for mailed questionnaires, shorter questionnaires are preferable to longer ones. The idea is that people will be more inclined to spend their time completing and returning shorter questionnaires than longer ones. Unfortunately, no one knows for sure what the guidelines are for determining whether any given questionnaire is long or short. For instance, **postcard questionnaires** have been used in the past for soliciting public opinion about various issues. Two or three statements can be printed on a self-addressed, stamped postcard, which can easily be mailed back to researchers. These are considered short questionnaires.

In another instance, I taught part time at a small college in Tennessee for several years. One semester, all faculty were required to complete a 110-page questionnaire, printed on both sides of each page. The questionnaire solicited information about their teaching duties, college functions, and numerous other items. It was administered as part of a general accreditation program for the college. One hundred percent compliance was obtained from all faculty, since completing and turning in questionnaires to the payroll office was the only way faculty could receive their paychecks. This type of questionnaire would be considered long. Most questionnaires are somewhere in between postcard length and 110 pages.

Questionnaire length is a matter of personal preference and standards. One consideration that provides a good standard for limiting questionnaire length is how long it will take to complete. Extremely lengthy questionnaires can cause some respondents to become test-weary. Tired respondents may become somewhat careless in the responses they give, and they may drift into response sets.

Questionnaire length is also influenced by organizational time constraints. If you approach a police department and attempt to get departmental approval to administer questionnaires to all officers commencing various shifts, you will not be particularly persuasive if you tell the watch commander that the questionnaire will take about an hour to complete. An investigator would be better off limiting questionnaire administration to 15 minutes or less. And even this short time interval may be considered lengthy by the target agency or department. Questionnaires sent to persons in their own homes and on their own time may be lengthier and take longer to complete. But again, you must balance questionnaire length against factors that would enhance the likelihood of increasing the rate of returns.

The length of the questionnaire is generally a function of the amount and type of information sought. If we assume that investigators are operating within a theoretical context and that the variables being studied are limited, then the length of the questionnaire will be determined by the inclusion of those scales necessary to measure the limited number of variables examined. Researchers should not "throw in" extraneous scales or include variables that are detached from or irrelevant for their theoretical schemes. But sometimes, novice researchers will add other variables simply because they are interesting. A good rule of thumb is to include only those relevant variables that enable you to carry out your research objectives fully. Leave out additional variables that might be more suitable for a subsequent investigation.

Selecting and Ordering the Questionnaire Items

Item Selection.   Because the primary functions of questionnaires are description and measurement, researchers have a variety of options for selecting items for inclusion. Several classic sources exist that either tell researchers where to find existing measuring instruments in questionnaire form or provide them with compilations of measures themselves (e.g., Miller & Salkind, 2002). Investigators will often want to combine several relevant existing measures with items of their own or even newly devised scales. Many existing scales are often dated culturally or contain questions using phraseologies that might have different meanings in the 2000s compared with their meanings in the 1980s or 1990s. Sometimes, the researcher may be able to adapt older existing scales to fit present problems by changing the wording of various statements. Basically, the originally devised scales are used, but they have been given an upbeat treatment by investigators who have modified certain statements to fit the present research problem.

Whenever any scale is used in research, whether it is a previously constructed scale or a newly devised one, researchers should perform various tests to determine whether the items are clearly worded or are fairly internally consistent with one another. Such tests are known as pretests, and they involve administering early versions of questionnaires to audiences similar to those targeted for one's research. For example, if researchers wanted to administer questionnaires to a sample of Indiana prison correctional officers, they might want to pretest their questionnaires by giving them to samples of jail correctional officers or to others who perform similar work. Jail correctional officers in the researcher's local community might be more accessible for study than prison correctional officers, where access to the prison environment is extremely limited. Sometimes, these pretests are designated as **pilot studies,** because they involve trial runs of questionnaires before audiences similar to those where the final form of the questionnaire is to be administered. Thus, pilot studies are small-scale implementations of the actual studies researchers are prepared to conduct. They enable investigators to detect faults associated with their research instruments and obtain ideas about how best to carry out the final project.

For example, these pretests are helpful, in that they help researchers to detect spelling errors, awkward question wordings or statements, or possibly irrelevant items that do not apply to correctional officer duties or functions. Also, investigators may expose their scales to preliminary tests in order to determine whether they provide accurate indications of the degree to which certain characteristics are possessed by respondents.

Including items whose primary function is description is a fairly easy task for seasoned researchers. But precautions need to be taken, particularly with reference to question wording. For instance, if investigators wanted to estimate the amount of marijuana consumption among an aggregate of college students, they might draw a probability sample and ask them the following question: "How often do you smoke marijuana per month?" or "How many 'joints' do you smoke per week?"

Each of these questions is presumptuous in that they both assume that these students smoke marijuana, when in fact, none of them may do so. Such questions are labeled "husband-beating-wife" questions, and are similar to the question, "When was the last time you beat your wife?" The ridiculousness of this question is apparent. First, it assumes that respondents are married (which may not be true). Second, it assumes that all respondents are male (which may not be true). Third, it assumes that all respondents beat their wives (which may not be true). It is important that researchers refrain from assuming too much about their target populations.

Provided that investigators have established or legitimized their research purpose with the target audience (particularly where information is requested concerning possible law violations by respondents), a safer and more reasonable approach to the marijuana question would be: "Have you ever smoked marijuana?" If the respondent's reply is "yes," then the researcher can use the follow-up question, "Do you smoke marijuana currently?" Again, if the respondent's answer is "yes," then the "frequency" question may be asked safely: "How often per week (or month) do you smoke marijuana?"

These are **contingency questions,** since the answer to the first question ("Have you ever smoked marijuana?) determines whether the respondent will answer subsequent questions about marijuana smoking or the frequency of marijuana use. If the respondent answers "No" to the "Have you ever smoked marijuana?" question, then he or she can skip the next question(s) relating to the frequency of marijuana use. Other types of contingency questions might be "Have you ever been assaulted?" or "Have you ever had any property stolen from your house or car?" Depending on respondent answers to either of these questions, they may be directed to other questions about the nature of the assault against them or what types of property were stolen from them.

Caution should also be exercised when interpreting answers persons give to questions or statements. For instance, several interpretations may be made about the extent of one's professionalism as a police officer, depending on the answer given to the following question:

"How many journals, periodicals, or other police officer–oriented materials do you subscribe to on an annual basis?"

_____ None

_____ One or two

_____ Three or four

_____ Five or six

_____ Seven or more

If some police officers do not subscribe to any journals or police-oriented periodicals, does this mean that they do not have professionalism or are not professional? Are officers who subscribe to "seven or more" periodicals more professional than those who subscribe to only "three or four" periodicals? We have no way of controlling for the types of periodicals referred to in the above item. Are these equipment magazines that advertise police officer weapons and accessories? Are these journals from a peace officer's association, such as *Police Chief,* that contain research articles about police work? Are these magazines about hand-to-hand combat or developing better public relations skills? We have no way of equating one's number of magazine subscriptions with one's degree of police officer professionalism.

We can ask police officers how professional they believe they are, relative to their work. Or we can ask certain officers to evaluate the professionalism of other officers. All of these questions are contingent upon what we mean by the term *professionalism.* But questionnaires are designed to function as indicators of the extent to which these various phenomena are possessed by our respondents. By probing and seeking answers to questions that relate logically to professionalism, such as membership in professional organizations, taking courses that improve one's performance on the job, or enrolling in workshops that are geared to enhance one's professional skills, we can acquire a fairly good understanding or impression of one's degree of professionalism. However, we don't know whether these officers will necessarily do better jobs at enforcing the law or refraining from using excessive force. Indicators of one's attitudes only suggest a possible propensity to behave in given ways. Often, there are discrepancies between what our indicators reveal on questionnaires and the ways people actually behave in the real world.

Ordering the Questionnaire Items.   Constructing questionnaires is not particularly difficult. Constructing good questionnaires is absorbing and requires much thoughtfulness on the part of researchers. A major problem for many researchers is how to begin their questionnaires. Much of the time, questionnaires are started by some type of identification, such as one's name, address, telephone number, or other personal information. While these items seem innocent enough, they may be viewed as intrusive by some respondents.

Better questionnaires begin with interesting questions that attract one's attention. For example, if we were studying the opinions of prison inmates and inmate rights, we might plan to distribute questionnaires to a sample of prison inmates. We might begin our questionnaire as follows.

"In recent years, more attention has been focused on the rights of inmates. Please indicate your agreement or disagreement with the following statements."

1. The constitutional rights of inmates should not be ignored.
   Check one:

   _____ Strongly Agree

   _____ Agree

   _____ Undecided, Probably Agree

   _____ Undecided, Probably Disagree

   _____ Disagree

   _____ Strongly Disagree

Most if not all prison inmates are going to check the "Strongly Agree" option, since they have a strong vested interest in this question. It attracts their attention. In some way, inmates may feel that by responding to these items, they may influence public policy about inmate rights. At least they have a chance to express their opinion to outsiders, such as criminological researchers. Other similar statements will follow. Eventually, researchers can insert more intrusive information about type of conviction offense, age, socioeconomic status, gender, and other personal information.

Response and Nonresponse: Some Considerations

Survey researchers who utilize questionnaires in their investigations are concerned about maximizing the number of respondents who are contacted initially. Also, they are concerned about the potential effects of nonresponse, if any, particularly in mailed-questionnaire situations. Below are listed some of the more important factors that affect the rate of response to questionnaires generally. Many of the factors identified are particularly relevant for mailed questionnaires, although most pertain to all types of questionnaire administration.

Questionnaire Length

Much attention has been given to questionnaire length. As we have seen, there are no clear-cut standards that distinguish short questionnaires from long ones. The common belief held by many researchers is that shorter questionnaires tend to be returned more often than longer ones. It is also true that shorter questionnaires may be regarded as more trivial or unimportant compared with longer ones. Therefore, respondents may reason, why should they be returned at all? Some investigators may consider any questionnaire under 10 pages to be short, whereas other researchers would use different length standards. It is safe to assume, however, that generally, keeping a questionnaire as short as possible, while including only the relevant scales and question items designed to accomplish one's research objectives, will elicit the highest return rates under most conditions.

Questionnaire Content and Wording: Possible Sources of Bias

Questionnaires that contain controversial material or request intimate details about the personal lives of respondents may influence response rates significantly, depending on the topics investigated and the target audience. It is quite likely that some persons will find material on some questionnaires to be offensive and immoral, whereas others will find the same material interesting, titillating, or arousing. It would be logical to expect different response rates from these diverse groups of persons.

Some people may view questionnaires as an invasion of their privacy and simply refuse to answer them. Others may see questionnaires as an opportunity to express their feelings about important issues, and therefore, the questionnaire functions as a means of tension release or frustration reduction, as well as a data-gathering tool.

For instance, a prominent married New Jersey governor resigned his office in late 2004 following a disclosure that he had had an affair with another man. If researchers wished to investigate New Jersey public opinion about this matter, they might formulate a questionnaire and mail it to a sample of New Jersey residents selected from the latest city directory information. Without a lot of thought given to questionnaire construction, some of the following items might be included:

1. What is your age?
2. What is your marital status?
3. What is your annual income?
4. Are you male or female?
5. How many times have you been married?
6. How many extramarital affairs have you had since you have been married?
7. How do you feel about homosexual experiences?
8. How many homosexual experiences have you had in the last 10 years?
9. Should married persons be allowed to have affairs outside of their marriages provided that the affairs are with same-sex persons?
10. How much do you think about having sex with another person of the same sex?
11. Do you rent or own your dwelling?
12. What is your residential monthly payment?

Chances are that if you asked these particular questions or others like them, the respondents would be offended. These questions pry into one's private sexual behaviors, finances, and other matters that if disclosed would be embarrassing admissions. A major reason that these questions will repel most persons is that you know and they know who they are. Also, several of these questions make assumptions about these persons and their behaviors that may not be true. Question #5 assumes a person has been married more than once or is or has been married. Question #8 assumes that a person has had at least one homosexual experience. Question #10 assumes that a person thinks about having homosexual experiences. None of these assumptions may be true. Even if we were to somehow change the wording of these items and make them less threatening to respondents, at the very least it would be good if we provided our respondents with some type of anonymity.

Double-Barreled Questions

Sometimes questions are asked that are really two questions in one, or **double-barreled questions.** For instance, a double-barreled question might be, "Are you a Republican and pro-choice?" Or, "Are you dissatisfied with your present work and thinking of quitting?" We need to think through these questions and determine whether they will confuse or confound our respondents. In double-barreled question scenarios, we need to break down the question into two or three items, such as: "What is your political affiliation?"; "Are you pro-life, pro-choice, or do you have no opinion in this matter?"; "Are you dissatisfied with your present work?"; "Have you considered quitting your present job?"

The Use of Certain Key Words

What may appear to be clear to us as questions or statements may be very confusing or unintelligible to others. For police officers we might ask, "I always do my job in a professional manner." What does that mean? What does the word *professional* mean to the officer? Does it have the same meaning for the officer that it has for us?

If we conduct a survey of halfway house parolee/clients, we may ask them if they feel if the halfway house staff are effective. What does "effective" mean? Does it have the same meaning for halfway house parolee/clients as it does for us? We may need to provide some specificity for these clients, such as "Do you think the halfway house staff does a good job at providing you with job referrals and employment opportunities?"

Anonymity

Respondents may be more likely to give more truthful answers on questionnaires to the extent that their anonymity is assured. Sensitive items related to racial or religious attitudes or to sexual behavior may appear to be less threatening if the responses are anonymous. However, because of certain psychological and/or social factors presently unidentified, persons may derive some gratification (e.g., ego, sexual prowess, deviance) from disclosing sensitive information about themselves to others. No consistent pattern is evident in the literature concerning the influence of anonymity on response rates.

Regardless of whether we provide anonymity to those who respond to our questionnaires, we must consider several possible problems that anonymity creates. First, if responses to our questionnaires are anonymous, we won't be able to identify the respondents. Perhaps a meaningful interpretation of questionnaire results depends on knowing the identities of the respondents. For instance, suppose we use the city directory to obtain a list of respondents. The city directory contains much valuable information about families, such as occupation/profession of household heads, whether the family has a telephone, and average property value of the neighborhood where the respondent lives. This information can be gleaned directly from the city directory. This means that we don't have to ask these types of potentially sensitive questions on our questionnaire. But we need to know *who* the respondents are in order to link their questionnaires to city directory information. While some researchers might consider the practice unethical, one study used invisible ink on questionnaires to identify respondents on a mailed questionnaire. Applying a special fluid to the paper of returned questionnaires enabled researchers to see the names of respondents, and therefore they could be traced to city directory information. The researchers did not consider this deception as serious, since the names of respondents were used only to associate their questionnaires with sociodemographic information in the city directory.

Second, the target sample of respondents may be so small that even though anonymity is assured, it would be easy for most anyone to identify all respondents. Suppose an investigator wanted to study a probation office. Questionnaires are administered to 30 employees in the office. Respondents are asked to indicate their job titles or positions, age, years on the job, and other salient job characteristics. With only a superficial knowledge of that work setting, researchers would know the identities of all respondents.

Third, some respondents may interpret assurances of anonymity from investigators as an indication that the questionnaire is unimportant or trivial. Respondents may assume that if researchers don't care who the respondents are, then the investigators probably don't care about what responses are given. There is no way for researchers to overcome this dilemma.

Self-Reports

Self-reports involve a data collection method that is an unofficial survey of youths or adults where the intent is to obtain information about specific types of behavior not ordinarily disclosed through traditional data collection methods, including questionnaires, interviews, polls, official agency reports, or sociodemographic summaries. The exact origin of the use of self-reports is unknown. However, the early use of the self-report method often targeted juvenile delinquents. In 1943, Austin L. Porterfield investigated hidden delinquency, or delinquency neither detected by nor reported to police. He surveyed several hundred college students, asking them to disclose whether they had ever engaged in delinquent acts. While all of the students reported that they had previously engaged in delinquent acts, most also reported that they had not been caught by police or brought to the attention of the juvenile court.

In 1958, James Short and Ivan Nye became the first investigators to conduct the first self-report study of a delinquent population. They obtained self-report information from hundreds of delinquents in several Washington State training schools. They compared this information with self-report data from hundreds of students in three Washington State communities and three Midwestern towns. Their findings revealed that delinquency was widespread and not specific to any social class. Furthermore, both the seriousness and frequency of juvenile offending were key determinants of juvenile court treatment of youthful offenders and public policy relating to delinquents.

Some of the popular self-report surveys conducted annually are the *National Youth Survey (NYS)* and the *Monitoring the Future Survey (MFS)*. These are large-scale surveys of high school students that focus on particular behaviors. In addition, the Institute for Social Research at the University of Michigan annually solicits information from a national sample of 3,000 high school students. These informative reports are frequently cited in the research literature, which attests to the integrity, reliability, and validity of this information among noted juvenile justice professionals.

These national surveys involve administering confidential questionnaires and checklists to high school students. Students are asked to indicate which behaviors they have engaged in during the past 6 months or the previous year. Assuming that their responses are truthful, researchers believe that the results are a more accurate reflection of delinquent behaviors than are official sources, such as the *Uniform Crime Reports (UCR)*.

High school students or others may be asked to complete a confidential questionnaire where lists of offenses are provided. Ordinarily, simple checklists are given to students and they are asked to identify those behaviors they have done, and not necessarily those for which they have been apprehended. Considered unofficial sources of information about delinquency and delinquency patterns, these self-disclosures are considered by many professionals to be more accurate than official sources. An example of such a checklist is shown in Figure 5.1.

Research Applications of Self-Reports

Self-reports enable researchers to determine whether there are changing offending patterns among juveniles over time. Substantial information exists that characterizes violent juvenile offenders and catalogs the many potential causal factors that are associated with violence.

How often during the past six months have you committed
the following offenses? *(Check whichever best applies to you.)*

Offense	Frequency				
	0 times	*1 time*	*2 times*	*3 times*	*4 or more times*
Sniffed glue	___	___	___	___	___
Shoplifted	___	___	___	___	___
Stole a car	___	___	___	___	___
Used marijuana	___	___	___	___	___
Used crack	___	___	___	___	___

FIGURE 5.1   A hypothetical checklist for self-report disclosures of delinquent or criminal conduct among high school students. (*Source:* Compiled by author)

Self-report data suggests that a sizeable gap exists between official reports of juvenile offenses and self-reported information. Generally, self-report disclosures reveal more delinquency than is reported by either the *Uniform Crime Reports* or *National Crime Victimization Survey* (Cashel, 2003; Yacoubian, Green, & Peters, 2003). Self-reports of delinquency are often referred to as hidden delinquency, largely because much of this delinquency is undetected through official data collection methods (Pepper & Petrie, 2003).

An application of these self-reports is found in the work of Cesar Rebellon and Michelle Manasse (2004), who have studied delinquency and romantic involvement among adolescents. They used data derived from self-reports and the first several waves of questionnaires from the *National Youth Survey (NYS),* a longitudinal study involving a national probability sample of 1,725 youths. The *NYS* includes a large amount of descriptive information concerning one's socializing and dating patterns. Surveyed youths indicated whether they had "lots of dates," "dated significant others," and/or "the number of evenings spent dating." This information can be correlated with different types and amounts of delinquency, which is also self-reported. Rebellon and Manasse found that on the basis of this self-reported information, delinquency serves to increase romantic involvement and that romantic involvement may provide vicarious, but not necessarily direct, reinforcement for delinquency among male adolescents.

Information about runaways is almost exclusively gleaned from self-report studies (Whitbeck et al., 1997). For example, it has been found that runaways compared with other types of status offenders have greater levels of family violence, rejection, and sexual abuse. Not unexpected, runaways were from families where there was less parental monitoring of juvenile behavior, warmth, and support.

Not all of this research is dependent upon recollections of one's childhood and familial past. For instance, 39 community-based organizations in Miami, Florida, have provided risk-focused delinquency prevention services for over 900 families (Kakar, 1998). These organizations provided families with parenting skills and counseled both adults and juveniles about how to cope with day-to-day family problems and stresses. Self-reports from family members indicated that the program was effective and accomplishing its goal of delinquency prevention.

In general, self-report investigations are not limited to juveniles and delinquency. Persons in any area of criminal justice, including law enforcement, the courts, and corrections, may disclose things about themselves through self-reports. The potential uses of self-report information are unlimited.

How Do You Know Respondents Tell the Truth? The Lie Factor

Much has been written about deception practiced by researchers when contacting and studying respondents. However, respondents may also be deceptive according to how they respond to questions. Some respondents may simply lie to investigators and give false information about themselves. We don't know all of the reasons why people lie to researchers. We suspect, for instance, that some juveniles lie in order to make themselves seem tough or adult-like. Maybe some adults lie for similar reasons. Maybe they think that if they admit to criminal or embarrassing activities, this information will be made available to others and they might get into trouble or suffer social ostracism.

Whenever investigators administer questionnaires to respondents, sometimes they include a few questions that will sensitize them as to whether respondents are lying. Essentially, researchers build into their questionnaires a lie factor, consisting of several general statements with almost universal answers. Some of these items are:

1. Sometimes I have thoughts that would be embarrassing if known to others.
2. Sometimes I feel anxious about a trivial incident.
3. I never lie for any reason.
4. Sometimes I feel insecure or underconfident.
5. I have never said anything that embarrasses others.
6. I have never had bad or unpleasant dreams.
7. I never worry about anything.

These and similar items are sometimes included together with other statements that describe one's self and personal characteristics. Respondents are asked to indicate whether these statements are true or false. Researchers assume that *every* one of these statements is true of most people. However, some persons deny that these statements characterize them. If a respondent gives a "false" response to most of these items, then their responses to other items on a questionnaire are suspect. Most everyone has worried about something at one time or another. Most everyone has felt anxious about a trivial incident or had an unpleasant dream. However, some persons want to convey a particular image to investigators. Maybe they think that "normal people" don't worry about things and are totally self-assured and confident. Maybe they think that it is "abnormal" to dream about unpleasant things or say something that embarrasses others. Therefore, they lie in order to appear normal. However, by lying, they appear abnormal. Thus, a lie factor is established and undermines the credibility of their responses to other items. Researchers are inclined to discard their questionnaires as useless if their lie factor is significantly high.

The Minnesota Multiphasic Personality Inventory (MMPI) is a personality assessment inventory. It consists of over 550 true–false statements and measures a multitude of personality characteristics. Some of the items above are found on the MMPI. It also has a built-in lie factor. When persons take the MMPI, they get a lie factor score in addition to an assessment of several salient personality characteristics. The MMPI is administered for many reasons, some of which pertain to applications for employment with different agencies. Some professions, such as probation or parole officer work, are stressful. Some persons may be unsuited for such work according to their personality characteristics. Perhaps it has been found that persons with certain personality traits do not deal well with stress. Prospective job applicants may or may not be selected, depending on how they respond on the MMPI and the personality profile they exhibit.

The Long Beach, California Police Department (LBPD) is one police organization that uses the MMPI as a part of its officer selection process. Once, an undergraduate student told me that he wanted to become an officer with the LBPD. He said that he had heard about the "personality test," and he wondered if I had a copy of it that he could study. I told him that I did not have a copy of it, that the measure (MMPI) was not available for general distribution, and that the MMPI was an assessment device and not something to prepare for, such as a math or verbal aptitude test. "Well then," he asked me, "is there a way I can respond that will make me look good to them [the LBPD selection committee]?" I said, "Tell the truth. Give truthful responses." Later, he reported that he took the MMPI and was not selected for the police officer position. I asked him about the responses he gave on the MMPI. "Well," he said, "I gave answers according to what I thought I ought to say." I told him to go back at the next available opportunity and retake the MMPI. This story has a happy ending. The student retook the psychological assessment and was eventually selected as a new LBPD police officer recruit. The most likely explanation for his "failure" to be selected as a police officer recruit the first time around is that the results of his MMPI score disclosed possible deception. His second chance with the MMPI was more truthful, and apparently the "fit" between the job itself and his personality was a good one.

Many researchers in criminal justice and criminology simply construct questionnaires and assume that their respondents will be truthful. Or these investigators may use questionnaires and scales previously used by others. Lie factors in these questionnaires are relatively rare and are most frequently associated with psychological inventories and educational testing. Nevertheless, lie factor items are certainly an option if researchers wish to use them.

Cultural Values and Questionnaire Wording

When questionnaires are administered to anyone, consideration should be given to the cultural values and differences of the target audience and how questionnaire items are worded. Non-English-speaking persons may be unable to read or understand questionnaire items. For example, there are large numbers of Hispanic persons in California, Arizona, and Texas.

Sometimes, researchers in these states construct bilingual questionnaires, anticipating that a significant portion of their respondents will prefer Spanish over English.

Comparative research or investigations of other cultures may require that we formulate questions that are culture-specific. If someone is studying the Russian mafia and their role in organized crime in the United States, there are English expressions and colloquialisms that are unfamiliar to Russians. Some terms and expressions used in the United States cannot be literally translated into Russian. Therefore, alternative phrases or other ways of asking about organized crime in the United States involving Russian immigrants must be considered.

Despite the best efforts of states to educate their citizens, the fact is that there is still a significant amount of illiteracy throughout the U.S. population. Some persons cannot read, while others read poorly. A **self-administered questionnaire** in the hands of an illiterate or semi-literate respondent is meaningless. Sometimes researchers may actually need to read questionnaires to respondents in a structured interview format face-to-face. However, if large numbers of questionnaires are mailed to anonymous respondents, this option is not feasible.

The educational level of target audiences varies greatly. Investigators may need to adjust the wording of their questionnaires depending on the composition of their respondents. For instance, when Sandra Hafley and Richard Tewksbury (1996) studied marijuana distribution in Bluegrass County, Kentucky, they exercised choices about how certain questions were asked. It probably would not be appropriate for them to ask local residents, "Can you please provide us with a description of the distributional patterns of cannabis and related paraphernalia in this socioeconomic milieu as well as the political and economic ramifications of such commerce for the affected populace?" More than a few Kentucky mountain folk would cock their heads and give Hafley and Tewksbury peculiar stares. Rather, the authors probably asked questions similar to these: "Who are the pot-growers? Where do they sell their stuff? How do people in this neck of the woods get by? Is everybody around here in on it?"

However, if we were investigating professional groups, such as medical examiners, coroners, and criminalists, we want to prepare questions that use jargon appropriate for these persons in their respective professional fields. Also, if we were to question police officers or corrections personnel, we might construct our questions so that they tend to fit these special audiences. Researchers must use their own best judgment about framing questions for specific target audiences.

Other Factors

If questionnaires are mailed to respondents, factors such as the type of postage used (i.e., metered, hand-stamped, special delivery), type of cover letter attached (appeals to respondent egoism or altruism), rewards for responding (money, turkeys, opportunities to express opinions), and the socioeconomic status of the target sample are considered to be influential to different degrees for eliciting greater rates of response. If questionnaires are administered on a face-to-face basis, such factors as the appearance or ethnic/racial origin of the investigator or questionnaire administrator, the readability of the questionnaire, and the types of responses required must be considered important in determining response rates. When questionnaires are administered on a face-to-face basis, many problems are encountered similar to those encountered by interviewers.

What about Nonresponse?

Two of the most frustrating questions investigators must deal with are "Who are the nonrespondents?" and "What would be the outcome of my results or findings if the nonrespondents were somehow added or included as a part of all the data analyzed?" There are various ways of identifying nonrespondents, particularly in a mailed questionnaire situation. Lists of individuals to whom questionnaires are sent are compiled. Those who respond and return the questionnaire are simply checked off of these lists. Those who do not return their questionnaires may be sent follow-up letters to remind them to return the questionnaires they received. Under such conditions, it is ethical to advise respondents that their identities are known in advance and that the researcher will know if they have not responded to the mailed questionnaire.

Another method is to simply code each questionnaire or the return envelope with a number that refers to specific respondents. However, respondents may notice the number. This absence of anonymity may inhibit their response, but it will also explain why they receive a follow-up letter from researchers later if they do not respond to the original questionnaire mailed. A questionable practice is using some sort of invisible ink or undetectable coding procedure on the questionnaires or return envelopes to identify all respondents. Respondents are unaware that their questionnaires have been coded so that if they are returned, researchers will know who they are. Various professional associations, such as the Academy of Criminal Justice Sciences, the American Society of Criminology, and the American Sociological Association, presently scrutinize these and other research practices and seek to provide ethical safeguards that will protect human subjects who are contacted by social investigators.

If researchers have made no provisions for identifying nonrespondents, they have little or no hope of being able to describe the characteristics (social, psychological, socioeconomic) of nonrespondents and contrast them with the characteristics of those who have responded. Obviously, the respondents and nonrespondents differ in at least one important respect—some of them returned the questionnaires and some did not return them. Would the inclusion of information from the nonrespondents be significant enough to change or alter one's research findings to any degree? We don't know. It would be wrong to think that the inclusion of the information from nonrespondents would have no influence on one's results. However, we have no way of calculating the impact of unknown information on our study findings. Considering that response rates to mailed questionnaires vary from 30 percent to 60 percent in a majority of investigations, nonresponse rates ranging from 70 percent to 40 percent would be expected as well. These are sizable numbers of respondents, and we could speculate that if they had been included in one's data analysis, their information probably would have made a difference to the study outcome and findings disclosed.

SUMMARY

Questionnaires are self-administered inventories that describe and measure information about people, their social characteristics, and their opinions about things. Questionnaires are perhaps the most popular data collection strategy researchers use to gather information about groups. They are used in all areas of criminology and criminal justice, and every component of the criminal justice system has been subjected to questionnaires of one type or another over the years. Each data collection strategy (e.g., questionnaires, observation, interviewing) has various weaknesses and strengths relative to other strategies, although researchers frequently employ multiple data collection techniques when conducting investigations and triangulate their findings by comparing the results obtained from these different strategies. Triangulation means simply to use multiple data-gathering methods when conducting a single study. Therefore, researchers may use questionnaires, interviews, observation, and even examine organizational documents when investigating a juvenile court or correctional facility. The use of several data collection methods at once involves more work, to be sure, but it provides much richer detail than is provided by a single data collection method. Also, one method of data collection can lend support to the consistency of information yielded by using other data collection methods.

The major functions of questionnaires are description and measurement. The descriptive function of questionnaires is quite important. Persons can check responses that best fit them or describe them in different ways. They can give researchers a fairly accurate view of who they are and what they think. Questionnaires also measure things. It is quite common for questionnaires to include one or more attitudinal scales that purport to measure one's attitudes or dispositions. It is believed by many researchers that if we know how people feel about different ideas or if we know about their attitudes, this will enable us to better understand their actions, whatever they may be. These attitudinal scales are measures of different phenomena. We won't worry yet whether these scales actually measure what researchers think they measure. The fact is that various scales that purportedly measure different phenomena are used and included on many questionnaires. Later, researchers tabulate the information from these questionnaires and can assign numerical values to attitudes they believe they have measured. Questionnaires frequently include numerous measures of different phenomena. The data gathered from these questionnaire instruments may be analyzed different ways and yield much insightful information about people and their behaviors or about the settings where people work.

Questionnaires can be classified different ways, depending on how we choose to construct them. Questionnaires may consist exclusively of fixed-response items, where all statements have previously designated fixed-answer options, and open-ended items, where respondents must provide more or less extensive written replies to questions asked. Fixed-response items are more easily completed by respondents, and many investigators feel such questionnaires have a higher rate of return compared with open-ended questionnaires that take more time and depend on a certain ability to express oneself in writing. Educational and socioeconomic factors may inhibit responses from less educated persons to open-ended items as well. One advantage of fixed-response items is that they are easier to score than open-ended items. If researchers have to read lengthy responses to questions in an open-ended format, it may take quite a while to know how to score what someone has written. These are subjective judgment calls that may lead to inaccurate interpretations of what persons have said about themselves and their work environments.

Another distinction between different kinds of questionnaires has to do with how they are administered. Questionnaires can be mailed to respondents or distributed to them under face-to-face conditions. Mailed questionnaires are the easier of the two questionnaire administration methods. Investigators merely place a questionnaire in an envelope and mail it to someone, hoping that the questionnaire will be completed and the respondent will mail it back, usually in an included self-addressed stamped envelope provided by the researcher. Or the investigator may go door-to-door, asking people to fill out questionnaires in their presence. This method is very time-consuming, and it does not afford respondents any anonymity while responding. It is much easier, and seemingly anonymous, to fill out a questionnaire in the privacy of one's dwelling, and then return the document later. Of course, if researchers administer questionnaires face-to-face, they can answer immediately any possible questions respondents might have, or they can clear up any confusion over questionnaire items that are unclear.

Constructing questionnaires is time-consuming and complex. Investigators should be sensitive to questionnaire length, to the inclusion of sensitive items that solicit intimate details of respondents' lives, and to the possible illiteracy of certain respondents, where English may not be understood by some of the target population or where some persons in the population may not be well educated. Also, some questions may be presumptuous and offensive. It would be improper, for instance, to ask a husband, "When was the last time you beat your wife?" This question presumes that the husband beats his wife, which he doesn't do. More than a few investigators ask similar questions of their research subjects. Also, some questions are contingency questions. Depending on one's answer to an earlier question, the respondent may be directed to one of several alternative subsequent questions that are contingent upon their first answer. Some questions are double-barreled in that they are actually two questions in a single sentence. "Are you a Republican and gay?" What if the respondent is a Republican but not gay? How can this type of question be answered? Thus, question content, wording, item ordering, and the cultural nature of the items are key considerations when putting questionnaires together for research purposes.

Frequently, researchers will conduct pretests and administer early versions of their questionnaires to others, simply to verify if the question wording is clear. Errors in wording, misspelled words, and other problems are often detected. In these cases, investigators conduct pilot studies or trial runs to see how their questionnaires might be regarded by their intended target sample later.

Some questionnaires are known as self-reports because they disclose important information about people that may be unknown to other agencies, such as police departments, probation departments, or the courts. The self-report is a data collection method where persons provide information about themselves and their behaviors. Self-reports have frequently been used with juveniles to disclose information about so-called hidden delinquency. Often such self-report information shows that certain delinquent behaviors occur more often than official sources reveal. But self-reports are not limited to juveniles. Their use for other populations is virtually unlimited.

Some amount of nonresponse is expected in most projects where questionnaires are used, although mailed questionnaires seem to generate the greatest amount of nonresponse. Anonymity, type of postage used, and types of cover letters that have egoistic or altruistic appeal may be used to increase response rates. Follow-up letters may be used to solicit questionnaires from those who were unresponsive to the initial mailings of questionnaires. No one knows about those who do not respond, although their inclusion in the final results might have profound effects on the findings. Another issue is the truthfulness of respondents. How do we know respondents tell the truth when they fill out a questionnaire? We don't. Some standardized personality measures have built-in lie factors, where items are included that may involve some unusual behavior or thought that almost everyone exhibits. If some persons deny that they have this common behavior or thought, then this is a fairly good indication that they are lying. If researchers believe that some persons are not being truthful with them, the researchers may discard their questionnaires and exclude those responses from their gathered data.

QUESTIONS FOR REVIEW

1. What are questionnaires? What are two important functions of questionnaires? Why are these functions important?

2. What is meant by triangulation? What are some primary purposes of triangulation?

3. What are two types of questionnaire administration? What are some of the weaknesses and strengths of each of these administration methods?

4. What are some key differences between fixed-response and open-ended items? What are the positive and negative features of each type of item?

5. What is a response set or set response? What types of questionnaires are more likely to contain set responses? Can researchers do anything to control for response sets and their occurrence when constructing their questionnaires? What can be done?

6. What are some primary drawbacks to using open-ended items on culturally diverse populations?

7. What are some limitations and advantages of using existing scales devised by other researchers?

8. What are mailed questionnaires? How much nonresponse is usually anticipated in mailed-questionnaire situations? What can be done to decrease nonresponse?

9. What are some important questions we must consider before constructing our questionnaires?

10. What are follow-up letters? What are their purposes? Are there any ethical considerations to be made when sending out follow-up letters?

6

Data Collection Strategies III: Interviews

CHAPTER OUTLINE

CHAPTER OBJECTIVES

As the result of reading this chapter, the following objectives will be realized:

1. Determining the value of the interview as a major data collection strategy for criminological research.
2. Determining the weaknesses and strengths of using interviewing as opposed to other data collection alternatives.
3. Distinguishing between unstructured and structured interviews and their relative value.
4. Differentiating between interview guides and interview schedules and the data quality yielded.
5. Determining the functions of interviews in criminology and criminal justice research.
6. Understanding how interviews are constructed and administered, including some of the major problems associated with the interview technique.
7. Describing alternative interviewing procedures including random-digit dialing and computer-assisted telephone interviewing.
8. Describing the process of conducting interviews, including making interview arrangements and appointments, attire, personality attributes that improve interviewing, videotaped or tape-recorded interviews, and some of the hazards of interviewing.

Introduction

A useful supplement and alternative to questionnaire administration is interviewing. Interviewing is a direct data-gathering tool that involves verbal communication between researchers and their respondents. This chapter examines the interviewing process and highlights different types of interviewing that may be conducted. Like questionnaire construction and administration, considerable planning is necessary for the purpose of implementing interviewing successfully. The planning of interviewing will be examined in some detail. Unlike questionnaires, a different kind of information is yielded from interviewing. Respondents are able to give verbal elaborations of answers that otherwise might have been given on more superficial questionnaire instruments. Interviewers themselves may probe further into the responses given by different subjects, seeking more detail and clarification for the answers yielded. Therefore, the first part of this chapter provides a preliminary contrast between information yielded from interviewing and questionnaire administration.

The second part of this chapter examines different types of interviews, including both unstructured and structured interviews. Unstructured interviews often employ interview guides, which are merely listed topics that interviewers will use to elicit general answers from respondents. Based on the answers given to these questions, interviewers can follow up with more specific kinds of questions. Therefore, a flow of information evolves and is influenced greatly by the nature of answers to previous questions provided by respondents. These unstructured interviews are useful in that they often yield serendipitous information that otherwise may not have been apparent to researchers when the investigation was planned and implemented. The advantages and disadvantages of unstructured interviewing are examined.

Structured interviews are more rigid in their composition, appearing a great deal like open-ended questionnaires. Such interviews use interview schedules, which are more structured than interview guides, that are typically used under unstructured interviewing conditions. However, in an interviewing scenario, researchers ask these questions of respondents and may freely depart from fixed question ordering at times to make additional and more in-depth probes into the answer to questions they are provided. Almost always there is some confusion about certain questions and the nature of information sought by investigators. Fortunately, trained interviewers can easily clarify aspects of questions that are confusing or misunderstood by different respondents. Both unstructured and structured interviews may occur under diverse conditions, including a respondent's workplace, home, or at a neutral location, such as a library or other public building. The time limitations of interviewing are highly variable, and it is unknown exactly how much time should be allocated to any particular interview. Much depends on the dynamics established between the interviewer and his or her subjects. Whether unstructured or structured interviewing is used depends greatly on how much is known in advance about the target population about which an investigator seeks information.

Besides unstructured and structured interviews, focused interviews are also examined. These types of interviews involve persons who have undergone particular experiences or have been involved in particular interventions or experiments. Former boot camp participants may be subjected to focused interviews to determine the nature and impact of boot camp experiences. Convicted persons who have served some of their time under house arrest may be subject to focused interviews that seek to capture what their home confinement or house arrest experiences have been like. Each of these types of interviews is described in some detail, and the weaknesses and strengths of each are examined.

Some interviewing occurs via telephone. The telephone interview is a relatively inexpensive way of gathering information. While the nature of such interviewing differs greatly from face-to-face interviewing experiences, researchers are still able to follow up questions asked with more in-depth probes to seek more information about responses subjects provide. Investigators lack considerable control over who they interview under telephone interviewing circumstances, however. They are not in a position to observe the body language of respondents, or signs that respondents are being truthful or untruthful about the answers they provide. At the same time, there is some degree of anonymity provided respondents giving information who may be more uncomfortable providing such information under face-to-face interviewing circumstances. Several telephone interviewing mechanisms are also discussed. These include random digit dialing and computer-assisted telephone interviews. These types of strategies for conducting interviews will be described, and their advantages and disadvantages will be described.

The chapter next examines the general functions of interviewing, which include description and exploration. Interviewers are able to take notes, mental or otherwise, about the information yielded through interviews. If interviews are tape-recorded, abundant details are provided by respondents that add to other information provided through questionnaires or simple observation of persons on their jobs or in their homes or other settings. Exploration and description are essential in providing rich background information for investigators who may seek to implement a more experimental study with the same or similar respondents at a later date. Some examples from the research literature are provided to illustrate the type of descriptive and exploratory information yielded.

The actual construction of interviews is a complex business. The chapter next explores some of the essential steps taken by investigators in the preparation of interview schedules and guides. Some of the preliminary steps of interviewing are described, including gaining access to organizations or groups where respondents may be contacted to provide interviewers with valuable information. Interviewing arrangements are discussed, as well as the training process for interviewers. Some of the characteristics of effective interviewers are described, including dressing for the interview, the nature of follow-up questions or probes and how such probes may be used to elicit more in-depth information, and whether it is feasible to use tape recorders or videotape equipment when conducting interviews. Under some conditions, experimental subjects as respondents may be asked to take lie detector or polygraph tests. These situations are infrequent, but since such interviews do occur occasionally, their application must be addressed.

Also, since interviewing involves direct contact with research subjects, it may be hazardous. Interviewers may have to enter dangerous neighborhoods to reach particular respondents. These neighborhoods may be dangerous because of high crime rates or because they are gang-controlled. Therefore, some of the dangers of interviews are discussed. The chapter concludes with an examination of some general advantages and disadvantages of the interviewing process and the use of interviews generally compared with other data collection methods.

Interviews as Instruments in Criminal Justice Research

The interview is a very time-consuming, yet valuable, data-gathering tool that can disclose much about various types of social settings and the people within them. Interviewers are at liberty to go well beyond the limited boundaries of questionnaires, even open-ended ones, and to probe respondents for additional, insightful information about themselves, their work, and those with whom they work. There are no restrictions relating to the conditions under which interviews may be conducted. If we consider each component of the criminal justice system, no single component is immune from an interviewer's questions.

For instance, we can interview police officers and their administrators to inquire about their work roles and how they are performed, how police officers react to job stress and life-threatening situations, their reactions to different patrol styles, and a host of other considerations. Prosecutors and judges may be interviewed to determine their prosecutorial and sentencing priorities, which types of cases are most and least preferred, and their reactions to different types of sentencing reforms. Defendants, inmates, probationers, and parolees may also be interviewed to determine their reactions to different types of prison or jail conditions, the quality of various community-based correctional programs, and their interpersonal relations with those who supervise them. Juvenile gang members may be questioned about their behavioral patterns, reasons for fighting other gangs, and their gang formative processes. The types of respondents and the ranges of questions they might be asked are virtually unlimited.

Most students are familiar with the results of several common interview applications, such as the *National Crime Victimization Survey* (where random households are targeted and occupants questioned about crimes they have experienced during the past year or some other time interval), the *National Youth Survey* (where samples of high school students disclose through interviews the incidence and types of crimes they have committed but have not been apprehended for committing), and the U.S. Census, where random samples of households throughout the United States are contacted and interviewed concerning specific demographic, social, and socioeconomic characteristics.

The characteristics of interviews include the following:

1. Questions are asked and responses are given verbally. The verbal nature of the questions emphasizes three points about interviews that are not sufficiently stressed in our original definition. First, interviews are not simply conversational exchanges between interviewers and interviewees. They are conversations wherein the major thrust is obtaining verbal answers to questions put verbally. Second, these verbal exchanges need not be on a face-to-face basis, even though they usually are. Sometimes, interviews with others are conducted over the telephone. Finally, interviewing may be conducted with more than one interviewee, such as interviews of partners, such as husband/wife, two patrol officers, or small groups of prisoners who cell together.

2. Information is recorded by investigators rather than respondents. The fact that interviewers record information provided by respondents underscores the greater accuracy of interviewing regarding information obtained. Interviewers may take notes, mark interview schedules or guides, or tape-record these verbal exchanges with audio or videotaping devices.

3. The relationship between interviewers and interviewees is structured. First, this relationship is transitory. It has a fixed beginning and a fixed point of termination. Second, the relation is one where the participants are usually strangers. Even if these persons are not strangers to one another, the nature of the interviewer–interviewee relation is one of scientific objectivity, where most, if not all, threats are removed that might otherwise hinder or frustrate honest responses to one's questions.

4. There is considerable flexibility in the interviewing format. Few other data collection tools offer such a large range of question-asking formats to investigators. It seems at times that the only limitation is the ingenuity of interviewers. Such an amount of structural variability allows for greater mutual understanding of both the questions by interviewers and the answers given by interviewees.

Some researchers deliberately choose interviewing, in part, because it permits them the opportunity of moving into unexpected or uncharted areas. Even the most standardized interviews do not prohibit such spontaneity of exploration both before and after the data have been compiled through the interview.

Interviews Contrasted with Questionnaires

Interviews are "Up Close and Personal": Survey Questions are Not.   Compared with mailed questionnaires used in surveys, interviews are "up close and personal" means of data collection. There is a close interaction between the interviewer and interviewee. This type of relation does not exist under most types of questionnaire administration. Thus, respondents are more inclined to have a conversation with and be interviewed by a researcher. They are also more likely to trivialize a questionnaire sent to them and throw it away.

Anonymity Doesn't Exist in Interviews.   Interviews are conducted face-to-face, and as such, **anonymity** does not exist. Under questionnaire administration, at least assurances of anonymity can be made to increase both the response rate and truthfulness of responses.

Questionnaires Yield Superficial Information, While Interviews Yield In-Depth Information.   Questionnaires, especially those mailed to respondents and returned anonymously, are often criticized for their superficiality. Respondents respond to checklists. There is no sound method for determining who completed the returned questionnaires, unless they are administered in face-to-face situations (e.g., "I'll wait here in the living room with you while you complete the questionnaire."). Researchers are usually not in a position to clarify or explain the meaning of certain questions. Nor can researchers see facial expressions of bewilderment or confusion or frustration. Interviews overcome the problems of superficiality and lack of clarity concerning how questions are formulated and presented. Interviews permit additional **probes** of respondents, in order to amplify or expand their answers verbally. There is little opportunity for such amplification or expansion when respondents complete a mailed questionnaire.

Interviews Permit Probing and Follow-Up Questions, Questionnaires Do Not.
Generally, interviews permit investigators to gather more in-depth information from respondents with **follow-up questions.** Interviewees can elaborate on their answers to certain

questions. Sometimes they add information that was not originally contemplated by researchers. Thus, there is an element of serendipity in many interview situations.

Interviews Generate Larger Response Rates.   Also, a greater rate of response is obtained through interviewing, provided research subjects allow themselves to be interviewed. Mailed questionnaires have considerable nonresponse, perhaps has much as 50 or 60 percent on the average. An estimate of the average response rate to interviews is about 80 percent.

Types of Interviews

Interviews are either unstructured or structured.

Unstructured Interviews

Unstructured interviews are much what their name implies. Investigators might be charged with finding out about parent–child relations relative to a sample of juvenile delinquents. They might conduct informal, unstructured interviews with several delinquents to determine what they can about how these juveniles define their relations with their parents. The interviews may vary greatly in the time taken to complete them, from one juvenile to the next. Furthermore, not all questions asked of one juvenile may necessarily be asked of another. Also, the order of questions is irrelevant, as long as interviewers "cover their bases" and get all relevant material they can from the youths they interview.

Another feature of unstructured interviews is that interviewers do not need special interviewing training. They may record any observations they make and their own interpretations or impressions of any answers given. The interviews are also characterized as free-flowing, with the direction and depth of interviews determined by situational factors. If certain juveniles are obviously reluctant to talk about certain background factors, interviewers can shift gears to discuss other areas of interest. Thus, unstructured interviews are the closest thing to the spontaneity inherent in natural conversation.

There are several advantages of unstructured interviews. First, the interview itself approaches natural conversation. Subjects interviewed might feel more at ease in responding to an interviewer's questions. Second, interviewers are guided in their questions by the types of responses given. Thus, there is less likelihood that interviewers will infuse their own values and biases into the interview itself. Third, unstructured interviews offer the greatest degree of flexibility and serendipity. Researchers can spend as much time as they wish **probing** certain aspects of answers persons give in order to develop certain emerging themes.

One problem with unstructured interviewing, however, is that there may be incomparability of information derived from one interview that might be contrasted with information derived from other interviews. Since there is no systematic control over the question-asking procedures, the reliability of data is thrown into serious question. Also, much wasted time may be spent with respondents who have little or nothing to add to the knowledge interviewers have already obtained from others. Sometimes, interviewers may engage in repetitive or unproductive conversations with respondents.

Another problem is that some respondents may choose this opportunity to use interviewers as therapists. For instance, one interviewer who studied employees in a large probation department reported that one older probation officer, a 63-year-old, was being singled out for early retirement. The probation officer didn't want to retire early, but probation office administrators were dissatisfied with his performance, which was diminishing rapidly. The officer continually forgot to keep appointments with various probationer/clients, failed to submit presentence investigation reports with the court, and failed to comply with other rules and regulations associated with probation officer work. In short, the administration wanted to get rid of him. Since civil service regulations were in effect at the time and mandatory retirement could not be enforced until one reached 70 years of age, one's early retirement was not mandatory. Therefore, the administration sought to make his life as uncomfortable as possible, hoping that eventually, he would take the "hint" and resign of his own accord.

The interviewer who interviewed this elderly probation officer found himself in the role of therapist, since the probation officer poured out his life experiences and disclosed what had been happening to him on the job. At one point, the probation officer broke down and cried. The interviewer was in an awkward situation, since it wouldn't be appropriate to simply get up and leave. The interviewer decided to hear him out, and this "interview," a tape-recorded one, lasted nearly 7 hours. The interviewer finally was able to "get away" by noting that the sun was setting, his wife had dinner waiting, and his tape-recorder had run out of tape.

Another drawback of unstructured interviewing is that there are no guarantees that the interview will be fruitful or insightful. However, this limitation may be a function of the original research enterprise implemented. If researchers have such poorly conceived research problems that unstructured interviewing is chosen as a data-gathering option, then the investigators' own lack of problem conceptualization may enhance any shortcomings of unstructured interviewing. This is not meant to suggest that such unstructured interviewing is chosen only when researchers have poorly conceived research plans. Rather, it is simply more likely that unstructured interviews will be used whenever researchers are uncertain of the information desired from target audiences or if they believe that something new or insightful will be disclosed.

Closely related to this possible drawback is the fact that considerable time must be allocated to devising categories into which one's responses from an unstructured interview can be classified. If several interviewers are involved in the data-collection effort, then problems may arise relating to interinterviewer reliability. Different interviewers may ask different questions, or they may code similar responses to the same questions differently. For these and other reasons, most researchers prefer more structured interviews to less structured ones, since greater ease in coding and systematization of information derived are achieved. Some unstructured interviews are given some structure by using an **interview guide.** Interview guides consist of lists of predetermined questions and/or topics about which researchers seek information. Since these questions and/or topic areas are anticipated in advance, some thought may be given to the codes devised for probable replies from respondents.

BOX 6.1   PERSONALITY HIGHLIGHT

CANDACE KRUTTSCHNITT
University of Minnesota

Statistics: B.A. (criminology), University of California, Berkeley: M.A., MPhil, Ph.D. (sociology), Yale University.

BACKGROUND AND INTERESTS

Virtually all of my research has focused on women offenders but I didn't enter the field of criminology with this topic in mind, or even enter college knowing I was going to major in criminology. I was at Berkeley and taking my university requirements for the B.A. degree and I found myself fascinated by a course I was taking in abnormal psychology. A friend of mine told me that if I liked that class, I should take Dr. Bernard Diamond's course, the Etiology of Crime from a Psychiatric Perspective. I did, and I never looked back. At that time, Berkeley had a school of criminology that admitted students in their junior year. I applied; I was admitted; and, I graduated with a degree in criminology 2 years later.

Thinking I could get a job with my B.A. in criminology, I applied after graduation for a number of positions but was turned down by all of them, except my application to serve as a VISTA (Volunteers in Service to America) worker was accepted and I was sent to work in New York City. There I was given the choice between working in a program for drug offenders or with a street-gang project in the South Bronx. I chose the latter. It was a wonderful experience and during that year, I decided that I wanted to go on with my studies in criminology. At that time, there were relatively few schools that offered doctoral degrees in criminology, so I applied to sociology departments that had strong faculty in the area of crime, law, and deviance. Yale University was very strong in this respect with a faculty that included Albert Reiss, Kai Erikson, Stanton Wheeler, and Donald Black. Like many students, I found graduate school arduous but Professor Black made the experience come to life for me. He encouraged me to read widely and to discuss my ideas with him. My dissertation topic came from reading the *New York Times*. A small article appeared on the noted increases that had occurred in women's crime rates. I thought it was fascinating and so did Professor Black but he suggested that perhaps I might want to think about these data from a different angle—that is, not what the statistics tell us about women's offending, but rather, what they tell us about women's social locations and the *behavior of law* in response to these social locations.

My dissertation set my research agenda squarely in the area of female offending where it has remained ever since. However, there have been important deviations along the way as I

BOX 6.1   CONTINUED

have moved from research on the criminal court sanctions accorded female offenders to the etiology of violent crime, child abuse, and female victims of violent crime. Most recently, I completed a monograph with Rosemary Gartner on women's experiences of imprisonment in California (*Marking Time in the Golden State: Women's Imprisonment in California,* forthcoming, Cambridge University Press). Our research replicates and extends the 1960s study Ward and Kassebaum conducted of the California Institution for Women. The study encompasses both the oldest and the newest prisons for women in California, but it started as a temporal study. We thought we would just return to the institution that Ward and Kassebaum had studied to see if "doing time" changed for women, as their lives in the free world had changed substantially over the past 30 years. However, as we began the study, it was clear that the women prisoners we interviewed were very fearful of being transferred to one of the newer prisons. We then realized that we needed to expand our methodological and theoretical approaches to control for time and study two prisons in the same era, operating under what has been called the neoliberal regime of crime control or the "new penology."

ADVICE TO STUDENTS

My advice to students is to take advantage of every opportunity that comes your way. The field of criminology offers lots of wonderful avenues for developing research and, especially, collaborative research endeavors. Throughout my career I have benefited tremendously from projects that have involved both graduate students and other faculty, including faculty outside my area of expertise. One of the strengths of criminology is its interdisciplinary nature and we have much to gain by drawing on the wisdom of our colleagues in sociology, psychology, history, law, and economics.

Structured Interviews and the Focused Interview

Contrasted with interview guides and unstructured interviews, **structured interviews** consist of a predetermined list of fixed-response questions or items. For the most part, interviewers adhere rather closely to the predetermined question list. Structured interviews reflect a high degree of interviewer control. Such interviewer control may be exercised over the time taken to complete the interview, interviewer clarification of any confusing questions or answers received from respondents, and limiting the questions only to those factors relevant for the problem being investigated. In contrast, unstructured interviewing lacks such controls. Often, it is important for those interviewed to know how much time the interview will take to complete. Interviewing is sometimes conducted on one's job. Sometimes, employers will allocate times when interviewing may be conducted. These infringements on a company's time must be carefully controlled, since researchers do not want to jeopardize their chances of studying the same setting at a later date. Telling interviewees that the interview will only take 15 minutes, and subsequently conducting an interview that takes 2 hours, will do nothing but antagonize respondents and make them resistant to being interviewed again. This method of interviewing has been referred to as the **foot-in-the-door technique,** since once the investigator has gained access to the respondent, the interviewing process stretches well beyond the original time limits suggested by the interviewer. During interviewing, time passes so quickly that 1–2 hours of interviewing seems like 15 minutes. The interviewer often knows that interviews will take longer than 15 minutes, but 15 minutes "sounds good" to respondents and they are often more willing to be interviewed if they don't think it will take too much time. And once the interview commences, respondent interest in being interviewed intensifies as they realize that others find their answers and opinions important. Many people simply like to talk about themselves and what they do. Additionally, research projects where the same samples are studied over several different time periods rely upon access to the same samples, and therefore, good public relations skills are essential to permit study completion.

BOX 6.2   PERSONALITY HIGHLIGHT

DAVID R. STRUCKHOFF
Executive Director, Justice Research Institute, Joliet/Chicago, Loyola University, Chicago

Statistics: B.A. (philosophy, psychology), Quincy University; M.S. (sociology), Illinois Institute of Technology; Ph.D. (sociology), Southern Illinois University–Carbondale; Graduate Research Fellow, U.S. Department of Justice, Law Enforcement Assistance Administration.

BACKGROUND AND RESEARCH INTERESTS

My research interests are related to the interview method of gathering data. I like to interview people. Indeed, my entire professional career has involved interviewing.

Specifically, I have a strong, ongoing interest in the motives and behaviors that lead to trouble with society and the law, interest in the people who actually do justice—police, judges, and correctional professionals—and interest in comparative views from colleagues from other nations. During consulting in and about jails, the sheriff has emerged as a fascinating topic for research.

During the completion of my bachelor's degree work at Quincy University, I worked with Illinois Youth Commission social workers and interviewed juveniles in street venues for prevention programs. For my M.S. degree at the Illinois Institute of Technology, I interviewed members of the Black P. Stone nation near Chicago's Hyde Park under the direction of sociologists at the University of Chicago. And for my doctorate, I interviewed prisoners and their

BOX 6.2 CONTINUED

wives. In the meantime, I had been hired by the Illinois Department of Corrections as a correctional sociologist. In this capacity I interviewed incoming prisoners, including a regular counseling assignment on death row for about 14 years. Interestingly, the great experience of prison has allowed many of us who have worked in these interviewing and diagnostic capacities to move to successful careers in academia and consulting. It was only natural to develop skill in the evaluation of programs and systems; case studies; policy analysis; advising police, corrections, and the judiciary; and providing expert testimony in court.

Interviewing as a research tool maximizes the depth of one's analysis. Qualitative work is intuitively appealing to me. The response rates are very high if you are trusted. As Professor Champion points out in the text, this type of work is not anonymous. There may be a script, but it can be deviated from to pursue interesting angles to one's research. On the downside is the potential for interviewee manipulation. Still, when I accumulate enough qualitative data and if I can keep it systematic, I can begin to do quantitative work with it. The more interviewing I do, the greater the database with which I can work and the more confidence I have in statistics used to describe and infer things from the data. I enjoy using nonparametric statistics as well as parametric statistics—and I really didn't appreciate them until I taught a series of graduate statistics courses for practitioners.

INTERESTING EXPERIENCES

Talking with so many people has led to exceptionally valuable networks in criminal justice. I once commented at a meeting of researchers that I serve on research boards and research panels because for me, it is "fun." A couple of my colleagues didn't think our work should be "fun," but I got some good networking contacts out of the meeting with others who enjoy what we're doing. Another offshoot of durable and intense personal contacts was the formation of the Justice Research Institute, which serves the field in a very discreet way with publishing and consulting assistance involving colleagues who are trusted in both the academic and the practice side of the field and who have reputations for credibility and integrity. We have evolved and are now often involved in curriculum reviews for criminal justice departments and programs.

The results of interviewing allow me to bring a wealth of firsthand data to students. This is primary data based on observation and interview. Some of it, such as work with Richard Speck and John Wayne Gacy and Chicago gang members, is rather sensationalistic, but it sure gets some points across as examples in the classroom. But all of the interviews with less spectacular clients in the criminal justice system and with all of the actors in the system cannot be minimized. As an aggregate, the men and women I have interviewed over the years have provided a wealth of lecture information as well as research leads. Moreover, these interviews have led me to see that those convicted are not inferior, deserve respect, have needs and problems, and in general, often exhibit "stinking thinking." As a consequence, I am concerned about cultural values. I enjoy sharing all of this with my students and they, in turn, reward me with high levels of performance and their trust.

BOX 6.2   CONTINUED

The contacts and clients in this kind of work have led to international travel and comparative studies. I really enjoy students learning about other cultures and seeing policing, courts, and corrections in other nations firsthand. My original interests here were shaped at Southern Illinois University–Carbondale in the International Visitor Program sponsored by the U.S. Department of Justice that elected me as a research fellow. This work also involved intensive talk and discussion both with our international visitors and with my mentors, Elmer Johnson and Thomas Eynon. Some of my best personal learning experiences have been during the leisurely sharing of meals with both guests and hosts during these international exchanges.

ADVICE TO STUDENTS

Follow your interests. Higher interest leads to better papers, increased energy, higher success, and grades. Shape your projects in language, history, philosophy, and other needed core experiences as much as possible to follow your interests. I believe in having the basic scientific skills, including observation, database searching, interviewing, writing, and logic. Hone people skills—criminology is working with people for your data. A wealth of information is available from the police, criminals, judges, defense counsels, prosecutors, correctional personnel, and others. Intern, volunteer, and participate in student organizations. Observe and talk. When possible, I make sure my doctoral and graduate assistants do it. Get out there. Dig in. Have a theory of behavior with which you are comfortable. Keep it open to new scientific evidence. Beware of media and popular mass productions. Enjoy them, but don't depend on them for reality and your science. And remember, poor theory results in poor policy.

Actually, a structured interview utilizes an **interview schedule.** An interview schedule is a questionnaire consisting of a predetermined list of questions and fixed-response replies that interviewers can fill in themselves when they conduct interviews. Often, a copy of the interview schedule is given to respondents so that they may read it along with the interviewer. If respondents think of answers that are not among those provided by fixed responses, then the interviewer can write in their verbal replies or tape-record them.

One type of structured interview is the **focused interview** (Merton, Fiske, & Kendall, 1956). Focused interviews are interviews with respondents who have shared some common experience that has, in turn, been carefully scrutinized by investigators to generate hypotheses about the effects of the experience on participants. The interview context focuses on the actual effects of the experience as viewed by the participants. Thus, applications of focused interviews may be directed toward samples of shock probationers or those who participate in electronic monitoring or home confinement in community-based correctional programs. Focused interviews may be conducted with police officers who have received special types of training relating to resolutions of marital disputes. It is apparent that focused interviews may be used in close conjunction with experimental types of research designs, where it is important to assess the effects of experiments on subject behaviors and attitudes.

Bahn and Davis (1991) were interested in describing the social psychological effects of the status of probationers. They wanted to learn from probationers themselves whether the probation experience was helpful and if it stigmatized them in their communities. Bahn and Davis used self-administered questionnaires and focused interviews with samples of probationers to learn about their feelings and attitudes toward their probation program. They obtained a sample of 43 probationers and exposed them to three data-gathering instruments: (1) a questionnaire, consisting of 16 open-ended questions, administered in an interview format; (2) a scalogram consisting of 15 items, with five choices for each item, which had been devised especially for the study by these authors; and (3) the Self-Attitude Inventory (SAI), a self-concept scale. The open-ended questions that comprised their focused interview are shown in Table 6.1.

Bahn and Davis (1991) were able to learn much about probationers and their feelings through the use of these questions. They found, for instance, that probationers generally received considerable assistance from their families and friends, and even from some employers. Interestingly, these researchers found that the stigma of being on probation was not as stigmatizing as many people think. For example, these probationers reported that most of their friends did not avoid them. However, they were hesitant to disclose their probationary status to employers for fear of being fired. They told the investigators that their behaviors had changed to the extent that they no longer associated with other criminals and that they tended to avoid using drugs and alcohol.

TABLE 6.1   Open-Ended Questions Administered to 43 Probationers by Bahn and Davis

1. Have you told your family, relatives, and friends that you are on probation? Why or why not?
2. Have any of your family, relatives, or friends been in trouble with the law?
3. Have the actions or what was said to you by your family or friends changed in any way after they found out that you were on probation?
4. Have any of your family, relatives, or friends helped you since you were on probation? In what way? How about before probation?
5. Have you told your boss that you were on probation? Why or why not?
6. Do you think about the fact that you are on probation very often? Is it something that's on your mind?
7. Is there anything you especially like about your probation?
8. Is there anything you especially dislike about your probation?
9. What would you like to go on between me and you? What would you like to talk about?
10. What do you think the purpose of probation is?
11. Has your life changed since you have been placed on probation? How?
12. Are you afraid or anxious about probation? Why?
13. Have you felt depressed since you have been on probation? Why?
14. Do you think of yourself as a criminal since you have been on probation? Why or why not?
15. Do you think your arrest was justified? Why or why not?
16. Do you think the judge should have placed you on probation for the offense? Why or why not?

Source: Questions from Bahn and Davis (1991, p. 24).

As an indication of how a scenario might develop between probationers and their probation officers, we might envision the following hypothetical interview, using one of Bahn's and Davis's questions:

P = Probationer
PO = Probation Officer

PO: "Are you afraid or anxious about probation?"

P: "Yes."

PO: "Why?"

P: "Well, for one thing, you know . . . you always think they're looking over your shoulder. Like, they might be looking for a reason to bust you, or to run you in for something. I don't know . . . it just makes me feel uncomfortable."

PO: "But you haven't broken the law. You've told me that probation helps you go straight. Do you feel like law enforcement officers might pick on you more than someone else if a crime occurs and you happen to be near there?"

P: "Yeah, well, not exactly. It's just that . . . well, what if you happen to run into somebody accidentally . . . you know . . . on the street . . . you are walking along one day, and this guy comes up to you, and he says, 'Hey, Joe, long time no see.' And suppose it's a guy you knew had committed crimes. You begin thinking, are they watching me, are they testing me? You don't really know for sure, whether its a test, or whether its just an accident . . . you know, you don't really have a whole lot of privacy . . . you want to feel like you're free, being on the outside and all . . . but they still have you . . . you are still controlled by the system . . . they can still put you away if they want . . . for any reason . . ."

PO: "But you have to do something pretty serious to get your probation revoked."

P: "Well, yeah, I know . . . but I suppose . . . I guess, it's like they might think the wrong thing, seeing you with someone else whose maybe a criminal or former criminal, like maybe, you are still doing your old thing and all . . . I don't know . . . there are just those times when I feel, like, I feel the system is looking at me and thinking I'm going to screw up . . ."

PO: "Are you afraid about your own willpower or will to avoid things that might get you into trouble?"

P: "Well, yeah. You know, like I might want a drink, or maybe I want to get high, or do some coke. But, you know, they got these checks, where they might come around and test me . . . I never know when to expect them . . . what if you only screw up once, have one little drink, and the next minute they're there wanting to test your pee. You don't know when they are coming around, or if they're watching . . . you get to where you don't trust anybody anymore, because there's so much at stake."

PO: "And so, being free on probation maybe doesn't mean that you are as free as everyone else?"

P: "Exactly. Anybody else, you know, they can get in a car and drive to Mexico, Canada, out of state, wherever, and who cares? But me, I drive out of the county and my PO might make a federal case out of it. I'm even afraid of the mail I get . . ."

PO: "What do you mean, 'Afraid of your mail'?"

P: "Well, you know, you're always getting things in the mail even if you didn't order them . . . well, once I got this sporting goods catalog from some company back East . . . there were guns advertised in there. . . . I was looking at the catalog one day when my PO paid me a visit . . . saw that magazine, about had a fit . . . wanted to know if I was going to order a gun by mail. . . . I said, 'Hey, not me, I don't want no trouble . . . I just got this thing in the mail . . . I didn't even ask for it . . . you know, it's the little things that really screw you up . . . you don't have to do anything, just be there in the wrong place at the wrong time. . . . I guess what really bothers me the most, why I worry, is that I never know when I am going to be in the wrong place at the wrong time. I don't even sometimes want to go out at night because of that."

While this exchange between a probation officer and a probationer is hypothetical, it is apparent that much enriching detail may be furnished the interviewer when the respondent is able to answer freely. The interviewer may probe at various points to seek clarification of particular points. We can learn from the above interview. For instance, probationers may feel certain pressures about being on probation that would be considered commonplace occurrences for most other people. Also, there is a psychological strain that persists among many probationers, no doubt owing to the possibility that they might be in the wrong place at the wrong time. Thus, there is a persistent threat to their freedom that is inherent in their probationer status. Although probation revocation today is much more involved than it once was, it nevertheless exists as an option available to probation officers and judges if probationers violate one or more of their program conditions.

There is little disputing the fact that greater precision is achieved as the investigator's knowledge of the target population increases. The more closely investigators can approach the narrow objectives of the focused interview, the greater likelihood that they will acquire more precise data. There is also a better chance that they might make full use of the advantages inherent in interviews generally.

There are three clear advantages of structured interviews. First, data from each interview may be compared and equated with data from other interviews. Second, there are fewer problems of recording and coding data. Thus, greater precision in measurement is achieved. Third, the more highly structured the interview, the less likely it is that attention will be diverted to extraneous, irrelevant, and time-consuming conversation.

On the other hand, as interviews become increasingly structured, they tend to lose the spontaneity of natural conversation. In addition, there is the danger that investigators have structured the interview in such a way that the respondent's views are minimized and the investigator's own biases about the problem are highlighted. Finally, the possibility of exploration and probing further, although not absolutely eliminated, is less likely to occur in structured interviewing compared with unstructured interviewing.

In-Depth Interviews

Similar to questionnaires, interviews may be somewhat superficial or they may be in-depth. For example, Peggy Giordano, Stephen Cernkovich, and Donna Holland (2003) studied the life histories of a sample of female and male offenders who were interviewed at the time they were incarcerated and then again 13 years later. These researchers wanted to learn more about life-course changes among these persons, such as their changing friendship choices, the influence of their past and present friendships with others, and how key events such as marriage may facilitate the desistance process, making such persons less susceptible to engaging in further criminal activity. Originally in 1982, Cernkovich conducted interviews with 254 delinquent boys and girls in state institutions in Ohio. Thirteen years later, 180 of these persons were located and reinterviewed, this time providing researchers with life history narratives of their experiences over time. Interviews with these persons were tape-recorded and transcribed. In their follow-up interviews, subjects were asked about how much time they spent with their friends or peers, perceived peer pressure, any continuing criminal involvement, and other pertinent information. They were also asked whether they were married or if any of their friends were married, and whether or not marriage was significant in altering their social relationships with one another.

One subject, "Debbie," was asked whether marriage for her was a significant factor in changing her behavior. She said,

> "I wanted to settle down and stay out of trouble and they are still doing those things." [She considers her life better than theirs because] "I think they are still doing a lot of things that they still did back then. I don't want to do any of that. Drinking, drugs, I just know where it got me and I don't want to get back into all that stuff. I am more secure in my life than they are, I think. I don't think they really got nobody to be really secure with . . . I got a husband." [Feels she is less likely to get into trouble because] ". . . I don't put myself in a position where I am going to get into trouble. I just stay away from trouble and people that I think is going to get me into trouble. I don't need it." (Giordano et al., 2003, p. 304)

In another instance, one subject, "Dan," has continued to maintain associations with some of his former delinquent peers who are now adult criminals. But he has developed a relationship with "Wendy," his wife. He was asked by interviewers if he has been contacted by his former delinquent buddies to commit a crime. The following dialogue occurred between the interviewer, Dan, and his wife, Wendy:

> Dan: "Yeah, I had one ask me yesterday . . . wanted me to go steal a Harley with him. He said, 'It's easy, man . . . all we got to do, it's in the alley . . . push it right down the alley.
> Wendy: "Ah hah?"
> Dan: "Six hundred dollars . . ."
> Wendy: "I know who that was. Wait until I see him!"
> Dan: (Laughs)
> Interviewer: "And you were like, no man?"
> Dan: "No . . . I ain't going. I don't want to be looking out those bars downtown saying damn, I wish I was home. I was like—you go do it. I ain't, I ain't touching . . . I'm not part of it anymore." (Giordano et al., 2003, p. 305)

These researchers say that this example is useful because it shows that, while it is probably not ideal, it is realistic to expect that some of these respondents will continue to have contact with potentially negative social influences. It is apparent from the above interview that

Wendy, Dan's wife, had no knowledge of this incident until the time of the interview. This indicates that Dan and others in similar positions will likely encounter situations outside of their spouse's ability to provide control or guidance for their potential conduct (Giordano et al., 2003).

Interviews similar to those conducted in the Giordano and colleagues study are undertaken by many investigators. Interview information provides insightful statements about why persons choose to act in particular ways. They are intended to embellish sterile tabular material that might be generated through surveys or fixed-response questionnaire data. In the Giordano and colleagues research, considerable interview data were collected, but only selected portions were provided for readers in their subsequent article, which summarized their research. These researchers theorized initially about the life course, about youthful offenders, and how different social experiences might influence their adult lives. Later, through interviews, they were able to see and provide some support for their earlier theorizing in the words of those interviewed.

In-depth interviews seek to discover intimate knowledge of research sites and respondents by the use of intensive and personalized questioning. In-depth interviews are most closely associated with qualitative research, where the objective is to gain greater understanding while certain social events transpire.

Investigators have made extensive use of **in-depth interviews** as a means of obtaining greater insight into various social phenomena. In 1997, for instance, Mary Ann Farkas studied the normative code among corrections officers. Farkas obtained permission to study the correctional officers at two Midwestern state prisons. Farkas could have sent these officers self-administered questionnaires in a survey. However, she believed that face-to-face interviews would provide her with greater detail, the nature of which would enrich her investigation. She focused on the correctional officer code, an informal abstract policy of conduct among officers, where a certain type of social solidary evolved. The dangerous nature of correctional work, together with low pay and scorn from inmates, caused many correctional officers to close ranks and devise informal ways for dealing with officer–inmate problems.

One identifying characteristic of in-depth interviews is dialogue between the interviewer and interviewee. Farkas's work was replete with quotes from various officers about their on-the-job experiences. One of the female corrections officers said:

> "One of the women I work with calls the inmates 'her guys." She'll walk in and say, 'How are my guys tonight?' I think that you have to keep a certain distance. This is not kindergarten and these are not choir boys. She thinks I am too tough with them [inmates]. If they want anything, they ask her and she'll give it to them, too."

Another officer said,

> "Don't *ever* tell inmates any details of your personal life. Don't mention names of your family members. Don't get too close with inmates. Remember that you are not their buddy. You can be nice, but remember that you have a job to do. You've got to keep your distance!" (1997, p. 28)

Farkas was able to identify several important informal social norms among corrections officers, including:

1. Always go to the aid of an officer in real or perceived physical danger.
2. Don't get too friendly with inmates.
3. Don't abuse your authority with inmates. Keep your cool.
4. Back up your fellow officers in decisions and actions; don't stab a coworker in the back.
5. Cover your ass and do not admit to mistakes.
6. Carry your own weight.
7. Defer to the experience and wisdom of veteran corrections officers. (pp. 27–31)

It is unlikely that Farkas would have been able to identify these and other officer codes of conduct from a training manual or survey questionnaire. The fact that she was able to record and reproduce dialogue between herself and those interviewed added a very interesting and insightful dimension to her study.

BOX 6.3   PERSONALITY HIGHLIGHT

LEWIS YABLONSKY
California State University–Northridge, Professor Emeritus
Legal Consultant, Psychotherapist, Expert Witness

Statistics: B.S. (sociology), Rutgers University; M.A. (sociology and criminology), New York University; honorary Doctor of Laws degree, Grand Valley State University.

BACKGROUND AND INTERESTS

I have been a research and group therapist for almost 50 years in the combat zones of crime and delinquency. In this context, my research and work has taken place in a variety of settings, including prisons, psychiatric hospitals, community crime prevention, and therapeutic communities. As the result of these explorations, some of my best friends are former addicts/criminals, and have revealed to me many secrets of the underworld of crime and delinquency that is valuable for students of this subject to understand.

My personal introduction to the phenomenon of senseless delinquent behavior happened to me as a victim at the age of 8. My family lived in the area of a black ghetto in Newark, New Jersey, and I grew up in the swirl of violence and rage that dominated our "hood." I attended Miller Street School, a predominantly black school, whose only claim to fame was that Sarah Vaughn, who later became a famous jazz singer, was an alumnus. At Miller I was in the white minority, and I was referred to as an "ofay" or "fayboy" (meaning "white boy") by the black gangs that dominated the school. During those years from age 8 to 12, I was victimized many times by the school's gangs for what I considered at that time as both rational and irrational mo-

BOX 6.3 CONTINUED

tives. The rational approach was a form of protection called "tech-taking" that involved the extortion of 15 to 20 cents a week—big money for a kid in those days. The "protection" was that you wouldn't be assaulted if you paid up.

In my high school years in the early 1940s, the school was self-segregated, with black students hanging out on one side of the school and whites on the other. I often integrated the black area of the school, largely because I was interested and entertained by male black students who played the "dozens." This was a verbal game, where a number of kids would encircle two main actors who would verbally spar with each other spontaneously and creatively rhyming nasty poems—that usually attacked the opponent's mother. (A one-liner I recall was "F..... your Ma in an alleyway, when I got through she thought she was Cab Calloway.") The adversary would counter with what was called a "backhap." If his retort was strong, the group would chant, "Man what a strong backhap!" Retrospectively, I believe the "dozens" was really the earliest form of what is now hailed as a new musical form known as "gangsta rap" or "hip hop."

Shortly after I graduated from high school, I was in the U.S. Navy for 3 years during World War II. Using the GI Bill, I graduated from Rutgers University and then became a graduate student in sociology and criminology at New York University. During my NYU graduate student days, I worked as a group supervisor for 2 years in a juvenile detention center attached to the juvenile court facility in Newark. Many of the youths, incarcerated in this juvenile jail, were gangsters from my old neighborhood and this connection was helpful to me in establishing rapport with them. There is no better training for an aspiring criminologist than to work directly with offenders in custody.

RESEARCH INVESTIGATIONS

My position in the juvenile jail, as a group supervisor, enabled me to learn more about the phenomenon of gangs and delinquency. I spent many hours informally talking with and researching the gang kids in custody. During those years, I learned a great deal about their motivation for participating in gangs, gang violence, and the structure of gangs. My first major, direct, and in-depth research into the function of gangs and delinquency was implemented in the period from 1953 to 1958 on the Upper West Side of Manhattan in a large area infested with crime and delinquency. This 5-year period of firsthand research with the problem was part of a job I acquired in 1953 as the Director of a Crime Prevention Program by a community organization known as Morningside Heights, Inc. During this period, I began my teaching career at Columbia and the City University of New York where I taught police officers sociology and criminology.

In my gang research, I had a strategic and understandable position vis-à-vis the gang youths in the area as the Director of the Morningside Heights Project. They had a good reason for understanding our work. To them we were not simply poking around in their lives for some vague research reason. Our agency was attempting to do something concrete to prevent and control the crime and delinquency of the area through various social, recreational, and family projects that we had developed.

BOX 6.3   CONTINUED

In my early research in New York into the phenomenon of gangs and delinquency in the context of the Project, I utilized a variety of approaches. These included (1) in-depth interviews with gangsters; (2) tape recordings and field notes; (3) written questionnaires; (4) the employment of two former gang leaders as paid interviewers; (5) various therapy groups; (6) unanticipated data from an unusual diary kept by a gang leader; and (7) a number of other research methods. My 5 years of gang research in New York City became the basis for my NYU doctoral dissertation. And my thesis was the foundation for writing my first book on gangs, *The Violent Gang* (1962).

My relationship to the delinquent youths in the neighborhood was similar to that of an anthropologist engaged in field work. During the 5-year period I directed the project, I lived and worked in the area. I bonded with many gangsters. It became natural for them to hang out in my office and under certain circumstances, visit my home. Phone calls and contacts at all hours from gang boys with special problems, youths in jail, citizen volunteers with emergency gang war problems, or the police, became a part of my daily routine.

My daily communications with the people and conditions I was trying to change were significant elements of my overall research with gangs. My efforts to produce change in criminals and delinquents was an intrinsic element in learning about the overt and underlying dynamics of their behavior. The social psychologist, Kurt Lewin, stated this concept simply—"If you want to truly understand something, try to change it."

In recent years, in addition to my professorial role, I have been a consultant and group therapist in the Synanon and Amity Therapeutic Community projects in the R.J. Donavan California Prison, a prison in Beaumont, Texas, and other correctional institutions. Over the past 7 years, I have been intensely involved in the criminal justice system as an expert witness in the courts. I have participated as an expert witness in over 135 cases. Most of them, around 120, are gang and homicide cases. This work has been an extraordinary learning experience into the dynamics of our criminal justice system.

INTERESTING EXPERIENCES

In my travels throughout the world of crime and delinquency, in addition to observing and knowing many difficult and violent individuals, I have also had the positive experience of observing the fact that given a chance in an effective treatment program, many youths seemingly trapped in their self-destructive lifestyle can change their behavior in many positive ways and facilitate positive change in their community. My efforts toward focusing on a solution are generated not only by my mind, but by my heartfelt and sympathetic emotions for the human waste and destructiveness that crime and delinquency produce in our society.

Perhaps I can explain my intensely felt emotions on this subject, more specifically, by describing the following recurring scenario that I observe whenever I enter a large California prison to direct group psychotherapy and psychodrama sessions with the men in custody. After being searched and checked out at the front gate of the prison that incarcerates around 5,000 men, I have to walk almost a mile through depressing "big-yards" to the hopeful therapeutic community cellblock where 200 prisoners in the program reside. As I pass through these several big-yards, I can't

BOX 6.3   CONTINUED

help observing hundreds of prisoners along the way. They are usually engaged in typical negative prison activities, including secretive small-group discussions on crimes they have committed or will commit, or simply strutting around the big-yard displaying their absurd macho posturing.

Most of these young men, all former delinquents, are from various minority groups, especially intelligent black and Chicano individuals between the ages of 18–30 who are wasting away in the cold storage of prison life. My heartfelt and emotional reaction is that the current prison system destroys the valuable human potential that exists in these unfortunate men.

All of them, even the worst-behaving sociopath, has a spark of motivation and compassion in him, and if given a chance through a humanistic treatment program, this positive spark can be ignited into a flame that would lead him into a law-abiding and satisfying lifestyle. I wholeheartedly agree with the often ridiculed comment attributed to the founder of Boy's Town, Father Flanagan, that "there is no such thing as a bad boy." It is my firm belief, that without exception, all individuals who are adjudicated delinquents and criminals, including the toughest sociopaths I have met, can with the proper humanistic treatment approach be salvaged from a life of self-destructive and other adverse behavior into responsible law-abiding adults.

ADVICE TO STUDENTS

My basic opinion is that any student who aspires to become a criminologist has to immerse him- or herself into the cauldron of our "correctional" and prison systems, especially if they plan to teach the subject.

SELECTED ACHIEVEMENTS, HONORS, AND AWARDS

Author of 17 books, including *The Violent Gang* (Macmillan); *Crime and Delinquency* (Rand-McNally); *Criminology* (HarperCollins); *The Hippie Trip* (Pegasus and Penguin); *The Therapeutic Community: A Successful Approach for Treating Substance Abusers* (Gardner Press); *Juvenile Delinquency* (Wadsworth); and *Criminology in the 21st Century* (Allyn & Bacon). Dr. Yablonsky has presented over 150 papers at regional and national professional conferences; was Director of the Crime Prevention Program for Morningside Heights, Inc., New York; has been an expert witness in over 100 criminal cases, many involving violent juvenile gangs; a member of numerous professional associations, including the American Sociological Association, Academy of Criminal Justice Sciences, and American Society of Criminology; past president of the American Society of Group Psychotherapy; a former editor of the *Journal of Group Psychotherapy;* received the Outstanding Professors Award from the California State University Board of Trustees; received the Frederic Thrasher Award from the National Gang Crime Research Center; and received the American Sociological Association's William Foote Whyte Distinguished Career Award for Sociological Practice. Dr. Yablonsky has received more numerous honors and accolades than space permits to list here.

Similarly, Paula and William Faulkner (1997) studied a sample of prison inmates to describe the inmate status system and how it might be affected by organizational change. The Faulkners engaged various inmates in in-depth interviews and learned much about how status among inmates is assigned. One inmate disclosed,

> "I remember when I was in Kansas and this guy never showered and no one ever said anything about it to him. He got a new cell mate and he came back to his cell and the new guy had cleaned his cell and he killed the guy for it. All the inmates respected him . . . "

Another inmate revealed some insight about toughness:

> "This is the way it is done. If you are a man, you must either kill or turn the tables on anyone who propositions you with threats of force. It is the *custom* among young prisoners. In doing so, it becomes known to all that you are a man regardless of your youth" (Faulkner & Faulkner, 1997, pp. 60–61).

Again, there are certain things about social situations, such as the lives of prison inmates, that you cannot know about through conventional survey research methods and self-administered questionnaires. In-depth interviews with selected inmates can reveal much about themselves and what they respect. Researchers using in-depth interviews can learn much from their respondents.

Interviewing was also used in a study by Robin Engel and Robert Worden (2003), who studied police officers' attitudes, behavior, and supervisory influences. A great deal of research has been conducted relating to police attitudes and behaviors, especially the tension between police officer discretion on the streets and the control of that discretion by police administrations in departments. Police supervisors play an important role in police discretionary policies as well. Furthermore, police work is stressful, and more than a few situational pressures arise, some of which originate within the bureaucracy of police departments. These investigators wanted to learn more about police discretion and officer attitudes toward others, such as their supervisors, as they engaged in day-to-day problem solving. Engel and Worden decided to study two police departments, the Indianapolis, Indiana Police Department (IPD) and the St. Petersburg, Florida Police Department (SPPD), respectively. One reason for their choice of these departments was that these organizations were in the process of implementing community policing, which would greatly modify police patrol styles and police–citizen encounters where discretionary decision making would be significant.

Engel and Worden and their assistants observed large numbers of police officers during their different shifts. Trained observers accompanied patrol officers during their shifts and took notes about what they observed. Besides observation, 398 (93 percent) IPD officers and 240 (98 percent) SPPD officers were interviewed by these researchers. According to Engel and Worden, these interviews captured information on officers' personal characteristics, training and education, work experience, perceptions of their beats, attitudes toward the police role, and perceptions of their department's implementation of community policing and problem solving. Participation was voluntary, and each respondent was promised confidentiality (Engel & Worden, 2003, pp. 141–142). Using triangulation, the authors were able to cross-validate their observations of police behaviors during different patrol shifts, and the interview information was quite useful in clarifying different officer actions taken and the discretion they exercised under different circumstances.

Telephone Interviews

An interview may be conducted by telephone, known as a **telephone interview.** To some extent, at least, a degree of anonymity between interviewers and interviewees is created. But because of this physical separation, interviewers may not see puzzled expressions on interviewee's faces, or they may not know the exact identity of those interviewed. Nevertheless, the telephone interview may be used as a relatively inexpensive way of obtaining information directly from respondents.

In one profitable use of telephone interviewing, this writer was hired by an attorney to conduct telephone interviews with various persons in an East Tennessee community. A local citizen had been arrested and charged with murder and conspiracy to commit murder. He had been linked with several others and was allegedly involved directly in the murder of a North Carolina man. His trial was scheduled soon in that community, but his attorney believed that the press had prejudiced prospective jurors. Thus, the attorney sought a change of venue for his client, so that the trial might be held in another community where publicity was not as significant.

This writer called approximately 300 persons in the community and asked them various questions about their knowledge of the case. Among the questions asked were whether those contacted were voting citizens, whether they could be called for jury duty, whether they had formed an opinion about the guilt or innocence of the defendant and if so, what was that opinion? Did they know any family members of the person charged with the murder? The results showed that most citizens had followed the case closely in their local newspapers. Furthermore, most citizens contacted had formed opinions. Most believed the defendant guilty of the murder and that he should be sentenced to death. On the basis of these telephone interview results, the attorney was able to convince the presiding judge to move the case to another county where it was believed a fair trial could be conducted.

Telephone interviewing has been used extensively in criminal justice and criminology. For instance, Tom Tyler and Cheryl Wakslak (2004) studied racial profiling by police, how frequently it occurred, and what were the consequences for citizens who thought they were being singled out because of their race. Samples of residents who lived in minority areas in Oakland and Los Angeles, California, were telephoned by these researchers and their assistants. All persons were screened according to whether they had had personal contact with the police or courts in the recent past. An initial sample of 1,656 persons was identified who had had recent personal contact with the police or courts. Subsequently, 521 persons were identified who were stopped by police. Of these, 163 were white, 186 were black, and 172 were Hispanic.

From these telephone interviews, Tyler and Wakslak were able to learn a great deal about citizen attitudes toward the police, including their willingness to accept police decisions in these police stops, the degree of satisfaction with the police officer, the amount of trust in their motives and authority, police respectfulness, and fairness of the outcome received from the police. Quite understandably, those contacted by Tyler and Wakslak reacted negatively to attributions of profiling. Some of their evidence suggested that minorities contacted through these telephone interviews believed that they had been singled out for police stops and had been treated unfairly by officers. One policy implication of their findings was that the idea of racial profiling by police is repugnant, and that the mere fact that people believe that it occurs seriously undermines police authority and respect. Interestingly, even among minority respondents, when police officers treated them respectfully, those citizens believed that they had been treated fairly and had not been racially profiled. Thus it is clear that police officers themselves can influence greatly how they are perceived by those they stop for whatever reason or according to whatever criteria, especially if they are respectful and considerate.

Telephone interviews have their limitations, however. Although large numbers of persons may be contacted by interviewers and large amounts of data can be compiled, it is impossible for interviewers to interpret facial reactions to questions asked, or to the body language of respondents. There is also little or no control over potential deception by respondents who give information over the telephone. In the study of racial profiling reported by Tyler and Wakslak above, these and other limitations of their research were noted. However, these researchers also said that much of what they learned through these telephone interviews was consistent with information and findings yielded by other studies. Thus, if other studies of racial profiling support what subsequent researchers discover in their own research, this other information is independent confirmation about whatever is later discovered and reported.

Random-Digit Dialing and Computer-Assisted Telephone Interviews.   Utilizing new technology, researchers who conduct telephone interviews can randomize the numbers dialed. Known as the **Computer-Assisted Telephone Interviewing (CATI)** system, any designated sample size of numbers to be dialed can be produced. More conventional methods of dialing persons might include using current city directories or telephone directories to obtain numbers. However, city directories and telephone directories are quickly dated as persons move and change their numbers. Also, increasing numbers of citizens have unlisted numbers. **Random digit dialing** overcomes these problems, since numbers, listed or unlisted, new or old, are dialed randomly. Once the connection is established, interviewers can seek to obtain essential information from randomly dialed respondents.

An example of using random-digit dialing for telephone interviewing is a study by Ted Chiricos, Kelly Welch, and Marc Gertz (2004). Their research investigated racial typification of crime and support for harsh punitive measures. These investigators wanted to assess public opinions about crime generally and how the public related race to different types of crime and the accompanying punishments. The American criminal justice system has sometimes been criticized as racist, inasmuch as disproportionately larger numbers of minorities, especially blacks, are incarcerated compared with whites. When larger numbers of persons are incarcerated, for instance, this may be interpreted by the public as more incarcerations of black offenders. This is racial typification of crime.

How can these researchers learn more about racial typification of crime, especially on a national scale? In their study, Chiricos and colleagues (2004) conducted a telephone survey of a national random sample of adults ($N = 885$), 18 years of age or older, in households throughout the United States using random digit dialing. The calls were made between January and April 2002. A subsequent description of some of the sociodemographic characteristics of the sample was provided, showing that about 56.5 percent were female, 80 percent were white, 11.4 percent were black, and 7.5 percent were Hispanic. College graduates accounted for 44 percent of all respondents, and the median age was 46.

Standard questions were asked of all respondents. Each respondent was asked to rate from "0" to "10" (where "0" is not at all supportive and "10" is being very supportive) the following list of things that have been suggested as ways of dealing with crime. The list included (1) making sentences more severe for all crimes; (2) executing more murderers; (3) making prisoners work on chain gangs; (4) taking away television and recreational privileges from prisoners; (5) using more mandatory minimum-sentencing statutes for repeat offenders; (6) locking up more juvenile offenders; (7) using the death penalty for juveniles who murder; and (8) sending repeat juvenile offenders to adult courts. Respondents were also asked the following questions:

> "What percent of people who commit violent crimes in this country would you say are black?"
> "When you think about people who break into homes and businesses when nobody is there, approximately what percent would you say are black?"
> "When you think about people who rob other people at gunpoint, approximately what percent would you say are black?"

Subsequently, Chiricos and colleagues (2004) found that respondents tended to exaggerate the amount of black involvement in different types of crimes. For instance, the respondents overestimated black involvement in violent crime, where respondent perceptions were that about 40 percent of violent crime is committed by blacks, although this percentage is less than 30 percent. But for robbery, respondents underestimated black involvement. Ultimately these investigators were able to glean much about racial typification of crime from these telephone responses. Furthermore, the apparent racism reflected by these respondents related closely with more severe punishments for different types of crime. These researchers were able to gain a great deal of insight into modern racism and how different sentencing and punishment policies are affected by such attitudes. And again, these researchers were able to compare their research results with previous studies where similar phenomena had been disclosed.

Techniques Used in Telephone Interviews.   In many respects, the techniques used in telephone interviews are the same as those used in conventional interview situations. The questions to be asked in telephone interviews are arranged in much the same fashion as a researcher would construct a questionnaire. An interesting, attention-grabbing question or two would be used to attract the respondent's interest. If respondents are going to hang up on an interviewer, it will probably occur during the first minute or two of the interview. The longer the amount of time an interviewer can keep the respondent on the line, the greater the likelihood that the entire interview can be conducted.

Sometimes interviewers will use a **branching technique** to narrow the range of response to a sensitive question. If the victim of a sex crime is being interviewed by telephone, it might be appropriate first to ask, "Have you ever been the victim of an assault?" If the victim says "yes," then the interviewer can ask, "Were the injuries sustained primarily psychological or physical?" If the victim says "physical," then the interviewer can ask, "Was the assault sexual or nonsexual?" The intent of branching is to gradually draw out the respondent to disclose more personal aspects of the victimization or incident. Branching is preferred to a direct question such as, "Have you ever been raped or sodomized?"

Criticisms of Telephone Interviews.   Telephone interviews are much cheaper than face-to-face interviews. Furthermore, researchers have the opportunity to draw out respondents and probe with follow-up questions. They can also explain complex or confusing terminology to those interviewed. However, it is difficult to verify whether the researcher is interviewing the true target of the interview. If the "head of household" is called, a son, other relative, or a family friend may answer the telephone and respond as though he or she were the head of the household. Also, there is no way to judge the validity of one's responses according to facial expressions or other physical criteria.

Telephone interviews contain some anonymity to the extent that the researcher is unsure of who the respondent is. It is possible for some deception to occur under these circumstances. More than a few respondents may resent the intrusion of interviewers into their homes via the telephone. For those with unlisted numbers, privacy is highly valued. Thus, interviewers who use random-digit dialing and connect with someone with an unlisted number are likely to be chastised with strong language. There are no precise figures about the average response rate to telephone interviews, although success rates reported by investigators who use telephone interviews for data collection suggest response rates of 75 percent or higher. Compared with the average response rates to mailed questionnaires, telephone interviewing yields a substantially higher rate of response.

Functions of Interviewing

The major functions of interviews are description and exploration.

Description

Information obtained from interviews is particularly useful for describing various dimensions of social reality. With certain exceptions, such as certain forms of observation, no other type of research data-gathering tool performs this descriptive function as well. Most people spend much of their time with others in some sort of verbal exchange or dialogue. Being able to capture the question-and-answer process as an unfolding dimension of this dialogue permits us to catch a glimpse of social life as it is lived. Compared with the relatively stale and abstract nature of statistical results, interviewing can yield a "gut-level" understanding of how people think and behave that is more reflective of social reality than summarizing certain survey questionnaire results.

Exploration

Another purpose of interviewing is to provide insights into unexplored dimensions of a topic. Surveys of work done usually only scratch the surface and yield only superficial details about the phenomena we wish to explain. However, interviews invite more in-depth probing and detailed descriptions of people's feelings and attitudes. For instance, evidence in the criminal justice literature suggests that private counsel as opposed to public defenders tend to have greater plea bargaining successes with prosecutors. Thus, if defendants charged with various crimes attempt to plea bargain or negotiate favorable sentences in exchange for pleas of guilty, they will probably receive more lenient treatment if they are represented by private counsels than by public defenders. Some of the logical reasons for this are that in many jurisdictions, public defenders are often new attorneys with little trial experience. Furthermore, private counsel probably have developed reputations and associations with various prosecutors so that their bargaining powers are favorably enhanced. Do prosecutors view public defenders different from private counsels, and if so, how will these different views influence prosecutorial decision making and the plea bargains eventually worked out between counsel?

Among the various studies examining prosecutorial decision making relative to plea bargaining, Champion (1988) examined prosecutorial discretion and the relative influence of private counsels and public defenders on their plea bargain decisions. In the jurisdictions examined, it was found that private counsels generally were able to negotiate more favorable plea bargains for their clients compared with public defenders. Furthermore, of those cases that eventually went to trial, private counsels had a greater success rate through client acquittals. Prosecutors in these jurisdictions were interviewed in order to see whether they view public defenders and private counsel differently. One interview proved illuminating in that it explained some of the informality associated with plea bargaining that is often hidden from public view. Behind-the-scenes plea bargaining is inherently secretive, since no one knows the final contents of a plea bargain until it is accepted by the presiding judge. Regarding his interactions with private counsel compared with public defenders, one prosecutor said:

> "One problem with public defenders is that they get stuck with a lot of cases they don't want. They don't get paid much for these cases. It's in their best interests to get their clients to cop pleas [plead guilty] and get it over with. Usually, they come to me and ask me what I recommend. If I say, 'I think a year in jail and 2 years' probation sounds good,' they often agree with that without making a counteroffer. But if defendants can get themselves some high-powered counsel, well . . . let's put it this way. I know most of the big criminal attorneys in this town on a first-name basis and associate with several of them regularly. They know what and how I think and I know how and what they think. They make me an offer, and you know, more often than not, they know I'll probably go for it. They're not pushovers. I don't bluff as much with them as I do with PDs [public defenders]."

In this interview, the intent of the interviewer was to find out whether prosecutors view public defenders differently compared with privately appointed counsel. It was apparent from these few statements what this particular prosecutor thought about public defenders. However, he said something else of interest that aroused the interviewer's curiosity. He said, "I don't bluff as much with them [privately appointed counsel] as I do with PDs." The fact that he brought up "bluffing" led the interviewer to try and find out more about prosecutorial bluffing. The interviewer said:

Interviewer: "What do you mean by 'bluffing'?"
Prosecutor: "Oh, you know. Whenever we have a weak case, perhaps a witness is unreliable, evidence is scarce, but, you know, we think we have the guy who

did the crime, because of other things . . . we might push them hard, the PDs . . . to get them thinking we have more against their clients than we actually do. You'd be surprised how much of the time it works. Not all of our cases are airtight. So we do a little bluffing."

Interviewer: "You said that you don't do that as much, bluffing, with private counsels. Why not?"

Prosecutor: "Well, most of them know me and how I operate. Some of them have even been PDs. I've been at this job for 9 years. Plus, they do their own research on a case, do their homework. They have a pretty good idea whether or not I've got a solid case. If they even smell a bluff, you can bet they'll call me on it. I've had 'em do it to me. But then, sometimes it backfires."

Interviewer: "What do you mean?"

Prosecutor: "Sometimes they think I'm bluffing and I'm not. They have pushed it in some cases, in really important cases, and they've gone to trial. I've got a perfect track record with them on that . . . when I really know down deep that I've got a solid case, and they're stupid enough to push it to trial, probably because they think I've got a weak case . . . I beat 'em."

Interviewer: "Why is it easier to bluff PDs?"

Prosecutor: "For one thing, none of them want to go to trial. They don't want to drag things out. Most of their clients are sleaze-bags anyway, and they're probably guilty, know they're guilty. We just let them think we're going to play hard ball with 'em, and most of the time, it works. We make an offer, they accept it. Bam! That's it!"

Interviewer: "Do you have many PDs call your bluff?"

Prosecutor: "Sometimes. We sit on the case for a few weeks, let them steam a little . . . then we drop it. So what? We didn't lose anything by trying. It works both ways, you know."

Interviewer: "What do you mean, 'It works both ways.'?"

Prosecutor: "Defense attorneys do it to us, bluff."

Interviewer: "Do you know when they're doing it?"

Prosecutor: "Some of the time. There are some attorneys in town that do a good job at it. If I've got a weak case, I'm not going to take the chance, I mean, I'm not going to lose something for nothing. We usually work something out."

Interviewer: "Plea bargain?"

Prosecutor: "Yeah. Some attorneys I know let me know up front what they have and what they think I have. They make me an offer. You know, it kind of shakes you up, they come to you and try to dictate their terms."

At this point, the interviewer learns something else about the prosecutor/defense attorney relation. This is "who" initiates the plea bargain offer and terms. A follow-up to this might be:

Interviewer: "Is there any pattern to this? I mean, do you get many defense attorneys coming to you with offers?"

Prosecutor: "Not too often. I'd say about 20–30 percent of the time."

Interviewer: "Is there any, do you think that those situations, where offers are made by these attorneys . . . are these situations the kind where they might have strong cases . . . as opposed to you going to them with an offer?"

Prosecutor: "Definitely. If they come to me with an offer . . . now I'm not going to say this as a policy thing . . . but if they come to me with an offer, I'll seriously consider it. I want to know what . . . I mean, I don't know what they have in their favor, but they must have something, you know, for them to come to me with the offer. If it is a "no time" deal . . . they don't want their client to do time . . . maybe probation, something like that . . . I'll probably think they've got a strong defense. It makes me think twice about pushing them."

Interviewer: "Now, let me see if I understand this. Would you say that, well, if you initiate a plea bargain, you've got a weak case, but if they initiate a plea bargain, they've got a weak case?"

Prosecutor: "No. It depends on when they bring me an offer. If they hit me with a plea bargain offer early on, like within a week or so after their client's been booked . . . they might have a weak case. But then again, we don't get approached that often. Most of the time, we approach them. I'll say this, and that is, if we approach them early with a plea bargain, we probably have a weak case. Not always, you know. But the sooner we send out an offer, well, we're hoping for a quick decision."

Interviewer: "So you think it makes a difference, who makes the offer to begin with, the attorney or the prosecutor?"

Prosecutor: "Definitely. You have to know these guys to figure out whether . . . you have to figure they've either got a weak case, and they might be bluffing, but they also might have a strong case. . . . I'll bet they have a strong case if they come out with an offer of probation for a cop [guilty plea] to a lesser charge."

Interviewer: "So, it's more likely that if you make a plea bargain proposal to some attorney, especially early in the case, you might not have a particularly strong case?"

Prosecutor: "Something like that. That doesn't mean that we have a weak case. It might mean that we don't have the kind of evidence we want to be sure about nailing 'em. We've got evidence, but a lot of it might be circumstantial. First, we believe their guy's guilty. We're not going to purposely set up some shmuck and bluff him into a cop. But we're not going to lay down either, especially when we've got incriminating stuff against the guy . . . also, you've got to understand . . . the longer you wait, well, the evidence might get cold. Witnesses might forget, move away, die. Attorneys are smart, too . . . they might try to delay things. . . . you know, delays almost never hurt their cases. We had one guy, a vehicular homicide case . . . a waiter at a local restaurant . . . he was crocked, driving home from work one night. Ran over two drunks fighting in the middle of the road near his apartment. Killed 'em both. They dragged that [case] out for a year and a half . . . never did come to trial . . . the girlfriend of the two guys he killed [who was watching the guys fighting when they were killed] moved out of state. We lost track of her, couldn't get her here if we wanted. Anyway, it turns out these two guys were always in and out of jail . . . long records. Trash. Whose going to get uptight about running over trash like that? We settled the damn thing by putting the guy on probation for 3 years . . . he plead guilty to reckless driving. Can you beat that? Anyway, there would have been a problem or two with vehicular homicide . . . for one thing, you know, he didn't leave work that night thinking, 'I'm going to go out and run over two drunks fighting in some road.' We had a real problem with intent. Also, there was contributory negligence. The street wasn't lit up, either . . . some problem with the street lights. The trial, if there had been one, would've been a mess. Turned out the kid's dad was a physician, plenty of money. Also got himself the best criminal attorney in town. We knew it'd be tough initially, but when he got that attorney . . . well, I wasn't going to push it."

This interview was one of the more interesting conducted. It is apparent that the prosecutor's answers often open up new areas previously unexplored by the interviewer. The prosecutor's comment about "hiring the best criminal attorney in town" could have led to questions about defense attorney quality and whether those who can afford the best attorneys receive more lenient treatment than indigent clients. Suffice it to say that the interview functions as an exploratory tool every bit as much as it functions as a descriptive instrument.

Interview Construction

Constructing interview items is comparable to constructing questionnaires. Investigators who plan to use interview schedules, more highly structured interviewing formats, and standardized items are included. Thus, interviewers must ask fixed numbers of questions, usually with fixed responses. If items are open-ended, then interviewers must either record a respondent's replies by hand or tape-record them in some fashion. More structured interviewing instruments may be coded more easily. Also, data from several different interviews may be compared directly.

Focused interviews, those that solicit information from subjects exposed to common stimuli or events, are structured to disclose specific details about one's experiences. The more investigators know about the target audience, the greater the precision that interviews may achieve. An excellent illustration of a structured, focused interview, with open-ended options and space for interviewer notes, is the survey instrument for the *National Crime Victimization Survey (NCVS)*.

Figure 6.1 shows a portion of the survey instrument used by the U.S. Department of Justice in its National Crime Survey. This instrument contains several parts, including a basic screen questionnaire that collects information about respondent characteristics. On the basis of respondent replies, a Crime Incident Report is completed, which is a lengthy, 28-page questionnaire. Observe that space is provided for interviewer notes and for open-ended replies by respondents. Subsequently, these data are easily coded and transmitted to computer programs for various types of analyses. These analyses yield numerous tabular data, cross-tabulating social and individual characteristics (age, race, victim–offender relationship) with different types of crime (robbery, assault, burglary, rape).

OMB No. 1121-0111: Approval Expires 10/31/2003

NOTICE – We are conducting this survey under the authority of Title 13, United States Code, Section 8. Section 9 of this law requires us to keep all information about you and your household strictly **confidential**. We may use this information only for statistical purposes. Also, Title 42, Section 3732, United States Code, authorizes the Bureau of Justice Statistics, Department of Justice, to collect information using this survey. Title 42, Sections 3789g and 3735, United States Code, also requires us to keep all information about you and your household strictly confidential.

FORM **NCVS-1**
(5-10-2001)

U.S. DEPARTMENT OF COMMERCE
Economics and Statistics Administration
U.S. CENSUS BUREAU

ACTING AS COLLECTING AGENT FOR THE
BUREAU OF JUSTICE STATISTICS
U.S. DEPARTMENT OF JUSTICE

NATIONAL CRIME VICTIMIZATION SURVEY

NCVS-1 BASIC SCREEN QUESTIONNAIRE

N C V S 1

BEFORE INTERVIEW – TRANSCRIBE FROM CONTROL CARD

Sample (cc item 1)	Control number (cc item 2) PSU	Segment	CK.	Serial	HH No. (cc item 3)
J ___					

ITEMS FILLED AT START OF INTERVIEW

1. Field representative identification
201 Code | Name

2. Unit status
202
1 ☐ Unit in sample the previous enumeration period – *Fill 3*
2 ☐ Unit in sample first time this period – ***SKIP** to 4*

3. Household status – *Mark first box that applies.*
203
1 ☐ Same household interviewed the previous enumeration
2 ☐ Replacement household since the previous enumeration
3 ☐ Noninterview the previous enumeration
4 ☐ Other – *Specify*

4. Line number of household respondent
204 ________ *Go to page 2*

AFTER INTERVIEW – TRANSCRIBE FROM CONTROL CARD

5. Special place/GQ type code *(cc item 6d)*
205 ________

6. Tenure *(cc item 8a)*
206 1 ☐ Owned or being bought 2 ☐ Rented for cash 3 ☐ No cash rent

7. Land use *(cc item 9)*
207 1 ☐ Urban 2 ☐ Rural

8. Farm sales *(cc item 10)*
208 x ☐ Item blank 1 ☐ $1,000 or more 2 ☐ Less than $1,000

9. Type of living quarters *(cc items 11c and 11d)*

Housing unit
209
1 ☐ House, apartment, flat
2 ☐ HU in nontransient hotel, motel, etc.
3 ☐ HU permanent in transient hotel, motel, etc.
4 ☐ HU in rooming house
5 ☐ Mobile home or trailer with no permanent room added
6 ☐ Mobile home or trailer with one or more permanent rooms added
7 ☐ HU not specified above – *Describe*

OTHER unit
8 ☐ Quarters not HU in rooming or boarding house
9 ☐ Unit not permanent in transient hotel, motel, etc.
10 ☐ Unoccupied site for mobile home, trailer, or tent
11 ☐ Student quarters in college dormitory
12 ☐ OTHER unit not specified above – *Describe*

Use of telephone *(cc item 26a and b)*
10a. Location of phone – *Mark first box that applies.*
210
1 ☐ Phone in unit . . . .
2 ☐ Phone in common area (hallway, etc.) . . .
3 ☐ Phone in another unit (neighbor, friend, etc.)
4 ☐ Work/office phone . . . .
} *Fill 10b*
5 ☐ No phone – ***SKIP** to 11a*

10b. Is phone interview acceptable? *(cc item 26d)*
211 1 ☐ Yes 2 ☐ No 3 ☐ Refused to give number

11a. Number of housing units in structure *(cc item 27a)*
212
1 ☐ 1 – ***SKIP** to 12a* 4 ☐ 4 7 ☐ Mobile home or trailer – ***SKIP** to 12a*
2 ☐ 2 5 ☐ 5–9
3 ☐ 3 6 ☐ 10+ 8 ☐ Only OTHER units

11b. Direct outside access *(cc item 27b)*
213 1 ☐ Yes 2 ☐ No 3 ☐ DK x ☐ Item blank

AFTER INTERVIEW – TRANSCRIBE FROM CONTROL CARD – Cont.

12a. Household Income *(cc item 28)*
214
1 ☐ Less than $5,000 6 ☐ 15,000 – 11 ☐ 35,000 –
2 ☐ $5,000 – 7 ☐ 17,500 – 12 ☐ 40,000 –
3 ☐ 7,500 – 8 ☐ 20,000 – 13 ☐ 50,000 –
4 ☐ 10,000 – 9 ☐ 25,000 – 14 ☐ 75,000 and over
5 ☐ 12,500 – 10 ☐ 30,000 –

12b. College/University *(cc item 8b)*
218 1 ☐ Yes 2 ☐ No

12c. Public Housing *(cc item 8c)*
219 x ☐ Item blank 1 ☐ Yes (public housing) 2 ☐ No (not public housing)

12d. Manager Verification of Public Housing *(cc item 8d)*
220 x ☐ Item blank
Able to verify: 1 ☐ Public housing 2 ☐ Not public housing
Unable to verify: 3 ☐ CATI/Telephone 4 ☐ Other – *Specify*

12e. Indian Reservation or Indian Lands *(cc item 8e)*
221 1 ☐ Yes 2 ☐ No

ITEMS FILLED DURING AND/OR AFTER INTERVIEW

13. Proxy information – *Fill for all proxy interviews*

a. Proxy interview obtained for Line No.	**b.** Proxy respondent Name	Line No.	**c.** Reason *(Enter code)*
301		302	303
304		305	306
307		308	309
310		311	312

Codes for item 13c
1 – 12–13 years old and parent refused permission for self interview
2 – Physically/mentally unable to answer } *FILL INTER-COMM*
3 – TA and won't return before closeout }

14. Type Z noninterview

a. Interview not obtained for Line No.	**b.** Reason *(Enter code)*
313	314
315	316
317	318
319	320

Codes for item 14b
1 – Never available
2 – Refused . . . .
3 – Physically mentally unable to answer — no proxy available
4 – TA and no proxy available . . . .
5 – Other . . . . . .
} *FILL INTER-COMM*
6 – Office use only

▶ *Complete 17—28 for each Line No. in 14a*

15a. Household members 12 years of age and OVER
321 ________ Total number

15b. Household members UNDER 12 years of age
322 ________ Total number
0 ☐ None

15c. Crime Incident Reports filled
323 ________ Total number of NCVS-2s filled
0 ☐ None

16. Changes in Household Composition *(cc item 25a)*

a. Line No.	**b.** Reason *(Enter code)*
324	325
326	327
328	329
330	331

Only transcribe changes discovered during the current enumeration

Fill BOUNDING INFORMATION

FIGURE 6.1

HOUSEHOLD RESPONDENT'S PERSONAL CHARACTERISTICS		
17. NAME (of household respondent)	**18.** Type of interview	**19.** Line No.
Last First	401 1 ☐ Per. – Self-respondent 2 ☐ Tel. – Self-respondent 3 ☐ Per. – Proxy ⎱ 4 ☐ Tel. – Proxy ⎰ Fill 13 on cover page	402 Line No.

AFTER INTERVIEW – TRANSCRIBE FROM CONTROL CARD										
20. (cc 13b) Relationship to reference person	**21.** (cc 17) Age last birthday	**22a.** (cc 18) Marital status THIS survey period	**22b.** (From previous enumeration) Marital status LAST survey period	**23.** (cc 19) Sex	**24.** (cc 20) Armed Forces member	**25a.** (cc 21a) Education -highest grade	**25b.** (cc 21b) Education -complete that year?	**26.** (cc 22) Attending school	**27.** (cc 23) Race	**28.** (cc 24) His-panic origin
403 01 ☐ Husband 02 ☐ Wife 03 ☐ Son 04 ☐ Daughter 05 ☐ Father 06 ☐ Mother 07 ☐ Brother 08 ☐ Sister 09 ☐ Other relative 10 ☐ Nonrelative 11 ☐ Ref. person	404 Age	405 1 ☐ Married 2 ☐ Widowed 3 ☐ Divorced 4 ☐ Separated 5 ☐ Never married	406 1 ☐ Married 2 ☐ Widowed 3 ☐ Divorced 4 ☐ Separated 5 ☐ Never married 6 ☐ Not inter-viewed last survey period	407 1 ☐ M 2 ☐ F	408 1 ☐ Yes 2 ☐ No	409 Grade	410 1 ☐ Yes 2 ☐ No	411 0 ☐ Regular school 1 ☐ College/ Univer-sity 2 ☐ Trade school 3 ☐ Voca-tional school 4 ☐ None of the above schools	412 1 ☐ White 2 ☐ Black 3 ☐ Amer. Indian, Aleut, Eskimo 4 ☐ Asian, Pacific Is-lander 5 ☐ Other	413 1 ☐ Yes 2 ☐ No

29. Date of interview ⟶ 501 ☐☐ ☐☐ ☐☐☐☐
Month   Day   Year

MOBILITY QUESTIONS	
Before we get to the crime questions, I have some questions that are helpful in studying where and why crimes occur. *If unsure, ASK OR VERIFY –* **33a.** How long have you lived at this address? *(Enter number of months OR years.)*	505 _____ Months (1-11) – **SKIP** to 33b **OR** 506 _____ Years (Round to nearest whole year) – *Fill Check Item A*
CHECK ITEM A How many years are entered in 33a?	☐ 5 years or more – **SKIP** to 34 ☐ Less than 5 years – *Ask 33b*
33b. Altogether, how many times have you moved in the last 5 years, that is, since _____, 19 ___?	508 _____ Number of times

BUSINESS OPERATED FROM SAMPLE ADDRESS	
34. Does anyone in this household operate a business from this address?	530 1 ☐ Yes – *Go to 35* 2 ☐ No – **SKIP** to 36a
PERSONAL – *Fill by observation.* TELEPHONE – *Ask.* **35.** Is there a sign on the premises or some other indication to the general public that a business is operated from this address?	531 1 ☐ Yes (Recognizable business) 2 ☐ No (Unrecognizable business)

Page 2

FORM NCVS-1 (5-10-2001)

FIGURE 6.1 *(continued)*

36a. I'm going to read some examples that will give you an idea of the kinds of crimes this study covers.

As I go through them, tell me if any of these happened to you in the last 6 months, that is since _____ _____, 20 ____.

Was something belonging to YOU stolen, such as –

(a) Things that you carry, like luggage, a wallet, purse, briefcase, book –

(b) Clothing, jewelry, or calculator –

(c) Bicycle or sports equipment –

(d) Things in your home – like a TV, stereo, or tools

(e) Things outside your home such as a garden hose or lawn furniture –

(f) Things belonging to children in the household –

(g) Things from a vehicle, such as a package, groceries, camera, or cassette tapes –

OR

(h) Did anyone ATTEMPT to steal anything belonging to you?

Briefly describe incident(s)

MARK OR ASK –

36b. Did any incidents of this type happen to you?

532 1 ☐ **Yes – What happened?**
Describe above
2 ☐ No – **SKIP** *to 37a*

36c. How many times?

533 _____
Number of times (36c)

37a. (Other than any incidents already mentioned,) has anyone –

(a) Broken in or ATTEMPTED to break into your home by forcing a door or window, pushing past someone, jimmying a lock, cutting a screen, or entering through an open door or window?

(b) Has anyone illegally gotten in or tried to get into a garage, shed or storage room?

OR

(c) Illegally gotten in or tried to get into a hotel or motel room or vacation home where you were staying?

Briefly describe incident(s)

MARK OR ASK –

37b. Did any incidents of this type happen to you?

534 1 ☐ Yes – **What happened?**
Describe above
2 ☐ No – **SKIP** *to 38*

37c. How many times?

535 _____
Number of times (37c)

FIGURE 6.1 *(continued)*

38. What was the TOTAL number of cars, vans, trucks, motorcycles, or other motor vehicles owned by you or any other member of this household during the last 6 months? Include those you no longer own.

536 0 ☐ None – *SKIP to 40a*
1 ☐ 1
2 ☐ 2
3 ☐ 3
4 ☐ 4 *or more*

39a. During the last 6 months, (other than any incidents already mentioned,) (was the vehicle/were any of the vehicles) –

(a) Stolen or used without permission?

(b) Did anyone steal any parts such as a tire, tape deck, hubcap or battery?

(c) Did anyone steal any gas from (it/them)?

OR

(d) Did anyone ATTEMPT to steal any vehicle or parts attached to (it/them)?

Briefly describe incident(s) ⬏

_____

MARK OR ASK –

39b. Did any incidents of this type happen to you?

537 1 ☐ Yes – **What happened?**
Describe above
2 ☐ No – *SKIP to 40a*

39c. How many times?

538 _____
Number of times (39c)

40a. (Other than any incidents already mentioned,) since _____, 20 ___, were you attacked or threatened OR did you have something stolen from you –

(a) At home including the porch or yard –

(b) At or near a friend's, relative's, or neighbor's home –

(c) At work or school –

(d) In places such as a storage shed or laundry room, a shopping mall, restaurant, bank, or airport –

(e) While riding in any vehicle –

(f) On the street or in a parking lot –

(g) At such places as a party, theater, gym, picnic area, bowling lanes, or while fishing or hunting –

OR

(h) Did anyone ATTEMPT to attack or ATTEMPT to steal anything belonging to you from any of these places?

Briefly describe incident(s) ⬏

_____

MARK OR ASK –

40b. Did any incidents of this type happen to you?

539 1 ☐ Yes – **What happened?**
Describe above
2 ☐ No – *SKIP to 41a*

40c. How many times?

540 _____
Number of times (40c)

FORM NCVS-1 (5-10-2001)

FIGURE 6.1 *(continued)*

41a. (Other than any incidents already mentioned,) has anyone attacked or threatened you in any of these ways *(Exclude telephone threats)* –

(a) With any weapon, for instance, a gun or knife –

(b) With anything like a baseball bat, frying pan, scissors, or stick –

(c) By something thrown, such as a rock or bottle –

(d) Include any grabbing, punching, or choking,

(e) Any rape, attempted rape or other type of sexual attack –

(f) Any face to face threats –

OR

(g) Any attack or threat or use of force by anyone at all? Please mention it even if you are not certain it was a crime.

Briefly describe incident(s) ↙
_____
_____
_____
_____
_____
_____
_____
_____
_____
_____
_____
_____

MARK OR ASK –
41b. Did any incidents of this type happen to you?

| 541 | 1 ☐ Yes – **What happened?** *Describe above* |
| | 2 ☐ No – *SKIP* to 42a |

41c. How many times?

| 542 | _____ |
| | Number of times (41c) |

42a. People often don't think of incidents committed by someone they know. (Other than any incidents already mentioned,) did you have something stolen from you **OR** were you attacked or threatened by *(Exclude telephone threats)* –

(a) Someone at work or school –

(b) A neighbor or friend –

(c) A relative or family member –

(d) Any other person you've met or known?

Briefly describe incident(s) ↙
_____
_____
_____
_____
_____
_____
_____

MARK OR ASK –
42b. Did any incidents of this type happen to you?

| 543 | 1 ☐ Yes – **What happened?** *Describe above* |
| | 2 ☐ No – *SKIP* to 43a |

42c. How many times?

| 544 | _____ |
| | Number of times (42c) |

43a. Incidents involving forced or unwanted sexual acts are often difficult to talk about. (Other than any incidents already mentioned,) have you been forced or coerced to engage in unwanted sexual activity by –

(a) Someone you didn't know before –

(b) A casual acquaintance –

OR

(c) Someone you know well?

Briefly describe incident(s) ↙
_____
_____
_____
_____
_____
_____
_____

MARK OR ASK –
43b. Did any incidents of this type happen to you?

| 545 | 1 ☐ Yes – **What happened?** *Describe above* |
| | 2 ☐ No – *SKIP* to 44a |

43c. How many times?

| 546 | _____ |
| | Number of times (43c) |

FORM NCVS-1 (5-10-2001)

FIGURE 6.1 *(continued)*

HOUSEHOLD RESPONDENT'S SCREEN QUESTIONS

44a. During the last 6 months, (other than any incidents already mentioned,) did you call the police to report something that happened to YOU which you thought was a crime?

Briefly describe incident(s) ⬐

_____
_____
_____
_____
_____
_____

547 1 ☐ Yes – **What happened?**
　　　　　　Describe above
　　　2 ☐ No – **SKIP** *to 45a*

548 | | | | | **OFFICE USE ONLY**
*

CHECK ITEM C Look at 44a. If unsure, ASK, otherwise, mark without asking. **Were you** (was the respondent) **attacked or threatened, or was something stolen or an attempt made to steal something that belonged to you** (the respondent) **or another household member?**

549 1 ☐ Yes – *Ask 44b*
　　　2 ☐ No – **SKIP** *to 45a*

◄

44b. How many times?

550 _____
　　　Number of times (44b)

45a. During the last 6 months, (other than any incidents already mentioned,) did anything which you thought was a crime happen to YOU, but you did NOT report to the police?

Briefly describe incident(s) ⬐

_____
_____
_____
_____
_____
_____

551 1 ☐ Yes – **What happened?**
　　　　　　Describe above
　　　2 ☐ No – **SKIP** *to INTRO at top of page 7*

552 | | | | | **OFFICE USE ONLY**
*

CHECK ITEM B Look at 45a. If unsure, ASK, otherwise, mark without asking. **Were you** (was the respondent) **attacked or threatened, or was something stolen or an attempt made to steal something that belonged to you** (the respondent) **or another household member?**

553 1 ☐ Yes – *Ask 45b*
　　　2 ☐ No – **SKIP** *to INTRO at top of page 7*

45b. How many times?

◄

554 _____
　　　Number of times (45b)

NOTES

Page 6

FORM NCVS-1 (5-10-2001)

FIGURE 6.1 *(continued)*

278

HOUSEHOLD RESPONDENT'S COMPUTER CRIME SCREEN QUESTIONS

FIELD REPRESENTATIVE – *Read introduction.*

INTRO: **The next series of questions are about YOUR use of a computer. Please include ALL computers, laptops, or access to WebTV used at home, work, or school for PERSONAL USE** *or* **for operating a home business.**

45c. During the last 6 months, have YOU used a computer, laptop, or WebTV for the following purposes *(Read answer categories 1–4) –*

Mark (X) all that apply.

100
*

1 ☐ **For personal use at home?**
2 ☐ **For personal use at work?**
3 ☐ **For personal use at school, libraries, etc.?**
4 ☐ **To operate a home business?**
5 ☐ None of the above – **SKIP** *to Check Item D*

45d. How many computers do you have access to for personal use or for operating a home business?

101

0 ☐ None
1 ☐ 1
2 ☐ 2
3 ☐ 3
4 ☐ 4 or more

45e. Do YOU use the Internet for personal use or for operating a home business?

102

1 ☐ Personal use
2 ☐ Operating a home business
3 ☐ Both
4 ☐ None of the above

45f. Have you experienced any of the following **COMPUTER-RELATED** incidents in the last 6 months *(Read answer categories 1–6) –*

Mark (X) all that apply.

103
*

1 ☐ **Fraud in purchasing something over the Internet?**
2 ☐ **Computer virus attack?**
3 ☐ **Threats of harm or physical attack made while online or through E-mail?**
4 ☐ **Unrequested lewd or obscene messages, communications, or images while online or through E-mail?**
5 ☐ *(Only ask if box 4 is marked in Item 45c)* **Software copyright violation in connection with a home business?**
6 ☐ **Something else that you consider a computer-related crime?**–*Specify* ↙

_____

_____

7 ☐ No computer-related incidents –**SKIP** *to Check Item D*

45g. Did you suffer any monetary loss as a result of the incident(s) you just mentioned?

104

1 ☐ Yes
2 ☐ No – **SKIP** *to 45i*

45h. How much money did you lose as a result of the incident(s)?

105

$ _____ .00 Amount of loss
x ☐ Don't know

45i. Did you report the incident(s) you just mentioned to *(Read answer categories 1–5) –*

Mark (X) all that apply.

106
*

1 ☐ **A law enforcement agency?**
2 ☐ **An Internet Service provider?**
3 ☐ **A Website administrator?**
4 ☐ **A Systems Administrator?**
5 ☐ **Someone else? –** *Specify* ↙

_____

_____

6 ☐ None of the above

HOUSEHOLD RESPONDENT'S CHECK ITEMS D AND E

CHECK ITEM D

Who besides the respondent was present when the screen questions were asked? *(If telephone interview, mark box 1 only.)*

555
*

1 ☐ Telephone interview – **SKIP** *to 46a*
   Personal interview – *Mark all that apply.*
2 ☐ No one besides respondent present
3 ☐ Respondent's spouse
4 ☐ HHLD member(s) 12+, not spouse
5 ☐ HHLD member(s) under 12
6 ☐ Nonhousehold member(s)
7 ☐ Someone was present – Can't say who
8 ☐ Don't know if someone else present

CHECK ITEM E

If self-response interview, **SKIP** *to 46a*

Did the person for whom this interview was taken help the proxy respondent answer any screen questions?

556

1 ☐ Yes
2 ☐ No
3 ☐ Person for whom interview taken not present

FIGURE 6.1 *(continued)*

46a. Now I'd like to ask about ALL acts of vandalism that may have been committed during the last 6 months against YOUR household. Vandalism is the deliberate, intentional damage to or destruction of household property. Examples are breaking windows, slashing tires, and painting graffiti on walls.

Since _____, 20 ____, has anyone intentionally damaged or destroyed property owned by you or someone else in your household?

(EXCLUDE any damage done in conjunction with incidents already mentioned.)

| 557 | 1 ☐ Yes |
| | 2 ☐ No – **SKIP** to Check Item G |

46b. What kind of property was damaged or destroyed in this/these act(s) of vandalism? Anything else?

Continue asking "Anything else?" until you get a "No" response.

Mark (X) all property that was damaged or destroyed by vandalism during reference period.

558	1 ☐ Motor vehicle (including parts)
*	2 ☐ Bicycle (including parts)
	3 ☐ Mailbox
	4 ☐ House window/screen/door
	5 ☐ Yard or garden (trees, shrubs, fence, etc.)
	6 ☐ Furniture, other household goods
	7 ☐ Clothing
	8 ☐ Animal (pet, livestock, etc.)
	9 ☐ Other – *Specify* ↙

46c. What kind of damage was done in this/these act(s) of vandalism? Anything else?

Continue asking "Anything else?" until you get a "No" response.

Mark (X) all kinds of damage by vandals that occurred during reference period.

559	1 ☐ Broken glass: window, windshield, glass in door, mirror
*	2 ☐ Defaced: marred, graffiti, dirtied
	3 ☐ Burned: use of fire, heat or explosives
	4 ☐ Drove into or ran over with vehicle
	5 ☐ Other breaking or tearing
	6 ☐ Injured or killed animals
	7 ☐ Other – *Specify* ↙

46d. What was the total dollar amount of the damage caused by this/these act(s) of vandalism during the last 6 months? (Use repair costs if the property was repaired.)

(EXCLUDE any damage done in incidents already mentioned.)

| 560 | $ _____ . | 00 | – **SKIP** to Check Item F1 |

x ☐ Don't know

o ☐ No cost – **SKIP** to Check Item F1

46e. Was the damage under $100 or $100 or more?

(INCLUDE total amount for all incidents of vandalism during the last 6 months.)

561	1 ☐ Under $100
	2 ☐ $100 or more
	3 ☐ Don't know

CHECK ITEM F1 Look at 46a. If unsure, ASK, otherwise, mark without asking. **In the vandalism just mentioned, were you** (was the respondent) **attacked or threatened, or was something stolen or an attempt made to steal something that belonged to you** (the respondent) **or another household member? (other than any incident(s) already mentioned)**

Briefly describe incident(s) ↙

_____

_____

_____

| 562 | 1 ☐ Yes – **What happened?** *Describe above* |
| | 2 ☐ No – **SKIP** to 46g |

46f. How many times?

| 563 | |
| | Number of times (46f) |

NOTES

FORM NCVS-1 (5-10-2001)

FIGURE 6.1 *(continued)*

HOUSEHOLD RESPONDENT'S HATE CRIME SCREEN QUESTIONS

46g. Hate crimes or crimes of prejudice or bigotry occur when (an offender/offenders) target(s) people because of one or more of their characteristics or religious beliefs.

Do you have any reason to suspect the vandalism just discussed was a hate crime or crime of prejudice or bigotry?

586	1 ☐ Yes – Ask 46h
	2 ☐ No . . . . } **SKIP** to Check Item G
	3 ☐ Don't know . .

46h. An offender/Offenders can target people for a variety of reasons, but we are only going to ask you about a few today. Do you suspect the offender(s) targeted you because of...

(a) Your race? . . . .   **564**   1 ☐ Yes   2 ☐ No   3 ☐ Don't know

(b) Your religion? . . . .   **565**   1 ☐ Yes   2 ☐ No   3 ☐ Don't know

(c) Your ethnic background or national origin (for example, people of Hispanic origin)? . . . . . .   **566**   1 ☐ Yes   2 ☐ No   3 ☐ Don't know

(d) Any disability (by this I mean physical, mental, or developmental disabilities) you may have? . . .   **567**   1 ☐ Yes   2 ☐ No   3 ☐ Don't know

(e) Your gender? . . . .   **568**   1 ☐ Yes   2 ☐ No   3 ☐ Don't know

(f) Your sexual orientation? . . . .   **569**   1 ☐ Yes   2 ☐ No   3 ☐ Don't know

If "Yes," SAY – (by this we mean homosexual, bisexual, or heterosexual)

46i. Some offenders target people because they associate with certain people or the (offender perceives/ offenders perceive) them as having certain characteristics or religious beliefs.

Do you suspect you were targeted because of...

(a) Your association with people who have certain characteristics or religious beliefs (for example, a multiracial couple)? . . . .   **587**   1 ☐ Yes –Specify ↙ 2 ☐ No   3 ☐ Don't know

588 _____

(b) The offender(s)'s perception of your characteristics or religious beliefs (for example, the offender(s) thought you were Jewish because you went into a synagogue)? . . . .   **589**   1 ☐ Yes – Specify ↙ 2 ☐ No   3 ☐ Don't know

590 _____

| **CHECK ITEM F2** | Are one or more boxes marked "Yes" in 46h OR 46i? | ☐ Yes – Ask 46j
☐ No – **SKIP** to Check Item G |

46j. Do you have any evidence that this vandalism was a hate crime or crime of prejudice or bigotry?

If "No" or "Don't know," ASK –

Did the offender(s) say something, write anything, or leave anything behind at the crime scene that would suggest you were targeted because of your characteristics or religious beliefs?

591	1 ☐ Yes – Ask 46k
	2 ☐ No . . . . } **SKIP** to Check Item G
	3 ☐ Don't know . .

FIGURE 6.1 (*continued*)

46k. The next questions ask about the evidence you have that makes you suspect this vandalism was a hate crime or a crime of prejudice or bigotry. As I read the following questions, please tell me if any of the following happened:

(a) Did the offender(s) make fun of you, make negative comments, use slang, hurtful words, or abusive language? . . . .

| 592 | 1 ☐ Yes | 2 ☐ No | 3 ☐ Don't know |

(b) Were any hate symbols present at the crime scene to indicate the offender(s) targeted you for a particular reason (for example, a swastika, graffiti on the walls of a temple, a burning cross, or written words)? . . . .

| 593 | 1 ☐ Yes | 2 ☐ No | 3 ☐ Don't know |

(c) Did a police investigation confirm the offender(s) targeted you (for example, did the offender(s) confess a motive, or did the police find books, journals, or pictures that indicated the offender(s) (was/were) prejudiced against people with certain characteristics or religious beliefs)? . . . .

| 594 | 1 ☐ Yes | 2 ☐ No | 3 ☐ Don't know |

(d) Do you know the offender(s) (has/have) committed similar hate crimes or crimes of prejudice or bigotry in the past? . . . .

| 595 | 1 ☐ Yes | 2 ☐ No | 3 ☐ Don't know |

(e) Did the vandalism occur on or near a holiday, event, location, gathering place, or building commonly associated with a specific group (for example, at the Gay Pride March or at a synagogue, Korean church, or gay bar)? . . . . .

| 596 | 1 ☐ Yes | 2 ☐ No | 3 ☐ Don't know |

(f) Have other hate crimes or crimes of prejudice or bigotry happened to you or in your area/neighborhood where people have been targeted?

| 597 | 1 ☐ Yes | 2 ☐ No | 3 ☐ Don't know |

(g) Do your feelings, instincts, or perception lead you to suspect this vandalism was a hate crime or crime of prejudice or bigotry, but you do not have enough evidence to know for sure? . . . .

| 598 | 1 ☐ Yes | 2 ☐ No | 3 ☐ Don't know |

CHECK ITEM G

Transcribe "number of times" entry for each of the following:

☐ No entries transcribed below – *Go to Check Item H*

(a) Screen Question, Item 36c, page 3   _____ Number of times (36c)

(b) Screen Question, Item 37c, page 3   _____ Number of times (37c)

(c) Screen Question, Item 39c, page 4   _____ Number of times (39c)

(d) Screen Question, Item 40c, page 4   _____ Number of times (40c)

(e) Screen Question, Item 41c, page 5   _____ Number of times (41c)

(f) Screen Question, Item 42c, page 5   _____ Number of times (42c)

(g) Screen Question, Item 43c, page 5   _____ Number of times (43c)

(h) Screen Question, Item 44b, page 6   _____ Number of times (44b)

(i) Screen Question, Item 45b, page 6   _____ Number of times (45b)

(j) Vandalism Screen Question, Item 46f, page 8   _____ Number of times (46f)

*FIELD REPRESENTATIVE – After completing Check Item G, fill a separate crime incident report for each screen question that has an entry of 1 or more. Do this **before** marking Check Item H.*

FORM NCVS-1 (5-10-2001)

FIGURE 6.1   (*continued*)

HOUSEHOLD RESPONDENT'S EMPLOYMENT QUESTIONS

Be sure to fill any incident reports before marking Check Item H.

CHECK ITEM H	Is the respondent 16 years or older?	1 ☐ Yes – *Ask 47a* 2 ☐ No – **SKIP** *to Check Item I*

47a. Did you have a job or work at a business LAST WEEK? (Do not include volunteer work or work around the house.)

(If farm or business operator in household, ask about unpaid work.)

576   1 ☐ Yes – **SKIP** *to 48a*
      2 ☐ No – *Ask 47b*

ASK OR VERIFY –
47b. Did you have a job or work at a business DURING THE LAST 6 MONTHS?

577   1 ☐ Yes – *Ask 47c*
      2 ☐ No – **SKIP** *to Check Item I*

47c. Did that (job/work) last 2 consecutive weeks or more?

578   1 ☐ Yes – *Ask 48a*
      2 ☐ No – **SKIP** *to Check Item I*

ASK OR VERIFY –
48a. Which of the following best describes your job?

PERSONAL INTERVIEW *(Show flashcard)*

TELEPHONE INTERVIEW – **Were you employed in the** *(Read main headings until you get a yes. Then read answer categories) –*

Mark (X) only one category.

579

Medical Profession – As a –
1 ☐ Physician
2 ☐ Nurse
3 ☐ Technician
4 ☐ Other – *Specify* _____

Mental Health Services Field – Are your duties –
5 ☐ Professional (Social worker/psychiatrist)
6 ☐ Custodial care
7 ☐ Other – *Specify* _____

Teaching Profession – Were you employed in a –
8 ☐ Preschool
9 ☐ Elementary
10 ☐ Junior high or middle school
11 ☐ High school
12 ☐ College or university
13 ☐ Technical or industrial school
14 ☐ Special education facility
15 ☐ Other – *Specify* _____

Law Enforcement or Security Field – Were you employed as a –
16 ☐ Law enforcement officer
17 ☐ Prison or jail guard
18 ☐ Security guard
19 ☐ Other – *Specify* _____

Retail Sales – Were you employed as a –
20 ☐ Convenience or liquor store clerk
21 ☐ Gas station attendant
22 ☐ Bartender
23 ☐ Other – *Specify* _____

Transportation Field – Were you employed as a –
24 ☐ Bus driver
25 ☐ Taxi cab driver
26 ☐ Other – *Specify* _____

OR
27 ☐ Something else – *Specify* _____

ASK OR VERIFY –
48b. Is your job with *(Read answer categories) –*

580
1 ☐ **A private company, business, or individual for wages?**
2 ☐ **The Federal government?**
3 ☐ **A State, county, or local government?**
4 ☐ **Yourself (Self-employed) in your own business, professional practice, or farm?**

If box 12 is marked in 48a, mark without asking.
48c. Are you employed by a college or university?

581   1 ☐ Yes
      2 ☐ No

48d. While working at your job, do you work mostly in *(Read answer categories) –*

582
1 ☐ **A city?**
2 ☐ **Suburban area?**
3 ☐ **Rural area?**
4 ☐ **Combination of any of these?**

CHECK ITEM I	Is this the last household member to be interviewed?	☐ Yes – *Ask or verify Control Card items. Then END interview.* ☐ No – *Ask or verify Control Card items. See note below before interviewing next household member.*

*FIELD REPRESENTATIVE – If the next household member to be interviewed is under 18, tell the household respondent that you will be asking the **same** questions you just asked him/her.*

FORM NCVS-1 (5-10-2001)

Page 11

FIGURE 6.1 *(continued)*

Conducting Interviews

Since interviews mean direct contact between the interviewer and one or more respondents, there is some strategy involved. A golden rule practiced in business is that "the customer is always right." This also applies in interview situations. The interviewee is always right. Researchers must cater to the convenience of respondents. This means that investigators must schedule their interviews in ways that maximize the successfulness of the interview and that accommodate interviewees.

Some of the major points to consider when conducting interviews are: (1) gaining access to organizations, (2) arranging interviews, (3) training and orienting interviewers, (4) how to dress for interview occasions, (5) determining when to probe with follow-up questions, (6) whether to videotape interviews, (7) whether polygraph or lie detector tests are used in certain situations, and (8) the dangerousness of interviewing.

Gaining Access to Organizations

Conducting interviews varies in formality, depending on the nature of the research, the sophistication of the interviewers, and the scope of the research plan. If employees are to be interviewed at their work settings, permission must first be obtained from superiors to interview these subjects. If jail or prison inmates are to be interviewed, permission must be obtained from the prison warden, county sheriff, or chief jailer. Inmates themselves must consent as well. If researchers are connected with a well-known sponsoring agency, such as the Bureau of Justice Statistics, National Institutes for Mental Health, or National Opinion Research Center, they stand a much better chance of gaining access to prospective interviewees than those investigators who are conducting research independently.

Sometimes, it is desirable to preface requests to interview employees with a letter, on official letterheads, indicating the purposes of the interviews and research objectives. It is advantageous to point out how the research might benefit those interviewed, or the organizations who employ them. A subsequent face-to-face meeting with higher-ups can clarify any misconceptions management might have about permitting interviewers access to their employees. Even then, access to employees may be denied. Perhaps the organization can be persuaded to permit investigators to interview employees at their homes, on their own time. This tactic has the advantage of leading subjects to believe that their organizations are sponsoring or condoning the interviews, and their cooperation with interviewers is enhanced.

If interviews are to be conducted on a door-to-door basis, there is no need to obtain permission beforehand. However, interviewers must spend considerable time visiting each home and explaining their research purposes. Again, such interviewing is enhanced to the extent that researchers have the sponsorship of well-known research agencies. While it may be ideal to contact subjects in advance by telephone, many subjects to be interviewed do not have telephones or may have unlisted numbers. Thus, investigators may have to take what they can get through door-to-door contacts. The best advice to interviewers is to expect the worse, but hope for the best, interviewing conditions. Poor weather, vicious dogs, and other distractions quickly transform one's ideal plans into reality, which often is far from optimum interviewing conditions.

Arranging the Interview

Where interviewees are selected in advance, especially outside of their work settings, a time must be arranged for the interview. It is important to work closely with the interviewee and schedule and interview time that best suits them. If they are on shiftwork schedules, the only convenient time for an interview may be between 2:00–4:00 A.M. Daytime interviewing is preferred, especially if persons to be interviewed live in high-crime or gang-dominated areas. The researcher's best strategy is to have the respondent name the time, and perhaps even the place. One's home or apartment is often the best location for an interview, but the close proximity of small children and relatives may prove to be too distracting. Sometimes a small restaurant or city park might be better locations. But researchers must anticipate that no matter where an interview is conducted, there are extraneous factors that may interfere with a smooth interview.

Interviewing persons at their workplaces may not be the best interview sites. Sometimes workers may suggest their organization lunch rooms for interviews. These areas have unusually high traffic, where other employees drift in and out. Again, there is too much potential for becoming distracted. Some employees may wander over to your table and look over your shoulder. "Hey, what's up? What is that? Are you being interviewed? Do you want to interview me? What are you wanting to know?" Interview areas are best where minimal distraction occurs.

In the case of interviews with jail or prison inmates, researchers literally have a captive audience. However, even under these circumstances, inmates can refuse to be interviewed. After all, what's in it for them? Researchers need to remember that no interviewee has anything to gain when granting an interview. The interview is an imposition and generally has relevance only for the researcher. However, interviewees have the information a researcher needs, information that will describe the setting and orientations of group members. If a theory is being tested or crime or delinquency interventions planned, interviewees are the sources for necessary data. Everything within reasonable limits should be done to cater to an interviewee's whims concerning when and where to be interviewed.

Training and Orientation for Interviewers

Depending on the magnitude of the study, researchers themselves may conduct interviews with various respondents. If large numbers of interviews are to be conducted, then it is increasingly likely that interviewers will have to be recruited for the task and trained. For example, J.L. Miller and Glenna Simons (1997) studied prospective jurors and the impact of news reports and media coverage of spectacular events on their opinions about defendants. Miller and Simons recruited eight graduate students at Purdue University in West Lafayette, Indiana, to conduct interviews with 117 persons. The students were trained at Purdue University and coached in various ways to minimize the chances of a refusal or a break in the interview. A role-playing exercise was conducted wherein a mock interview was completed. This enabled the interviewers to practice interviewing techniques and provided them with an opportunity to ask questions (Miller & Simons, 1997).

When interviews are conducted in face-to-face situations, sometimes sensitive questions are asked. Interviewers should be trained in ways that enable them to be unmoved by things they might hear from respondents. The best way to end an interview is to ask a sensitive question, hear the answer, look shocked, and say, "Oh, my!" Or the interviewer may ask about one's income. If the respondent says, "$200,000 a year," the interviewer might say, "That's a *lot* of money!" This and other judgmental reactions turn off interviewees. At the very least, the interviewer will cause the interviewee to be less than candid and more guarded for the remainder of the interview. Interviewers should refrain from looking surprised or shocked at anything the interviewee might disclose. Interviewers should look interested and somewhat detached. This mode of behavior is acquired through interviewing experience. There is no such thing as the perfect way to behave when conducting interviews.

What Makes a Good Interviewer? Personality Factors

It is impossible to set forth a set of personality characteristics to suit all interviewers. Interviewers cannot be rigidly standardized like cans of peaches on a store shelf. There is considerable variety among persons and their personalities. Some general recommendations can be made, however. First, interviewers should be friendly and cordial. They must be familiar with the subject matter of the interview. Thus, when interviewees have questions about the meaning of certain questions or statements, interviewers should be competent enough to provide answers.

The key to a good interview is developing rapport. The interviewer can influence the rapport of any social situation. If the interview is conducted at the interviewee's home, the environment may include trappings, such as awards or plaques, that can be used to start the conversation. Perhaps a comment about one's automobile or neighborhood would help to make everyone comfortable before commencing the interview.

More successful interviewers must be able to think on their feet, to make instant assessments of situations and respond accordingly. Your objective is to blend in with the immediate social surroundings and not appear to be overly conspicuous. If you're interviewing farm families in Kansas or isolated persons in places like Rafter, Tennessee, wearing a three-piece suit from Brooks Brothers is out of the question. The interviewer's attitude should reflect an interest in the interview and respect toward the interviewee. Interviewers should relax and attempt to be comfortable, regardless of the circumstances in which they find themselves.

Dressing Appropriately

It is important for interviewers to adapt to the settings they are investigating. If executives of a large organization are being interviewed, it would be advantageous for interviewers to dress rather formally, in attire similar to those being interviewed. However, if interviewers are conducting interviews in run-down neighborhoods, formal attire is inappropriate. Casual attire is less likely to arouse suspicions of those interviewed. Detectives often wear coats and ties, and interviewees may suspect interviewers of being law enforcement personnel. This may cause prospective respondents to become uncooperative and refuse to answer an interviewer's questions.

Since much research is conducted by investigators working independently, it is unlikely that they will have an adequately trained interviewer pool. Only major research organizations have this degree of sophistication and training capability. Assuming, then, that most interviewers will enter the field relatively untrained, their "training" will often consist of learning some general guidelines, or dos and don'ts, associated with conducting interviews.

An interviewer's primary objective is to obtain the most accurate data from respondents. It is important, therefore, to put respondents at ease during the interview. Even the most unskilled interviewers become more at ease themselves when conducting interviews after they have participated in 10 or 20 of them. The more experienced the interviewer, the easier it becomes to create good interviewer–interviewee rapport and obtain desired information. Interviewers, therefore, should not over- or underdress in relation to those interviewed. Furthermore, interviewers should remain interested in one's answers yet relatively neutral, depending on an interviewee's responses. For instance, if the interviewee discloses some sexual indiscretion or admits to a crime, the interviewer should refrain from smiling, laughing, frowning, or deeply inhaling suddenly. These are some of the "don'ts" of conducting interviews. It is also possible to get too close to those interviewed. The objectivity of the interview may be impaired when either the interviewer or interviewee becomes overly friendly. Offers of alcoholic beverages or soft drinks during the interview should probably be avoided.

Probing

One of the positive features of interviewing is the fact that interviewers can seek clarification or amplification whenever respondents give one-word answers or are somewhat vague. For instance, if you are interviewing probationers about the effectiveness of probation officers who supervise them, you might ask:

Q: "Is your probation officer helpful in providing you with job contacts and referrals?"
A: "Yeah, he's OK."
Q: "What does the probation officer do to help you in that regard?" (Probe)
A: "He gives me job leads, you know, names and addresses of people to see, you know, people who might hire me."
Q: "Does your probation officer provide any other type of assistance?" (Probe)
A: "Well, beyond that, I don't know. What do you mean?"
Q: "Well, does he help you fill out job applications, or does he provide you with ideas to put on a job application?" (Probe)
A: "Ohhhh, yeahhh. That, too. He's real good at helping me fill out those forms. One time, I had forgot something I done a long time ago, and it was important for some job I was applying for. He just, you know, sort of worked with me, and helped me remember that and other things. I never would have thought of some of that stuff. He's real smart like that. Yeah, come to think of it, he was really helpful. I got the job!"

The above scenario reveals the value of probing questions. Rather than allow the probationer to simply brush off the interviewer with a "Yeah, he's OK" answer to whether the probation officer is effective, the subsequent probes permit additional elaboration concerning the nature of the probation officer's effectiveness, especially regarding job assistance. This may be important for depicting areas where probation offices can improve their various services. Probes also permit investigators to gain insight into the subject matter of their investigation.

Another feature of probing is to uncover areas of inquiry previously neglected by the researcher. There is an element of serendipity associated with probing, meaning that one or more issues, topics, or ideas may be elicited that were not previously thought of by the investigators when the interview was originally constructed. Researchers can't think of everything meaningful to be included in their questionnaires or interviews.

Videotaping or Tape-Recording Interviews

In some situations, it may be important to videotape or tape-record interviews. This method of data collection totally eliminates the anonymity factor and jeopardizes the truthfulness or candor of respondents. However, it may be an important feature of the interview to see the interplay between interviewer and interviewee or to hear the dialogue as it transpires. Vocal inflections and the interview tempo may be important and suggest that the interview is properly or improperly conducted. Tape-recording or videotaping the interview memorializes the event as well. The option is to rely on one's memory of events and what was said. A tape recording permits a transcription to be generated. This transcription can be consulted at any time later to authenticate what actually was said.

When police interrogate suspects or interview witnesses, videotaping and tape-recorded interviews are most helpful and reliable. Suspects will have a difficult time later recanting confessions if those confessions are videotaped. Allegations of coercion or officer failures to Mirandize suspects can be overcome with a videotaped or tape-recorded account of the interview. Video or audio tapes are also effective when played back to juries in courtrooms.

The Use of Lie Detectors or Polygraph Tests

Although the results of **polygraph tests** or **lie detector tests** are inadmissible in criminal court proceedings, the results of these devices may provide exculpatory evidence for criminal suspects. Polygraphs are devices that measure several physical characteristics and sensory responses of someone responding to a focused interview, such as heart rate and perspiration. The most frequent use of polygraphs is to determine the veracity or truthfulness of someone who is either a criminal suspect or a witness to a crime, although polygraphs may also be used in civil proceedings. "Passing" a polygraph test is interpreted as possibly excluding that person from suspicion of lying. But polygraph tests are not 100 percent accurate and reliable. Some persons may be able to lie without exhibiting any physical characteristics indicating that they are lying. Sometimes, taking certain types of drugs or narcotics prior to responding to a polygraph test will drastically alter the results.

Interviewing May Be Dangerous

A rule cannot be written to cover every interview situation or contingency. Even the most seasoned interviewers encounter unusual situations for which there are no ready-made solutions. For instance, this writer interviewed 33 women who worked in a large Indiana bank. The interviews were conducted at the women's homes on Saturdays and Sundays, when they would be available to answer questions. One woman in her late 40s was interviewed on a Sunday afternoon. The interviewer placed a tape-recorder in the middle of the floor, started it, and then sat on a sofa in the woman's living room, opposite the woman who sat in a chair.

The purpose of the interview was to solicit these women's opinions about certain job changes that were occurring at their bank. Their work roles were changing because of the introduction of new computer equipment. The researcher wanted to know how their individual work roles would be affected. As the interviewer asked the woman various questions about her job and her interpersonal relations with other coworkers, a man burst through her front porch screen door into her living room. He cursed at the woman, calling her a whore and other unflattering names. He turned to the interviewer, called him things that would make a sailor's ears burn, and began ranting and raving about the house, breaking lamps and ceramic objects. The interviewer discreetly packed up his notes and tape-recorder and quickly left. The man burst from the house and jumped into his car. He followed the interviewer for miles, at high speed, throughout the city, until the interviewer finally lost him in a back alley. Later, the woman called the interviewer, apologized, and explained that the man was her ex-husband who had been in the war. It seems he was suffering from shellshock and had other mental problems. She had divorced him a few years back, but he continued to visit her occasionally. The interviewer had indeed picked the wrong day to conduct his interview.

In another case, a young male interviewer agreed to meet with and interview a woman in her trailer park at 7:00 A.M. one morning before she went to work. When the interviewer arrived, the 30s-something woman was dressed in a see-through negligee. She insisted on having the interviewer sit with her at the small breakfast table and have coffee. During the interview, the woman frequently changed the subject of the interview, asking whether the interviewer was married, what he did apart from interviewing, and other personal questions. She also appeared to sit provocatively. This situation made the interviewer extremely uncomfortable. The woman continued, saying that she was unhappily married to a Marine recruiter. At that point, the interviewer found some excuse to terminate the interview and made a hasty exit. While this situation was potentially compromising and conceivably dangerous, the problem was averted by the interviewer's retreat. The point is that situations like this one may occur. Interviewers may need to familiarize themselves with the exits as they might do when entering a movie theater.

Hazards are also encountered by those who conduct research in high-crime areas. More than one interviewer has been mugged or assaulted in the course of conducting research. Perhaps one reason mailed questionnaires are so popular is that they avoid certain problems that may arise in face-to-face interview situations, especially in areas of high crime or under circumstances that may jeopardize their safety. For example, some interviewers who have interviewed delinquent gang members have reported receiving threats or obscene telephone calls from various gang members subsequent to those interviews. Physical damage to an interviewer's property, such as their automobile, might occur, if interviewees suspect that the information they provide might be used against them in some way.

Advantages and Disadvantages of Interviews in Criminal Justice Research

The major advantages of interviews are:

1. They enable investigators to obtain desired information more quickly than data-gathering methods such as mailed questionnaires.

2. They permit investigators to be sure respondents understand questions and interpret them properly.

3. They allow greater flexibility in the questioning process.

4. They permit much more control over the context within which questions are asked and answers given.

5. Information is more readily checked for its validity on the basis of nonverbal cues from respondents.

It is clear that other forms of data collection, such as observation and questionnaire administration, share certain of these advantages. However, none of these offers such a unique combination of advantages as interviews. But interviewing is not without flaw. Several disadvantages of interviewing are as follows:

1. Whenever persons are asked questions in a face-to-face situation, any anonymity of response is lost. It is generally believed that anonymity heightens one's objectivity in responses given, such as is the case with self-administered questionnaires mailed to strangers. But interviews are direct. If some of the questions pertain to intimate details of persons' lives, then there is the possibility that they will not disclose some of this information to interviewers. Or if any information is disclosed, it may not be true. One of the more frequent contaminators that interferes with accurate information about people is social desirability. Social desirability is giving false, but favorable, information about oneself, either to the interviewer or on paper in a self-administered questionnaire situation. Thus, a respondent may be prejudiced toward some minority group, but if the respondent is asked whether he or she is prejudiced, he or she might say "no" simply because it is undesirable to say "yes." Therefore, respondents may say what they think the interviewer wants to hear.

2. Interviewers may become tired as they conduct several interviews during the day. Their minds may wander or they might be distracted by environmental factors. Therefore, their own reliability in recording responses accurately may not be consistent from one interview to the next.

3. If unstructured interviews are used, there is the real possibility that interinterviewer reliability may be poor. This is because each interviewer will give different priority to or show greater interest in certain topics compared with others. This makes it difficult to compare interview results from different interviewers.

4. Interviews may take different amounts of time to complete. Each respondent may prolong the interview by becoming enmeshed in certain questions or by unnecessary elaboration on particular topics. It takes considerable tact on the part of interviewers to terminate one's responses without appearing rude or disinterested.

5. If interviewers tape-record their interviews, transcribing these recordings takes time. If they make notes about one's responses, they may distract respondents with their notepads and pens.

SUMMARY

Interviewing is perhaps the most direct way of gathering information about people and their opinions. Some of the characteristics of interviews are that questions are asked directly of human subjects and their responses are given verbally. Also, this verbal information is often recorded by interviewers themselves rather than the respondents. This situation stands in stark contrast to questionnaire administration, where respondents fill out blank questionnaires and provide information under more anonymous conditions. The relationship between interviewers and their respondents is somewhat structured as well. Interviews also allow for considerable flexibility in the interviewing format, as informative dialogue often occurs between interviewers and their respondents. Unclear questions may be clarified by interviewers, or follow-ups to unclear answers provided by respondents may be made by those conducting interviews. This give-and-take feature of interviewing says much about the flexibility of the interviewing process.

Compared with questionnaires, interviews are up close and personal. Interviewers know who they interview, can observe body language and facial expressions, and can function to clarify certain information or questions. Interviews provide more in-depth information about persons that is not ordinarily provided through questionnaire administration. Interviewing also has larger response rates compared with questionnaires. Once someone has consented to be interviewed, it is rare that respondents will cease being interviewed in midstream. Thus, more information is yielded through the interviewing process, as well as a richer type of information, compared with more anonymous and superficial questionnaires, which are often mailed to respondents.

Three types of interviews are unstructured, structured, and focused. Unstructured interviews use interview guides, which are often nothing more than general topics about which researchers seek information. Interviewers require no special training in conducting such interviews, where their questions are more general and they follow the course of the interview in very much the same way that they would carry on conversations with others. Unstructured interviews may more often be associated with exploratory research, where little or nothing is known about the research subjects providing information.

Structured interviews use interview schedules or a combination of fixed-response and open-ended items and where interviewers ask respondents verbally to indicate which answers best fit them. Where open-ended items are used, interviewers ask respondents to explain certain events or behaviors, and answers may often be followed up with probes, or questions requiring more elaboration and detail. Structured interviewing usually occurs under conditions where more is known about research settings where respondents are found. Sometimes such interviews are conducted in the confines of one's workplace or home. There are no fixed time limits for interviews generally. Some interviews may take 15 minutes, while other interviews may take up to several hours. The constraints of each situation dictate how much time an interview will take to complete. If researchers are asking questions of persons in work settings, then the amount of time for interviews will be severely limited, since employers do not want their employees spending too much time away from their jobs.

A third type of interview that is sometimes used is known as a focused interview. Often investigators may wish to learn more about the effect of an intervention or the impact of an experimental variable on a particular group of research subjects. Focused interviews may probe respondents who have been supervised on electronic monitoring or home confinement, and how they felt about such supervisory methods. Innovative programs such as youth courts or drug courts may be implemented in different jurisdictions. Interviews with persons who have experienced youth courts, sometimes known as peer courts or teen courts, will yield much descriptive information about these types of programs and whether or not they are effective. Drug courts are used increasingly in different jurisdictions to alleviate criminal courts of the larger numbers of drug cases that clog court dockets. Convicted drug offenders who have participated in the therapeutic milieu of drug courts can provide much valuable information about the effectiveness of these courts in their lives. Thus, focused interviews can accomplish much, especially in evaluation research, as different interventions and programs are implemented to deal with various types of problems pervasive throughout the criminal and juvenile justice systems. Interviewing generally elicits greater in-depth information about research subjects and their particular situations or circumstances.

An alternative to traditional interviewing is conducting interviews by telephone. During the last few decades, telephonic interviewing has been used increasingly as a cheaper way of contacting research subjects and obtaining information from them. Apart from the obvious bias that only persons with telephones are contacted and that persons without telephones are excluded, telephone interviews permit investigators to conduct much of their data gathering in the privacy of their own homes or offices. Some attempt has been made to randomize telephone interviews. Therefore, random digit dialing and computer-assisted telephone interviewing (CATI) have been used. While the representativeness of samples drawn from different city and state populations is not guaranteed, such telephone interviewing strategies have made it possible for investigators to increase the plausibility that their generalizations from gathered information telephonically is more typical of the general population than attempting to call persons at random from often out-dated telephone directories. While economy and generalizability are strengths of such telephone interviewing methods, some weaknesses include the facts that interviewers do not know for sure who it is they are interviewing, and investigators are not present to observe facial reactions or other body language from respondents when particular questions are asked. Nevertheless, telephone interviews have high rates of response, as much as 75 percent or higher.

Two general functions of interviewing include description and exploration. Interviews provide enriching detail to otherwise sterile and superficial information disclosed through questionnaires. Also, areas of interest to researchers may be probed in great depth in the course of interviewing. Such probing is typically absent under standard questionnaire administration conditions. A great deal of descriptive information is yielded through questionnaires and new ideas often emerge in the course of interviewing that suggest alternative answers to investigators' questions.

Interview construction is similar to questionnaire construction. Much depends on how much information is known about the settings and persons investigators study. Researchers may opt to go with interview guides if they don't know much about their prospective respondents. Or they may add a great deal of detail and specific types of questions to interviews if they know much about the subjects to be interviewed.

The process of conducting interviews sounds simple, but it often involves careful planning and implementation. Before any information is gathered from certain research subjects, it is important for investigators to know that they have access to organizations where their respondents are employed. Sometimes this problem does not occur, if interviewees are going to be interviewed in their own homes or at neutral locations, such as public parks or buildings. Time must be taken to arrange interviews, and estimates must often be made about how much time is needed to gather the requested information. These estimates are important if there are time limitations, such as when employees are interviewed in their workplaces. Furthermore, interviewing involves some amount of training. Interviews must acquire certain skills and learn how to ask potentially sensitive questions. Also, they need to learn how to follow up certain questions with strategic probes to elicit further and more detailed information from respondents.

Sometimes field training sessions are conducted to provide interviewers with the necessary training they need to become competent interviewers. Interviewers learn what to do and more importantly, what not to do during interviews. Dressing appropriately, avoiding unpleasant mannerisms such as gum-chewing or eye-rolling, and using proper language for target audiences are important interviewer traits. Certain personality characteristics are highlighted by training coordinators as they seek to equip prospective interviewers with interviewing skills to maximize their data-gathering potential.

Under certain conditions, some investigators may use polygraphs when conducting interviews, especially with convicted persons or job applicants. While polygraph results are not admissible in court, they do give investigators general information about whether their respondents are giving truthful answers to their questions. Also, interviewing itself involves entering areas of the community where certain hazards may exist. Sometimes interviewing can be dangerous. Dangers may arise from muggers on city streets as interviewers travel to and from locations where interviews will be conducted. Sometimes those interviewed may dislike certain questions they are asked and become violent. Even relatives of those interviewed may pose dangers to interviewers if they are in close proximity to the interviewing site. Thus, interviewers are often trained on how to act and how to defuse potentially volatile situations before they result in injuries to one or more parties.

The major strengths of interviews are that they permit researchers to gather desired information more quickly and directly from respondents compared with questionnaires. Also, interviewers are there to provide instant clarification if certain questions are misleading or confusing to respondents. Greater flexibility is achieved through interviews, and interviewers exercise more control over the interviewing process. Body language and various nonverbal cues are apparent to trained interviewers so that they may judge the validity and reliability of the information disclosed by respondents. Some of the disadvantages of interviews are that they are usually not anonymous. When some persons are confronted with questions under face-to-face conditions, they may be less than candid with investigators and give false answers to questions asked. Social desirability is a likely contaminant in the interviewing process.

Other disadvantages are that if interviewers are conducting numerous and lengthy interviews during several days or weeks, they may tire of asking the same questions of respondents, and their own body language and behaviors may alienate respondents. Interviews are highly variable in terms of the amount of time taken to complete them. Thus, one disadvantage is that some interviews take too much interviewing time, making it impossible for researchers to interview others at specified times. Furthermore, transcriptions of notes or tape recordings are time-consuming. And such information is not as easily coded compared with information provided by fixed-response self-administered questionnaires.

QUESTIONS FOR REVIEW

1. What is the focused interview? What are some examples of how focused interviews may be applied?

2. What are some general differences between unstructured and structured interviews? Under what circumstances would investigators want to use each type of interview? What general kinds of research plans might be associated with these two types of interviews?

3. What is social desirability, and how might it emerge to influence respondent truthfulness during an interview?

4. What are some major functions of interviews?

5. What are some major disadvantages of interviewing?

6. What kinds of things can interviewers do to make the interviewing process go more smoothly for targeted respondents?

7. What are some characteristic features of interviews?

8. What are some differences between interview schedules and interview guides? Under what kinds of circumstances might each of these instruments be used?

9. What is a telephone interview? What are some purposes and advantages of telephone interviews? What are several potential problems with telephone interviews?

10. What are some potential hazards faced by interviewers, especially those who conduct research in high-crime neighborhoods?

11. What is random-digit dialing? How is it useful and what types of problems does it overcome?

12. What are probes? What advantages are associated with probes?

13. What is meant by in-depth interviewing?

14. What are some general guidelines for dressing and preparing for interviews? What are some of the characteristics of good interviewers?

15. What are some potential problems facing interviewers who wish to interview persons at their workplaces? How is gaining access to organizations problematic for interviewers?

16. How much time should be taken to conduct interviews? How does the interviewing process itself modify any time constraints that may exist?

CHAPTER

7

Data Collection Strategies IV: Observational Techniques and the Use of Secondary Sources

CHAPTER OUTLINE

CHAPTER OBJECTIVES

As the result of reading this chapter, the following objectives should be realized:

1. Understanding the major purposes of observation as a data-gathering tool.
2. Describing different types of observation, such as participant and nonparticipant observation.
3. Learning about the advantages and disadvantages of observation, as well as different forms of observation.
4. Understanding the various functions and purposes of observation.
5. Discussing the mutual impact of the observer on the observed and the observed on the observer.
6. Learning about the various types of secondary source analysis.
7. Describing the importance of autobiographical and biographical information about persons as data sources.
8. Describing the nature and usefulness of content analysis and its importance for disclosing information about persons and organizations.
9. Understanding the usefulness of canned data sets available to researchers for hypothesis testing and theory verification purposes.
10. Describing meta-analysis and its advantages and disadvantages as a data-gathering tool.

Introduction

This chapter focuses on two broad classes of data-gathering tools available to researchers. The first set of techniques involve observation, usually of persons in their natural settings such as workplaces or in social groups. Observation is generally known as field research. Whenever researchers immerse themselves in the settings they observe, they are engaged in field research. They may either participate in the activities they are observing, or they may observe from a distance, independent of the activities they observe. Thus, either participant observation or nonparticipant observation may be used.

The second class of data-gathering tools covered in this chapter involves the examination of information yielded from secondary sources. Such information may include public documents, letters, autobiographical works, research articles from journals, newspaper reports or opinion pieces, and any other published or written information compiled. This information may or may not parallel closely the investigators' own research interests. Nevertheless, examining such information may yield considerable data that has research value. Such information is usually free and thus attracts the interest of investigators who are working with limited budgets. Furthermore, research subjects seldom need to be contacted directly in order to access such information. Investigators have the advantage of learning about the existence of all types of documents and other published information, and they can tailor their own research objectives to fit whatever information exists for analysis.

Rivaling interviewing as the most direct access to information people possess is observation. In the broadest sense, researchers are constantly observing human conduct. Whether investigators are distributing questionnaires in the classroom or listening to remarks made by interviewees, they watch others and their expressions. They carefully scrutinize the circumstances under which their investigations are conducted. Sometimes, these researchers learn more by watching people than by recording whatever they say.

This chapter opens with an examination of observation as a major data collection tool. For criminologists and other social scientists, observation is much more than sitting in some social setting watching others and their behaviors. Criminologists using observation for data collection purposes are often trained to look for certain kinds of behaviors and to structure their observations of others according to specific guidelines or rules. Therefore, scientific observation differs from casual observation in that it is focused and linked closely with one's research objectives. Like marks made by respondents on questionnaires, observers code and classify their observations in order to make sense out of whatever they observe. Observers may either participate in the activities they are observing, often as actual group members, or they may be nonparticipant observers looking at the actions of others. Thus, a distinction is drawn between participant and nonparticipant observation. Each of these types of observation is examined and their respective weaknesses and strengths as research tools are listed and described.

The next part of this chapter examines data collected by others, usually for purposes unrelated to immediate investigator interests. Besides observing others, researchers may inspect various resource materials in libraries or elsewhere. Government publications, especially those produced by the Bureau of Justice Statistics and other federal agencies, are quite useful to investigators as information sources. Any information compiled by others, including public, government-sponsored, research publications or reports or analyses made by private organizations, is lumped under the umbrella term **secondary source analysis.**

Usually, public or private data have been collected for other purposes by different agencies, and such information may not necessarily coincide with the immediate interests of investigators. These sources may include statistical information about different segments of the population (e.g., the police, probation/parole officers, agency expenditures, types and numbers of court cases processed and case outcomes, and labor turnover rates for different organizations or institutions) and any other available, published material.

The major purposes of secondary source analysis are presented. Several important types of secondary sources are listed and described. Some of these types of secondary sources include archives and historical accounts of events. Other types of secondary sources may encompass autobiographical and biographical information, letters, diaries, and various types of governmental or private organizational records. During the last several decades, the Freedom of Information Act (FOIA) has been used to enable investigators to obtain copies of information that was once unavailable to the public. However, changing laws and political pressures have made some of this information available to research scrutiny and analysis. The general advantages and disadvantages of secondary source analysis are described.

The chapter next examines content analysis, or the intensive perusal of documents in systematic ways to glean information from document contents. More than a few investigators are using content analysis today as a method of acquiring insightful information about people and events. Content analyses of different kinds of documents and publications enable researchers to track interesting topical trends over time. The general uses of content analysis will be identified as well as the advantages and disadvantages of this data collection method.

Increasingly made available free or at minimal cost to the general public and criminologists are canned data sets. These are large data sets containing much valuable information about certain populations, such as juvenile delinquents, prison inmates, probationers and parolees, corrections officers, police agencies and personnel, and the courts. Much of this data have not been analyzed, simply because it is so time-consuming and costly. Therefore, government organizations are hopeful that criminologists and others will assist them in deriving much valuable information from these data sets compiled from previous years. The advantages and disadvantages of using information from canned data sets will be listed.

The chapter concludes with an examination of meta-analysis, a technique that involves an analysis of a large number of published articles on specific topics. Although some quantification is used in meta-analysis, interesting patterns and trends concerning various persons and organizations are disclosed. The major strengths and weaknesses of meta-analysis are discussed.

What is Observation?

In order to appreciate the distinctiveness of **observation** as a data-gathering tool, we must distinguish between observations of a casual nature or those that might be by-products of one's investigations, and observations that are used exclusively and fundamentally for data-gathering purposes. It has often been said that those using observation are probably seasoned, which means that they know pretty much what to expect in advance of their observations. This comes from having been there before, regardless of the types of studies being conducted. Most serious observers have some firsthand, on-the-scenes contact with studies they are conducting. If properly conducted, observation is characterized by the following:

1. Observation captures the natural social context where persons' behaviors occur.
2. Observation grasps significant events or occurrences that might influence the social interactions of participants.
3. Observation determines what makes up reality from the worldviews, the outlooks, and the philosophies of those observed.
4. Observation identifies regularities and recurrences in social life by comparing and contrasting data obtained in one study with those obtained in studies of other natural settings.

These characteristics of observation set it apart from casual, sporadic, and spontaneous observations made by researchers as they conduct their investigations with other types of data-gathering tools. These characteristics also highlight the distinction between **observational research** and experimental social research. In experimental research, observations are made, but events have been deliberately manipulated to effect certain results. Observational research, in contrast, seeks to preserve the natural context within which observed behaviors occur.

Major Purposes of Observation

The major purposes of observation in criminological research are:

1. To capture human conduct as it actually happens, to permit us to view the processual features of behavior. Whenever persons are interviewed or respond to questionnaires, these are more or less static glimpses of how people think and feel about things. Most observers claim that the difference between what people say and do is great. Observation reflects a dimension of reality that is untapped by other data-gathering methods.

2. To provide more graphic descriptions of social life than can be acquired in other ways. Thus, observation supplements the factual information disclosed from other data-gathering methods. For example, we may describe delinquent behavior in terms of its incidence or frequency. However, observational methods may reveal what delinquents actually do to get into trouble. How do juveniles go about vandalizing businesses and homes, taking drugs, or stealing automobiles? Observation enriches our descriptions of social life and enables us to illustrate behaviors more graphically. Triangulation involves the application of two or more data-gathering tools (e.g., combining interview data with questionnaire and observational information) when investigating a particular subject area. Observation may be combined with other data-gathering strategies to provide us with a more complete picture of the behaviors of others.

3. To learn, in an exploratory sense, those things that should receive more attention by researchers. Often, observational findings suggest topics for future research that were unanticipated by investigators when their studies were commenced.

Types of Observation

Two major types of observation are described here. These are participant observation and nonparticipant observation.

Participant Observation

Participant observation is the structured observation of social settings of which the observer is a part. This is a popular form of observation, since researchers may find it convenient to describe the settings wherein they work or the groups in which they have membership. One of the best illustrations of participant observation is some research by James Marquart (1986).

Marquart (1986) participated in a project designed to evaluate correctional officer training, supervision, and turnover in the Texas prison system. While working on his doctorate in sociology in 1979, Marquart met with officials connected with the Texas Department of Corrections (TDOC) and explained his interests. The TDOC had recently been involved in highly publicized litigation involving allegations of brutality against inmates. One of Marquart's study objectives was to observe actual officer–inmate interactions to determine whether these allegations were true. Also, he wished to describe the "building tender system," or the pattern in many prisons of using more dominant/aggressive inmates to control other inmates.

Marquart became a prison guard in the Eastham Unit (a pseudonym), a maximum-security facility housing 3,200 prisoners over age 25 who had been incarcerated three or more times. Although Marquart acknowledged some difficulty being accepted by the prisoners and other prison guards, he was eventually able to build rapport and acquire both guard and inmate trust. An example of one of his guard experiences describes the enriching detail that can only come from participant observation. In this case, the use of force by other guards was obviously excessive, but both prisoners and guards alike seemed to accept its occurrence. One of Marquart's guard associates recalled the following:

> "I was sitting at the Searcher's desk and Rick [convict] and I were talking and here comes Joe [convict] from 8-block. Joe thinks he knows kung-fu, hell he got his ass beat about 4 months ago. He comes down the hall and he had on a tank top, his pants were tied up with a shoelace, gym shoes on, and he had all his property in a sack. As he neared us, Rick said, 'Well, Joe's fixing to go crazy again today.' He came up to us and Rick asked him what was going on and Joe said they [staff] were f---ing with him by not letting him have a recreation card. I told him, 'Well, take your stuff and go over there to the Major's office,' and there he went. Officer A went over and stood in front of Joe, so did Officer B who was beside Joe, Officer C was in back of A, and two convicts stood next to Officer A.
> Inmate James, an inmate who we 'tuned up' in the hospital several days before, stood about 10 feet away. All of a sudden Joe took a swing at Officer A. A and B tackled Joe. I ran over there and grabbed Joe's left leg while a convict had his right leg and we began kicking his legs and genitals. Hell, I tried to break his leg. At the same time B was using his security keys, four large bronze keys, like a knife. The security keys have these points on them where they fit into the locks. Well, B was jamming these keys into Joe's head. Joe was bleeding all over the place. Then all of a sudden another brawl broke out right next to us. Inmate James threw a punch at Officer D as he came out of the Major's office to see what was going on. James saw Joe getting

beat and he decided to help Joe out. I left Joe to help Officer D. By the time I got there (about 2 seconds), Officer D and about six convicts (building tenders) were beating the s--- out of James. Officer D was beating James with a blackjack. Man, you could hear the crunch noise every time he hit him. At the same time, a convict was hitting him in the stomach and chest and face. These other inmates were kicking him and stomping him at the same time. It was a wild melee, just like being in war.

I got in there and grabbed James by the hair and Officer D began hitting him, no love taps. He was trying to beat his brains out and yelling, 'you mother------, you think you're bad, you ain't bad, you mother------, son of a b----, you hit me and I'll bust your f-----' skull.' I think we beat on him alone for 10 minutes. I punched him in the face and head. Then Officer D yelled, 'Take him [James] to the hospital.' Plus we punched and stomped him at the same time. At the hospital, Officer D began punching James in the face. I held his head so D could hit him. Then D worked James over again with a blackjack. We then stripped James and threw him on a bed. D yelled at James, 'I'm going to kill you by the time you get off this unit.' Then D began hitting him in the shins and genitals with a night stick. Finally, we stopped and let the medics take over. James had to leave via the ambulance. Joe required some stitches and was subsequently put in solitary."

This was clearly a dimension of prison life Marquart saw that most researchers with conventional research instruments might never see. Can you imagine a formal interview in the home of one of these officers: "Do you hit inmates with your blackjack?" "Do you use excessive force on any inmate to obtain his compliance with prison rules?" How many officers are going to admit to that? Few, if any.

Marquart's participation as a prison guard made him very much aware of some of the shortcomings of participant observation. As a guard, his relationships and rapport with inmates was changed accordingly. Because of his status, he would not become privy to certain types of inmate information. Interestingly, he might have acquired some "guilty knowledge" about drug use or other rule violations, but he did not report such infractions to authorities. He believed that this "guilty knowledge" created an ethical dilemma, although he attempted to walk the fine line of civility and legality. Additionally, much of the brutality he witnessed was difficult for him to accept emotionally. Also, since others knew that he was not "really" a guard, his views of what occurred may have been manipulated by other guards to a degree. However, Marquart believed that he had acquired sufficient credibility and was honest enough to solicit true reactions from those with whom he worked.

Nonparticipant Observation and Unobtrusive Observation

Another type of observation is **nonparticipant observation.** Nonparticipant observation is structured observation of others with or without their knowledge, and without actually participating in the behaviors and activities being observed. In this situation, researchers conduct observations of various social settings from the sidelines. Their observations of others may or may not be known to those being observed.

For example, Humphreys (1970) and his associates observed homosexual exchanges that occurred in the restrooms of public parks. They secreted themselves in these restrooms where they had a vantage point to see possible homosexual interactions. They observed numerous occurrences of homosexual behavior, followed certain persons and obtained their automobile license numbers, and determined their identities and residence information. Later, some of those who had been seen committing homosexual acts were visited by researchers on some other pretext. Humphreys claimed that although this type of observation raised certain ethical questions, it nevertheless provided him with valuable data about attitudes concerning homosexuality from those he observed.

Many nonparticipant observers believe that the naturalness of the settings they observe yields more accurate information about social reality than what we might expect from contrived experiments in laboratory settings. Observing persons in their natural habitats is certainly not demanding on any investigator, and **field notes** may be taken to record one's observations. Field notes are simply written entries in a field diary to refresh one's memory about what has been observed. Field research, or any research conducted in the natural habitat of those observed, builds upon whatever is observed and the interpretations we make of these observations.

In recent years, for example, criminologists have focused increasingly on citizen fear of crime and how it affects citizen behaviors, such as feeling safe in one's neighborhood; traveling from one location to another, especially during evening hours; and a general contentment with life in the community. Irene Carvalho and Dan A. Lewis (2003) decided to study the phenomenon of fear of crime by conducting interviews and field observations of 69 welfare recipients in the greater Chicago area. They selected these persons because they were most likely to live in less prestigious neighborhoods where crime might be most prevalent. According to previous research, these persons might be expected to exhibit a high fear of crime. Actually, the research of Carvalho and Lewis subsequently identified several unexpected reactions to neighborhood crime among those observed. Although some fear of crime was found, most residents observed and interviewed exhibited either anger or an ordinariness that tended to dilute the dangers of crime, so that many residents tended to feel safe even in crime-ridden and gang-controlled neighborhood environments. For instance, two subjects' responses typified the responses of others who tended to regard neighborhood crime and violence as something that is prevalent everywhere. One 36-year-old resident said,

> "I don't think I need to move. All neighborhoods are dangerous in one way or another. I used to think I should move to the suburbs, but really, they have the same things going on here . . . it's just more secret."

Another respondent, reflecting anger, said,

> "I don't like this neighborhood. I don't like my neighbors. There's always something going on outside my house. But I guess that's how it is wherever you go. It ain't safe nowhere. I just don't like it. I like the suburbs better."

Several persons said they feel safe in their gang-controlled neighborhoods, and that gang members may actually protect them from other dangers that otherwise might exist if it were not for the gang presence. When asked if she were afraid of the neighborhood, two residents said,

> "I like this neighborhood. This is a beautiful park, but sometimes, people cross . . . some guys don't like these guys here and they come and shoot. . . . Kids can come out and play, no problem with that. But if you mess with them, turn to them, call them names. . . . Nobody likes that."

"No, not of anything! If I'm scared, I'd move! The guys (gang members) are very protectful, they don't hurt you. What they do, they do, sell their things, but they have respect for the elders, no matter what color you is. 'How are you, ma'am?' and all. They watch who comes in the neighborhood. They keep this safe. They fight in the weekends because it's when they have parties. Otherwise, they don't bother anyone. They're cool." (Carvalho & Lewis, 2003, pp. 792, 795–796)

As nonparticipant observers, a team of trained researchers conducted in-depth interviews with and observations of a sample of welfare recipients in a conversational style, after reassurance about the confidential nature of the conversation. The purpose of their observation and discussions with residents was to understand the place and role of specific events in respondents' lives by prompting recounts in the first person and positioning these events within the context of daily experiences. The following topics were selected for observation and casual conversation and were included in extensive field notes that were compiled: daily routine, concerns for life, experiences with welfare, sources of satisfaction, and goals for the future. Extensive notes were taken by these researchers that characterized the physical and social settings of respondents' neighborhoods of residence; descriptions of the block and immediate surroundings (adjacent blocks); litter on the ground; condition of buildings; lawns and yards; block physical upkeep; vacant lots; abandoned houses and cars; visible people; and social activity (Carvalho & Lewis, 2003).

As we have advanced technologically, it is now possible to record what is observed through video cameras. Such observations may be done secretly, so that those observed will be unaffected by the intrusion of cameras into their social interactions. Several different law enforcement agencies, such as the FBI, have used videotaping to record illegal activities. The effectiveness of sting operations has been enhanced through videotaping, as criminals are filmed in the act of committing various crimes. Criminologists have used videotaping for diverse purposes. For example, some criminologists have videotaped citizen reactions to vandalism. In one instance, an unattended automobile parked on the street was broken into by paid stooges of the researchers, and reactions of passersby to this breaking and entering were photographed. Several interesting observations were made about citizen apathy or noninvolvement in events that affect others. Certain theories about victimization and public response to being victimized can be recorded and tested.

Advantages and Disadvantages of Observation in Criminological Research

Both participant and nonparticipant observation are not physically demanding on investigators. Some amount of skill is required, however, in order to record whatever is observed accurately. Nonparticipant observers may choose their settings at will, as well as the times when their observations will be conducted. Thus, there is great flexibility associated with this data collection method. Observed behaviors may be either anticipated or unanticipated. Unanticipated observations may form the basis for new research into previously unexplored areas. Observing what is anticipated may enhance theory verification. Observation is also a cheap method of acquiring data. It costs little or nothing to look at others.

An investigator's choice of participant or nonparticipant observation often depends on the nature of the research being conducted. If private clubs, gangs, prisons, or other "closed"

BOX 7.1   PERSONALITY HIGHLIGHT

JAMES W. MARQUART
Sam Houston State University

Statistics: B.S. (law enforcement administration), Western Illinois University; M.S. (sociology), Kansas State University; Ph.D. (sociology), Texas A & M University.

BACKGROUND AND INTERESTS

At this time I am pursuing several research interests that involve victimology, underage drinking, recidivism among institutionalized delinquents, and racial integration in prison organizations. My foremost interest, however, involves anything related to staff and inmate behavior in prison settings.

As a part of my undergraduate work, I was required to do an internship in a criminal justice agency of my choosing. I opted for a co-ed juvenile facility not far from my home in the Chicago area. I was absolutely fascinated by the staff, the delinquents, and the society that they created. I learned many things and I am, by the way, a total advocate of student internships.

I took this experience and pursued my master's degree at Kansas State University. I worked as a graduate assistant in an Introduction to Sociology class and one of the students had a relative who was the warden at the Missouri State Penitentiary in Jefferson City. Arrangements were made for me to work as a guard during my first summer of graduate school. I worked the cell houses, prowled the yard, and supervised inmates in various work areas. This was an amazing experience. I saw firsthand how the guards and cons got along in an old-style "American Big House." For my thesis, I interviewed a number of prison officers at the Kansas State Penitentiary and had a chance to talk with several old-timers who participated in the Hickock and Smith executions described in Truman Capote's work, *In Cold Blood.* Hickock and Smith were drifters who murdered a farm family, including the mother, father, daughter, and son, in Kansas in a most brutal way. They mistakenly believed the father, who was a successful businessman, had considerable money hidden in his home. They were wrong. In anger and to leave no witnesses behind to identify them, they systematically murdered the four innocent persons with guns and knives. Subsequently, they were apprehended, tried, convicted, and hanged for their crimes.

BOX 7.1   CONTINUED

RESEARCH INVESTIGATIONS

It was at Texas A & M University that I took full advantage of my growing interest in prisons. My mentor, Ben Crouch, opened my eyes and many doors, especially in the Texas prison system. We were both fascinated by the Texas prison culture and why these prisons had low rates of violence. He encouraged me to work as a prison officer, which I did for nearly 2 years. My doctoral dissertation was based on my time spent in a correctional uniform. I collected over 2,000 pages of field notes, and the bulk of these notes detailed the structure of formal and informal social contact within a Texas penitentiary.

I continued to study how prisons work, how they change, and the consequences of imprisonment on inmates and staff. I researched the impact of judicial intervention on prisons, staff use of force to control inmates, and inmate snitch networks. I returned to Texas in 1986 and Dr. George J. Beto, former head of the Texas Department of Criminal Justice, suggested to me an idea that I regard to this day as "one in a million." Whatever happened to the capital offenders who received commutations as the result of the *Furman* decision? [*Furman v. Georgia* (1972) was a landmark U.S. Supreme Court case that led to a 4-year suspension of the death penalty in all jurisdictions because of irregularities and racial discrimination in how the death penalty was imposed by juries in capital cases. One result of *Furman* in many jurisdictions where the death penalty was used was that inmates on death rows had their sentences commuted to life, with the possibility of parole. Many former death row inmates were subsequently paroled. The death penalty was reinstated in many jurisdictions following another landmark U.S. Supreme Court case, *Gregg v. Georgia* (1976), where a bifurcated trial procedure was implemented to minimize or eliminate the impact of racial factors in death penalty cases.]

Several colleagues and I conducted extensive research on these former death row offenders, as well as those whose sentences were commuted to life under the post-1976 capital punishment statutes. My interest in prisons still remains, and most recently I conducted research for the Texas Department of Criminal Justice about inappropriate staff–inmate relationships. Findings from this research formed the basis for a training video for new correctional officers. Also, a colleague of mine and I produced a research report for the Texas Youth Commission that was used by the state legislature.

I have never had a "pet theory" to guide my work. I follow and advocate one theme—do research that matters. My career is based on conducting research that impacts public policy. Above all, relax and have fun, because it is only a career, not your complete life.

ADVICE TO STUDENTS

My advice to students is to "keep your options open." Learn about interviews, agency data, secondary data, primary data, surveys, experiments, and any other datadredging methodology. Learn and understand qualitative and quantitative methods and get to know as many statistical techniques for data analysis as possible. The more tools you have in your box, the greater chance to make a contribution to public policy.

organizations are to be studied, it is necessary to penetrate these settings either obtrusively or unobtrusively. James Marquart became a prison correctional officer temporarily in order to gather information about officer–inmate interactions. Frequently, researchers will go "underground" to infiltrate groups or organizations they plan to study. This may be the only way such phenomena may be studied scientifically. On other occasions, researchers may have to solicit the help of others to become informants for them as group or organization members. Juvenile gangs may be studied, for instance, by enlisting the cooperation of one or more gang members to report on gang activities and member behaviors. The use of key informants is one method whereby researchers may obtain access to restricted organizations and acquire greater knowledge about them.

The researcher's gender may influence what is studied and how it is studied. For example, Jackie Wiseman (1970) was interested in studying Skid Row alcoholics. Wiseman had several choices. She could walk up and down Skid Row, make random observations, conduct random interviews with alcoholics and street people, and generally conduct conventional interviewing and nonparticipant observation. She could pretend to be an alcoholic and attempt to "blend in" with other Skid Row inhabitants as one of them. Or she could enlist the aid of one or more Skid Row people and use them as key informants. Wiseman's observations are insightful here, as she explains how she resolved this data-gathering problem:

> "On Skid Row, observations were made both by myself in the company of a paid 'guide,' and by paid male observers. My observations were confined to those activities in which a woman can take part on the Row without causing undue comment—walking around during the day, sitting in bars, eating in cafeterias, cafes, and shopping in grocery stores.
>
> Four male observers walked the streets of Skid Row with the men at night, stood talking to them on the street, drank in taverns with them, and met them at the bars returning from jail. These observations were spread in time through one year. Findings were further supplemented by published observations of the Skid Row area by other researchers.
>
> On Skid Row, I passed as a woman friend of a presumed resident there, as a woman looking for a lost boyfriend, and as a woman who had returned to the area after some absence and was looking for a bartender friend. In Christian Missionary prayer meeting and in free soup lines, I merely joined the men and few women recipients. At the various screening sessions held at stations on the loop, [police officers] were kind enough to allow me to sit in and pass as a secretary who was taking medical notes.
>
> In the Jail and the State Mental Hospital, no attempt to pass was made for two different reasons: in an all-male world like the jail, it would be virtually impossible; in a calmly coeducational and research-oriented environment like the State Hospital, it seemed unnecessary. The first night at the Hospital, when I was introduced to the men in one of the alcoholic wards, they gallantly included me in a late night party based on food raided from the kitchen. From then on they treated me as one of the family.
>
> However, while there were a greater many scenes I could observe, it became apparent that as a woman, or as a researcher, access was denied to some areas of the loop. Especially acute problems were presented by the County Jail and the Christian Missionaries (in addition to Skid Row at night where a woman attracts attention no matter how innocuously she is dressed).
>
> For these three areas, as well as a fourth (the courts) where time was at a premium, observers were hired. In jail, at the Christian Missionaries, and on Skid Row they were participant observers, unknown to their subjects as researchers. Recruiting observers for the Jail posed several problems. Obviously, I could not ask someone to commit a crime so as to be sentenced to the County Jail. On the other hand, there was a need for someone who could participate unnoticed in prisoner activities. The decision was to recruit within the jail. Young men who were

not in jail for alcoholism were selected. There were four observers in all. These men were not used simultaneously, but two were observing and recording for three weeks and then two others working for the same period of time approximately six months later—some time after the first two had been released. In this way, it was hoped that collusion between observers would be prevented." (1970, pp. 276–277)

Therefore, Wiseman effectively blended several different strategies—use of key informants, participant observation, the use of volunteers, and simple nonparticipant observation—to obtain her data. She was able to collect considerable data from her own observations and experiences as well as from those she paid to observe others.

Some of the limitations of observation as a data-gathering tool are that (1) the desired events to be observed may not occur; (2) certain actions of those observed may be wrongly interpreted by observers, since they are not directly involved with what is going on; (3) the observed behaviors may be atypical of the normal behaviors of those observed, given the time when the observations are conducted; and (4) it is impossible to ask those observed for explanations of their conduct, with disclosing one's identity as an observer. Two additional limitations are (5) the impact of the observer on the observed; and (6) the impact of the observed on the observer.

Impact of the Observer on the Observed

The Hawthorne Experiments.   A classic illustration of the impact of the observer on those being observed is the small-group experiment conducted in two rooms. One room, the experimental setting, contains a small group seated around a table. A one-way mirror is on one wall in the room, and it is known by those observed that one or more observers are viewing them from an observation booth or room on the other side of the mirror. Theoretically, those being observed eventually ignore others that are watching them, and thus, they behave more naturally. Critics of such experimentation indicate that those observed cannot possibly ignore that they are being observed. Thus, their actions are restrained or inhibited. They cannot act normally, since they are not in a normal setting, unhindered by observations made of them by others. A major criticism of such small-group research is that it is contrived and not indicative of real-world conditions. Experimenters counter by arguing that such settings are ideal, since they are uncluttered with extraneous factors that might otherwise jeopardize the naturalness of actions or behaviors of those observed. Both views have some validity.

An early study where observation was used, and where the influence of the observer on the observed was significant and eventually apparent, was the classic **Hawthorne experiment.** This experiment consisted of a series of studies conducted at the Hawthorne, Illinois, plant of the Western Electric Company. This company manufactured telephone components. One experiment involved observations of workers who were wiring telephone equipment. Experimenters manipulated the number of rest pauses of these workers, the times when they took their lunch breaks, and even room temperature.

One experiment, known as the illumination experiment, involved the use of a dimmer switch in the work area. Experiments believed that worker productivity would increase if the lighting intensity in the room was raised. An observer sat in the room and watched workers perform their jobs. As the room was made brighter by raising the lighting intensity, worker productivity climbed. Experimenters argued accordingly that if the room lighting were decreased, productivity would drop also. Thus, they dimmed the lights, although productivity continued to increase. Eventually, the room was lighted with the equivalent of moonlight, and worker productivity hit an all-time high. Later, workers disclosed in interviews that, while they didn't know the purpose of these experiments, they believed the company wanted them to produce as much as possible, even under conditions of moonlight. They believed that the entire company was watching them as an example. Thus, they deliberately worked hardest when conditions of work were most adverse to them. This phenomenon became known as the **Hawthorne effect,** and currently, such an effect is used to explain certain behaviors of those observed when they know they are being observed by researchers.

Too Up Close and Personal.   Another dimension of the impact of observers on the observed occurs whenever observers are actual participants in the social events observed. If observers are a part of the social situation they are observing, they may be too close to the situation to retain their objectivity about it. Furthermore, their own input into what is going on may actually influence the behaviors of others in ways that detract from the naturalness of these settings. Therefore, participant observers may (1) develop friendships with certain group members they are observing, and these friendships, in turn, may prevent them from accessing information about others; or (2) observers may profess to believe various things about group ideas and goals, and these beliefs may alter the belief systems of those being observed.

   In most groups, group members have closer attachments to certain persons in the group more than others. If observers become accepted by and closer to specific group members, this association may automatically restrict them from close access to other group members. For example, John may like Allen and Fred, but John may dislike and be disliked by Gene and Gary. If the observer, Tom, becomes close to John, he may be able to learn much from John, as well as Allen and Fred. But Gene and Gary see Tom's association with John, Allen, and Fred as choosing sides. Gene and Gary will not disclose anything to Tom, simply because of his associations with others Gene and Gary do not like. Gene and Gary may have important information about the group that Tom needs to know, but Tom will never acquire this information because of his previously developed friendships with John, Allen, and Fred. This oversimplification illustrates an important point about participant observation. That is in the normal course of social interaction, the observer becomes co-opted into certain cliques or groups. These cliques or groups may be socially isolated from other cliques or groups in the social setting. While it is an objective of the observer to get close to those being observed, such closeness may become a social liability for interactions with others in the same group.

Impact of the Observed on the Observer

Observers may cause those observed to say and do things that are strictly for the benefit of the observer. It is presumed that if persons know they are being observed, then they may behave according to whatever they think the observers expect to see. For example, if school teachers are being evaluated by their principals or supervisors, they may dress especially nice for these occasions. Furthermore, they may prepare canned lectures or lessons that highlight their particular teaching skills. Thus, observers develop impressions of these teachers that may or may not be accurate portrayals of their average teaching conduct. There is every reason to believe that if observers make their presence known to others, the validity of whatever is observed may be seriously questioned. This is a phenomenon similar to social desirability, where those observed behave in ways they believe are anticipated or expected by observers.

Although this problem was not addressed in their research of police officers on patrol in two large cities, Robin Engel and Robert Worden (2003) conducted fieldwork by using trained observers who rode along with police officers during their entire shifts in the Indianapolis, Indiana, and St. Petersburg, Florida, police departments. These researchers wanted to find out whether the officers they observed actually put into practice certain principles of community policing that the departments were attempting to implement. Furthermore, these investigators attempted to glean from officers' comments and behaviors certain attitudes toward their departments, their supervisors, and community policing generally. The investigators found only weak support for the view that how officers do their jobs is positively related with their occupational attitudes. Apart from these findings, the situations under which these officers were observed and interviewed by civilian researchers raise interesting questions about the accuracy of data yielded. It is unknown whether these officers disclosed to Engel and Worden or their research associates information that was deliberately doctored by these officers to fit what the citizen observers wanted to see or hear. But in an era where police conduct is under continuous social scrutiny, it is possible that officers being observed by civilian researchers might behave differently or say things that are different from their real thoughts or beliefs simply because of the fact that they are not alone but in the company of "outsiders."

Observers may cause those observed to exaggerate or distort their natural behaviors. Another type of influence observers exercise upon the observed is that their own presence may reinforce certain behaviors. If observers are attending a political rally or religious meeting, their own presence may in fact heighten the emotionally charged gathering. Therefore, whatever is observed may be an exaggerated form of behavior that would not occur but for the presence of the observer. These types of behaviors may or may not occur, depending on the circumstances. There are no direct ways of assessing how observers influence the behaviors of others in these contexts. The same phenomenon occurs in conventional, face-to-face interviewing as well.

For instance, in a study previously cited in an earlier chapter, Giordano and colleagues (2003) investigated a sample of serious male and female officers who were incarcerated as juveniles and studied by these investigators 13 years later. Among other of their research objectives, these researchers wanted to know whether one's peer contacts over time had changed their behaviors from crime to more law-abiding activities. It was evident from the questions these different respondents were posed by researchers that the focus of attention was on the influence of significant others in the lives of these persons and whether their lives had changed as a result.

From the outset, respondents quickly learned what these researchers were interested in learning. One question posed by researchers was whether marriage (for those persons who had married) was influential in changing their lives toward more law-abiding modes of social conduct. The conditions under which interviewing was conducted were not necessarily ideal. More than a few respondents were interviewed with their spouses present. In some of these cases, former delinquents disclosed things about themselves and their former delinquent peers that were previously unknown to their spouses. Some spouses reacted with shock, although the "shock" reaction was downplayed with playful dialogue or joking retorts, such as, "Just wait until I see your friend, Jack, again!" While it is unknown whether the presence of spouses or others during these interviews influenced the responses given, we can't help but wonder whether respondents may have been pressured to say things that they thought interviewers wanted to hear.

Investigators who use observation of any kind as a data-gathering tool should be sensitive to their own influence upon those who are observed. Attempts should be made to inform readers about any influence their presence as observers may have had on reported findings. As we have seen, observation can be an excellent source of enriching detail to supplement otherwise drab statistical presentations and summaries of tabulated information from questionnaires. One general vulnerability of observation is that it often lacks well-established, coherent, methodological protocol for its implementation. The benefits of its use in criminological research are realized only to the extent that its users are skilled and aware of its potential as well as of its limitations.

Analysis of Secondary Sources

It is possible to engage in research projects without having any direct contact with human subjects. Some investigators spend their entire professional careers studying secondary sources. Secondary sources are any information originally collected for purposes other than their present scientific one.

The Major Features of Secondary Sources

Secondary source materials are characterized by the following:

1. Secondary source materials are ready-made. Any student may visit a local school or public library to discover a vast amount of ready-made data available for analyses of any kind.

2. Secondary source materials have been collected independent of an investigator's research purposes. Researchers seek out secondary sources that contain some or all of the information they might need to answer their research questions. Often, research projects are designed around available information from secondary sources. Thus, one's research is tailored to fit existing data sets. This is different from formulating a research project in advance, and not knowing whether data are available that can answer one's research questions.

3. Secondary sources are not limited in time and space. This means that investigators who use such sources did not have to be present when and where these data were gathered.

Types of Secondary Sources

Archival Records.   One of the most common sources of information are historical archives. Libraries maintain vast records and archival data available to interested researchers. Governmental agencies also compile and maintain records of criminal acts and other relevant information. For example, Marc Riedel and Tammy Rinehart (1996) studied murder clearance rates for Chicago during the period 1987–1991. They determined that murder records and homicide reports are sent to the Illinois Department of State Police. These reports, known as Supplementary Homicide Reports (SHRs), are maintained as Victim Level Murder (VLM) files. The Department of State Police is the state repository for crime statistics. Riedel and Rinehart eventually studied 3,066 single-victim murder cases reported by the Chicago Police Department.

Riedel and Rinehart searched these murder archives conducting an **archival analysis** in an effort to determine whether the murders were committed concomitant with another felony, such as a burglary, robbery, or rape. Sometimes this research is referred to as the **historical method.** Information was also obtained about whether the murders occurred as the result of brawls or arguments. These investigators cross-tabulated murders where concomitant felonies were committed with those in which the circumstances were unknown. Clearance rates were compared with these variables as well. Riedel and Rinehart eventually established several interesting correlations. For instance, they found that if the conditions that govern the acquisition of information about victim race, gender, and weapon are independent of those that govern information about circumstances, then:

1. Clearances will not be related to victim race, gender, and weapon, but will be related to circumstances.
2. The relation between circumstances and clearance status will remain generally unchanged when victim, race, gender, and weapon used are introduced as controls.
3. The presence or absence of circumstances information will not be related to victim race, gender, and weapon (1996, p. 98).

Riedel and Rinehart (1996) concluded that cases involving missing data on circumstances may represent a variety of murders characterized by a lack of clearance-relevant information. However, the limitations of the data set prevent further testing of hypotheses drawn from these interpretations.

The Riedel-Rinehart study utilizing the Chicago Police Department archival information about murders highlights an important disadvantage of using archival information generally. That is, the information has not been collected for research purposes, such as those contemplated by Riedel and Rinehart. Therefore, these investigators could only proceed so far with their analysis of the data. While they wanted to learn more about the phenomena they were studying, they were limited to existing recorded information.

Another study involving the use of historical documents was conducted by Mitchell Chamlin and Steven Brandl (1998). Chamlin and Brandl were interested in studying the historical evolution of vagrancy laws. They focused on Milwaukee, Wisconsin, largely because of the facts that Milwaukee is an older city; has experienced rather typical changes in its ecological structure; the records collected and maintained by the city and police department are unusually detailed and complete; and longitudinal data for vagrancy arrest are not readily available for other cities.

Chamlin and Brandl examined historical records from 1930–1972. They correlated vagrancy arrests with unemployment and available sociodemographic information. They were interested in testing several propositions generated by the research of William Chamblis and his associates. Chamblis has argued, for instance, that vagrancy statutes and their

BOX 7.2   PERSONALITY HIGHLIGHT

SALLY S. SIMPSON
University of Maryland

Statistics: B.A. (sociology), Oregon State University; M.A. (sociology), Washington State University; Ph.D. (sociology), University of Massachusetts.

BACKGROUND AND INTERESTS

Most of my research has been conducted in three interrelated areas: corporate crime, gender and crime, and criminological theory. Although it may not be obvious, what ties these interests together is a fundamental interest in social stratification. While an undergraduate at Oregon State University, I became interested in what was then a subfield of sociology—criminology. This was also a time of student protests (the Vietnam War, gender and race discrimination) and in my studies I was introduced to conflict theory, theories of social stratification, and minority relations.

It was not until graduate school, however, that my long-standing criminological interests began to encompass gender and corporate/organizational behavior. At Washington State, I had a wonderful organizational theory class that made light bulbs go off. I also wrote a paper on women's prisons that lead me to the early feminist writings of Dorie Klein, Meda Chesney-Lind, and Chris Rauche (among others). What a find! When I took a break from graduate school after receiving my M.A., this budding interest in women's prisons helped me gain a temporary teaching position at Gonzaga University in Spokane—where I developed a Women and Society course.

Returning to graduate school in Massachusetts after 2 years of teaching (8 months at Gonzaga and 1 year in Spain for Troy State University), I had the opportunity to work with Anthony Harris who had written an insightful piece on gender and deviance theory in the *American Sociological Review* (1977). Harris argued that the "sex variable in some form has not provided the starting point of all theories of criminal deviance has been the major failure of deviance theorizing in this century." Indeed! My own work in criminological theory (some with coauthor Lori Elis) has explored similar themes, challenging mainstream theorists as well as those on the left to consider the ways in which gender, race, and class intersect to affect behavior (*Criminology,* 1989, 1991, 1995; *Journal of Criminal Law and Criminology* 1994). I have also used Harris's typescripts theory to explain gender differences in juvenile justice processing (Sealock & Simpson, *Justice Quarterly,* 1998) using data from the second Philadelphia cohort study.

Also at U-Mass, I began to apply organizational theory to the criminal behavior of corporations. My dissertation research examined the relationship between firm, industry, and national economic indicators and antitrust offending. Specifically, I wondered whether some of

BOX 7.2 CONTINUED

the common explanations for criminal offending (poverty and strain) were applicable to corporations (profit-squeeze) and, if so, for what types of offenses (e.g., mergers, price-fixing, advertising violations)? I put together a database that tracked the antitrust offending of 52 randomly selected U.S.-based manufacturing companies over 55 years of economic activity, drawing from a variety of archival and secondary sources (e.g., FTC Case Decisions, Trade Cases Blue Book, Moody's, Census of Manufacturers, and the Historical Statistical Abstract of the United States). What I found was that industry-level economic growth *and* decline affected offending levels, with growth associated with more trivial offenses and decline predicting serious antitrust criminality (*American Sociological Review,* 1986). I also discovered that macro economic indicators (e.g., unemployment rates and aggregate stock prices) and political regime (Republication administrations) increase aggregate antitrust behavior (*Social Forces,* 1987). When I joined the faculty at the University of Maryland, a graduate student (Chris Koper) and I updated and refocused the dissertation research to examine specific deterrence among these firms. Corporate deterrence is a subject that has drawn much discussion and speculation but very little empirical investigation. Our results found little support for the deterrence model (*Criminology,* 1992). We then turned our attention to intraorganizational characteristics of firms by identifying the CEO or president of the company and tracking his or her background and training; how long he or she had been with the company, the goverance structure of the firm, when the CEO/president took control, and so forth). Overall, we found that antitrust offending increased when firms were headed by CEOs with finance and administrative backgrounds (relative to sales and marketing, legal, and other training), a turnover in top management decreased offending while the pursuit of produce dominant strategies increased antitrust levels (*Journal of Quantitative Criminology,* 1997).

All of my corporate crime research up to this point involved either the analysis of secondary/archival data or the development of case studies (archival data coupled with some interviews with top- and middle-level managers). This work convinced me that more theoretical and empirical work was needed to understand the etiology of corporate crime. I also realized that data are sparse in this area and, when data do exist, the quality is poor. This realization led me to conduct a series of vignette studies using corporate managers and managers in training to learn more about what perceptual factors are taken into consideration when criminal opportunities arise.

The vignette research not only emphasized etiological factors related to offending, but crime prevention and control as well (Simpson & Elis, *Journal of Research in Crime and Delinquency,* 1995; Paternoster & Simpson, *Law and Society Review,* 1997). Results from both vignette surveys are reported in *Corporate Crime, Law, and Social Control* (Cambridge University Press, 2002). Generally, this research has found that managers are more sensitive to informal sanction threats such as loss of reputation or discipline while on the job than formal sanction risks (i.e., getting caught and sent to jail). Many will not offend because they are morally dissuaded from doing so. I also learned that managers care more about their own sanction and discovery risks than those of the company, but both sets of risks affect decision making. Finally, situational factors—such as being ordered to violate the law by a supervisor or gaining a market advantage over competitors—also factor into the offending decision. The theoretical im-

BOX 7.2   CONTINUED

plications of this research suggest that explanations for corporate offending must take micro, organizational (meso), and structural (macro) considerations into account. Popular explanations for corporate offending, such as low self-control or greed, are overly simplistic and lack empirical support (Simpson & Leeper-Piquero, *Law and Society Review,* 2002).

ADVICE TO STUDENTS

Be actively engaged in your studies. Find something that piques your interest and explore as much as you can about the topic. Discover the ways in which other disciplines make sense of the topic. Interdisciplinary approaches will enhance your understanding of a phenomenon. Develop an appreciation for different theories, methodological approaches, and epistemologies. You will be a better and more critical scholar for it. Finally, do not work in isolation. Collaborate with others. Share your ideas and enthusiasm for a subject.

codification and subsequent modification reflect changes in the social and economic structure of political units. Specifically, vagrancy laws have been used throughout history to control the criminal propensities of those who refused to accept low-wage employment.

Chamlin and Brandl (1998) examined all vagrancy arrests during the 1930–1972 period as recorded in the *Directory and Report of the City of Milwaukee, 1930–1973.* They consulted other concomitant records for population data, including the *Population of Milwaukee, City, County, and Minority: 1800–1990* and *The U.S. Census.* On the basis of their analysis, they concluded several things about vagrancy statutes. They found, for instance, that where demand for labor is low, vagrancy arrests decreased. They also found that during World War II, a 68 percent reduction in arrests for vagrancy occurred in Milwaukee. Several other interesting propositions were tested using this archival data.

Personal Documents and Biographies.   Other sources for data include various historical documents, biographies, autobiographies, letters, and other writings. This information doesn't always have to be historical. Contemporary biographies of criminals and influential political figures can provide interesting insights into the motives that promote criminal behaviors. But biographies are not always used to portray famous or infamous personalities. Sometimes studies, such as **biographical information** about persons who are institutionalized in mental hospitals, might enable investigators to test certain psychosocial theories. Alison Brown (2003) studied numerous biographies of disturbed persons, including certain prison and jail inmates who were punished for reasons related to their psychological conditions or states. Brown was able to investigate different punitive responses toward criminal offenders by examining their biographies. She studied the influence of antisocial tendencies and conscience upon the processes of criminalization and conflict. Her work has led to a greater understanding of the social and structural location and construction of crime.

Brenda Geiger and Michael Fischer (2003) used the biographies of eight female ex-prisoners, ages 32 to 52, who were living in a hostel for released female inmates under the auspices of the prison rehabilitation authority. The investigators wanted to learn more about the process of identity negotiation among female inmates who were separated for long periods from their young children, and who eventually lost them. The women were asked to reconstruct their biographies retrospectively to account for their crimes and drug addiction, with regard to the sexual, physical, and economic abuse they had endured, and to the offspring for whom they are expected to provide. When these women were required to acknowledge their failings as mothers, all biographical reconstruction, external blame, and accusation collapsed. Viewing themselves through their children's eyes, these female offenders were unable to negotiate the identity of incompetent mothers. They were generally unable to confront the anger of their children toward them or explain why their children have abandoned them. Considerable insight into their criminality and the consequences of it was derived as the result of studying their individual biographies.

Another use of biographical information is to understand the various habits of inmates from previous eras, and the relation between their personal habits and what eventually led them to lives of crime and incarceration. For instance, Philip Gura and colleagues (2001) studied the biographies of 300 inmates from the Massachusetts State Prison who had been incarcerated between 1829 and 1831 in an effort to understand them and their criminal motives. Records of these inmates were preserved over time and transcribed and annotated by prison officials. Details of their ages, races, upbringing, education, drinking habits, and types of offending were insightful in accounting for their incarceration and subsequent adaptation to prison life. Gura and colleagues were able to relate their experiences to Jacksonian America and disclosed significant details about 19th-century prison reforms. Furthermore, these biographies, which portrayed prison conditions and daily prison regimens of prisoners, were useful in understanding the reorganization of the Massachusetts State Prison that occurred in 1829.

Sometimes biographies of interesting criminal personalities serve to enlighten us about existing social and economic conditions. For instance, John Touhy (2001) studied the biography of Roger Touhy, who was a Chicago gangster. Roger Touhy was heavily involved in organized crime and ruled a strong criminal empire in Chicago during the 1920s. Subsequently, he was convicted in 1933 for a crime he didn't commit, and he eventually escaped from prison 11 years later. He was recaptured and again imprisoned. Eventually he was released, but he was murdered by rival gang members to prevent him from reclaiming his former power. Explicit depictions of the Chicago underworld were disclosed by his biography, particularly during the period known as the Prohibition Era.

Biographies might also be used to describe particular types of prisoners in institutional settings. For example, Diana Medlicott (2001) examined the biographies of various prisoners housed in a large British prison during the 1990s. She wanted to learn more about the high suicide rate of the prison and the conditions that may have contributed to these rates. Through her collection of biographies of prisoners who knew many of the inmates who committed suicide, she learned a great deal about the process whereby inmates become suicidal and transform their thoughts into action. Her research led to the development of a **typology** of suicide behavior, including how time and spatial deprivations affect an inmate's sense of self.

Autobiographical information has also been used to characterize and describe pedophiles and their sexual behaviors. The work of Feierman (1990) is an anthology demonstrating a cross-cultural, cross-species, and cross-historical approach to adult/nonadult sexual behavior that gives new insights into the biosocial roots of pedophilia as it occurs in industrialized societies. Feierman includes several autobiographies and clinical assessments of known pedophiles as a means of depicting their actions and providing explanations for them.

Social events can be explained or interpreted by paying attention to autobiographical information. For instance, Jack Henry Abbott, twice-convicted murderer and former inmate of a Marion, Illinois, federal penitentiary calls the facility "the belly of the beast" (Abbott, 1981). His autobiographical depiction of his confinement is most illuminating for researchers who wish to characterize prison settings and describe the lives of certain inmates. Other autobiographies of prisoners have led to illuminating details of their lives while incarcerated. For instance, the Feminist Press (2002) has examined the extensive autobiographies of women confined in different prisons throughout the world. Through an analysis of the writings of 37 female inmates confined in prisons in different countries, the investigators were able to learn a great deal about how these women not only survive but also transcend the prison experience.

Not all biographical and autobiographical research is related to criminals and their experiences. For instance, Tom Tripodi and Joseph DeSario (1993) wrote their autobiography describing the efforts of American special agents working for the CIA, Drug Enforcement Administration, Federal Bureau of Narcotics, and the Bureau of Narcotics and Dangerous Drugs to combat organized crime and illegal drug trafficking. They described the French Connection, government corruption, the FBI under J. Edgar Hoover, and anti-Castro operations.

Also, Helen Stapinski (2001) conducted a detailed study of the autobiography of a young girl who grew up among swindlers, bookies, and other types of criminals in New Jersey during the mid-20th century. She learned a great deal about how the girl coped in this extensive criminal milieu and avoided becoming a criminal herself.

Using autobiographical materials, Walter Rucker (2001) examined various conjurers among slaves during the early 1800s in the United States. He discovered that many of these conjurers claimed to possess supernatural powers, including the ability to communicate with the spirit world, the power to heal the sick, and other feats that garnered for them both fear and respect among many slaves. Interestingly, these conjurers played an important role in inciting American slaves to revolt and to resist their subjugation at the hands of powerful land owners and merchants. Thus, through an examination of autobiographical records, Rucker learned a great deal about the revolutionary consciousness among slaves during the pre-Civil War period.

Some persons have written about their lives as members of notorious youth gangs. Reymundo Sanchez (2000) has written about his daily gang life on the streets of Chicago, and his personal reasons for joining the Latin Kings, a notorious gang with national connections. He has provided much insightful information into why youths join gangs, what they derive from gang associations, how the gang rules and rituals serve to bind members to the gang for life, street survival tactics, and the gang's relationship with the police.

Finally, some autobiographical information has been examined to chart trends over time relating to social problems and public policies. For instance, Ian Loader and Aogan

BOX 7.3   PERSONALITY HIGHLIGHT

Peter Kirby Manning
Northeastern University

Statistics: B.A. (sociology), Willamette University; M.A., Ph.D. (sociology), Duke University; M.A. hons., Oxford University.

BACKGROUND AND INTERESTS

Art, it is said, is a matter of choices—what to show, what to leave out. And bad art is thus a series of bad choices about omission and commission (de Botton, 2004). Ethnography based on fieldwork is often like that, too—observations, stories, side involvements, and other commitments are left out. The author hides behind the data. To be an ethnographer, nevertheless, is to situate oneself in a world with others. Perhaps one wants to understand the place of selves or being in relation to other things in the world rather than the place of oneself in the world (Levi-Strauss, 1973).

What does this mean for a qualitative researcher? Partial revelations. I heard once that field workers write about or reveal the second worst thing that happened to them in the field, and so any report is selective. Most ethnographic work, close-up observation of doings, is based on occasioned insights, writing about a series of recalled images. If *X* is the case, what were the conditions producing it? Life must be lived forward, Kierkegaard wrote, but unfortunately is understood, like ethnography, backwards. Written ethnography in this sense is a backward glance that at best dimly illustrates an imagined future. The idea of coherent, detailed, factual, and orderly sets of field notes is a useful fiction, but it rarely exists in my experience.

It has taken me considerable time to realize that the world is an awesome, mysterious, and complex place that no one does or can understand. The writers who have most captured my attention and passions have accepted this as a fundamental premise. Yet, what we do as social scientists is a kind of doubling act—we are creating and constructing a meaningful world while accepting the limits of insights and the constraints of worlds beyond our control and understanding.

Studying sociology for me was both a freeing and coruscating process—freeing from my father's distance; my mothers' confusing, complex, ambiguous haze of words and emotions; and my western upbringing. I consumed it until it consumed me. Anything beyond the Rocky Mountains, for a person born and living in Oregon, was the East. I found out later that people in the East referred to anything west of Nebraska as "out West." The East was so distant, known only through stories of visits by others (there was no television in Portland at this

BOX 7.3   CONTINUED

time), that it could have been Mars. A series of schools east of the Rockies shaped my life: post-Oregon Duke, Oxford, and Michigan State. In schools, I learned to be a scholar and an academic. I was 24 with two young children when I was granted a Ph.D. As a close friend once told me at a party, "Most people learn by experience, Peter, but you have to figure something out intellectually and return to the world to locate its truth."

I was not trained in graduate school to do field work. Three major ideas have given me hope—the dynamic psychology of Freud (I keep a picture of his study including his cluttered desk on my own desk); the complexity of situated performance drawn from Erving Goffman (this idea highlights tensions between appearance and reality); and the limits of illusion of authority. I traced out some of the variations and interdigitation of these ideas first in Peru, then in London, and again in Oxford. When I was asked first to write about my career (in 1975—the book never saw print), I found a central question troubled me: How do people make authoritative decisions in conditions of uncertainty? In that circumstance, answers are neither factually available nor impossible to identify. A social situation of interest for me as a scholar must contain risks, and the probability of unwanted negative consequences. I like being around risk-takers. Some risks, of course, are sought with glee. Remembering the past, I realize that my fascination with the peasants in the highlands of Peru, English police officers, the engineers and mathematicians who were ensuring the safety of nuclear reactors in the United Kingdom, arose because they were mysterious figures, performers. Their words conveyed little to me (I did not trust words), and I sought to connect words to actions. I work back from actions, accounts, displays, and recipe knowledge, not forward from a theory or a preconceived paradigm. Social scientists cannot predict, and when they try to do it, the result is often disastrous. But we can capture a moment well.

Some of my literary heroes were vulnerable and adventurous men who lashed out at the world in a lonely fashion—Gustave Flaubert, T.E. Lawrence, and Ernest Hemingway—their words connecting them to others at times, and at other times, failing them completely. I admire, too, Proust, the voice of memory, who wrapped himself in a cork room with his words. He was a most sensitive and yet ironic observer who could little tolerate the world at large yet wrote the most penetrating fiction of the past century. These writers scorned those around them as frightened, untrustworthy, and at times devious. Their words built a slightly comforting yet shabby protection for them, as I think my words have given me. Erving Goffman, our most brilliant social scientist, darted in and out of life, peeking up across the trenches at little performances, seeing their deeply requisite situational features (deference, compliance, contriteness, forgiveness), while arguing for the temporarily meaningful configuration as our ground.

As a person, I appear to be upbeat at times, and at other times, distant. My oldest daughter Kerry once said "my dad sometimes disappears." I find at parties I either must dominate or shrink, finding the edges to observe, watching and listening unobtrusively. Painful experiences lead me to retreat as I did to England for most of the 1980s and in so doing, I almost lost my career as I had lost my marriage. I read works of profound and profoundly lonely men—T.E. Lawrence (1936) and Saint Exupery (1932, 1940, 1942), searching for clues, trying to figure out how to live the good and just life.

BOX 7.3   CONTINUED

These exposures, drifts through time and place, have become part of my data over the years as are the notes I take from books, my memory, which serves me well, my field notes, and of late the reflections upon books I expected to read (classics, for the most part) earlier but did not. Reading is relaxing because I manage only a few tracks of thinking when reading (the pages of the book, the books' ideas, the sounds and colors around me, and other things, great and small, that are troubling). Otherwise, I often find I am managing several tracks, and appear distant from others and distracted. I am rarely fully in the world, and resist engagement powerfully.

I like probing the connections between lies and trust, the fragile shell that keeps us in chaotic motion, and I seek to analyze a little patch of order and ordering. A sentence. A little conversation. An aporia or an epiphany, a momentary connection. Doing this allows me to combine innocence with distrust, and ultimately, requires a leap of faith. This "leap," or maybe it is merely a hop, is based on the assumption that I can make sense of these "patches" in ways that communicate to others and so connect myself. I feel a desperate sense of pessimism about the raging, ravaging, ongoing injustices of this society, but feel little capacity to alter them.

The idea of a reputation was an unfamiliar one to me until I was well into my career. Reputation, such as it is, seems to me to be more consuming than elevating; more erosive and insidious than comforting, and more a burden than a blessing. Having said that, I think I do what I do because I cannot do otherwise. Although I believe in the idea of choice, it is an elusive one. I am an aesthete, yet I disdain this pose. I see a figurine of Freud on my home desk, a gift from my youngest daughter, see his cigar in his outstretched hand, and know that he died a very painful death of cancer of the jaw. Above my desk at school is a wooden carved Simon Bolivar and he speaks to me with the words of Marquez from his labyrinth.

ADVICE TO STUDENTS

Advice? A young scholar ideally should obtain a classic liberal arts education, including language, history, some philosophy, and literature. Learning to write is also necessary. It is a craft and refining it takes time, effort, and patience. Sustain a critical attitude toward the world. We live in an ideologically shaped, belief-sodden world that requires mature distance and scrutiny, but a questioning posture must be gained from the ground up, not the other way around. Go out into the world and listen, watch, inquire, and keep your eye on things that are out of sight. If this is not bad art, perhaps I have left out the right things.

References: Alaine de Botton (2004), *On the Art of Travel.* New York: Vintage International; T.E. Lawrence (1936), *Seven Pillars of Wisdom.* New York: Doubleday Doran; Claude LeviStrauss (1973), *Tristes Tropiques.* London: Penguin; Gabriel Marquez (1936), *The General in His Labyrinth;* Antoine de St. Exupery (1932), *Night Flight.* New York: Harcourt and Brace; Antoine de St. Exupery (1940), *Wind, Sand and Stars.* New York: Reynal and Hitchcock; Antoine de St. Exupery (1942), *Flight to Arras.* New York: Reynal and Hitchcock.

Mulcahy (2001) examined the autobiographies of 10 chief constables, either serving or re- tired, who were affiliated with either the Metropolitan Police of London, or the Cheshire, or Greater Manchester Constabularies. The chief constables disclosed information dating back to 1945, and chronicled events from post–World War II England to the present. These investigators found, for example, that chief constables were regarded during the 1950s and 1960s as police heroes, and they were powerful and essential local figures. Subsequently, during the 1980s, a more corporate and generally liberal police voice was established. De- spite these different depictions of how chief constables have been viewed over time, it is clear that chief constables, at least in the jurisdictions studied, continue to rise above political debate and argue for or against social policies and crime on the basis of their professional expertise and judgment, and that the citizenry continues to respect their views.

Gaining Access to Records: The Freedom of Information Act.   Not all public records are open to the public. When President John F. Kennedy was assassinated in 1963, for in- stance, records about that incident were subsequently sealed. One important reason for seal- ing these records was to protect the identities and respect the privacy of witnesses who gave testimony. When Martin Luther King, Jr., was assassinated in 1968, the records surround- ing his assassination were similarly sealed. Subsequently, the **Freedom of Information Act (FOIA)** was passed. The FOIA permits private citizens to access information about them- selves, others, and certain events, including assassination data.

Among the various provisions of the Act, agencies that collect data on individuals are required to inform the individuals that such information is being gathered, to explain the pur- poses for the data collection, to tell them whether disclosure of information by them is mandatory or voluntary, and to provide them with other similar protective warnings (National Association of Attorneys General Committee on the Office of Attorney General, 1976).

There are several restrictions and exemptions. For instance, investigatory records com- piled during civil and criminal enforcement proceedings are exempt if their production would deprive a person of a fair trial or impartial adjudication. Some information may con- stitute an invasion of privacy. Other exempted material would be the disclosure of inves- tigative techniques and procedures, disclosure of confidential sources of information (informants), or any information that might endanger law enforcement personnel (McIn- tyre, 1986; Riedel, 2000).

Under the FOIA, information about former FBI Director J. Edgar Hoover has been dis- closed to researchers. The secret files maintained by Hoover demonstrate his interest in col- lecting derogatory information about prominent Americans, such as Eleanor Roosevelt, John F. Kennedy, Martin Luther King, Jr., and others (Theoharis, 1991). New revelations about Hoover's investigative techniques reveal his obsession for retaining his position and discrediting his critics. Interestingly, certain sociologists and other social scientists were once targeted for intensive FBI scrutiny at the direction of Hoover. W.E.B. DuBois and C. Wright Mills were among several prominent social scientists who espoused a Marxist tra- dition in American sociology that thrives today. But at the time, these individuals were sin- gled out for intensive investigation, and as a result, they were marginalized from mainstream society because of FBI excesses (Keen, 2004).

Inmates and others also have a right under the FOIA to obtain their presentence in- vestigation reports, although some of the contents of these reports may be censored because of confidentiality provisions relating to probation personnel or informants (Shockley, 1988).

Ordinarily, access by prisoners to their presentence investigation reports has been tightly restricted by federal courts and government officials.

There is practically no limit to the sorts of materials that can serve the purposes of scientific exploration. From the most private items, such as personal letters, diaries, logs, and appointment books, to the most systematically accumulated and distributed documents such as the publications of the U.S. Census Bureau, a bewildering array of information awaits investigators.

Secondary sources may be either public or private. Public data sources are most frequently national agencies and departments that publish and distribute information relative to their functions and goals. All types of data are compiled. Any public information source is directly accessible by researchers, and ordinarily, research costs associated with obtaining their data are low. Private sources include voluntary agencies or associations, bureaus, and societies. These organizations also publish and distribute data about their functions and goals, usually as technical reports or bulletins. Such information may or may not be distributed to all libraries. Often, researchers must do some detective work to determine whether certain types of information are available and where such data may be obtained.

Advantages and Disadvantages of Secondary Sources

The major advantages of analyzing secondary sources are:

1. There is considerable savings of time and money, since ready-made data are analyzed and are accessible to the public.

2. Information compiled often pertains to large aggregates of people and their characteristics. Thus, generalizations to larger populations have greater legitimacy than those based on relatively small samples of elements.

3. Information from secondary sources may be triangulated with information obtained through interviews, observation, and questionnaires to yield more reliable data.

4. Researchers avoid potential ethical problems and harm to human subjects by studying documents rather than people directly.

The major disadvantages of secondary source analysis are:

1. Data have been collected for other purposes and may be incidentally related to the researcher's goals and interests. Specific questions that researchers would prefer to ask may not be included in available data.

2. There is no way researchers can reconstruct missing data in available secondary sources. Nonresponse in secondary source materials is a "given," and the incompleteness of information may be an important limitation that can affect data reliability.

3. Researchers must often speculate about the meaning of phraseology in various documents, and they lack the opportunity of obtaining further clarification from respondents.

4. Researchers must devise codes in order to classify the contents of documents analyzed. If their analyses are conducted over time, it is possible that missing information may exist to frustrate their coding efforts.

In sum, the use of secondary sources in criminological research is widespread. The strengths of using secondary sources far outweigh any limitations or disadvantages. Secondary source materials are often used to supplement one's research efforts where alternative data collection procedures are used. Therefore, an additional, inexpensive mechanism exists for bolstering a study's internal and external validity. External validation is important because it pertains to a study's generalizability to other settings and elements. A close correspondence between what is generally known about a given topic as revealed by data in secondary source materials and the information disclosed by a given study attests to the study's generalizability. Internal validity reflects the study's quality and internal consistency. Thus, information derived from questionnaires may be compared with various secondary source materials as a means of verifying its accuracy and dependability.

Content Analysis

When investigators have targeted their research objectives, and if these objectives may be achieved in full or partially through the analysis of secondary sources, these researchers may engage in **content analysis.** Content analysis is the systematic qualitative and quantitative description of some form of communication. Thus, the contents of communications of different kinds are examined for the purpose of discovering patterns and meanings.

Some Examples of Content Analysis

Shadd Maruna's Study of Desistance from Crime. Content analysis is used frequently in criminological research. For instance, Shadd Maruna (2004) used content analysis to investigate transcriptions of tape-recorded interviews with 100 British citizens who had formerly spent time in prison for a variety of crimes, mostly drug-related and property-offending. Life story interviews were given by these persons and their oral replies were tape-recorded and subsequently transcribed, thus yielding a vast amount of written information. Each session lasted approximately 2 hours, and investigators subsequently used the Content Analysis of Verbatim Explanations (CAVE) system to analyze the subjects' responses. The CAVE system has been used in studies of depression, precursors of mental illness, and the success of presidential candidates. It is an innovative method for measuring the cross-event consistency in the explanations provided by individuals for both positive and negative events in their lives.

In Maruna's (2004) research, he wanted to understand more about the various events in one's life that would cause ex-offenders to cease their criminal activities and become law-abiding. Thus, his research investigated the desistance process. What is the psychological mindset that seems to best support efforts to go straight and maintain a desistance from crime? Based on self-report information, Maruna found that of the 100 participants, 55 of them had been classified as desisting from crime. All of these persons were former long-term, habitual offenders, but who at the time of their interviews with investigators had been crime-free and drug-free for over a year. These persons also reported that they have no future plans to engage in criminal activities. At least 34 of the remaining 45 persons indicated that they were persistent offenders, still active in their criminal behavior. They reported recent criminal activity and their explicit plans to continue selling drugs, robbing convenience stores, and other criminal activities.

Maruna (2004) and his research associates coded collected material according to certain rules, and from his observations of the contents of these transcriptions, he was able to learn much about persisters and desisters. He recorded negative and positive events and made interpretations of them. For instance, a positive event might be, "I love working with computers." The explanation given was, "Because it's like I can be myself now." A negative event and the explanation included, "I wanted to get a job when I got out of prison, but I went back to crime." The explanation given was, "'Cause it's the only way I know how."

Thus, Maruna (2004) used these narratives to provide support for his idea about why persons desist from criminal activity. One interesting facet of Maruna's research was that the replies given by these respondents suggested that subsequent research on this topic should focus on offender neutralization, where offenders' attributions for positive life events can be explored and linked with criminal desistance. Within the context of neutralization theory, for instance, criminologists have long been interested in whether offenders accept internal responsibility for their actions or blame these events on external factors. His findings from the content analysis made of these offenders' narratives suggest that equal attention ought to be paid to other dimensions of cognition related to controllability.

Green, Gabbidon, and Ebersole's Study of African American Presence in Delinquency Textbooks.   Frequent use is made of content analysis relating to the contents of textbook materials and differences in topic coverage. A study by Helen Green, Shaun Gabbidon, and Myisha Ebersole (2001) was conducted of some of the leading textbooks in juvenile delinquency published between the years 1997 and 2000. These investigators wanted to know about the amount of African American scholarship present in these texts, whether portrayals of African Americans was negative or positive, and interpretations made of African American youths involved in delinquency.

The researchers noted in their literature review of available materials and similar analyses of such textbooks in previous years that much content regarding African Americans was influenced by racism and prejudice, and that the social, economic, and political impact on the lives and treatment of these people has been deemphasized by mainstream scholarship. These authors noted, for example, that previous examinations of textbook contents relating to African American representation and portrayals of such persons with photographs and other depictions have disclosed that African Americans have been underrepresented, and that coverage of racial variations in crime and delinquency has been inadequate. Five issues were examined by these investigators. They included conceptualization of race, visual depictions of African Americans, interpretations of black crime, inclusion of African American scholarship, and African American issues related to the administration of justice.

Using content analysis, these investigators conducted searches by topic of electronic versions of delinquency textbooks in print. The available database yielded 21 textbooks. Several of these textbooks were excluded for various reasons, and the investigators eventually narrowed the scope of their content analysis to eight delinquency texts published between 1997 and 2000. Several trained researchers examined each book's contents according to the different criteria outlined above. Thus, **interrater reliability** was evaluated to ensure that different reviewers of a book's contents were consistent.

Some of the findings of their content analysis were quite interesting and show how content analysis can yield insightful information about the contents of different types of literature or writing. For instance, researchers found that all eight textbooks published scholarship from African Americans. Regarding photographs as illustrations, 114 photos were of African Americans. Forty percent of these photos were positive portrayals of African Americans, while 43 percent were negative portrayals. About 17 percent were neutral, while the remainder could not be classified according to the adopted content analysis scheme. It was disclosed that the most common explanations provided for African American delinquency stressed racial bias and socioeconomic status. These explanations were followed by social disorganization and family structure considerations. Very little discussion of the historical context of African American involvement in the juvenile justice system was provided by any of the books analyzed, although most had a section dealing with race/ethnicity and delinquency.

On the basis of their content analysis of these textbooks, these investigators concluded that there were adequate discussions of the social dimensions of race, more negative than positive images, and inadequate coverage of African American scholarship. More negative than positive images of African American juveniles seemed to reinforce stereotypical depictions of racial/ethnic relationships with delinquent behavior generally. Glaring omissions of significant work by minority authors, such as Becky Tatum, were detected. Thus, content analyses can disclose not only what a book contains and how minorities are portrayed, but it can also disclose important omissions as well. One negative depiction of African Americans was the photo of a young African American boy in a casket with the following caption: "African-American males are five times more likely than white males to be homicide victims. This young boy was the victim of a drive-by shooting." In the opinions of these investigators, they believed that the photo was used for "shock value" and had no place in an academic-oriented textbook. One general conclusion reached by these investigators was that authors of juvenile delinquency textbooks as well as other types of texts for academic markets should present more balanced portrayals of African Americans and other minorities already suffering from excessively negative portrayals in American society. These writers propose that if the present trend continues, it might be better for publishers of these textbooks to either carefully screen or exclude photos from these textbooks altogether.

Content analysis is conducted under a variety of circumstances and for different research purposes. For instance, Aysan Sev'er (2002) used content analysis to study women who left their abusive partners using a sample of 39 survivors of domestic abuse from Toronto, Canada. Contents of in-depth, face-to-face interviews with these women were examined to disclose important information and insights into women's experiences of abuse; children as targets and witnesses of abuse; general strategies used by these women for survival; positive and negative social support systems; and debates about women's own aggression against their partners.

Phyllis Gerstenfeld, Diana Grant, and Chau Pu Chiang (2003) conducted a content analysis of 157 extremist websites on the Internet, where two raters were used to analyze different sites that promoted racism, violence, hatred, and other extremist views. Some sites were operated by groups or organizations, while other sites were established and maintained by particular individuals. Interestingly, these investigators found that almost all of these sites had links to other extremist sites where persons could easily find and read similar extremist materials. About half of all sites analyzed contained racist symbols. Although a third of all sites disavowed racism or hatred, one-half of all sites included multimedia content and a third contained supremacist literature. The authors concluded from their content analysis of these sites that the Internet is an extremely powerful tool for extremists as a means of reaching potentially large extremist audiences and reinforcing their stereotypical views.

Content analysis was used by Klaus von Lampe, who studied the conceptual history of organized crime in Germany and the United States during the 20th century. He conducted a content analysis of the *New York Times* and *Der Spiegel* during the period 1896–1995 and determined that the term *organized crime* was coined in 1919 in Chicago. Germany included organized crime in its ongoing policy debates during the 1960s. He found that both the content and meaning of organized crime has undergone transformation over the last 50 years. He identified two important trends. One is the extension of the geographical scope of organized crime from a local to a global frame of reference. The second trend was the narrowing down of the social scope from a systemic to a dichotomic view of organized crime and society. von Lampe found also that while initially organized crime was perceived to be an integral facet of big-city life, eventually organized crime and society came to be viewed as antagonistic entities, culminating in the image of global criminal players who challenge even the most powerful countries. But he added that the imagery of global mafias that dominate public perception stands in stark contrast to the very broad conception of organized crime that appears in criminal statutes and law enforcement guidelines.

Alejandro del Carmen and Elmer Polk (2001) applied content analysis to some information they had collected relating to academic employment trends in criminology and criminal justice. They did a longitudinal content analysis, where they surveyed job listings for criminology and criminal justice positions during the 1995–1999 period. The primary purpose of their research was to identify areas of specialization and expertise most commonly desired by hiring departments and agencies or required by employing institutions. They also wanted to explore trends in employment by geographical region, timing of advertisements, department or program area, type of employer, and type of position available. They analyzed a total of 636 job advertisements from the *Chronicle of Higher Education,* a weekly publication containing a comprehensive source of employment advertisements in an array of academic disciplines.

On the basis of their content analysis of these advertisements, they disclosed the facts that individuals seeking an assistant professor position are likely to encounter employers seeking a minimum academic qualification of a Ph.D. Employers are also likely to seek assistant professors with no specific area of concentration, or generalists. Also, employers are likely to be housed in criminology/criminal justice departments located at 4-year universities. Individuals seeking employment as an assistant professor are most likely to find job advertisements and openings during the months of October–November of any given year, and from academic institutions located in the eastern part of the United States. These investigators suggested that those interested in conducting similar analyses of job advertisements might want to focus on recruitment techniques employed by community colleges and whether the advertisements are the same or different from those placed by 4-year universities.

Yet another study using content analysis was conducted of fraudulent practices by health care physicians and was conducted by Brian Payne and Charles Gray (2001). Payne and Gray studied detailed reports of 246 reported home health care offenses and abuses between 1993 and 2000. These reports were compiled as part of a general Medicaid fraud report. These researchers found that home health care professionals commit offenses that are similar to, yet different from, those committed by doctors. Fraud control units appeared to be using traditional policing strategies to detect and investigate home health care abuses. Furthermore, these investigators found that the process for prosecuting and sentencing these workers is similar to the process for handling other offenders. Ultimately, these investigators were able to provide support for both conflict and general systems theory. Thus, content analysis may be used as a method to investigate the predictive utility and accuracy of particular criminological theories that purport to explain criminal conduct or any type of illegal activity.

An interesting use of content analysis has been applied by Stephen Webster (2002), who examined the contents of victim apology letters written by convicted child molesters and rapists. Webster obtained a random sample of apology letters from convicted child molesters and rapists and analyzed them. The letters were written by sex offenders in the English Prison Service Sex Offender Treatment Program. A total of 32 child molesters and 31 rapists participated in the research. An integral part of the treatment program for these offenders consisted of writing letters of apology to their victims and families. These letters were prepared during the 9th and 10th weeks of offender programming. Webster was able to identify and assess changes in sex offenders' levels of victim-specific empathy following the therapeutic intervention of the sex offender treatment program.

Finally, an example of content analysis used to investigate public and media reactions to a widely publicized tragedy is found in the work of Glenn Muschert (2002), who studied mainstream news coverage of the Columbine High School shootings of 1999. Two youths armed themselves with semi-automatic weapons and killed or wounded numerous students at Columbine High School in Littleton, Colorado. The data for Muschert's content analysis consisted of 728 articles from ABC, CBS, CNN, PBS, the Associated Press, *New York Times, Time,* and *Newsweek.* An online database search over the Internet provided article contents for Muschert's analysis.

Muschert (2002) found, for example, that the media appeared to be more interested in covering the reactions to the crime, such as the police investigation and community reactions, rather than the crime itself. Other significant themes disclosed by content analysis included commentaries, consequences of the shootings, and discussions of the Columbine event. He was able to identify at least two contradictory themes in discussions about the shooters. One theme seemed to suggest, "How could this have happened?" Another suggested, "Someone should have known." Muschert concluded that on the basis of his content analysis of these articles and commentaries, the story about the Columbine shootings is an evolving narrative, bound by institutional and rhetorical conventions. He suggests that the work of reporting, and the corollary effort of news consumption, is intimately connected with the social construction of reality. Therefore, consumers of media would be wise to understand that, rather than receiving a version of an external reality, their consumption of news media content contributes to the construction of reality itself. He suggested that future research should extend to including media coverage of other school shootings, which would allow for comparisons and assessments of how the discourse of school shootings in general emerge and develop.

Advantages and Disadvantages of Content Analysis

Content analysis is an inexpensive way to collect data. No one needs to be interviewed. No surveys need to be prepared. Questionnaires do not have to be mailed. Permission is not required for access to documents, such as newspapers and televised media excerpts, in order to conduct content analyses of them. Lengthy periods of time can be covered by content analysis. Researchers can conduct content analysis on their own, without the assistance of others. Human subjects' permission is not required. Content analysis is perhaps the most unobtrusive data collection method that exists. Contemporary use of computers and software make it possible for researchers to scan documents and conduct word searches to facilitate their content analysis of specific materials.

However, content analyses of documents, articles, or other materials are difficult to replicate by others who are interested in studying the same events. It is also possible for two or more researchers who examine the same documents independently to arrive at totally different conclusions about the contents examined. Each researcher may devise a particular code for classifying article or document content. There is a strong subjective element present here. Codes for particular content are devised that may reflect researcher bias. The subject matter of content analysis is fixed. This means that whatever the form of material examined, it is in print or on videotape. It is not subject to cross-examination or probing or follow-up questions. The clarification inherent in any document is there for the researcher to interpret.

Official and Criminal Justice Agency Records

For criminal justice professionals and criminologists, much use is made of publications generated by the U.S. Department of Justice Bureau of Justice Statistics. The *Uniform Crime Reports,* published annually by the Federal Bureau of Investigation, is also tapped as a primary crime information source.

Since 1977, the National Archive of Criminal Justice Data has been operating at the Interuniversity Consortium for Political and Social Research in Ann Arbor, Michigan. This archival network makes available substantial information to analysts, policymakers, and researchers in all criminal justice fields. Data from the archive are made available to over 350 colleges and universities throughout the United States without charge. Private researchers are charged modest fees to access this information for their own investigative purposes (National Archive of Criminal Justice Data, 1990).

In 1998 the *Sourcebook of Criminal Justice Statistics* was made available to interested persons and researchers on CD-ROM, including editions for the previous years 1994–1996. This extensive annual compendium of updated statistical information has made it possible for instantaneous data retrieval and analysis. Today, the *Sourcebook* is available to interested persons on hard copy or CD-ROM for a nominal fee.

Canned Data Sets

Increasing numbers of national and state data sets are being made available to researchers for different types of analyses (Woodiwiss et al., 2003). These are **canned data sets.** For instance, the National Judicial Reporting Program distributes data files for various states. The National Center for Juvenile Justice distributes data disks as well, including an extensive number of variables and records relating to juvenile delinquency characteristics and juvenile court data. This information can be cross-tabulated and analyzed in many different ways. Each year new sources of information are being established and distributed to researchers for nominal costs. In some instances, this information is freely dispersed (Bouffard, 2003).

Certain data sets are based on prior information collected on birth cohorts, or persons who were born in earlier years and tracked over time. One frequently cited and studied data set is the Philadelphia Birth Cohort Study of 1958 (Brame, Bushway, & Paternoster, 2003). This information has yielded much insight into the onset of delinquency and adult criminality, as follow-up investigations of persons in the original cohort have been made. For instance, the "chronic 6 percent" has been taken from this cohort and suggests that a core number of persons, 6 percent, have accounted for over 50 percent of all delinquency and crime exhibited by the entire cohort. Many other types of information have been disclosed by investigators who have analyzed different dimensions of the data collected. This information is still being analyzed in different ways by contemporary researchers. Along similar lines, the National Consortium on Children, Families, and the Law provides various data sets containing much information about the victimization of children and youths in American society (Finkelhor & Wells, 2003).

Meta-Analysis

Meta-analysis is the quantitative assessment of a large number of articles and research that focus on a particular issue or research question (Dowden & Teller, 2004). This definition may sound like the definition of a literature review. However, a literature review is an examination and synthesis of information about a specific research question and what generally has been found out about it. Those conducting literature reviews summarize the studies examined and describe the similarities and differences. However, in meta-analysis, the quantitative findings of individual studies are themselves quantified and examined for patterns or trends.

A study by Brian Spitzberg (2002) illustrates a typical application of meta-analysis. Spitzberg was interested in the phenomenon of stalking, which became more widely known in the media during the 1990s through various celebrity victimizations. Spitzberg wanted to know more about the stalking phenomenon, how many victims of stalking were women, what conditions initiated the stalking behavior, and the nature of the relationship, if any, between the stalker and his/her victim. Spitzberg investigated 103 studies, which studied 108 samples of stalkers and victims, representing approximately 70,000 persons. On the basis of his meta-analysis of these studies, he found that the prevalence of stalking was 23.5 percent for women and 10.5 percent for men, with an average duration of stalking behavior of 2 years. He also found that the average **proportion** of female victims across studies was 75 percent.

A total of 77 percent of the stalking incidents involved some former acquaintance, with 49 percent involving former romantic relationships. Across 42 of these studies, violence occurred in 33 percent of the cases. Sexual violence occurred in about 10 percent in 17 of these studies. Restraining orders were issued according to published results in 32 studies, and that 40 percent of the time, these restraining orders were violated by stalkers. Spitzberg subsequently developed a new typology of stalking behavior, including coping responses to stalking by victims, as well as a detailed description symptomology due to stalking.

Another study where meta-analysis was more aggressively used was conducted by John Archer (2002) who studied different physically aggressive acts between heterosexual partners during the period 1976–1998. He surveyed the contents of 800 articles having to do with physical aggression and abuse. On the basis of his meta-analysis, Archer found that women were more likely than men to throw something at the other person, slap, kick, bite, or punch, or strike the other with some object. Men were more likely than women to beat up their partners, and to choke or strangle them. The meta-analysis was also used to track physical abuse trends over time. Using a Conflicts Tactics Scale (CTS), Archer observed that increases in male physical aggression toward their female partners increased during the 1976–1998 period. However, samples of student partners showed growing physical aggression among women than men.

Michael Dreznick (2003) conducted a meta-analysis of heterosexual competence of sex offenders. He examined 14 studies of sex offenders, involving 119 rapists and other sex offenders. He found that among sex offenders, heterosexual competence was lower compared with non-sex offenders. Rapists in prison differed from non-sex offenders who were not in prison. He also found that the difference in heterosexual competence between child molesters and non-sex offenders is significantly larger than between rapists and non-sex offenders. His research was subsequently used to further research in the understanding and treatment of sex offenders and the etiology of sex offending generally.

Meta-analysis was also used by Theodore Cross and colleagues (2003), who examined 21 studies of the prosecution of child abuse. The authors studied the rates of child abuse referrals to prosecution, filing charges, and subsequent incarceration. Rates of carrying cases forward without dismissals were 72 percent or greater. For cases subsequently prosecuted, plea bargaining occurred in 82 percent of these cases, and conviction rates were 94 percent. Compared with other types of crime, child abuse is less likely to lead to filing charges and incarceration and more likely to be carried forward without dismissal.

Diversion, plea bargaining, and trial and conviction rates are about the same for child abuse as they are for other types of felonies. Thus, Cross and colleagues found that prosecuting child abuse cases is not considered reckless. Furthermore, the high rate of convictions and incarcerations suggest that prosecution successes in such cases are often underestimated by the general public.

Another application of meta-analysis by Craig Dowden and Claude Teller (2004) investigated job stress among corrections officers. Information from 38 studies of corrections officers yielded much information about job stress, work orientations of human service/rehabilitation and counseling, and various demographic variables and job characteristics (e.g., security level, punitiveness, custody orientation, social distance, and corruption). Overall work attitudes, such as participation in decision making, job satisfaction, commitment, and turnover intention were examined and correlated with specific correctional officer problems (e.g., perceived dangerousness and role difficulties). Dowden and Teller found that job stress was generated the most by role difficulties and perceived dangerousness of the correctional officer role. Moderate correlations were found related to job stress and involved one's work orientation and disposition toward inmates.

Finally, Craig Dowden and S.L. Brown (2002) used meta-analysis to examine the utility of several substance abuse factors in predicting general and violent recidivism. A total of 45 studies were analyzed during the period 1950–1998, producing 116 individual effect size estimates. The principal finding was that substance abuse and recidivism were highly related. A combined alcohol and/or drug problem tended to be highly associated with recidivism, followed by drug abuse, parental substance abuse, and alcohol abuse. It was interesting to note that Dowden and Brown did not find that substance abuse convictions were strongly related to recidivism.

Advantages and Disadvantages of Meta-Analysis

Meta-analysis is not new. It has the advantage of statistically synthesizing a large number of research articles and separating better predictor variables from poor ones. Meta-analysis has been used extensively in psychological studies, but its use in criminal justice and criminology is increasing. A survey of *CJ Abstracts* reveals that meta-analysis has been used in 119 articles during the 1990–2004 period, almost double the 60 articles using meta-analysis reported by the same *CJ Abstracts* for the period 1990–1998.

Meta-analysis works best where considerable data are available on particular research subjects. The examples of meta-analysis applications cited above pertained to recidivism. Much work has been done over the years to explain why recidivism occurs. Thus, when researchers have large numbers of studies to examine, perhaps as many as 50 or more, meta-analysis is an effective method for assessing this research and isolating the best predictors of recidivism or whatever phenomena are of interest to researchers. But not every research question is investigated aggressively. Some topics, such as the use of K-9s in law enforcement, are less intensively investigated. As a result, where few studies exist, meta-analysis would not be appropriate. Thus, it is highly dependent upon popular research questions rather than less popular or infrequently studied events.

Meta-analysis involves the application of sophisticated statistical techniques. Those who use meta-analysis must be familiar with a wide variety of statistical applications. This is because they must be familiar with the different statistical procedures used in each of the studies they examine, and they must also have the capability of translating statistical findings in the various studies into a common statistical format for use in their own meta-analysis of predictor variables. More than a few investigators may not understand the complexities or significance of meta-analyses reported in the research literature.

Additionally, there is little uniformity among studies investigating a common research question. Both qualitative and quantitative investigations are conducted. Different samples of persons are studied. Many extraneous factors are uncontrolled. Researchers may not report their numerical results. Thus, important information may be missing from certain articles subjected to meta-analysis. Despite these limitations, meta-analysis is considered a highly effective means of quantitatively synthesizing large amounts of research data where available.

SUMMARY

Observation is a data-gathering tool involving the direct observation of persons under different conditions and circumstances. Observation permits investigators to capture the natural social context where the behaviors of others occur. Observers are able to see occurrences or events that might influence those being observed. Observation provides a different dimension of the real world of others that is otherwise unavailable through either interviewing or questionnaire administration. Observers usually focus on and look for personal and social behaviors or incidents that help to explain what is going on and why.

Observational techniques employed by researchers provide enriching detail for their investigations. Scientific observation is systematic and controlled. Criminologists who observe others engage in controlled or structured observation, where they seek to discover patterns of behavior and interaction.

Two types of observation are participant and nonparticipant. Participant observation occurs when observers are a part of the group or situation they are observing. They may be employees in work settings where they are in strategic positions to observe those with whom they work. Or they may be members of social groups. They may join groups for the exclusive purpose of being able to observe others to obtain important information about them. Participant observers make casual acquaintances of other group members during normal social interaction. Thus, these acquaintances may obscure their objectivity in their views of others around them. At the same time, participant observers themselves actually may influence the behaviors they observe, since they belong and contribute to the group dynamic and social interaction.

When nonparticipant observation is used, observers are set apart from the groups or settings they are observing. They are outsiders looking in. They only understand what they are seeing from their own subjective interpretation of events. Since they do not directly participate in a group's activities, they are unable to understand fully the reasons for why people behave in particular ways or why certain events occur. Furthermore, their observations may or may not be known to those being observed. They may place themselves in work settings and observe the behaviors of employees going about their day-to-day work tasks. Or they may secret themselves in places where their presence is unknown to those being observed. The nature and type of information yielded by these different nonparticipant observational methods varies considerably.

The weaknesses and strengths of nonparticipant observation are several. If persons know they are being observed, they may act differently from how they would act if they weren't being observed. Or they may alter their conduct to fit what they think the observer wants to see. This is the observational equivalent to social desirability that insinuates itself into and contaminates interviews and questionnaires.

Observers usually take notes of their observations of others and dutifully record them. The accuracy of note-taking may be flawless, but the meaningfulness of such information may be impaired by factors unknown to the observer. Thus, investigators must cautiously gauge the impact of the observer on the observed as well as the impact of the observed on observers. During the classic Hawthorne Experiments, for instance, observers watched groups of employees at the Western Electric Company plant in Hawthorne, Illinois. While the purpose of the observation was to observe the impact of rest pauses and breaks on worker productivity, the workers themselves pushed harder to work more rapidly because they thought the observers were company officials who were singling these workers out for special observation and treatment. Thus, the Hawthorne Effect was created, which is now used as an explanation for why some observed subjects will engage in socially desirable actions for the benefit of those observing.

Once observations have been concluded and field notes are compiled, it is sometimes difficult to code this information in ways similar to how questionnaire information is coded. There is so much observational information available. Investigators may face difficult decisions about how to interpret or make sense out of this mass of information.

On the positive side, observation is cheap. It costs very little or nothing to observe others. Anyone can do it, and at almost any time of the day or night. However, there may be hazards that arise if observers are watching certain types of people. If observers are observing a group of homeless persons during evening hours, or if they are sitting in parked cars in high-crime areas of neighborhoods looking for signs of gang activity, they may become crime victims of the very persons they are observing. They may be assaulted or harassed by certain persons who object to being observed. Observers may even attract the attention of police officers, who may mistake their observational conduct as related to some future criminal activity, such as casing a neighborhood for the purpose of committing a burglary or robbery. More than one observer has had to explain him- or herself and his or her reasons for being in particular places at particular times.

Another important data-gathering tool is secondary source analysis. The analysis of secondary sources is widespread throughout criminology and criminal justice. Available documents from the Bureau of Justice Statistics and other government agencies is exploited extensively by researchers. The inexpensive accessibility of large amounts of data, together with the low cost of information retrieval, make the analysis of secondary sources an attractive investigative option for those investigators with limited research funds. But secondary sources have been collected for other purposes, and investigators must often adjust their own studies to conform to the limitations of secondary sources they analyze. Despite these flaws, secondary source materials provide much enriching information to supplement data derived from questionnaires, interviews, and other data collection strategies.

Different types of secondary sources include archival records, which often contain historical accounts of events and extensive documentation about them. Personal documents, such as autobiographies and biographies, may contain much rich information about persons and their behaviors and thoughts. Some documents, particularly politically sensitive information, may be difficult to access, even by legitimate social researchers or investigators. In the last few decades, the Freedom of Information Act (FOIA) has enabled criminologists and others to obtain previously sealed documents, often compiled by governmental sources. Sometimes certain types of information are sought for political advantage and not especially for direct research. In the 2004 presidential election, for example, the FOIA was used by Democrats to obtain the military service records of President George W. Bush. Although some information about Bush was disclosed, officials declared that other information about Bush's service record was either lost or missing. Needless to say, Democrats made considerable use of subsequent references to this missing information.

Information from secondary sources is almost always unrelated to an investigator's specific research purposes. Therefore, adjustments need to be made by researchers to tailor their research interests to fit information from secondary sources that already exists. Also, much information from secondary sources is aggregate information, usually about large numbers of persons, and specific information about personal characteristics or behaviors is simply not available. If the researcher needs such personal information, then other methods will need to be used to gather it. Positively, however, information from secondary sources may assist researchers in verifying information they may have gathered through questionnaires, observation, and/or interviews. Thus, triangulation may occur for cross-authentication purposes. Another advantage of analyzing secondary sources is that most of the time, research subjects are not harmed by discovered information. Again, this is because of its aggregate characteristics. However, secondary source information may have missing or incomplete records that frustrate the coding efforts of those conducting their investigations.

An important data collection method that is frequently used by researchers is content analysis. This involves the systematic qualitative examination of different sorts of documents, such as books, journals, book reviews, biographical materials, and other published and/or written records. Content analyses of different sorts of published materials may yield important trend information or the existence of particular policies or agendas of various persons, groups, or organizations. Content analyses have been conducted of college textbooks in an effort to compare them and their effectiveness at covering different topics or literature. Such content analyses have influenced professors and others in their text selections for college classes. Many other uses of content analysis are possible. One common disadvantage of content analysis, however, is that the coding process is hampered because there may be great variation among documents being analyzed.

Increasingly used are canned data sets made available either freely or at nominal cost to researchers. Because the federal government and certain private organizations cannot possibly analyze the vast amounts of information compiled annually about agencies and their employees or clients, criminologists and others may use these canned data sets for their own research purposes. Usually researchers will tailor their own research to fit the available data provided in these canned data sets. Then the data are analyzed in different ways, thus enabling researchers to test their theories and various hypotheses derived from them. The primary strengths of canned data sets are that they are usually free, large amounts of data are available, researchers do not have to contact persons directly to obtain vital information, and much of this information has already been coded and processed. But canned data sets may lack specific information of interest to some researchers. They may be forced to compromise their own research to fit the parameters of information available in such data sets. But the low cost factor and ready data availability more than offset these research objective inconveniences that some investigators may suffer.

Finally, a novel research technique used in recent years is meta-analysis. Meta-analysis is a quantitative examination of a large body of information, usually a large number of articles that are devoted to a particular research topic. Often compared to a massive literature review, meta-analysis seeks to quantify the findings yielded by large numbers of research projects and demonstrate certain consistencies or inconsistencies in the research literature.

Meta-analysis assists researchers in determining which factors may be most significant in causing particular events or behaviors, such as recidivism. The identification of certain predictor variables is certainly advantageous to theorists who wish to advance their own theoretical schemes and develop more sophisticated explanations of events. However, meta-analysis is faulted because it cannot control for different settings studied, or for different samples selected. There is a great deal of qualitative variability among research studies. Different data-gathering methods are used, with accompanying variability in research findings. Thus, those using meta-analysis urge that readers should interpret their findings with the same degree of caution they would otherwise use when reading about the findings of investigators in a single study. Meta-analysis offers considerable promise, however, as a heuristic device for theory-building and problem formulation.

QUESTIONS FOR REVIEW

1. What is meant by secondary source analysis? What are some examples of public secondary sources?

2. What is nonparticipant observation? What are some limitations of nonparticipant observation regarding the reliability of whatever is observed and its meaning?

3. What is participant observation? How can researchers who engage in participant observation "get too close to" their subjects being observed? What can be done to avoid this problem?

4. Who is a key informant? What are some purposes of key informants? What are some problems that can be anticipated from using key informants in research?

5. What is content analysis? How can content analysis be used to affect policy decision making? What are two examples of content analysis?

6. What are some major problems associated with content analysis?

7. If you plan to use content analysis over a lengthy period, such as 5 or 10 years, what types of problems might occur to interfere with your coding of data?

8. In what sense is observation a source of enriching detail to supplement questionnaire information?

9. How does observation conducted by criminologists differ from everyday, random observations by others?

10. In what ways are participant and nonparticipant observation structured?

11. What are some hazards of doing participant observation with criminals and street people?

12. What are the major limitations and strengths of secondary source analysis?

13. What is meta-analysis? What conditions maximize the usefulness of meta-analysis?

8

Measurement of Variables in Criminal Justice and Criminology

CHAPTER OUTLINE

CHAPTER OBJECTIVES

As the result of reading this chapter, the following objectives should be realized:

1. Understanding the fundamental purposes of scientific measurement in social research.
2. Determining the relation between measurement and theory verification.
3. Learning about the process of operationalization and how social and psychological phenomena are brought into the empirical realm.
4. Distinguishing between nominal and operational definitions and their functional utility in the research process.
5. Differentiating between concepts and constructs.
6. Understanding the differences between four measurement levels, including nominal, ordinal, interval, and ratio.

7. Learning about set responses and social desirability as major contaminants of measures and scales.
8. Describing Likert, Thurstone, and Guttman scales, their applications, and their weaknesses and strengths.
9. Learning about measures of crime and crime rates.
10. Examining several important measurement issues, including the attitude–action relation, captive audiences, social desirability, and response sets.

Introduction

When a police department implements a sensitivity training program to encourage their officers to become more professional in their interactions with citizens, how do we know that police officer professionalism improves over time following the implementation of the program? If a probation department reduces its client–officer caseloads to enable probation officers a greater chance to offer their clients more personalized assistance, how do we know whether there are favorable attitudinal changes among clients as the result of these reduced caseloads? If morale among correctional officers in a prison is low and we seek to raise their morale by allowing them greater participation in decision making over matters affecting their work, how do we know their morale is improved over time?

Each of these questions involves potential relationships between variables. There are possible relationships between sensitivity training programs and police professionalism; between caseload reductions among probation officers and attitudinal changes among clients; and between morale and decision-making participation. An infinite number of questions about variable interrelationships are asked by those in criminal justice and criminology in an effort to discover how different variables impact other variables. In order to answer these and other types of questions about variable interrelationships, we must be able to measure the variables of interest to us.

This chapter investigates the measurement process and delves into the intricacies of how variables are conceptualized for purposes of social research. Measurement is the assignment of numbers to various psychological and/or social properties of persons and groups according to rules and for the purpose of differentiating between these persons or groups. The chapter opens with a general discussion of measurement, what it is, and what its important functions are. Our theories contain several variables, and these variables are defined in different ways. We seek to test our theories by examining persons from different populations and studying their characteristics. In order for our theories to be tested adequately, the variables we have incorporated into them must be conceptualized in certain ways so as to make them amenable to measurement. As we have seen in earlier chapters, theories generate numerous hypotheses that can be empirically tested. Testing hypotheses derived from our theories will either provide support or fail to provide support for the theories from which they were derived. Over time, repetitive tests of hypotheses derived from theories will yield some amount of consistent information about various events we seek to explain.

This chapter next explores the process whereby our variables are defined. A distinction is made between nominal definitions of variables, which are conventionally used in our theoretical schemes, and operational definitions of these same variables, which are directly useful in testing our hypotheses derived from these same theories. Operational definitions of the variables we use in our theories are created through the process of operationalization. This process will be examined and described. Because many of the variables we examine in criminology, such as attitudes, cannot be seen directly, their existence in the real world must often be inferred, usually by referring to an indirect **indicator** of one or more of these phenomena. These indicators are known as epistemic correlates of the variables we wish to measure. Therefore, a distinction is made between concepts and constructs as we create different measures of the variables we use in our theoretical schemes.

Following this discussion is a description of levels of measurement. All variables may be classified according to different measurement levels. Respectively these are nominal, ordinal, interval, and ratio levels of measurement. These categorizations mean that each variable may be given numerical values, but these numerical values have different meanings depending on the variables they represent. Numbers assigned to "male" and "female" to distinguish between these subclasses of gender have quite a different meaning from the numbers assigned to subclasses of income, social class, prejudice, or job satisfaction. These different measurement levels will be described and their importance for criminologists and social scientists in general will be explained.

Next, the chapter examines several popular scaling methods. Scales represent ranges of scores that portray varying amounts of different variables. For example, a scale of job satisfaction will usually contain different scores representing different amounts of job satisfaction among a group of persons. Two popular and important scaling procedures for measuring attitudinal phenomena are Likert and Thurstone scaling. These scaling procedures will be defined, discussed, and explained in some detail, together with several examples provided from the research literature concerning their practical application in the measurement process. The weaknesses, strengths, uses, and limitations, together with the advantages and disadvantages of these respective scaling procedures, will be discussed.

Several other less popular scaling procedures will be examined as well. These include Guttman scaling, the semantic differential, the Q-sort, the Sellin–Wolfgang Index, the Salient Factor Score (SFS 81), and Greenwood's Rand Seven-Factor Index. A few of these scales seek to portray variables as unidimensional phenomena, where essentially the same characteristics of each variable are measured by different scale items. Most other scaling procedures are multidimensional, meaning that different scale items for these measures represent different dimensions of a variable. Job satisfaction is usually measured with multidimensional scales, for instance, as items are used that relate to one's satisfaction with work pay, work associates, retirement benefits, the degree of interest in work performed, supervision, work content, the clients assisted, working hours, and other rewarding experiences associated with one's job. The phenomena of unidimensionality and multidimensionality will be described.

The final part of this chapter examines several important measurement issues. One issue examined is the attitude–action relation. It is often assumed by researchers that if we know one's attitudes about things, then actions consistent with those attitudes will be observed among those persons we study. But sometimes actions are exhibited by persons that are not necessarily consistent with the attitudes these persons express. Considerable work has been done to examine and explain the nature of the attitude–action relation and why inconsistencies occur from time to time. Another measurement issue is the social desirability factor. Often, particularly on attitudinal measures, respondents may give answers that they believe researchers want to hear. Or respondents may give answers to questions that are not necessarily true of them but are nevertheless socially desirable answers. Social desirability is a major contaminating factor in all attitudinal measuring instruments and will be discussed in some detail.

Another measurement issue discussed is the matter of response sets. A set response is frequently associated with responses to questionnaire items, and is indicated by response patterns suggesting that respondents have not taken the time to read questions or statements about them or their attitudes. Response sets occur when persons mark the same responses to all questions, such as "strongly agree," regardless of whether these responses are consistent or inconsistent with other responses they have given. If someone marks "strongly agree" to an item that says, "I like my job," and then if that same person later marks another item "strongly agree" and the item says, "I hate my job," this is evidence of a set response. Usually, though not always, set responses occur when respondents are in hurry and wish to get through a questionnaire quickly, to get it over with. Hurried responses are not accurate responses, and they do not represent a person's true feelings or attitudes toward things. Response sets affect the validity of any measure, and whether that measure actually measures whatever the researcher intends to be measured. In short, questions arise about whether we can trust the answers persons give on questionnaires they complete and whether the information yielded from those particular questionnaires can be relied upon or trusted.

Another measurement issue examined involves relating particular measurement levels (e.g., nominal, ordinal, interval, or ratio) with different statistical test choices. Statistical tests are used in social research to yield numerical results that can be interpreted. Probabilities are assigned these numerical results, and our hypothesis tests can be judged according to their likelihood of being true, at least in their present study circumstances. More than a few researchers pay little or no attention to the measurement levels they have achieved with the scales they use to portray different variables. One result is that they may use statistical tests that assume one level of measurement, but that level of measurement has not been achieved with the scales they use to measure certain variables. This situation renders the application of certain statistical tests less meaningful or even meaningless. This issue is examined and its relevance for hypothesis testing is discussed.

Measurement of Variables in Criminology and Criminal Justice

Variables are quantities that assume more than one value, and they may be discrete, continuous, dependent, or independent. All attitudinal phenomena are variables. Race, ethnicity, gender, political affiliation, religious affiliation, income, age, education, occupation/profession, and nationality are variables in the sense that they may assume different values. The persons we study have these and many other characteristics. Our attempts to describe persons and differentiate between them according to these and other characteristics involve measurement.

Some of the earlier definitions indicated that it is "the correlation with numbers of entities that are not numbers" (Cohen & Nagel, 1934, p. 6), or "the assignment of numerals to objects, events, or persons, according to rules" (Stevens, 1951). A subsequent definition referred to measurement as "the procedures by which empirical observations are made in order to represent symbolically the phenomena and the conceptualizations that are to be explained" (DiRenzo, 1966, p. 14).

Bailey (1987, p. 60) has added to these previous definitions by saying that measurement is "the process of determining the value or level, either qualitative or quantitative, of a particular attribute for a particular unit of analysis." Bailey distinguishes between qualitative and quantitative measures by whether labels or names are applied to variables or whether numbers are applied to them. If labels or names are applied, such as eye or hair color, religion, political affiliation, or gender, he would describe these variables as qualitative. Descriptions of prison inmates, including "real man" or "punk," would also be qualitative. Age, income, years of education, and all attitudinal phenomena could be expressed in quantitative terms, and numerical values would be applied to them.

For our purposes, measurement is the assignment of numbers to social and psychological properties of individuals and groups according to rules, and correlating these numbers with these properties symbolically. Another way of viewing measurement is the process of using numerical expressions to differentiate between people and groups according to various properties they possess. These properties are largely behavioral and attitudinal characteristics that are amenable to measurement.

Functions of Measurement

The primary functions of measurement are to:

1. Describe social and psychological phenomena empirically.
2. Render data amenable to some kind of statistical manipulation or treatment.
3. Assist in hypothesis testing and theory verification.
4. Enable researchers to differentiate between people according to various properties they possess.

Conceptualizations of Social and Psychological Phenomena

Exploratory and descriptive studies of criminological phenomena depict both social settings and characteristics of persons in those settings. For example, jail overcrowding is sometimes used to explain the incidence of inmate suicides or unrest. Overcrowding is conceptualized in different ways, such as the amount of cell square footage available to inmates, the number of beds per cell, the number of inmates confined per cell, and the actual capacity of the jail facility in relation to its rated capacity. Different quantitative expressions of this phenomenon can be correlated with suicide rates, inmate anxiety, and the incidence of rioting. Describing the characteristics of burnout can help us acquire a better understanding of the effectiveness or ineffectiveness of police officers or others exposed to hazardous or life-threatening situations.

Rendering Data Amenable to Statistical Treatment

Another function of measurement is to bring various phenomena into a form that enables researchers to manipulate it statistically. In order to make sense out of data collected from different sources and respondents, it is often helpful to transform the data into numerical quantities. Once data have been cast into some kind of numerical form, we can apply various statistical tools and analyze the data more effectively.

Suppose researchers inspect recidivism rates of probationers (i.e., their arrests or convictions for new crimes while on probation) in a given state. They note that in some cities, the recidivism rate among probationers is higher than in other cities. Believing that these different rates of recidivism among probationers might be attributable, in part, to differences in the ways these probationers are managed or supervised, these researchers place themselves in several probation offices for 2 weeks and observe what is going on around them. They observe interactions of probation officers and their clients, supervisory practices, and the general office setting. They probably take notes about what they observe. Furthermore, they might ask questions of officers about different ways their jobs are performed or how they feel about their work. At the end of their observation, interviewing, and questionnaire administration, they will have compiled a good bit of information about the persons in the probation office. What can they do with this data they have collected? In order to make sense out of their observations of probation officer behaviors, they may find it helpful to classify their observations into different categories.

Perhaps one result of their investigation is the finding that in those cities with higher probationer recidivism rates, the caseloads of probation officers generally seem much higher compared with caseloads of officers in cities with lower probationer recidivism rates. Probation officer caseloads are easily quantified. We can count the numbers of probationers each officer is assigned. What about less obvious dimensions of the probation officer–probationer relation? What if there are certain probation offices with lower client caseloads but higher probationer recidivism?

Observations made by these researchers may lead them to conclude that in these particular offices, probation officers do not seem especially interested in probationer problems. Probation officers in these departments may relate to probationers in an impersonal fashion, whereas in other comparable departments, probation officers may seem to take more of a personal interest in their clients. If we are going to make sense out of these observations, we are going to have to translate "appears more impersonal or distant" or "seems to take more personal interest in probationers" into numerical quantities. We are going to have to measure these probation officer–client interactions in some way. Once we have measured these types of interactions, we can compare them with different office policies about how offenders ought to be supervised, or caseloads of officers, or size of office, or any other relevant variable. After these variables have been quantified in some way, it will then be possible to apply various statistical procedures to these data in order to enhance our understanding of what is going on and why.

Assisting in Hypothesis Testing and Theory Verification

Hypotheses Defined. An important function of measurement is to permit us to verify theories and test hypotheses derived from them. Conventionally, investigators proceed in their scientific inquiry by theorizing about events. Why does recidivism occur? What causes labor turnover in probation agencies? What causes burnout among correctional officers? How does jury nullification occur? Why do we have sentencing disparities? Why do persons support the death penalty? Researchers conjecture about why these events occur. Different explanations are considered. These explanations are translated into hypotheses, where a stated relation between an event and an explanation of it is made. Hypothesis statements may be, "The greater the alcohol use, the greater the recidivism among probationers." Or, "Whites receive shorter sentences compared with blacks where both are convicted of the same offense." Or, "The stress of correctional work increases job burnout for corrections officers." Or, "Punishment-centered citizens favor the death penalty, while rehabilitation-centered citizens are opposed to the death penalty." Or, "White jurors will tend to acquit white defendants, despite extensive inculpatory evidence." Or, "Probation officers who have to travel great distances to meet with their probationer clients will be more likely to leave their probation agencies." These are examples of different kinds of hypotheses, and they are not necessarily good ones.

Hypotheses are tentative statements, usually derived from theories, that may be refuted. Hypotheses are alternatively defined as statements of theory in testable form. Hypotheses may be assertions of a relationship between two or more variables. Hypotheses may contain a single variable. One research objective is to test various hypotheses. Initially, researchers believe that their hypothesis statements are true. However, they must test these hypotheses in some way in order to support or refute them. The logic is that if one or more hypotheses are supported by data collected by the investigator, then the theory from which those hypotheses was derived is also supported.

Perhaps investigators learn from their investigations of various probation offices that each is somewhat autonomous from the others, and that chief probation officers administer office procedures and policies according to their personal discretion. Researchers may suspect that the probation officer–client relation is influenced greatly by office policy. Perhaps certain offices are more rule-oriented and bureaucratic than other offices. Perhaps caseload assignments are quite different from one office to the next. These investigators may conjecture about the degree of formality in probation office operations and the relation of formality–informality to probation officer–client interactions. Certain organizational theories may be used to explain probation officer behaviors and conduct. Measurement of the degree of formality–informality as well as the nature of probation officer–client interactions will permit researchers to test hypotheses about these variable interrelationships. Tests of hypotheses derived from theory are also tests of the theories from which those hypotheses were derived.

The nature of caseload assignments may have some explanatory value and account, in part, for probation officer–probationer interactions. In some offices, caseloads are determined by dividing the total number of probationers by the number of officers. This method gives each probation officer a caseload equivalent to other officers. But in another probation office, caseloads may be more specialized. Some probation officers may be assigned principally those probationers who have serious drug or alcohol dependencies. Other probation officers may be assigned violent offenders to supervise, including convicted rapists and robbers. Specialized caseload assignments such as these are often determined on the basis of a probation officer's skills and interests. Thus, it may be that where caseloads are specialized and tailored to fit particular officer interests, the probation officer–client relationship may be more personalized. The officer takes greater interest in those clients supervised and relates better to their individual problems and needs. In more generalized caseload assignment situations, probation officers may have such diverse clientele that they cannot conceivably relate to all probationer problems and needs. These officers may feel frustrated and overworked. In order to insulate themselves from the complexities of these diverse relations, they may bureaucratize their behaviors and relate to their clients impersonally, on a "strictly business" basis.

BOX 8.1   PERSONALITY HIGHLIGHT

SUSETTE M. TALARICO
Albert Berry Saye Professor of American Government and
Constitutional Law, University of Georgia

Statistics: B.A., Diocesan Sisters College; M.A., Ph.D. (criminology), University of Connecticut.

BACKGROUND AND INTERESTS

I never paid much attention to crime or criminal justice until graduate school. Prior to that, I was primarily interested in politics and law. When studying political science, I took a course from George Cole on the criminal justice system in the context of my broader study of courts and law. From that time, I was hooked. I analyzed criminal sentencing and parole decision making for my dissertation, and I have really stayed true to my criminal justice origins ever since, with the exception of my current study of civil litigation.

Interestingly, until my generation of scholars, few in political science paid much attention to crime or criminal justice. This has continued to astonish me because criminal law and criminal justice are governmental functions and focus on one of the most important dimensions of political power, namely the authority to define what is criminal and to administer the related and sweeping powers of criminal arrest, conviction, and punishment. I can think of few dimensions of government and law that are more appropriate for political science consideration.

I have served on the faculty at the University of Georgia (UGA) since 1977 where I have twice won the Josiah Miegs Award for Excellence in Teaching. Additionally, I won the Creative Research Award, a Special Sandy Beaver Teaching Award, and a Sandy Beaver Professorship, among other awards for research and teaching. Additionally, I was the recipient of an award for outstanding national contributions to the advancement and professional development of criminal justice administration from the American Society of Public Administration. As of this writing, I am editor of the *Justice System Journal,* which is published by the National Center for State Courts.

RESEARCH INVESTIGATIONS AND PUBLICATIONS

My research is primarily directed to studies of state trial court systems. I have done a great deal of writing on criminal sentencing, which has led to an outstanding scholarship award from the Society for the Study of Social Problems for my coauthored book (w/Martha A.

BOX 8.1   CONTINUED

Myers), *The Social Contexts of Criminal Sentencing.* Presently, I am studying tort litigation in Georgia courts. Some of the articles related to this research have appeared in journals such as the *Georgia Law Review* and *Yale Law and Policy Review/Yale Law Journal on Regulation.* I am also completing a study on discovery abuse in state and federal trial courts. Both of these projects are being conducted with UGA School of Law faculty, Thomas A. Eaton, and C. Ron Ellington, respectively.

I have authored several other books and journal articles, including several book reviews, government reports, and book chapters. Among these publications are a report to the Committee on the Judiciary of the U.S. House of Representatives, *Explorations in Crime and Justice,* and contributions to several encyclopedias. I have been fortunate to have my research funded by the Georgia Civil Justice Foundation, the National Science Foundation, and the National Institute of Justice. I have also received several research and conference grants from various UGA programs.

I believe that it is important to present my research through various outlets besides journals. Over the years I have presented numerous papers about different aspects of my research endeavors at regional, national, and international conferences, and most recently I served as a faculty-in-residence at the SPIA at Oxford program. I have also been involved as an officer in the Law and Courts Section of the American Political Science Association, the Criminal Justice Section of the American Society for Public Administration, the American Society of Criminology, and the Academy of Criminal Justice Sciences. I have served in various professional positions in the Southern Political Science Association and other regional associations. Presently, I am a member of the editorial board of the University of Georgia Press, *Criminal Justice Review,* and *State Constitutional Commentaries,* and I have served in the capacity of a reviewer and associate editor for a variety of journals and book publishers. My involvement in this activity has also resulted in my inclusion on various research award panels for the National Science Foundation, as well as a consultant for various research, public service projects, and community programs, including the State Bar Committee on Court Filings.

ADVICE TO STUDENTS

I would advise anyone interested in doing what I do to complete at least one degree in political science at a university where there are faculty who are interested in the social scientific study of law and courts. If one aspires to teaching and research in this area of political science and criminal justice, a law degree is also very useful and one of the things I regret not undertaking. In terms of the broader discipline of political science, study of law and courts, public administration, or even comparative politics would help prepare one for a career that concentrates on the role of law and the courts in the criminal justice system.

Measurement permits us to evaluate these settings and the personnel within them. We can characterize office settings and caseload assignment policies according to various criteria and correlate these factors with other variables. In the general case, if a hypothesis is about the relation between two variables, X and Y, and is of the form,

"As X increases, Y increases."

then we should conceptualize variables X and Y in such a way so that this hypothesis can be tested. If variable X is "office formality" and variable Y is "recidivism rates," a hypothesis might be as follows:

"As the formality of probation office policy increases, recidivism rates among probationers will increase."

Both formality of probation office policy and recidivism rates of probationers will have to be measured. Also, if variable X is the nature of caseload assignments and variable Y is probationer recidivism rates, we might develop the following hypothesis:

"Recidivism rates among probationers will be lower where specialized caseload assignments are made for probation officers compared with offices that use generalized caseload assignment models."

For both of these hypotheses, we can measure probationer recidivism by the proportion of those probationers who are arrested for new crimes. If there are 100 probationers and 20 are arrested for new crimes, then the recidivism rate based on this measure is $20/100 = .20$. If there are 300 probationers and 90 of them are arrested for new crimes, then the recidivism rate would be $90/300 = .30$, a higher rate of recidivism. We might develop the following tables:

	Office Procedures	
	Formal	Informal
Recidivism rate of probationers	.40	.30

OR

	Nature of Caseload Assignment	
	Specialized	Generalized
Recidivism rate of probationers	.15	.30

In each of these tables, we have created categories for office formality/informality and for the nature of caseload assignments. In each table, we have supplied hypothetical recidivism rates for aggregates of probationers. From the ways these data are arranged, it would seem that probation office formality is associated with higher probationer recidivism rates of probationers, while informality is associated with lower probationer recidivism rates. Also, those offices making specialized caseload assignments seem to have less probationer recidivism associated with them compared with those offices making generalized caseload assignments. These tables are relatively simple, but they illustrate how we might translate office characteristics into categorical expressions and contrast them with offender recidivism rates. Measurement would help us test our hypotheses about the influence of office environments on client recidivism.

Differentiating between People According to Properties They Possess

A primary function of measurement is to make distinctions between people according to certain properties they possess. Suppose we are looking at five large tables in a room. Each table is slightly different from the rest and of a different color. We might wish to know which table is longest, which is heaviest, which is widest, and which is tallest. One solution to our problem is to grasp a ruler as our measure of length, width, and height and compare the five tables. We can bring in scales and weigh each table as well. These two measuring instruments, the ruler and the scales, help us answer our questions about the different properties of length, width, height, and weight shared by these five tables.

However, what if we are looking at several people and wish to know whether they differ regarding their age, educational attainment, job satisfaction levels, morale, stress and burnout, job proficiency, and attitudes toward supervision? The ages and levels of educational attainment for these persons are not difficult to determine. We may have access to employee information that tells us their ages and amounts of formal education. Or these persons may tell us their ages and amounts of education when asked. The remaining variables of job satisfaction, morale, stress and burnout, job proficiency, and supervisory attitudes are more difficult to conceptualize. True, each of these persons may tell us how they feel about their work, whether they feel stressed or burned out, whether they have high or low morale, whether they are proficient at their work, and whether they approve of how they are supervised. What if they all say they like their jobs and have high morale? What if they all deny that they are stressed or burned out? What if they all say they are proficient in the performance of their work tasks? What if they all like their supervisor and approve of how they are supervised? Are we to assume that all of these persons surveyed are equal on each of these variables? While all of these persons may be equivalent to one another on each of these properties, social scientists generally assume that for any group, there will be differences among individual members pertaining to their behavioral and attitudinal characteristics. These differences may be either great or small, depending on the variables or characteristics examined.

Thus, depending on how we choose to conceptualize job satisfaction, some of these persons will have higher levels of it compared with other persons. Variation in the level of morale will also be observed among these individuals. They will differ in their job performance, with some persons performing better or worse than others. We may even find that although all appear to like their supervisors and how they are supervised, some of these persons may not like these supervisors as strongly as the other persons. Typically, we will create a measuring **instrument** for each of these different variables. These measures will likely consist of questions or statements, and these persons will differ in their agreements or disagreements with these statements. We will make an inference from their responses about whether they possess these characteristics or properties to high or low degrees. This is a basic task of measurement that will permit us to classify people differently and make distinctions between them on various dimensions.

Hypotheses: Operationalizing Variables

Nominal and Operational Definitions

The process whereby variables are brought into the empirical world where they can be manipulated or controlled is **operationalization.** An **operational definition** is the result of operationalization. Operational definitions of variables may be understood by comparing them with nominal definitions.

The explication of theories is heavily dependent upon extensive use of the **nominal definition.** Nominal definitions are those we might find in a dictionary. All attitudinal terms are defined by other terms that are considered synonymous with them. This establishes a circularity or merry-go-round of terms that is confusing, since these terms are seldom defined in a uniform fashion. No consistent meaning is assigned to many of these terms, so that one, and only one, meaning of a term can be measured by independent investigators. An attitudinal example is *anxiety*. Using the latest version of *Webster's New World Dictionary, anxiety* is defined as the state of being uneasy, apprehensive, or worried about what may happen; misgiving; a thought or thing that causes this; an eager and often slightly worried desire. If we look up the word *misgiving,* we find that it means a disturbed feeling of fear, doubt, apprehension. When we look up the word *apprehension,* we find that it means foreboding, fear, dread. And when we look up the word *fear,* we find that it means to be uneasy, anxious, or doubtful, to expect with misgiving. And when we look up the word *uneasy,* we find that it means disturbed by anxiety or apprehension. In other words, according to this dictionary, *anxiety is defined as anxiety.* Such circularities in nominal definitions of things are commonplace. Nominal definitions assist us by linking different ideas in a logical fashion. For instance,

> "Bureaucratic settings are characterized by adherence to rules and impersonality. The greater the bureaucratic operations, the greater the impersonalization. Probationers often require personalized treatment in order to complete their probation sentences satisfactorily. Personalized treatment is less likely to occur in a highly bureaucratized probation office. The greater the bureaucracy of a probation office, the less individualized and personalized the treatment received by probationers from their probation officers. The less personalized the treatment received by probationers, the more likely they will reoffend or recidivate."

All of this theorizing is done using nominal definitions of terms. Seemingly, we know or understand what "impersonal relations" implies and what "individualized treatment" means.

We can understand how probation office policies may inadvertently contribute to greater rates of probationer recidivism. But all of this theorizing is articulated through the use of nominal definitions of terms.

Theories are constructed mostly of nominal definitions and logical abstract linkages between different concepts. Logical interrelationships between variables are outlined, largely through the use of nominal terms and how they are intrinsically associated with other nominal terms. However, in order to test our theories, we must bring our terms into the empirical realm. The term *empirical* means "amenable to our senses" in some respect. If we can see something, smell it, taste it, touch it, or hear it, it is said to be in the empirical realm. Translating terms into empirical reality most often involves the measurement process, or the assignment of numbers to different amounts of personal and/or social properties. Transforming nominal definitions into an empirical form or rendering them measurable quantities is operationalizing them. Thus, operational definitions are quantifications of nominal definitions. Kerlinger (1965, p. 34) defines an operational definition as "one that assigns meaning to a . . . variable by specifying the activities or operations necessary to measure the . . . variable."

For example, if we wanted to devise an operational definition of anxiety, we would come up with something like, "Anxiety is what an anxiety test measures." The anxiety test we might devise consists of agreement or disagreement with several statements that appear logically related to our nominal definition of anxiety. Certain responses are designated as anxious responses, whereas other responses would be nonanxious responses. For instance, Janet Taylor (1953) investigated anxiety and formulated an operational definition of it. Prior to creating this definition, however, she examined numerous psychoneurotic patients at a large state mental hospital. She reasoned that one of the best places to find anxious people would be a mental hospital. The patients she investigated had previously been diagnosed by psychiatrists as either psychotic or neurotic and suffering from considerable anxiety. Taylor observed these patients, their behaviors, and their ailments. On the basis of her observations of large numbers of anxious persons and their behaviors, she created a manifest anxiety scale consisting of 50 statements with "true–false" responses. A few of the 50 items Taylor used to measure anxiety are shown below. "True" or "anxious" responses are indicated in parentheses following each item:

1. I am often sick to my stomach. (True)
2. I am about as nervous as other people. (False)
3. I blush as often as others. (False)
4. I have diarrhea once a month or more. (True)
5. When embarrassed, I often break out in a sweat, which is very annoying. (True)
6. Often my bowels don't move for several days at a time. (True)
7. At times I lose sleep over worry. (True)
8. I often dream about things I don't like to tell other people. (True)
9. My feelings are hurt easier than most other people. (True)

The rationale underlying this scale and others like it is that the greater the number of anxious responses, the greater the degree of anxiety. Taylor's anxiety scale ranged from "0" (low or no anxiety) to "50" (high anxiety). This score range was achieved by assigning one point (1) for each "anxious" response, and assigning no points (0) to a nonanxious response. When administered to samples of persons in different social contexts, most of their anxiety scores generally range from 14 or 15 to 35 or 40. Few persons ever have scores below 10 or above 40. Notice that the nine items above are related with different attitudes and behaviors. Psychological, social, and biological dimensions of anxiety are tapped by this measure. Irregular bowel or bladder functioning, loss of sleep, excessive worry, and greater sensitivity about one's thoughts and dreams seem to be closely correlated with anxiety. These characteristics are called concomitants of anxiety, primarily because they have been found to be closely correlated with it.

Taylor used psychoneurotic patients at a mental hospital exclusively for the purpose of identifying characteristics of anxiety and to devise her scale items. Later, she administered the scale to persons outside of the hospital setting, in work environments and elsewhere. She found that anxiety could be used as an indicator of personal and social reactions to changes in one's work environment or family stability. The same principles that pertained to the development of Taylor's anxiety scale are also generalizable or applicable to constructing scales of burnout, stress, the nature of the probation officer–probationer relation, or any other attitudinal variable of interest to criminal justice professionals and criminologists. The nominal definition–operational definition distinction is also exemplified by the use of concepts and constructs.

Concepts

Concepts are terms we use that have direct empirical referents. When we say the terms *book, desk,* or *blackboard,* we can point to specific objects that these terms represent. Thus, any book may be a direct **empirical referent** of the term *book.* We would say that the term *book* is a concept, because it has a tangible object as its direct empirical referent.

Constructs

Constructs are terms we use that do not have direct empirical referents. All attitudes are constructs, since we must rely on indirect empirical evidence to determine their existence. When we say the word *anxiety,* we cannot point to some specific referent of it. However, we can point to an anxiety scale as a referent for the term *anxiety.* The scale itself contains specific items that depict behaviors that are concomitants of the term. Occasionally, the term *epistemic correlate* has been used to characterize the components of operational definitions. Thus, it is likely that underlying many attitudinal phenomena are numerous epistemic correlates. As an example, Taylor's manifest anxiety scale described above consisted of 50 **epistemic correlates** of anxiety.

The work of criminal justice professionals and criminologists involves the widespread investigation of constructs. Some variables, such as recidivism rate, age, gender, fractured family, or race/ethnicity, are more directly defined and amenable to measurement than other variables, such as anxiety, psychotic-aggressive personality, stress and burnout, political conservatism, offender dangerousness, reactive depression, extroversion, and acceptance of responsibility. These are just a few of the many constructs that have been gleaned from recent issues of *Criminal Justice Abstracts,* and they reflect the diversity of subject matter studied by social scientists.

BOX 8.2   PERSONALITY HIGHLIGHT

KIMBERLY KEMPF-LEONARD
University of Texas at Dallas

Statistics: B.S. (criminal justice), University of Nebraska; M.S. (sociology), Pennsylvania State University; M.S., Ph.D. (Social Systems Sciences: Criminology and Criminal Law), University of Pennsylvania.

BACKGROUND AND INTERESTS

In my research, I like to address measurement issues of conceptualization and operationalization of indicators, and policy issues of reducing inequality and improving effectiveness within systems of justice. I favor original data collection because when I supervise data collection, I know what the data represent, including both the strengths and weaknesses. For this same reason, I focus data collection efforts within a single location; data collection is easier to manage and, when the research has a policy focus, it is easier to influence reform at the local level.

WHAT INITIALLY ATTRACTED ME TO CRIMINAL JUSTICE

Like many criminal justice students today, I first became interested in criminology while pursuing what I thought would be a career in law. Like students today, my expectations were affected by media images of criminal justice. However, unlike today's images of cutting-edge technology used by police to apprehend heinous offenders, the news, television drama, and movie images I saw more often depicted police and judicial corruption, defendants who were unjustly convicted, jail suicides, prison riots, and women and minority groups demanding social equality. When a professor tried to steer me toward a career in juvenile probation, I was irked by his gender-bias and steered clear of anything related to delinquency. Ironically, it is the research area that most interests me now. Through an undergraduate internship experience, I was able to work briefly as a "paralegal." That experience serving indigent Native American clients convinced me that the system needed more help than an attorney could then provide.

I didn't actually decide to pursue criminology instead of law until the summer after graduation, but I knew I'd chosen wisely my first semester as a research assistant for the Pennsylvania Sentencing Commission. It was my first exposure to Gottfredson and Gottfredson's theoretical framework for effective decision making that has guided a lot of my work. The research took place in a small house on the edge of campus, but it was more important than any "silk stocking" lawyer's office. My desk was in the basement and my contribution was small,

BOX 8.2   CONTINUED

but I was there when the legislature first required every judge in the state to sentence in the same way. I was totally enthralled by criminology and have been ever since.

INTERESTS IN CURRENT AND PAST RESEARCH

I'm sort of a generalist in my research because many topics interest me, but justice is what I think most important, so that is a frequent topic of my research. I wrestle with what the concept of justice means and how we want systems of justice to achieve this surprisingly inexplicit goal. Within the United States, equal application of the law is a fundamental part of the socially constructed definition so I examine inequality or disparity issues based on race, ethnicity, sex, socioeconomic status, age, family status, and location. I also study discretion and how it can be structured to avoid abuse of power. These two fit nicely with my personal views on due process.

My interest in justice has been affected by new federal and state government requirements of uniform criminal justice responses based on criteria of offense. The intuitive appeal of these mandatory policies has been the visceral appreciation of equal application of the law and the control of judicial discretion. To understand dimensions of crime that are important, I have studied sequential patterns of offending among a large cohort population to understand issues of onset, recidivism, specialization, escalation, and desistance. I was lucky to help in the final coding of these Philadelphia data and from them have learned the importance of longitudinal designs. Some patterns of offending involve very young children who are processed by systems in which justice is conceptualized very differently. I now focus most of my attention there because effective early interventions should reduce the need for later efforts.

Within criminal justice, the mandatory policies have been popular because they meet the face validity requirements for equal application of the law, but turn out to lack construct validity, which is more important. Offense alone cannot accurately define similarly situated offenders because the processes by which defendants are accused and their offenses are defined are unequal. This remains an area that fascinates me, especially now as efficient expenditure of resources has become a dimension of justice, along with effective crime reduction and retribution.

I first started studying juvenile justice because the concept of justice in these legal venues seemed consistent and clear. Each state code was explicit that justice systems should meet the needs of individual youths. Crime wasn't traditionally a requirement for children to receive justice. I was naive, and quickly found that what constitutes justice here involves an important tension between due process and effectiveness. It is trying to reconcile these dimensions to understand justice that keep my attention. Systems have changed to include crime and retribution, and even more recently, efficiency has become a factor here too.

DATA COLLECTION TECHNIQUES USED

I pursue methodological strategies that enable me to approach the topics I study from multiple sources. Generally, the primary method involves archival data from case files from a criminal justice organization. I try to supplement these data with interviews, questionnaires, or focus

BOX 8.2 CONTINUED

groups with subjects who can represent offender populations and justice system personnel. Quotes available from the second sources always help to suggest meaning in the statistical results from the first source that I might not have considered in their absence. Many methodologists recommend this "triangulation" of method or indicators for the obvious benefit that two sources of evidence are better than one.

TYPE OF RESEARCH PLAN I PREFER AND WHY

My single most preferred method is to conduct primary data collection so I know what the data represent and the extent to which they will suffice to support the analyses, interpretations, and recommendations I hope to glean from them. For most of my career, funding sources and journal publications have seemed to favor secondary analyses of macro-level data testing crime etiology. This baffles me. When I have examined data collected by someone else, I have encountered confusing coding schemes, errors, and lack of documentation that has made substantive questions about the data difficult to answer. When the study requires aggregation or comparison across diverse locations, it is extremely difficult to be confident in the accuracy and consistency of the data. Secondary data analysis leaves the researcher vulnerable to the documentation, expertise, and similarity in purpose of the original effort.

ADVICE TO STUDENTS

First, have a plan, and study something that interests you. Don't just follow the funding streams, as funded research is what's politically popular but not necessarily what's important. I also can't emphasize enough how important it is to understand the research question before you begin collecting the data. Second, consider options for primary data collection. Too many researchers rely on big data sets collected by other people. Most of the time secondary data analysis suffers because an important concept can't be measured or the original design is not well suited to the research you want to do.

Third, think about collaboration. An academic career can be a lonely business, and it is usually more fun and better research if the project is a joint effort. Triangulation of methods and research crossover between disciplines is how many advances to science occur. Of course, just like the group projects you are familiar with as students, there can be frustration to collaborative efforts when responsibilities aren't evenly divided. Fourth, please realize that most of what we know about research design and methods comes from "rules of thumb" rather than clearly delineated procedures. I pass along from Travis Hirschi the following advice that has helped me to keep research fun: "Avoid the fallacy fallacy. When a theorist or methodologist tells you you cannot do something, do it anyway. Breaking rules can be fun!" (1973, pp. 171–172). [Sources: Hirschi, Travis. (1973). "Procedural Rules and the Study of Deviant Behavior," *Social Problems* 21 (2): 159–173.]

While most of the instruments that are devised to conceptualize these and other variables are of the paper-and-pencil variety and are often administered in a questionnaire format, some attitudinal variables may be measured through other creative means. For example, Thompson, Dabbs, and Frady (1990) studied 17 adult male first-offenders who were exposed to a 90-day shock incarceration program. The program was modeled after a military boot camp, and offenders were examined over time regarding their stress levels and self-concepts pertaining to social status. These researchers found, for instance, that these offenders' stress levels were lowest and their perceptions of social status were highest at the time of their admission to the boot camp. However, stress for most program participants heightened during the first 4 weeks, and their social status perceptions decreased during the same period. Eventually, their stress levels dropped and social status perceptions increased.

These researchers were able to chart these changes by testing saliva samples and varying levels of testosterone concentrations. Levels of testosterone appeared to decrease in response to increased stress and loss of social status, coincidentally during the first 4 weeks of boot camp. Eventually, testosterone levels for most participants increased, varying positively with decreased stress and higher perceptions of social status. Although this particular means of tracking stress is not unique, it is imaginative and suggests alternative ways of evaluating attitudinal dimensions. Furthermore, precise levels of testosterone can be measured or gauged.

Briefly summarizing, we construct our theoretical schemes and use nominal definitions liberally as a way of logically relating attitudes and behaviors and developing explanations for events. When hypotheses are derived for empirical testing, we must devise operational definitions for the terms used in our hypotheses. Operational definitions of terms are created by using epistemic correlates or observable characteristics that can be empirically determined. While some of our terms used may be concepts, inasmuch as they have direct empirical referents, other terms we use must be conceptualized as constructs. Constructs involve the use of indirect indicators of phenomena of interest to us. Operationalization is the process of developing operational definitions from nominal ones. Operationalization is also described as establishing constructs for some of the less empirical terms used in our theories.

Some variables are more a part of our empirical world (concepts) than other variables (constructs). Concepts and more elusive variables (constructs) are brought into the empirical world through quantification, where numbers are ultimately assigned. The fact that some of these variables are less tangible than others (e.g., attitudes, the psyche, stress), the numbers assigned to such intangible phenomena will vary in their meaning. Four different meanings have been assigned to numbers that represent social and psychological phenomena. These meanings are described as levels of measurement and are crucial to our data presentation, analysis, and interpretation.

Levels of Measurement

Four **levels of measurement** have been determined. These are the nominal, ordinal, interval, and ratio levels. Some investigators use other labels to describe these levels of measurement, such as classifiables or countables, rankables, and measurables (Peatman, 1963).

BOX 8.3   PERSONALITY HIGHLIGHT

MELISSA J. SPELCHEN
Research Associate, Rural Crime and Justice Center, Minot State University

Statistics: B.A., M.S. (criminal justice), Minot State University.

BACKGROUND AND INTERESTS

My interest in the field of criminology can be traced back to my childhood; I absolutely adored reading true-crime novels. At a young age, I would stay up way past my bedtime because I could never put the books down. And this was surprising, considering none of the extra time I had because of all the sports that I played in junior high and high school. I never focused on one type of true-crime book either, be it serial killing, domestic violence, or white-collar crime. As long as it was true crime, I would be enthralled. The turning point in my future career path occurred when I was in the 10th grade and began reading a book regarding convicted murderer Colin Thatcher, a former Canadian politician and son of former Saskatchewan premier Ross Thatcher. Thatcher was convicted in 1984 of the brutal murder of his ex-wife Joann Wilson in the garage of her upscale Regina, Saskatchewan home, near the Saskatchewan Legislative building. The book, *A Canadian Tragedy: Joann and Colin Thatcher—A Story of Love and Hate,* which was over 1,000 pages in hardcover, had my attention from page one and I remember taking it everywhere, just so I could finish reading it. In most cases, a vibrant 16-year-old usually has something better to do than read such a large book for enjoyment, but I did and it changed my life. From that moment I realized that I wanted to get into the minds of violent offenders and understand what made them "tick" and act so brutally. So my first chosen career direction was forensic psychology.

I had two main college options coming out of high school, either attend the University of Calgary in Calgary, Alberta, and take their law or psychology program, or Minot State University, where I was being recruited to play volleyball and take their Criminal Justice Program. I chose the latter and have been extremely happy with that decision ever since. Not only did I meet and have a chance to learn from Dr. Dean Champion, but I also have been mentored by two other incredible researcher/academics, Dr. Gary Rabe and Dr. Harry Hoffman. These three men have made my academic life at Minot State an absolute joy and I have learned most of my knowledge regarding academia and research from them. I completed my undergraduate degree, as well as my volleyball eligibility, in 4 years and I decided to stay at Minot State and get my master's degree in criminal justice. This is where my career path veered off. I was

BOX 8.3 CONTINUED

asked to teach an intro to criminal justice class in my second year and I fell in love with teaching. I have gone on to teach two more classes, juvenile justice and victims and victimology, and I really feel that I have found my calling. Also, since 1999, I have been involved with a research grant within the Criminal Justice Program at MSU. The initial research grant has turned into many grants incorporated in the Rural Crime and Justice Center (RCJC). And what started out as a founding graduate assistantship has turned into a full-time research associate position within the RCJC at Minot State University. So I have found my other calling, and since academia and research go hand-in-hand, I am set in life . . . after I complete a Ph.D. and find a job, of course.

My main interest throughout my latter years of my undergraduate degree and early years of my graduate degree has been researching juvenile justice, from both the criminal and psychological perspectives. So naturally, the theme of my thesis was centered on this interest and perspective.

I conducted an exploratory and descriptive study of 400 files (100 cases from the decades of the 1960s, 1970s, 1980s, and 1990s—50 female, 50 male) at the North Dakota Youth Correctional Center in Mandan, North Dakota. My mode of observation was content analysis, more specifically a qualitative form of content analysis entitled historical/comparative analysis, which is the researching of historical documents to describe a particular set of events or patterns that recur in different times. I asked four research questions: (1) Have treatment strategies and philosophies at the North Dakota Youth Correctional Center changed between the periods of 1960–1999? (2) Has there been a change in the pattern of offenses committed by juvenile offenders over time and has this affected the types of treatment offered? (3) Have the background characteristics and family history of juvenile offenders admitted to the NDYCC changed over time and has this affected the types of treatments offered? and (4) Have the types of diagnoses applied to juvenile offenders at the NDYCC changed over time and has this affected the types of treatment offered?

What I found is that many treatment strategies have remained stable due to consistency of certain attributes of juvenile offenders. These strategies and their affecting attributes included: attending school/GED because of a rising age yet lowered education level in juvenile offenders; and structured living, learning to respect authority, and emphasis on understanding behavior because of a consistency of status offenses, a lack of control by parents, and more diagnoses of conduct disorder among juveniles admitted to the NDYCC. The two treatment strategies that evolved most significantly were chemical abuse therapy and family therapy. Chemical abuse therapy was affected by consistency in alcohol and drug related offenses, the increase of drug and alcohol abuse by the juvenile, the increase and consistency of drug and alcohol problems among family members, and the increase of diagnoses of alcohol and cannabis abuse for the juvenile offender. Family therapy was affected by an increase of the juvenile offender's issues within the family and more specifically problems with the relationship between the juvenile and the parent; an increase of physical, drug, and sexual abuse by parents; a consistency of status offenses that should be controlled by the parents; and increasing divorce rates. The increase of a more serious and experienced offender in relation to both offense numbers and treatment experience has also affected the need for these strategies in terms of their detailedness.

BOX 8.3   CONTINUED

Within the Rural Crime and Justice Center, I currently work under the Nationwide Rural Area Law Enforcement Study (NRALES). The purpose of our study is to evaluate, on a nationwide scale, the Small Town and Rural Training programs put on by the National Center for State and Local Law Enforcement. The National Center falls under the umbrella of the Department of Homeland Security and the Federal Law Enforcement Training Center in Glynco, Georgia.

Our data is collected through the administering of onsite pre- and post-surveys as well as 3- and 6-month follow-up surveys. The type of research conducted within the NRALES is evaluation-based, giving us the opportunity to make suggestions on how to better training programs that are given to rural law enforcement and other agencies. The suggestions we make are through identifying issues such as: the type of criminal behaviors that are prevalent in small town and rural areas; what training, education, and prevention strategies are required to address these issues; what type of training law enforcement personnel would like to receive as well as what type of training should be provided related to homeland security. Through this grant, not only am I hands-on in conducting important and career building research, but I am also given the opportunity to travel across the United States and network, meeting various law enforcement and special-interest agency personnel.

In terms of preference, I don't feel that I have enough experience in the research field to be able to tell you which methods I like and don't like. But I look forward to the day when I do. My aspirations in the future are to complete a Ph.D., and conduct more criminal justice research with a psychology flavor on different aspects of juvenile justice including juvenile sexual assaults and the relationships between juvenile offenders and their parents.

ADVICE TO STUDENTS

- Don't be afraid of change. I really thought that I wanted to study the criminal mind and become a forensic psychologist, but that all changed when I taught a class. Let your research and your academia lead the way!
- Never give up and be persistent. Although it took me a long time to complete (besides driving 3 hours to Mandan, ND, and back, I spent hours in an enclosed room with no window going through 400 cases), I was determined to finish my thesis fully and properly, even with numerous distractions and unsupportive colleagues.
- Find a mentor. It is important for every graduate-level student to have one professor that shapes and guides your academics, your research, and sincerely cares about your future work. I was fortunate to have two, and I am forever indebted to them, for their intelligence, their professionalism, and their faith in me as a researcher and a future academic.

Happy Studying!

In a sense, numbers pretty much mean the same thing from one application to the next. For instance, higher level mathematics uses numbers in a consistent way, regardless of their application. In another sense, numbers mean different things, depending on what they are used to represent. When numbers are assigned to social and psychological variables, they take on different meanings, depending on how the variable has been measured. If we assign a "1" to a male and a "2" to a female, for example, the "1's" and "2's" will have a different meaning compared with the "1's" and "2's" we use in our description of ages. We will not be able to average the "1's" and "2's" assigned to gender categories, for example, since these numbers are simply used to distinguish males and females in our sample from one another (e.g., classifiables). Numbers assigned to different socioeconomic statuses or basketball ratings can be ranked (rankables). And numbers assigned various ages can be summed and averaged (measurables). Thus, numbers are interpreted differently depending on whatever they stand for in criminological research.

In this section, several popular levels of measurement are presented. This arrangement of levels moves from low to high, beginning with the nominal level and ending with the ratio level. The importance of distinguishing between different levels of measurement is that researchers have a greater range of data analysis and statistical test options where higher measurement levels can be assumed to underlie the data they have obtained. The fewest statistical and analytical options are associated with the nominal level of measurement, whereas the greatest number of options would be associated with the ratio level of measurement. Each of these levels of measurement is described below.

Nominal Level of Measurement

The lowest form of measurement is the **nominal level of measurement.** This level involves the classification or categorization of variables into nominal subclasses. Gender, for instance, has two nominal subclasses: male and female. Religious affiliation has numerous nominal subclasses, although they are generally divided for social research purposes into Protestant, Catholic, Jewish, and Other. Delinquency is most often treated as a nominal-level variable, where different types of delinquent conduct can be distinguished. "Felony" and "misdemeanor" are two nominal subclasses on the "type of crime" variable. "Urban" and "rural" serve to nominally categorize persons in terms of where they were reared or what they consider their home background to be. Different types of deviant behavior also may be placed into nominal subclasses. Each of these variables is a **categorical variable.** When numbers are assigned to these nominal subclasses, the numbers mean nothing more than to differentiate one subclass from another. Thus, nominal-level measurement is highly qualitative, and serves to distinguish between people according to discrete attributes.

Ordinal Level of Measurement

A higher level of measurement compared with the nominal level, the **ordinal level of measurement** not only allows researchers to distinguish between persons according to certain attributes, but the numbers assigned certain attributes are considered either higher or lower compared with one another. Socioeconomic status is generally considered measured according to the ordinal level of measurement. Federal court judges may be ranked higher than university professors or probation officers. The numbers assigned these various professions or occupations permit researchers to say that a "1" is higher or lower than a "2," which may be higher or lower than a "3," and so on. Other variables that might be measured according to an ordinal scale might be amount of force used by police when making arrests of suspects, juvenile probation officer labor turnover, delinquent peer group influence, level of jail officer training and professionalism, and job burnout among pretrial service officers. Most attitudinal variables are measured through the use of ordinal scales.

Assignment of numbers to data measured according to an ordinal scale permits researchers to make "greater than" or "less than" distinctions between different scores. However, we cannot know or determine actual distances between scores on a scale. Consider the intensity continuum of police professionalism below:

Nonprofessional   Professional

——— / —— / —————————— / – / —————————————————— / ——

　15　　25　　　　　　　26　30　　　　　　　　　　　　　　　　31

Points or units to the far left are toward the "nonprofessional" end of the continuum, whereas points or units toward the far right are toward the "professional" end of the continuum. Therefore, some police officers are more professional than others. Some officers are less professional than others. However, we cannot say how much more professional or less professional these officers are from each other. Observe that these points are not equidistant from one another. The scores of 15 and 25 are close together, while the scores of 25 and 26 are far apart. There is a great distance between 30 and 31, yet there is only a small distance between 26 and 30. This is the nature of ordinal scales. Ordinarily, we can say that one score is higher or lower in relation to other scores, but we are not permitted to say "how much higher" or "how much lower" these scores are from other scores. The magnitude of differences between scores on an ordinal scale has little meaning other than to locate scores relative to others along a continuum. There is no standard distance between units along the horizontal axis of an ordinal continuum.

This particular feature of ordinal scales limits the statistical and data analysis options available to researchers. Some statistical procedures require that we can specify the magnitude of score differences for certain arithmetic operations, such as averaging, square root functions, summing, multiplying, and dividing. Thus, averaging numbers derived from ordinal scales is not a legitimate arithmetic function. However, there are conventional applications of certain statistical measures to ordinal data even though a higher level of data is required. There are several reasons for these conventional misapplications of statistical procedures, and they will be discussed subsequently.

Interval Level of Measurement

Data measured according to the **interval level of measurement** are also assigned numbers. These numbers permit nominal differentiations between values. Furthermore, these numbers permit determinations of "greater than" or "less than." Additionally, these numbers have equal spacing along an intensity continuum, and researchers may say that there are specified distances between units. In the study by Thompson and colleagues (1990), for example, levels of testosterone in saliva specimens provided by several boot camp "shock probationers" would be measurable according to an interval scale. Thus, if we had several boot camp participants' testosterone levels indicated by scores on a testosterone scale, we might see something like this:

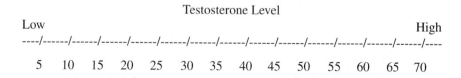

This hypothetical testosterone level continuum is graduated according to five-point intervals. These intervals are considered equal distances from each other. The distance between 5 and 10, for example, would be identical to the distance between 50 and 55. The distance between 10 and 30 would be equal to the distance between 50 and 70. This equal spacing of interval scales is desirable, because it permits us to use statistical procedures and other data analysis techniques that involve arithmetic operations such as averaging and square rooting. Comparing our hypothetical police professionalism scale with this hypothetical testosterone level scale, we would not be able to determine meaningful average police professionalism scores, whereas we would be able to compute meaningful average testosterone level values.

Ratio Level of Measurement

The **ratio level of measurement** is identical to the interval level of measurement with one exception. The ratio level of measurement assumes an absolute zero on some ratio continuum. Income is a ratio-level variable, since income may be measured according to a scale having an absolute zero. Persons can have no money. Where an absolute zero is assumed, values may be proportionately related to other values. Therefore, $50 is to $100 as $10,000 is to $20,000. Interval scales lack an absolute zero, and therefore, ratio statements are not permissible with such scales.

However, no procedure discussed in this book and in most other texts in statistics and methodology requires levels of measurement beyond the interval level. For instance, while income is actually measurable according to a ratio scale, it is treated as though it were interval. Since income has ratio-level properties, it also embraces properties of all other lower levels of measurement, including the interval level, the ordinal level, and the nominal level.

Various statistical measures and techniques are associated with different levels of measurement. Therefore, it is important to know how variables are measured initially before we decide which statistical procedures to apply. If a particular statistical procedure required that our data be measured according to an interval scale, it would not be considered appropriate to apply this statistical measure if our underlying levels of measurement achieved were either nominal or ordinal. Table 8.1 describes various permissible arithmetic actions that can be performed with numbers assigned to variable subclasses, depending on the level of measurement assumed and associated with these variables.

TABLE 8.1   Levels of Measurement and Statistical Applications

If the measurement level required by our statistical tests is:	Then, we may apply:
1. Nominal	1. Nominal-level procedures
2. Ordinal	2. Nominal- and ordinal-level procedures
3. Interval	3. Nominal-, ordinal-, and interval-level procedures
4. Ratio	4. Nominal-, ordinal-, interval-, and ratio-level procedures

Table 8.1 says that analytical tools and statistical procedures may be used according to whether certain levels of measurement have been achieved. The characteristics of all lower levels of measurement are embodied within higher levels of measurement. Therefore, the interval level of measurement may also be treated as an ordinal scale, and it may be divided nominally. However, if we choose to divide interval scales according to some lower-level-of-measurement standard, we lose a certain amount of information. In the case of reducing an interval scale to a nominal one, we lose the equal spacing between units as well as the "greater than" or "less than" qualities it possesses. This is throwing away valuable data. Researchers may be faulted for "underutilizing" analytical techniques if they have the data to warrant applications of procedures suitable for higher measurement levels. A case of underutilization would be to take various age scores for some sample of elements and divide them into two categories, "old" and "young." By dichotomizing such values, we destroy the interval features of the scores. The statistical measures we might apply to such dichotomies may not be as sophisticated as those measures that require the interval level of measurement for their application.

Alternatively, some researchers attempt to do too much with the data they have collected. If they apply statistical techniques or analytical procedures to data measured according to an ordinal scale, and where those statistical procedures require at least an interval scale, then they are violating at least one important assumption underlying those techniques or procedures. In the social sciences, this is a common occurrence and has come to be regarded as conventional. The frequent application of averages or means to data measured according to ordinal scales, such as attitudinal scores, is typical of such a violation. If we observe police professionalism scores of 10, 20, 25, 30, and 15, for example, their sum is 100. The average score would be 100 divided by the number of scores. Since there are five scores, the average score would be computed as follows: 100/5 = 20. The average professionalism score is 20. What does 20 mean? Not much. Again, the reason is that in order for averages to be computed, scale scores must be equal distances from one another along a continuum. We can see above that the hypothetical police professionalism continuum does not have equal spacing along the intensity continuum. Nevertheless, attitudinal scores are frequently averaged by researchers. Therefore, two major pitfalls to be avoided by researchers are:

1. Underutilizing information collected by using lower-level-of-measurement tests and procedures with higher-level-of-measurement data, and
2. Overanalyzing data by applying tests requiring higher levels of measurement to data measured according to lower levels of measurement.

Types of Scaling Procedures for Measuring Variables

Measuring social and/or psychological variables may be accomplished by applying several popular methods devised by researchers. These include (1) Likert scaling or the method of summated ratings and (2) Thurstone scaling or the **method of equal-appearing intervals.**

Likert-Type Scales

Rensis Likert (1932) was instrumental in devising the **method of summated ratings** as a means of distinguishing between persons according to differing degrees of ordinal-level characteristics. Subsequently labeled a **Likert scale,** this procedure is probably the most popular attitudinal scaling method used in criminology and other social sciences today. Likert scales are widely used in criminological research. A survey of articles in the database of the *Criminal Justice Abstracts* shows 300+ studies where Likert scaling was mentioned in summaries of research investigations. This is probably a gross underestimate, since article abstracts typically do not include specific scaling methods used to measure attitudinal and sociodemographic variables.

Likert scales are easy to identify in the research literature. We may identify them according to the response patterns that accompany attitudinal items in questionnaires geared to measure ordinal-level attitudinal phenomena. Respondents are provided a list of statements with which they agree or disagree to vary degrees of intensity. For example, the following items are typical Likert-style items:

SA = Strongly agree
A = Agree
U,A = Undecided, probably agree
U,D = Undecided, probably disagree
D = Disagree
SD = Strongly disagree

CHECK (OR SELECT) THE RESPONSE THAT BEST FITS YOU.

1. Firearms ownership in the United States should be limited to law enforcement officers and military personnel.
   (SA) (A) (U,A) (U,D) (D) (SD)

2. The right to bear arms is fundamental for all U. S. citizens.
   (SA) (A) (U,A) (U,D) (D) (SD)

3. When guns are outlawed, only outlaws will have guns.
   (SA) (A) (U,A) (U,D) (D) (SD)

4. There is a high relation between access to firearms and violent crime.
   (SA) (A) (U,A) (U,D) (D) (SD)

5. Firearms don't kill people; other people kill people.
   (SA) (A) (U,A) (U,D) (D) (SD)

6. Children should receive firearms instruction when they are very young.
   (SA) (A) (U,A) (U,D) (D) (SD)

These items obviously have something to do with firearms ownership and use in the United States. The categories, "Strongly agree," "Agree," "Undecided, probably agree," "Undecided, probably disagree," "Disagree," and "Strongly disagree" comprise a graduated pattern indicative of **weighting.** Respondents choose the response that best fits them. These responses are weighted numerically. Depending on the choices one makes, the **item weights** of selected responses are summed to yield a raw score, hence the term *summated ratings.*

An assumption made by researchers is that those persons who favor or disfavor gun control to varying degrees will select more or less intense responses for each question. Those strongly in favor of gun control and limiting firearms possession only to law enforcement officers and military personnel would tend to agree with items #1 and #4, and they would tend to disagree with the other items. Those favoring gun ownership and private use of firearms would tend to agree with items #2, #3, #5, and #6, and they would probably disagree with items #1 and #4. This scheme is not foolproof, however, since those favoring private ownership of firearms may not want small children to be exposed to them. Also, persons who agree that constitutional guarantees mandate private ownership and use of firearms may not agree that when guns are outlawed, only outlaws will have guns or that there is a strong relation between accessibility of firearms and violent crime.

A prevailing belief of researchers is that there is a fairly constant correspondence between the attitudes manifested by people and their behaviors. Therefore, it is often assumed that

$$\text{Attitude } X \longrightarrow \text{Behavior } X'$$

where X is a particular attitude expressed and X' is the behavior that corresponds with that attitude. Thus, if some persons indicate strong prejudicial attitudes toward members of some minority group, it is assumed that they will probably discriminate or act differently toward those minorities. The attitude–action relationship is not consistent, however. Currently, considerable controversy exists about how accurately attitudinal measures actually forecast behaviors corresponding with those attitudes.

Police Professionalism Scale.   To illustrate the application of Likert scaling, we must begin with a nominal definition of some phenomenon. Suppose we wish to measure police officer professionalism. We might define police officer professionalism nominally as the adoption of a set of attitudes and values by police officers, where those attitudes and values are consistent with a professional ideology (Crank et al., 1987, p. 1). Professionalization has been conceptualized as the process of legitimation an occupation goes through as it endeavors to improve its social status. Crank and his associates indicate that efforts toward conceptualizing police professionalism have focused on recruitment and training practices as well as management policies of police departments.

It is significant to note that a clear, concise nominal definition of police professionalism does not exist in the above paragraph. This is not intended to be critical of Crank and colleagues, since their extensive research efforts have been designed to devise such a concept and measure it. The fact is that many nominal definitions, including the one for police professionalism, are elusive, vague, and nonspecific. We might suspect as much, considering our earlier attempt to define anxiety using the *Webster's New World Dictionary* as our source. Furthermore, this author researched at least 20 separate articles where police professionalism was studied and was used in different article titles. No article contained a definition of police professionalism, not even a vague, elusive, or nonspecific one. It was as if everyone knew what it meant and it didn't need to be defined. Nevertheless, these articles discussed police professionalism at length, including factors associated with it, how it develops, and how it influences officer performance and police–citizen interactions.

However, from the statements about police professionalism provided by Crank and colleagues, we can glean that police professionalism has something to do with rigorous selection and training procedures for police officers. Perhaps acquiring more education is regarded by many as evidence of police professionalism, or achieving high scores on various fitness and situational tests.

In any case, once we have given a term a nominal definition, the next step is to give the term some substance through the creation of an operational definition of it. Regoli and colleagues (1987) attempted this particular task, although they were primarily interested in exploring the relation between police professionalism and cynicism. They devised various statements believed to be indicative of police professionalism. Some of the statements they devised are shown below:

Police Professionalism Scale

1. I systematically read the professional journals (e.g., *Police Chief*).
2. I regularly attend professional meetings at the local level.
3. Although I would like to, I really don't read the police journals (e.g., *Police Chief*) too often.
4. Some other occupations are actually more important to society than mine is.
5. Other professions are actually more vital to society than mine is.
6. The importance of being a police officer is sometimes overstressed.
7. There is really no way to judge fellow police officers' competence.
8. There is not much opportunity to judge how another police officer does his or her work.
9. My fellow police officers have a pretty good idea about each others' competence.

Thus, a strict operational definition of police professionalism would be "police professionalism is what the Regoli et al. police professionalism scale measures."

Accompanying each item might be the following responses and numerical weights:

Strongly Agree	Agree	Undecided, Probably Agree	Undecided, Probably Disagree	Disagree	Strongly Disagree
6	5	4	3	2	1

or

Strongly Agree	Agree	Undecided, Probably Agree	Undecided, Probably Disagree	Disagree	Strongly Disagree
1	2	3	4	5	6

These two response patterns are designed to accompany positively worded and negatively worded statements, such as "I like my job" or "I hate my job." Regarding the police professionalism scale above, items #1, #2, and #9 appear favorably worded, while the other items are somewhat negatively worded. If a police officer strongly agrees with statement #1, "I systematically read the professional journals," then we might interpret this response as a sign of the officer's professionalism or commitment to the profession of policing. Also, if the police officer's response is strong disagreement to item #7, "There is really no way to judge fellow officers' competence," this response suggests that "professional" criteria exist whereby officers may be evaluated objectively. We might interpret agreements with items #3, #4, #5, #6, #7, and #8 as indicative of low professionalism, since the importance of the police officer role compared with other professions and occupations is played down, or perhaps objective criteria do not exist to evaluate this role.

The weights associated with each response reflect different intensities of agreement or disagreement with these statements. This particular weight arrangement is a six-point response pattern. The reversed weights shown in the example above are useful whenever we wish to interrupt the monotony of the same response pattern. Also, those who answer these statements may do so with little interest or enthusiasm. Sometimes, respondents don't read the statements carefully, and they rush through the questionnaire checking the first answers to all questions. A careful inspection of item weights associated with the responses they select may tell the researchers whether their responses are valid or whether they should be questioned. For instance, if someone says "Strongly agree" to the statement, "I love my job," and later, that same person says "Strongly agree" to the statement, "I hate my job," this suggests a problem. Specifically, it suggests a response set or set response, where respondents rush through their questionnaires and check the first responses they encounter. They do this simply to "get it over with quick." For all practical purposes, their responses to the questionnaire are worthless to the researcher, because they didn't take any interest in completing it and giving truthful responses. This issue will be addressed later in the section dealing with measurement issues.

Returning to our example of police professionalism and the scale items that comprise it, we have hypothetically assigned a six-point response pattern to the nine items above. This means that the most points one may receive per item answered is "6," while the least number of points is "1." If there are nine items that comprise the scale of police professionalism, we may quickly calculate the range of raw scores officers may receive when they respond to these scale items. We may multiply the largest weight, 6, by the number of items on the scale. This is (6)(9 items) = 54. Multiplying the number of scale items by the smallest weight, 1, will give us (1)(9 items) = 9. If we designate 6 to be indicative of a high degree of professionalism and 1 to be indicative of a low degree of professionalism, then the range of responses for this particular set of items will be from 9 (low professionalism) to 54 (high professionalism).

For example, if 10 officers respond to these nine items, they might receive the following raw scores: 14, 22, 25, 29, 32, 33, 33, 40, 44, and 49. These are ordinal-level scores, since they were derived from a Likert scale. These raw scores may be grouped into different categories (low professionalism, 9–25; medium or moderate professionalism, 26–35; and high professionalism, 36–54). This categorization is mostly arbitrary, depending on the number of officers who respond and the overall raw scores they receive for this measure.

So far, what steps have we taken to measure police professionalism?

1. We devised a nominal definition of police professionalism.
2. We created several items or statements that appeared to correlate highly with the nominal meaning of the term.
3. We devised a six-point response pattern for all items.
4. We assigned item weights to the different responses.
5. We administered the set of items to 10 police officers.
6. We summed each officer's weights for the nine items and determined their total scores.
7. We devised three intensity categories to portray police professionalism, according to the distribution of their raw scores.

There is nothing magical about any of this. The items that have been created were literally the products of the researchers' thoughts. They formulated items that they believed would closely parallel what they meant by police professionalism. But this doesn't necessarily mean that they derived the best items or the only items.

Numbers of Items. This nine-item scale is only one of many scales we might construct to measure police professionalism or any other attitudinal variable. We might create 35 statements or 100 statements. We might even use one statement to measure this and other phenomena. We might furnish officers with the following statement: "I consider myself a true police professional." The response might be a simple "Yes" or "No." Of course, not many police officers are going to say that they are not professional. We will expand the number of items used to measure any phenomenon in order to create a wider range of response over which these officers may be distributed. This will enable us to obtain some meaningful variation on this variable and correlate the raw scores with scores on other variables. There is no limit to the number of items researchers may use whenever they create Likert scales. Of course, larger numbers of items may wear out respondents. They may approach a 50-page questionnaire with apathy or resistance, whereas they might feel more comfortable with a 10-page or shorter questionnaire.

Forms of Response. The particular form of response for Likert scaling is not restricted to the agree–disagree variety. Any response pattern that can be graduated (very strongly/very weak, increasing/decreasing, very positive/very negative, more/less) may be adapted to fit the Likert pattern. The most common response pattern is the agree–disagree format shown above, however.

There is little uniformity pertaining to the number of response categories, and there is no uniformity regarding the number of statements researchers may use to measure things. Decisions about the number of items and the particular response patterns to be used are made by the researcher. Consideration is made for the size of the group where the measure will be administered. If the researcher's intention is to administer the measure to thousands of people, then more statements will be required to render a desirable degree of precision regarding the raw scores obtained. Perhaps more responses per item will be required as well.

For example, if we expand the number of items from 9 to 25, then our range of response becomes $(1)(25) = 25$ (low) to $(6)(25) = 150$ (high). If we expand the number of items to

50, we have a range of from 50 to 300, using a six-point response pattern. Or we can devise a 10-point response pattern with 10 items and have a low score of 10 and a high score of 100 (1×10 and 10×10).

Sometimes the Likert format may be used to characterize attitudes of persons toward particular issues or programs. Kaci and Tarrant (1988) studied the attitudes of prosecuting attorneys and probation departments toward diversion programs for persons charged with spousal abuse in domestic violence cases. They were able to solicit opinions from district attorneys' offices in two California counties concerning various attitudes toward diversion programs. They devised categories such as those shown below:

Very High Rating of Diversion,
Highly Effective

Good Opinion of Diversion,
Somewhat Effective

Guarded Opinion of Diversion,
Possibly Effective

Totally Negative Opinion of
Diversion, Ineffective Program

No Opinion of Diversion

The proportion or percentage of responses of district attorneys were charted for each of these categories. In the study by Kaci and Tarrant, they found that a majority of district attorneys rated diversion programs as highly effective or somewhat effective, on the basis of these percentage distributions. This is a type of Likert pattern that appears to have some utility in portraying respondent opinions.

Another version of a Likert-type scale is the Multidimensional Anger Inventory devised by Judith Siegel (1985). Her inventory consists of 38 statements with a five-response pattern per statement. Each response is weighted as follows: 1 = completely undescriptive; 2 = somewhat undescriptive; 3 = descriptive; 4 = rather descriptive; 5 = completely descriptive. Siegel asked respondents to rate themselves on each of the items below.

_____   1. I tend to get angry more frequently than most people.

_____   2. Other people seem to get angrier than I do in similar circumstances.

_____   3. I harbor grudges that I don't tell anyone about.

_____   4. I try to get even when I am angry with someone.

_____   5. I am secretly quite critical of others.

_____   6. It is easy to make me angry.

_____   7. When I am angry with someone, I let that person know.

_____   8. I have met many people who are supposed to be experts who are not better than I.

_____ 9. Something makes me angry almost every day.

_____ 10. I often feel angrier than I should.

_____ 11. I feel guilty about expressing my anger.

_____ 12. When I am angry with someone, I take it out on whoever is around.

_____ 13. Some of my friends have habits that annoy and bother me very much.

_____ 14. I am surprised at how often I feel angry.

_____ 15. Once I let people know I'm angry, I can put it out of my mind.

_____ 16. People talk about me behind my back.

_____ 17. At times, I feel angry for no specific reason.

_____ 18. I can make myself angry about something in the past just by thinking about it.

_____ 19. Even after I have expressed my anger, I have trouble forgetting about it.

_____ 20. When I hide my anger from others, I think about it for a long time.

_____ 21. People can bother me just by being around.

_____ 22. When I get angry, I stay angry for hours.

_____ 23. When I hide my anger from others, I forget about it pretty quickly.

_____ 24. I try to talk over problems with people without letting them know I am angry.

_____ 25. When I get angry, I calm down faster than most people.

_____ 26. I get so angry I feel like I might lose control.

_____ 27. If I let people see the way I feel, I'd be considered a hard person to get along with.

_____ 28. I am on my guard with people who are friendlier than I expected.

_____ 29. It's difficult for me to let people know I'm angry.

_____ 30. I get angry when someone lets me down.

_____ 31. I get angry when people are unfair.

_____ 32. I get angry when someone blocks my plans.

_____ 33. I get angry when I am delayed.

_____ 34. I get angry when someone embarrasses me.

_____ 35. I get angry when I have to take orders from someone less capable than I.

_____ 36. I get angry when I have to work with incompetent people.

_____ 37. I get angry when I do something stupid.

_____ 38. I get angry when I am not given credit for something that I have done.

Siegel has devised various subscales on this instrument to measure specific aspects of anger, such as hostile anger and situations that evoke anger. Raw scores received by respondents can be compared with other variables, such as gender, prior record, or probationer/parolee designation. Researchers such as Delores E. Craig-Morehead have used this scale to measure anger levels of inmates. Craig-Morehead found, for instance, that anger levels vary according to the conviction offense of inmates in a large penitentiary in a Midwestern state. Interestingly, property offenders had the highest anger scores compared with other inmates in her study, including those convicted of violent crimes.

The Meaning of Raw Scores Derived from Likert Scales.   Provided that the items on a Likert scale are true indicators of the phenomenon to be measured, what do the **raw scores** mean that are yielded? Raw scores by themselves mean relatively little. Raw attitudinal scores are of the greatest value whenever they are compared with one another. Thus, persons who receive raw scores of 50 or lower on some attitudinal scale may be predicted to behave differently in some social situation compared with those who receive raw scores greater than 50.

A hypothetical example illustrates how we might use scores from a Likert scale. Suppose we administer our nine-item police professionalism scale to a random sample of 100 police officers of the Los Angeles Police Department, and that they receive raw scores ranging from 9 to 54. Further suppose that we determine that approximately 50 of these officers have scores of 32 or lower, while the other half of our sample has scores above 32. If we decide to see whether professionalism is associated with the rate of citizen complaints filed against these police officers, we might devise a table such as the one shown in Table 8.2.

Table 8.2 is a hypothetical cross-tabulation of police professionalism with citizen complaint filings against officers. A cross-tabulation is where two or more variables are compared with one another in tabular form. One variable is placed across the top of the table, while the other variable is located down the lefthand side. The more influential variable is placed across the top of the table. In this case, police professionalism is believed to effect changes in citizen complaint filings. Thus, it is placed across the top of the table. Police professionalism has been divided into two categories or dichotomized, according to "high" or 33 points or more on the police professionalism scale and "low" or 32 or fewer points on the scale. The number of citizen complaint filings is depicted down the lefthand side. Complaint filings by citizens have been divided into two categories, high and low, based on three or more filings (3+) or two or fewer filings.

TABLE 8.2   Hypothetical Distribution of Citizen Complaints Field Against Police Officers Who Have High and Low Amounts of Professionalism

	Police Professionalism*		
	High (33+)	Low (32 or less)	Totals
High Citizen Complaint Filings (3+)	5	35	40
Low Citizen Complaint Filings (2 or less)	45	15	60
Totals	50	50	100

*Measured by nine-point professionalism scale, where 32 or lower means low professionalism, while 33 or higher means high professionalism.

Researchers who read this table will understand from this tabular arrangement that police professionalism influences citizen complaint filings. Had we placed citizen complaint filings across the top of the table and police professionalism down the lefthand side, this may have meant that we believe that citizen complaint filings determine or influence one's police professionalism. We are merely following an accepted conventional tabular arrangement here by placing the variables where one variable is the more influential cause of the other variable.

According to Table 8.2, we might expect to find that officers with high professionalism scores tend to have low numbers of citizen complaints filed against them, whereas officers with low professionalism scores tend to have high numbers of citizen complaints filed against them. In Table 8.2, 45 out of 50 officers with high professionalism scores have low numbers of citizen complaints filed against them, while 35 out of 50 officers with low professionalism scores have high numbers of citizen complaints filed against them. These findings strengthen our belief that we have measured police professionalism with these items. In short, the more professional the police officers, the less likely they will engage in the types of behaviors that cause citizen complaints. This is one way these Likert-type scores can be used and interpreted.

The cutting points we used to determine high and low police professionalism and high and low numbers of citizen complaint filings were not magically determined. Usually, researchers determine these cutting points where the samples can be conveniently divided in logical ways. If our 100 police officers are distributed widely from scores of 9 to 54, we can use the point that divides them into halves as our cutting point. Perhaps that dividing line is the raw score of 32, where half of our officers are below this point and the other half of them are above this point.

Also, suppose we tally the number of complaints for all officers and determine that there is an average of three complaints filed against officers during the year. We might note that some officers have 10 complaints filed against them, while some officers have no complaints filed against them. Thus, we might arbitrarily say that those officers who have three or more complaints filed against them will be in the "high complaint" group, while those receiving two or fewer complaints will be in the "low complaint" group. This distinction will enable us to cross-tabulate these results as shown in Table 8.2. Thus, the five officers with high professionalism scores also have high numbers of complaints filed against them, or three or more. The 45 officers with high professionalism scores also have low numbers of complaints filed against them, or two or less.

"Don't Know" or "Undecided" Responses.   The response scenarios provided in the examples above did not contain "don't know" or "undecided" response options. The major concession to the "undecided" category was two "middle-of-the-road" categories designated as "undecided, but probably agree" and "undecided, but probably disagree." This arrangement was deliberate. The reason is as follows.

Typically, many Likert scales contain "undecided" or "don't know" categories. Thus, we might see a response pattern like this:

Strongly Agree	Agree	Undecided	Disagree	Strongly Disagree
5	4	3	2	1

Notice that the "undecided" category above has been "weighted" with a "3." The same would be true of a "don't know" response. Some of the social sciences have reported a general trend in America toward noncommittal responses or middle-of-the-road opinions about things. Thus, if persons are presented with a "don't know" or "undecided" option, they will probably take it. It is a safe response. Unfortunately, it has no weight or value. Persons who honestly don't know or are undecided about some statement are neither in agreement or disagreement with it. When these categories are assigned weights, the resulting point totals or raw scores lose some of their meaning.

Suppose someone responds to a scale with 10 items, where the five-point response pattern shown above is used. A possible score range exists of 10 to 50. It is possible for someone to obtain a score of 30 strictly on the basis of checking the "undecided" response category for each of the 10 scale items. This score is contrasted with others near it, where persons have received individual item weights of 4, 5, or 2. These other weights are meaningful, reflecting one's intensity of attitude toward something. Rather than run the risk of winding up with meaningless "30" scores in a scale such as this, the "undecided, but probably agree" and "undecided, but probably disagree" options are created. This gives persons an opportunity to say they are undecided, but it also gives them a chance to lean one way or another in terms of their attitudinal intensity.

This means forcing them to make a choice one way or another. While many respondents apparently have no serious objections to these forced choices, a few respondents have been known to write "don't know" or "undecided" in capital letters in the margins of their questionnaires, or perhaps a string of profanity in response to these forced-choice scenarios. The presumption made by researchers who study attitudes, however, is that people generally have attitudes, one way or another, about various issues. The "undecided, probably agree/disagree" choices simply make it easier for them to make a middle-of-the-road decision with some degree of commitment. Furthermore, it permits researchers to give meaningful weights to these middle categories.

Several elaborate techniques have been proposed to deal with "don't know" or "undecided" responses, such as assigning these items the "average" weight otherwise assigned to the other items where persons actually express "agree" or "disagree" choices. This is tantamount to putting words in the respondents' mouths and creating artificial scores for them. Thus, this alternative is discouraged. It is preferable to provide "forced-choice" responses and risk offending a few respondents while obtaining meaningful responses rather than to use "don't know" categories and assign meaningless weights to these choices.

What do you do when respondents leave certain items blank and fail to answer them? First, don't put words in their mouths by creating artificial responses for them based on their responses to the completed items. There are different kinds of "missing item" situations. Did the respondent skip one item in a 10-page questionnaire? Did the respondent skip one page of a 10-page questionnaire? Did the respondent skip four pages of a 10-page questionnaire? Any respondent who skips one or more pages when completing a questionnaire is rushing through it and probably not taking it seriously. One page skipped may be accidental. Two or more pages skipped is apathy and carelessness.

The recommended solution when one page is skipped is to survey the contents of the page. If a portion of a scale is printed on the page, then that scale should be dropped from the questionnaire. If several key questions are on the page, such as age, years of education, gender, and socioeconomic status, it might be a good idea to discard the entire questionnaire. It is better not to have the additional questionnaire as a part of your collected data, where strong evidence exists that the respondent did not take the study seriously. Skipped pages or numerous skipped items should tell you something. Dropping such questionnaires from your study makes your study better and more reliable anyway.

The recommended solution when one or two items are skipped is to determine if those items are a part of a scale. If they are part of a scale, drop the scale from the questionnaire. This type of omission frequently accounts for odd sample analyses in articles and reports. A researcher may indicate that 600 persons were surveyed and responded. But a table included in the report may show income averages for 590 persons. This probably means that 10 persons did not disclose their incomes to the investigator. The same thing may happen with other variables in other tables. Don't be disturbed when reading reports and different sample sizes are reported for different tabular analyses. Omissions of questions by respondents are common occurrences.

Strengths and Weaknesses of Likert Scales.   Some of the major advantages of summated rating scales are:

1. Likert scales are easy to construct and interpret. Because researchers combine their professional experience with logic to derive items from an abstract theoretical universe of some trait, it is not too difficult to construct a questionnaire as a measure. Researchers are at liberty to word statements derived in any manner they choose, provided that they adhere to some logical standard of continuity between the trait being measured and the items used to measure it. Scoring Likert scales is easy also. Furthermore, statements can be worded negatively or positively, and numerical weights can be assigned to any common Likert response format. It is a simple matter to sum the responses to individual statements and derive a total score or raw score that may be compared with other scores from the same scale. The larger (or smaller) the score, the more (or less) the subject possesses the attribute being measured, according to the logic underlying this scaling procedure.

2. Likert scaling is the most common scaling format used in criminology and criminal justice. Likert summated rating measures are most frequently applied in social research. The ease of application and simplicity of interpretation are factors that make this scaling procedure especially attractive. The popularity of this measurement form is evidenced by its widespread conventional use in criminology and criminal justice.

3. Likert scaling is flexible. The flexibility of these scales is unattained by any other attitudinal scaling procedure yet devised. Researchers are at liberty to include as many or as few items in their measures as they choose. Because each item is presumed to count equally in the measure of some phenomenon, increasing the number of statements or responses to statements will increase the instrument's ability to disclose differences in the trait measured as group size increases.

4. Summated rating scales lend themselves to ordinal-level measurement. Numerous ordinal-level statistical procedures exist for assessing variations and patterns in social and psychological phenomena.

5. Likert scales are similar to other forms of attitude measurement such as Thurstone scaling or Guttman scaling. Inspections of scores derived by other scaling procedures show that Likert scaling yields raw scores that are roughly equivalent with those obtained by alternative means.

Weaknesses of Likert scales include the following:

1. There is no consistent meaning that can be attached to the raw scores derived by such measurement. There is little that can be said about raw scores by themselves. Raw scores vary according to the number of statements devised and the extensiveness of response patterns used. This adds to the inconsistency of things as well. Summated rating measures are primarily useful when they permit comparisons to be made between individuals.

2. It is assumed that each item in the measure has identical weight in relation to every other item. This is not necessarily a valid assumption. Certain statements compared with other statements may have greater meaning or relevance to the trait being measured. Different persons may possess a given attitude to the same degree, although they may respond differently to common items on the measure.

3. Persons receiving the same score on a measure do not necessarily possess the trait or attitude to the same degree. This means that our measures are never as precise as they could be. Raw scores are crude estimates of peoples' locations on intensity continuums.

4. The validity of summated ratings is questionable. Because the process of deducing items from an abstract universe of traits is a logical one, the possibility always exists that some items may be wrongly included in the measuring instrument at any given time. How do we know that we are measuring what we say we are measuring? The validity of our measures is generally determined by comparing score results with manifest behaviors of respondents in prediction situations. This is not an infallible process.

Thurstone Scales and Equal-Appearing Intervals

A second type of measuring technique is **Thurstone scaling.** Another term for it is equal-appearing interval scaling (Thurstone & Chave, 1929). This technique probably rates second in overall social science usage to Likert scaling, although probably fewer than 10 percent of all researchers might be inclined to use it. A survey of article abstracts between 1968–2004 from *Criminal Justice Abstracts* showed that approximately 70 studies cited Thurstone scaling in their abstract summaries, although it is likely that Thurstone scaling was more widely used during this time period. This is because article abstracts are somewhat sketchy, particularly about details of methods used to measure critical research variables.

Thurstone scaling differs from the Likert summated rating format by supplying each attitudinal statement with a specific scale value that stands for the intensity of the statement itself. Thus, instead of deriving a total score from accumulated item weights in the case of Likert scales, Thurstone scales would use intensity values associated with two or three items selected by respondents from a larger list of items. Consider the five statements below:

(10.5) **1.** Life imprisonment might be an acceptable punishment for child sexual abusers.
(2.1) **2.** Convicted child sexual abusers should be treated like any other convicted felons.
(3.4) **3.** Most child sexual abusers suffer from psychological problems and should be hospitalized rather than imprisoned.
(1.8) **4.** I would allow former convicted child sexual abusers to work as custodians in large apartment complexes with large numbers of children.
(8.3) **5.** Child sexual abuse is itself an aggravating factor in any prosecution for child sexual abuse.

The five statements above are hypothetical items that might be used to measure district attorneys' attitudes toward prosecuting child sexual abusers. Supposedly, these items are designed to reflect different intensities or degrees to which persons hold one view or another toward some idea, issue, person, or group. The values in parentheses are item weights or intensities assigned through a simple, but rather elaborate, judging procedure. In this hypothetical example, the larger the value, the more intense one's position toward the prosecution of child sexual abusers. Persons who would select item #1, for example, would probably press the prosecution of alleged child sexual abusers more vigorously than those who might select item #4.

Consider several statements designed to measure one's degree of racial prejudice:

1. I would consider living next door to members of race *X*.
2. I would consider marrying a member of race *X*.
3. I would bar members of race *X* from my church.

It is apparent that each of these items reflects a different degree of acceptance or hostility toward members of race *X*. We might consider the most accepting item as #2, where one might agree to marry persons from race *X*. The least accepting item might be #3, where respondents would not permit members of race *X* to belong to their churches.

Therefore, instead of furnishing respondents with a questionnaire consisting of various Likert-type items with which they must agree or disagree, researchers using Thurstone scales would provide them with a list of items from which they would choose two or three that they agree with the most. These items would already have weights assigned that reflect each item's intensity.

How do researchers devise these Thurstone scales? Thurstone recommended that investigators begin by creating a large number of statements that they believe closely correlate with the trait to be measured. Thurstone recommended that about 100 statements should be constructed. Next, at least 25 judges should inspect these items and sort them into various intensity categories. Thurstone recommended 25 judges, although he later indicated that fewer judges could accomplish the task adequately. The intensity categories into which these items might be sorted would consist of seven, nine, or eleven categories.

Who are the judges and how are the categories conceived? Originally, Thurstone envisioned using university professors who taught psychology courses as judges. He believed they would be able to sort items of different intensities into appropriate categories, largely because of their training and expertise in attitudinal measurement. Since it was quite difficult to get these individuals to perform such sorting chores, this qualification was later relaxed. Currently, anyone may be a judge and sort these items, including introductory students in criminology courses. Sorting was simplified by providing "judges" with boxes containing various numbers of slots. Judges would be handed items individually typed on strips of paper. They would be asked to read each item and place it in one of seven, nine, or eleven categories, ranging from "low intensity" to "high intensity." These slots or categories would be numbered, and it would be easy to calculate the average for each item, according to the categories it was assigned by the judges.

Consider the following simplified example. Suppose we were to ask 25 judges to sort ten statements into seven categories. We might designate each statement by letters, including items A, B, C, D, E, F, G, H, I, and J. We would hand each judge slips of paper containing each statement. Each judge would sort the statements into the various categories or slots, according to each item's intensity (in the judge's opinion or "judgment"). Below is Statement A and the number of judges who sorted it into various categories.

STATEMENT A

Category	Number of Judges Placing Item in Category	Category Multiplied by Number of Judges
1	5	5
2	2	4
3	6	18
4	8	32
5	3	15
6	0	0
7	1	7
Totals	25	81

Hypothetical Statement A, whatever it might be, has been rated by 25 judges and placed into one of seven categories as shown. The categories into which it has been placed by these judges are used to "weight" Statement A. Thus, category numbers are multiplied by the number of judges placing Statement A into those categories. These are the products shown in the far right column. To determine an item's "average weight," we compute a simple average, or $81/25 = 3.2$. Statement A's weight is 3.2.

After all items have been sorted and assigned numerical weights, it is possible to select approximately 20 or 30 of these statements for use in our final questionnaire. Some statements will have weights in the 6–7 range, while others will have weights in the 1–2 range. The objective in our statement selections is to include statements having weights that span the spectrum of them, from 1 to 7. For instance, suppose we select the following statements shown in Table 8.3 from an original list of 100 statements.

The different weights accompanying the 20 items in Table 10.3 are derived from judges' ratings measured by us earlier. Note that there is a broad diversity of weights, ranging from a low of 1.2 to a high of 6.8.

The next step is to ask a sample of respondents to select two or three statements from this list that best reflect their position, attitudes, or sentiments. Thurstone recommended that respondents should select at least three statements. Theoretically, if these statements are accurate reflections of one's sentiments, then persons will select statements having similar

TABLE 8.3   Twenty Hypothetical Statements Taken from an Original List of 100 Statements, with Item Weights

Statement	Weight	Statement	Weight
1	6.8	11	3.9
2	6.2	12	3.4
3	5.9	13	3.2
4	5.6	14	2.8
5	5.2	15	2.7
6	5.0	16	2.2
7	4.8	17	1.9
8	4.6	18	1.8
9	4.2	19	1.6
10	4.1	20	1.2

weights. For instance, persons who select item #1 as closest to their opinion about something might also be expected to select items having weights close to that item's weight, or 6.8. These items are nearest the person's attitude. It is unlikely that persons will select item #1, with a weight of 6.8, and item #20, having a weight of 1.2, since these weights are at such different points on the intensity spectrum. According to these different weights, they indicate basically different points of view.

Suppose a female respondent selects items #1, #5, and #6 as the three statements that best suits her. We would take the weights associated with these statements and average them. Respectively, the weights would be 6.8, 5.2, and 5.0. Average these values, we would have (6.8 + 5.2 + 5.0)/3, or 17/3 = 5.7. Thus, 5.7 would be the final raw score we would use for this person.

Equal-Appearing Nature of Intervals.   Individual raw scores may be compared with one another and are theoretically reflective of differences in the degree or intensity of the attitude expressed. Thurstone believed that the weight assigned each scale item is a better way (e.g., compared with Likert scaling) of assessing attitudinal variations among people and plotting their differences along some attitudinal continuum. One assumption he made was that the resulting weights would enable researchers to approximate the interval level of measurement with the collected data. He used the term **equal-appearing intervals** to describe positions of these points along a continuum. To Thurstone, his scale of attitudinal intensity would look something like this:

Low 1 —— 2 —— 3 —— 4 —— 5 —— 6 —— 7 High

Subsequently, Thurstone changed his mind about the equal-appearing nature of spacing between items on these scales. He said that the interval level of measurement would be approached or approximated rather than actually achieved by such a scaling method. A subsequent comparison of Likert and Thurstone scales and their relative accuracy for measuring the same variables was made by Edwards (1957). Edwards reported no significant differences in the accuracy of the two scaling methods. Therefore, the greater time and effort required to formulate Thurstone scaling doesn't result in greater accuracy of attitudinal measurement as Thurstone had originally anticipated. Likert scaling is much easier and has accuracy equivalent with that of Thurstone scaling.

Three points should be made about applying Thurstone scaling in criminological research. First, it is not acceptable to place item weights on questionnaires so that respondents can see them. Many researchers who use Thurstone scaling to measure attitudes often include such weights, since this makes the scoring process much easier for them. But to include these weights conspicuously causes respondents to focus more on the weights than on the items. Some bias may be incurred as a result.

A second problem pertains to the items subsequently selected by respondents as most typical of them. There are some disturbing patterns that may result. For instance, suppose persons A and B chose the following items as most typical of them from Table 8.3, items #1, #6, and #20. These items have weights of 6.8, 5.0, and 1.2, respectively. These weights sum to 13.0, and the average for persons A and B would be 13/3 = 4.3. Next, suppose persons C and D picked items #8, #9, and #10, with respective weights of 4.6, 4.2, and 4.1. These weights, summed, equal 12.9. The average of these three weights would be 12.9/3 = 4.3. The two average weights for persons A and B and for persons C and D would be 4.3. However, if we compare the actual distribution of weights for both pairs of subjects, it is apparent that there is less homogeneity in response weights among C and D compared with A and B. The greater the differences among item weights selected by various persons, the greater the unreliability of the Thurstone scale. It is presumed that no such wide variations among weights will occur. However, they do occur occasionally.

Finally, when Thurstone scaling is used, some researchers are inclined to believe that they have actually achieved the interval level of measurement with their scales. This is not so. The scale scores are at best ordinal.

Advantages and Disadvantages of Thurstone Scales.   Thurstone scales have the following advantages and strengths:

1. Thurstone-derived scales enable researchers to differentiate between large numbers of people regarding their attitudinal positions. When item weights are averaged, a greater variety of attitudinal positions is revealed compared with Likert-type scale values. This would seemingly have the advantage of making more precise distinctions between people according to the attitudes they possess.

2. Another argument in favor of using Thurstone-derived scales is that judges—usually professional persons and sometimes students—have achieved a high degree of agreement on the items used, and hence, they perform a screening function by eliminating the bad or poor items that produce little or no agreement. Researchers might apply such scales with increased confidence that the items used have a greater claim to reliability than would be the case in Likert scale construction.

Thurstone scaling procedures have the following weaknesses and limitations:

1. Thurstone scales are time-consuming to construct. Investigators must solicit judges who must take the time to sort numerous items. Then scale values must be determined. Then respondents' item selections must be averaged in order to place them on some attitudinal **intensity continuum.**

2. It is possible to derive identical scores based on widely divergent attitudinal views. This is the problem noted above, where two different persons might receive identical scale scores, but where the scores are made up of widely dispersed scale items with different intensity weights. Do these persons with the same scores actually hold the same attitudes to the same degree? We don't know. The fact that greater variation in score values results from one subject compared with another subject would seem to place the validity of this scale in question.

3. There is no way of controlling the influence of a judge's bias in item sorting. The personal biases of judges might interfere with their objectivity in making item categorizations. However, repeatedly Thurstone scaling has yielded a high degree of consistency among judges when attitudinal items have been sorted.

4. In reality, Thurstone scale values are no better at predicting behavior compared with Likert-based measures. Because Likert measures are so much easier to construct and score, the logical preference would be to use Likert scaling over Thurstone-derived methods.

Other Types of Scaling Procedures

Several other types of attitudinal scaling procedures exist. It is beyond the scope of this book to cover all other types of procedures, but six alternative procedures will be mentioned here because of their utility in criminology and criminal justice. These include (1) Guttman scaling or the Cornell Technique, (2) the semantic differential, (3) the Q-sort, (4) the Sellin–Wolfgang **Index,** (5) the Salient Factor Score (SFS 81), and (6) Greenwood's Rand Seven-Factor Index.

Guttman Scaling

Another scaling method is called **Guttman scaling** or cumulative scaling. Although it is used far less than either Likert or Thurstone scaling, it used enough in criminological research to feature it here. For instance, a survey of the methodology of studies during the period 1968–2004 in the *Criminal Justice Abstracts* database revealed that at least 11 studies used Guttman scaling or had mentioned the scaling procedure in the accompanying article abstracts. More frequent use of this scaling method is likely, however, since article abstract information is notoriously sketchy relating to the measures used for variable conceptualization in different research investigations. Other popular terms that refer to it are the **Cornell technique** and **scalogram analysis.** Guttman (1944) devised a method of scaling that permits researchers to determine whether the items they use in their scales are actually unidimensional. **Unidimensionality** means that the instrument items measure the same dimension of the same phenomenon. Thus, a **unidimensional scale** would consist of several items that would assess one, and only one, dimension of an attitude.

By comparison, Likert and Thurstone scales are **multidimensional scales,** since several different dimensions are measured by various items included on these scales. The police professionalism scale, for instance, contained items that tapped whether officers read police journals, whether assessments of officer competence can be made, and whether officers attend professional meetings. These are obviously different dimensions of professionalism, and it is possible for someone to agree with one item but not the others. With Guttman scaling, however, it is assumed that all items reflect a single dimension of the trait measured. Applied to our police professionalism example, items on a Guttman scale of police professionalism might focus on professional meeting attendance, how often such meetings are attended, whether papers are presented at those meetings, whether police officers hold various positions at those meetings, and so on. All items would focus on one specific dimension of professionalism.

Edwards (1957, p. 172) defines a unidimensional scale as follows: "In the case of attitude statements, we might say that this means that a person with a more favorable attitude score than another person must also be just as favorable or more favorable in his response to every statement in the set than the other person. When responses to a set of attitude statements meet this requirement, the set of statements is said to constitute a unidimensional scale."

Using aspects of the **Bogardus social distance scale,** suppose we were to ask respondents to either agree or disagree with the following five statements:

1. I would marry a member of race *X*.
2. I would allow a member of race *X* to attend my church.
3. I would allow a member of race *X* to live in my neighborhood.
4. I would allow a member of race *X* to live in my community.
5. I would allow a member of race *X* to live in my country.

All of these statements are indicative of the amount of social distance we will permit or accept between ourselves and members of race *X*. Guttman would argue that if we agree with item #1, it makes sense that we would also agree with items #2, #3, #4, and #5. Guttman said that if we assign a "1" to all agreements, a person's score on this scale of five items would be 5. Knowing the score of 5 would enable us to predict the person's responses to all items. Knowing the score on the scale is 4 would allow us to predict their responses as well. We would probably say that the person with a score of 4 picked items #2 through #5 and disagreed with item #1. Knowing a person's score is 1 would mean agreement with item #5 only. Using these five statements, Guttman scaling or scalogram analysis may be illustrated. Table 8.4 shows these five statements of different attitudinal intensity for 15 persons. We have provided hypothetical responses for all 15 persons according to whether they agree or disagree with each item.

The far lefthand column in Table 8.4 shows each individual, from 1 to 15. The next five columns show x's for either agreement or disagreement for each of the five items listed across the top of the table. In the far righthand column of the table are total scale scores, ranging from a "high" of 5 to a "low" of 0. Horizontal lines have been drawn underneath the pattern of agreements for each item. When agreements end, lines are drawn. These are cutting points based on how these 15 persons have responded to the five items. The statements have been arranged in the table, from left to right, according to "most intense" to "least intense." Thus, persons who agree with item #1 will likely agree with the other four items. This is the case for persons 1 and 2. However, persons 3 and 4 do not agree with items #1 and #2. But

TABLE 8.4   Illustration of the Guttman Cornell Technique[a]

Individual	Statement 1 A	1 D	2 A	2 D	3 A	3 D	4 A	4 D	5 A	5 D	Score
1	X		X		X		X		X		5
2	X		X		X		X		X		5
3		X	X		X		X		X		4
4		X	X		X		X		X		4
5		X		X	X		X		X		3
6		X		X	X		X		X		3
7		X		X		X	X		X		2
8		X		X		X	X		X		2
9		X		X		X		X	X		1
10		X		X		X		X	X		1
11		X		X		X		X	X		1
12		X		X		X		X	X		1
13		X		X		X		X		X	0
14		X		X		X		X		X	0
15		X		X		X		X		X	0

[a]The horizontal lines (dashes) in the body of the table are defined as "cutting points" for each statement.

they do agree with item #4. They also agree with the remaining items of lesser intensity. When items for a perfect scale vary in a graduated fashion such as those five items in Table 8.4, Guttman calls the scale a perfectly reproducible one. Reproducible scales are those where one's individual item responses can be reproduced fairly accurately with a knowledge of one's overall scale score. A perfect, error-free response pattern is illustrated in Table 8.5.

Few perfectly reproducible scales actually exist in reality, however. Thus, Guttman devised a coefficient of reproducibility, which would enable him to calculate the amount of error

TABLE 8.5   Error-Free Scalogramatic Presentation

	Statement[a]					
	(Most Intense)			(Least Intense)		
Individual	1	2	3	4	5	Score
1	+	+	+	+	+	5
2	−	+	+	+	+	4
3	−	−	+	+	+	3
4	−	−	−	+	+	2
5	−	−	−	−	+	1

[a]A plus indicates acceptance or agreement with statement; a minus, rejection or disagreement with statement.

TABLE 8.6   Scalogramatic Presentation of Errors

| | Statement[a] | | | | | |
| | (Most Intense) | | | (Least Intense) | | |
Individual	*1*	*2*	*3*	*4*	*5*	Score
1	+	+	⊖	+	+	4
2	+	⊖	+	+	+	4

[a]A plus indicates acceptance or agreement; a minus, rejection or disagreement. Circled responses indicate errors.

involved in reproducing any individual's response pattern to a set of items through **reproducible scales.** This would ultimately tell Guttman whether he was measuring a single dimension of the variable or whether multiple dimensions were being measured. What does a scalogram with errors look like? Table 8.6 shows a pattern of responses with several errors for a sample of two persons.

In this small-scale example, two persons have identical scale scores of 4. However, notice that person #1 has agreed (indicated by a +) with items #1, #2, #4, and #5 but has disagreed with item #3. By the same token, person #2 has agreed with items #1, #3, #4, and #5 but has disagreed with item #2. These are errors, according to Guttman. We have circled them and will later refer to such errors in the computation of the **coefficient of reproducibility.** The coefficient of reproducibility is as follows:

$$\text{Coefficient of reproducibility} = 1 - \frac{\text{Number of errors}}{\text{Number of Responses}}$$

where the number of responses = the number of people times the number of statements. A larger-scale example illustrates this computation more clearly. Suppose we observe a response pattern to five items for 10 people as shown in Table 8.7.

In Table 8.7, five errors have been circled. In order to detect errors, we usually arrange persons by ranking their overall scale scores. Persons who have the same scores can be moved upward or downward among one another in order to minimize errors. Thus, in Table 8.7, persons #2, #3, and #4 can be moved upward or downward in relation to each other to minimize errors. Note what would happen if we switched persons #2 and #3. Two errors in their response patterns would occur instead of one. Suffice it to say that the way they are presently arranged yields minimal errors in their response patterns. If we were to draw imaginary horizontal lines underneath each item cutting point, minuses (−) above those lines and pluses (+) below those lines would be errors. These are illustrated in Table 8.7. A total of five errors are shown in this table and have been circled. We may compute the coefficient of reproducibility as follows:

$$\text{Coefficient of reproducibility} = 1 - \frac{5}{(10)(5)}$$

$$= 1 - \frac{5}{50}$$

$$= 1 - 0.10 = .90.$$

TABLE 8.7   Error Illustration of Scalogram Analysis

Individual	Statement[a] (Most Intense) 1	2	3	(Least Intense) 4	5	Score
1	+	+	+	+	+	5
2	+	⊖	+	+	+	4
3	−	+	+	+	+	4
4	−	+	+	+	+	4
5	−	−	+	+	+	3
6	−	−	+	+	+	3
7	−	⊕	−	−	+	2
8	−	−	−	⊕	+	2
9	−	−	−	⊕	−	1
10	−	−	−	−	⊕	1
Errors	0	2	0	2	1	

[a]A plus indicates acceptance or agreement; a minus, rejection or disagreement. Circled responses indicate errors.

The coefficient of reproducibility would be .90 in this case. This would mean that we can reproduce these persons' individual scores with 90 percent accuracy. Guttman believed that 90 percent is an acceptable cut-off point, and that coefficients below 90 percent were simply not reproducible or nonreproducible. Later, he changed his mind somewhat and allowed unidimensionality to be declared if scales could be reproduced with 80 percent accuracy. He called these quasi-reproducible scales. Apparently, not too many researchers were developing unidimensional scales with reproducibility coefficients of .90 or higher and this rigorous standard was relaxed somewhat.

Guttman believed that unidimensional scales are superior to multidimensional scales for several reasons. First, if we really develop a true measure of something, then the scores yielded by the measure should reflect the attribute consistently. Also, if several dimensions are being tapped by the measure, it is entirely possible that items from some other attitudinal universe (the imaginary place from which items are derived or thought of by researchers in their construction of scale items) may be included in our multidimensional scales. Therefore, our multidimensional measures, including Likert and Thurstone scales, may suffer some inaccuracy. This is a debatable point and one beyond the scope of this text.

The reality of the situation suggests that most attitudes are multidimensional anyway. If someone is satisfied with their work, for instance, they usually are satisfied with it because of several desirable features, such as good working hours, long lunch breaks, good supervision, extensive fringe benefits, good work content, challenging tasks, good work associates, and reasonable commuting distances. Presently, it is unknown how extensively Guttman scaling is used in criminology and criminal justice. An inspection of a wide assortment of current criminal justice and criminology journals shows several articles where Guttman scaling procedures are used, however.

For example, David Klinger (1995) used a Guttman scale to measure force patterns used by police officers in arrests during police–citizen encounters. Officers indicated various verbal and nonverbal degrees of force that were used to obtain suspect compliance. Klinger noted that a high coefficient of reproducibility was observed in his particular application of this attitudinal measure. And in a study conducted by William Cook (1990), scalogram analysis was used to examine the effects of terrorism on executives' willingness to travel abroad. Cook studied 408 executives and gave them different hypothetical scenarios that would influence their decision to travel. The Guttman scaling procedure he used also disclosed high reproducibility, indicating that his study results had strong validity and reliability.

Advantages and Disadvantages of Guttman Scaling.   Some of the advantages and strengths of Guttman scaling are:

1. Guttman scaling demonstrates the unidimensionality of items in an attitudinal measure. Guttman considers this feature of scalogram analysis desirable, although it remains to be seen whether Guttman scaling yields scores that are any more accurate compared with Likert or Thurstone scale scores.

2. Assuming a scalable set of items used in an attitudinal measure, the researcher is in a good position to identify inconsistencies in responses of subjects and possible untruthful replies. This desirable feature could enhance a researcher's confidence in the quality of information furnished by respondents.

3. Guttman's procedure is relatively easy to use when applied to small numbers of items. However, when the number of items exceeds 12, the technique becomes unwieldy.

4. A person's response pattern may be reproduced with a knowledge of one's total raw score on the scale. Likert and Thurstone scale scores are not reproducible, although this should not detract from their usefulness as attitudinal measures.

Some of the weaknesses of Guttman scaling are:

1. The Guttman scaling technique fails to provide as extensive an attitudinal continuum as the Likert and/or Thurstone methods. Thus, if we were to attempt to apply Guttman scaling to a sample of 100 or more persons, there would be an excessive number of tied scores. The error rate for these tied scores would be quite difficult to determine, and the researcher would not know whether the scale items were truly reproducible.

2. The Guttman procedure is most easily applicable to situations where the researcher has few items with dichotomous responses. Although Guttman scales may be constructed where there are more than two responses, the complexities of scoring such instruments outweigh their usefulness as unidimensional measures.

The Semantic Differential

The **semantic differential** consists of a series of bipolar characteristics, such as hot–cold, popular–unpopular, witty–dull, cold–warm, and sociable–unsociable. The semantic differential has been cited as a useful attitudinal measure in at least 46 studies abstracted by the

Criminal Justice Abstracts for the period 1968–2004. It is likely that more frequent use of this measurement method has occurred in criminological research, since article abstract information is somewhat sketchy and doesn't always specify the methods used to measure critical variables studied.

Osgood (1965) says that the semantic differential is a useful measure of psychological, social, and physical objects to various respondents. According to these researchers, the semantic differential should represent three basic dimensions of a person's attitude toward another person, group, or object. These dimensions are (1) potency, the strength or physical attraction of the object; (2) evaluation, the favorableness or unfavorableness of the object; and (3) activity, the degree of movement of the object. These researchers originally devised a list of 50 pairs of terms, called scales, and arranged them on a continuum, such as:

Neutral

Witty ————————————————————————————— Dull

    1   2   3   4   5   6   7

Friendly ———————————————————————————— Unfriendly

    1   2   3   4   5   6   7

and so on. Persons responding to the semantic differential would check the point on each of the continuums that described their particular feelings toward the object, person, or group. The marks can be scored easily.

Criminologists might apply the semantic differential and make up terms to suit their particular needs. Studies of juvenile delinquents may make use of the semantic differential to evaluate the desirability or repulsion of school or peer groups. Personality assessments can also be made. Subjects are asked to portray themselves as they believe they are at present, and how they would like to view themselves in the future. Treatment programs in community corrections agencies might benefit from such applications, since insight may be gained about various clients. The primary usefulness of the semantic differential is to assess the subject's perception of the attractiveness of social and personal objects according to several dimensions. This assessment, in turn, may lead to specifying reasons for certain behaviors manifested in relation to those objects, groups, or persons, to the extent that attitudes and behaviors coincide with reality.

One application of the semantic differential is found in the work of Thomas Austin and Don Hummer (1999), who studied college student impressions of police women. Both male and female criminal justice majors were surveyed in a sample of 835 undergraduates regarding their attitudes toward women in policing. Male and female undergraduates disclosed polar opposite impressions of women in policing, with male students viewing women in policing more unfavorably and female students having more positive views. The investigators found that having a family member or relative in law enforcement seemed to promote less favorable views of women in police officer roles. The investigators speculated that these attitudinal differences may be reflective of perceptions of the dangers posed by police work generally and the greater exposure of female officers to physical assaults and other dangers associated with law enforcement.

In another study where the semantic differential was used, James Fox, Kevin Minor, and William Pelkey (1995) investigated the perceptions of a sample of juvenile offenders who participated in a Kentucky diversion program between 1992 and 1993. Social and self-perceptions, measured with the semantic differential, enabled researchers to determine the effects of a law-related education program on offender attitudes about themselves over time. Program participation resulted in significantly changed self-perceptions as measured by the semantic differential. Self-perceptions tended to improve as juveniles advanced through their law-related educational programming. Recidivism among graduates of the program was very low, about 10 percent.

Q-Sort

The **Q-sort** is a variation of Thurstone scaling. It is seldom used in research. A survey of the *Criminal Justice Abstracts* found six articles where the Q-sort was used as a methodological tool between 1968 and 2004. Using the Q-sort involves presenting research subjects with a number of slips of paper or cards. These slips of paper or cards contain descriptors or statements that each respondent is asked to rate. Respondents are asked to sort these descriptors or statements into various categories, ranging from "strong" to "weak" or "high" to "low." Depending on how the respondents sort the statements or descriptors, individual scores can be assigned to each subject and they can be differentiated from one another for possible experimental purposes.

An early application of the Q-sort involved a study of juvenile offenders committed to Japanese training schools for short terms. The delinquents were compared with nondelinquents of comparable age. The results of an attitude test indicated that the average test scores for nondelinquents were somewhat higher than those for delinquents. Juveniles were given several items and asked to sort them according to how they were viewed by their parents and others, either positively or negatively. The results of the Q-sort test revealed a significant difference between nondelinquents and delinquents in how they are viewed by their parents and other persons (Hashimoto et al., 1968).

The National Council on Crime and Delinquency (1979) used the Q-sort technique to determine informational needs in juvenile justice. Numerous members of state juvenile advisory groups and related staff or members of analogous ad hoc state groups were given questionnaires and asked to rate 99 different topics on a 5-point Likert scale. Additionally, these members were asked to rank, by means of a Q-sort, 15 major topics according to desire for more information. Based on the rankings generated by these group members, prevention and diversion were selected as the two topics about which most information was needed, followed by juvenile status offenders and serious juvenile offenders. The need for information about violent crimes was ranked relatively low.

A more recent application of the Q-sort was done by Trevor Josephson and Wally Unruh (1994), who used a Q-sort personality instrument administered to four subgroups of male delinquents. A trait analysis revealed two interpretable factors, which were labeled "normal, adjusted, responsible, positive self-concept" versus "abnormal, alienated, psychotic tendency, and outer-directed." The results of the Q-sort led to certain modifications in treatment programming for delinquents with personality disorders.

Sellin–Wolfgang Crime Severity Index

Thorsten Sellin and Marvin Wolfgang (1966) established an index of crime seriousness as applied to youthful offenders. The **Sellin–Wolfgang Crime Severity Index** is a rating system that assigns values to different crimes. Point values are generated for both offense quality (offense seriousness) and quantity (financial loss attributable to the offense). The scale includes different weights for offenses such as homicide or voluntary manslaughter, forcible sexual intercourse, aggravated assault, armed robbery, burglary of an occupied residence, larceny/theft of more than $1,000, auto theft in which the vehicle was not recovered, arson of an occupied building, kidnapping, extortion, or illegal sale of dangerous drugs.

On the basis of scale scores for different offender aggregates, crime seriousness may be tracked over time and compared. Thus, violence escalation and other crime trends might be noted using the Sellin–Wolfgang index. This crime seriousness index has been used extensively in the research literature. Reliability studies have shown that the measure has considerable stability.

For example, Elmer Weitekamp and Hans Kerner (1995) used the Sellin–Wolfgang Crime Severity Index to examine the actual dangerousness of chronic youthful offenders from data analyzed in the Philadelphia Birth Cohort Study of 1945. From their application of the Q-sort, these researchers determined that chronic offenders were not as serious as other writers have claimed. Rather, much of their offending consists of petty crimes or property offenses that are essentially nonviolent. Furthermore, they did not find support for the view of some criminologists that increasing career length as offenders escalates offense severity. Instead, these investigators found strong consistency over time among offenders relative to the nonviolent crimes most committed. However, some criticisms have been leveled against this index by researchers who believe that crime seriousness scores portrayed by the index should have a greater degree of standardization. Some criticism has also been directed at how certain types of crimes are scored (Collins, 1988).

The Salient Factor Score (SFS 81)

The **Salient Factor Score (SFS 81)** is an actuarial device used by the U.S. Parole Commission as an aid in assessing federal prisoners' likelihood of recidivism after release. The SFS was designed to assist parole board members to make fair parole decisions. Departures from these guidelines by parole boards were to be accompanied by written rationales outlining the reasons for such departures. At the federal level, the salient factor score was made up of seven criteria and was refined in 1976. This was referred to as SFS 76. In August 1981, the salient factor scoring instrument underwent further revision and a new, six-factor predictive device, SFS 81, was constructed (Hoffman & Beck, 1985). A comparison of the revised SFS 81 with its previous counterpart (SFS 76) was made according to validity, stability, simplicity, scoring reliability, and certain ethical concerns.

Both instruments appeared to have similar predictive characteristics, although the revised device possesses greater scoring reliability (Hoffman & Beck, 1985). Of even greater significance is that SFS 81 places considerable weight on the extent and recency of an offender's criminal history (Hoffman & Beck, 1985). Seven points can be earned by having no prior convictions or adjudications (adult or juvenile), no prior commitments of more than

30 days, and being 26 years of age or older at the time of the current offense (with certain exceptions). Figure 8.1 shows the six-item federal Salient Factor Score instrument, **SFS 81.**

Scores on the SFS 81 can range from "0" to "10." The following evaluative designations accompanying various score ranges:

Salient Factor Score Index

1. Prior convictions/adjudications (adult or juvenile):

   None (3 points)
   One (2 points)
   Two or three (1 point)
   Four or more (0 points)

2. Prior commitments of more than 30 days (adult or juvenile):

   None (2 points)
   One or two (1 point)
   Three or more (0 points)

3. Age at current offense/prior commitments:

   25 years of age or older (2 points)
   20–25 years of age (1 point)
   19 years of age or younger (0 points)

4. Recent commitment free period (3 years):

   No prior commitment of more than 30 days (adult or juvenile) or released to
   the community from last such commitment at least 3 years prior to the
   commencement of the current offense (1 point)
   Otherwise (0 points)

5. Probation/parole/confinement/escape status violator this time:

   Neither on probation, parole, confinement, or escape status at the time of the
   current offense, nor committed as a probation, parole, confinement, or escape
   status violator this time (1 point)
   Otherwise (0 points)

6. Heroin/opiate dependence:

   No history of heroin/opiate dependence (1 point)
   Otherwise (0 points)

   Total score = _____

FIGURE 8.1   Salient Factor Score Index, SFS 81. (Source: U.S. Parole Commission, *Rules and Procedures Manual.* Washington, DC: Author, 1985.)

Raw Score	Parole Prognosis
0–3 ———————	"Poor"
4–5 ———————	"Fair"
6–7 ———————	"Good"
8–10 ———————	"Very Good"

The paroling authority next consults a table of offense characteristics consisting of categories varying in offense severity. Adult ranges in numbers of months served are provided for each category and are cross-tabulated with the four-category parole prognosis above. The SFS 81 retains predictive power when the follow-up period is extended to 5 years and the definition of recidivism is restricted to cases that sustain a new sentence of imprisonment exceeding 1 year, an outcome measure that focuses on the most serious type of recidivism. Many uses have been made of this instrument in criminological research (Lucente et al., 2001; Yeager, 2002).

Greenwood's Rand Seven-Factor Index

Peter Greenwood, a researcher who works for the Rand Corporation in Santa Monica, California, has spent considerable time developing various scales to measure an offender's dangerousness and potential for recidivism. One of the measures developed by Greenwood is known as the **Rand Seven-Factor Index.** This index consists of seven items. These include:

1. Prior conviction for same charge
2. Incarcerated more than 50 percent of preceding 2 years
3. Convicted before age 16
4. Served time in state juvenile facility
5. Drug use in preceding 2 years
6. Drug use as a juvenile
7. Employed less than 50 percent of preceding 2 years (Greenwood & Abrahamse, 1982).

Using a simple yes–no answer format, a score is derived that ranges from "0" to "7." A score of "7" for any offender indicates that the offender poses the greatest risk, while a score of "0" means that the offender poses the least amount of risk. Risk refers to one's success potential for either probation or parole.

Greenwood's seven-factor scale has been constructed on the basis of actuarial information about chronic recidivists. For instance, it is widely known that recidivists often have problems with drugs and/or alcohol. Furthermore, unemployment is frequently associated with committing new offenses. Most scales purporting to predict one's risk or dangerousness use percentage of employment preceding one's arrest and conviction as a predictor variable. Also, the earlier the onset of criminal behavior, the more serious it is regarded. This is probably why Greenwood included information about one's juvenile record on the scale. If certain adult offenders were previously adjudicated as delinquent offenders prior to age 16, this is a serious concomitant of future adult offending. Greater weight is given to the earlier onset of delinquency or criminal conduct.

Essentially, a profile of specific criminals is devised using the seven-factor index. Therefore, a prediction is made about the potential of any given offender for recidivating in the future. Parole boards and judges can consider information from the Rand Seven-Factor Index as one of several criteria for evaluating offenders for parole or probation eligibility. The index serves as a "successfulness forecast," where the score is indicative of future conduct. For instance, Scott Decker and Barbara Salert (1987) have used the index as a means of predicting high rate offenders among inmates of various state correctional facilities. They have found the instrument to be highly reliable in forecasting recidivism.

Some Issues of Measurement

Several measurement issues are discussed below. These include the following: (1) the attitude–action relation; (2) social desirability as a contaminating factor; (3) response sets and validity; and (4) the level of measurement–statistical choices relation.

Attitude–Action Relation

Social scientists presume that behind every action is an attitude related to it. The logic is that if these attitudes can be identified in advance and measured accurately, then actions or behaviors can be predicted or anticipated. Sounds easy, doesn't it? It isn't. Unfortunately, the attitude–action relation is far from certain. For example, it is possible for persons to possess certain attitudes and not express behaviors consistent with those attitudes. Those who may be prejudiced toward certain racial or ethnic groups may not discriminate against those groups, since discrimination is prohibited by law. Also, persons may behave in certain ways that suggest they possess certain attitudes when they don't possess them.

Criminologists do not terminate their investigations of factors that explain criminal behavior or delinquent conduct or spousal assault, simply because there are questions about the attitude–action relation. The attitude–action controversy actually began many decades ago. An early article about the relation between attitudes persons express and their accompanying actions was written by Richard LaPiere (1934). LaPiere was interested in determining whether people behave in ways consistent with the attitudes they express. He planned a research project where he traveled throughout various parts of the country. He questioned hotel and restaurant owners about whether they would serve certain minorities, such as blacks and Asian Americans. Overwhelmingly, the hotel and restaurant owners indicated to LaPiere and his assistants that they would not serve such persons. Several months later, LaPiere instructed black and Asian American couples to travel to these same hotels and restaurants and attempt to be served. LaPiere expected that in most instances, they would be refused accommodations or food services because of their minority status. Interestingly, over 90 percent of the minority couples said that they were served or accommodated without incident. This finding caused LaPiere and others to critically evaluate their earlier thoughts about attitudes and how behaviors might be affected or influenced by their presence or absence.

Despite the uncertainty of the attitude–action relation, a prevalent belief among criminologists and others is that attitudes should be studied. A majority of empirical investigations in criminology and criminal justice reveal attitudinal factors that appear related to actions or behaviors observed. However, replication research or repeating studies under different conditions and in different time periods contributes to our knowledge stockpile. As we learn more about people and their behaviors, we refine our instrumentation and theoretical schemes to more sophisticated levels. Interestingly, several complex statistical tools have been useful in helping us to understand how numerous variables affect behavior. Multiple correlation, path analysis, and other correlational techniques have proved valuable in assisting us in building our theories of criminal behavior.

If attitudes precede certain types of social conduct, then it is imperative that we develop sound measures of these attitudes. Not only must we identify those attitudes most relevant in explaining certain behaviors, but we must measure these attitudes accurately and reliably. The validity of measures, or the extent to which our instruments actually measure what we say they are measuring, as well as the reliability of measures, or their consistency for applications over time, are discussed in the following chapter. Several conventional procedures will be described that enable researchers to demonstrate whether their instruments are accurate and consistent attitudinal measures.

Because we deal largely with quantities that cannot be observed directly, many of our attitudinal measures are challenged by competing instruments. It is not unusual to see numerous ways of conceptualizing and measuring police officer professionalism, or burnout and stress among probation officers. Every researcher is potentially capable of devising new instruments to measure virtually any attitudinal phenomenon. However, some attitudinal instruments have acquired some popularity and are used frequently to measure certain attitudinal dimensions. In the area of personality assessment, for instance, criminologists and others rely heavily on measures of personality such as the Minnesota Multiphasic Personality Inventory or MMPI, or Cattell's 16 Personality Factor Inventory, or 16 PF. Subparts of both of these personality assessment devices have been used by many researchers to assess one's ego strength, self-concept, self-assurance, and other personality dimensions for selected purposes. Treatment programs in community-based corrections agencies, mental hospitals, and prisons often rely on such measures for preliminary assessments of patients or inmates. Some of these devices are used for classification purposes, in order to segregate more potentially violent patients and prisoners from less violent ones.

Because there is no single device to measure any attitudinal phenomenon that has 100 percent acceptance in criminal justice and criminology, we must constantly be aware of the strengths and weaknesses of all measures as we use or develop them. Better instruments stand the test of time, through repeated applications. Few, if any, professionals are prepared to declare a moratorium on questionnaire construction and instrumentation. The field is expanding rapidly and maturing. Experimentation is vital to its growth, and we must constantly subject our theories devised and measures created to empirical testing.

Social Desirability as a Contaminating Factor

When attitudinal measures are constructed, we rely on the honesty of respondents to provide us with truthful information about themselves. The more sensitive the questions, however, the more difficult it may be for others to disclose their personal thoughts and feelings to us. An example of measuring anxiety was provided earlier. That example contained excerpted items from Janet Taylor's Manifest Anxiety Scale. Some of these items were personal statements about one's bowel and bladder habits. Some items required that persons disclose things about their dreams or worries or manners of sleep. All of these personal items are, to one extent or another, related to anxiety. However, respondents may be inhibited and hesitate to give honest responses about themselves. Who wants to say that their sleep is fitful and disturbed, that the palms of their hands perspire frequently, or that they have bowel or bladder trouble frequently? These traits are undesirable. Few persons want to be undesirable. Therefore, people may say things about themselves that are not true but desirable. Methodologists refer to this behavior as **social desirability.**

Social desirability is saying things or disclosing things about yourself in writing that you want others to hear or see or that are favorable or self-serving. Social desirability is perhaps the most important contaminating factor affecting any attitudinal measure. We have no way of preventing social desirability. No foolproof remedies exist to detect it. Some standardized personality assessment tools have built-in "lie" factors that seek to detect the influence of social desirability. Thus, persons are suspected of giving socially desirable responses when they deny behaviors or thoughts that most persons experience at one time or another. Asking people whether they worry about things or think about trivial matters may prompt some respondents to deny that they worry about things or think about trivial matters. Almost everyone worries about things from time to time, and it is rare for anyone to avoid thinking about trivial things occasionally. The thinking behind the inclusion of such items on personality assessment devices is that if people lie about commonplace traits, they will probably lie about less commonplace traits, such as frequent bowel or bladder trouble or frequent fitful and disturbed sleep.

Therefore, any measure of attitudinal phenomena must be considered a candidate for **contamination of data** by social desirability the more it delves into deeply private and personal matters and opinions. Giving responses that you think the researcher wants to hear or that make you look good tend to detract from the accuracy and reliability of measures.

The experiences of numerous criminologists and other social scientists suggest that social desirability occurs in their investigations frequently, and that it contaminates their research results. For instance, George Bonanno and colleagues (2003) studied 103 women who had previous histories of documented child abuse. A longitudinal study was conducted of these women and their attitudinal changes on different variables over time. Because these women were subjected to face-to-face interviews, the likelihood of social desirability influencing their responses to interviewer questions was increased, especially relating to disclosures by these subjects about their former abusive behaviors toward their own children.

In another study conducted by Su Boatwright-Horowitz, Kristen Olick, and Robert Amaral (2004), various persons were investigated and questioned by interviewers about domestic abuse and what might constitute serious grounds to justify calls for police intervention. Samples of men and women were given hypothetical scenarios about different persons who had suffered physical injuries as the result of domestic violence. Each scenario called for some type of police intervention or outside assistance. Research subjects were asked in interviews how they would respond if confronted by these different situations. Again, social desirability was considered influential in modifying their replies.

In yet another study of 733 police officers in the San Jose and Oakland areas of California, Akiva Liberman and colleagues (2002) asked them various questions about different factors that might produce occupational stress. Many police officers were asked to relate stories or incidents that would ordinarily produce stress or anxiety. They were asked to describe traumatic events that had happened to them. They were also asked how they handled such incidents and the stress the incidents produced. Again, social desirability was a significant factor. How likely are police officers, who learn to cultivate macho images of themselves to the outside world, to disclose that they are stressed by one incident or another? How truthful can they be concerning whether certain incidents were personally upsetting to them and caused them considerable anxiety or stress? The fact is that social desirability is always a possible contaminant when sensitive subjects are breached through interviews or questionnaire administrations. It is difficult to know when research participants are being truthful or whether they are giving responses they think investigators wish to hear.

Response Sets and Validity

Another contaminating factor is the response set or set response (Maguire & Mastrofski, 2000). Set responses occur whenever respondents check all "agree" or "disagree" responses or use some other systematic response pattern in a self-administered questionnaire, regardless of statement or question content. Therefore, if respondents were presented with obvious contradictory statements, such as: "My job completely lacks challenge and intrinsic interest" or "My job is intellectually rewarding, challenging, and intrinsically interesting," a response set would be indicated if "Strongly Agree" were checked for both items. Usually, there is a systematic response pattern throughout one's entire questionnaire. A male respondent, for instance, may check "Female," if "Female" is the first space to be checked among the information items included in the questionnaire. The best thing to do with questionnaires where response sets are strongly suspected is to throw them out. The researcher's concerns should be about the quality of data collected, not the quantity of data collected. Detecting response sets whenever they occur is fairly easy, if researchers have constructed their questionnaires creatively. This usually means that they have interrupted phrasings of items that purportedly measure the same thing with reverse phraseology suggested by the two items above. The decision to reject questionnaires or data because of the strong likelihood of set responses rests with the individual researcher and is a judgment call that depends on each situation.

In an actual research situation, Michaela Heinze and Arnold Purisch (2001) studied a sample of 57 criminal defendants who claimed that they were incompetent to stand trial. The American Psychological Association defines malingering as the intentional production of false or grossly exaggerated symptoms motivated by external incentives. Such incentives might be prosecutorial or sentencing leniency under the circumstances of this research. These defendants were subjected to a battery of psychological tests, where they were asked to disclose a wide range of information about their psychological states. Some scales they were given were intentionally created to disclose intentional fabrication of symptoms to detect socially desirable responses or even response sets. Heinze and Purisch were able to detect response sets among many of these study participants. Thus, substantial evidence was generated to support the idea that many of these persons were demonstrating symptoms of malingering behavior.

And in a study of community policing by Edward Maguire and Stephen Mastrofski (2000), several large police agencies that had implemented community policing or were in the process of implementing it responded to mailed questionnaires. Many of the questionnaire items in these surveys had fixed-response answers, and thus these similar response patterns made it easier for police officers and administrators to respond more quickly to them by giving set responses. The investigators found that some evidence of response sets existed, although the precise extent to which it existed could not be determined.

The Level of Measurement–Statistical Choices Relation

Much has been made of levels of measurement and a researcher's efforts to measure attitudinal phenomena at the highest measurement levels. This is because we normally convert our data collected into numerical quantities for subsequent analysis. We want our analyses of collected data to be legitimate analyses. The scientific community has generally agreed upon the rules by which the scientific game should be played. If one or more of those rules are violated in the course of our research efforts, then our research is perhaps weakened in terms of its scientific contribution and significance.

The most typical rule violation relating to attitudinal measurement is the use of certain statistical procedures that involve particular arithmetic operations, such as summing and averaging. The facts are simple. Regarding the data you have collected and how you measured the different variables, you either have achieved the required level of measurement to conduct these arithmetic operations or you haven't achieved the required level of measurement. The following hypothetical scenario illustrates a common occurrence in the social sciences, whenever attitudinal variables are investigated.

Suppose researchers study two samples and collect data about certain attitudes they possess. Suppose that Likert-type scales have been used to operationalize each of the attitudes investigated. At best, these researchers have achieved the ordinal level of measurement by using Likert scaling. They now have numerous raw scores over some range from low to high. How should these scores be analyzed?

Perhaps these data have been coded and stored in a computer. A subsequent statistical program package is run for these data, and much descriptive material about the two samples is generated. Since the computer package usually features programming that computes assorted statistical values for the data to be analyzed, the results of the analysis may be the equivalent of data overload. In other words, even if the researchers are interested in only one particular computation, the computer package churns out all sorts of additional information not otherwise requested or desired by these researchers. They didn't ask for additional data analyses, but the computer gave it to them anyway.

Perhaps they scan the data analyzed by the computer and notice that the program computed sample means or averages for all variables, including the attitudinal ones. Of course, the computer also computed modes, medians, ranges, standard deviations, and other miscellaneous descriptors for the same data. It is sometimes difficult to resist the temptation to do something with the additional data not originally requested from the computer.

Suppose that Attitude *X* was measured according to Likert scaling and became a part of the data the computer analyzed. Subsequently, Attitude *X* for the two samples was examined, and the researchers determined the following about Attitude *X:*

Attitude *X*		Group 1	Group 2
Mean (Average)	=	55.2	51.6
Mode	=	50.0	49.3
Median	=	54.7	52.1
Standard deviation	=	4.6	4.9
Range	=	29.0	31.0

The first three values reported above are called measures of central tendency, because they describe points around which scores in the distribution tend to focus. The standard deviation and range are "measures of dispersion or variability," because they depict how the scores are distributed around those central points. The mean or average for each sample on Attitude X is shown, together with the mode and median, respectively. These are other central tendency measures that reflect different things about the central tendency of distributions. For instance, the mode indicates which scores are most popular or occur most frequently. The median defines that point separating the distribution of scores into two equal parts. In the example above, the median for group 1 of 54.7 divides group 1 into two equal parts, so that 50 percent of sample 1 is below 54.7 while 50 percent of sample 1 is above 54.7.

Now, how does this relate to rule violations? Likert scaling procedures produce ordinal-level raw scores. These are rankables, where raw scores may be placed along an intensity continuum from low to high. Scores at one point on the continuum are either higher or lower than other scores, but we cannot say how much higher or lower. If we wanted to say how much higher or lower these scores were from others, we would need to achieve the next highest level of measurement with these scores, or the interval level of measurement. If we had achieved the interval level of measurement for Attitude X, then it would be arithmetically permissible to say how much higher or lower these scores were from each other. Unfortunately, we have only achieved the ordinal level of measurement with these scores using our Likert-type instrument to measure Attitude X. The central tendency measure of choice should be the median. The median fits ordinal-level data well. The mean doesn't fit, because averaging ordinal-level scores is meaningless, something similar to averaging Social Security numbers.

As the researchers examine their data, they observe arithmetic similarities between the means and medians of scores for these two groups on Attitude X. For group 1, for instance, the mean of 55.2 isn't much different from the median of 54.7. Likewise, the average of 51.6 for group 2 isn't all that different from the median of 52.1. Since there is an obvious similarity in the two values, and since other investigators are more likely to be familiar with the mean or average rather than median, it might be considered harmless to report the means for these groups instead of the medians.

If researchers regard this as harmless, they might also regard as harmless the idea of using a "difference between means" test to evaluate the significance of differences between these two groups, particularly now that they have two means to work with. There is such a test, and it, too, requires that researchers have interval-level data at their disposal. Thus, bending the rules in one instance may lead to other instances of rule-breaking.

How important is all of this for the measurement of attitudes? There are mixed opinions among professionals about this matter. Some researchers do not consider these data treatments as serious. In a conventional sense, considerable rule-breaking can be detected in many professional journals. Thus, if we gauge the incidence of this type of rule-breaking according to what professional researchers do, then we will conclude that it is generally acceptable. Convention often compels us to follow procedures that have been used by others. Beyond this, some professionals contend that if we were to comply fully with all requirements for statistical applications, we would never be able to do research. This is because our investigations are imperfect in various respects. Seldom are all requirements of tests and procedures actually achieved. Therefore, some information (where some rules are violated) is better than no information (where no rules are violated). In sum, the importance of this section is that it cautions us to recognize the various limitations of our data collection and instrumentation and view our findings accordingly.

SUMMARY

Measuring variables in criminal justice and criminology is a complex task, especially when the variables to be measured cannot be seen directly and must be inferred from other traits or characteristics. Virtually all attitudinal phenomena cannot be observed, although they exert significant influence on our behaviors in different ways. Measurement is the assignment of numbers to social and psychological properties according to rules. Another way of viewing measurement is to consider it as a way of differentiating between persons or groups according to different properties they possess. Some variables are easier to measure than others. Gender, race/ethnicity, religious affiliation, political affiliation, and years in school are easily conceptualized and measured. However, police professionalism, group morale, job satisfaction, anxiety, fear of crime, and peer group influence are less easily conceptualized and measured.

Four important functions of measurement are to describe social and psychological phenomena empirically; to render data amenable to scientific treatment and statistical manipulation; to assist in hypothesis testing and theory verification; and to enable researchers to differentiate between persons according to the different properties they are believed to possess. Hypotheses, which are most often derived from theories for the purpose of testing, consist of one or more variables. These variables must be measured in some way before hypotheses containing them can be tested.

Ordinarily theories are made up of different assumptions, propositions, and definitions of variables that are related in ways that help us to explain and predict relationships between variables. Theories utilize nominal definitions of variables, which are associated with the types of definitions of things we might find in dictionaries of terms. Although nominal definitions of terms are useful and permit us to have a heuristic understanding of how different variables are related theoretically and logically, such definitions are of little value to social scientists. Usually social scientists must convert nominal definitions of terms into operational definitions, where numbers can be assigned to represent important theoretical variables. Numbers are assigned nominal definitions through the process of operationalization. Operational definitions can assist investigators by enabling them to conduct tests of hypotheses and verify theories from which they were derived. Operational definitions of terms also enable researchers to compare persons and groups according to different amounts of certain variables they are said to possess. Often, operational definitions of variables utilize epistemic correlates of various phenomena, or indicators of variables and the degree to which they exist.

A distinction is made between concepts and constructs. For purposes of this discussion, concepts are considered to be terms that have direct empirical referents, or objects that represent the term. Constructs are terms we use that have indirect empirical referents. All attitudes are constructs, because they consist of numerous indirect empirical indicators of different variables. Whenever attitudes are operationalized, they are converted into constructs so that they may be used conveniently in hypothesis tests. Testing hypotheses assist us in verifying the predictive utility of our theoretical schemes that are intended to explain and predict relationships between variables.

When variables are measured, numbers are assigned different variable subclasses. Because there are so many different variables, and because some variables are more easily and directly measured than others, the numbers we assign to variable subclasses have different meanings depending on the variables they represent. Therefore, several different measurement levels have been identified. These are nominal, ordinal, interval, and ratio levels of measurement. The nominal level of measurement, or lowest level, involves the assignment of numbers to subclasses of discrete variables, such as gender, race, religion, or political affiliation. The numbers assigned serve to differentiate one variable subclass from another, and nothing more. We cannot say, for instance, that a "1" assigned to the gender subclass "male" is greater or less than a "2" assigned to the gender subclass "female." The ordinal level of measurement means that the numbers assigned to different variable subclasses mean that we can not only differentiate between these subclasses, but we can also say that a "1" is higher (or lower) than a "2," and so forth. But we cannot say how much higher (or lower) these numbers are from one another. Only when we achieve the interval and ratio levels of measurement are the actual distances between assigned numbers to variable subclasses meaningful. Thus, numbers themselves differ in meaning depending on the different variables and variable subclasses to which they are assigned. Different levels of measurement entitle investigators to manipulate numbers in different ways. Usually, the higher the level of measurement, the more mathematical functions can be performed. This means also that a greater variety of statistical tests and procedures are available to researchers for hypothesis testing and theory verification.

Two popular scaling procedures for operationalizing variables are Likert scaling and Thurstone scaling. Likert scaling, which accounts for probably over 90 percent of all scaling in the social sciences, is also referred to as the method of summated ratings. Using a wide variety of items that are statements about how people feel about themselves or some issue or topic, usually in combinations of 10 or more, response patterns are configured that range from low to high intensity. Different intensities are given numbers. Common categories of different item intensities are "strongly agree," "agree," "disagree," and "strongly disagree," although these labels can be changed to fit different situations or variables to be measured (e.g., "favorable" and "unfavorable," "pleasant" or "unpleasant," "very strong" or "very weak," and so forth). These responses are weighted from "1" to "5" or "6" and then summed, depending on the responses a subject selects. The sum of item weights yields a raw score representing how strongly a person feels about one issue or another. Typically, attitudinal variations are reflected by different summed weights for comparison purposes. Persons with similar summed scores may be grouped into different intensity categories and compared. These scores may also be cross-tabulated with other scores on other attitudinal dimensions or characteristics to see whether any relationships between variables are apparent.

Thurstone scaling, which is considerably more complicated than Likert scaling, involves judges who determine weights associated with different items. After a laborious series of steps, different items or statements are presented to research subjects and they are asked to pick which statements best typify them. The weights associated with these selected items are summed and averaged, yielding an attitudinal position similar to that derived from Likert scaling. Similar groupings and comparisons with Thurstone scales can be made comparable to those derived from Likert scales. Research comparisons of the effectiveness and accuracy of Thurstone and Likert scales suggest that both types of scaling are about equal at representing the degree to which persons possess various measured attitudes. Because Likert scaling is much simpler in design and implementation, it is widely preferred as an attitudinal measure compared with the more complicated Thurstone procedure.

Other attitudinal measures include Guttman scaling, also known as the Cornell Technique and scalogram analysis; the semantic differential; the Q-sort; the Sellin–Wolfgang Index; the Salient Factor Score (SFS 81); and Greenwood's Seven-Factor Index. Guttman scaling is the only scale that purports to measure a single dimension of a given variable, and it is thus regarded as a unidimensional scale. Other scales, such as Likert and Thurstone scaling, are multidimensional, in that several different characteristics of particular variables are represented in these scaling procedures. There is no particular advantage for having a unidimensional scale as an attitudinal measure, and thus, Guttman scaling is used infrequently by researchers.

The semantic differential purports to measure bipolar characteristics, such as hot–cold, witty–dull, popular–unpopular, and sociable–unsociable. This scale is widely used in personality assessments and may be associated with different forms of delinquency or criminality. The Q-sort, a variation of Thurstone scaling, also is used to represent varying degrees of different attitudinal characteristics exhibited by research subjects. The Sellin–Wolfgang Index is a rating system used to assign values to different types of crimes. Thus, using such an index enables researchers to track increases or decreases in crime violence over time. The Salient Factor Score (SFS 81) is used as a measure of parole eligibility and potential adjustment. Used most frequently by the U.S. Parole Commission for parole-eligible federal inmates, this scale uses background information about one's juvenile and adult criminal and/or delinquent history and other factors in determining one's eligibility score. The resulting scores from the SFS 81 are used to assist parole commission members in early-release decision making. Peter Greenwood's Rand Seven-Factor Index also assesses one's potential for recidivism and thus may be used to indicate one's eligibility for probation or parole.

Several important issues relating to measuring attitudinal variables include the attitude–action relation, social desirability, response sets, and the measurement–statistical choices relation. It is widely assumed by criminologists and others that knowing one's attitudes in advance will enable investigators to forecast particular actions consistent with attitudes expressed or measured by different attitudinal scales. While this consistency has been amply illustrated by different studies, there are exceptions where one's actions fail to follow one's expressed attitudes. Thus, the attitude–action relation is not always a consistent one. Furthermore, because attitudinal scales ask people to agree or disagree with different statements that may characterize them, respondents may be inclined to select descriptions of themselves that are socially desirable and not necessarily accurate in reflecting their true thoughts or perceptions. Or they may select responses that they think researchers want to see that may or may not be true of these respondents. Social desirability is probably the greatest contaminating factor influencing the credibility of attitudinal measures in the social sciences.

Another issue involves set responses, especially evident when persons complete self-administered questionnaires. Many questionnaires contain Likert scales measuring one or more attitudes. The response patterns are the same throughout these different scales, and persons may get into a habit of selecting the first response for each item just so that they can complete the questionnaire quickly. This "get it over with quick" response to one's questions is a set response, and often it yields inconsistencies. Deliberate steps are taken by investigators to include both positively and negatively worded statements throughout their questionnaires to detect set responses whenever they are given. For example, a statement such as "I would recommend this job to my friends." might be accompanied by another statement on the same scale such as, "I hate this work." If someone says "strongly agree" to both of these statements, this is an inconsistency and suggests the possibility of a set response. This renders the scale meaningless. Also, it may mean that other information yielded by the questionnaire is essentially undependable or unreliable. The investigator may choose to simply throw out the entire questionnaire rather than risk using it as a part of his or her collected data.

Finally, the level of measurement–statistical test choice relation means that statistical test selections should be decided according to whether or not researchers have complied with various assumptions that are closely associated with these tests. One assumption associated with all statistical tests is that a particular level of measurement (i.e., nominal, ordinal, interval, or ratio) should be achieved in order for the statistical test to be used properly. Statistical tests manipulate numbers in different ways, through division, addition, multiplication, subtraction, and square rooting. Thus, attention must be paid to what the numbers represent before they are manipulated and averaged by particular statistical tests. It is meaningless to average numbers that stand for "male" or "female" categories, for example. This is a critical issue that influences one's choice of statistical tests when data are subsequently collected and analyzed. Usually the method chosen to measure different variables, such as Likert or Thurstone scaling, will determine which level of measurement has been achieved. Most attitudinal measures are closely associated with the ordinal level of measurement, and thus, investigators are limited in their statistical test choices to those procedures where the ordinal level of measurement is a basic assumption of the test's appropriate application.

QUESTIONS FOR REVIEW

1. What is measurement? What are several important functions of measurement?

2. What are Likert scales? How are they constructed? What are some general strengths and limitations of Likert scales?

3. What are Thurstone scales? How does their accuracy compare with Likert scales that purportedly measure the same attitudinal phenomena? Which scales seem more accurate to you? Why?

4. What are some general limitations and strengths of Thurstone scales?

5. What are some important differences between concepts and constructs? How do these terms relate to operationalization?

6. What is the difference between an operational definition and a nominal definition? What are the purposes of each in social research?

7. What are three important issues relating to measurement? Why are these issues important to criminologists and others?

8. What are Guttman scales? What is meant by the coefficient of reproducibility?

9. What are some contrasts between multidimensional and unidimensional scales? Which types of scales are easier to construct? Why?

10. What are the respective contributions of nominal and operational definitions in theory construction, verification, and hypothesis testing?

11. What are four levels of measurement? Which levels of measurement permit averaging and division?

12. Why are levels of measurement important in relation to statistical applications to collected data? How can misapplications of statistical procedures influence the meaningfulness of scientific findings? What are two examples of different levels of measurement from the research literature?

13. What are two major contaminating factors in self-administered questionnaires? How does each factor function as a contaminating factor? Of the two factors, which is probably more important and why?

14. What is the semantic differential? What are some possible applications of it in criminology?

15. How can social desirability be detected in a questionnaire? How can a set response be detected? In what ways do these different phenomena affect the dependability and validity of one's attitudinal information?

9 Validity and Reliability of Measures

CHAPTER OUTLINE

CHAPTER OBJECTIVES

As the result of reading this chapter, the following objectives should be realized:

1. Learning about validity and how it is measured or determined.
2. Describing four different kinds of validity checks, including face or content validity, pragmatic validity or concurrent or predictive validity, and factorial validity.
3. Defining reliability and how it is measured or determined.
4. Describing four different kinds of reliability checks, including the split-half method, test–retest, parallel forms of the same test, and item discrimination analysis.
5. Determining the complementarity between validity and reliability.
6. Examining various factors that influence a test's reliability and validity, such as mechanical, environmental, and personal factors, the instrument's contents, and researcher's interpretations.

Introduction

Whenever we measure attitudinal variables or any other social or psychological characteristic, we want to know whether our measures are accurate and dependable. All measures of criminological phenomena possess at least two important characteristics. These characteristics are validity and reliability. Validity is the property of a measure or scale that enables us to say that our measure of a particular variable is actually measuring that variable. Reliability is the property of a measure or scale that allows us to say that the variable we are measuring is dependable and consistent. It is important that our scales exhibit high degrees of both validity and reliability.

This chapter focuses exclusively on validity and reliability as attitudinal scale properties. The chapter opens with a definition and examination of validity and how it is assessed. Whenever we measure any variable, especially an attitudinal variable we cannot see, we are concerned whether or not we are measuring that attitudinal variable accurately. Several procedures have been devised to enable us to test the validity of our attitudinal measures. Validity can be examined and determined through the use of at least four different procedures.

The first type of validation procedure examined is content or face validity. This procedure is highly dependent upon the correlation between the scale items and the variable being measured. This procedure is explained in some detail. A close association between the scale items and variable being measured suggests that content or face validity exists. On its "face," the measure appears to be valid. This is an exclusively logical process involving the linkage of scale items with the variable and how it has been conceptualized or defined.

A second validation procedure is predictive validity. It is one of two types of pragmatic validity, where again logical criteria are used to demonstrate the relation between scale items that purport to measure a variable and personal or social behaviors that are consistent with these scale items. In a predictive validity scenario, scale items are used to forecast some type of future behavior or conduct. Thus, a time lapse must occur between the time a variable is measured and the predicted behavior consistent with the scale items is exhibited. The second type of pragmatic validity, and the third type of validation procedure, is concurrent validity. Concurrent validation of an attitudinal measure is demonstrated at the same point in time. Items purportedly measuring some variable or personal or social characteristic are usually correlated with other measures, presumably of the same phenomena. Both of these types of pragmatic validity will be discussed and examples will be provided. These particular procedures utilize both statistical correlations and logic in determining a scale's validity.

The fourth type of validity is construct validity or factorial validity. This validation procedure rests on the premise that various scales, such as personality assessment devices, yield different scores reflecting one's position on a variety of personality dimensions. Through a complex statistical technique, a measure is statistically divided into multiple parts, where each part reflects one personality or attitudinal characteristic or another. Construct validity is defined and illustrated. In all four types of validation, the applications, advantages and disadvantages, and weaknesses and strengths of these procedures are explained.

The chapter next examines reliability. Reliability is assessed at least four different ways. Reliability is defined and discussed. Two methods for determining a measure's reliability are internal procedures, while two methods are external. The two internal reliability methods of checks include the split-half method and item discrimination analysis. Both of these procedures examine the internal consistency of a measure's or scale's items and the degree to which they correlate with one another. External reliability procedures or checks include using test–retest and parallel forms of the same test. Each of these reliability procedures is discussed. In all instances, applications of the different reliability checks or procedures are explained and applications are provided. The advantages, disadvantages, weaknesses, and strengths of all four methods are discussed.

Next, the chapter examines several important functional relationships between validity and reliability. There are several important implications for the validity of the test depending on the reliability of it. Accordingly, several important implications exist for a test's reliability, again depending on the validity of it. These interrelationships are illustrated and explained.

Both validity and reliability are affected by different factors and circumstances. The chapter concludes with an examination of an array of different factors that influence these important scale characteristics. These factors include measuring instruments and their contents; environmental circumstances; personal factors; interpretations of scale scores by investigators; certain testing effects; selection bias; experimental mortality; the Hawthorne effect; the halo effect; the placebo effect; and the influence of diffusion of treatment with control and experimental groups. Each of these potential effects on a measure's validity and reliability is examined, explained, and illustrated.

Validity Defined

Validity is the property of a measuring instrument that allows researchers to say that the instrument is measuring what they say it is measuring (Selltiz et al., 1959). An instrument is said to be valid whenever it measures what we say it measures. If we say that an instrument measures trait X, an attitudinal variable or otherwise, then our measuring instrument is valid to the extent that it truly measures trait X. If our instrument measures trait Y and not trait X, then it is not a valid measure of trait X, even though we might think it is. Thus, it is possible for instruments to be valid indicators of certain unknown variables when they are not particularly valid indicators of those variables we wish to define.

Measuring instruments are created by people. For example, our standards of weight and length are previously agreed-upon standards. In early times, primitive cultures used the distance from the tip of one's thumb to the first thumb joint as a length standard. However, it was soon apparent that some people received more than others because their thumbs were longer. More objective measures were subsequently employed to measure length and weight. Currently, rulers are universally used to measure feet, inches, meters, and millimeters; assorted weights and scales are used to measure pounds, ounces, and grams.

The use of such objective measures leaves little room for dispute among most people. They have agreed that certain measuring instruments will be used to take into account various properties of objects, such as length and weight. We say that a ruler is a valid measure of feet to the extent that it is patterned after some commonly agreed-upon standard that has been determined to measure feet. If the ruler is constructed of wood and if the wood gets wet, there is the possibility that due to shrinkage and warping of the instrument, the measure will not accurately reflect feet as it did previously. All of our measuring instruments, without exception, are vulnerable to contamination from various sources outside (external) or inside (internal) to the instrument itself. Various weights may become worn, and their precision as measures will be affected. The validity of any measure, therefore, is a variable property.

Validity is a relative term, inasmuch as there are serious doubts among some social scientists that there is anything such as absolute validity. Rather, we determine the degree of validity, and validity has little meaning apart from particular operations by which it is determined. Some measures of things have higher validity, some have moderate validity, and some have lower validity, relative to other measures.

Assessing the validity of weights and measures is accomplished rather easily, since it is not difficult to compare certain instruments with those already in existence and accepted as standards. If certain rulers and weights correspond to the accepted standard measures, then we conclude that our measuring instruments are valid. In criminology and other social sciences, however, it is somewhat more difficult to establish the validity of instruments that assess nonempirical phenomena such as attitudes, prestige, power, or peer group pressure. Because many types of attitudes are said to be important in predicting human behavior in various social contexts, it is necessary for social scientists to devise measures of these attitudes so that their usefulness as predictors can be assessed empirically.

Once a measure has been constructed for some attitude, there is usually no objective standard whereby it may be evaluated. We have no universally acceptable measure of burnout and stress, or of police officer professionalism. If we devise scales for these variables, what good would it do to compare them with other scales of these phenomena already in existence? These other measures must also be assessed in their own right, in terms of the degree of validity they happen to manifest. How do criminologists know whether their measures possess validity?

Before we examine several ways of tapping this elusive instrument property, we need to consider the relation between the items included on a paper-and-pencil questionnaire measure and the theoretical universe of traits and items that may be used to measure that phenomenon. Figure 9.1 shows a theoretical universe of items that measure some

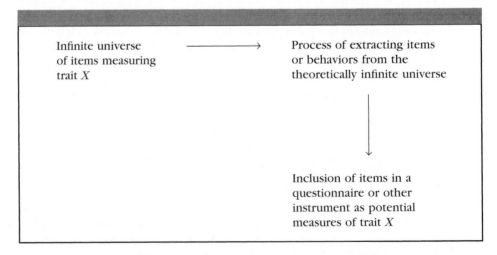

FIGURE 9.1   An illustration of the process of extracting items from an abstract and infinite universe of traits measuring phenomenon X.

variable, in this case, Trait *X*. The universe of items does not exist in the real world; it is merely an abstraction. Thus, it comprises an infinite universe of items and traits for any variable that has been nominally defined. Also theoretically, abstract universes of items and traits exist for all other variables that currently remain unknown or that we have not, as yet, nominally defined.

Consider the illustration in Figure 9.1. Researchers extract items from this abstract universe, almost wholly arbitrarily, although logic is an integral feature involved in their method of item or trait selection. Researchers have no way of proving that those items extracted are indeed from the universe of items that theoretically measures Trait *X*. Thus, investigators are in the difficult position of attempting to illustrate to others that the measures they have devised actually measure what they say they are measuring. The main arguments they cite supporting the validity of their instruments are founded almost entirely on logic and/or statistical support.

Types of Validity

There are four major methods for establishing a test's validity. These include (1) face or content validity, (2) predictive validity, (3) concurrent validity, and (4) construct validity. The labels applied to these types of validity are not uniformly used throughout the social sciences. Alternative terms are sometimes used, such as criterion validity and pragmatic validity. Where appropriate, alternative terms will be noted where they might be substituted for some of the labels used to describe types of validity here.

Content Validity

Content validity or **face validity** is based on the logical inclusion of a sampling of items taken from the universe of items that measure the trait in question. Sometimes such scales are known as **arbitrary scales,** since they are developed on the basis of individual discretion. The only way content validity can be demonstrated is by examining the test or instrument items and comparing them with the universe of items that could theoretically be included, if known (Suris et al., 2001). Researchers judge, on the basis of the items that comprise the instrument, whether the test or instrument is valid according to its representative content. On the basis of the contents of the measure or on the face of it, do the items included seem logically related to the trait measured?

Content or face validity is exclusively a logical type of validity that any given measuring instrument may possess. For example, in the construction of verbal or quantitative tests such as the Graduate Record Examination (GRE), it is important that this test has content validity. It is essential that the items included on the test should reflect the abilities and achievements of the persons taking the test or their personal experience and professional background. If the examination were to emphasize a rather narrow treatment of mathematical skills rather than cover a broad spectrum of mathematical items (e.g., if the emphasis were on trigonometry rather than algebra, calculus, and/or simple arithmetic), then the content validity of the measure as an index of general mathematical knowledge would be called into question. Specifically, we would challenge the test as a valid measure of general quantitative aptitude. And accordingly, if the verbal portion of the GRE emphasized only grammatical rules exclusive of reading comprehension and word understanding, we would seriously question whether it was a valid measure or indicator of one's verbal aptitude as that is generally understood or defined.

Therefore, for any given test or measuring instrument to have content validity, researchers must endeavor to ensure that the instrument contains a logical sampling of items from the so-called universe of items that presumably reflects the characteristic to be measured and correspond with it in some consistent fashion. In the classroom, for example, students might rationalize poor performance on an examination by arguing that the instructor selected test items from book chapters that were not emphasized as important in class. If the test is supposed to cover the first five chapters of a book but only Chapter 1 has questions drawn from it, then the test lacks content validity. It fails to have a representative sampling of items from the **universe of items** that could be utilized in the test's construction, or any text material from the other four chapters.

Applied to attitudinal measures, face or content validity would be applied by simply inspecting a measure's content. On the face of the instrument, does the measure contain logical items that seem related to whatever the instrument purports to measure? If work satisfaction of probation officers is being assessed, the following items might appear on such an instrument administered to probation officers:

1. I would recommend this probation agency to my friends as a good place to work.
2. I would like to continue my present work arrangement for an indefinite time period.
3. If I had the opportunity, I would leave this work to work in another organization doing entirely different things.
4. It would take a sizable change in pay to get me to move from my present position.
5. I don't get along well with my work associates.
6. I like my job more than most of my work associates like theirs.
7. My work assignments are boring and repetitious.
8. There are many things about my job that should be changed to make it more interesting to me.
9. There are many things about my job that I don't like.
10. My work is challenging and interesting.

It is apparent on the face of this instrument that these items are directed at one's work satisfaction and at different dimensions of one's work environment. These are just a few of the items that could be selected from the universe of items that purportedly measure job satisfaction. Our direct inspection of these items suggests that the instrument has at least content validity. This is a strictly logical analysis and conclusion.

Criticisms of Content Validity. The fact that a measure appears to have content validity doesn't necessarily mean that we are indeed measuring the trait. In the previous chapter, problems occurred relative to social desirability and response sets as contaminating factors in attitudinal measurement. Certainly these factors may be involved to varying degrees with the administration of any attitudinal scale, and we must expect a certain amount of social desirability to influence one's personal responses. If measures contain items that are so obvious

BOX 9.1   PERSONALITY HIGHLIGHT

STEVEN A. EGGER
University of Houston at Clear Lake

Statistics: B.S. (police administration), Michigan State University; M.S. (criminal justice), Michigan State University; Ph.D. (criminal justice), Sam Houston State University.

BACKGROUND AND INTERESTS

I certainly didn't start off by thinking that I'd ever work as a criminologist. When I first went to college, I was primarily concerned with football and fraternity life. This didn't last very long, since my studies got the short end of the stick, so to speak, and I was encouraged to look elsewhere for an education. I chose military service and spent most of my 3 years as a military police officer in Germany. This experience fostered my interest in crime and crime control, and upon leaving the military, I enrolled at Michigan State University (MSU) in Police Administration while working as a Flint, Michigan, police officer. From there I was accepted for employment with the Ann Arbor Police Department where I worked as a patrol officer and homicide investigator.

After direct involvement in a serial murder investigation in Ann Arbor, I realized that college was important to my career and that if I didn't do something about it soon, I would never finish my education. And so I resigned from the Ann Arbor PD and started pursuing the police administration degree at MSU. I completed my degree with high honors and went to work for a consulting firm specializing in criminal justice. From this position I went on to direct a police academy in the upper peninsula of Michigan, and my future became focused on crime control research. After completing my master's degree in criminal justice at MSU, I became involved in a number of criminal justice consulting projects, after which I accepted an Instructor position in criminal justice at Jackson Community College in Jackson, Michigan.

After 7 years of teaching at the community college, I realized I wanted to do research and write. The best path to reach this goal was to obtain a Ph.D. I was accepted into the Criminal Justice Program at Sam Houston State University and completed my Ph.D. in 1985, during which time I wrote my dissertation on serial murder in the world. Shortly thereafter, I became Project Director of the development of a computerized system to track and identify serial killers in New York. Upon completion of this project, I accepted a teaching position in the Criminal Justice Program at Sangamon State University (later to become the University of Illinois at Springfield), where I taught for 15 years and wrote and did research on the phenomenon of serial murder.

BOX 9.1   CONTINUED

RESEARCH INVESTIGATIONS

My research and writing on serial murder and violent crime has continued to the present with the completion of a number of articles, book chapters, and encyclopedia entries. My published books are *Serial Murder: An Elusive Phenomenon* (1990); *The Killers Among Us: An Examination of Serial Murder and Its Investigation* (1998, 2002); and *The Urge to Kill* (2004). I am currently working with my wife, Kim, on an encyclopedia of serial killers and coediting a book on police corruption and misconduct.

My research and writing has primarily concentrated on policing and control of violent crime that includes my consulting and training. My background, education, and experience have exposed me to all facets of the criminal justice system. Results of my research have led to my coining two new terms related to serial murder and crime control: "linkage blindness," or the lack of networking and sharing information among law enforcement on unsolved crimes, and the "less-dead," which are those people who are at the greatest risk of becoming victims of a serial killer.

ADVICE TO STUDENTS

The best advice I can give students is to get as much and varied experience as possible while attending college. This not only adds to your résumé and increases your chances of getting a job, but it allows you to choose the area of criminal justice you want to work in. One of the ways to get some experience is to participate in an internship program at your community college or university. I have known a number of students whose internship has evolved into a full-time position in the same agency. This won't always happen, but it will give you an advantage over students with no criminal justice work experience. This advice applies whether you are interested in going into law enforcement, probation, corrections, parole, or criminal law.

about what they measure, it is relatively easy for respondents to fake their responses to these items or alter them in favorable ways. Therefore, some researchers resort to indirect means of assessing certain attitudinal variables. For instance, rather than asking persons if they are afraid of being confined in small places or of heights, they might ask persons whether they would like to be either a forest ranger or an accountant working in a small office. The indirect nature of this and other similar questions enables researchers to prevent respondents from knowing what the researchers are trying to measure. But the more indirect the questions or items, the greater the chance that some universe of items will be tapped other than the one associated with the variable to be measured. This criticism will be discussed in a later section dealing with construct validity.

Another criticism of content validity is that it is subjectively determined. Because content validity is dependent upon the subjective professional judgment of the researcher to a large extent, what one person regards as high content validity might be regarded by another as low content validity. Consider the divergent views of teachers and students about the content validity of the same examination. The teacher may feel strongly that the test has high content validity, but the student may take issue with this belief because of what are felt to be good reasons.

Content validity depends heavily upon the quality of judgment of researchers. Whoever devises the measuring instrument must be careful to include as much as possible of a representative set of items that will measure the particular trait, whether it be verbal or quantitative aptitude, the degree of anxiety, or socioeconomic level.

Another criticism concerns the reality of defining the universe of items from which the measuring instrument will be constructed. The universe of items may consist of all facts included in specific chapters of some textbook students have been assigned. Or the universe of items may consist of all biological, social, and/or psychological features of anxiety. How does one go about identifying all of these features? For all practical purposes, anxiety has an infinite number of physiological, psychological, and social factors that may be extracted and included on an anxiety scale. Again, the judgment of researchers permits them to draw reasonably representative sets of items that measure the trait.

It is difficult to argue that a test does not have content validity, primarily because there is usually some resemblance of the items in the test to the trait presumably measuring it. Few measuring instruments, if any, are perfectly valid indicators of social and psychological traits. The general content validity of any test rests to a great extent on the skill and judgment of the constructor of the test. If poor judgment has been exercised (a factor that always exists as a possibility), then the test or measure will likely have low content validity or no validity at all.

Pragmatic Validity

Perhaps the most useful and popular indicators of validity are **predictive validity** and **concurrent validity.** Both of these types of validity are forms of **pragmatic validity.** Pragmatism suggests that the validity of something can be assessed by whether or not it works. Does a particular attitudinal measure work in assessing a specific attitude? Two ways of demonstrating whether a measure works are to use the measure to forecast some future behavior consistent with scores on the instrument, or correlating these instrument scores with some other concurrent activity at the same point in time (Hemple, Webb, & Reynolds, 1976). These two types of validation are called predictive validity and concurrent validity.

Predictive Validity.   Predictive validity, also known as **criterion validity,** is based on the measured **association** between what an instrument predicts behavior will be and the subsequent behavior exhibited by an individual or group (Ayres & Donahue, 2002). For example, if we obtain from persons their attitudinal scores that purportedly reflect their degree of prejudice toward minority group members (written expressions of what these persons might do if placed in a social situation requiring interactions with minority peoples), the relationship between their scores on the measuring instrument and their subsequent behaviors toward minority group members will provide us with the necessary evidence of the predictive validity of the measure. If their scores indicate discriminatory behaviors, and if these

BOX 9.2   PERSONALITY HIGHLIGHT

MITCHELL B. CHAMLIN
University of Cincinnati

Statistics: B.A. (history), University at Albany; M.A. (criminal justice), University at Albany; Ph.D. (sociology), University at Albany.

BACKGROUND AND INTERESTS

I am a macro-criminologist. That means I spend my time trying to figure out why some places have more or less crime (e.g., violent and property crime rates) and crime control (police per capita, arrest rates) than others. Individual behavior is a mystery to me. I do not know why anyone does anything, including engaging in illegal activities. I always supposed that people committed crimes because they wanted to and left it at that.

What had always fascinated me, and continues to intrigue me to this day, is how and why the characteristics of communities can influence patterns of crime, independently of the characteristics of the people who live there. Put a little differently, I wanted to understand and predict how the racial, economic, and social composition of places can influence behavior above and beyond the attitudes, beliefs, dreams, and fears of individuals.

Toward this end, I spent the first few years or so of my career extending, clarifying, and testing existing macro-social theories of crime and crime control. My early work as a graduate student, especially with my late mentor Al Liska, focused on the pluralistic conflict perspective. The basic problem we grappled with was trying to "explicate the linkages" (Al's favorite admonition to his graduate students) from the racial and economic structure of macro-social units to various indicators of crime control. We had some modicum of success (see especially Liska & Chamlin, 1984).

Eventually I earned my Ph.D. and moved on to the University of Oklahoma [OU]. I was fortunate to have three excellent colleagues in my area of specialization, Bob Bursik, Harold Grasmick, and John Cochran (my primary collaborator since 1992). Although I continued to apply pluralistic conflict theories to the study of various dimensions of macro-social control, my research also took a new direction: the study of general deterrence theory.

RESEARCH INVESTIGATIONS

A series of accidents, coincidences, and dumb luck led me to the study of macro-level deterrence theory. While I was at the 1982 ASC meetings in Toronto I met Dick McCleary. He convinced me to take his time series (ARIMA) statistics course during the spring of 1983. When

BOX 9.2   CONTINUED

I came to Oklahoma, I met Harold Grasmick who, as it turns out, is one of the leading scholars in perceptual deterrence theory. Lastly, the last student of Gwilym Jenkins (the co-creator of ARIMA procedures), Jim Horrell, who happened to be a professor in the business department at OU, had the only copy of Jenkins's mainframe (yes, we still used mainframe computers back then) ARIMA time series program in North America. Cutting to the chase, these occurrences led me to begin a number of articles, rooted in general deterrence theory, examining the reciprocal effects, over time, between measures of crime (property offenses) and crime control (arrests, arrest clearances, and the number of police). Perhaps more importantly, within the context of this essay, this new line of research led me to more fully comprehend the interplay between theory and research.

Consider, for example, how one goes about "falsifying" general deterrence theory. At a minimum, a researcher must make a priori decisions about: (1) the appropriate unit of analysis (census tracts, cities, or states); (2) how to measure the threat of punishment (arrests, arrest clearances, sentence length); (3) how to measure crime (property, violent, or total index crimes); (4) how to disentangle the potential reciprocal relationship between measures of crime and punishment (assume them away or use longitudinal data); and (5) the best way to estimate the time lag between changes in the risk of being punished for a crime and changes in the level of crime (ARIMA techniques or panel designs). As you complete this course, it should become more and more apparent that the best way to make these methodological determinations is to be guided by theory.

In 1994 I moved on to the University of Cincinnati and continued my study of interrelationships between macro-criminological theory and research. Within a few years my interests diverged into two distinct, yet complementary, directions. First, I began to think more seriously about Al Liska's advice to "explicate the linkages" and decided to attempt to devise my own theoretical schema to explain the influence of macro-structural and macro-cultural conditions on crime. This led to two publications. The first, which was published in *Criminology,* focuses on how the willingness of community members to help the less fortunate (what we call "social altruism") promotes cultural values that lower the crime rate (Chamlin & Cochran, 1997). The second, which is forthcoming in *Homicide Studies,* is a theoretical piece that draws on both conflict and functionalist models of society to explain how and why economic inequality affects crime rates across nation-states. In brief, we argue that ascribed economic inequalities reduce the legitimacy of a society's system of stratification, thereby weakening the norms and values that discourage the performance of illegal and deviant acts (Chamlin & Cochran, 2004).

Second, I became increasingly convinced that the biggest problem with macro-criminology is not that we lack sufficient theory or statistical techniques to advance our understanding of the root causes of crime. Rather, the chief problem is one of measurement. All too often the key theoretical constructs remain unmeasured intervening variables in our statistical analyses. Therefore, I, along with my colleague John Cochran, decided to try and come up with improved measures of macro-social constructs. For example, we published an article in the *Journal of Quantitative Criminology* that offered an alternative to the traditional Bureau of Labor Statistics measure of civilian unemployment: the capacity utilization rate. As we antic-

BOX 9.2   CONTINUED

ipated, this nontraditional measure of the demand for labor proved to be a better predictor of property crime than the conventional unemployment rate (Chamlin & Cochran, 2000).

In the immediate future, I plan on continuing to refine my theoretical ideas and apply them to construct more valid and reliable measures of the abstract constructs that connect background structural conditions to rates of criminal behavior among macro-social units.

ADVICE TO STUDENTS

My advice is simple. Never forget that theory construction and theory testing are flip sides of the same coin. My knowledge of theory helps me make better decisions when I design an empirical evaluation of some macro-social explanation for criminality. Similarly, my knowledge of realities of empirical research, such as whether or not it might be possible to operationalize abstract constructs that one might want to incorporate into a conceptual schema, informs my attempts to develop my own theoretical ideas. So, do not be tempted to believe the myth that one can ignore methods and be a "pure" theorist or that one can engage in empirical research without a rich understanding of theory. Both myths are wrong.

subjects exhibit discriminatory behaviors toward one or more minority group members, this is evidence that the test is measuring what we say it measures.

Suppose we devise a measure of male chauvinism among personnel officers of several companies and find that some officers possess male chauvinistic attitudes to a high degree while others possess this characteristic to a low degree. A comparison of their subsequent hiring practices and their respective chauvinism scores might disclose much about the predictive utility of our measure. If those officers with high chauvinism scores have hiring records that show some gender discrimination (e.g., low numbers of female hires), and if those officers who have low chauvinism scores have hiring records showing more equitable hiring practices, then our measure of male chauvinism would seem to have predictive validity. Predictive validity is the simple correlation of predicted behavior with subsequent exhibited behavior. A high correlation or relationship between the predicted behavior and the behavior exhibited means that the measure possesses predictive validity.

Concurrent Validity.   Concurrent validity differs from predictive validity in that the scores of predicted behavior are obtained simultaneously with the exhibited behavior (Paschall et al., 2001). For instance, if we obtained manual dexterity and work efficiency scores from drill press operators in a factory, we might also obtain from their supervisors their productivity records. We can compare directly their productivity records with the manual dexterity and work efficiency scores to determine if there is concurrent validity. Again, as in the case of predictive validity, a high correlation or relation between the dexterity scores and high drill press productivity suggests that our measure has concurrent validity. Therefore, predictive validity forecasts expected behaviors in some future time period, while concurrent validity is assessed by comparing test results with some simultaneous behavior. Consider some hypothetical scores in Table 9.1.

In the example of hypothetical scores shown in Table 9.1, two measures have been obtained from a sample of delinquent boys. One measure we have presumably constructed is self-esteem, while the other is perceived peer pressure. Wishing to validate our self-esteem scale, we might predict that those boys with lower amounts of self-esteem might be more receptive to peer pressures. Accordingly, we might suspect that as their scores on self-esteem increase, their perceived peer pressure scores might decrease. Also, as their self-esteem scores decrease, their perceived peer pressure scores might increase. Table 9.1 has been deliberately configured to demonstrate this. If these were actual scores of self-esteem and perceived peer pressure, we would consider this relation supportive of our theorizing. Also, our measure of self-esteem would appear to be validated by its correlation with perceived peer pressure.

Both predictive and concurrent validity are determined largely by statistical correlations, although we might conclude that our measures have these types of validity by visually inspecting the patterns of scores such as those displayed in Table 9.1. If there is a logical relation between these sets of scores, this is logical evidence of predictive and/or concurrent validity.

Criticisms of Predictive and Concurrent Validity.   One criticism of predictive and concurrent validity is that simply observing a numerical association between a test score and some actual individual or group behavior is no guarantee that the measuring instrument is a valid indicator of the trait we have nominally defined. It could be, for example, that our measure really is a valid indicator of something else closely related with the phenomenon we are investigating. Therefore, we might be led to suspect that our instrument is a valid measure of what we say it is, when in fact it may be a measure of something else. This problem always exists, whenever attitudinal measures are constructed. There is no way we can ever be sure that we are measuring what we say we are measuring regarding attitudinal

TABLE 9.1   Self-Esteem and Peer Pressure Scores for Ten Delinquent Boys

Delinquent	Self-Esteem	Perceived Peer Pressure
1	42	28
2	45	27
3	47	25
4	49	24
5	52	23
6	55	21
7	56	20
8	58	20
9	59	19
10	61	16

scales. However, we do consider as evidence of the potential validity of the instrument the relationship between the predicted and the observed behavior in question. This should actually serve as a caution. Researchers must always be aware of the potential limitations of their measures. They should not be overconfident that they are measuring what they say they are measuring, strictly on the basis of high correlations between predicted and observed behaviors (Suris et al., 2001).

In the case of gender and racial discrimination, another criticism is apparent. Since it is illegal to discriminate on the basis of gender and race, it is entirely possible to tap a gender or racial prejudice dimension with our devised instruments but not observe discriminatory behaviors. Thus, people may have an amount of gender or racial prejudice, but they may not exhibit illegal behaviors of discriminating against persons because of their race or gender. Even if certain behaviors are not prohibited by law, social constraints exist to prevent certain discriminatory behaviors from being observed.

Another criticism of pragmatic validity is the researcher's interpretation of exhibited behaviors by respondents as representing the predicted behavior. Some attitudinal measures are so abstract that several different kinds of interpretations of given behavior patterns could be made according to a variety of social researchers who define the situation. Again, the judgment of the researcher is a crucial element in determining the degree of pragmatic validity that exists.

Construct Validity

Construct validity, sometimes known as criterion validity, is both a logical and a statistical validating method (Kleck, 2004). Also known as factorial validity, construct validity is useful for measuring traits for which external criteria are not available, such as latent aggressiveness. This type of validity is determined through the application of **factor analysis.** Factor analysis is a statistical technique designed to determine the basic components of a measure (Blalock, 1972). For example, if we were to factor analyze a measure of police professionalism, we might find that the variable consists of three predominant factors—formal educational attainment, supervisory expectations, and promotional ambitions. Factor analysis is beyond the scope of this text, although we can discuss briefly what it does. If we devised a police officer professionalism scale that consisted of 50 items, the application of factor analysis might cause our scale to factor in three major parts corresponding to educational attainment, supervisory expectations, and promotional ambitions. Thus, we could see three distinct clusters of items that focus around these dimensions. An inspection of the individual items within each cluster should bear directly upon those particular factors. We could determine this relation in much the same way that we would use content or face validity to evaluate the contents of a scale.

A popular personality assessment device is Raymond Cattell's 16 Personality Factor Inventory, developed at the Institute for Personality and Abilities Testing in Champaign, Illinois. Designated as the "16 PF," Cattell's inventory purportedly measures 16 separate personality dimensions. When factor analysis is applied to this measure, which consists of 187 questions, it factors into 16 separate parts, with 16 separate clusters of items. This is evidence of **factorial validity.** More advanced sources may be consulted for how factor analysis might be applied (Dozois & Kelln, 1999).

Criticisms of Construct Validity.   Construct validity can be used to demonstrate whether or not a measuring instrument is in fact measuring a particular phenomenon. If a measure is supposed to reflect only one dimension, and if factor analysis shows that more than one dimension of the variable is being measured, then this raises serious questions about the instrument's validity.

Another criticism is that construct validity requires a rather sophisticated statistical background on the part of the researcher in order to apply it manually. While statistical programs exist and have been adapted for computer use to facilitate one's computations, we must still possess interpretive skills to make sense out of what has been computed.

Furthermore, because construct validity pertains almost exclusively to traits that are not directly observable, there is a greater risk that the instrument is actually measuring some other phenomenon closely related to the trait being investigated rather than the actual trait itself. Compared with predictive validity, for instance, there is no direct means to correlate actual behaviors with test scores as a way of demonstrating the construct validity of the instrument.

It was mentioned earlier that often, researchers will devise items that are indirect indicators of the traits they investigate. Thus, rather than asking persons whether or not they like their work, researchers may ask them whether they would recommend the job to others as an indirect way of assessing their own job contentment or work satisfaction. For more deep-seated personality characteristics such as acrophobia (fear of heights) or claustrophobia (fear of small, enclosed places), indirect items are preferable. The use of indirect items is to discourage respondents from making socially desirable responses. We might ask someone if they are anxious or claustrophobic, for instance. It is likely that they will not be perfectly honest with us and say things that are socially desirable. However, if we ask indirect questions, they cannot easily determine what it is we are trying to assess. This is a case of the test-taker trying to outwit the tester. Indirect questions involve the tester attempting to outwit test-takers. Consider the following item as an example:

> 121. I would rather:
> (A) grow flowers; (B) add columns of numbers; (C) in between.

Presumably, if someone selects (A) and prefers growing flowers over adding numbers, then an inference might be made from this. Since "growing flowers" is a largely out-of-doors activity and "adding columns of numbers" is associated with in-door work, we might use this item to assess one's claustrophobic tendencies, if any. Bear in mind that we do not limit our inferences about one's behaviors to one item such as is indicated above. We might use multiple items, perhaps as many as 15 or 20, in order to ensure that our behavioral and attitudinal inferences are more valid ones. We are not going to conclude that because someone says they like to grow flowers, they must be claustrophobic.

But the further we depart from the actual traits or characteristics we want to measure with the items we construct, the more likely it is that we might not be tapping variables closely related to those we are investigating. Thus, our indirect indicators of variables are helpful in the sense that they discourage test-takers from making socially desirable responses, but they are detrimental in the sense that we may be losing touch with the variables purportedly measured.

Reliability Defined

Another important test property is reliability. Reliability is the ability of a measuring instrument to consistently measure whatever it is designed to measure (Selltiz et al., 1959). Reliability refers to test consistency. Suppose we develop a measure of police professionalism. We believe our measure is reliable. If we administer our police professionalism scale to a sample of police officers in time 1 and record their scores, and then if we wait a month and measure these same officers again on our police professionalism scale in time 2, the officers' scale scores should be the same or very similar between the two time periods. This fact presumes that nothing happens to these officers between the two time periods that might otherwise change their scores. No differences between officers' scores between the time 1 and time 2 administration of our police professionalism scale is evidence of the reliability of this measure.

Why is it Important to Have Reliable Measures?

It is important to have reliable measures for at least two reasons: (1) reliability is a prerequisite for measuring an instrument's validity and (2) researchers want to assess the impact of certain variables on other variables. Reliable measuring instruments will enable researchers to draw tentative conclusions about causal relationships between variables.

Reliability as a Prerequisite for Validity.   In order for a measuring instrument to be valid, it must be demonstrably reliable. Any measuring instrument that does not reflect some attribute consistently has little chance of being considered a valid measure of that attribute. For example, suppose persons have conservative political views. A measure of conservatism would be regarded as unreliable if, after repeated measures for the same persons, widely different conservatism scores were reported. This assumes, of course, that other variables did not intervene to cause changes in their score results.

Determining Whether One Variable Affects Other Variables.   If it can be reasonably determined that individuals are relatively uninfluenced by extraneous variables that are a part of their environment from one instrument administration to the next, then the chances for a measure to be considered unreliable are greatly increased if significant score differences are observed. The reliability of a measuring instrument is seldom, if ever, determined by examining responses from a single individual to that measure. Most often, evidence of reliability is gathered from large aggregates of persons.

Scores on a reliable measuring instrument will fluctuate only in response to some independent factor or condition causally associated with it directly or indirectly. Caution should be exercised in interpreting apparent relationships between two or more variables as causal relationships. If researchers observe a change in a person's score on some attitudinal dimension from one time period to the next, they want to be able to say that the score change is empirical evidence of the potential effect of one variable upon the other.

Generally, if factor X is introduced between two time periods, then theoretically, certain changes in specific attitudinal dimensions that relate meaningfully to factor X should occur. For example, in many police departments in the United States, films and videotapes dealing with human relations skills are shown to units of officers as a part of their training and to enhance their interactions with the public. If officers manifest poor human relations skills in dealing with the public prior to seeing these films or videotapes, then they are much improved in this respect after viewing the films and videotapes, this is considered to be tacit support for the assumption that the audiovisual aid helped to account for their behavioral change. Taken by itself, this does not prove that the audiovisual aid caused the changes in human relations skills, but it is nevertheless strong support for this contention. Figure 9.2 illustrates a conventional independent–dependent variable pattern, where one variable purportedly causes changes to occur in another variable.

While Figure 9.2 shows only one score, most real-world applications utilize numerous scores in before–after research. In this hypothetical example, however, measures are taken in time 1 (t_1) and time 2 (t_2). Score differences are noted in a column to the far right. In this case, one score of 50 is observed for the dependent variable Y in time 1 and the score of 25 is recorded on the same measure of Y administered in time 2. The score difference of -25 is recorded. Between the two time periods, an experimental variable X is introduced. The score difference of -25 is presumed attributable to the introduction of variable X, if our measure of Y is reliable. Again, some caution must be exercised when drawing causal inferences among variables. Several other factors may have accounted for this score difference. We will examine several phenomena that influence a measure's reliability and validity in a later section of this chapter.

Types of Reliability

Four methods for assessing an instrument's reliability are presented here. These are divided into internal and external reliability checks or methods. Internal checks establish reliability by examining the internal consistency of items, while external checks use the measure

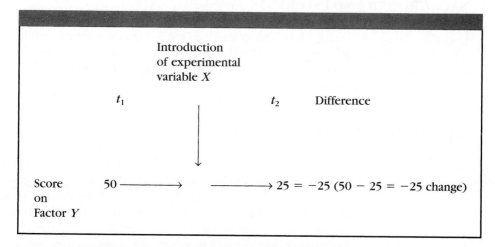

FIGURE 9.2   The effect of an experimental variable X on factor Y.

against itself over time or a comparison of two or more equivalent measures of the same phenomena. **Internal reliability checks** include the split-half method and item discrimination analysis. **External reliability checks** include test–retest and parallel forms of the same test.

Internal Reliability Checks

One way of attacking the reliability problem of instruments is to examine the **internal consistency** of items used to construct them. Items that measure the same phenomenon should logically cling together in some consistent pattern. Persons who like their jobs are unlikely to give responses that would typify persons who don't like their jobs. The argument is that persons with particular traits will respond predictably to items affected by those traits.

BOX 9.3   PERSONALITY HIGHLIGHT

FRANK R. SCARPITTI
Edward and Elizabeth Rosenberg Professor, University of Delaware

Statistics: B.A. (social science), Cleveland State University; M.A., Ph.D. (sociology), Ohio State University.

BACKGROUND AND INTERESTS

Over the course of my career, I have done research on and written about mental health, juvenile delinquency, female crime, rape, group therapy, corrections, organized crime, and substance abuse. Most recently, I have been researching the impact of drug courts on those who appear before these unique judicial bodies.

WHY CRIMINOLOGY?

My family moved to Cleveland, Ohio, when I was 12 years old and settled in a rapidly changing neighborhood. Within a few years, our area of the city changed almost completely in terms of class, race, employment, safety, and crime. The number of youth getting into trouble with the law grew rapidly, gangs flourished, and pressure to be one of the group, to fight, to be delinquent was felt by all of the boys in the neighborhood. Although some of my friends did get into trouble with the law, I somehow resisted, did well in school, and graduated from high school without a delinquency record. These experiences did, however, generate a curiosity in me about

BOX 9.3   CONTINUED

delinquency and crime, and why some of us were able to avoid illegal behavior, or at least avoid being caught.

As a "college boy" commuting to an urban campus while still living in the neighborhood, I took a course in criminology, and thought it was the most fascinating course I had yet taken. The text was written by Walter C. Reckless, and addressed many of the issues I had wondered about pertaining to my experiences growing up, friends who had gotten into trouble, illegal activities I saw in the neighborhood, and much more I wanted to know about crime. In addition, after my second year of college, I took a night job as a supervisor in the local juvenile detention home, working the midnight to 8:00 shift 6 days a week. Here I had an opportunity to talk with a large number of teenagers who were bound for court or for the state industrial school, asking them about their experiences, their motivations, their expectations for the future, and so forth. I tried to "apply" what I was learning in my sociology and psychology courses, but found my charges to be confused, inarticulate, and unaware of their motivations. Nevertheless, I was hooked, and when my professors encouraged me to consider going to graduate school in sociology, I knew there was only one area of the discipline I wanted to focus on, criminology.

RESEARCH INVESTIGATIONS

I was fortunate to attend graduate school at Ohio State University and study with Walter C. Reckless. Reckless had each of his graduate students work on an aspect of a large, ongoing study testing the efficacy of his containment theory. My assignment was to follow up in the community so-called "good" and "bad" boys living in high delinquency areas and their mothers, interviewed some 4 years earlier. I learned to do field work in this way, tracking down respondents, visiting them in their homes, and convincing them to be interviewed by me. Sometimes the interviews took 45 minutes, sometimes 2 hours, usually depending on how talkative the boy and his mother were. After doing over 200 of these interviews, I knew a great deal more about delinquency, the difficulty of staying out of trouble, and the daily lives of youngsters living in troubled areas of a large city. Since then, I have always made it a point of getting to know the subjects of my research by spending time with them, talking about the issues that they see as influencing their behavior, and generally attempting to get a "feel" for their world as they see it.

In the years since graduate school, I have conducted research on the first community mental health project in the United States, a treatment program for delinquent boys, the long-term effects of removing status offenders from the juvenile court, the effectiveness of therapeutic communities on incarcerated substance abusers, and the efficacy of therapeutic jurisprudence as practiced by drug courts. These have all been forms of evaluation research, studies designed to see whether or not programs actually work as intended. This form of research is consistent with my desire to do what I refer to as "meaningful" research, that which may actually make a direct contribution to the betterment of the human condition. While the testing of abstract principles and theory is essential for the advancement of science, it doesn't bring personal satisfaction to everyone. I enjoy the research endeavor more when I believe that what I'm doing will improve the world just a little bit, and soon enough for me to see it.

BOX 9.3   CONTINUED

While these projects and others that I haven't mentioned have all involved the use of structured instruments with large samples, as well as the application of reasonably sophisticated statistical analyses, I have also done research that is more akin to investigative journalism. A few years ago, a colleague and I became interested in the role of organized crime in the disposal of toxic waste in the United States. Although it had long been known that organized crime was involved in the solid waste industry, little was known at the time about their role in the more dangerous business of toxic waste disposal. We set out on a 5-year search for information by examining thousands of pages of documents, interviewing officials, visiting disposal sites, talking with truck drivers, and even securing the cooperation of illegal dumpers. It was a different kind of research, not subject to statistical analysis, but very rewarding and consistent with my attempt to do research that makes a difference.

ADVICE TO STUDENTS

I have always wanted to be a detective, but not a police officer. That is, I want to do what detectives do, confront problems, look for clues, investigate relationships, pose questions, seek answers based on fact. A career as a criminological researcher has provided me with the opportunity to do all of those things. Students who share my fascination with mystery, puzzles, the unexplained, why we act as we do may also find research in criminology and criminal justice to be a worthwhile career choice.

To prepare for a career in criminology and criminal justice, either as a practicing professional in law enforcement or corrections, or as a researcher, students should study the broad principles of social behavior found in the theory and research of various disciplines devoted to understanding human behavior. In effect, one's preparation should be interdisciplinary, drawing on the perspectives of many fields of study to obtain the most comprehensive picture possible.

Interdisciplinary, theory-based college training of this sort can still prepare students for applied careers in criminal justice if that is what one wants. It assumes that the best way to prepare students for these careers is through broadly based educational experiences that qualifies them to learn and assume diverse professional roles. Those aspiring to a career in law enforcement, for example, are better served by learning the dynamics of human behavior than crime scene investigation, which may be learned at a training academy if one does eventually end up as a police officer.

It is my belief that the best education for those who major in criminology and criminal justice consists of sampling many disciplines and getting a broad knowledge of the many intellectual pursuits available to them. No one discipline or orientation has a monopoly on understanding crime and criminals. The criminal justice professional, whether an applied practitioner or an academic researcher, should be an eclectic thinker with insight into those aspects of the physical and social world that influence our behavior. The opportunity to develop those critical intellectual skills necessary to succeed in the field of criminal justice is available in every college course a student takes.

Suppose we were to construct a measure of some attitude and include 20 items in our instrument. These 20 items are statements with Likert-type agree–disagree responses. Ten of the items are positively worded, whereas the other 10 statements are negatively worded. Persons who have the attitude to either a high degree or a low degree should respond to all 20 items consistently, provided that each of these items has been extracted from the same attitudinal universe. Examining the internal consistency of the instrument enables researchers to determine which items are not consistent with the rest in measuring the phenomenon under investigation. The object is to remove those inconsistent items from the measure to improve its internal consistency. However, one preliminary caution is in order. Since most of our attitudinal measures are multidimensional, it may be possible for respondents to give positive responses to some items and negative responses to others. They might like their pay but not their work associates. Thus, internal consistency may be more or less difficult to create, depending on the potential for these complex variations in item responses. Two categories of internal checks for reliability include the split-half method and item discrimination analysis.

The Split-Half Technique.   The **split-half technique** is designed to correlate one half of the test items with the other half of them (Melvin et al., 1985). For instance, if we devised a 30-item scale, a suitable procedure for establishing the internal consistency of the test would be to divide the items into two equal parts and correlate them. Some researchers recommend numbering the items from 1 to N, and then correlating the odd-numbered items with the even-numbered ones.

There are no conventional standards that prescribe how to interpret the results of these correlations. One rule-of-thumb that might be applicable is to regard correlations of .90 or higher as indicative of high test reliability. The Kuder–Richardson 20 procedure may be applied here. Step-by-step directions for applying this advanced statistical procedure are presented in Magnusson (1967).

Applied to Likert-type scaling, recall that item weights are assigned on five- or six-point response patterns from "Strongly Agree" to "Strongly Disagree." If we took one half of all test items and correlated them with the other half of the test, we would be correlating item weights with one another. Theoretically, if a person receives lots of "6's" and "5's" on one half of the test because of the responses given, then there should be lots of "6's" and "5's" on the other half of the test, if it is internally consistent. The Kuder–Richardson 20 procedure produces a correlation coefficient of the magnitude of relation between these two test halves.

Item Discrimination Analysis.   The second internal method of determining a test's reliability is called **item discrimination analysis,** sometimes simply **item analysis.** It is relatively simple to illustrate and understand, and complex statistical manipulations of data are not required.

For instance, let's assume that researchers have administered an attitudinal instrument to 100 persons. Further assume that the instrument contains 10 items, each having a six-point Likert-type response pattern of attitudinal intensity (i.e., strongly agree, agree, undecided, probably agree, undecided, probably disagree, disagree, and strongly disagree). If we weight each response per item according to a 1, 2, 3, 4, 5, and 6 intensity pattern (or, 6, 5, 4, 3, 2, and 1 in the case of positively worded items), it would be possible for a person to obtain a maximum high score of $10 \times 6 = 60$ and a minimum low score of $10 \times 1 = 10$. These would be the number of items times the largest and smallest weights for a single item. The scoring range would be between 10 and 60.

Logically, persons with larger overall scores on the instrument (e.g., 60, 59, 58, 56, and so on) would tend to respond to each item in such a way that the weight assigned each item response would probably be either a 4, 5, or 6. Persons with smaller overall scores of 10, 12, 15, and so on, would probably have small weights of 1, 2, or 3 associated with particular item responses. Sometimes, persons with overall larger scores will respond to an item and receive a 1, 2, or 3 instead of a 4, 5, or 6. By the same token, those with overall smaller scores might receive an item weight of 4, 5, or 6 instead of 1, 2, or 3. These response deviations are inconsistencies. If there are too many inconsistencies in any given response pattern for particular items, then those items become suspect. An inconsistent item may not be from the same universe as the other items. Possibly the inconsistent item may be excluded from the rest in order to improve the internal consistency of the measure and thereby improve its reliability. To illustrate item inconsistencies, consider the hypothetical response patterns of 12 research participants to 10 items in a questionnaire designed to measure variable X. These are shown in Table 9.2.

The body of Table 9.2 consists of weights assigned to each of the 10 items. Each column consists of the response pattern of different individuals to the 10 items. Note the consistency of subject #1 to all items except item #5. Note also the consistency of subject #2 (with opposite response patterns and indicating low attitudinal intensity) to all items except #5. Subject #3 is equally consistent in responses with the exception of item #5. When certain items stand out from the rest as being inconsistent, this may be considered evidence to challenge not only the reliability of the particular item, but also its validity. If items are to be discarded and total attitudinal scores are recalculated on the basis of the new item composition and arrangement, the resulting score would be considered a more reliable estimate of the person's attitude X.

TABLE 9.2   Example of Item Discrimination Analysis

	Subject											
Item	1	2	3	4	5	6	7	8	9	10	11	12
1	6	1	3	2	5	1	6	4	1	4	1	6
2	5	1	2	1	5	1	6	4	1	4	1	6
3	6	2	2	1	5	2	6	4	1	5	2	5
4	6	1	3	1	4	2	6	4	1	4	2	6
5	2	5	6	4	2	4	2	2	5	2	4	3
6	6	2	1	1	5	2	6	4	1	3	2	5
7	6	1	2	2	6	2	5	4	2	5	1	6
8	5	1	3	3	5	2	5	4	3	5	2	4
9	5	1	3	1	5	2	6	4	1	6	2	5
10	6	1	2	1	5	1	6	4	3	6	2	4

It is important to note that items having consistently inconsistent response patterns, such as item #5 in Table 9.2, may not be unreliable items. If they are consistently inconsistent, we must examine the weight pattern we have assigned them. It may be that we mistakenly applied the 6, 5, 4, 3, 2, and 1 pattern to this item weight pattern when it should have received a 1, 2, 3, 4, 5, and 6 pattern. The wording of the item should be considered in relation to the weights we have assigned. In short, we may have a reliable item. It may be that we simply assigned the wrong weights.

Another way of spotting inconsistent items is to deal with the discriminatory power of each item and reject those items that fail to discriminate between individuals possessing the attitudinal trait to a high or a low degree, respectively. This method is as follows. We would first obtain responses from N individuals and rank them according to their total raw scores on the measuring instrument from high to low, or from the largest to smallest scores. Next, we would divide the total scores into the upper and lower quartiles. The upper quartile would contain the upper 25 percent of all raw scores, while the lower quartile would contain the lower 25 percent of all raw scores. Those individuals in the center of the distribution or the central 50 percent of it would be excluded from further consideration according to this particular internal consistency procedure. The argument favoring their exclusion is that if the item discriminates, then it is most observable in the case of extreme attitudinal intensity scores.

We now have two groups of respondents representing both extremes of attitudinal intensity. As one example, suppose we evaluated the hypothetical data presented in Table 9.2. Taking one item at a time on the measure, we could construct a table identifying the response weights of all individuals in the upper and lower quartiles. In Table 9.3, all responses to item #1 have been recorded for two groups of subjects in the upper and lower quartiles, considering their overall scores. This table has been constructed, based on an overall sample of 40 persons. Thus, the upper and lower quartiles would consist of 10 persons each, since 10/40 = 25 percent. In this particular instance, note that the weights of persons in the upper quartile are considerably larger collectively compared with the weights shown for the subjects in

TABLE 9.3   Illustration of Item Discrimination Analysis for a Single Item: Responses of Upper and Lower Quartiles to Item 1

$N_1 = 10$ Upper Quartile	$N_2 = 10$ Lower Quartile
6	1
5	3
4	2
5	3
4	4
5	3
6	4
6	1
5	2
5	1
Sum of item scores = 51	Sum of item scores = 24
$\overline{X}_1 = 5.1$	$\overline{X}_2 = 2.4$

the lower quartile. This is what we would expect logically for an item that discriminates be-tween individuals possessing varying degrees of some attitudinal characteristic.

On the basis of the total scores persons receive for a set of attitudinal items, we may infer that their response for each item should be consistent with their overall responses. Therefore, persons identified as belonging to the upper quartile should have consistently larger weights assigned their responses for each item in the questionnaire, and those who belong to the lower quartile on the basis of their total score should have consistently smaller weights assigned each item. In the case illustrated in Table 9.3, item #1 (any item taken from the set of items in our measure of some attitude) appears to discriminate. We must verify this statement further, however.

The next step is to determine the average weight for item #1 among the subjects of the upper and lower quartiles. Averaging the weights of both groups, we have a mean or $\overline{X}_1$ (the average score for the upper quartile on item #1) = 5.1. The average or $\overline{X}_2$ for the lower quartile on the same item is 2.4. A visual inspection of the difference between the means of both groups would reveal that the item appears to discriminate between those who possess the trait to a high degree and those who possess it to a low degree.

We may continue our item analysis by selecting item #2, recording the response weights for all individuals in the upper and lower quartiles, determining the average re-sponse for both groups, and so on. Finally, we would generate a table containing the means and mean differences of the upper and lower quartiles of subjects for all 10 items as is shown in Table 9.4.

In Table 9.4, the column to the far right contains mean differences between the aver-age weights of the upper and lower quartiles of respondents based on total scores to a mea-sure of attitude X. Notice that items #1, 4, 5, 7, 8, and 9 appear to discriminate between the two groups to varying degrees. These averages are consistent with what we would expect them to be. Note also that items #2, 3, and 6 do not appear to discriminate at all. In fact, item #6 contradicts slightly the way the average weights should logically be arranged in relation to one another. Predictably, averages for each item among the upper quartile of respondents

TABLE 9.4   Comparison of the Upper and Lower Quartiles

Item	Upper Quartile $\overline{X}_1$	Lower Quartile $\overline{X}_2$	Mean Difference $\overline{X}_1 - \overline{X}_2$
1	5.1	2.4	+2.7
2	4.6	4.5	+0.1
3	3.3	3.3	0.0
4	5.5	3.1	+2.4
5	4.8	1.8	+3.0
6	3.9	4.1	−0.2
7	5.0	4.0	+1.0
8	4.8	2.5	+2.3
9	4.9	2.8	+2.1
10	1.3	5.4	−4.1

should be larger compared with the averages of item weights for members of the lower quartile. Finally, observe that item #10 discriminates, but it does so in reverse!

There are several reasons why the item fails to discriminate as predicted. First, it could be a poor item and should not be included with the other items. It does not measure the phenomenon under investigation. Second, it may be that the researchers assigned the wrong weights to that particular statement. They must double-check the statement and response pattern assigned to it before throwing the item out altogether. It can be observed that if response weights have been assigned inappropriately to that item, then a correction will reinstate the item as a discriminating one. The function of item discrimination analysis is to improve the reliability of a test by eliminating those items that are inconsistent with the other items.

If researchers were to use item discrimination analysis, it would be advisable to begin by including a large number of items, at least in excess of 20. When item analysis is completed, several of the statements will be eliminated from the list because of their inability to discriminate between those individuals possessing variable amounts of the attitudinal trait under investigation. As a result of eliminating items, the range of response that is possible to achieve is narrowed. Considering the above response pattern of 6, 5, 4, 3, 2, and 1, a 20-item questionnaire would yield a total response range of from 20 to 120. Decreasing the number of items from 20 to 10 will narrow the range of response from 10 to 60. Decisions to eliminate items are based in part on the following considerations:

1. The degree to which the item discriminates
2. The number of individuals to whom the instrument is administered
3. The degree to which precision is desired by researchers in their attempt to measure the attitudinal phenomenon

If researchers reject too many items, then this increases the likelihood of larger numbers of tied scores among respondents. This narrows the latitude of flexibility in the data analysis stage and will affect tabular construction and significantly eliminate statistical test options. On the other hand, if too many items are retained, then the chances increase of including items that discriminate poorly.

Choices as to which items should be retained and which ones should be excluded are almost always made arbitrarily by the researcher. Again, no specific conventional guidelines exist for making these kinds of decisions. Some researchers have advocated conducting statistical tests of significance of difference between two means as a way of introducing probability theory into their decision making to accept or reject specific attitudinal statements, but this is not recommended. Nevertheless, in Table 9.4, for example, items #1, 4, 5, 8, and 9 would probably be included in the final form of the measure of attitude X. The other items would either be excluded entirely or modified and reexamined within another subject situation. The decision to include specific items from Table 9.4 was based on an arbitrary mean difference of + 2.00 or greater in the expected direction. This was purely arbitrary.

When the final items are chosen, it is possible to rescore the entire sample according to the remaining items. The results for all persons involved should be more reliable than before item analysis was applied. At least the internal consistency of the instrument has been significantly improved. And to that extent, the overall reliability of the instrument was strengthened.

A question may arise about why the middle 50 percent of persons was excluded from the original item analysis. The reason these persons are not included is that the upper and lower quartiles represent the extreme attitudinal intensities in either direction. Those persons in the middle of the distribution in terms of their overall scores are more likely to have responses weights of 3 or 4 associated with each item. Thus, the discriminatory ability of each item would be obscured by using these middle-of-the-road persons and their scores.

Strengths and Weaknesses of Item Discrimination Analysis.   Some advantages of item discrimination analysis are that it assists researchers in eliminating those unreliable items that are inconsistent with the rest. Also, internal consistency of any measure is strengthened. On the negative side, item discrimination analysis may result in the exclusion of items that truly measure the trait investigated. Some of those excluded items may be among the best indicators of the trait measured.

External Reliability Checks

External reliability checks utilize cumulative test results against themselves as a means of verifying the reliability of the measure. Test results for a group of people are compared in two different time periods, or two sets of results from equivalent, but different, tests are compared. Two major methods of determining the reliability of a test by external consistency are test–retest and parallel forms of the same test.

The Test–Retest Method.   The method of **test–retest** as a reliability measure is perhaps the most popular of all procedures discussed in this section. To determine the reliability of a measuring instrument using test–retest, an attitudinal measuring instrument is administered to a sample of persons at a given point in time. After a given time interval lapses (perhaps 2 to 4 weeks), the instrument is administered again to the same persons. The two sets of test results are correlated, and the resulting correlation coefficient is a measure of the reliability of the attitudinal measure. The higher the correlation between the two sets of scores, the more reliable the instrument. All of this assumes that nothing intervenes to influence test scores of these subjects between the two time periods. The logic is that if the measure is reliable, the score results should be equivalent or nearly equivalent in both time periods (Walters, 2003).

A reliable measure will reflect the characteristic to the same degree over two different time periods where no intervening variables can interfere significantly with test scores. A high correlation or similarity between the two sets of scores for the same individuals is considered as evidence of the instrument's reliability. Then, if researchers wish to use the instrument in an experimental situation, where some experimental variable is anticipated to elicit changes among respondents, then the use of the reliable measure may yield score differences between the two time intervals that will most likely be attributable to the experimental variable rather than to the unreliability of the instrument.

The test–retest reliability method is useful primarily in stable social situations where it is unlikely that the environment will change significantly from one test administration to the next (particularly over relatively short time periods such as a few months) (Turner & Piquero, 2002). Ideally, for a measuring instrument to be demonstrably reliable, the researcher expects a situation similar to that shown in Table 9.5.

TABLE 9.5   Scores for Ten Individuals on Measure of Attitude A

Individual	t_1	t_2	Difference in Scores $t_1 - t_2$
	Experimental variable absent		
1	45	45	0
2	35	35	0
3	27	27	0
4	50	50	0
5	46	46	0
6	31	31	0
7	29	29	0
8	30	30	0
9	41	41	0
10	45	45	0
	Experimental variable present		
1	45	20	−25
2	35	18	−17
3	27	22	−5
4	50	31	−19
5	46	40	−6
6	31	22	−9
7	29	26	−3
8	30	29	−1
9	41	40	−1
10	45	38	−7

In Table 9.5, scores are shown in the upper half of the table for 10 individuals in a test–retest situation with no intervening variable occurring between the two test administrations. There are no differences between scores comparing the two time periods. In the lower half of the table, score changes over two time periods are illustrated. Researchers want the measure to be reliable so that any observed score differences following the introduction of the experimental variable can tentatively be attributable to it. Score differences from one time period to the next should reflect actual differences in the trait being measured rather than the result of some chance fluctuation of an unreliable instrument.

Criticisms of the Test–Retest Method.   Some of the major strengths of the test–retest method for determining reliability are that test–retest permits instruments to be compared directly against themselves. An instrument that performs unreliably in a test–retest situation may require some kind of item-by-item analysis, such as item discrimination analysis, in order to determine which items discriminate between those who possess the trait to varying degrees. Test–retest also most directly reveals the continuity of the measure over time. It is easiest to use in an external reliability check compared with other methods designed to perform the same function. Test–retest is quick and easy to apply, and it offers researchers the greatest degree of control over extraneous factors that might otherwise interfere with the instrument's reliability.

Alternatively, test–retest means that respondents will be able to see the same items again and perhaps recall how they originally responded. There is often a strain for consistency among respondents, and therefore, even if they really feel differently in another time period, they will attempt to recreate their original responses from the first instrument administration. There is little researchers can do to prevent respondents from recalling their original responses to questions. One way of dealing with this problem is to lengthen the time interval between test administrations to several months. However, changes might occur among these persons over time as the result of natural causes and maturation. Conventionally, 2 to 4 weeks is considered an appropriate time interval between test administrations when applying the test–retest reliability check. There is no prescribed time interval that is universally accepted by all criminologists.

Another weakness of test–retest is that it is not foolproof. It is difficult for researchers to assess the impact of extraneous factors that might otherwise affect one's scores in two time periods. A high correlation between two sets of scores is not absolute proof of the test's reliability, since consistencies may be the result of chance fluctuations. Also, when researchers enter social settings to administer their instruments, their entry into these settings acts as an intervening variable that must be considered. Sometimes, after persons have had an opportunity to observe one's questionnaires and scales, they may not be receptive to reentry at a later date to complete the second phase of the test–retest sequence.

Parallel Forms of the Same Test.   A second major reliability check is the use of **parallel forms of the same test.** When researchers use parallel forms of the same test, they actually devise two separate measures of the same phenomenon (Schauer, 1990). Previously mentioned was the 16 PF, a personality inventory developed by Raymond Cattell. This instrument has two versions, A and B. Both versions consist of 187 questions each that purportedly both measure 16 different personality dimensions. Both versions of the 16 PF are considered equivalent. Whenever factor analyses of these instruments are conducted, they "factor" into 16 different parts. Interestingly, those items on Form A that purportedly measure certain personality dimensions factor into the same areas as those items on Form B that supposedly measure the same dimensions. Thus, the two versions of the measure help to validate each other as well as to verify the reliability of each.

Criticisms of the Parallel Forms of the Same Test Method.   The chief advantage of devising two separate tests of the same attitudinal variable is that the instruments may be administered to the same audiences over different time periods without having to worry about recalling previous responses. The two versions of these measures are made up of entirely different items. It is impossible to recall how you responded to items you haven't seen. Furthermore, it is unnecessary to have "waiting periods" between test administrations in order to evaluate the measure's reliability. Basically, two forms of the measure are administered and their results are correlated.

On the negative side, it is quite difficult and time-consuming to create two separate measures of the same attitudinal phenomenon. Some researchers have difficulty creating one measure. By doubling the number of items, the problems of establishing test validity and reliability are compounded, since more items are involved. Finally, it is difficult to establish the equivalency of two instruments that purportedly measure the same phenomena. What if the two measures correlate highly with one another? Does this mean the measures are reliable? What if they measure different attitudes, although those different attitudes may be related to a degree? One test may measure factor *X,* while the other measures factor *Y.* A high correlation between the two measures doesn't mean automatically that the two instruments are measuring identical phenomena.

Some Functional Relationships between Validity and Reliability

Of the two properties of measuring instruments, validity and reliability, the more important is reliability. There are several reasons for this. Before we examine these reasons, four general statements about the relation between validity and reliability may be made.

1. Valid instruments are always reliable instruments. This statement says that if you *really are* measuring whatever you say you are measuring, then you are also measuring it consistently. All valid measures are also reliable measures.

2. Instruments that are not valid measures of a specific variable may or may not be reliable. This means that if you are not really measuring variable *X,* then you *may or may not* be measuring something else, such as variable *Y.* If we say we are measuring variable *X,* such as job burnout, but in fact, we are *really* measuring variable *Y,* which may be job stress, then we don't have a valid measure of *X* (burnout) but we *do* have a valid measure of *Y* (stress). We just don't know that we have a valid measure of *Y* (stress).

3. Reliable instruments may or may not be valid for measuring specific variables. What this means is that if we are measuring something consistently such as variable *X* (job stress), then the instrument is a valid measure of job stress. However, the instrument may actually be measuring something else, such as job burnout. We don't know we're measuring job burnout, since we think the instrument is measuring job stress. In short, we really don't know what we're measuring, but at least it is significant. We can rely on it. The same thing is true about reliability. If our instrument exhibits reliability, we are measuring something. We may or may not be measuring what we think we are measuring, but we are definitely measuring something consistently.

4. Unreliable instruments are never valid. This statement means that if we do not have a reliable measure, then we most definitely do not have validity either. Reliability is fundamental to an instrument's validity. Reliability is the more important measure characteristic, therefore, since validity is very much dependent upon the instrument's reliability. If any measure lacks reliability, then it also lacks validity. However, any measure that lacks validity for measuring a specific phenomenon may or may not lack reliability.

Factors that Affect Validity and Reliability

Thus far, we have examined validity and reliability in considerable detail and have considered several ways these instrument properties may be assessed or determined. In this section, we focus on several factors and conditions that affect significantly the validity and reliability of measures. These factors are as follows: (1) the instrument and its contents;

(2) environmental factors; (3) personal factors; (4) researcher interpretations; (5) testing (pretest) effect; (6) selection bias; (7) experimental mortality; (8) Hawthorne effect; (9) halo effect; (10) placebo effect; and (11) diffusion of treatment with control and experimental groups.

The Instrument and Its Contents

Whenever the validity and reliability of attitudinal measures are assessed, the first aspect to be critically scrutinized is the list of items included in the instrument. Are the items valid? Have they been drawn from the universe of traits and characteristics that measure the phenomenon under investigation? If the researcher has been careless and included items from a universe other than the one consistent with the variable designated in the theoretical scheme, the validity of the test will be seriously undermined. Apart from the logical and theoretical connection between the items included in the measure and the trait to be measured, other aspects of the test emerge as crucial as well. Some of these factors are: (1) the length of the test; (2) the cultural date of the test; (3) open-ended versus fixed-response questions; and (4) mechanical factors.

The Length of the Test.   A lengthy instrument will sometimes cause respondents to give answers based on convenience rather than how they really feel about things. Longer tests may become boring, and respondents begin to check the first responses they come to, as is the case with set responses (Heinze & Purisch, 2001).

The Cultural Date of the Test.   A test that uses words or phrases not used conventionally becomes increasingly unreliable and hence, not a valid indicator of the trait in question. Using terms such as "ice box" to refer to "refrigerators" may create a misunderstanding between the meaning intended by the statement (defined by the researcher) and the way it is understood by respondents. The American Correctional Association and the American Jail Association have done much in recent years to improve the professional image of correctional officers who work in jails and prisons. In recent years, the term *guard,* earlier used to refer to those who perform jail duties and monitor inmates, has been rejected as archaic and derogatory. In its place, the term *jail officer* is more respectful and dignified. The use of *guard* on a questionnaire to be administered to jail officers may be considered offensive by them. Thus, unwittingly, researchers may evoke hostility from respondents because of the terms they use to characterize them and their work.

Open-Ended versus Fixed-Response Questions.   Measures that utilize open-ended questions (questions that have respondents furnish written answers rather than check specific fixed alternatives) place a strong emphasis on the ability of respondents to express themselves in writing. One's educational sophistication becomes an important consideration. Because the type of response provided to open-ended questions determines the degree of intensity of some attitude possessed by respondents, it is clear that the ability to express themselves may seem to reflect differences in attitudes by persons of varying educational backgrounds when actually there are no differences.

Mechanical Factors.   Mechanical factors refer to instrument problems, including misspelled words, illegible words, missing pages, and poorly phrased items. All of these mechanical factors may cause some misunderstanding of instrument content, and this misunderstanding will detract from the instrument's validity and reliability. The same is true of face-to-face interviews. If researchers leave certain statements off of their list of questions or if they use alternative words at random, the information solicited becomes less reliable, since respondents may make different interpretations of the questions asked. Ideally, the same administration conditions should prevail for each respondent. This uniformity would tend to minimize the possibility of errors due to differences in the way various subjects are approached by the investigator. Usually, pretests of instruments in smaller-scale pilot studies help to eliminate most of the mechanical deficiencies of measures.

Environmental Factors

Environmental factors describe the conditions under which instruments are administered. These include (1) face-to-face interviews versus self-administered questionnaires and (2) the clarity of instructions for completing the instrument.

Face-to-Face Interviews versus Self-Administered Questionnaires.   Varying the degree of anonymity or confidentiality under which the instrument is administered may generate score differences for the same person under various test administration conditions. Persons sometimes report feelings about things to an interviewer face-to-face that are quite different from those feelings they would otherwise disclose in a more confidential, self-administered questionnaire situation where considerable anonymity exists.

The Clarity of Instructions for Completing the Instrument.   If investigators fail to clarify the procedures to be followed in the completion of the instrument, there is a good chance that subjects will provide misleading information unintentionally.

Personal Factors

Some of the more relevant personal characteristics that impinge upon the validity and reliability of measures include (1) the socioeconomic status of respondents; (2) age, gender, and maturity level; (3) ethnic/racial background; (4) memory or recall ability; and (5) social desirability.

The Socioeconomic Status of Respondents.   Occupation, educational level, income, and race/ethnicity are primary components of socioeconomic status. These factors may influence one's performance on any attitudinal instrument. Researchers should attempt to construct their questionnaires and other measures to closely approximate the socioeconomic level of the audiences they investigate. The cultural aspects of any measuring instrument will limit the generalizability and utility of it to particular social aggregates.

Age, Gender, and Maturity Level.   Like socioeconomic status, age and gender are important considerations in any instrument administration. Closely associated with age and gender are differences in maturity levels among respondents. The maturity level of intended respondents may influence the manner in which researchers are accepted and the degree of cooperation and interest demonstrated by participating subjects.

Ethnic/Racial Background.   Although ethnicity and race are conventionally regarded as a part of socioeconomic status, it is worthwhile to note that ethnic background may account for certain misunderstandings pertaining to word choices in questionnaires. Different words may have different meanings and convey different ideas to people from different ethnic backgrounds as well as to persons of different socioeconomic statuses. In testing and measurement, researchers are increasingly moving toward the development of culture-free measures. They are learning more and more to appreciate the fact that tests often have built-in cultural biases that affect significantly our interpretations of results for different ethnic audiences.

Memory or Recall.   The ability of subjects to recall earlier responses on a before–after test administration may elicit responses consistent with earlier ones, regardless of whether or not the respondent's beliefs are the same in both time periods. Parallel forms of the same test are used frequently to overcome the effects of memory or recall in test–retest situations, particularly if the span of time between test administrations is short.

Social Desirability.   Many questionnaires have social desirability measures incorporated into them to ascertain the effect of this important variable on a subject's overall response pattern. Social desirability, or responding in accordance with what subjects believe to be a desirable set of traits rather than what might be true of them, frequently contaminates questionnaires and obscures how respondents really feel about things. There is no way to prevent social desirability from occurring.

Researcher Interpretations

Another important consideration in assessing an instrument's validity and reliability is the kind of interpretation made of results by researchers. Under this heading are included (1) the coding procedure and (2) interpretations of raw scores.

Coding Interpretations.   Researchers may code their information any way they wish. The validity and reliability of instruments often hinge, in part, on the coding pattern followed by investigators. Although this opportunity varies considerably from study to study, it is possible for researchers to code their information in such ways so as to increase the chances of supporting one particular theoretical perspective or another. Objectivity in coding is encouraged, and it is recommended that researchers compare their own coding procedures with those used by other researchers who investigate similar phenomena. This will not guarantee that their coding procedures will be foolproof, but at least researchers can minimize the possibility that their own values and biases will enter the picture significantly when data are interpreted.

The Interpretation of Raw Scores.   Raw scores on any attitudinal measure are seldom meaningful apart from their comparison with other scores on the same scale. When researchers extract raw scores from a list of them, they run the risk of assigning meanings to scores that are quite different from the practical meanings those scores have in a comparative sense. Single-score interpretations should be made conservatively and tentatively. Sometimes, previous norms exist for specific instrument applications to certain types of audiences. These norms may be used for evaluations of scores on subsequent administrations, although researchers should not rely too much on such previous norms. It is likely that each test administration is somewhat different from previous test administrations, and that the norms applicable in one setting may not be applicable in another setting.

Testing (Pretest) Effect

Respondents who are given the same self-administered questionnaires over several different time periods may be influenced by the fact that they have previous experience with or exposure to the same questionnaire. For instance, suppose you wanted to chart or track the influence of a type of counseling intervention for juvenile offenders over time. Your intent is to see whether juvenile offenders develop more positive self-concepts as the result of exposure to an innovative counseling method. Therefore, you administer a self-concept questionnaire to these youths in time 1, prior to the counseling, and then at successive time intervals throughout the duration of the counseling, which may be 6 months. Each month you administer the same self-concept questionnaire to these juveniles. Each month they are exposed to the same questionnaire items. After the counseling therapy, you compare the juvenile offenders' scores across the different time periods to see if there are marked improvements in their self-concepts.

Now you may or may not find differences in these youths' self-concept scores from the different questionnaire administrations. After all, these youths have been given the same self-concept questionnaire at least six or seven times. You presume that each time they have responded to the same questionnaire, they have been truthful. If there have been improvements in their self-concepts, these changes should be evident from the different test or questionnaire administrations. If there are few changes or small changes in self-concept, these may be due to the effects of repeated testing.

Investigators label these effects as **pretest effects** or **pretest bias.** Interestingly, under repeated questionnaire administrations, many respondents in different studies have reported changes in their attitudes and behaviors. However, sometimes respondents do not report changes in their behaviors or attitudes even though they have actually changed. When asked about *why* they don't report changes in their behaviors on these questionnaires, some respondents reply that they "wanted to be consistent with how they responded in earlier questionnaire administrations." This strain for consistency seems illogical to researchers who expect respondents to tell the truth and report differences in their behaviors and attitudes as they occur over time. Despite our best efforts to elicit truthful answers from respondents, the fact is that they may not be truthful for various reasons. This fact is attributable to pretest bias or the testing effect.

Selection Bias

Selection bias refers to deliberately designating two groups for comparison where the two groups are not equivalent in various salient characteristics (Santiago, Galster, & Pettit, 2003). For instance, if an investigator wished to study the effects of electronic monitoring, two samples of probationers might be selected for comparison. Beforehand, the investigator knows that 100 probationers differ according to a risk assessment instrument they have been given. The risk assessment instrument measures their potential dangerousness and community risk. The researcher divides the probationers into two groups of 50 probationers each according to those receiving the highest and those receiving the lowest risk scores. Those with the highest risk scores are monitored in the community for one year under standard supervision, which involves minimal probationer/client contacts with the probation office. Those with the lowest risk scores are placed on electronic monitoring for one year and are otherwise expected to comply with other standard probation conditions. At the end of one year, the different samples of probationers are compared according to their recidivism rates and numbers of program infractions. The sample of electronically monitored probationers has a much lower rate of recidivism and fewer program infractions compared with the sample of standard probationers who were not electronically monitored. The researchers conclude that electronic monitoring caused the lower recidivism rates and fewer numbers of program rule infractions.

Do you believe that this comparison is a legitimate one? Don't you think it is peculiar that the high-risk offenders would be placed on standard probation, while the low-risk offenders would be placed on electronic monitoring? We are not dealing with a level playing field here. This comparison is flawed. The researcher deliberately contrived a situation for comparison where those least likely to reoffend, those with low risk scores, were placed in an electronic monitoring program, where their whereabouts could be verified 24 hours a day. However, the high-risk group of probationers was virtually *unsupervised* much of the time, reporting perhaps monthly to the probation office. Thus, the high-risk group of probationers was far more likely to recidivate than the low-risk group. In fact, we would have expected the high-risk probationers to reoffend at a greater rate and have more program infractions compared with the low-risk group. This is known as "creaming" in the probation profession, where only the best candidates are selected for inclusion in client community management programs, such as electronic monitoring. These are the very persons who do not need to be electronically monitored. Thus, it is very unclear whether the fact of electronic monitoring resulted in lower recidivism rates and fewer program infractions, or whether the fact of the low-risk nature of the probationer sample resulted in lower recidivism rates and fewer program infractions. More legitimate comparisons of groups require that groups should be equivalent. Selection bias should be eliminated in order for valid comparisons and evaluations to be made (Lundman, 2003; McCollister et al., 2003).

Experimental Mortality

In any experiment, especially a longitudinal study over time, the same sample of respondents may be studied. The researcher's intent is to compare these respondents at different time periods to determine the effects of an experimental variable. But experimental mortality may occur. This means that some attrition occurs among the sample of respondents. Fewer respondents exist in later time periods compared with those existing in previous time periods. **Experimental mortality** may occur for a variety of reasons. Persons may move away, be transferred, or refuse to participate in subsequent experimental periods (Doerner et al., 1976). In fact, some respondents may die.

Suppose an investigator were studying the effects of a new inmate management method for elderly inmates in a federal prison. Elderly inmates were previously housed in isolated cells. Many of these inmates were morose and moody, depressed, with low self-esteem levels. Under a new inmate management method, elderly inmates were transferred to dormitory-like housing, where they were celled in pairs. Investigators believed that these new accommodations, especially for elderly offenders, would result in improved self-esteem, and that fewer elderly inmates would be depressed, moody, and morose. Researchers planned to study elderly inmate attitudes over a 2-year transition period. They started out with 200 elderly inmates in 1996, but by 1998, only 124 of the original elderly inmates were still housed in the federal prison. Attrition resulted in a 76-inmate reduction of the original sample. Attrition was caused by 40 inmate deaths from old age or fatal diseases, and 36 other inmates were paroled. Thus, this is literally a hypothetical case of experimental mortality.

But experimental mortality occurs in other ways besides death. Suppose you are studying a sample of 500 male delinquents in Compton, California. These are adjudicated delinquents who are gang members. You plan to study these 500 delinquents over a 1-year time period. Your experiment contemplates exposing these youths to a Big Brother program, where each youth is assigned to an adult male who will work with each youth on a one-to-one basis. As a part of the program, the "Big Brother" will take the youth to sports events and to other activities on weekends. The intent of the experiment is to decrease one's delinquent propensities by providing social alternatives to delinquency. Furthermore, the Big Brothers are supposed to provide a caring and interpersonally supportive environment for these youths.

At the beginning of the year, 500 male delinquents are designated by the Compton Juvenile Court and Big Brothers are assigned each of the youths. However, by the end of the year, only 260 of the youths are still participating in the Big Brother program. The remaining 240 youths moved away from Compton to other cities or out of the state and could not be located. This is an example of experimental mortality.

Experimental mortality poses a serious problem for researchers. The characteristics of those who drop out of the study are unknown, other than the scant information from the superficial juvenile records that have been maintained about them. Had these juveniles remained in the Big Brother program, then the significance of the Big Brother program as a delinquency prevention mechanism could be more adequately assessed. With about half of the delinquents remaining in the program, we are only able to report on the successfulness of the Big Brother program only as to how these 260 delinquents were affected. Therefore, experimental mortality causes the same difficulty for researchers that nonresponse to mailed questionnaires poses. We don't know who the nonrespondents are. We have no way of calculating the impact of the nonrespondents on our final results and study findings had they been included in our data analysis. The same is true about dropouts through experimental mortality. We have no way of assessing the impact of the study on these persons, since they were not a part of our final data analysis. Researchers can exert little or no control over experimental mortality. Rather, they must make the best of study findings based on those respondents who are present throughout the entire research process.

Hawthorne Effect

The Hawthorne effect derives its name from the Hawthorne Plant of the Western Electric Company in Chicago. The Western Electric Company manufactures telephone equipment, including relays and other parts. A series of experiments was conducted during the late 1920s, where certain groups of workers were measured according to their productivity rates.

One study involved adjusting the lighting in a room where workers were assembling telephone relays. It was believed by researchers that a brighter room would result in higher productivity rates because workers could see better than in a poorly lit room. Thus, a dimmer switch was installed that enabled researchers to increase room lighting. As the lighting in the room increased, worker productivity increased. The researchers were ecstatic. Next, they reasoned, if room lighting were dimmed, productivity would go down. They adjusted the lighting so that darker work conditions were created. However, worker productivity continued to increase. Even under moonlight conditions, where workers were barely able to see what they were doing, worker productivity hit an all-time high. Investigators were very bewildered. Later, they interviewed workers to find out why they were producing at such high rates under moonlight conditions. Workers replied that they were disregarding the changes in lighting. They (the workers) "knew that they were 'special,' and they were determined to show management that they could produce more no matter what conditions were imposed on them." Thus, the fact that workers "felt special" and were shown special treatment by management caused productivity increases. Lighting had nothing to do with it. This phenomenon was later termed the *Hawthorne effect.*

In any type of social experimentation, the potential for the Hawthorne effect exists. If workers or employees know that they are being observed or singled out in some way, they may behave in superlative ways apart from their natural work behavior. Thus, investigators should allow for the occurrence of the Hawthorne effect whenever experiments are conducted in the natural settings of research subjects.

Halo Effect

The **halo effect** is the bias toward observed subjects based on preconceived opinions of the observer (Accordino & Guerney, 1998). Perhaps a researcher has been advised that there are two groups of inmates. One group, Group A, has participated in a self-help G.E.D. program and other prison educational and vocational services while incarcerated. The other group, Group B, has not made use of the self-help G.E.D. program or the other prison educational and vocational services. If the researcher knows who the individual inmates are from both groups and later conducts experiments between the two groups, some bias may exist toward Group A, where these inmates participated in prison self-help services. If the investigator must rate the two groups of inmates later on some variable, such as improvement in self-esteem or self-worth, Group A inmates may be designated as having improved more than Group B inmates. In fact, neither group has changed in self-esteem or self-worth during the investigator's experiment. The halo effect occurs when the researcher attributes greater self-worth and self-esteem to a group of inmates known to have participated in self-help prison programs.

Another example might be a study of police officers in a precinct where citizen complaints against the police are low or infrequent. The investigator perceives that the police officers in the precinct must be better, on the average, compared with officers in other precincts, since they have fewer citizen complaints filed against them. Later, if the investigator observes these officers as they implement a community policing program and attempt to foster better public relations between themselves and community residents, the investigator may believe that these officers are superior to or more effective than officers in other precincts where community policing and public relations improvements are attempted. In reality, the officers of all precincts are equivalent in their community policing and public relations effectiveness. However, because one precinct has the lowest numbers of citizen complaints, their effectiveness is rated more highly. The researcher simply believes that these officers are inherently better than other officers. The investigator's perception of their effectiveness will carry over and influence their performance in other tasks.

The halo effect is a dangerous phenomenon, since it can nullify the objectivity of any experimental situation. Researchers must guard against such preconceived opinions about any group they study. In Knoxville, Tennessee, for example, the Knox County Sheriff's Department had a volunteer auxiliary unit known as the Organized Reserve. The Organized Reserve was an unpaid organization, and it performed valuable work such as guard duty at the Knox County Jail. Some Organized Reserve officers performed cruiser work and assisted regular sheriff's deputies in their patrols. However, because these Organized Reserve officers were volunteers, they were regarded as second-class citizens in the Sheriff's Department. Their uniforms differed from regular deputies' uniforms only by the inclusion of "OR" on the county sheriff patch worn at the shoulder. There was no basis for these biased perceptions from regular deputies, since Organized Reserve officers went through officer training and participated in numerous law enforcement exercises regularly. Had any experiment been conducted involving police professionalism and comparing Organized Reserve officers with regular sheriff's deputies, it is likely that Organized Reserve officers would have been downgraded in their professionalism despite the existence of few if any differences in the two groups of officers. The halo effect compromises the validity and reliability of any study where preconceived biases exist about groups to be studied.

Placebo Effect

The **placebo effect** originated with biochemical experiments on human subjects. A **placebo** is a harmless, unmedicated substance, usually given to patients merely to humor them. In experiments, placebos are used as controls in order to test the efficacy of another medicated substance (Nunn, 2001). Groups receiving placebos are control groups and are usually matched with another group, the experimental group, that receives the actual medication intended to produce a specific result. In experiments comparing two groups on motor skills, for instance, one group receives a stimulant drug designed to accelerate one's reaction time, while the other group receives a pill, the placebo, composed of some bland substance. The placebo has no effect whatsoever on one's body chemistry. However, researchers instruct both groups that they are both being given drugs to accelerate their motor skills.

Later, the two groups are compared on some motor skills activity. Accelerated motor activity is detected among the experimental group members who actually received the drug. However, the control group, the group receiving the placebo, exhibits little or no change in their motor skill behavior. There may be *some* improvement in their motor skill behaviors, simply because these persons *believe* they have received a drug to accelerate their motor skills. Thus a placebo can have an effect even though it is not intended to have any effect.

The placebo effect may obscure the effects of social experiments, since both persons in the experimental and control groups may exhibit changes in their behaviors and attitudes (Schoenthaler et al., 1997). Sometimes persons have been given placebos, but which were described as hallucinogenic drugs, such as LSD. They have reported feeling "funny" and having distorted perceptions of their surroundings, similar to someone who has taken LSD. In fact, these persons were given absolutely nothing to cause distortions in their perceptions.

Placebos are not always tangible sugar-coated pills. Sometimes placebos may be suggestions or instructions. When criminologists conduct experiments with two or more groups, control groups may be given certain instructions or suggestions. These instructions may be that as a result of exposure to some educational course or experience, the group should feel a certain way or have noticeable increased skills. Subsequently, the control group is exposed to a mundane lecture about general leadership skills. Afterwards, the group members report that they have increased skills or feel in certain ways anticipated by the researcher. Thus, these control subjects are conforming their behaviors to fit how researchers expect them to behave or think. The validity and reliability of studies is impaired to the extent that a placebo effect exists among control groups (Berkowitz, 1975).

The Diffusion of Treatment with Control and Experimental Groups

Sometimes diffusion of treatment may occur between the experimental and control groups. **Diffusion of treatment** occurs whenever the experimental stimulus is partially or totally adopted by both the experimental and control group. The likelihood for diffusion of treatment is heightened to the extent that the experimental and control groups are in close proximity and may interact with each other.

Suppose researchers study the effects of more frequent face-to-face visits of probation officers with their probationer-clients. Perhaps two probation departments in communities of equal size in the same state are studied. The probation officers from both probation departments in the two cities, Probation Department A and Probation Department B, are involved in an experiment to determine whether greater frequency of face-to-face visits reduces recidivism and improves program success of probationer-clients. In one probation department, Probation Department A, probation officers are instructed to have five face-to-face visits with 30 different probationers for a period of 1 year. In the other agency, Probation Department B, probation officers are instructed to conduct their visits with probationers as usual, meaning perhaps one face-to-face visit per month. At the end of the 1-year study, recidivism rates and program success measures will be obtained from probationers in both communities. It is expected that more face-to-face visits will reduce probationer recidivism and improve their program success.

However, suppose probation officers in Probation Department B determine that the experiment is some sort of evaluation of their performance as officers. If they make this determination, they may decide to outperform the probation officers in Probation Department A. They can do this by visiting their own probationers at least as often or more often than the probation officers in Probation Department A. Therefore, for the next year, probation officers in Probation Department B conduct seven face-to-face visits with their probationers. At the end of 1 year, the investigators compare the recidivism and success rates of the two aggregates of probationers in the two communities and find that there are no differences. They conclude, erroneously, that increasing the numbers of face-to-face visits with certain probationers has no effect on their recidivism or success rates. In fact, the probation officers in Probation Department B obscured the study results by deliberately competing with Probation Department A. This was a clear diffusion of the treatment variable, the number of face-to-face visits with probationers. When diffusion of treatment occurs, we cannot rely on our study results as valid indicators of the impact of the experimental variable on probationer recidivism or program success rates.

The numbers and types of factors that can influence the validity and reliability of studies is endless. Maturational changes in juveniles may cause many of them to grow out of delinquency between the ages of 15 and 17. Studies of delinquency career escalation may be affected by maturational changes. Personality changes or significant disruptions in the social lives of experimental or control group members may cause changes in their reactions to experiments that are not expected or anticipated.

S U M M A R Y

Two important instrument properties are validity and reliability. Validity is the property of an attitudinal scale or measuring instrument that enables researchers to specify what it is they are measuring. Reliability is the property of an attitudinal scale or measuring instrument that enables investigators to say that their measures are dependable and render consistent results over time.

Validity can never be proved. It can only be inferred on the basis of logical and/or statistical criteria. Four types of validation include content or face validity, predictive validity, concurrent validity, and construct validity. Content or face validity is a logical type of validity, depending largely on the close proximity of the items on the measuring instrument to the variable being measured. Thus, researchers can examine the instrument and its contents and know that a specific variable is probably being measured.

Predictive and concurrent validity are two types of pragmatic validity. Pragmatism suggests that the effectiveness of a measure depends on how well it works at predicting the occurrence of some anticipated behavior. Predictive validity is assessed by comparing individual or group attitudes and/or behaviors at a future point in time with the scores on a measuring instrument or scale that suggest the future occurrence of those behaviors or attitudes. Thus, Graduate Record Examination (GRE) scores on verbal, quantitative, and analytical skills suggest one's future skill level in those areas as graduate students. Subsequently, if graduate students exhibit skills commensurate with their earlier GRE scores, then predictive validity has been demonstrated. Predictive validity is demonstrated both logically and statistically, through correlations between predicted behaviors and attitudes and subsequent manifestations of those behaviors or attitudes.

Concurrent validity is closely related to predictive validity, except that one's behaviors or attitudes as evidenced by some scale or measuring instrument are indicated contemporaneously with the variable measured. Concurrent validity is often demonstrated by matching one's score on a measuring instrument or attitudinal scale with some existing behavior exhibited by the research subject. Another way of demonstrating this type of validity is comparing the scores from one attitudinal scale or measuring instrument with scores on another instrument that purportedly measures the same variable. A close correspondence between scores suggests that both scales are consistent with one another insofar as they in-dicate the existence of the variable being measured.

Construct validity or factorial validity is most conveniently demonstrated by attitudi-nal measures or scales that contain multiple variables. Factor analysis, a complex statistical technique, is applied to scores on these multidimensional scales, and the measuring instru-ment factors separate into various subparts consistent with different dimensions or variables being measured. Personality measures are frequently amenable to construct validation.

Reliability is the property of a measuring instrument that refers to its consistency to yield dependable scores over time. Compared with validity, which is always inferred, reli-ability is directly assessed or determined through one of several methods. Two internal meth-ods and two external methods for demonstrating reliability have been illustrated. Individual items on an attitudinal measure are correlated with one another through the split-half method as the first way of internally testing the scale's reliability. Usually the odd-numbered item responses or weights are correlated with the even-numbered item responses or weights. A close correlation between the two halves of the measure suggest the measure's reliability. The second internal method is known as item discrimination analysis. This method involves determining the discriminatory power of individual measure items. Usually persons are di-vided into high and low categories depending on their overall scores on a measuring in-strument. Then their individual item weights (from their responses) are averaged and compared. The greater the difference between the average item weights of those with the largest scores compared with those with the smallest scores, the more reliable the items are for measuring the variable.

External measures of reliability include test–retest and parallel forms of the same test. Under the test–retest method, one's overall scale score is compared in one time period with one's score in a second time period. This over-time comparison should yield similar over-all scores for each research subject, provided that no intervention occurs between the two time periods to affect one's scale score. The greater the consistency between a group's scale scores from one time period to the next, without an experimental or intervening variable pre-sent, the greater the reliability of the measure. Thus, when an intervening variable is sub-sequently introduced later under the actual research conditions of an experiment, changes in one's scale score are more likely indicative of an actual change in the variable being mea-sured rather than some chance fluctuation in scale scores. Tentative conclusions may be drawn about the influence of intervening variables on other variables, such as the ones being measured by different attitudinal scales.

Parallel forms of the same test are used from time to time, particularly where frequent measures of the same phenomenon are made over different time periods. If a group of re-spondents sees the same scale items several different times over several weeks or months, they may recall how they responded to these measures. These recollections may cause them to attempt to recreate how they originally responded. Thus, the results of the scale scores may be affected simply by one's memory or recall ability and thus lack reliability. Defeat-ing this particular possibility is accomplished by creating several alternative scales consist-ing of different items that purportedly measure the same variable. Thus, when respondents see a scale or measuring instrument in some subsequent time period, they cannot possibly recall how they responded initially in an earlier time period, since the scale is comprised of fresh items. However, constructing multiple measures of the same variable is time-consuming. Establishing the validity of different versions of scales is also problematic and difficult. Large organizations that have developed standardized personality assessment scales often engage in such parallel scale construction, however.

Several important relationships between validity and reliability have been established. Scales that are valid or that measure what we say they are measuring are always reliable. Scales that are reliable are always a valid measure of something, probably of what we believe they measure. Scales that are not a valid measure of one characteristic or variable may in fact be a valid measure of some other closely related characteristic. Therefore, we say that scales that are not valid may or may not be reliable. Finally, scales that are not reliable indicators are never valid measures of anything. This is because a key prerequisite of a measure's validity is reliability. In order to be a valid measure, the measure must be demonstrably reliable.

Several factors influence the validity and reliability of measures. The instrument and its contents provide one source of problems that may affect a scale's validity. The length of the scale, the cultural dating of the measure, whether the items are fixed-response or open-ended, and/or whether there are mechanical problems, such as missing items, pages, or poorly worded items, affect a measure's validity and reliability. Environmental factors also influence a measure's validity. If questions are asked face-to-face in interview situations, responses may vary greatly compared with responses to the same or similar items asked on a self-administered questionnaire under more anonymous conditions. Also, instructions about completing the scale or questionnaire generally will vary, depending on whether the administration of items is through an interview or a mailed questionnaire.

Several personal factors may influence the validity and reliability of scale values as well. A respondent's socioeconomic status may suggest lower or higher amounts of education, which in turn affect one's understanding of questionnaire contents and readability. One's age, gender, and maturity level are also critical. The ethnic/racial background of respondents, their memory or recall ability, and the prevalent problem of social desirability may affect a respondents' answers.

Another important factor influencing a measure's validity and reliability has to do with the researcher's interpretation of the results of scale scores for different groups. The coding procedure may vary among investigators, as well as their individual interpretations of scale results. The pretesting effect of giving the same scale to the same group of persons over time may decrease a measure's reliability. As a direct result of changes in a measure's reliability, test validity will also be affected. This is known as the testing effect.

Some amount of selection bias may be present when persons are selected for study. If investigators know in advance of questionnaire administrations certain characteristics of their research subjects, and if they wish to compare one group of subjects with other groups, they may inadvertently influence their research results by grouping certain respondents together who share certain variables to high degrees and who differ greatly from groups of persons who have lower amounts of these variables. In probation studies, for example, those clients known for their high degree of law-abiding behavior and low risk may be placed in an experiment designed to determine the effectiveness of home confinement or electronic monitoring. They have the greatest likelihood of succeeding in such programs. Thus, when their success rates are evaluated later, the programs in which they have been situated are credited with influencing their success rates. This is known as selection bias.

Experimental mortality may occur. This happens when experiments are conducted over time. Natural attrition may occur, as some persons leave their jurisdictions, die, or simply become unavailable for subsequent study. To the extent that these persons cannot be contacted for further research investigation, their earlier responses to questionnaires are essentially useless. Also, the Hawthorne effect may cause investigators to misinterpret whatever they observe and how the scores on different scales are interpreted. If persons know they are being observed for some scientific purpose, they may exhibit unnatural behaviors or attitudes in order to impress researchers, saying or doing things they believe investigators wish to hear or see. This is the Hawthorne effect. A closely related factor is the halo effect. This occurs as the result of preconceived biases of investigators. If volunteers in a probation department are studied, for example, and they are assessed according to their altruistic feelings toward their clients, they may be contrasted later with a sample of salaried employees of the same probation department. The fact that investigators know that volunteers are motivated to help others in altruistic ways compared with salaried employees may cause these investigators to make unwarranted assumptions about volunteers and view their altruism differently when it is measured or assessed.

Another factor interfering with a measure's validity and reliability is the placebo effect. In experiments where persons are administered doses of safe medicines designed to improve their alertness or comprehension of material to be learned, some research subjects may be given harmless tablets containing no drug substances. These are placebos. Some persons believe they are taking performance-enhancing medications, and thus they may strive to perform better despite the fact that they have not consumed any performance-enhancing drugs. This is the placebo effect.

Finally, diffusion of treatment with the control and experimental groups in an experiment may influence reliability and validity. If the control and experimental groups are permitted to have contact with one another during the course of an experiment, they may exchange ideas and information that contaminate one's experimental results.

QUESTIONS FOR REVIEW

1. What is reliability? How is it measured or determined? What are two internal reliability methods?

2. What are four general relationships between validity and reliability?

3. What is validity? How is it measured or determined? What are four different methods for determining test validity? How can validity be proved, if at all?

4. What are two external methods for determining a test's reliability?

5. What is the importance of social desirability and how it might influence the results of attitudinal measures? How are reliability and validity influenced by social desirability?

6. What are meant by environmental factors that impinge on a test's validity and reliability? What are two of these factors and why are they important?

7. What are five personal factors that influence the validity and reliability of tests?

8. Is it possible to have a valid test that is not reliable? Why or why not?

9. What is meant by a mechanical factor as it pertains to questionnaire construction?

10. How would the cultural dating of a test or measure influence its validity or reliability? What are two examples of the cultural dating of an attitudinal measure?

11. What are some contrasts between test–retest and parallel forms of the same test as reliability checks? What are the respective weaknesses and strengths of each?

12. What is the Hawthorne effect and how does it differ from the halo effect?

13. What is meant by diffusion of treatment?

14. What are some general differences between external and internal validity? How can internal validity be improved?

15. What is experimenter mortality? What is the placebo effect?

10 Data Coding, Presentation, and Descriptive Techniques

CHAPTER OBJECTIVES

As the result of reading this chapter, the following objectives should be realized:

1. Understanding what is meant by graphic presentation, including its value as a descriptive tool.
2. Examining the functions of graphic presentation in criminological research.
3. Understanding the basics of tabular construction and ways of collapsing tabular information.
4. Learning about cross-tabulating data and understanding the phenomenon known as spuriousness.
5. Learning about how best to present data that have been collected.

Introduction

This chapter is about coding, tabulating, and presenting data researchers have gathered. Researchers must code or assign numerical values to the different variables used in their research. Coding makes it easier to analyze the data we have collected. It involves the assignment of numbers to different subclasses of variables we have measured from scales and questions included in our interviews and questionnaires. If statistical tests are going to be applied in the course of our data analysis, then coding data in particular ways enables investigators to easily apply a variety of quantitative methods to the collected information. The coding process also includes a description of data cleaning and verification. When numerical data are entered into a computer for subsequent analysis, it is important for investigators to know that this information has been entered and recorded accurately. The data cleaning process will be explained.

The chapter next examines the general process of data presentation. Any introduction to a criminology or criminal justice course will involve a variety of charts, tables, and graphs and other visual materials to supplement an investigator's findings. The idea that "a picture is worth a thousand words" is appropriate here. The *Uniform Crime Reports,* compiled by the FBI and published by the Department of Justice, is filled with graphic material about crime and crime trends. One glance at a well-illustrated graph or table can tell you much about whether certain crimes have increased or decreased over different time intervals.

Graphs and tabulated data presentations are not limited to scientific research journals. Popular periodicals, such as *U.S. News & World Report, Time, Newsweek,* or *The Reader's Digest,* feature numerous illustrations that inform us about such things as drug flow from South American countries, illegal immigration, violence among juveniles, prison and jail overcrowding, and public opinion or sentiment. These tables, graphs, charts, figures, and diagrams enhance our understanding of written material. Furthermore, our efforts to build theories and test hypotheses are advanced through the strategic use of these materials. Graphic presentation is illustrated and explained. The functions of graphic presentation are examined.

We should learn about this material for at least two reasons. First, we will be exposed to a great deal of written material where illustrations are used to highlight important points. We should be informed about how these illustrative materials should be interpreted and how they enhance our understanding of subject matter. Second, we will be preparing reports, articles, and other writings ourselves. We want to maximize the reader's understanding of our own work, and graphic materials can assist us in achieving this objective.

Criminologists are interested in measuring crime and charting crime trends over time. Thus, it is important to learn about crime rates and their computation. Ratios are also discussed as ways of determining probation or parole officer caseloads and other variables. Crime rates and ratios are discussed and described.

The next part of this chapter illustrates the construction and use of tables in our research work. Tabular construction is presented and discussed. Often we create tables consisting of differing numbers of rows and columns. Tables most frequently represent cross-tabulations of variables. When our data are distributed certain ways in the tables we have created, they are amenable to various interpretations, and certain statistical tests may be applied for quantitative analyses. Also, certain distributions of frequencies in tables of different sizes allow us to draw tentative conclusions about variable interrelationships and enable us to provide support for our theoretical schemes. In some cases, however, tabular arrangements of our collected information may not lend support to our theories. Unusual tabular distributions will be illustrated, and a discussion of these possible outcomes and interpretations we might make of our findings will be presented.

Throughout this chapter, conventional rules guide much of our graphic and tabular construction. It is important to recognize the power of convention as we construct our graphs and tables to illustrate the data we have collected. For instance, sometimes we are confronted with very large tables from computer-generated numerical information. We must reduce the size of these large tables to more manageable table sizes. There are conventional procedures to be followed when larger tables are collapsed into smaller ones. The process of collapsing tables will be described. The chapter concludes with a discussion of how researchers determine how their data ought to be presented and the criteria they might use in this process.

Coding Variables

Whenever we construct a questionnaire or design an interview, we will need to code the questions or statements as well as the responses in certain ways. Even if we are conducting content analyses or investigating secondary sources for new information, we usually devise a code to give some structure to our analysis. In order to facilitate our processing of information, we often precode our data collection instruments. Perhaps we have a questionnaire that includes the following:

1. ID _____ [For research use only]
2. What is your gender? [Check one]   _____ Male _____ Female
3. What is your age? [Check one]
    _____ Under 21
    _____ 21–23
    _____ 24–25
    _____ 26–28
    _____ 29 or over

4. What is your education? [Check one]
    _____ Some elementary school, not completed
    _____ Completed elementary school
    _____ Some high school, not completed
    _____ Completed high school
    _____ Some college, not completed
    _____ Completed college
    _____ Graduate work or degree

5. What is your political affiliation? [Check one]
    _____ Democrat
    _____ Republican
    _____ American Independent
    _____ Other

These are four simple questions. We want to know the respondent's gender, age, educational level, and political affiliation. The "ID" refers to an identifying number we will assign to the questionnaire. The above information as it is presented is uncoded. If we were to code the information, we might have something like the following:

Column	Item
1,2,3	1. ID [For research use only] <u>0</u> <u>0</u> <u>1</u>
4 1	2. What is your gender? [Check one]
	1 ___X___ Male
	2 _____ Female
5 3	3. What is your age? [Check one]
	1 _____ Under 21
	2 _____ 21–23
	3 ___X___ 24–25
	4 _____ 26–28
	5 _____ 29 or over
6 5	4. What is your education? [Check one]
	1 _____ Some elementary school, not completed
	2 _____ Completed elementary school
	3 _____ Some high school, not completed
	4 _____ Completed high school
	5 ___X___ Some college, not completed
	6 _____ Completed college
	7 _____ Graduate work or degree
7 2	5. What is your political affiliation? [Check one]
	1 _____ Democrat
	2 ___X___ Republican
	3 _____ American Independent
	4 _____ Other

The columns identified above are categories designated to contain each variable. Notice that the first three columns, **1, 2, 3,** are used for the respondent's identification. "001" refers to the first person who completes the questionnaire. The next column, **4,** is for recording one's gender. We have recorded a "1" to indicate that the person checked the "male" subcategory of gender. The next column, **5,** is for recording one's age. The person indicated "24–25," and so we coded this response with a "3." The next column, **6,** is for recording the person's education. We have recorded a "5" for column **6,** since the person answered "Some college, not completed." For column **7,** we record a "2" to stand for "Republican," the choice indicated by the respondent.

For more complicated coding, such as coding a scale that measures anger intensity or police professionalism, we might have a set of statements with Likert-type responses. For a 10-item scale and a six-point response pattern (Strongly Agree = 1; Agree = 2; Undecided, Probably Agree = 3; Undecided, Probably Disagree = 4; Disagree = 5; Strongly Disagree = 6), we would have possible responses from a low of 10 to a high of 60 (e.g., $1 \times 10 = 10$; $6 \times 10 = 60$). We might record one's raw score in *two* columns, such as columns **8** and **9.** The score might be "36." Or we might decide to *code* the *range of responses* to our anger intensity or police professionalism scales, such as:

$$10–15 = 1$$
$$16–20 = 2$$
$$21–25 = 3$$
$$26–30 = 4$$
$$31–35 = 5$$
$$36–40 = 6$$
$$41–45 = 7$$
$$46–50 = 8$$
$$51–55 = 9$$
$$56–60 = 0$$

Coding a scale in this way will enable us to use a single column, such as column **8,** for one's scale score. Thus, someone with a "3" on column **8** means a raw score of 21–25. A "0" on column **8** would mean a raw score of 56–60. Let's assume the person responded with a raw score of "28," and therefore we will code column **8** with a "4." So far, we may have coded eight columns as follows:

Columns

| 1 | 2 | 3 | 4 | 5 | 6 | 7 | 8 | 9 | 10 | 11 | 12 | 13 | 14 | 15 ... |

We may assign one or more columns to each variable in our study. There are no re-strictions on the numbers of variables we can measure. However, it is unusual for studies to contain more than 50 variables. Besides sociodemographic and personal information, several attitudinal scales, and other included measures, there is not a whole lot more that investigators can include in their questionnaires and interviews. In most cases, researchers are interested in explaining criminological phenomena by limiting their analyses to those variables that have the greatest explanatory power. Even complex research designs will yield fewer than 10 explanatory variables that have the greatest predictive power.

Another consideration is that as we add more variables to our study, we increase the length of our questionnaires and stand a greater chance of wearing out our respondents. Few persons want to sit down and fill out a 100-page questionnaire. Some novice researchers want to add as many variables as possible to their questionnaires, thinking that certainly something significant will emerge from all of those variables. Some persons refer to this as shotgunning. Fortunately, we have the guidance of criminological theory. Theories tend to limit our explanations of criminal behaviors, attitudes, and social events to several key variables.

Developing a Coding Manual.   After we have constructed our questionnaire or interview schedule, we may want to construct a **coding manual** or **codebook.** A coding manual contains all columns we are going to use and the information to be recorded in each column. The coding manual explains exactly how each column is to be coded and how the codes are to be interpreted. Our coding manual for the variables coded above might be as follows:

Column	Variable	Question #s	Code
1,2,3	Respondent ID	1	As indicated
4	Gender	2	1 = male
			2 = female
			9 = no answer
5	Age	3	1 = under 21
			2 = 21–23
			3 = 24–25
			4 = 26–28
			5 = 29 or over
			9 = no answer
6	Education	4	1 = Some elementary school, not completed
			2 = Completed elementary school
			3 = Some high school, not completed
			4 = Completed high school
			5 = Some college, not completed
			6 = Completed college
			7 = Graduate work or degree
			9 = no answer
7	Political Affiliation	5	1 = Democrat
			2 = Republican
			3 = American Independent
			4 = Other
			9 = no answer
8	Police Professionalism	6	1 = 10–15
			2 = 16–20
			3 = 21–25
			4 = 26–30
			5 = 31–35
			6 = 36–40
			7 = 41–45
			8 = 46–50
			9 = 51–55
			0 = 56–60

9. . .

It is apparent from the abbreviated version of the coding manual above that we may construct our manual as simply as we choose. The purpose of this manual is to enable us or anyone else to review the column codes and determine what specific numbers mean. If we administer our questionnaire to 100 persons, then we would have coded information for these 100 persons transferred to coding sheets. Coding sheets contain all of the columns we are using in our research. Coding sheets summarize the numbers assigned based on each respondent's answers.

Columns

1	2	3	4	5	6	7	8	9	10	11	12	13	14	15	16	17	18	19	20	21	22
0	0	1	1	3	5	2	4	6	4	2	1	7	3	6	5	3	4	2	4	2	3
0	0	2																			
0	0	3																			
0	0	4																			
0	0	5																			
0	0	6																			
0	0	7																			
0	0	8																			
0	0	9																			
0	1	0																			
0	1	1																			
0	1	2																			
0	1	3																			
0	1	4																			
0	1	5																			
0	1	6																			
0	1	7																			
0	1	8																			
0	1	9	2	3	2	9	0														
0	2	0																			
0	2	1																			
0	2	2																			
0	2	3																			
0	2	4																			

The coding sheet above contains the answers for the first respondent to our questionnaire. In the above coding sheet example, we have used 23 columns. The coding manual will enable us to determine what the number in each column means. Notice that the first 24 persons in our sample have been identified in the first three columns. As we record information for each of our respondents, the coding sheet will fill with values. Later, the numbers from the coding sheet can be entered into various statistical computer programs, such as the Statistical Package for the Social Sciences, or **SPSS.** Once this information has been entered into our SPSS program, various kinds of statistical analyses are possible. For the time being, it is important to know how to transmit data from our questionnaires and interview schedules/guides to the coding sheets and how to develop a coding manual.

What to Do about "Don't Know" Responses or No Responses.   In a perfect world, everyone we contact about completing our questionnaires will do so happily. In a perfect world, our respondents will be truthful in their responses. Additionally, they will fill out the questionnaires completely. All questions will be answered. All scales will be completed. Unfortunately, it is not a perfect world. Bad things happen to researchers. Some information on questionnaires is missing. Some items are skipped. We have noted some of these problems in earlier chapters. How should these situations be handled when we are coding data?

BOX 10.1   PERSONALITY HIGHLIGHT

SCOTT DECKER
Curator's Professor of Criminology and Criminal Justice, University of Missouri–St. Louis

Statistics: B.A. (social justice), DePauw University; M.A., Ph.D. (criminology and criminal justice), Florida State University.

BACKGROUND AND INTERESTS

My primary research interests are in criminal justice policy, gangs, violence, and juvenile justice. This might seem like a set of diverse and unrelated interests. But I see them as unified by a couple of common themes, including understanding how institutions affect individuals. The majority of my recent research has been focused on gangs, whether it has been studying gang members in the community, as they pass through the police department and juvenile court, or evaluating comprehensive intervention programs. The fascinating thing to me about gangs is what they add to normal adolescent behavior. We know that during gang membership, involvement in crime increases both in frequency and seriousness. And that once an

BOX 10.1   CONTINUED

individual leaves a gang, their involvement in crime declines. This makes understanding gangs very important for learning more about delinquency, violence, and other forms of illegal behavior like drug sales.

There has been a lot of research through the years on gangs and gang crime. I have often wondered why this is the case. It seems to me that gangs have been studied so often because they integrate knowledge from a variety of different areas. For example, the study of gangs includes paying attention to the role of gender, neighborhoods, race and ethnicity, the impact of the economy, cultural transmission, urbanization, adolescence, prisons, police, social development, and marriage and the family. This list, while not exhaustive, includes most of the major subareas of sociology. The reliance of the study of gangs on traditional areas of sociological interest, combined with high levels of crime, have combined to make the study of gangs a staple throughout the past century.

I was initially attracted to criminology by a couple of factors. First, like many students, I was influenced by an outstanding undergraduate teacher, Dr. Paul Thomas. He made criminology interesting to me by integrating knowledge from a variety of areas of sociology and psychology. In addition, it seemed to me that criminology addresses some of the most fundamental questions about a society. These questions include:

> Why do people conform?
> Why do some people choose not to conform?
> How does a society organize itself to respond to individuals who fail to conform to the laws and norms of that society?

These seemed to be the essential questions about how civil societies live together, or fail to. And in the area of gang members, you have the study of many adolescents and the way that they are influenced not only by adult and juvenile justice systems, but also by such important institutions as the family, school, polity, and economy.

I went to Florida State University (FSU) in 1972 as a graduate student hoping to pursue my Ph.D. and was met there by a small cadre of excellent instructors, particularly Charles Wellford, who made a lasting impression on me. Charles taught me never to accept the easy answer or the first answer, and to push for other explanations. He also taught me that understanding the response to a problem (in this case, criminal behavior) may be more interesting than understanding the behavior itself.

RESEARCH INVESTIGATIONS

Of course, I remain interested in the study of gangs and the response to gangs for many of the reasons noted above. Gangs have changed considerably since I started to study them in the late 1980s, and that is one reason it remains of interest as a topic of study. But I have been even more interested in how cities organize and respond to gangs. The ability of different groups, often

BOX 10.1 CONTINUED

with different interests, orientations, cultures, and structures, to address a common problem is an issue of considerable interest and importance. The inability of communities to come together and form an effective response to this problem has been a source of personal frustration, especially in my hometown of St. Louis, but it is also an opportunity for more study.

Two research developments I have watched with interest have been the use of statistical methods that build in the influence of communities on individuals as well as their individual characteristics. Too much research, it seems to me, has lost sight of the context within which the individual lives. The second development has been the use of longitudinal research designs that allow for the study of individuals throughout their life course.

I have used a host of data collection techniques throughout my career. These have included primary data collection, secondary records, observation, and interviewing. Most interesting to me has been my collaboration with Richard Wright and Barrik Van Winkle in the use of field research techniques in interviewing and observing active offenders. This technique was used profitably to study residential burglars, armed robbers, and gang members. The ability to hear in their own words, and then fit these words into a theoretical perspective, has been a challenging and interesting part of my career. I have applied theoretical perspectives from several different areas, including social movements, interactional theory, and some components of labeling theory. I have not been an advocate of a particular theoretical approach, but rather, I have tried to find the theory most appropriate for the data at hand.

ADVICE TO STUDENTS

For students interested in pursuing criminology, the study of the making of law, the breaking of law, and the social reaction to law-breaking, I offer the following advice:

1. Look for the "off-diagonals" to confirm your larger observations. That is, sometimes when you only look at the model category of a behavior, you are apt to miss the most interesting aspects or the exceptions that often prove the rule. For example, while male gang members dominate the news, female gang members' lives may be more interesting, and in some ways, more important to study.

2. Ideology can be useful for many things, but research is not one of them.

3. Don't be fooled or enamored of techniques; after all, they are only tools.

4. Don't rely on technology alone for your analysis. There is no substitute for reading the transcripts. On the quantitative side, knowing the data well, starting with solid descriptive statistics, can prevent you from making serious errors in analysis and interpretation down the road.

5. Use one research opportunity to address many goals. It may not be the case that the express purpose of a study or data collection effort is all that interesting. However, that data can be used to address a variety of purposes and may lead to future access.

6. Be sure to draw from a broad range of perspectives. Criminologists can become far too insulated, to their detriment I think.

In our example above, digits ranging from "1" to "0" were used to represent different responses for each variable. However, if someone leaves the "gender" item blank or refuses to tell us their political or religious affiliation, there isn't much we can do about it. When there is no response to a given item, or when a scale measuring some variable is incomplete, we need to indicate this in some way in our coding manual. Sometimes, investigators will use either "9" or "0" as "No response," or "Not ascertained," or "Not given." Notice that the police professionalism scale used a "9" as well as a "0" for different score intensities. If we decided to use "9" or "0" to indicate "No response" or "Not ascertained," then we could code this and other scales in a way that would only utilize eight or fewer categories. Perhaps we could code our police professionalism scale as follows:

10–19 = 1
20–29 = 2
30–39 = 3
40–49 = 4
50–60 = 5
No response or incomplete response = 9 (or "0")

Accordingly, we could expand our categories for gender, education, political affiliation, and other variables to allow for nonresponse. Thus, gender would be:

1 = male
2 = female
9 = not ascertained

Our political affiliation responses would be coded as follows to allow for nonresponse:

1 = Democrat
2 = Republican
3 = American Independent
4 = Other
0 = Not ascertained

Therefore, either "9" or "0" functions as an indication that there was no response to that particular item, or a scale score could not be calculated. For instance, on a 10-item scale, if the respondent failed to answer one or more items, we could not calculate a meaningful raw score for the variable, such as police professionalism. We would record a "9" or a "0" in the column designated for that variable. Notice respondent #19. Hypothetical entries have been made in several columns. Columns **7** and **8** contain "9" and "0," indicating that the person either did not respond to the item or the person failed to give responses to all of the items comprising the scale.

Verification and Cleaning Data

Data-cleaning and **verification** means to closely examine all numerical information taken from questionnaires or interviews and determine that it is accurate. Thus, data-cleaning is an error-detection process, most often used in connection with questionnaire data and data coding sheets. Once researchers and their assistants have entered data on coding sheets, called **data entry,** this information will be transmitted to some type of computer software program for statistical analysis. The type of program to be used is unimportant at this point. The fact is that data will be transmitted to a computer. There are possible errors that may be prevalent or occur during the transmittal process. For instance, suppose one or more mistakes were made when entering data and numerical information on the coding sheets. Suppose erroneous numbers were entered on these sheets. Instead of entering a "1" for "male," the coder may have entered a "2," "female," in error. Or perhaps an entry of "5" was given for this variable. There is no gender as "5," but the "5" appears anyway. Suppose other numerical errors occurred as information was copied from questionnaires to the coding sheets. If left undetected, these errors will be transmitted to computer programs, and once computer programs have erroneous information, the results these programs produce will be somewhat unreliable, depending on the nature and extent of the erroneous information entered.

Erroneous information can be minimized by following a few simple steps. These steps are not foolproof, but errors can be detected in data entries and corrected easily. The first step is to be particularly careful if you are copying information from questionnaires to coding sheets. Second, have another coder examine your copied information and authenticate it. This is done by having another coder examine each questionnaire and your own coding sheet. The numerical information recorded by you is double-checked by another person. If the transmitted information survives two inspections, you have fairly accurate data recorded.

Some computer software programs, such as SPSS, require that users first create the categories into which data will be recorded. All variable titles are created as well as the subclasses of all variables. The subclasses for "male" and "female," the "1" and "2," will be recorded by the program. Later, if the researcher attempts to enter a digit other than a "1" or "2" (or a "9" or "0" in the case of no response) into that particular category, an error message will appear, questioning the possibly erroneous entry. But not all software programs for analyzing data have this capability.

There is nothing particularly complicated about cleaning data. Basically it is a process of verifying the accuracy of recorded information. In the event that coded information is erroneous and was not detected, sometimes there are clues about errors when data have been tabulated. If researchers prepare a distribution of age categories for their sample of respondents, the expected range is 1 through 5 (or a "9" or "0" for no answer). Perhaps the distribution shows the following:

1 = 22
2 = 32
3 = 15
4 = 26
5 = 16
7 = 1
8 = 1
9 = 3

This distribution says that 22 persons answered with a response that was coded with a "1," 32 persons answered and were coded with a "2," and so on. But our attention is immediately directed to categories "7" and "8." These categories simply don't exist. The age range went up to "5," and after that, a "9" was used for no response. Thus, the two responses of "7" and "8" are errors. Once detected, these errors are corrected and the data can be analyzed. These types of errors are fairly common, especially if there are large numbers of respondents being analyzed.

Simple Data Presentation

Researchers have lots of options when reporting whatever they have found. The most frequent option is to prepare a written account of what was done. The investigator can write an article about the research, what was studied, and what was found. This written account will be more or less lengthy, perhaps 20 or more pages. The style of the report varies greatly depending on the intended purpose of the written work. If the work is submitted to a professional journal for publication, there are journal guidelines that dictate the format to be followed. This formatting includes how to list citations and bibliographical entries. If the work is a report to a federal agency or some other organization providing funds for the research, the researcher will prepare it differently from an article format. Many studies are originally submitted and published as technical reports to different organizations or agencies. The Appendix contains additional descriptions of various types of papers and reports that are prepared by persons who do different types of research and writing.

The written word provides much enriching detail about one's study and what was found. However, supplemental charts, tables, and graphs can help to illustrate one's findings in creative ways. If one's research involves extensive analysis of data and statistical computations, some of this information may be tabled or graphed to enhance reader interest. Some numerical information, such as crime rates and population ratios, can be reported as a part of the written document.

Measures of Crime and Crime Rates

An important dimension of measurement of variables pertains to charting crime, delinquency, and other criminological phenomena over time and describing diverse components of the criminal justice system.

Crime Rates

What is the crime rate in the United States? The crime rate is reported by the FBI in the *Uniform Crime Reports* and other sources. It is given for different states, cities and towns, counties, and rural and urban areas. It is also provided for different types of crime and for crime generally. The crime rate is computed as follows:

$$\text{Crime Rate} = \frac{\text{Number of Crimes}}{\text{Population}} \times 100{,}000$$

For example, in 1988 there were 245,807,000 persons in the United States. During the year, there were 12,356,865 property crimes reported to the FBI, including burglary, larceny, and vehicular theft. Using these figures, we have

$$12{,}356{,}865 \,/\, 245{,}807{,}000 \times 100{,}000 = .0502706 \times 100{,}000 = 5027.06.$$

BOX 10.2   PERSONALITY HIGHLIGHT

DAVID C. MAY
Division of Public Affairs, Indiana University/Purdue University, Fort Wayne

Statistics: B.A. (criminal justice, sociology), University of North Alabama; M.S., Ph.D. (sociology), Mississippi State University.

BACKGROUND AND INTERESTS

I have numerous articles in professional journals and have published a book examining the causes of gang membership, weapons possession, and violent crime among serious juvenile male offenders. I am a member of the American Society of Criminology, the Academy of Criminal Justice Sciences, the American Sociological Association, and five regional sociological and criminal justice societies. My primary areas of research interest include the fear of crime, firearms, causes of juvenile delinquency, and the effectiveness of alternative sanctions.

My interest in criminal justice and criminal justice research began in a unique manner. At age 18, I joined the U.S. Army with the intention of being a career soldier. Three days into my tour, I realized that the Army was not my calling, although I spent the next 3 years and 362 days waiting for my honorable discharge in October 1988. During that time, I made two decisions that impacted the rest of my life. First, I decided to become a federal law enforcement agent; second, I developed an interest in guns.

My question for federal law enforcement took me to the University of North Alabama, where I completed my B.A. in criminal justice and sociology in the fall of 1992. During the spring of 1993, I learned that none of the federal agencies with positions available at that time were interested in hiring me. As such, I decided to pursue my master's degree with the hope that I would be more qualified after its completion. I then embarked on a graduate career in sociology at Mississippi State University. As a part of my coursework at Mississippi State University, I was required to complete a number of courses that involved research papers on topics of our own interest, as well as a master's thesis with the same criteria. It was this coursework and thesis that sparked my interest in research. For the first time (as I did not apply myself very well at the undergraduate level), I discovered the library and the hundreds of books and articles about my topic of interest, effectiveness of firearms policies and the causes of firearms ownership. The research methods courses and statistics courses I enrolled in further stimulated that interest, and gave me the tools necessary to do scientific research. I have maintained that interest in causes of gun ownership until this day.

BOX 10.2 CONTINUED

My other research interests developed from that initial research into causes of firearms ownership. As I was particularly interested in why adolescents carried and used guns, I began an exploration of the adolescent fear of crime literature, which was virtually nonexistent, as well as the causes of delinquency in general. Thus, the articles I have published and continue to develop largely fall into one of these three categories.

RESEARCH INVESTIGATIONS

My experiences with research have been both positive and negative. In my experience, there is nothing more frustrating than spending an entire summer working on a grant proposal that doesn't get funded, or having journal editors or reviewers reject your work without comment over a year from the date of the original submission. On the other hand, it is also very gratifying to develop hypotheses, acquire a sample, and realize that your countless hours spent reading and studying your topic allow you to predict exactly what will happen, and publish those findings in a scientific journal or book. The numerous places I have been, people I've met, and friendships I've forged as the result of my research have made it a worthwhile effort, far outweighing the frustrations that are bound to occur in the process of "doing science."

ADVICE TO STUDENTS

I would advise any student thinking about a career in criminal justice to become proficient early in their academic career in the area of research. Research skills are not easily acquired; thus, if you wait until the end of your academic career to begin research, you will not fully maximize that potential. If I had it to do over again, I would apply myself as an undergraduate, particularly in my criminal justice courses. Like many of you, I waited until the last semester of my senior year to enroll in research methods because I thought it would be difficult. Learn from my mistakes. Find a professor in your department or on your campus doing research; approach them and become involved. Learn to research and write well, but more importantly, learn to think well. The research process will allow you to acquire critical thinking skills that you might never be able to develop without that background in research.

This means that there were approximately 5,027 crimes against property per 100,000 persons in 1988. There were 20,675 murders reported in 1988. Therefore, $20{,}675/245{,}807{,}000 \times 100{,}000 = .00084 \times 100{,}000 = 8.4$ murders per 100,000 persons.

Caution should be exercised when interpreting any official statistics such as crime rates. The limitations and strengths of these statistical compilations are extensively documented elsewhere. Most introductory criminal justice texts summarize the pitfalls of such measures. There are seasonal variations in different types of crime. Crime varies from city to city and from state to state. Reported crime does not reflect the amount of unreported crime, which is known to be extensive from independent victimization reports. Large numbers of arrests do not represent large numbers of convictions. Crime waves may be politically created. When law enforcement agencies report crime to the FBI annually, only the most serious crime is reported, even if more than one crime was committed during a particular incident. These are only a few of the sources of error that interfere with the accuracy of these crime figures.

Suppose we wished to determine whether particular types of crime were increasing or decreasing, from one year to the next. Hypothetically, suppose that in 1995 there were 11,722,700 property crimes reported in the United States. Also, there were 241,077,000 persons in the United States as provided by Bureau of the Census estimates. What was the amount of increase in property crime between 1995 and 1999? We can calculate the percent change by using the following formula:

$$\text{Percent change} = \frac{(\text{quantity at time 2}) - (\text{quantity at time 1})}{(\text{quantity at time 1})} \times 100$$

$$= \frac{12,356,865 - 11,722,700}{11,722,700} \times 100$$

$$= 634,165/11,722,700 \times 100$$

$$= .054 \times 100 = 5.4 \text{ percent.}$$

There was a 5.4 percent increase in reported property crimes from 1995 to 1999. Was this particular percent increase equivalent with the general population increase during the same time period? The same formula may be used to answer this question. The population of the United States in 1995 was estimated to be 241,077,000. In 1999, it was estimated to be 245,807,000. Therefore,

$$\text{General Population Increase} = \frac{245,807,000 - 241,077,000}{241,077,000} \times 100$$

$$= 4,730,000/241,077,000 \times 100$$

$$= .0196 \times 100 = 1.96 \text{ percent.}$$

Thus, between 1995 and 1999, the general population was estimated to increase slightly less than 2 percent, or 1.96 percent. Compared with the 5.4 percent increase in property crimes, it would appear that property crimes are increasing at a greater rate between 1995 and 1999 than the growth of the general U.S. population. At least reporting property crimes is increasing at a greater rate than U.S. population growth.

Ratios

Ratios are commonly used by criminal justice professionals and others for various purposes. Suppose we wished to determine the ratio of prison inmates to prison correctional officers. If the prison population consisted of 1,500 prisoners and there were 500 correctional officers, the ratio of prisoners to correctional officers would be

[1,500 to 500] to 1 or 1,500/500 to 1 or = 3 to 1.

Thus, there would be three prisoners per correctional officer. This might also be expressed as 3:1. Reversing this ratio, we might consider the number of correctional officers to prisoners, or [500 to 1,500] to 1, or 500/1,500 to 1 or .33:1. A 1:1 ratio would mean one correctional officer per prisoner. If this type of arrangement actually existed, which it doesn't, no doubt it would be found in a close-custody, maximum-security facility. In 1999 there was an average of six inmates per corrections officer in all jails and prisons in the United States.

Graphic Presentation

Graphic presentation consists of all tables, charts, illustrations, figures, and line drawings that depict how collected data are distributed or arranged. Usually, graphics are limited to the most important features of studies that deserve to be highlighted. Charts and graphs can show trends over time regarding the incidence of different types of crime and other variables. The "spread" or distribution of frequencies throughout tables can show the influence of certain variables on other variables, and whether associations exist. Informative summaries of statistical information, such as the proportionate distribution of race, gender, age, and type of offense associated with jail or prison inmate populations, enable researchers to design their own studies more effectively by isolating the most crucial factors for investigation. Below is a summary of some of the more important functions of graphic presentation.

Functions of Graphic Presentation

The major functions of graphic presentation include: (1) enhancing articles, reports, and data summaries; (2) testing hypotheses derived from theories; (3) illustrating relationships between variables; (4) depicting trends and proportionate distributions; (5) influencing statistical test selections and applications; and (6) influencing policy decision making.

Enhancing Articles, Reports, and Data Summaries.   It is helpful to provide line drawings and other illustrations to highlight the written words in technical reports. Those who read articles often analyze charts and graphs before digesting the written material. Much can be gained by paying attention to how variables are distributed. Readers may quickly grasp whether certain variables are important as explanatory factors and deserve to be studied further.

Testing Hypotheses Derived from Theories.   Often, data are presented by researchers in tabular form for the purpose of testing hypotheses derived from theories. Depending on how graphs and tables are constructed and arranged, investigators may be able to influence the significance of whatever they find. As we will see, it is fairly easy to "lie with statistics," and the manipulation of the same data in graphs and tables by two different researchers may yield opposite and contradictory results when analyzed. Several objective rules or conventional procedures have been established to minimize the bias that may be introduced by the different vested interests of researchers. However, not everyone adheres strongly to convention when presenting their data to others. At appropriate points in this chapter, conventional guidelines will be presented that are calculated to enhance the objectivity of data presentation.

BOX 10.3   PERSONALITY HIGHLIGHT

HOWARD N. SNYDER
National Center for Juvenile Justice

Statistics: B.S. (physics and mathematics), Westminster College; M.S., Ph.D. (social psychology), University of Pittsburgh.

BACKGROUND AND INTERESTS

I have always been amazed by the quality of data available for secondary analysis to researchers who are able to exploit them. My original dissertation proposal described a research effort based on an analysis of hundreds of thousands of automated records copied from juvenile court management information systems that, when combined, documented the complete court careers of tens of thousands of youth. My department denied the proposal because it believed that Ph.D. students should collect their own data. And so I interviewed a few hundred eighth graders in a local middle school about their feelings toward their white and black classmates, wrote up the findings, earned the Ph.D.—and gave the data to a fellow graduate student for him to prepare and publish as a journal article. Even though the article was published in a leading journal, I doubt if more than 100 people ever read it. Afterwards I analyzed the juvenile court case records. That report was published in the mid-1980s by the U.S. Department of Justice, and I still see references to it today in academic and criminal justice articles.

In 1998 I attended a meeting honoring the 30th anniversary of the landmark work, *The Challenge of Crime in a Free Society.* This report, written by President Lyndon Johnson in response to the urban unrest in the 1960s, was based on over 2 years of work by a large team of the best researchers in the country. When asked in 1998 how the world had changed in the last 30 years, one team member said that the high school student with an Internet connection could learn more about crime patterns and trends in 30 minutes than the team learned in 2 years of intense effort.

RESEARCH INVESTIGATIONS

While at times we seem buried in information, so many entities (from federal agencies to your local food store) compile databases loaded with untapped information. Often the data were originally collected at great cost and burden to serve a specific purpose. A clever researcher can look beyond the original purpose and see other research studies embedded in the data. With a

BOX 10.3   CONTINUED

sound knowledge of available data, the ingenuity to see how the data can be applied to the research question at hand, and with the necessary technical skills, a researcher can build a career uncovering facts and relationships that support policy and program development, testing theories, and answering unanswered questions without ever going through the cost and tedium of collecting new data.

The trick is to find data to address your research needs. For example, in the early 1990s, juvenile violent crime was on the rise. One commonly held solution (the type of solution that is often wrong) was "midnight basketball," or programs that gave kids something other than crime to do during these hours. The popularity of midnight basketball in the media and in the minds of legislators led many communities to consider establishing juvenile curfews. In reviewing the constitutionality of these laws, the courts said that to limit the rights of a subgroup, there had to be strong evidence that the limitation benefitted the community. In other words, the courts asked lawmakers to show that juvenile violent crime was high during the proposed curfew hours.

We were asked to do one of these analyses. At the time, the FBI's new National Incident-Based Reporting System (NIBRS) was being installed in police departments across the country. Its primary purpose was to keep count of crimes reported to law enforcement agencies and the arrests they made. The system also collected the time of occurrence of each incident and the victim's description of the offenders, whether or not an arrest was made. We already had the data in our archive, and so in a very short period of time, we analyzed records on tens of thousands of crimes, simply graphing the number of violent crimes that occurred each hour of the day.

We found that crimes committed by adults did peak around midnight. However, crimes committed by juveniles peaked at about 3:00 P.M. A closer look at the juvenile pattern showed that there was a 9:00 P.M. peak during summer and weekend days, and an extremely high peak at 3:00 P.M. on school days. The analyses did not support the assumptions underlying proposed curfew legislation, but they did point to the crime reduction potential of after-school programs. Over the years the media have reported these findings so often that most people see them as common knowledge. More importantly, in the 10 years following the publications of these findings, over a billion dollars has been allocated for after-school programs in the United States—based in large part on an analysis that cost no more than a few thousand dollars to conduct because the data were already collected and awaiting analysis.

ADVICE TO STUDENTS

On the wall of my office is a poster that reads, "The world doesn't need another crummy theory, it needs better data." This may be too strongly worded, but it does highlight a basic weakness in criminology and criminal justice research. Most research is limited by the data underlying it. Data are expensive to collect, and so most research must settle for minimal information from small samples. Instead of having the exact information needed to test a theory or answer a policy question, most researchers "make do." Modern researchers must become students of avail-

BOX 10.3   CONTINUED

able data, learning their intricacies. Then, when a research need presents itself, the researcher can consider the range of the available information, select the best candidate, and restructure and analyze it. Unlike 30 years ago, to prepare tomorrow's researchers, I believe that colleges and universities must train their students to exploit the information potential of existing data. The best conceptualized and implemented research design can't overcome poor quality or inadequate data. For any research project, the data are at least as important as the research design.

Illustrating Relationships between Variables.   Tabular materials may illustrate relationships or associations between two or more variables. Thus, we may be able to point at the distribution of tabular frequencies to show that one or more variables are related with each other in meaningful ways. Statistical tests may be applied to furnish independent numerical objectivity to our visual interpretations of tabular material.

Depicting Trends and Proportionate Distributions.   Certain line drawings and graphs help to show whether variables change in certain directions over time. Is crime in the United States increasing? What is the proportion of mentally ill inmates among the entire U.S. jail population? How does the incidence of property crimes compare with violent crimes over time in specific cities or geographical regions? Which states have the highest execution rates? Graphic presentation illustrates this material easily.

Influencing Statistical Test Selections and Applications.   In order for certain statistical tests to be applicable for our data analyses, various assumptions about score distributions may be required. Some statistical procedures require that the sample data be distributed in the form of a bell-shaped curve or normal distribution. If our line drawings of raw scores show curves or distributions other than "normal" ones, then we have failed to meet at least one statistical test assumption. Our choices of central tendency and dispersion or variability measures often depend on how our data are distributed or arranged as well. If some raw scores among our collected data are quite different from the others or are "deviant scores" (e.g., most of 100 scores in some hypothetical distribution fluctuate between 10 and 30, but three of these scores are 80, 85, and 90, and are considered "deviant scores"), then we would want to apply the central tendency measure that works best with these deviant scores. Otherwise, applications of the other central tendency measures to our data with deviant scores would be distorted or misleading. Visually inspecting the distribution in graphic form influences our statistical test selections.

Influencing Policy Decision Making.   Intervention programs that are intended to change behavior may be adopted on a large scale by communities if positive results can be illustrated by investigators. For example, researchers may believe that a particular elementary school juvenile counseling and therapy method for youths considered "at risk" is useful for reducing their inclination to become delinquent. Graphic presentations of samples of "high-risk" youths exposed to the intervention program or therapy may eventually illustrate low numbers of delinquent youths over time. Thus, the community may adopt the intervention in schools as a general policy. Low recidivism rates among parolees and probationers may be attributable to lower probation and parole officer caseloads and more intensive supervision. Therefore, attempts may be made to keep officer caseloads low in an effort to decrease recidivism among clients.

Types of Graphic Presentation

Two types of graphic presentation will be illustrated: pie charts bar graphs.

Pie Charts

Pie charts are circular graphs that portray either portions of 100 percent of some aggregate or the frequency of incidents. Figure 10.1 shows a crime clock of the incidence of burglary every six minutes in the United States, while Figure 10.2 illustrates the proportion of minimum-, medium-, and maximum-security U.S. state prisons.

The FBI has considered dropping **crime clocks** from its publication, the *Uniform Crime Reports,* because it is possible to easily misinterpret them. When certain crimes are represented as occurring every few minutes, this refers to the total number of those crimes during the year divided into the total number of minutes in that same time interval. It does not mean that if there is a rape every 20 minutes in the United States, that rapes occur in Denver, Colorado, or Sioux Falls, South Dakota, every 20 minutes. Rather, *national* figures are portrayed. There are *seasonal fluctuations* in these crime rates as well. More rapes occur in warm summer months compared with cold winter months. One reason is that less clothing worn by potential rape victims in summer months attracts attackers.

Few restrictions exist pertaining to pie charts, their construction, and their application. The major shortcoming of them is the number of segments into which they may be divided conveniently. Too many segments create a "cluttered" pie chart. A rule of thumb governing

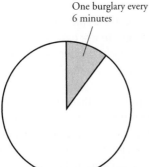

One burglary every
6 minutes

Figure 10.1   Crime clock. [Source: From the *FBI Uniform Crime Report Bulletin* (Washington, DC: U.S. Government Printing Office).]

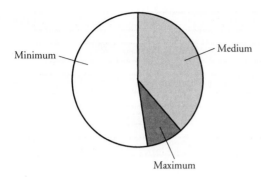

Figure 10.2   Pie chart showing proportion of minimum-, medium-, and maximum-security state prisons in the United States.

the maximum number of divisions for portraying data would be six. Beyond six divisions, it is difficult for researchers to label each sector in the chart adequately. Their use may be extended to virtually any variable and its subdivisions.

Bar Graphs

Bar graphs are either vertical or horizontal bars that portray the frequency of values on some variable. Figure 10.3 shows the percent of capacity of state and federal prison facilities occupied for a particular year, according to various prison sizes.

All state and federal prisons are rated by officials according to the maximum number of inmates each institution is designed to hold. These rated population sizes are considered maximum sizes by officials who conduct such ratings. Figure 10.3 discloses, however, that for different categories of prison sizes, these maximum capacities are exceeded by different percentages. First, we can determine at a glance that with one exception, state facilities are operating at a lower percent capacity compared with federal facilities. Overall, state facilities are operating at 3% above capacity, while federal facilities are operating at 24% above capacity. As the size of state and federal prison sizes increase, federal prisons operate

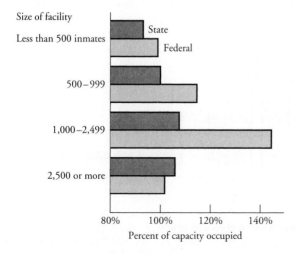

Figure 10.3   State facilities operating at 3% above capacity; federal facilities, 24% above.

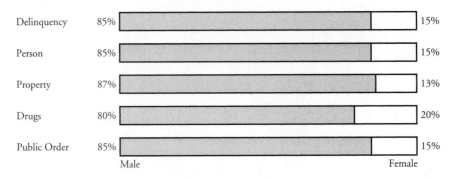

Figure 10.4   Offense characteristics of delinquency cases by gender.

at greater percents in excess of their rated capacities. The prison size, 1,000–2,499, seems to operate at the greatest capacity well in excess of rated maximum capacities, while facilities of less than 500 inmates operate below these maximum capacities. Figure 10.3 enables us to understand at a glance the magnitude of state and federal prison overcrowding in the United States.

Bar graphs can be used to illustrate trends, such as increases or decreases in crime rates over time. An imaginative use of bar graphs is the portrayal of various forms of delinquent conduct for both males and females. Figure 10.4 shows proportionate distributions of male and female juveniles for overall delinquency and for specific types of offenses within uniformly drawn horizontal bars. Much like pie charts, the area within each bar represents 100 percent of each type of offense. Shaded areas are used to represent proportions of either males or females within each offense category.

Bar graphs do not need to consist of uniformly drawn bars. For example, we might construct a bar graph such as the one shown in Figure 10.5 to depict the incidence of crime across various social classes.

In this instance, we have simply constructed vertical and horizontal axes, with high and low crime rates illustrated on the vertical axis, and social class, arranged from low to high,

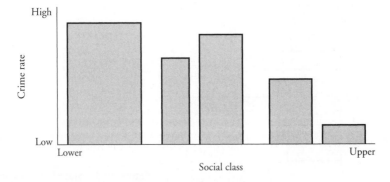

Figure 10.5   Bar graph reflecting social class and crime.

across the horizontal axis. The widths of the vertical bars in this case reflect either smaller or larger proportions of persons in different social classes. The wide flexibility of bar graphs and their lack of restrictions for any particular measurement level (e.g., nominal, ordinal, interval, or ratio) make them attractive illustrative devices in research reports and articles.

Tabular Presentation and Cross-Tabulation

Tables and How to Read Them

Tabular presentation is the most popular method of presenting data in research articles and reports, where tables of various sizes are used for descriptive and other informative purposes. Tables may be small or large, simple or complex, depending on the research purposes of investigators and the elaborateness of the data they are presenting. Tables consist of various rows (r) and columns (c), designated as size $r \times c$. These **rows and columns** are designated variables, and the particular divisions on the rows and columns depict the subclasses of these variables, or the variable subclasses. If the variable is gender, then two subclasses on the gender variable are male and female. If the variable is political affiliation, then several subclasses on this variable might be Republican, Democrat, and American Independent. If the variable is police professionalism, the variable subclasses may be high, moderately high, moderately low, and low.

BOX 10.4   PERSONALITY HIGHLIGHT

JAMES AUSTIN
President, JFA Associates

Statistics: B.S. (sociology), Wheaton College; Ph.D., University of California–Davis

BACKGROUND AND INTERESTS

I got involved in the study of prisons by accident. Raised in a white, middle-class culture (Wheaton, Illinois, the home of *Washington Post* journalist Bob Woodward and the late comedian John Belushi), I graduated from Wheaton College in 1970 in search of work and a career. One of my sociology professors was a consultant for the Illinois Department of Corrections at its Joliet and Stateville maximum-security prisons. He knew that I was in search of em-

BOX 10.4   CONTINUED

ployment after graduating from college with less than a stellar academic record. He mentioned that the prison system was hiring college graduates to work as counselors, and so I applied and was quickly hired along with several naive college graduates and a few middle-aged men with college degrees and a checkered past in search of a new mission.

My first impression of prisoners was how normal they were. Like most persons with no exposure to prisons, I had expected to see a high level of violence, aggression, and other forms of pathology. Instead, I saw a "city of captives" that depended almost exclusively on the inmates to prepare the food, type up the forms, repair the locks, and in general, run the prison. I rarely encountered inmates who were criminal as most people perceive them to be or as portrayed in HBO's *OZ* series. Rather, they seemed to express conventional values and aspirations, such as settling down, getting married, having children, owning a home, having a regular job, and going straight. What was different about them from the "rest of us" was the color of their skin and the lack of social, educational, and employment skills that would allow them to reach those shared middle-class goals. And it became increasingly clear to me that their incarceration would do little to help them make it. Finally, I was impressed with how boring it all was—that is, the daily routine of prison life, both for prisoners and for the staff.

I spent a total of 4 years bouncing between the Joliet and Stateville prisons (they had been relabeled as "correctional centers"), helping to provide the illusion of rehabilitation and treatment. These were real persons with a rich history of American penology. Most of the inmates were uneducated, youthful, streetwise blacks being managed by uneducated, middle-aged, white males from the rural farms of Illinois. It was truly a culture clash.

During those 4 years I saw it all, including a couple of major prison riots; working on death row, one of the country's first high-security control units designed by Karl Menninger and Norval Morris; spending time with James Jacobs as he wrote his book on Stateville; and watching inmates "volunteer" for experimental drugs for tuberculosis, malaria, and who knows what else (they received about $25 a month). I also had the opportunity to get to know some of Chicago's most notorious gang members who were then being sent to prison in record numbers by an aggressive Chicago prosecutor and who were wreaking havoc on the way prisons used to be run. I even saw the famous convict-turned-college-professor John Irwin make a cameo appearance at Stateville peddling his book, *The Felon*. But like so many "experts" before him, he came and went, but nothing really changed at Stateville and Joliet.

RESEARCH INVESTIGATIONS

After 4 years of the same routine (i.e., working in a prison can be like doing time), I had grown bored and escaped to San Francisco out of the fear that I would end up doing 30 years at Stateville, owing the prison credit union a ton of money, and slowly losing my mind. I soon was hired by the National Council on Crime and Delinquency (NCCD), a well-known liberal think tank, where I mastered the craft of writing successful proposals, which allowed me to live off of "soft money" for the next 25 years.

BOX 10.4 CONTINUED

While working at NCCD, I gingerly navigated my way through the University of California–Davis Sociology Department where I had the opportunity to study with Travis Hirschi and Ed Lemert (two extremes in criminological theory), and I received my Ph.D. in 1980 with Professor Lemert as my dissertation chair. My claim to fame as a criminologist was that I had actually worked in a prison—a rare attribute for almost all criminologists.

Today, I have my own consulting firm (JFA Associates) that works with state and local correctional agencies to help improve the conditions of prisons and advise politicians about how to save money by safely reducing their inmate populations. I have had the good fortune of working with a talented group of devoted colleagues and researchers who help me study who should be incarcerated and for how long. I spend each week traveling to some state that needs help in figuring out how best to reform current sentencing laws and release practices.

Throughout my career, I have marveled at how many of our most distinguished criminologists who have so little firsthand knowledge or experience with prisons and inmates are able to dominate the discourse on criminal justice policy. In my view, criminologists have become increasingly distant from what they are supposed to have expertise in—criminal behavior and the criminal justice system. They are spending less time observing firsthand the behavior in question, and they are increasingly relying upon official records despite the rich sociological history of the bias inherent in relying exclusively on agency-constructed records.

This trend toward armchair quantitative criminology has resulted in what I believe is a flawed and incomplete understanding of criminal behavior and the so-called benefits of imprisonment. Unfortunately, this knowledge has contributed mightily to the historic imprisonment binge in the United States. When I first entered Stateville there were only 7,000 prisoners in the entire Illinois prison system, and there were less than 200,000 prisoners in the entire U.S. prison system. Some three decades later there are over 45,000 Illinois prisoners and over 1.4 million in the United States. My hope is that the next generation of criminologists will pay more attention to the destructive nature of incarceration and how it can actually serve to worsen public safety. I hope that the next generation of criminologists does a better job reducing this harm than my generation has done.

The smallest tables used in research contain either one row or one column, divided into two subclasses. Thus, these smallest tables are either of size 2×1 or 1×2. For illustrative purposes, some fictitious data have been presented that portray the distribution of conviction offenses for a sample of state prison inmates. Tables 10.6 and 10.7 show examples of these smallest table sizes. In Table 10.6, one column is used to show inmates divided according to property or violent conviction offenses. The column represents the numbers of inmates in each of the conviction offense categories. The two rows show whether the conviction offense is a property crime (r_1) or a violent crime (r_2).

Table 10.7 is arranged differently. In this table, we have arranged the two types of conviction offenses in different columns with a single row. The row, r_1, shows the number

TABLE 10.6   The Distribution of a Hypothetical Sample of State Prison Inmates, by Conviction Offense, Illustrated with a 2 × 1 Table

	Conviction Offense	N	%	Row numbers
Column number	c_1			
Rows	Property	250	68.4%	r_1
	Violent	115	31.6%	r_2
	Total	$N = 365$	100.0%	

of persons in each conviction offense category. The two columns, c_1 and c_2, represent the two conviction offense categories.

Notice for each of these tables, percentages have been calculated for the property and violent inmate categories. An inspection of articles and reports in a wide array of professional journals will disclose several stylistic differences in how data are arranged in tabular form. While each journal has specific requirements about how to construct tabular material, there is a convention often followed regarding how to percentage one's data. This convention is that we should percentage in the direction of the independent variable. In Tables 10.6 and 10.7, only one variable has been portrayed—conviction offense. In one-variable tables, it makes little difference whether we percentage in one direction or the other. However, for larger tables where **cross-tabulations** are involved, it does make a difference. There are a few conventional rules that most researchers follow.

Cross-tabulations of Variables.   **Cross-tabulations of variables** represent arrangements of two or more variables in tables of size 2 × 2 or larger, and where one of the variables has been designated as independent. Table 10.8 shows some fictitious data arranged in a **2 × 2 table.**

In Table 10.8, gender has been cross-tabulated with type of delinquent offense and has been designated as the independent variable. Notice also that the table has been percentaged in the direction of the independent variable, gender. Had the table been constructed where type of delinquent offense had been placed across the top of the table

TABLE 10.7   A Distribution of a Sample of State Prison Inmates, by Conviction Offense, Illustrated with a 1 × 2 Table

	Conviction Offense		Totals
	Property	**Violent**	
Column numbers ———>	c_1	c_2	
Row (r_1) N's =	250 (68.4%)	115 (31.6%)	$N = 365$ (100%)

TABLE 10.8 A 2 × 2 Table

Dependent Variable		Independent Variable (Gender)		
		Males %	Females %	Totals %
Type of	Property	30*a* (17%)	120*b* (75%)	150 (44%)
Delinquent	Violent	150*c* (83%)	40*d* (25%)	190 (56%)
Offense	Totals	180 (100%)	160 (100%)	340 (100%)

and gender down the lefthand side of it, type of delinquent offense would be treated as influencing one's gender. As Table 10.8 is currently presented, however, gender is the variable used to account for variation on the type of delinquent offense variable. This particular presentation of the data is conventional and makes more sense, although not all researchers follow such a convention. If several professional journals were scanned, they would disclose a variety of tabular styles, although a majority of tabular styles would probably be consistent with the conventional independent–dependent variable layout shown in Table 10.8. Thus, following this particular convention permits readers to make easier and more systematic interpretations of tabular material. Again, not all researchers follow this tabular style.

Table 10.8 also shows that four table cells have been identified with the letters *a, b, c,* and *d.* This is because several statistical tests and measures of association are constructed, especially for data presented in 2 × 2 tabular form, and these letters have symbolic significance in various statistical formulae. When reading Table 10.8, we can see that of our 340 juveniles, they are almost evenly distributed according to gender (180 males and 160 females). Property offenders account for 44 percent of our sample, while violent offenders account for 56 percent of it. However, we have percentaged in the direction of the independent variable, gender, and therefore, we can say that 83 percent of our male juveniles are violent offenders, whereas 75 percent of our female juveniles are property offenders. Our initial impression is that our sample of female juveniles commits more property offenses than violent offenses. Just the opposite impression is drawn about our sample of male juveniles, where most appear to have committed violent offenses. Tentatively, gender appears to explain whether or not one will tend to be a violent or property offender.

Although caution has been recommended about drawing conclusions about cause–effect relationships between variables, we may at least infer that some causality exists between gender and type of delinquent offense in Table 10.8. Our rationale for making this inference about a possible relation between these two variables is based on the particular arrangement of frequencies throughout the cells in this table. Notice that the largest numbers of **cell frequencies** are found in cells *b* and *c.* The fewest frequencies are found in cells *a* and *d.* This **diagonal distribution of frequencies** is important as well as desirable, since it permits us to make direct inferences about how the variables might be related to each other. The other desirable diagonal arrangement that would permit such relational inferences would be for the largest numbers of the cell frequencies to accumulate in cells *a* and *d*. Using the 2 × 2 tabular case to illustrate desirable and undesirable distributions of frequencies, we have the following two desirable distributions:

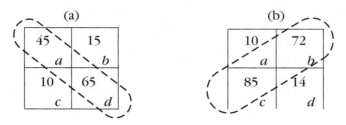

These distributions are considered desirable not only because tentative causal inferences between variables may be drawn, but because of the direction of the relationship between variables may be determined. In the case of the data distributed in (*a*) above, cells *a* and *d* contain the most frequencies. If these frequencies were placed in Table 10.8, we would conclude tentatively that male juveniles and property offenses appear related, while female juveniles and violent offenses appear related. Note that the distribution of frequencies in table (*b*) is more similar to the actual distribution shown in Table 10.8, where the largest numbers of frequencies are found in cells *b* and *c*.

The following four tabular arrangements of frequencies are less desirable:

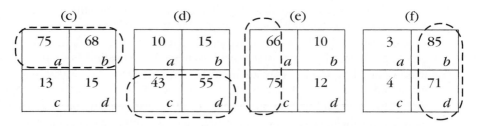

The primary reasons these four tabular arrangements are undesirable are because the largest numbers of frequencies are found in the subclasses of either the independent or dependent variables, and the direction of the relationship between the two variables cannot be determined easily. Thus, there is little variation on either the independent or dependent variables. For instance, in the first table (*c*), the largest numbers of frequencies are found in the first subclass of the dependent variable, cells *a* and *b*. In the table (*d*), the largest numbers of frequencies are found in the second subclass of the dependent variable in cells *c* and *d*. In the latter two tables (*e*) and (*f*), the largest numbers of frequencies are found in either the first or second subclasses of the independent variables (cells *a* and *c* and cells *b* and *d*, respectively).

This lack of variation in either the dependent or independent variable fails to provide us with an adequate opportunity to evaluate the impact of either variable on the other. This would be the same as commencing a study by declaring that we want to observe the impact of an intensive supervised probation program on recidivism among probationers compared with a program involving standard probation. We might obtain a large sample of probationers, but in creating our tables for these probationers and identifying their degree of recidivism, we may find that only a small proportion of probationers are involved in intensive supervised probation programs. Alternatively, we might find that the particular sample we have collected exhibits a low rate of recidivism across the board. Thus, it is imperative for researchers to ensure that ample representations of elements will be available to have more desirable tabular distributions. Statisticians recommend that proportionate breakdowns on the independent variable should be approximately 50–50, or close to it. Equal divisions on the dependent variable are also desirable, although dependent variables are often more difficult to control compared with independent variables.

Whenever less desirable tabular distributions of frequencies are encountered, and the preponderance of frequencies is found on one or the other subclasses of independent or dependent variables such as those illustrated above, researchers may make proportionate analyses of their data, and determine whether greater proportions of persons with specific characteristics share other designated attributes. For example, suppose we investigated two samples of 100 first-degree murderers each in selected states that use the death penalty as the maximum punishment. One sample consists of convicted offenders who killed police officers during the commission of their crimes, whereas the other sample consists of convicted offenders who killed store clerks, innocent bystanders, or relatives during the commission of their crimes. We observe the results of jury deliberations in all cases and cross-tabulate both samples of convicted murders with the nature of punishment imposed. Keeping our problem simplified, suppose only two punishment options exist. These options are life without parole and the death penalty. Perhaps our belief is that those convicted of murdering police officers will be more likely to receive the death penalty compared with those convicted of killing non-police officers. Our data might appear as shown below:

		Victim of Convicted Murderer		
		Police Officer	Non-Police Officer	Totals
Punishment Imposed by Jury	Life without parole	14	26	40
	Death penalty	86	74	160
	Totals	100	100	$N = 200$

Perhaps we are disappointed at first because there is no diagonal relation between the punishment imposed and whether the murder victim was a police officer. For both samples, the death penalty was imposed, and our cell frequencies accumulated on the second subclass of the dependent variable, the death penalty as punishment. However, we can examine the proportionate distribution of the imposition of the death penalty and see whether or not those convicted of murdering police officers received it more frequently than the other sample of convicted murderers. In the table above, we can see that 84 percent of those convicted of murdering police officers received the death penalty, whereas only 74 percent of those convicted of murdering non-police officers received it. This is an obvious proportional difference and is generally consistent with what we originally anticipated, despite the fact that both samples of murderers tended to receive the death penalty anyway. Statistical tests may be applied to this table to determine whether 84 percent is significantly different from 76 percent. After all, this difference may be due to chance, and not to whether police officers were the murderer's victims. In this case, a statistical test, the Z test for differences between two proportions discussed elsewhere (Champion, 1981; Siegel, 1956), could be used as a numerical measure of the significance of difference between these two proportions in a statistical sense. Thus, if diagonal relations between variables are nonexistent, we can usually adopt "Plan B" methods to evaluate proportionate differences. Alternative problem solutions are useful whenever tables such as (c), (d), (e), and (f) above are encountered.

It is relatively easy to illustrate direction and association between variables by using the 2 × 2 tabular case for our example. However, when tables are constructed larger than 2 × 2, it becomes increasingly difficult to detect relations between variables or to infer the direction of an association. An example of this more difficult chore might be illustrated by a 5 × 5 table. Consider the following hypothetical table, where data have been distributed across five rows and five columns:

Independent Variable

	(Low) Col. 1	Col. 2	Col. 3	Col. 4	(High) Col. 5	Totals
Dependent Variable (Low)						
Row 1	18	28	36	15	19	116
Row 2	31	22	19	45	28	145
Row 3	16	18	18	14	21	87
Row 4	31	29	20	15	12	107
Row 5 (High)	16	19	30	40	60	165
Totals	112	116	123	129	140	620

It is quite difficult to determine whether any directional relation exists between the independent and dependent variables in this table. The frequencies appear scattered and do not seem to occur in any patterned relation. Not all larger tables exhibit this much disarray, however. Below is a 5 × 5 table where direction is more visually apparent:

Independent Variable

	(Low) Col. 1	Col. 2	Col. 3	Col. 4	(High) Col. 5	Totals
Dependent Variable (Low)						
Row 1	6	15	19	30	50	120
Row 2	8	16	20	28	31	103
Row 3	10	6	20	16	15	67
Row 4	30	16	12	10	8	76
Row 5 (High)	70	40	20	16	3	149
Totals	124	93	91	100	107	515

In this particular 5×5 tabular scenario, we can see that as we move across the five columns on the independent variable from left to right, there are few frequencies in the first few columns, but these frequencies increase in successive columns as we move to the right (e.g., 6, 15, 19, 30, and 50 as frequencies across Row 1, and 8, 16, 20, 28, and 31 as frequencies across Row 2). However, in Row 3, there is an inconsistent pattern in the distribution of frequencies across the five columns (10, 6, 20, 16, and 15, moving from left to right). In Rows 4 and 5, however, there are initially larger numbers of frequencies to the far left, although these frequencies systematically decrease as we move to the right across other columns (30, 16, 12, 10, and 8 in Row 4, and 70, 40, 20, 16, and 3 in Row 5, moving from left to right).

We would be able to say that for this particular table, higher scores on the independent variable are associated with lower scores on the dependent variable, while lower scores on the independent variable are associated with higher scores on the dependent variable. A rough line has been drawn around the preponderance of frequencies in the table, showing an approximately diagonal relation. Unfortunately, relationships between variables in many of these larger tables are not seen as clearly whenever real data are presented and discussed in articles, reports, or research summarizations.

When we increase the number of variables to be cross-tabulated, we make it possible to control for the influence of these additional variables on the remaining variables. We may observe a tentative association between some hypothetical variables in the following 2×2 table:

		Status of Mother		
		Works	Does Not Work	Totals
Status of	Delinquent	100	50	150
Children	Nondelinquent	50	100	150
	Totals	150	150	300

When we first inspect this table, it seems that it makes a difference whether mothers work or do not work and whether their children are or are not delinquent. While it is entirely possible that the working/nonworking status of mothers affects whether their children become delinquent, we may wish to explore other factors to evaluate their potential impact on our initial observation. Perhaps we want to consider the influence of continuous adult supervision on the incidence of delinquency among the children involved in this research. Maybe research suggests that continuous adult supervision of children is a more important determinant of a youth's delinquency or nondelinquency rather than the working/nonworking status of mothers. We can reconstruct the data above in the following rearranged table:

		Adult Supervision of Children				
		Yes		No		
		Mother Works	Mother Does Not Work	Mother Works	Mother Does Not Work	Total
Status of	Delinquent	0	0	100	50	150
Children	Nondelinquent	50	100	0	0	150
	Totals	50	100	100	50	300

An entirely different pattern of the role of working mothers in relation to the delinquency/nondelinquency of their children emerges. After we added the third variable, continuous adult supervision, it seems that the more important factor is whether the children are continuously supervised by adults, regardless of whether their mothers work. This also illustrates spuriousness, or the presence of a supposed association between two variables that is actually the result of a third, perhaps unknown, variable. Notice that all of the delinquent children are found under the category where children are not continuously supervised by adults, and that all of the children who are not delinquent are under the continuous adult supervision category. While this finding does not prove a relation between the continuity of adult supervision and delinquency/nondelinquency, it nevertheless seems to rule out the status of working mothers as an explanatory factor.

In the event that our tables are too large and unwieldy, such as the first 5 × 5 table above containing 620 frequencies in disarray, it is possible to collapse these tables to create smaller and more meaningful ones. **Collapsing tables** means to reduce either the number of rows or the number of columns or both and combine the total frequencies into smaller numbers of cells. Suppose that the column designations for the first 5 × 5 table were "Strongly Agree," "Agree," "Undecided, Probably Agree," "Disagree," and "Strongly Disagree." Further suppose that the row designations were "Very Favorable," "Favorable," "Undecided, Probably Favorable," "Unfavorable," and "Very Unfavorable." We could collapse the data into a 3 × 3 table to see whether our results are more meaningful. We might decide to collapse the columns as follows: place the "old" Columns 1 and 2 into "new" Column 1, the "old" Column 3 into a "new" Column 2, and the "old" Columns 4 and 5 into a "new" Column 3. Furthermore, we might decide to collapse our rows as follows: We will combine our "old" Rows 1, 2, and 3 into a "new" Row 1, the "old" Row 4 into a "new" Row 2, and the "old" Row 5 into a "new" Row 3. These collapsed data would be illustrated below (the old row and column totals are shown in parentheses in each of the nine cells of the new, collapsed 3 × 3 table):

(Collapsed Table) Independent Variable

Dependent Variable	(Agree) Col. 1	Col. 2	(Disagree) Col. 3	Totals
(Favorable) Row 1	(18+28+31 +22+16+18) = 133	(36+19+18) = 73	(15+19+45 +28+14+21) = 142	348
Row 2	(31+29) = 60	= 20	(15+12) = 27	107
Row 3 (Unfavorable)	(16+19) = 35	= 30	(40+60) = 100	165
Totals	= 228	= 123	= 269	= 620

The above pattern has simplified the task of perceiving relationships between these variables, if any. However, an inspection of the distribution of frequencies shows no meaningful pattern. There are 133 elements (persons) who tend to "agree" on the independent variable, while they are "favorable" on the dependent variable. However, 142 persons who "disagree" on the independent variable also are "favorable" on the dependent variable. It is possible that we might collapse these data differently and generate more meaningful patterns of frequencies. But collapsing of categories on either the independent or dependent variables should be done in a logical fashion. It would be illogical, for instance, to combine "unfavorables" with "favorables" on the dependent variable or to combine "agrees" with "disagrees" on the independent variable.

Other Forms of Tabular Presentation

Many other forms of tabular presentation exist. Often, these tables illustrate trends or present informative figures. *The Sourcebook of Criminal Justice Statistics 2003* (Maguire & Pastore, 2004) contains hundreds of tables about all aspects of the criminal justice system, including crime trends and case information. For example, Table 10.9 shows the average and median number of days between arrest and conviction for various crimes disposed of by state courts.

An inspection of Table 10.9 breaks this data down into cases by type of offense and method of conviction (i.e., whether a jury or bench trial was conducted, and whether a guilty plea was entered through plea bargaining). Both average (mean) and median figures are presented, expressed in numbers of days from arrest to conviction. Explanatory notes in the table indicate the meaning of the median for purposes of reading the table as well as the meaning of other tabular notations. Murder cases seem to take the longest to resolve, with an overall average of 354 days from arrest to conviction. Larceny convictions account for those cases most rapidly resolved, taking an average of 196 days from arrest to conviction. In almost every type of criminal case, the mean number of days to dispose of each case was higher than the median number of days. This suggests that jury trials for a portion of these cases may have prolonged the length of time needed to conclude them. Averages are influenced greatly by deviant scores or, in this case, a few extraordinarily long, drawn-out trials.

Tables may present **trend information,** such as the rates associated with the use of plea bargaining over time, or the proportion of civil and criminal cases in federal courts across several decades. *The Uniform Crime Reports* publishes tabular information about index crimes in most U.S. cities and counties on an annual basis.

Deciding How Best to Present Your Information

There are no definitive guidelines about how much graphic material is best for any research report or article. One guideline is that such materials should not appear to be thrown in or frivolous. Editors of professional journals generally favor shorter publications rather than longer ones. Excess graphic presentation and use of tabular materials may be distracting. Many articles are written without any graphic material in them. Qualitative research projects rely heavily on interpretations of social actions and descriptions of attitudes. In short, it is not a requirement of social scientific writing that such materials must always be supplemented with tables or graphs.

TABLE 10.9   Average and Median Number of Days between Arrest and Conviction for Felony Cases Disposed by State Courts

By offense and method of conviction, United States,
(In days)

Most serious conviction offense	Number of Days between Arrest and Conviction for Cases Disposed by:		
	Trial		
	Jury	*Bench*	*Guilty plea*
Average number of days			
All offenses	273	235	165
Violent offenses	285	252	203
Murder	356	398	307
Rape	295	347	214
Robbery	263	218	193
Aggravated assault	245	214	201
Other violent offenses	346	262	178
Property offenses	249	229	158
Burglary	263	219	151
Larceny	205	229	155
Fraud	320	259	171
Drug offenses	271	232	155
Possession	245	218	142
Trafficking	279	242	163
Weapons offenses	279	215	159
Other offenses	231	236	159
Median number of days			
All offenses	219	167	116
Violent offenses	233	185	148
Murder	309	364	253
Rape	254	247	159
Robbery	232	167	151
Aggravated assault	173	146	144
Other violent offenses	319	219	122
Property offenses	200	154	111
Burglary	200	154	110
Larceny	175	167	107
Fraud	224	154	114
Drug offenses	202	162	108
Possession	181	159	98
Trafficking	202	164	112
Weapons offenses	203	161	120
Other offenses	191	181	113

The median marks the point below which and above which 50% of all cases fall. The grand total column includes all cases, whether or not conviction type was known. Some estimates are based on as few as one case and are therefore unreliable.

Source: U.S. Department of Justice, Bureau of Justice Statistics, *State Court Sentencing of Convicted Felons, 1994,* NCJ-164614 (Washington, DC: U.S. Department of Justice, 1998), p. 52.

Decisions about the inclusion of graphs or tabular materials depend, in large part, on the nature of one's research. If samples of elements are studied and described, summary tables are helpful for portraying various features of the sample, including average age, prior record, educational training, gender, and a host of other factors. This material is also presented in written form, as authors describe the essential aspects of their graphic and tabular presentations. Studies that investigate trends, such as whether there is a rise in juvenile violence or female criminality over time, might profit from including summary tables of crime rates across several years.

SUMMARY

Coding variables, especially information derived from questionnaires, is an important step in the data-gathering process. Coding means to assign numerical values to responses given to individual items on questionnaires or some other medium, or to statements given in response to interview guides or interview schedules. Typically researchers will devise coding manuals with varying degrees of detail and sophistication. These coding manuals are useful in determining the meanings of numbers assigned different variables and scores. Coding facilitates the data analysis process by permitting rapid information retrieval via computer and various data analysis programs, such as the Statistical Package for the Social Sciences (SPSS). Data cleaning and verification are also integral parts of the coding process, as sometimes coding errors may be made and erroneous numbers may be entered. A relatively simple process of detecting erroneous entries is conducted, as investigators seek to improve the accuracy of their data and how it is tabulated or recorded through data entry.

In order for data to be interpreted meaningfully, several common strategies are used for data presentation. Graphs, charts, and different types of tables are used for different illustrative purposes. Graphic presentation consists of all tables, charts, illustrations, and line drawings that depict how collected data are distributed or arranged. The functions of graphic presentation include enhancing articles and reports, testing hypotheses derived from theories, providing evidence of relationships between variables, depicting trends and proportionate distributions, influencing statistical test selections, and influencing policy decision making.

Two types of graphic presentation include pie charts and bar graphs. Pie charts are circular graphs that portray either proportions of 100 percent or the frequency of incidents such as burglary or robbery. Bar graphs may be either vertical or horizontal bars that portray the frequency of values on some variable. Other graphics include maps of geographical territories and line charts superimposed upon one another to connote crime trends or other data that vary over time.

Another way of portraying data is to use rates and ratios, particularly where different types of crime are reported. Crime rates reflect how much crime is committed in a given time period, such as every 6 months or year, and crime trends may be charted by comparing crime rates across several time intervals. Ratios may assist investigators in their studies of caseload distributions among probation or parole officers, or they may be used to indicate the number of cases scheduled per judge in a given state or federal jurisdiction. Rates and ratios are vital components of data presentation in many research investigations.

The most popular form of data presentation is the use of tables and cross-tabulations of variables. The smallest table sizes, represented by the expression, $r \times c$, are 1×2 or 2×1, where r designates the number of rows in the table and c designates the number of columns.

The smallest cross-tabulated table is 2×2, or a table having two rows and two columns. Larger tables with more rows and columns may be constructed. Sometimes, larger tables are unwieldy and may be collapsed. Collapsing means to reduce the number of cells in tables and combine the frequencies from the collapsed cells into fewer cells. Collapsing is done in accordance with a logical plan, where blended categories are meaningfully related with one another. Collapsing helps researchers to gain a clearer perspective about how frequencies in tables are distributed.

The most fruitful distributions of frequencies in tables are diagonal ones. This is because diagonal distributions of frequencies in the cells of these tables enable researchers to identify possible relationships between variables and help to establish possible causality. Sometimes, additional variables are introduced in tables as control variables, in an effort to see which variables have the most explanatory value. Desirable diagonal relationships between variables may not always be observed. Frequencies may bunch up on one variable subclass or another. Both independent and dependent variables in tables may reflect such "bunching up" of frequencies. Researchers often use alternative analytic strategies whenever less desirable distributions of frequencies in tables are found. These analyses often become proportional analyses, where differences between proportions on different variable subclasses are examined. Some research is conducted without relying on graphic presentation. Reasonable use should be made of tables and graphs, and only to highlight the most important aspects of one's research.

QUESTIONS FOR REVIEW

1. What is coding? Why is coding important in the research process?

2. What is a coding manual? What are its uses for social research?

3. What is meant by data entry, data cleaning, and data verification? Why are these steps in analyzing data important?

4. How should investigators deal with "Don't Know" or "Uncertain" types of answers on fixed-response items on questionnaires? What sorts of problems do such types of answers pose for researchers? What solutions have been proposed to deal with these types of responses?

5. What is a crime rate? How is it determined for particular categories of crime?

6. What is a ratio? What are some of its research uses?

7. What is meant by graphic presentation? What are two popular forms of graphic presentation? What are some of their advantages for expressing one's research findings?

8. What is meant by tabular presentation? Why is it important to present some of an investigator's collected data into tables of various sizes?

9. What is meant by $r \times c$? What is meant by collapsing? What are some hypothetical examples of collapsing from the research literature?

10. What is meant by cross-tabulating data? How are cross-tabulations of value to researchers?

11. What conventions are followed in terms of the placement of independent and dependent variables in any $r \times c$ table?

11 Hypothesis Testing and Theory Verification

CHAPTER OBJECTIVES

As the result of reading this chapter, the following objectives should be realized:

1. Understanding how hypotheses are derived and constructed so that theories may be tested.
2. Distinguishing between several different kinds of hypotheses, including research hypotheses, null hypotheses, and statistical hypotheses, and their respective functions.
3. Understanding the purposes of null hypotheses and hypothesis formulation.
4. Understanding the functions and relative weaknesses and strengths of different types of hypotheses.
5. Learning about one-variable, two-variable, and *k*-variable hypotheses and how these can be tested.
6. Learning how theory verification is related to hypothesis testing.

Introduction

This chapter examines hypotheses, or various testable statements that are derived from our theories. Hypotheses are the means whereby our theories are usually tested. The chapter opens by examining the relationship between the theories we create and the types of hypotheses that may be derived from them.

Hypotheses vary in their complexity and wording, and thus, several different kinds of hypotheses will be described. The conventional use of hypotheses in research suggests that these statements should be implicitly or explicitly presented in pairs or in hypothesis sets. Hypothesis sets, including the conventional pairing of research and null hypotheses, will be examined and several examples from the research literature will be provided. Traditional categories of hypotheses include research hypotheses, which are directly derived from theories. Subsequently, null hypotheses are constructed from these research hypotheses and subjected to different types of empirical tests. Mathematically expressed forms of these hypotheses, statistical hypotheses, will be illustrated and examined. Examples from the research literature will be used. Several reasons will be given for why hypothesis sets are developed and used when investigators conduct their research projects.

There are an infinite number of hypotheses that may be devised from the various theories investigators use in their criminological research. Some attention will be given to hypothesis formulation. It is important that hypotheses should be formulated in particular ways in accordance with how the variables in these hypotheses have been related theoretically. Some hypotheses are more informative than others in that they have greater specificity. Sometimes this is a function of how much or how little we know about the settings or persons we study. Also, some hypotheses predict how different variables will fluctuate in relation with one another. Some hypotheses are directional, while others are nondirectional. The more we know about the variables investigated, the more specific we can be about how variables ought to be related. Directional and nondirectional hypothesis statements will be examined as well as the circumstances under which these statements are used. Different types of hypothesis formulation will be examined and explained.

Next, the chapter explores several important functions of hypotheses. Their use in criminological research signifies more elaborate or sophisticated research plans, where investigators are interested in description and experimentation. Hypotheses may contain single variables, two variables, or more than two variables. As we add variables to hypothesis statements, these statements become increasingly complex and they are more difficult to test empirically. Both one- and k-variable hypothesis statements will be illustrated.

This chapter subsequently examines the ways in which hypothesis tests are interpreted. Hypotheses are intended to be tested scientifically. In most research projects, several hypotheses are tested. Depending on one's particular research outcome, hypothesis test results are not always favorable, in that whatever the investigator believes is true about his or her theory may not be supported by some or all of those hypothesis tests. How should researchers interpret these hypothesis test outcomes? Different types of outcome scenarios will be presented and different interpretations will be explained.

The chapter concludes with a discussion of different types of factors that can influence the results of one's hypothesis tests. Several considerations must be made when interpreting our hypothesis test results. Areas of interest to us in this regard include theoretical considerations; sampling considerations; considerations made for measuring the variables we have used in hypotheses; considerations for data collection methods we have used; and the amount and nature of participation we have had in the study itself.

Hypotheses and Theory

Hypotheses are tentative statements about something, the validity of which is generally unknown. For example, to declare that "upper-class people have fewer delinquent children than lower-class people" might be construed as an hypothesis concerning the effect of social class on delinquent behavior. Whether or not this is a statement of fact or an hypothesis depends on how much we know about the social class–delinquency relation and whether the declarer actually knows if the statement is true. If the statement reflects the investigator's "hunch" about the social class–delinquency relation, then the statement is largely a hypothetical one. However, if census data exist to show clearly that large proportions of delinquents are found in lower-class families and small proportions of them are found in upper-class families, then these data provide empirical support for the authenticity of the statement.

Many facts that we recite today were hypotheses in earlier times. For example, we know a great deal more about marijuana today than we did in the 1930s. Some persons believed that marijuana caused irreversible mental illness and insanity. Others believed that it led to sexual promiscuity. Today, although it is unlawful to use marijuana in any U.S. jurisdiction, we understand that it impairs our judgment and depth perception, although it doesn't appear to cause irreversible mental illness, insanity, or sexual promiscuity.

Another example pertains to the relation between broken homes and delinquency. Children from broken homes (either by desertion or divorce) were believed to be likely candidates for delinquency. Religious leaders promoted the importance of family stability and unity as a way of preventing children in those families from acquiring delinquent behaviors and characteristics. Single-parent adoptions of children were unheard of in most jurisdictions, because the conventional, two-parent family was believed most therapeutic for children. Today, however, several states permit single-parent adoptions of children, since the evidence that single-parent families are unhealthy for child-rearing has been inconclusive and contradictory.

Many of our present beliefs have been shaped by previous verifications of theories about things. Much uncertainty remains about different types of behaviors and social events, however. Below are several examples of hypotheses that have been drawn from recent research articles and may be tested in criminological and criminal justice research:

1. Persons convicted of white-collar crimes come from upper socioeconomic classes (Piquero & Benson, 2004).
2. Blacks and Hispanics are more likely than whites to support reforms in policing (Weitzer & Tuch, 2004).
3. Chronic truant juveniles processed through a community Truancy Center Intervention Program will have lower recidivism rates compared with chronic truant juveniles who are formally processed through juvenile intake (Bazemore et al., 2004).
4. Females of Asian descent are less likely than white females to report spousal assaults (Kingsnorth & Macintosh, 2004).
5. Convicted drug users processed by drug treatment courts will remain drug-free for longer periods compared with convicted drug users processed through traditional criminal courts (Gottfredson, Najaka, & Kearley, 2003).
6. The District of Columbia Curfew Law will decrease the overall number of juvenile arrests (Cole, 2003).

7. Membership in a gang will be associated with higher levels of delinquency compared with nongang membership (Gordon et al., 2004).
8. Reformed criminal offenders view their lives as the result of positive internal and stable events compared with active criminals who view their lives as the result of negative external and unstable events (Maruna, 2004).
9. Prison inmates who are denied visitation rights with their children will have greater numbers of misconduct reports compared with prisoners who are granted visitation rights with their children (Dow, 2004).
10. Parolees under the supervision of parole officers with caseloads of 50 or less will be more successful in their community transitions compared with parolees under the supervision of parole officers with caseloads greater than 50 (Binder, 2003).

Hypotheses can pertain to anything. There are no restrictions concerning what variables can be hypothesized. Hypotheses do not necessarily have to be true, however. In fact, the truthfulness of most hypotheses formulated by investigators is usually unknown. Hypotheses, therefore, are tentative statements about things that researchers either wish to support or refute.

The 10 hypotheses listed above have been studied and subjected to verification by various researchers in recent years. Some of these statements have been investigated more often than others. Thus, our degree of certainty about any given statement is based, in part, on the amount of confirming evidence we can compile about it. Also, each of these statements is derived from a larger theoretical scheme. If we are examining the effectiveness of various parole programs, for instance, we might theorize about the therapeutic value of parole officers in relation to their parolees by using the size of a supervising parole officer's caseload as a predictor variable. One statement we might test would be whether those under supervision where parole officers' caseloads are 50 or fewer parolee-clients might be more likely to adjust to living again in their communities compared with parolee-clients supervised by parole officers with caseload sizes greater than 50. In this instance, we don't know for sure whether the size of a parole officer's caseload makes any significant difference in a parolee's community adjustment, but we might believe that it does. Only through research and testing one or more hypotheses about caseload sizes of parole officers and parolee community adjustment can we acquire greater certainty about the relationship between these variables.

It might also be believed that fining offenders might function to reduce their recidivism. Currently, the Internal Revenue Service and Drug Enforcement Administration, together with the U.S. Department of Justice, seize assets of drug dealers and others who traffic in illegal drugs. These assets might include automobiles, boats, airplanes, homes, and other types of property, in addition to large sums of money used for illicit drug transactions. In 2004, for instance, the Department of Justice claimed that several billion dollars had been used to improve law enforcement effectiveness, and that much of this money was from illegal drug transactions and property seizures. It might be hypothesized, therefore, that seizing tangible property assets of drug traffickers might have a deterrent effect on their criminal behavior.

All hypotheses are connected with some theoretical scheme that provides an explanatory and predictive framework for them. The theories from which hypotheses are

BOX 11.1   PERSONALITY HIGHLIGHT

RAY PATERNOSTER
University of Maryland

Statistics: B.A. (sociology), University of Delaware; M.A. (administration of justice), Southern Illinois University; Ph.D. (criminology), Florida State University.

BACKGROUND AND INTERESTS

My research interests over 25 years have been fairly consistent. I have been and continue to be interested in deriving hypotheses from criminological theory and empirically testing them. As an essential part of this process, I am interested in the application of quantitative statistical methods to criminological issues and questions. Currently, I am particularly interested in explaining criminal offending and cessation from offending over the life course, and the role of adolescent employment in delinquency. In a recent series of papers with some colleagues of mine, we found, contrary to years of research, that adolescents who work long hours while in high school (more than 20 hours of work per week) are not at greater risk of problem behaviors (e.g., delinquency, substance and alcohol abuse). This was surprising because for over 20 years there had been a consistent belief that working intensively during the school year was detrimental for youth. Through our work, we became convinced that this was not the case. Over the years I have also been consistently interested in the possibility that criminal conduct is rational behavior and is guided by principles of cost and benefit. In our field, deterrence theory and rational choice theory presume that human beings are influenced by the outcomes of their behavior. If this is true, then offenders and would-be offenders should be affected by their assessment or perception of the costs and benefits of offending. This rational calculation of costs and benefits, however, may be affected by more long-term dispositions of people, such as how impulsive they tend to be, and short-term factors, such as whether or not they are under the influence of alcohol or strong emotional states. Over the years I have been interested in examining the role of rationality in offenders' decision making.

I also have an interest in what is called procedural justice theory. The notion of procedural justice is that people are more likely to comply with rules if they are given fair treatment and are treated with dignity and respect by authorities. While it may be common sense to believe that people will be more likely to think favorably about and comply with authorities when the outcomes they receive are favorable (e.g., they don't get a ticket when they are caught speeding), it is less intuitively believable that both legitimacy and compliance can occur when one is treated fairly even if the outcome is unfavorable. Procedural justice theory hypothesizes

BOX 11.1   CONTINUED

that subjects will think authorities are more legitimate and more deserving of compliance when they are treated in a procedurally fair manner, even when they don't get the outcome they want. In one experiment we found that subjects who were randomly assigned a lawyer at a bail review hearing (a lawyer can tell the arrestee's side of the story to the judge, an important component of procedural justice) had a substantially more favorable perception of the bail process than those not provided with lawyers. Since this research involved a random experiment, we were fairly confident that the different perceptions of the bail process by those with versus those without lawyers was due to the presence of an attorney rather than some other factor.

In addition to my work in testing criminological theories, over the course of my career I have been interested in investigating issues pertaining to capital punishment. My interest in the death penalty came about almost by accident. I was an assistant professor at the University of South Carolina when a friend, who also happened to be one of the best capital defense lawyers in the state, asked me to get involved in a death penalty case. From this initial involvement, I conducted a very controversial investigation of the death penalty in that state. I found that the decision of the local prosecutor to seek a death sentence was substantially influenced by the race of the offender and the victim, and where in the state the crime had been committed. I also found that the state supreme court had completely abandoned its required duty to examine each death sentence for the influence of racial factors and proportionality. The South Carolina Supreme Court was virtually rubber-stamping the decisions at the trial court level, rather than conducting an independent review. More recently, I conducted a study of the imposition of capital punishment in Maryland where I now work. This study was commissioned by then-Governor Parris N. Glendening, who imposed a moratorium on all executions in the state until the completion of the study. This research also found that the decision to seek a death sentence and the decision to impose one was influenced by the race of both the defendant and the victim, as well as the jurisdiction where the crime had occurred. In fact, we found that the chance of a death sentence in one jurisdiction was over 20 times higher than in an adjacent jurisdiction! One could substantially increase their chances of getting sentenced to death, therefore, if they moved a few feet, crossed a county line, and committed capital murder. As in other parts of the country, the death penalty remains a very controversial topic in the state of Maryland.

ADVICE TO STUDENTS

I must confess that I didn't start out in college to become a criminologist or even a college professor. When I was an undergraduate student at the University of Delaware, I was academically lost. I thought I was an English/Political Science/Mathematics/Sociology major for most of my undergraduate "career," without the faintest clue about what I wanted to do with my life. I probably had more credits in more potential majors than any other Delaware student at the time, but I completely lacked any direction. When I was a junior, however, I took a criminology class that was offered by Professor Frank Scarpitti, one of the most eminent crime schol-

BOX 11.1   CONTINUED

ars in the country. His teaching and his class convinced me that I wanted to research crime, and that I wanted to teach at the college level. It was only late in my undergraduate days, therefore, that I discovered what I wanted to do, and only after sampling many possibilities. I have never regretted the decision to become a criminologist, study crime, and become a university professor.

My advice to any student would be the same. First, don't worry if you don't immediately have a career plan in mind. Keep your mind open to new learning experiences, and at least for the first few years of college, take courses in many different fields. What you like won't fall from the sky into your lap; you have to go out and look for it. Second, and most important, have a passion for whatever you do. Most people reserve passion for the bedroom only and sleep-walk their way through life. Life is meant to be attacked every day. Work hard when you are working, play hard when you are playing, and don't take any day or any moment for granted. Whatever you decide to become, make sure that you enjoy it—that you love your work, and that you wake up each morning with a feeling of excitement and enthusiasm.

derived may be loosely or tightly integrated or explicit in one's research. Hypotheses derived from them are similar to advance forecasts, since particular outcomes are anticipated or expected if those theories are true. The theory itself is designed to explain and predict how it came to be so that the hypotheses derived from it may be true.

Types of Hypotheses, Hypothesis Construction, and Hypothesis Sets

There are several different kinds of hypotheses used in criminological research. The primary types of hypotheses examined here are (1) research hypotheses, (2) null hypotheses, and (3) statistical hypotheses.

Research Hypotheses

Hypotheses that are derived from the researcher's theory are called either **research hypotheses** or **working hypotheses.** Social scientists believe that their research hypotheses are true, since they are derived logically from theoretical schemes constructed by these researchers. These hypotheses are believed true to the extent that the theories from which they were derived are true.

Because theories are, in a sense, suppositions about the true nature of things and thus considered tentative statements about reality until they have been verified to the scientist's satisfaction, the hypotheses derived from theory must also be regarded as tentative suppositions about things until they have been tested. Testing hypotheses means to subject them to some type of empirical confirmation or disconfirmation. For example, testing the hypotheses, "The average income expectation of boys in a poverty area is $1,000 per month as adults," might be done by entering a poverty area, obtaining a sample of male youths, and asking them questions about their monthly income expectation as adults. If most of the boys tell us that their income expectation is around $1,000 per month, then our hypothesis about their income expectation is confirmed, at least in this instance. If their reports are substantially more or less than $1,000, then our hypothesis is refuted, not confirmed, and not supported. It is important to know that hypothesis tests under any condition or in any situation, regardless of a study's magnitude or breadth, are not conclusive proof of the truthfulness of any hypothesis. Replication research is strongly advised, where one's research is repeated over and over under different settings with different samples, and in different geographical areas. If sufficient numbers of samples of boys continue to report income expectations of $1,000 as adults, then our hypothesis gradually becomes a factual statement. In time, there will be no further need to test it.

Null Hypotheses

In a sense, a **null hypothesis** is the reverse of a research hypothesis, although this is not entirely accurate. Null hypotheses are also statements about the reality of things, except that they serve to refute or deny whatever is explicitly stated in a given research hypothesis. To continue with our example above, if investigators state in their research hypothesis that the average income expectation of boys in a poverty area is $1,000 as adults, then the appropriate null hypothesis to accompany this research hypothesis is "The average income expectation of boys in a poverty area is not $1,000 as adults." If investigators subsequently find out that boys in a poverty area have income expectations considerably more (or less) than $1,000 as adults, then the null hypothesis can be rejected and the research hypothesis will be supported.

Another way of looking at research and null hypotheses is that both statements are directly contradictory of one another and cannot coexist as true. Therefore, if one of the statements is true, then the other statement must be false. If one of the statements is false, then the other statement must be true. If we show that the statement, "The average income expectation of boys in a poverty area is not $1,000 as adults" is false, then this statement can be rejected. Then we conclude that it must be true that "The average income expectation of boys in a poverty area is $1,000 as adults" is true and should be supported. Confirming one statement denies the other. Denying one statement confirms the other.

Null hypotheses are usually paired with specific research hypotheses into sets of hypotheses. These statements were listed earlier in this chapter and have been recreated below, with accompanying null hypotheses devised for each research hypothesis presented. Pay particular attention to the wording of both the research and null hypotheses in these various **hypothesis sets.**

Hypothesis set 1:

1. Research Hypothesis: Persons convicted of white-collar crimes come from upper socioeconomic classes.
1'. Null Hypothesis: Persons convicted of white-collar crimes come from all socioeconomic classes or from lower socioeconomic classes.

Hypothesis set 2:

2. Research Hypothesis: Blacks and Hispanics are more likely than whites to support reforms in policing.

2′. Null Hypothesis: Blacks and Hispanics are equally likely or less likely than whites to support reforms in policing.

Hypothesis set 3:

3. Research Hypothesis: Chronic truant juveniles processed through a community Truancy Center Intervention Program will have lower recidivism rates compared with chronic truant juvenile offenders who are formally processed through juvenile intake.

3′. Null Hypothesis: Chronic truant juveniles processed through a community Truancy Center Intervention Program will not differ in their recidivism rates compared with chronic truant juvenile offenders who are formally processed through juvenile intake; if there are differences in recidivism rates, chronic truant juveniles processed through a community Truancy Center Intervention Program will have higher recidivism rates compared with chronic truant juvenile offenders who are formally processed through juvenile intake.

Hypothesis set 4:

4. Research Hypothesis: Females of Asian descent are less likely than white females to report spousal assaults.

4′. Null Hypothesis: Females of Asian descent will not differ from white females in reporting spousal assaults; if females of Asian descent differ from whites, females of Asian descent will be more likely to report spousal assaults.

Hypothesis set 5:

5. Research Hypothesis: Convicted drug users processed by drug treatment courts will remain drug-free for longer periods compared with convicted drug users processed through traditional criminal courts.

5′. Null Hypothesis: Convicted drug users processed by drug treatment courts will remain drug-free for the same or shorter periods compared with convicted drug users processed through traditional criminal courts.

Hypothesis set 6:

6. Research Hypothesis: The District of Columbia Curfew Law will decrease the overall number of juvenile arrests.

6′. Null Hypothesis: The District of Columbia Curfew Law will either have no effect on or increase the number of juvenile arrests.

Hypothesis set 7:

7. Research Hypothesis: Membership in a gang will be associated with higher levels of delinquency compared with nongang membership.

7′. Null Hypothesis: Membership in a gang will not be associated with higher levels of delinquency compared with nongang membership; if there is a difference, gang members will have lower levels of delinquency compared with nongang members.

Hypothesis set 8:

8. Research Hypothesis: Reformed criminal offenders view their lives as the result of positive internal and stable events compared with active criminals who view their lives as the result of negative external and unstable events.

8′. Null Hypothesis: There is no difference between reformed criminal offenders and active criminals regarding how they view their lives as influenced by either positive or negative internal or external events; if there is a difference, reformed criminal offenders will view their lives as the result of negative external and unstable events while active criminals will view their lives as the result of positive internal and stable events.

Hypothesis set 9:

9. Research Hypothesis: Prison inmates who are denied visitation rights with their children will have greater numbers of misconduct reports compared with prisoners who are granted visitation rights with their children.

9′. Null Hypothesis: Prison inmates who are denied visitation rights with their children will not differ in their numbers of misconduct reports compared with prisoners who are granted visitation rights with their children; if they do differ, prison inmates denied visitation rights with their children will have fewer numbers of misconduct reports than inmates who are granted visitation rights with their children.

Hypothesis set 10:

10. Research Hypothesis: Parolees under the supervision of parole officers with caseloads of 50 or less will be more successful in their community transitions compared with parolees under the supervision of parole officers with caseloads greater than 50.

10′. Null Hypothesis: Parolees under the supervision of parole officers with caseloads of 50 or less will be equally successful in their community transitions compared with parolees under the supervision of parole officers with caseloads greater than 50; if there is a difference, parolees under the supervision of parole officers with caseloads of 50 or less will be less successful in their community transitions compared with parolees under the supervision of parole officers with caseloads greater than 50.

In each of the hypothesis sets above, the null hypothesis was constructed directly from the wording of the research hypothesis. Notice that if we refute any of the null hypotheses or show that they are not true under the existing circumstances of our research and the relevant information or data we have collected and analyzed, then the accompanying research hypothesis will be assumed true, at least under those specific test circumstances.

Why should we do all of this in the first place? After all, we have an adequate theory that has been constructed. We have derived various hypothesis statements from our theory logically and subjected these hypothesis statements to empirical testing. Why not just test these research hypotheses and not bother with formulating null hypotheses?

Before these questions are answered, we must first accept the fact that null hypotheses are strictly hypothetical models used to test research hypotheses indirectly. Thus, null hypotheses were never intended to exist, on their own, in reality. We make up null hypotheses directly from research hypotheses. Then, we test null hypotheses. As the result of our tests of null hypotheses, we make decisions about research hypotheses. Rejecting a specific null hypothesis, or throwing it out, or refuting it, or disconfirming it, means that we support the specific research hypothesis that was used originally for the formulation of a specific null hypothesis. If we fail to reject a null hypothesis, then we fail to support the specific research hypothesis from which that null hypothesis was created. We never accept or support or confirm null hypotheses, simply because they do not exist in reality. In effect, null hypotheses are artificially contrived statements derived from our research hypotheses. Their existence is based solely on the specific wording of research hypotheses, which were derived logically from the theories we constructed. The following relation is helpful in understanding what is meant by rejecting and failing to reject null hypotheses:

Our decision about the null hypothesis is: **Our decision about the research hypothesis is:**

"Reject It" ⟶ "Support It"

"Fail to Reject It" ⟶ "Fail to Support It"

Many students want to know, "Why do criminologists bother with null hypotheses anyway?" "Why don't they just test their research hypotheses directly and be content with that?" There are four reasons why null hypothesis models are used, most of which may not answer these questions to your satisfaction. These reasons are:

1. Because criminologists and other social scientists define their roles as being more detached and objective about phenomena compared with laymen, it would appear as though they were not behaving objectively if they sought to prove true those statements they believed to be true initially. Therefore, attempting to show the truthfulness of research hypotheses would imply some bias toward trying to confirm one's suppositions and possibly ignoring facts or findings that refute one's beliefs. Null hypotheses assist researchers, therefore, because such hypotheses are denials of what is believed to be true. If investigators are able to reject or refute null hypotheses, then their case for supporting their research hypotheses is strengthened as a result.

2. It seems easier to prove a statement false than to prove it true. There are those who contend that it is easier to find fault with something (i.e., an idea, belief, or hypothesis) than to look for facts or evidence that would support it. Whatever the merits of this argument, the null hypothesis is assumed to be true until proven otherwise.

3. It is conventional to use null hypotheses in criminological and criminal justice research. The key word here is *convention*. It is conventional in social research of any kind to use null hypotheses in conjunction with research hypotheses. Most social scientists use null hypotheses in their own research and in their articles published in professional journals.

4. Null hypotheses fit the probability model underlying hypothesis testing. This is the best of the four reasons. Under a probability theoretical model, hypotheses have a likelihood of being either true or false. The null hypothesis is an expression of one possible alternative outcome of our social observations. The probability model specifies that the null hypothesis may be either true or false, but not both simultaneously. Another **alternative hypothesis** about our social observations is the research hypothesis. Research hypotheses are grounded in and derived from theory. Research hypotheses also have a probability of either being true or false. Thus, the null hypothesis is a statement that may or may not be true, but it is subject to empirical verification or refutation. Neither the research hypothesis nor the null hypothesis is absolutely true or false for any given hypothesis test we conduct. There is always a probability that both types of hypotheses are true or false at the same time.

Statistical Hypotheses

A third type of hypothesis exists, which is known as a **statistical hypothesis.** Statistical hypotheses are statements about statistical populations that, on the basis of information obtained from observed data, one seeks to support or refute (Winer, 1962). Statistical populations refer either to people or things. It is generally the case when testing hypotheses that our observations about people or things are reduced in some way to numerical quantities and symbolic expressions. For instance, suppose we are concerned about age differences between two groups of persons. We hypothesize that one group is older than the other. In order to test our research hypothesis, which might be "Group 1 is older than group 2", we first create a null hypothesis, which becomes "Group 1 is the same age as or younger than group 2."

To subject these hypotheses to an empirical test, we would obtain age values for Groups 1 and 2, average the ages, and assess the average age difference by applying a statistical test of significance. In effect, we are transforming both our research and null hypotheses into statistical hypotheses so that they can be tested by numerical means.

A statistical hypothesis concerning the difference in average ages between Groups 1 and 2 can be represented symbolically. Below are both verbal and symbolic expressions of the above hypotheses:

Verbal expression:

Null Hypothesis: H_0: Group 1 is the same age as or younger than group 2.
Research Hypothesis: H_1: Group 1 is older than group 2.

Statistical expression:

Null Hypothesis: H_0: $\overline{X}_1 \leq \overline{X}_2$
Research Hypothesis: H_1: $\overline{X}_1 > \overline{X}_2$

where H_0 is the symbol for the null hypothesis and H_1 is the symbol for the research hypothesis;

$\overline{X}_1$ = (read "X bar sub one") is the mean or average age of group 1
$\overline{X}_2$ = (read "X bar sub two") is the mean or average age for group 2

The symbols ">" and "≤" mean "greater than" and "equal to or greater than."

In the examples above, H_0 denotes the null hypothesis, which says that the mean or average age of group 1 is equal to or less than the mean or average age of group 2. The research hypothesis, H_1, says that the average age of group 1 is greater than the average or mean age for group 2. Sometimes, the designations H_1 and H_2 are used to signify the null and research hypotheses. The notation systems or symbolic portrayals of such statistics such as the average or mean, and even research and null hypothesis designations, differ from one textbook to the next. Most textbooks use the H_0 and H_1 designation, however, and thus, this format is considered conventional.

Notice in the example above that the null hypothesis does not say simply that group 1 is younger than group 2. Rather, it says that group 1 is either younger or the same age as group 2. Think about which hypothesis would be supported if an investigator rejected a null hypothesis that said: Group 1 is younger than group 2. If this statement were not true, then it would be true that either group 1 is older than group 2 *or* that group 1 is the same age as group 2. In order to prevent this imprecision, the null hypothesis is carefully worded as follows: "Group 1 is the same age or younger than group 2." This is an "equal to or less than" type of arrangement between the two samples, and thus, the symbol ≤ (equal to or less than) is used. If this statement is rejected, the single remaining option is that "Group 1 is older than group 2," and the symbol ">" (greater than) would be used.

Two conventional symbol combinations used by criminologists and others are intended to illustrate direction and nondirection. Direction is intended to signify that one value is greater or less than another, whatever the values happen to be. Anytime the "greater than" (>) or "less than" (<) signs are used in any hypothesis set, it can be safely assumed that a **directional hypothesis test** is being made. That is, the researcher is interested in saying whether or not two or more values differ in specified directions. If the hypothesis set contains "equal to" (=) or "not equal to" (≠) signs, this means the hypothesis test is nondirectional. In this case, investigators are only interested in whether differences exist among observed values, not in whether they differ in any particular direction. Thus, in the hypothesis set above relating to the average ages of two groups, the hypothesis set was directional, since "greater than" (>) and "less than" (<) signs were used. A nondirectional hypothesis set is the following:

H_0: Group 1 is equal to group 2.
H_1: Group 1 is different from group 2.

Symbolically expressed, these hypotheses become:

$$H_0: \overline{X}_1 = \overline{X}_2$$
$$H_1: \overline{X}_1 \neq \overline{X}_2$$

Nondirectional hypothesis tests are also known as **two-tailed tests,** while a directional hypothesis test is designated as a **one-tailed test.** The tails refer to areas of sampling distributions of statistics. The subject of sampling distributions of statistics can be examined in greater detail in other works (Champion, 2000). Statistical hypotheses are usually established to indicate (1) differences between two or more groups regarding some trait or characteristic that they possess; (2) associations between two or more variables within one group or between several groups; and (3) point estimates of certain population characteristics such as average values.

Summarizing briefly, three classifications of hypotheses are important to us. These are research hypotheses, null hypotheses, and statistical hypotheses. As a result of theorizing, research hypotheses are derived. Null hypotheses are established conventionally in accordance with how various research hypotheses are stated. Null hypotheses are hypothetical models established so that research hypotheses may be tested indirectly. Numerical and symbolic expressions of research and null hypotheses are called statistical hypotheses. Statistical hypotheses are those ultimately subjected to some sort of empirical test. On the basis of one's observations and the test of statistical hypotheses, tentative conclusions are reached about null hypotheses, and ultimately, about research hypotheses. If certain null hypotheses are not refuted by evidence found by researchers, then the certain accompanying research hypotheses are not supported. However, if certain null hypotheses are rejected by evidence found by investigators, then certain accompanying research hypotheses are supported. Supporting any research hypothesis derived from some theory is considered partial support for that theory.

Hypotheses are composed of variables. Hypotheses may contain a single variable, two variables, or k or more than two variables. Hypotheses containing more than two variables are considered complex hypotheses and are more difficult to test. This is because the interrelatedness of more than two variables acting simultaneously is more difficult to assess quantitatively and theoretically. Table 11.1 shows the general relation between research, null, and statistical hypotheses.

Where Do Hypotheses Come From?

Scanning various professional journals will expose any student to a wide variety of studies, each with its array of hypotheses and theory. People often ask, "Where do those hypotheses come from?" Quite simply, hypotheses come from our thoughts about things. Hypotheses are generated in graduate student "bull sessions," conversations and discussions between students and faculty, from random observations and reflections about life as people go to and from work, and of course, they are deduced from theory. Because of the diverse circumstances under which hypotheses are formulated, it stands to reason that there will be a wide variation in the quality of hypotheses.

TABLE 11.1   Relation between Research, Null, and Statistical Hypotheses

H_1	H_0	H_1 and H_0
Research Hypothesis	Null Hypothesis	Statistical Hypothesis (Symbolically Expressed)
Two groups differ according to age.	Two groups do not differ regarding age.	$H_0: \overline{X}_1 = \overline{X}_2$ $H_1: \overline{X}_1 \neq \overline{X}_2$
↓	↓	↓
Derived from theory	Created from research hypothesis	If conclusion is to reject null hypothesis, research hypothesis is supported

BOX 11.2   PERSONALITY HIGHLIGHT

ROLAND CHILTON
University of Massachusetts–Amherst

Statistics: B.A. (philosophy), Monmouth College; M.S. (sociology), University of Wisconsin; Ph.D. (sociology), Indiana University.

BACKGROUND AND INTERESTS

Perhaps the best way to explain my interests is to describe my background. Born in Chicago in time for the Great Depression, I was educated in that city through the first 2 years of college. When I encountered Shaw and McKay and their maps in a criminology class at Monmouth College, I realized that I had grown up in a set of high school delinquency neighborhoods. This is why I usually explain my interest in criminology by saying, "I grew up on the west side of Chicago." However, it is closer to the truth to say that I drifted into criminology through an interest in social work that grew out of my contact with religiously oriented settlement house workers. They came into the city to save souls, but for some of us, they saved our lives instead. As I drifted along, I was greatly influenced by a set of criminologists and one great law professor.

At Wisconsin, Michael Hakeem's hard-nosed realism, Marshal Clinard's enthusiasm for teaching, and Robert McGinnis's insistence that data collection and analysis should be guided by ideas and research questions started me in the right direction. McGinnis also put me in touch with electronic data-processing machines, a development that tremendously expanded the kind of work I was able to do. Although all three of these men had an impact, I think that Jerome Hall, in Indiana's School of Law, and Karl Schuessler and Albert K. Cohen, in Indiana's Sociology Department, were major influences on the direction of my work. Most of what I have done was shaped by Karl Schuessler's insistence on careful empirical work. Al Cohen's fascination with theory, and Jerome Hall's view that the best criminology will be a fusion of theory, fact, and values. Alfred Lindesmith's lifelong interest in drug addiction, drug addicts, and the need for humane responses to this problem reinforced this realization that values are an essential component of any balanced study of crime.

RESEARCH INVESTIGATIONS

As a result of these influences, I can see myself as a "values-driven empiricist." Almost everything I have done involved the use of some kind of factual information. In most cases, the information is drawn from administrative records, such as the FBI's Age, Race, and Sex Arrest

BOX 11.2   CONTINUED

Data, and more recently, the FBI's National Incident-Based Reporting System (NIBRS). An early study used data culled from juvenile court records and the U.S. Census to examine the relationship of social class and juvenile delinquency in urban areas. This interest in replication and continuity has been another constant in my approach to crime. Other studies have focused on age structure and crime, gender and crime, and race and crime. Some of these studies looked at the impact of race- and gender-specific changes in the age structure on overall crime rates. Other studies looked at the extent to which increases in arrest rates of women have been influenced by arrests of black women. Another set of studies looked at the impact of the changing age and race composition on city crime rates. As a result of these studies and the work of many others, I am now convinced that race, class, and crime are linked in some obvious ways and that the impact of class and race has been amplified over the last 30 years by a set of harsh and inflexible drug laws. These are the issues I plan to explore in the next 5 to 10 years.

ADVICE FOR STUDENTS

Focus on facts but be especially skeptical of suggestions that a values-free criminology is possible or even desirable. Crime is defined by law and laws reflect values. Be equally skeptical of suggestions that a theory of crime in general is possible or sensible. What is called crime is too variable, too subject to the influences of fad and fashion in law to be explained by a single theory. Follow your interests but try not to be a slave to professional ideology or political correctness. If you enjoy puzzles and challenges and have any interest at all in trying to make the world a better place, there is no better work than in criminology.

Also, there is variety associated with the standards criminologists employ to determine whether hypotheses are good or bad, useful or not useful. It is possible, for example, for two different researchers working independently to derive similar hypotheses from a common theory, although they might word their hypotheses differently and/or they might select different circumstances under which to conduct their empirical tests. The evaluation of hypotheses is quite often a relative matter. What one social scientist might regard as a good hypothesis might be judged as bad by another social scientist. We don't want to convey the impression that social science advances purely on the whims and personal preferences of criminologists or criminal justice professionals. What is important to understand here is that there are flexibility and latitude that enable social investigators to design studies in unique ways and to give hypothesis wording their personal style. Furthermore, investigators may design their studies any way they wish and specify the empirical tests to be conducted in accordance with their personal and professional standards. Although personal standards of researchers vary, there are conventional guidelines followed by most investigators. And so despite the diversity in methodological inquiry, there is a high degree of uniformity regarding the application of certain methodological guidelines.

Hypothesis Formulation: Good, Better, and Best

The informative value of any particular hypothesis is dependent upon the circumstances of the theory from which it was derived. One way of evaluating hypotheses is in terms of the amount of information they specify about phenomena. Consider the example below of three statements, each stating a simple relationship between two variables, X and Y.

> Hypothesis A: X and Y are related.
> Hypothesis B: X is related to Y.
> Hypothesis C: As X increases, Y decreases.

Notice that for hypothesis A, a simple statement of relationship is provided. Nothing else is indicated about the relationship other than the fact that X and Y are associated. From the way this statement is worded, we know little or nothing about which variable, X or Y, has more of an impact on the other in a causal sense. Anyway, we are cautious about making statements of a causal nature, since causality is so difficult to establish in any type of social research. Clues about which variables tend to influence others may, of course, be found in the theoretical scheme. This explanatory framework shows linkages among variables and specifies how each relates with the others. However, examining statement A above gives us no clue as to which variable might be independent or dependent.

Statement B is more informative, "X is related to Y," since it mildly implies that Y influences values of X. If we wished to mildly imply that X influences Y, we might rephrase this hypothesis, "Y is related to X." Statement B is considered an improvement over statement A. Statement C, however, is the most informative of the three statements. This statement indicates that increasing values of X seem to elicit changes on the Y variable, namely, Y values decrease as X values increase.

Which of these hypotheses is best? Ordinarily, we might choose the most informative hypothesis, if specific direction of the relationship between the two variables is indicated. The objectives of one's research come into play here as well. If the research is primarily exploratory or descriptive, then statements A or B might be suitable, given our immediate lack of awareness of how X and Y are related with one another. However, if extensive investigations have been conducted of variables X and Y, then statement C would be best, since it is the most informative. Investigators would tend to select hypothesis statements such as statement C, since their research designs would be more experimental in nature.

Functions of Hypotheses

Theories are relatively elaborate tools we use to explain and predict events. Social scientists develop theories to account for social and psychological phenomena, and then they devise a means whereby these theories can be tested and subjected to verification or refutation. Seldom do researchers actually test their entire theories directly. Most of the time, they conduct tests of specific hypotheses derived from theory. These hypotheses pertain to different parts of the theory, and if they test out and are supported by the evidence researchers find, then their theories are supported in part.

Usually, it takes many tests of different hypotheses derived from the theory in order to adequately test it and determine its predictive value and its adequacy as a tool of explanation for events. One major function of hypotheses, therefore, is to make it possible to test theories. In this regard, an alternative definition of a hypothesis is a statement of theory in testable form. All statements of theory in testable form are called hypotheses.

Sometimes, certain hypotheses are not associated with any particular theory. It could be that as a result of some hypothesis, a theory eventually will be devised or constructed. Consequently, another function of hypotheses is to suggest theories that may account for some event. Although it is more commonplace that research proceeds from theories to hypotheses, occasionally the reverse is true. Social investigators may have some idea about why a given phenomenon occurs, and they hypothesize several things that relate to it. They judge that some hypotheses have greater potential explanatory value than others, and as a result, they may construct a logical system of propositions, assumptions, and definitions linking their explanation of the event to the event itself. In other words, they create a theory. Working from hypotheses back to some theory is not necessarily poor methodology. Eventually, investigators are going to have to subject their resulting theory to empirical testing anyway to determine its accuracy. The predictive value of the theory may be evaluated at that time.

Single-Variable, Two-Variable, and *K*-Variable Hypotheses

Hypotheses are distinguished according to whether they contain single variables, two variables, or *k* variables.

Single-Variable Hypotheses

Single-variable hypotheses are often known as **point estimate hypotheses.** Researchers are interested in forecasting certain values associated with populations of elements. This is known as **point estimation.** They might predict various population values, such as the average age of some population. This predicted average age is known as a **point estimate.** Subsequently, they might obtain a sample of persons from that population and make a comparison of their sample mean with the hypothesized population mean. These are single-variable hypotheses, since the only variable is the predicted mean value for the population. An example of a single-variable hypothesis might be,

The average age of the inmate population of prisons is increasing.

Two-Variable Hypotheses

If we add a second variable and construct new statements, we will have two-variable hypotheses. All of the 10 hypotheses presented earlier in this chapter are examples of **two-variable hypotheses.** If we wanted to make a two-variable hypothesis out of the one-variable hypothesis above, we might differentiate inmates according to whether they are in prisons or jails. Our new two-variable hypothesis might be:

The average age of jail inmates is decreasing, while the average age of prison inmates is increasing.

Another way of phrasing this is:

Jail inmates tend to be younger than prison inmates, or
The average age of jail inmates is less than the average age of prison inmates.

However, these last two statements are not exactly equivalent with the first statement. The first statement indicates a "trend" in inmate age—upward for prison inmates and downward for jail inmates. But the last two statements merely indicate average age differences between prison and jail inmates, not trends over time.

K-Variable Hypotheses

When we construct hypotheses with three or more variables, these are designated as **k-variable hypotheses.** The letter, *k,* technically means "two or more." In this book, however, we will use *k* to mean "three or more," since there are so many specific statistical tests for *two* samples and measures of association for *two* variables. Distinctions are subsequently made, therefore, between two- and *k*-sample tests and between two-variable and *k*-variable hypotheses. In the general case, *k*-variable hypotheses are very difficult to test. For example, we might have the following *k*-variable hypothesis:

Correctional officer job effectiveness varies according to one's job satisfaction, which varies inversely with the closeness of supervision officers receive from their correctional officer supervisors.

This hypothesis is difficult to test for several reasons. First, we may find that job effectiveness and job satisfaction may be related as we have predicted. However, it may be that the type of supervision may have nothing to do with job satisfaction or with job effectiveness. To solve the problem of testing this hypothesis, it is recommended that this hypothesis should be broken down into two separate hypotheses, where each can be tested independently. These two hypotheses would be:

Correctional officer job effectiveness and job satisfaction are related.

Correctional officer job satisfaction varies inversely with the closeness of supervision received from correctional officer supervisors.

If a third hypothesis is desirable linking job effectiveness with closeness of supervision, we can state:

Correctional officer job effectiveness varies inversely with the closeness of supervision received from correctional officer supervisors.

Hypothesis Testing

When we engage in **hypothesis testing,** this means that we subject them to some kind of empirical scrutiny to determine if they are supported or refuted by collected evidence. If we are testing hypotheses about delinquents, we usually will need to go out and study a sample of delinquents to collect evidence relative to our hypotheses about them. If we are studying correctional officers or probationers, we will need to obtain samples of correctional officers from a prison or prisons or probationers from one or more probation programs.

Actually, testing hypotheses involves several tasks. These are listed below:

1. A real social situation is needed that will provide a reasonable testing ground for the hypotheses. Testing grounds are actual social settings where data exist pertaining to the hypotheses to be tested. These "grounds" may be probation agencies, jails, community corrections agencies, city or county courts, or any other location containing people with information we need to test our hypotheses.

2. Investigators must make sure that their hypotheses are testable. This means that only empirical phenomena should be selected for study. It makes no sense to ask questions that cannot be answered with our present instrumentation. Hypotheses containing variables that cannot be measured are also not amenable to empirical testing. For example, if we hypothesize that "evil spirits cause delinquency," this statement is incapable of being refuted. It cannot be supported either, but it cannot be refuted. This and similar statements are outside of the realm of scientific inquiry, because one or more variables are simply not amenable to empirical measurement.

For instance, in 1947, Hans Von Hentig wrote about western outlaws and observed that some of them had red hair. Von Hentig presented some spectacular observations about red hair and law-breaking behavior to a convention of psychologists, and he claimed to identify an internal motivator that, he said, precipitated abnormal and even criminal behavior. This phenomenon, he said, was "accelerated motor innervation," some mystical central nervous system phenomenon that seemed closely associated with red body hair. However, Von Hentig never outlined clearly how accelerated motor innervation could be measured or taken into account by other scientists. Thus, there was no way to refute Von Hentig's claims.

Many social scientists regarded Von Hentig's research as far-fetched, and some even suggested that his work might even aggravate the unfavorable stereotype of the "hot-tempered redhead." Von Hentig's work clearly rested outside the realm of scientific inquiry. This does not mean that we can never discover ways of measuring accelerated motor innervation empirically. For the time being, however, we must reject his explanation, since it lies outside of the realm of **empiricism.** The lesson to be learned here is to confine theorizing to only those phenomena that can be taken into account empirically.

3. Investigators should devise and use measures of the phenomena of interest so that these phenomena may be quantified easily. Each variable must be operationalized in order that objective, numerical assessments may be made of the hypothesis's worth. An assortment of statistical tests exists for hypothesis-testing purposes.

Interpreting the Results of Hypothesis Tests

Whenever hypotheses in one's research are tested, it is usually the case that several hypotheses are either confirmed or refuted rather than single-hypothesis tests. There is no fixed number of hypotheses that researchers must test, since different theories vary in their detail and sophistication. Some theories are more elaborate and yield more testable hypotheses than other, less elaborate theories. An extreme might include tests of 100 or more hypotheses in a single study. More often, however, are hypothesis test situations involving 10 or fewer hypotheses. Again, there are no conventional rules about how many hypotheses we should test.

BOX 11.3   PERSONALITY HIGHLIGHT

RICHARD HARTLEY
University of Nebraska–Omaha

Statistics: B.S., M.S. (criminal justice), Minot State University; Ph.D. (criminal justice), University of Nebraska–Omaha.

BACKGROUND AND INTERESTS

My research interests include prosecutorial and judicial discretion, disparities in sentencing practices, sentencing for narcotics violations, guideline sentencing, and departures under a guideline sentencing scheme. I am currently working on my doctoral dissertation, which assesses the effect of attorney type (public defenders vs. privately retained attorneys) across eight criminal justice outcomes.

Most of my research endeavors have been spurred by the amount of readily available data sets that are accessible online and especially through the Inter-university Consortium for Political and Social Research (ICPSR) at the University of Michigan website (*www.icpsr.umich.edu*). As such, my research consists mostly of secondary analysis because I utilize already existing data that has been collected by others. My research is also empirical in nature, and looks at what variables are predictors of criminal justice outcomes. Using appropriate control variables can help us uncover any disparities that may be present in the criminal justice system, especially regarding demographic variables such as age, gender, or race. These ICPSR data sets are easily downloadable in SPSS or SAS format, and the research possibilities and studies that can be undertaken are virtually endless.

BOX 11.3   CONTINUED

I became interested in academia and conducting research in criminal justice because of a research project I worked on while I was getting my master's degree. I was a graduate research assistant on the Rural Law Enforcement Education Project, which focused on bringing in federal experts to train rural law enforcement officers in various topics from traffic stops to gathering quality evidence and building better cases to methods in detecting different types of narcotics. After the officers went back to their departments, the research team conducted follow-up interviews to see whether or not the officers had utilized any of the training they had received. The results were very positive and the officers relayed how much better they were able to do their jobs because of the training. They also informed us of areas in which the training could be improved and also topics on which they would like to see further training. We would then adjust the training sessions appropriately. I remember the feeling I got when I realized that collecting this type of information and maintaining databases on it could actually help numerous persons in their day-to-day jobs. After that I realized the broader purpose of research. I was hooked. Research is not only a way to explore answers to questions that we have a personal interest in, or a way to further our discipline, but also a way to disseminate the findings of that research to spur further research and to help practitioners make decisions that have implications for policies that will affect people in their day-to-day lives. I believe the hope that we as researchers can somehow influence decisions that will make society a better place keeps us inspired to do what we do.

I have also had the opportunity to teach several courses from Survey of Criminal Justice to Criminal Courts to Research Methods at both a traditional university campus and a city university campus. Teaching is also something I find very important and rewarding. It is important to impart new knowledge to students and to shed preconceived notions about the criminal justice system they may have picked up from the media. But it is also important that I as an instructor can learn from students as well. What they expect from me as an instructor, which techniques work in the classroom, and ultimately how I can become a better teacher.

ADVICE TO STUDENTS

First of all, nothing is unattainable if you are willing to put in the time and effort. Second, never stop asking questions, there are no stupid questions. A professor I had always told me . . . the only stupid question is the one asked after the exam. Lastly, if students are seriously considering academia and conducting research, it would be wise to begin boning up on both statistics and research methods. Also, pay particular attention to the Wheel of Science as first proposed by Walter Wallace. All research whether practical or theoretical should follow some version of this as a template.

In order to illustrate how we might judge the results of hypothesis tests in the general case, let's assume that we are testing 10 hypotheses from a given theory in our research project. We have constructed a theory to explain relationships between certain variables, we have collected relevant data, and on the basis of our analysis of that data, we have tentatively concluded certain things about our findings. Since hypotheses are predictions of what we believe will be found, based on the validity of our previous theorizing about phenomena, either some or all of our hypotheses may test out and be supported, or some or all may not test out and be refuted.

Three possible outcomes or scenarios might be anticipated:

1. All of our hypotheses tested are supported by whatever we find.
2. None of the hypotheses we are testing are supported by whatever we find.
3. Some of the hypotheses we are testing are supported by our findings, while the remaining hypotheses are not supported.

Neophyte researchers will probably make the following interpretations of these outcomes:

Outcome #1: If all hypotheses being tested are supported, it might be assumed that the theory from which the hypotheses were derived is also supported.

Outcome #2: If none of the hypotheses tested are supported, it might be assumed that the theory from which these hypotheses were derived is refuted, or at least, not supported.

Outcome #3: The most perplexing outcome, partial support of the theory through supporting some hypotheses and refuting others, might be interpreted as "faulty theorizing." Perhaps our theory is faulty in certain respects, particularly those respects relevant to those research hypotheses that were refuted rather than supported.

We must be careful not to attach too much significance to any outcome of a hypothesis test. After all, we are testing our hypotheses, using various samples of elements that may or may not be representative of the general population about which we seek information. A few researchers blindly claim that their theories are valid, proved, or true if all of their hypotheses are supported. Other researchers are very dejected and negative, thus proclaiming that their theories are not true if the hypotheses they have tested are all refuted. Neither of these particular conclusions is warranted. This is because there are so many factors that influence hypothesis test outcomes. The adequacy of one's theory is only one factor. We may have a perfectly good theory but poor methodology. We may have perfectly good theory, perfectly good methodology, but a poor, unrepresentative sample. We may have perfectly good theory, perfectly good methodology, and a perfectly good sample, but poor instrumentation and measures of our phenomena studied. We may choose the wrong statistical tests to apply when analyzing our data. We may apply interpretive standards that are too rigorous. Suffice it to say that we may unintentionally commit any number of errors or experience any number of problems in the course of implementing our research plans. Generally, all of the threats to both a study's internal and external validity may affect anyone's research results under any given set of circumstances.

If someone examines various professional journals and inspects the contents of different articles, he or she will find that often, the authors of those articles have incorporated various safeguards into their studies. These warnings are similar to products liability statements, where manufacturers want consumers to know, in advance, whether their products contain substances that have been known to produce adverse side effects, whether some assembly is required, or whether there are sharp edges that might be harmful to children. Products' liability-type statements in criminological research warn "consumers" or readers about a study's flaws. Some common phrases are, "These findings should be cautiously viewed," "Further study is recommended," or "Some suggestions for future research include . . ." Specific drawbacks of the research or study limitations are cited, such as "The sample analyzed in the present study consisted of only 35 percent of the original 500 persons randomly selected. Thus, there is a question about how reliable the sample is in relation to its parent population." Or, "Evidence was disclosed to indicate that our measures lacked reliability. Further research is needed where more precise indicators of these phenomena can be constructed and applied." These writers are calling our attention to one or more faults or limitations of their studies. This is both acceptable and recommended, since no study is perfect.

The point is that we should not attach too much importance to any specific study, regardless of its magnitude. It is best to interpret research findings conservatively in a more general context. Thus, how do these study results compare with the findings of other similar studies? Considering several studies of the same topic, how does any new study support, refute, or modify what is generally believed about the phenomena under investigation? Regardless of the outcome of any given test of hypotheses (i.e., outcomes #1, #2, and #3 above), therefore, researchers should always raise questions about each of the following problem areas: theory, sampling, measurement, data collection, statistics, and participant involvement. Raising such questions will enable researchers to:

1. Improve the quality and meaning of the interpretation of any hypothesis test;
2. Evaluate the relative importance of a given hypothesis test for theory-building;
3. Determine the degree to which the study supports the work of others;
4. Determine the reliability of the explanation of events that are either explicitly or implicitly stated by the hypotheses.

Theoretical Considerations

Judging the results of one's hypothesis tests involves evaluating the adequacy of the theory from which the hypotheses were derived. Was the theory coherent, logical, and meaningful, and did it include measurable phenomena? Was it too broad or too narrow? Was the theory comprehensive enough to take into account certain intervening variables, but narrow enough to be fruitful as a predictive tool? Was the theorizing consistent with what has been found in the research literature on the subject? Were the hypotheses formulated correctly and did they contain variables that were included in the theory?

Sampling Considerations

How representative was the sample of the population from which it was drawn? How large was the sample? How many of the respondents from the original sample drawn were available at the time of the study? If questionnaires were mailed to respondents, how much nonresponse occurred? What importance would such nonresponse have on the hypothesis test outcomes, if any? Was the sample adequately selected? Did sample elements posses the necessary information relative to the hypothesis tests and theoretical questions?

BOX 11.4   PERSONALITY HIGHLIGHT

KAREN HEIMER
University of Iowa

Statistics: B.A. (psychology), Florida Atlantic University;
M.A. (psychology), Ph.D. (sociology), University of
Wisconsin–Madison.

BACKGROUND AND INTERESTS

I have been fascinated by social deviance, crime, and social control as far back as I can re-member. As a child, I recall becoming upset when some children were labeled "deviant" and picked on by more powerful peers. The injustice of these situations bothered me so much that I often tried to intervene in instances of bullying on the way home from school. (One of my brothers was often a target in these situations, so sometimes intervening was simply part of my "job" as the big sister.) During my teenage years, I became curious about how rules and laws are constructed and violators punished, and how injustice creeps into official or institutional re-sponses to deviance. Maybe this fascination with rule/law violations and injustice developed because I grew up just outside a very large city during a time of high crime and social unrest. Maybe it developed because I had family and friends who got into "trouble" with the law or were themselves victimized. Whatever the source, I always have had a passion for under-standing crime and social control, and a strong reaction to injustice.

In college, I eventually settled on psychology as a major, mainly because I was intrigued by my social psychology classes that addressed deviance, norm violation, and aggression. After fin-ishing college, I worked for a time in the juvenile justice system in an urban area in Florida and then in a psychiatric institution. These work experiences further heightened my interest in crime and deviance, and gave me a new interest, social control institutions. This, together with urging from my former undergraduate advisor, led me to think about graduate school. As I was finishing my master's degree in psychology at Wisconsin, studying human aggression in the laboratory, I took a couple of criminology courses in the sociology department. I soon knew that this was the field for me. So, I entered the Ph.D. program in sociology, with a specialization in criminology.

RESEARCH INVESTIGATIONS

Generally speaking, my research interests center on the impact of gender, race, and social class on criminal offending and imprisonment. More specifically, my research has taken three path-ways. The first focuses on better understanding gender, race, and class differences in delin-

BOX 11.4 CONTINUED

quency. Here I have conducted statistical analyses of existing self-report survey data, using the National Youth Survey, Monitoring the Future Survey, and, most recently, the National Longitudinal Survey of Adolescent Health. In these studies, I have been particularly concerned with how social structural positions (gender, race, and class) influence social psychological processes (e.g. cognition, relationships with families and peers), which in turn influence the chances of offending. Most of my research in this area has been rooted in culture conflict theories, especially differential association and interactionist theories.

I have a special interest in gender differences in offending. A couple of years ago, I started to feel that I could not pursue my interests in gender and crime fully enough by continuing to rely only on existing self-report data. So, I embarked on a second research pathway, focused on the potential association between changes over time in women's offending and the feminization of poverty. I compiled data on the gender ratios (or gender difference) in arrests for the 100 largest U.S. cities, since 1960, and then linked these data with various measures of the socioeconomic well-being of women (as compared to men). We currently are using the data to examine whether the feminization of poverty and changes in welfare policies are associated with changes in the gender ratio of offending. This new line of work has required becoming familiar with data sources and data analytic techniques with which I previously had only passing familiarity. It has been time-consuming, but I have learned a great deal. And, the opportunity to approach questions from different perspectives using new techniques is one of my favorite things about being a social science researcher.

In a third line of research, I am studying economic and political factors that are associated with changes in imprisonment in the United States, over time and across regions. Working in a couple of "total institutions" as a young adult stimulated an interest in imprisonment, especially with regard to issues of inequality; this was an interest that I never lost. Recently, I have been able to incorporate this interest into my research. I am collaborating on these studies with Thomas Stucky and Halime Unal, former students with whom I worked. In this line of research, we are especially interested in gender and race differences in imprisonment. Our analyses show that gender and race differences in criminal offending cannot explain patterns of imprisonment over time and space. Thus, we are examining whether variables capturing political processes, the economic marginalization of women, and racial threat contribute to our understanding of imprisonment patterns in the United States.

ADVICE TO STUDENTS

When students ask me what I think is the key to success in criminological research, I answer, simply, "passion and hard work." I firmly believe that these are the two essential ingredients for success at anything in life, including criminological research. This means that finding a research question (or set of questions) that excites *you* is key. Then, honing theoretical and

BOX 11.4   CONTINUED

methodological skills to answer these questions is critical. This takes persistence and hard work, of course, but contributing to knowledge on a topic that excites you makes all the hard work worthwhile. Finally, I think that it is important to consider our research questions from a variety of perspectives—theoretical and methodological. Being open to learning different viewpoints and methodological approaches can only enrich our understanding of crime and justice and make us all better scholars.

Measurement Considerations

Were the measures used valid and reliable? What tests were conducted by the investigators to demonstrate the reliability and validity of the measures and other instrumentation? How closely connected were the operational definitions of terms to the nominal definitions devised in the theory? Were measures of particular variables used from previous research, or were new scales devised? What steps were taken to determine the validity and reliability of our prior or newly developed attitudinal measures, given the present sample where these measures have been applied?

Data Collection Procedures as a Consideration

Were the data collection procedures necessarily the best ones to use, given the problem investigated? Would other data collection methods have yielded more fruitful results? If secondary sources were used, how reliable were those secondary sources? Was any triangulation employed by investigators to improve their data accuracy and validity?

Statistical Considerations

Were appropriate statistical tests selected for data description and analysis, given the quality and randomness of the sample obtained? Was the level of significance appropriate, given the sample size and generalizability desired? Were all statistical assumptions satisfied so that the meaning of the measures applied was maximized?

Participant Observation as a Consideration

Were respondents coerced into participating in the study or was their involvement voluntary? What degree of anonymity was provided by researchers to enhance response objectivity? Was there anything unusual about how respondents were questioned, observed, or otherwise studied that might interfere with our appraisal of the findings?

These are just some of the issues that are raised during the process of hypothesis testing in any research enterprise. Other issues may arise, depending on the extensiveness or restricted nature of the research project.

S U M M A R Y

Hypotheses are testable statements that are derived from theories. Varying in their complexity and tentativeness, hypotheses describe relationships between variables and predict various social and psychological outcomes. Hypotheses are capable of being refuted or rejected, making inferences about population values, specifying differences between two or more samples, and depicting variable interrelationships. Good theories are those that yield numerous hypotheses to test. It is unlikely that any specific hypothesis test will suffice as a test of the general theory itself, but rather, each hypothesis will likely test a portion of the theoretical scheme. Through repeated testing, hypotheses can eventually assist us in assessing the adequacy of a theory in relation to a problem or event we wish to explain.

There are no restrictions on what may be hypothesized. Virtually an unlimited number of hypothesis statements may be derived from theories to be tested. The research process includes various methods whereby relevant information can be used in different hypothesis tests. Eventually sufficient information is compiled through replication research and repeated study so that our certainty about events is increased.

Several different kinds of hypotheses exist. Hypotheses are most often derived directly from the theories we have formulated. Hypotheses that are derived from our theories are called research hypotheses or working hypotheses. Because of convention and other factors, investigators formulate alternative hypotheses to test in their research activities. These hypotheses are derived from research hypotheses and essentially refute them. These are called null hypotheses. As the result of tests of null hypotheses, research hypotheses are either supported or refuted.

Null hypotheses are frequently used in social research because it is conventional to use them; because it may seem easier to prove something false than true; because null hypotheses suggest greater objectivity; and because these types of hypotheses fit the probability model used by social investigators and science generally. Both research and null hypotheses can usually be expressed symbolically. These symbolic expressions of research and null hypotheses are called statistical hypotheses. Sometimes research and null hypotheses are provided in research as hypothesis sets. Usually, however, researchers may present the hypotheses they are testing in less direct ways. Published research articles may include the hypotheses being tested in a general discussion of what the investigator believes or is attempting to do.

The origins of hypotheses are diverse. Hypotheses are formulated from reading what others have written in the research literature. Or some hypotheses can be devised from one's own particular experiences. Depending on the hypotheses to be tested, different social settings must be chosen and accessed. Testing hypotheses almost always involves a real social situation and/or investigating empirical phenomena that can be measured or quantified.

Hypotheses vary in the degree of information they provide about relations between variables. Less descriptive hypotheses are associated with exploratory and descriptive research, while more descriptive hypotheses are associated with experimental research. Therefore, hypotheses may state simple relationships between variables where the wording makes it difficult if not impossible to understand which variable is independent or dependent. Other hypotheses may be stated in a way so that the independent or dependent use of the variable can be determined. The most informative hypotheses specify that as an independent variable changes in one direction, a dependent variable will change in the same or opposite direction, and to varying degrees. If readers want to know how particular variables are used in one's research, usually the theoretical scheme will disclose how these variables are being treated.

Several important functions are performed by hypotheses. Hypotheses test theories, suggest theories, and describe social phenomena. Also, they may contain single variables and act as hypotheses of point estimation, or they may contain two or more variables. Those hypotheses containing three or more variables are considered complex and difficult to test.

The process of hypothesis testing involves several tasks. First, a social situation is required where valuable information exists that is relevant to the hypothesis being tested. Second, the hypotheses must be testable or capable of being refuted. Some hypotheses contain variables for which there are no measures, or where developing measures for these variables would be extremely difficult. Hypotheses must be capable of being refuted, and this means that they must be empirical. Therefore, measures of phenomena of interest to researchers should be devised that are consistent with scientific inquiry. Outcomes of hypothesis tests depend on many factors, including theory adequacy, representativeness of the sample, type of respondent involvement, the validity and reliability of measuring instruments, and statistical sophistication. Data collection procedures also influence the quality of data obtained as well as hypothesis test results. Subsequent investigations of the same or similar phenomena are ordinarily recommended, since single studies rarely are conclusive about variable interrelationships.

QUESTIONS FOR REVIEW

1. What are hypotheses? How are hypotheses used in social research?

2. What are some major functions of hypotheses?

3. What are three different kinds of hypotheses? What is an hypothesis set? What are three examples of hypotheses different from the book and selected from your inspection of the research literature?

4. What is the relationship between hypotheses and theory?

5. Where do hypotheses come from?

6. What is the basic rationale for using null hypotheses instead of testing research hypotheses directly?

7. Does any particular study stand as the definitive work in any given subject area? Why or why not?

8. How should research hypotheses be interpreted if:
   a. particular null hypotheses are rejected?
   b. particular null hypotheses are not rejected?

Why don't we "accept" null hypotheses?

9. What are three kinds of statistical hypotheses? What are some examples?

10. Using X and Y as two variables, what are three different kinds of relationships between X and Y that reflect three different degrees of knowledge about their relation?

11. Below are several research hypotheses. What are the null hypotheses that we might formulate for each?
   a. The mean for group 1 equals or exceeds 20.
   b. Two groups of juvenile probation officers differ in their average professionalism.
   c. Police officers have higher job satisfaction compared with sheriff's officers.
   d. Rates of violence are the same between jail inmates and prison inmates.
   e. There is a positive relation between variables X and Y.

12. What are three complex hypotheses, where more than two variables of your choice are related? Compared with either one-variable or two-variable hypotheses, why are k-variable hypotheses more difficult to test?

13. What are some major considerations that must be made regarding outcomes of hypothesis tests?

12 Ethics in Research

CHAPTER OUTLINE

CHAPTER OBJECTIVES

As the result of reading this chapter, the following objectives will be realized:

1. Defining ethics and how codes of ethical conduct are formulated by groups and organizations.
2. Distinguishing between ethical dilemmas encountered in social research and the ethical issues emerging in professional organizations.
3. Understanding the relation between ethics and social responsibility.
4. Delineating several important ethical problems in social research, including plagiarism, fraudulent research, unethical statistical data manipulation, and conducting research that is potentially harmful to human subjects.
5. Learning about the practice of deception or deceiving research subjects.
6. Understanding some of the problems of accessing confidential or privileged information.
7. Learning about the Nuremberg Code and the importance of informed consent as a prerequisite to involving human subjects in research projects.
8. Understanding several ethical issues relating to research sponsorship, the rights of human subjects, and how gathered information will be used.

Introduction

This chapter is about ethics in the research process. First, ethics is defined and ethical practices in research are distinguished from ethical dilemmas in criminal justice organizations. Whenever human subjects are involved in one's research, ethical issues inevitably arise. These issues often pertain to how information about persons is gathered, how such information will be used, and whether the data-gathering process itself is potentially harmful to those from whom information is gathered. Ethical issues also emerge as organizational concerns. Often such concerns pertain to ethical practices related to one's work with others. Many service organizations that deal with the public in different ways, such as legal aid clinics, psychiatric and social services, and child protective services, articulate ethical codes or codes of professional responsibility by which the memberships of these organizations agree to be governed. These ethical codes will be examined. There is a close relationship between ethics and social responsibility. This relationship will be described and discussed.

Criminological research cuts across all areas of both the criminal and juvenile justice systems. A wide variety of persons is involved in different types of social investigations, including employees, clients, or inmates. Gathering information from these different populations is sometimes made difficult because of inaccessibility or organizational reluctance to external scrutiny by outside researchers. Even where information about these persons is obtained easily, questions may arise about how that information will eventually be used. Some of these questions will be examined.

Several types of ethical problems in the research process are highlighted, including the production of fraudulent research; engaging in research that might harm human subjects; deceiving respondents in various ways; accessing and studying confidential records and information; studying sex offenders; and gaining access to subordinates, potentates, and juveniles. The Nuremberg Code is presented and discussed. The ethical codes of conduct of different professional associations are described, including the evolution of ethical research standards and university guidelines for projects that involve human subjects.

The last section of this chapter examines selected ethical issues, including sponsored research and investigator interests; informed consent and the use of personal information, including victims, arrestees, defendants, and prisoners; fraudulent research; objectivity and research; ethics and public policy; and ethics and evaluation research. The chapter concludes with a consideration of alternative remedies for ethical violations.

Ethics Defined

Ethics are the standards of professional groups or organizations, the normative behaviors of right and wrong. Ethics involve the prescription of a moral **code of conduct** that is normatively binding on the members of a professional group or organization. It is implicit that by accepting membership in an organization, a member agrees to abide by the ethical standards of the organization. Violating one or more ethical standards is not necessarily illegal, although other members of the organization would define **unethical conduct** as immoral and improper. Various sanctions, including exclusion from the group or organization, are applied whenever ethical standards or the code of conduct is violated in any way. For instance, the Academy of Criminal Justice Sciences (2004) states that "violations of the[ir] **Code of**

Ethics may lead to sanctions associated with membership in the Academy of Criminal Justice Sciences, including restrictions on or termination of that membership."

Ethical Practices in Criminal Justice Organizations Distinguished From Ethical Dilemmas in Research

The focus of this chapter is on the array of ethical practices of researchers who identify potential research topics and conduct investigations. There are many situations that occur which involve different types of unethical behavior committed by persons conducting research. There are existing ethical standards that apply to research conducted by members of different professional organizations, such as the Academy of Criminal Justice Sciences and the American Society of Criminology. Fairly clear guidelines exist for all investigators to follow. Both acceptable and unacceptable conduct is outlined.

Ethics and ethical issues involved in the research process are substantively different from the ethics and ethical issues of law enforcement organizations, the courts, and corrections. In law enforcement organizations, for example, there are codes of professional responsibility. If some police officers engage in misconduct, such as roughing up suspects during routine arrests, these incidents should be reported. When such incidents are observed by other officers and not reported, this is a violation of one of their ethical standards or codes. Officers should testify truthfully on the witness stand in any criminal case. When one or more officers lie on the witness stand, they not only commit perjury, but they also violate one of their ethical codes of conduct (Frank et al., 1995; Prenzler, 1994).

Defense attorneys as well as prosecutors are expected to abide by American Bar Association (ABA) codes of professional responsibility. Defense attorneys are obligated to uphold the **confidentiality** between themselves and their clients. Any conflicts of interest involving any attorney or court officers are prohibited by certain ABA codes of conduct. If a defense attorney discusses a case with others and discloses confidential information about his or her client, this is considered unethical and a violation of ABA standards (Elliston & van Schaick, 1984). If a prosecutor has reason to believe that a defendant is innocent and has exculpatory information but decides not to disclose it and persists in the criminal prosecution, this behavior is considered unethical and inconsistent with ABA standards. If the prosecutor asks a prospective prosecution witness to give misleading testimony against a criminal defendant, testimony that will tend to incriminate the defendant, this practice may not be illegal but it is considered immoral and inconsistent with the canons of professional responsibility outlined by the ABA (Anderson & Winfree, 1987; Brannigan, Levy, & Wilkins, 1985). If a judge in a criminal case has a relative (e.g., uncle, brother, son, cousin) on the jury and does not disclose this relationship to all parties, this conduct is considered improper. Judges are expected either to dismiss these jurors or recuse themselves from the case. If they don't, then they are violating the ethics of their profession. They may also be violating the law.

In corrections settings, if prison administrators hire their relatives or close friends to perform correctional officer functions or lower-level administrative tasks, such nepotism, though not necessarily illegal, is probably unethical and/or immoral. If jail or prison correctional officers ask certain prisoners to snitch on other prisoners concerning institutional rule violations, or if these officers smuggle contraband to certain prisoners and overlook rule violations, such conduct is often a violation of their code of professional responsibility as outlined by the American Correctional Association (1993).

Whether we are discussing law enforcement, the courts and court officers, or corrections, we are dealing with professional codes of conduct and responsibility that govern the behaviors of persons performing different organizational roles. The performance of each role in these different types of organizations will involve either ethical or unethical conduct.

BOX 12.1   PERSONALITY HIGHLIGHT

MARVIN D. FREE, JR.
University of Wisconsin–Whitewater

Statistics: B.B.A. (management/marketing), M.B.A., M.A. (sociology), Baylor University; Ph.D. (sociology), University of Denver.

BACKGROUND AND INTERESTS

I am interested in racial disparity in criminal justice and the impact of race, gender, and social class on offending and the administration of justice. As one can discern from my academic credentials, I took a circuitous route to the field of criminal justice. After beginning my undergraduate career at two community colleges, I transferred to Baylor University where I pursued a degree in business administration. By the conclusion of my junior year I realized that I was fascinated by the social sciences. Nevertheless, the number of specialized courses in business that I had already accumulated precluded a change of major to sociology without a loss of substantial coursework.

Given the job market in 1970, I was unable to obtain professional employment upon graduation and consequently I returned to college to work on a master's degree in business. After completing my second degree I began working for Texas Instruments as a supervisor of an experimental line producing integrated circuits for computers, which at the time were still in their infancy. The realization that I was not particularly well suited for a business career occurred when I began to question the disparity in management/worker remuneration. Given this "revelation," I decided that I was going to save my money and return to school. The rest, as they say, is history. I returned to Baylor University and began taking the requisite courses to qualify for entry into a master's program in sociology. Upon completion of my Master of Arts degree, I began doctoral work at the University of North Texas (then known as North Texas State University) before eventually transferring to the University of Denver.

BOX 12.1   CONTINUED

The same concerns over social issues that drove me to sociology also fostered an interest in race and criminal justice. While in the first grade, my family moved from Southern California to Waco, Texas. Being raised in Texas in the 1950s and early 1960s, I had little exposure to persons of color as there was a "white" side and a "black" side of the city. It wasn't until my college years that I became cognizant of the prejudice and discrimination toward people of color that had permeated my childhood and adolescence. I attribute these early experiences to my intense interest in the impact of race on criminality and criminal justice that I have today.

RESEARCH INVESTIGATIONS

My earliest research in race culminated in the publication of a book, *African Americans and the Criminal Justice System.* This was succeeded by articles on the portrayal of African Americans in contemporary criminology textbooks and the impact of the U.S. Sentencing Guidelines on racial disparity in sentencing. Most recently, I have been examining the impact of race on presentence decision making.

Undoubtedly the most interesting moment in my career came during my preparation of *African Americans and the Criminal Justice System.* While doing some background work I became aware that some of my African American colleagues were (understandably) concerned about a "white man" writing about the African American experience in America. The honesty of a black female colleague (who shall remain anonymous) truly "opened my eyes" to the racial distrust that is still prevalent in American society. This earnest discussion further piqued my interest in this arena.

I have since expanded my research to include gender- and class-related issues. Having recently coauthored a criminology textbook with two colleagues whose research tends to focus on gender and class, I have learned to appreciate the intersection of these variables more fully in a future anthology.

ADVICE TO STUDENTS

The field of criminal justice is in need of individuals who can put aside their own stereotypes and examine relationships from as "neutral" a perspective as possible. We need both qualified people of color as well as nonminorities. An open discussion of our differences (and our many similarities) will be necessary if our knowledge is to advance.

An appropriate place to begin one's career in criminal justice is through active involvement in a regional association. I have had numerous positive experiences at the various criminal justice conferences that I have attended. Moreover, students in attendance appear to have an enjoyable and productive time. I would point out that it is never too early to start nurturing the professional affiliations that will continue throughout one's career.

These forms of ethical or unethical conduct are not relevant for this chapter. The only forms of ethical or unethical conduct examined here include any behavior in relation to the research enterprise.

Ethics and Social Responsibility

All ethical matters pertaining to the research process involve social responsibility. Each of us assumes that if we engage in research, we will be socially responsible and not do anything that departs markedly from the boundaries of professional propriety. We expect that others who do research will behave similarly. The product of one's research is eventually going to be consumed by others. When we read the research of others, we have a legitimate expectation that the investigators followed certain rules throughout the entire research process. Thus, we can rely on the evidence they have presented as genuine.

Does the End Justify the Means?   However, those of us who conduct research of any kind eventually realize that different persons have different interpretations of what it means to be socially responsible. Social responsibility is a relative term. Some researchers will condone minor or drastic departures from codes of accepted conduct, while other researchers will be intolerant of any departure from accepted standards of behavior. For example, an investigator mailed a survey questionnaire to several thousand persons in different states. The cover letter said that "all responses are confidential and anonymous." A self-addressed stamped envelope was conveniently enclosed in order to encourage those contacted to respond. But the investigator was interested in knowing the identities of the respondents. In a seemingly unobtrusive way, the investigator used invisible ink to mark the insides of return envelopes. Thus, when each questionnaire was returned, a chemical was used to reveal the numerical code on the inside of the envelope, and each respondent's identification code was written on their questionnaire by the researcher. This deception seemed innocent enough. The investigator considered the written assurance of anonymity a necessary white lie, since the only purpose was to identify respondents and utilize public information available from city directories. Later, such information could be correlated with respondents' answers on the questionnaires. However, several other researchers learned about this deception and were openly critical of it on moral grounds. Was the investigator who engaged in this deception immoral or unethical? Were any respondents harmed by this deception? It is unlikely that any respondent was ever harmed. But this ignores the fact that a lie was told in order to induce research subjects to return their questionnaires.

Does a Large Response Overwhelm Minor Departures from Scientific Procedure?   In another research project, an investigator collected 400 10-page attitudinal questionnaires from students in a large introductory criminology class. The researcher discovered that among the questionnaires, several revealed missing information. For instance, some of the pages on some of the questionnaires were simply blank, as though the pages had been skipped. In truth, some of the student respondents were in a hurry to answer questions and careless, simply turning two or three pages at once, not recognizing that they had skipped pages. Approximately 15 questionnaires had missing information. Instead of throwing out these questionnaires, the researcher merely filled in the blank spaces with fictitious choices. Later these questionnaires and responses were combined with the other 385 questionnaires and research results were yielded. While less than 4 percent of all questionnaires contained small portions of fictitious information, the study was eventually published in a popular criminological journal. No mention was made of the incident involving the missing data or the manufacture of fictitious information. The investigator later admitted, "Well, I didn't think it'd hurt anyone. What I did made no difference to the final result anyway!"

What if the researcher had reported just the information from the 385 valid questionnaires, where false information had not been manufactured? Suppose that this information was very similar to that reported where the false responses had been filled in by the researcher. Suppose the researcher was right, and that the inclusion of these false responses made no difference to the final result anyway. Was this an unethical act? Was this a violation of any particular code of professional responsibility or conduct? Yes and yes. Did it hurt anyone? Probably not. But whether anyone is injured by these particular actions of researchers misses the point of the results of these unethical behaviors. The point is that proper procedures were violated and conventional research rules were not followed. The reported research evidence was unreliable to the extent that these violations occurred.

It is apparent that whenever unethical research conduct occurs, it is seldom evident and detected. Often this misconduct occurs behind closed doors in secret, and the researcher is the only one who knows whether proper research procedures were followed. Unless the researcher tells others about not following proper procedures or admits to the misconduct, there is little that can be done by any professional organization.

Several reasons exist for why it is difficult to detect unethical research practices. The major reason is that it is customary to present findings in an anonymous context. A study of plea bargaining might occur in "a large southern state" or "in a large, urban western county." Prisoners may be studied at "a large state prison in the Midwest." Thus, some unscrupulous researchers are protected from discovery by the very guarantees of anonymity that are extended to most research subjects. If lawyers in "a large Midwestern state" are interviewed, how do we know which lawyers in which state? We don't know. If we don't know, we cannot verify or authenticate any of the reported information.

Another reason why it is difficult to detect unethical research practices is that much of the time, data analysis, interpretation, and dissemination is directly within the absolute control of the individual investigator. If the investigator chooses to be deceptive or dishonest, who is going to know about it?

Sometimes, the findings reported by unethical researchers are so outrageous and inconsistent with the research reported by others that we are alerted to possible research dishonesty. But here again, we are prevented from verifying or authenticating one's research since we don't know who was contacted and interviewed. Furthermore, contradictory and inconsistent findings are endemic to criminological research and social research of any kind. No subject is free from inconsistencies. We have no way of knowing whether an anomalous finding is the product of deception and dishonesty or an actual research inconsistency compared with other studies.

No one knows how much dishonesty occurs among any organization of professionals where research is conducted. By far the majority of researchers engage in reputable projects that are often sponsored by legitimate organizations, such as the National Institute of

Justice or the Office of Juvenile Justice and Delinquency Prevention Programs. But such sponsorship does not immunize any researcher from misrepresenting or massaging data in ways that slant research findings one way or another. Much research is also unsponsored. This fact does not mean that unsponsored research is inherently inferior to sponsored research. Most persons who conduct independent investigations of criminological phenomena do so in scrupulously ethical ways. Ultimately we must have faith in other investigators who report their findings to us in diverse outlets.

Ethics and Criminological Research

Criminological research and studies of the criminal justice system and those processed by it are ideal breeding grounds for a variety of ethical issues. Criminal behavior is interesting to study. However, investigations of criminal behaviors and criminals are often intrusive. Whether juveniles or adults are studied, the matter of confidentiality arises. It is imperative in many investigations that criminologists and criminal justicians have access to information that only criminals can provide. If criminals are interviewed, observed, or surveyed, they may disclose potentially damaging information about themselves to researchers. Researcher integrity becomes the safeguard to protect a respondent's anonymity and the information shared with investigators.

A few examples are in order to illustrate some of the ethical problems that are created in the process of studying criminals and delinquents. Suppose you are conducting interviews with various probationers and parolees. As a researcher you want to know how these probationers and parolees are responding to their probation and parole programs. You ask these offenders about themselves, about their use of drugs and alcohol, and their general conformity to program rules. In the course of your interviews, you might ask these clients whether they have committed new crimes. Thus, through self-reports, these clients disclose considerable information about themselves. Some of this information might get them into trouble if it came to the attention of their probation or parole officers. Suppose a probation officer asks you how your study is progressing. In your conversation with the probation officer, you might say that some of the clients are having trouble complying with program rules. The probation officer may push you to reveal if any program violations have occurred that have previously been undetected. Under this pressure, you might reveal what you have been told by others. This information could have serious implications for certain probationers.

In a study of delinquent youths in Provo, Utah, during the early 1960s, for instance, the Ford Foundation funded research about the subculture of delinquency. Researchers worked with the juvenile court in Provo to obtain over 200 juvenile participants in a delinquency prevention experiment over a 3 year period. In small groups, delinquents were encouraged to share their delinquent experiences with other group members, and then they were to introspect and determine why they had committed these delinquent acts. Open conversation among these youths was encouraged by researchers who promised total anonymity and confidentiality, regardless of whatever was said or disclosed in these group sessions. All group sessions were tape-recorded.

One goal of the group therapy was to enable these youths to understand the etiology of their delinquent conduct and form close social bonds with other delinquents. As they came to understand why they had committed their delinquent acts, they could actually un-learn their delinquency in the same group milieu where they originally acquired their delin-quent attitudes and behaviors. This method of creating substantial attitudinal change was premised in part on the confidentiality of the situation. However, researchers were pres-sured by police and the courts to reveal whatever these boys had said in the context of their closed group discussions. Researchers learned much from the boys about unsolved com-munity crimes and who had committed them. Some of the perpetrators were participants in these groups. But despite the pressure to disclose, the investigators respected the boys' con-fidentiality and refrained from reporting them to police. It would have been highly unethi-cal of these researchers to violate the confidences of these boys, and such behavior probably would have defeated an otherwise successful delinquency intervention program.

The fact is that criminologists are thrust into many situations where they are obligated to respect the confidentiality of others they examine. If they wish to study the cultural con-text of marijuana production in the hills of Kentucky, or if they want to examine the attitudes and opinions of prisoners at Leavenworth, or if they want to study a delinquent gang and un-derstand gang operations, they must be prepared to honor their code of ethics and respect the confidentiality of their respondents. Information yielded by respondents in different sit-uations can be quite damaging to them if made available to the wrong persons, agencies, or organizations. Thus, it is imperative that persons used as respondents in research and ex-perimentation should be made fully aware of the implications of their involvement. Their informed consent is essential as a respondent right.

Types of Ethical Problems in Research

Several types of ethical problems in research have been described. These include (1) pla-giarism; (2) fraudulent research and statistical manipulation; (3) research potentially harm-ful to human subjects; (4) deception or lying to respondents; (5) accessing confidential records and information; (6) studying sex offenders, including an examination of their sex-ual histories and conducting stimulus–response experiments; and (7) granting permission to study subordinates, potentates, and juveniles.

Plagiarism

Plagiarism means to use someone else's published work and represent it as your own. It is a type of fraud, where the ideas and/or work of others is used without acknowledgement. If you borrow a term paper from another student, put your name on it, and submit it to a pro-fessor as something you have written, this is plagiarism. If you quote from one or more sources and do not cite these sources, this is plagiarism. In the early 1990s at California State University–Long Beach, for instance, some graduate students in the Department of Criminal Justice obtained an "A" term paper from a California Highway Patrol officer. All of the term papers for a given class were placed in a tray outside the professor's office so that students could claim them. Another student merely picked up the officer's paper surrepti-tiously. The other students tore off the cover sheet containing the name of the officer and put in their own names. The same paper was recycled at least half a dozen times in subsequent criminal justice courses before this plagiarism was discovered. The highway patrol officer had been unwittingly exploited by other students. Once the plagiarism was detected, the students received failing grades in the courses where the officer's paper had been recycled.

Double-Duty Papers.   Another form of fraud is to use the same paper you have written in more than one course. More than a few students write a term paper for one course, and then they decide to replace the cover sheet with a new course title and submit the paper again. Thus, the student obtains course credit by using the same paper again and again. However, some professors may accept papers prepared originally for other courses. But many professors would consider this practice unethical on the part of students.

Plagiarism by Professors.   Students aren't the only ones who commit plagiarism. Various investigators have used the work of others without proper citation or referencing. Sometimes the author of an article submitted to a professional journal will replicate lengthy passages from articles written by others. This is also plagiarism. If detected, the plagiarist may be barred from publishing in the journal where the article was submitted for publication or published. Professional organizations may also sanction the plagiarist in different ways, such as withdrawing their membership and other privileges. If the plagiarist is a faculty member at a university, the university may consider such plagiarism as grounds for dismissal or reduction in academic rank.

Mail-Order and Internet Papers.   In an increasing technological age of computers and information access, numerous paper services exist on the Internet and elsewhere, offering papers on a variety of subjects for different college courses for a fee. Thus, anyone can order one or more papers from these sources. The papers are represented as original and properly referenced. The usual marketing strategy is to offer papers on different topics, noting the number of references used. Some students order these papers and submit them in their courses. It is increasingly difficult to detect this type of plagiarism whenever it occurs. Any type of plagiarism is clearly unethical in every context.

Dual Submissions of Articles to Different Journals and Other Outlets.   Another unethical practice committed by article writers is simultaneously submitting the same article to two or more journals. The article review process is time-consuming. Sometimes it takes up to 6 months or more for an article to be reviewed. With increasing pressure on professors to publish, time is precious. Some professors do not want to wait for these reviews. Furthermore, the rejection rates for certain high-quality journals are high. As many as 95 percent of all journal articles submitted to *Criminology* and *Justice Quarterly* are rejected annually. The *Journal of Crime and Justice* has a rejection rate of 75–80 percent. With these high rejection rates, more than a few authors might be inclined to submit their research articles to more than one journal at a time. The major problem is that two (or more) journals may decide to publish the same article at the same time. Sometimes these decisions are made without proper notification of the article author(s). When the article eventually appears in two different journals, this causes readers to label the article author as unethical. Thus, most journals today have a **dual-submission policy,** advising that it is against journal policy to review any submitted article that is presently under review by another journal.

Fraudulent Research and Statistical Manipulation

Fraudulent research occurs when the study or significant parts of it are fabricated or falsified. An investigator might invent a population and sample to study. Fake data are collected and analyzed. Perhaps no analysis ever occurs. The researcher simply invents tables and inserts fictitious data in them. Statistical tests are applied to these fictitious data, and meaningless results are yielded. Conclusions and implications for future research are discussed. The significance of the research is described. The research is published in different outlets, such as journals and periodicals. Other professionals may reproduce these fake studies in books of readings.

The "publish-or-perish" pressure generated by virtually every university causes some professors to resort to falsifying studies or study findings. If professors don't publish, or if they don't publish significant results, they may not be promoted or granted tenure at their collegiate institutions. They may even be terminated for failing to publish. When one's livelihood is seriously threatened under these "publish-or-perish" conditions, this may lead to the production of fraudulent research.

Or an investigator may actually carry out a legitimate research project. He or she may collect data from real human subjects. He or she may actually tabulate and analyze the data. However, the actual results yielded by the study may not be significant or worthwhile to anyone. Interestingly, editors of most journals are reluctant to publish studies where nothing significant was found. Thus, they become silent co-conspirators with universities and colleges by rejecting articles lacking significance or originality. (In past years, some journals have been established that make fun of the more prestigious journals. At least two journals operated for a time, called *The Journal of Insignificant Findings* and *The Journal of Irreproducible Results,* which continues to be published.)

Where insignificant, nonsignificant, or other such circumstances exist, an investigator may change the distribution of responses in tables and graphs so that statistical significance increases or occurs. As a major consequence, the investigator can write up the study, showing that the findings are very significant in different respects. The fact that the study findings are now "significant" enhances the chances of the article being accepted for publication in some journal or periodical. And the chances of promotion and tenure for the professor are also greatly improved.

Research Potentially Harmful to Human Subjects

Some research may be harmful to **human subjects.** The research may be either biologically or physically harmful or psychologically harmful, or both. During World War I, the U.S. military experimented with various types of noxious gases to determine their debilitating effects. Inmates from different prisons were typically used as human guinea pigs in these experiments. At the time, prisoners had few rights and could not effectively challenge the legality of their forced participation in these experiments. Some inmate deaths occurred, and more than a few inmates suffered chronic or serious side effects of exposure to these gases and other substances.

Well into the 1940s, many male inmates of prisons in Oklahoma and Virginia were routinely sterilized or castrated. It was believed at the time that criminal behaviors were genetically transmitted. Thus, if criminals were castrated or sterilized, then they could not reproduce these criminal characteristics to a new generation. Mass sterilization and castration of male prisoners was considered a valuable means of future crime prevention. Prevailing criminological beliefs suggested that these practices were fully warranted as aggressive measures to prevent future criminality. Today, these practices are considered unlawful and no longer used. However, from time to time, a judge will offer sex offenders, both male and female, the option of sterilization as an alternative to hard prison time. Such judicial actions were eventually declared unconstitutional.

Often major universities are used as conduits through which unethical research is conducted. For instance, during the 1940s Vanderbilt University in Nashville, Tennessee, exposed 800 pregnant women to radiation to determine its effects on fetal development. During the 1970s, various patients with leukemia and other cancers were exposed to extremely high doses of radiation to determine its therapeutic effects at the Oak Ridge, Tennessee, National Laboratory. At Columbia University and Montefiore Hospital in New York during the 1950s, 12 terminally ill cancer patients were injected with radioactive substances to determine the rate at which these substances were absorbed by various types of tissue. A program was operated during the 1950s and 1960s at the University of Cincinnati to develop more effective cancer treatments and how much radiation military personnel could endure before becoming unable to function effectively in combat. Subjects as volunteers were treated with high doses of radiation, and some of these subjects developed colon cancer later. And at the University of Rochester, University of Chicago, and University of California, San Francisco Hospital injected different subjects with varying amounts of plutonium, many without their knowledge or consent, for various medical purposes. None of these investigations were made public until 1993, when the Freedom of Information Act led to their disclosure (Lewis, 1994).

Several studies have emerged as landmarks in unethical research in the medical, psychological, and social fields. Some of these are described below.

The Tuskegee Syphillis Study.   One of the most notorious medical experiments of the 20th century occurred during the period 1932–1970. It has become known as the **Tuskegee Syphilis Study,** carried out at the Tuskegee Institute under the auspices of the U.S. Public Health Service. At the time, little was known about syphilis, a sexually transmitted disease. It was known that if left untreated, syphilis would cause degeneration of the bones, heart, and nerve tissue. Death usually results. Penicillin was available as a known treatment for syphilis at the time, although investigators were uncertain about how penicillin worked. They succeeded in soliciting nearly 1,000 black male laborers as volunteers. All of these volunteers had syphilis. Researchers treated one-half of all subjects with penicillin, while about 400 of these laborers were not given anything to treat their syphilis. At least 425 blacks died from syphilis. While experts concede that the study yielded much information about how penicillin acts on spirochetes, parasitic bacteria that cause syphilis, the study itself was a most inhumane biomedical experiment (Brandt, 1978).

The Tearoom Trade.   Some research is unobtrusive, where the researcher observes others without their knowledge. In the late 1960s, Laud Humphreys investigated male homosexual behavior. He secreted himself in certain locations in public restrooms and observed numerous homosexual encounters. On some occasions, he represented himself to homosexuals as a voyeur who wanted to watch others perform sex acts. Later, he followed these persons and wrote down their automobile license plate numbers. Using his connections with the police department, he learned where these persons lived and later visited them, pretending to be a mental health professional.

Humphreys discovered much about persons who carry on homosexual liaisons with others in public restrooms. His investigation revealed much about the sociodemographic characteristics of homosexuals. Humphreys defended his research by claiming that no one was ever harmed by his unobtrusive observations of their behaviors. He never disclosed the names of any of the homosexuals to the media, and he scrupulously maintained their anonymity. However, his research was widely criticized as unethical, inasmuch as he failed to disclose to those he observed that he was a social scientist who was studying homosexuals. He never gave these persons the option of refusing to participate in his research. Humphreys (1970) contended that he was under no obligation to disclose his research intentions to those he observed. In fact, he said, these persons were more than willing conspirators in his observation of them as a voyeur. Admittedly, it is unlikely that Humphreys would have obtained such extensive information about homosexual behavior patterns if he had advised all of those he observed of his true research intentions. But did this fact necessarily justify his actions and deceit? Did the ends justify the means used to gather important information?

The CIA's ARTICHOKE Program.   The Central Intelligence Agency (CIA), an intelligence-gathering organization of the U.S. government, has disclosed that for many decades, it has been involved in different means of controlling human behavior. A CIA memo dated January 25, 1952, indicated that a program, ARTICHOKE, was underway and that its primary objectives were the evaluation and development of any method by which we can get information from a person against his will and without his knowledge (Greenfield, 1977). Although ARTICHOKE was terminated sometime between 1952 and 1975, several memos disclosed through the Freedom of Information Act in 1977 lists ARTICHOKE methods, which included the use of drugs and chemicals, hypnosis, and total isolation as forms of psychological harassment. Another component of the control of human behavior included chemical and biological materials capable of producing human behavioral and physiological changes; radiology; electroshock; various fields of psychology, psychiatry, sociology, and anthropology; graphology; harassment substances; and paramilitary devices and materials.

Specific examples from the CIA's own files indicated:

1. Giving LSD to unwitting citizens, some of whom were literally picked up in New York and San Francisco bars.
2. Using hypnosis and drugs in interaction.
3. Attempting to recruit a neuroscientist to find the pain center of the human brain.
4. Shopping for methods to induce amnesia.
5. And looking for methods to make persons subvert their principles.

In 1963 the CIA was confronted by different news agencies about their work in human behavioral control. A representative said that research in the manipulation of human behavior is considered by many authorities in medicine and related fields to be professionally unethical. However, an extensive network of nongovernmental scientists and facilities was compiled that engaged in such activities, almost always without the knowledge of the institutions where the facilities were situated.

Professional organizations, such as the American Psychology Association and the American Sociological Association, have pursued avenues to discover how ARTICHOKE could have persisted for so long without public knowledge about its existence. How were psychologists and other social scientists enlisted by the CIA? What did they do? What, if any, is the scientist's responsibility for the applications of research? How are social scientists affected by social and political forces? What are the implications of covert funding?

Some of the psychologists affected by ARTICHOKE, with or without their knowledge, were Carl Rogers of the Center for the Study of the Person, La Jolla, California; Edgar Schein of MIT's Sloane School of Management; Martin Orne, a psychiatrist at the University of Pennsylvania; and Charles Osgood of the University of Illinois. The CIA's principal instrument for sponsoring basic research in psychology, sociology, and anthropology during the 1960s and 1970s was the Society for the Investigation of Human Ecology, later called the Human Ecology Fund. The origins of Human Ecology lie in a friendship between Allen Dulles and Harold Wolff, a prominent Cornell neuropsychiatrist who had cared for Dulles's son following a war injury. The return of American prisoners of war who had served in Korea evoked governmental and popular concern about the possible existence of brainwashing. As Director of the CIA, Dulles asked Wolff, an expert on stress, to find out what had happened to the prisoners of war, and the Society for the Investigation of Human Ecology was established at the Cornell Medical College to address this question through research on Chinese and Soviet methods of interrogation and indoctrination. Lawrence Hinkle, one of the Society's founders, said that he as well as the Dean of the Cornell Medical School were aware of the Society's CIA origins.

Obtaining cooperation from social scientists has been a relatively easy task for the CIA. For instance, Carl Rogers disclosed to an interviewer how he became involved with Human Ecology. He said that Colonel James Monroe, one-time head of the Psychological Warfare Research Division of the U.S. Air Force, came to him and advised that Dr. Harold Wolff, a neuropsychiatrist who he had a lot of respect for, was heading up an organization to do research on personality and so on. Rogers agreed to participate, attracted in part by the prospect of obtaining substantial funding for his own research interests. Rogers said that they did get a few grants from the government to do research on psychotherapy. It was research that Rogers had been wanting to do for a long time. Rogers believed at the time that the Human Ecology organization was doing legitimate things, and that it did not seem improper for him to be involved with an intelligence outfit at that time. But in later years, Rogers said that he looks at it quite differently now: He would not touch covert funding with a 10-foot pole (Greenfield, 1977).

Another social scientist, Charles Osgood, noted for his development and use of the semantic differential for attitudinal research, told interviewers that some of his work was funded by Human Ecology. He said that although some of the people working on his projects aroused his suspicions, none of their behaviors influenced or attempted to influence his research. Osgood had been studying the cross-cultural study of meaning, and how people in 31 societies attribute feelings to different aspects of culture. Human Ecology funded his research, which tested the cross-cultural generality of evaluation, potency, and activity as dimensions of affective meaning.

One researcher, Wilse Webb, a member of the American Psychological Association's Board of Directors, indicated that he, too, was a beneficiary of Human Ecology funding during the 1960s. Webb said that as a beginning researcher, he searched for money to do his job, and that any source willing to fund what he wanted to do would be attractive. He said that most social scientists don't think in particular terms as to where the money comes from. Researchers think about what they're going to do with the money (Greenfield, 1977).

ARTICHOKE raised numerous ethical questions about how social scientists could become involved, often unwittingly, in questionable social and psychological research with the ultimate purpose of learning more about interrogation methods, mind control, and other forms of social and psychological manipulation. The highly secretive nature of any organization makes it extremely difficult if not impossible to obtain accurate and credible information about its activities, regardless of how unethical those activities might be. Particularly in times of war or global conflict, there is always a suspicion that some type of covert activity or research is taking place that social scientists would find ethically offensive in various ways. Few procedures or protocols are in place that govern agency accountability, particularly an agency that rigorously protects its privacy and operations.

Obedience Research.   In the 1970s Stanley Milgram, a professor at Yale University, conducted several experiments involving obedience to authority. Milgram was interested in explaining why so many Germans and others routinely carried out orders from superiors in World War II and executed millions of Jews in death camps.

At Yale University, Milgram (1974) constructed a small laboratory where he could conduct obedience experiments. He hired a middle-aged man to act as his stooge and pretend to react in certain ways in response to how other persons treated him. The experiment involved 40 student volunteers who would sit at an electrical panel and administer a series of progressively severe shocks to the stooge, who was sitting in a chair and hidden from view on the other side of the electrical panel. The experimenter explained to his volunteers that the study involved a word-association learning test. An electrical shock would be administered to the stooge each time he gave an incorrect answer. Each time an electrical shock was administered, the intensity of the electrical shock would be increased by 15 volts. The shock range was from 15 to 450 volts. The electrical panel showed various levels of volts, with printed words showing "Slight Shock" to "Severe Shock." In reality, the electrical panel was fake, and there were no shocks administered to the stooge. However, each volunteer believed that he was administering increasingly severe electrical shocks to the stooge, referred to as the "learner." Each time the learner gave an incorrect answer, an electric shock would be administered by the volunteer at the direction of the experimenter. A red light on the instrument panel would blink as the "shock" was administered to the stooge. The experiment was structured so that the learner would give sufficient numbers of "incorrect" responses so that excessive shock voltages would have to be administered.

Milgram wanted to see how far these volunteers would go when ordered to administer progressively severe electrical shocks to the stooge. As each volunteer sat at the instrument panel and administered increased electrical shocks to the stooge, the stooge would cry out or hit the wall with his fists, as though he were responding to the painfulness of the shocks. Although the volunteers were reassured that the shocks, regardless of their severity, would not cause any permanent tissue damage or scarring, the situation created severe emotional conflicts for many of them.

Milgram found that five volunteers refused to administer any shocks beyond the 300-volt range. However, he found that 26 out of the 40 volunteers administered the most intense 450-volt shock when ordered to do so. Milgram concluded that his study supported the idea that even when senseless orders were given to inflict pain on anonymous test subjects, many persons would obey these orders without hesitation and administered seemingly severe shocks. Thus, the study helped researchers to understand the motivations and responses of subordinates in death camps in Nazi Germany during World War II.

More than a few critics contended that Milgram's **obedience research** was unethical in several respects. Deceit was practiced when experimental subjects, volunteers, were not advised that they would not actually be harming anyone. Of course, had they been advised of this fact, it would have defeated the whole purpose of Milgram's experiment. Therefore, some deception was essential if the experiment was to be considered valid. Other critics took issue with the whole idea of subjecting persons to an emotionally exhausting experience, where they thought that they were causing injury to a test subject. Was such an experiment ethical? Could Milgram have studied his theory of obedience in ways that would not have been controversial? Probably not.

Zimbardo's Simulated Prison Study.   Philip Zimbardo, a professor at Stanford University, conducted an experiment that was perhaps as controversial as Milgram's. Zimbardo (1972) solicited and paid student volunteers to act as either prison guards or prisoners. A "prison" was constructed in several rooms in the basement of a building on the Stanford University campus. Some students were designated as "guards," while others were designated as "prisoners." The experiment was designed to last 2 weeks. Prisoners were issued inmate jump suits, while guards were issued guard uniforms, nightsticks, and other guard-related equipment. Prisoners were fed regularly, and they had bathroom facilities and cots. Zimbardo wanted to study the interaction patterns of prison guards and inmates through this **simulation.**

After the student volunteers were chosen, either as prisoners or guards, they began to play out their roles. Guards became increasingly abusive, both physically and verbally. Prisoners were dehumanized and began to act both passive and hostile toward their keepers. The experiment was short-lived, however, when the emotional strain became too much for some of the prisoners. After only 6 days, Zimbardo terminated the experiment because of certain adverse effects observed among the various student participants.

Zimbardo was criticized for this research, since the emotional states of experimental subjects were altered in different ways. Zimbardo defended his research, observing that the students had knowingly volunteered for the experiment and were, in fact, being paid well for their participation. He contended that it was never his intention that anyone would be physically injured or psychologically abused as the result of the experiment. However, evidence to the contrary suggested that several students emerged from the experiment with serious emotional scars.

It is clear that social research of any kind may generate harmful effects upon human subjects. We cannot possibly know all of the potential adverse consequences of conducting experiments involving human subjects, regardless of how innocent our research objectives and procedures may appear. Certainly Zimbardo, Milgram, and Humphreys never expected that others would cast aspersions on their research and label them as unethical in various ways.

The Oregon Prisoner Experiments. During the 1960s and 1970s, at least one state, Oregon, was involved in different research projects designed to determine the effects of radiation on male reproductive functions (U.S. Department of Energy Advisory Committee on Human Radiation Experiments, 1996). In 1963 Dr. Carl Heller, an internationally known medical scientist, wanted to test the effects of radiation on the somatic and germinal cells of the testes, the dose of radiation that would produce changes or induce damage to spermatogenic cells, the amount of time it would take for cell production to recover, and the effects of radiation on hormone excretion. Human subjects would be required to agree to be vasectomized because of a small risk of chromosomal damage that could lead to their fathering genetically damaged children. Dr. Heller estimated that his research would cost $1.12 million over a 10-year period.

At the time, Oregon was targeted as a possible research site. This is because under the laws of the state, prisoners could be used as research subjects and that this was accepted practice. Oregon law permitted prisoners to give their consent to obtaining vasectomies. At the time, Heller knew little about any long-term adverse effects of different doses of radiation on testes, and thus he was unable to provide prisoners with assurances about their ultimate health benefits or liabilities arising from this research. Some prisoners were given vague references to the possibility of tumor growths resulting from irradiating testes, but not cancer. Often prisoners were informed that there was one chance in a million of getting cancer from their research participation. In reality, acute risks of these exposures to radiation included skin burns, pain from the biopsies, orchitis (testicular inflammation) induced by repeated biopsies, and bleeding into the scrotum from the biopsies. Prisoners were paid 25 cents per day for their participation in these experiments. Inmates were also paid $25 for each testicular biopsy, and they averaged five of these over the course of their involvement in Heller's research. A bonus was paid for those who had a vasectomy at the conclusion of the program. An obvious ethical question is whether the money constituted a coercive offer to prisoners.

Between 1963–1973, 67 inmates from the Oregon State Prison were irradiated. Subsequently in 1973, Amos Reed, Administrator of the Oregon Corrections Division, terminated Heller's program when he concluded that prisoners had not given their consent to participate in this research freely. In 1976 several Oregon inmates filed lawsuits alleging poorly supervised research and a lack of informed consent. Among other things, inmates alleged that other inmates had sometimes controlled the radiation dose to which they were exposed; that an inmate with a grudge against a subject filled a syringe with water instead of Novocain, resulting in a vasectomy performed without anesthetic; and that the experimental procedures resulted in considerable pain and discomfort for which they were not prepared. All lawsuits were subsequently settled out of court (U.S. Department of Energy Advisory Committee on Human Radiation Experiments, 1996).

Sex Reassignment Studies. In the recent past, several medical studies have been conducted of sex reassignment, which is surgically converting *XY* males with absent or minuscule penises into anatomical females, then raising them as girls (Lewis, 2000). In 1995 William Reiner, a child and adolescent psychiatrist and urologist at the Johns Hopkins Children's Center, reported on 14 *XY* genetic male cases, with an intersex appearance of no penis but normal testicles, and normal male hormone levels at birth. Twelve of the children were reassigned female, yet the parents reported that all displayed typical male behavior throughout childhood. Six of the 12 switched themselves to the male gender between the ages of 5 and 12 years, and that two children not subjected to the surgery were psychologically well-adjusted males who do not have penises.

The ethical concerns about sex reassignment have ranged from nature/nurture considerations, to good intent, to the practical matter of surgical expediency. No scientific evidence exists about what is the right way to do things. Many surgeries have been conducted according to what seemed the right thing to do. Some of the assumptions for sex reassignment are questionable. One assumption is that sexual intercourse is the most important thing that a human does. Another assumption is that the penis is the most important sexual organ. Also the traditional timing of female sex reassignment tends to raise ethical problems. During the 1960s, for instance, sex reassignment was done within 2 days following birth, where males were castrated and converted into anatomically correct females. Subsequently it has been determined that gender identity is a very complicated matter, and it appears that results vary greatly from among different individuals. Some medical experts and social scientists have suggested that the medical treatment of intersex and traumatic loss of the penis has been a 40-plus year, poorly run, unethical experiment, and that someday this will rank up there with the Tuskegee syphilis experiments. But with new knowledge of long-term outcomes, improved surgical techniques, and patient choice, sex reassignment for the future promises to be a more carefully considered option (Lewis, 2000).

The Fernald Cereal Nutrition Studies.   During the 1950s professors from MIT and Harvard University conducted a series of radiation experiments. These experiments took place at the Walter E. Fernald State School in Waltham, Massachusetts, which housed numerous mentally retarded patients. The late Professor of Nutrition, Robert S. Harris, studied the absorption of calcium and iron by feeding 125 mentally retarded patients from the Fernald school milk and cereal that contained radioactive tracers (Vaishnav, 1994). The purpose of the research was to improve understanding of the nutritional processes in order to promote health in young people, and that radiation was allegedly within today's safe limits.

Public disclosure of this research did not occur until 1993 when Energy Secretary Hazel O'Leary declassified thousands of government documents about radiation and radiation testing. According to the report, no significant health effects were incurred by the research subjects as the direct result of these nutritional studies in which radioactive calcium and iron tracers were used. Nevertheless, the parents of the youths at the Fernald school were not informed about the experiments, particularly about the fact that their children would be exposed to radiation in cereal. The informed consent issue was never raised when the study was initially implemented. Some officials from MIT and Harvard University commented that they were sorry to hear that at least some of the young people who participated in the radiation research and their parents were unaware that the study involved radioactive tracers (Vaishnav, 1994).

It is likely that if these studies were to be conducted today, informed consent would be an integral feature of the preamble to any research taking place. The potential risks, however minimal, would likely discourage most if not all persons from participating in such a study. Few persons in the world willingly wish to expose themselves to radiation, especially in their cereal, and even in low doses. Some radiation exposure occurs in the normal course of medical examinations and dental work, for instance. These low doses of exposure to radiation do not seem to have any long-term or adverse effects on patients. But the unethical methods used by MIT and Harvard University medical personnel and involving mentally retarded children to radiation exposure in their milk and cereal are certainly questionable and raise important issues about informed consent.

Who Is Harmed by Unethical Research?   These and other studies raise questions about the harm accruing to different persons and/or organizations resulting from unethical practices. From the participant's perspective, there is possible physical harm, mental harm, an invasion of privacy, and loss of confidentiality. Researchers stand to lose their reputations or have them damaged more or less extensively. There is also the possible guilt that may arise over having conducted a study that may injure some or all research subjects in different ways. Sponsors of research, like MIT, Harvard University, the CIA, and other organizations, suffer possible embarrassment and unfavorable publicity. Society itself becomes increasingly apprehensive toward researchers in any field where human subjects are studied.

In 2001 a study was conducted of the degree to which unethical behaviors are evidenced in different professional journals. In American medical journals, for instance, it was disclosed that over 40 percent of all articles involving human subjects failed to report ethical approval or informed consent, despite the fact that all of these journals advise their authors to document human subjects' approval before publication. Some of this nonreporting may be deliberate, while some of it may be unintentional. For instance, some of the reporting requirements appear confusing to article authors. Thus, whether to report informed consent of research participants or fail to report such consent is unclear or unknown. In some instances, however, there has been deliberate disregard for the protocol that exists for documentation. This research raises serious questions about the protection of human subjects in clinical trials and related research (*British Medical Journal,* 2001).

Journals published in criminal justice and other social sciences have inconsistent and unarticulated policies, if any, concerning whether to report or disclose whether human subjects studied have been informed of the potential harm they may incur as the result of research conducted. Organizations, such as the Academy of Criminal Justice Sciences, the American Sociological Association, and the American Society of Criminology, have established codes of ethics to guard against unscrupulous research practices. It is probably the case that these codes of ethics are believed to be sufficiently regulatory in an effort to prevent human subject abuses of any kind. Also, most universities and colleges have human subjects committees that oversee and approve research conducted by their faculty and where human subjects are studied. However, much research is conducted by investigators acting independently and where such approval by university authorities is not sought.

Deception: Lying to Respondents

Deception is used in social research projects as a means of obtaining unbiased research results. In several studies, human subjects are advised that their responses are anonymous, when in fact the researcher knows exactly who they are. This type of deception is justified by these researchers as a way of preserving the objectivity of respondents' reactions (Vohryzek-Bolden, 1997).

Deception is also used whenever investigators infiltrate social groups that they wish to examine. If someone wishes to study juvenile gangs, they might hire certain juveniles to join these gangs and report gang activities and behaviors to them. On other occasions, social scientists might pose as bikers and join biker's groups such as the Hell's Angels for a period of time. The intent of these researchers is to describe behavior patterns of close-knit gangs of either juveniles or adults. Access to these gangs would ordinarily be restricted, and conventional requests to study these gangs by social scientists would be rejected.

At the University of California–Riverside, a married couple joined a swinger's club in Southern California, where persons would routinely swap spouses for sexual intercourse. The couple joining the swinger's club was actually a pair of sociologists who wanted to study the behavior of swingers and describe the culture of swinging. They participated in the swinger's club for a year. At no time did they advise the club that they were researchers collecting data. Eventually, they left the club and wrote a book about their swinger experiences, detailing the culture of swinging and swinger norms and behaviors.

Is any of this deception justified? If we were to be totally truthful with the groups we wanted to study, would we be permitted to study them? If these groups knew who we really were and were aware of our true research purposes, would *they* deceive *us* by behaving differently? Under what circumstances, if any, is deception warranted for certain research purposes? While deception is generally disapproved by professional codes of ethics, the fact is that deception is practiced by at least some researchers every year. No precise figures are available to indicate the extent of deception in the research process, although it is probably relatively infrequent.

Accessing Confidential Records and Information

An incredible amount of information is available about people through the Internet and various official sources. Public statistics are published on a regular basis by different governmental agencies and organizations. However, much information exists that is privileged and confidential.

Governmental Safeguards to Ensure Confidentiality.   In 1973 the federal government established confidentiality provisions to shield persons from the prying eyes of researchers. Under the Omnibus Crime Control and Safe Streets Act, the government proclaimed that no officer or employee should disclose to anyone any research or statistical information of a personal nature, including any research sponsored and funded by the federal government. The intent of this provision was to protect research subjects from having personal details of their lives disclosed to others apart from those actually conducting the research. Thus, it would be both illegal and unethical to disclose specific information about research participants where they could be easily identified by name. However, such a provision would not preclude any legitimate governmental agency, such as the Internal Revenue Service, a U.S. District Court, or U.S. Probation Office, from securing personal information about any person targeted for investigation.

Thus, it would be unethical for a researcher to disclose personal information about research subjects involved in a study sponsored by the National Institute of Justice or the Office of Juvenile Justice and Delinquency Prevention. In almost every case where researchers

BOX 12.2   PERSONALITY HIGHLIGHT

WILLIAM F. MCDONALD
Georgetown University

Statistics: A.B. (liberal studies), University of Notre Dame; M.Ed., Boston College; D.Crim. (criminology), University of California, Berkeley.

BACKGROUND AND INTERESTS

The two main focal points of my current writing are (1) the nexus between immigration and crime and (2) the development of the institutions of global law enforcement and judicial cooperation. Beyond those I have several other interests that could be rekindled at any moment: criminal prosecution systems; criminal victimization; pretrial release; repeat offender laws; and conceptual schemes like social network theory, social trust, McDonaldization, and implosion.

The first topic is actually a cluster of distinct topics that are connected by virtue of the intersection of the two subject matters: crime and immigration. It includes various subtopics: the criminality of immigrants; public beliefs about the criminality of immigrants; the criminality against immigrants; the criminalization of immigrants; the challenge of immigrants to law enforcement and criminal justice; and immigrants and terrorism.

Putting this bundle together in one place (such as a book manuscript) is a bit unconventional. It concerns me slightly that some might see it as a crazy quilt. The more traditional approach would be to devote an entire book or article to each of these topics separately. This allows you to organize your presentation according to some theoretical perspective throughout the entire work—something that wins points in academic quarters.

Indeed I have already done that. What I am seeking to do now is to pull them together in a way that satisfies my personal desire to see a larger whole in my work and to express certain ideas and perspectives that I think are missing in the literature. How I arrived at this bundle of topics and this conception of how to fit them together represents a case study into one scholar's intellectual journey. It reveals the combination of expediency and opportunism as well as the principled development that have marked my career. It also reflects changes in Western culture as well as the discipline of criminology.

RESEARCH INVESTIGATIONS

In 1989 I spent my sabbatical at Georgetown University's villa in Fiesole, Italy. For a decade I had been involved in studies of plea bargaining and police–prosecutor cooperation. I exam-

BOX 12.2   CONTINUED

ined prosecutorial decision making with a modified version of a decision-simulation method developed by my professor, Leslie Wilkins. During that federally funded research I traveled to many jurisdictions to do field work. I could not help noticing that things are done differently in different jurisdictions. All prosecutors' offices are not the same.

In order to capture these differences, I wrote an article, titled "The Prosecutor's Domain," borrowing the concept of "domain" from the literature on formal organizations (in *The Prosecutor* [1979]). It was a useful way for describing the differences and for challenging the simplistic descriptions of the office of the prosecutor. This got me involved in researching the history of the office of the American public prosecutor as well as looking at criminal prosecution systems in other countries. Two findings stunned me: (1) our public prosecutor system did come from England; the English did not have one; and (2) public prosecutors in European countries that follow the Civil Law tradition are not allowed to exercise any discretion. The latter seemed incredible because American prosecutors have virtually absolute discretion. They need it to plea bargain and manage their caseloads.

I was intrigued by the finding of a law professor and colleague from Yale (Abraham Goldstein and Marvin Marcus) who had done an empirical study of judicial discretion in Italy, France, and Germany. They raised doubts about whether prosecutors and judges in those systems do not exercise discretion. They implied that discretion must be operating *sub rosa* because large caseloads were being managed.

And so I proposed to take a look for myself. OK, I admit that I was partially motivated by the urge to spend a sabbatical living like a Medici in a villa overlooking Florence. But I also paid my dues. I began learning Italian, reading about Italian law, and collecting the names of good contacts. While there I interviewed the American attorney from the U.S. Department of Justice who was working with the Italian-American Working Group Against the Mafia. That discussion turned my head. He was engaged in something I knew nothing about, namely, transnational law enforcement cooperation. The Italian-American Working Group was the first of its kind.

When I returned I began looking at the literature on this topic. It was very scarce. In the 1980s more and more academics had been stressing the importance of globalization and incorporating that idea into their textbooks and courses. Criminologists had not yet joined the trend. It occurred to me that I was on the frontier of an emerging new specialization in criminology. I began writing on the topic and edited a volume of original articles (*Crime and Law Enforcement in the Global Village* [1997]). Every year I responded to one of the National Institute of Justice's (NIJ) Requests for Proposals. My proposals always had an international dimension to them that caused them to be rejected, because NIJ did not fund studies of federal law enforcement agencies.

Eventually my next sabbatical was approaching and I desperately wanted to get funding to be able to study a transnational law enforcement issue for a full year rather than a half-year leave from teaching. In order to get NIJ funds for that purpose, I had to find a way to link the transnational issue to local law enforcement. It was the mid-1990s. Illegal immigration was a hot issue and also a transnational issue. And so I proposed to study the role of local law enforcement in dealing with illegal immigration and other transnational matters. The strategy worked!

BOX 12.2   CONTINUED

For decades immigrant criminality was addressed in every criminological textbook until the late 1960s when it disappeared. America was no longer vexed by immigrant criminality but by then Europe was, and has become more so as immigrants and refugees have flooded in from Eastern Europe, Africa, the Middle East, and Asia. Meanwhile, criminology had changed. Conflict theorists and left-leaning scholars shifted attention away from the criminality of people and toward the labeling, excluding, criminalizing, and labor-controlling policies of powerful forces in societies. Victimology, hate crime, and feminism happened. The Soviet Union came and went. Travel and communication technologies were revolutionized. Massive legal and illegal worldwide migrations were happening as was trafficking and smuggling of human beings.

It was not simply a matter of being politically incorrect to focus on the criminality of immigrants. It was a matter of recognizing that the problem is much larger than that. Reasonable, feasible, and humane answers to the problem will have to address this larger complexity. I am guided by one of H.L. Menchen's quips: "For every complex problem, there is a simple solution, and it is wrong."

In the meantime, "going global" has paid off for me. I have just returned from the University of Florence (Italy) where I was lecturing (in Italian) on comparative criminal justice. Dante probably turned over in his grave; but for me, it was sheer joy. In addition, I am now involved in a study of prosecutorial discretion in Hungary. One of the students in Florence was a Ph.D. candidate from Hungary. She offered to administer my decision simulation cases to prosecutors there.

ADVICE TO STUDENTS

If you have curiosity, you can get excited about many different topics. Pick something and work at it. Theory is more important than you now imagine. Fieldwork is the source of enthusiasm, insight, and motivation. It's the fun side of empirical research. Making a living doing empirical research is a privileged career of personal growth and satisfaction that most workers will never experience. Be grateful.

obtain sensitive information for their research, they refer anonymously to the research subjects studied. It is not their intent to name individuals or their characteristics. Also, **shield laws** have been passed to protect researchers from being compelled in court to reveal their sources of information.

Creating Anonymity and Disclosing Confidential State Data.   Some confidential information may be provided where personal identification characteristics have been obliterated. In 1994, a woman was completing her master's degree at a North Dakota university. She telephoned officials at two juvenile detention facilities in Mandan and Minot. The Mandan facility was a secure juvenile institution containing about 150 juveniles, while the Dakota

Boy's Ranch in Minot contained about 75 boys. The graduate student was interested in examining only "closed files," files of boys who were no longer in confinement. Authorities permitted the researcher to inspect 250 records of juveniles, where the names of juveniles had been omitted. Thus, even though this information was originally confidential and privileged, it was released to the woman with the provision that the identities of all the boys would not be known. Subsequently, the student wrote a master's thesis detailing the use of risk or dangerousness scores of youths and the varying lengths of their placement in these secure facilities. It was unnecessary to know the names of these boys to realize her specific study objectives. No ethical codes were violated.

On Ethics and Dating.   In another case involving juvenile records, a graduate student at California State University–Long Beach was dating a woman who oversaw juvenile records for the city of Long Beach. The graduate student was also a Long Beach police officer. He was interested in collecting data for a master's thesis and wondered if his female companion could assist him in inspecting juvenile files. The woman agreed to let him inspect these files, which had been maintained in a secure area of a city building since the early 1960s. Ordinarily, these files are closely guarded, and few persons are granted access to inspect them. She even let him xerox numerous files and prepare them for research analysis. He was also allowed to carry these files from the building and study them for several weeks. This was a very questionable action on the woman's part. No doubt the fact that she and the police officer were dating was the sole reason for her action to permit him to inspect and use otherwise confidential juvenile information.

Because of a shift change in his work schedule, the police officer had to postpone his graduate work for a few months. In the interim, he ceased dating the woman and returned the juvenile files. About 3 months later when his shift schedule was changed again, he decided to pursue an inspection of some of these juvenile files he had earlier examined. When he went to the city building and department where these records were maintained, a new woman was on duty. She advised that his previous acquaintance had been transferred to another department. When the officer asked to inspect the juvenile records, the new woman said that under no circumstances, excepting a court order, could he examine these sensitive records. Furthermore, she said, she was going to report the other woman for permitting him to illegally inspect these records on an earlier occasion. According to the police officer, he finally got the new woman to agree to forget about the incident. He did not study these juvenile files for his master's thesis research.

Sex Offenders: Sexual Histories and Stimulus–Response Experiments

Studies of sex offenders and the methods used to treat them have raised several ethical issues. Public sentiment against sex offenders was heightened when a New Jersey sex offender stalked, sexually assaulted, and murdered a young child. New Jersey passed Megan's Law, a significant piece of legislation requiring that all sex offenders must register in the communities where they reside; notify community leaders of their residency; and suffer lengthy civil commitments if they are regarded as serious, dangerous, and mentally ill (Brooks, 1996). Considerable attention has also been directed toward the treatment of sex offenders and preventing them from committing new sex crimes.

In the 1970s researchers conducted experiments with sex offenders using aversion therapy. Sex offenders would be exposed to various visual sexual stimuli (e.g., graphic sexual photos and scenes), and then they would receive electrical shocks or chemical injections that would tend to make them ill or nauseous. These and other similar treatments were largely unregulated and unstandardized. The result was that some sex offenders were permanently injured or suffered psychological traumas well beyond the scope of the intended treatment and sex crime prevention (Wardlaw, 1979).

In the 1990s experiments with sex offenders continued, with greater regulation and control. For male sex offenders, one method of charting their reaction to sexual stimuli was phallometry, or penile plethysmorgraphy, which measured erectile function of their penises resulting from exposure to visually stimulating sex scenes. Such methods have been deemed well suited to challenge sex offender denials that they are stimulated by sexual deviance of any kind. Investigators have used phallometry and other methods to assess a sex offender's treatment needs and to predict future deviant sexual behavior (Launay, 1994).

Despite the effectiveness of these and other treatment methods, several investigators have raised ethical questions about the assessment and treatment procedures used and the amenability of patients to counseling. Relatively little has been done to provide aftercare for sex offenders in communities. Furthermore, professional guidelines have been espoused by some of those treating sex offenders, including the development and design of more standardized stimulus material to discourage patient faking; providing more reliable data; and carrying out validation studies with forensic and nonforensic populations, including detailed analyses of subjects' sexual histories, motivations, and fantasies (Launay, 1994).

Granting Permission to Study Subordinates, Potentates, and Juveniles

Often, researchers contact heads of organizations and agencies for the purpose of studying their employees or obtaining different kinds of information about them. Investigators who study inmates in prison settings, for example, will contact prison administrators to obtain their permission to study prisoners. Prison wardens and others of authority will want to know how much time will be taken and what type of inmate involvement will be required. Do researchers wish to interview certain inmates? Do researchers want to distribute self-administered questionnaires to inmates for their reactions to certain questions? Do researchers want to study prisoners on death row or who are maintained in maximum-security areas? Who is sponsoring the research?

Granting Permission to Study Subordinates.   If investigators wish to study probation officers, they may contact probation agencies and discuss their contemplated research plans with agency heads. Sometimes agency heads or administrators will consent to have the researcher study their agency personnel. Investigators are at liberty to exploit every potential resource and contact to their research advantage. If a researcher has a friend who is politically connected with others in agencies or organizations where certain information is desired, then these contacts can make appropriate introductions. This doesn't mean that permission will automatically be granted to study persons in these settings, but at least the researcher has an opportunity to make a pitch for why the study should be conducted.

Investigating Potentates.   Some investigators want to study the characteristics of law enforcement administrators, chiefs, commissioners, and other functionaries. These persons are often insulated from the public. They are **potentates** or very powerful people. Gaining access to these people is difficult. It is helpful if the researcher is connected with an established agency, university, or research institution. Using agency, university, or research institution letterheads and auspices, researchers can often get their foot in the door of offices that would otherwise be closed to them. Before any researcher decides to study special samples of potentates, it is a good idea to determine whether or not they can be accessed by conventional research methods.

Studying Juveniles and Their Records.   Juveniles pose particularly difficult problems. Numerous protections and safeguards are in place to shield juveniles from research investigations. If a researcher were to show up at an elementary school and ask the principal to distribute a questionnaire to all fifth-grade students concerning their possible delinquent conduct, there is no doubt that the researcher would be turned away and flatly refused admission to fifth-grade classrooms. If investigators wished to inspect juvenile court records and study delinquency trends, they would quickly find that these records are safeguarded from the general public, including social scientists.

   Most juvenile courts have retained their status as civil bodies. Adjudications of juveniles are civil in nature. When juveniles are declared delinquent by juvenile court judges, they are not convicted of crimes. Rather, they are adjudicated delinquent in a civil proceeding, and at a later date when they become adults, their records will likely be sealed or expunged. Many authorities believe that youths who get into trouble should not have their juvenile records count against them as adults. Thus, in a majority of states, the records of juvenile offenders are either expunged or sealed. This means that only a limited number of agencies or officials can gain access to these records at some later date. These records are not available for public inspection. This is largely because of their civil nature and origins.

   However, increasing numbers of states are changing their policies concerning the privacy of and restricted access to these juvenile records. In some states these juvenile records are maintained for many years beyond one's age of majority or adulthood. Removing the cloak of anonymity from juveniles and their records is a relatively new strategy used to combat delinquency and crime. Traditional methods for dealing with delinquency have been ineffective, and many juveniles express contempt toward juvenile courts because of their known leniency. The get-tough movement has extended to juveniles so that accountability for their actions has been heightened. Making juveniles increasingly visible to the public is one way of making them take a new look at the law and their own responsibilities. Despite the get-tough movement and its effects, it is still difficult to obtain juvenile records or study juveniles in most jurisdictions.

The Nuremberg Code

During World War II, Nazi Germany engaged in mass genocide against Jews and others. The German dictator, Adolf Hitler, believed in the purity of Aryan and Nordic ethnicities and thought that Germany should be ethnically cleansed of all non-Aryan persons. Numerous death camps were established in several European countries controlled by German troops, and routine executions and exterminations occurred over a period of years. During World War II it is estimated that over 6 million Jews were put to death in these camps.

At the same time that Jews were being executed, more than a few Nazi physicians were conducting inhuman experiments calculated to change less desirable biological characteristics and features of prisoners to more desirable features. Consistent with the blond, blue-eyed Nordic ideal envisioned by Hitler and his close associates, German physicians injected the eyes of brown-eyed patients/prisoners with blue dye in the fruitless effort to change their eye color. Thousands of Jews were sterilized, where testicles and ovaries were removed surgically, and without anesthetic. Some of these experiments were designed to discover how much pain human beings could endure before dying. Other experiments were conducted, where men, women, and children were made to stand nude in rivers during the cold winter months. These experiments were calculated to test how long it would take for persons to freeze to death under varying conditions of exposure to the elements.

These atrocious experiments were subsequently revealed and described at the Nuremberg, Germany trials of war criminals following World War II. Many surviving victims testified against those who tortured them in the name of medical science. When the trials of war criminals were concluded, several countries including the United States adopted what popularly became known as the **Nuremberg Code,** a set of principles specifying conditions under which human subjects could be used in social and medical experiments. The critical provisions of the Nuremberg Code that have become widely adopted by virtually every research institute are: (1) any experimental subject must participate in any research project on a voluntary basis and give their **informed consent;** and (2) any potential research participant must be advised of any known or anticipated harmful effects arising from the contemplated experiment before the research is undertaken.

Despite these standards and potential safeguards, some agencies and individuals have conducted subsequent research where unethical and illegal experiments have been conducted. During the Vietnam war in the early 1970s, for example, several experiments were conducted by various military investigators. These experiments involved knowingly exposing selected samples of American soldiers to different chemical agents. For example, Agent Orange, the code name for a highly toxic herbicide, was used extensively in the jungles of Vietnam. Numerous soldiers were exposed to Agent Orange and contracted serious illnesses. More than a few soldiers died because of their exposure to Agent Orange. Other experiments were conducted with LSD and other drugs to determine their behavior-altering effects on soldiers. Later in the early 1990s, American soldiers were once again exposed to toxic chemicals in Operation Desert Storm, a military action against Iraq. Other types of controversial experiments have been conducted by U.S. researchers in recent decades involving hundreds of thousands of participants, where it is questionable whether these experimental subjects were involved through informed consent or advised of the social, psychological, and/or biological risks.

Professional Associations and the Development of Ethical Standards for Research

Most national social and criminological professional organizations in the United States have evolved codes of ethical standards for researchers to follow. Because of the diverse views and opinions of persons in these different organizations, consensus has been difficult to achieve and some codes of professional responsibility and conduct are in different revision

BOX 12.3   PERSONALITY HIGHLIGHT

DORIS LAYTON MACKENZIE
University of Maryland

Statistics: B.A., M.A., Ph.D. (psychology), Pennsylvania
State University.

BACKGROUND AND INTERESTS

When I first started college at the University of New Hampshire I became interested in psychology and social psychology. I thought I would learn to understand people and why they do what they do. After all these years I am still hoping to learn why people do what they do. In particular, the focus of my research has been on understanding criminals and how to change their behavior.

I began to study offender behavior when I started working on a research project with Lynne Goodstein, John Hepburn, and John Kramer. I traveled to several prisons where I interviewed and surveyed prison administrators, staff, and inmates. I became interested in understanding corrections, correctional programs, and offender behavior. I completed my Ph.D. and moved to Louisiana State University (LSU) where I had a joint appointment in the Departments of Experimental Statistics and Criminal Justice. From then on my major professional association was criminology and criminal justice. I was in Louisiana when the large increases in prison populations began in the late 1970s. State correctional administrators began to have serious problems because they didn't know how long the increase would continue. For this reason I began to develop models for predicting prison populations and to study factors that led to the massive increase in prison populations.

While in Louisiana, I also continued to study inmate adjustment to prison and correctional programs. One day I received a phone call from a psychologist who worked at a prison. He said they were developing a new program and he was concerned about it. He asked if I would be interested in evaluating the program. It was one of the first correctional boot camps in the country. I said I was interested in conducting the study. I applied to the National Institute of Justice (NIJ) for money to fund the study and I was granted the funding. This began my research in correctional boot camps. At first, I was very much against the concept. But my task as the researcher was to try to be objective and to not let my feelings influence the results. I was surprised to find that the attitudes of the inmates in the correctional boot camp were more positive than a comparison group of inmates in traditional prisons. However, the recidivism was the same for the two groups. As I studied the boot camps that were being developed throughout the United States, I realized that the camps were very different. Some emphasized rehabilitation and treatment, others emphasized punishment and hard labor. I proposed to the NIJ that we study a variety of

BOX 12.3 CONTINUED

programs so we can determine whether the effects were due to the military atmosphere or to characteristics of the programs offered in the boot camps. NIJ awarded me a Visiting Scientist position to assist them with program management and to conduct a multisite study of boot camps. I stayed at NIJ 4 years and was able to continue my research during this time. With Gaylene Styve, I just completed a book on correctional boot camps (2004). The book gathers together the research I have conducted through the years. I have continued to be interested in examining a large variety of correctional programs to identify effective programs. At the University of Maryland I had the opportunity to work with Larry Sherman on a grant I received from the NIJ. The grant required us to prepare a report for the U.S. Congress evaluating the effectiveness of crime prevention programs. I work on the chapter examining programs in the courts and corrections. Working with graduate students, I reviewed a large number of correctional programs such as drug courts, drug treatment, correctional boot camps, juvenile residential facilities, electronic monitoring, and cognitive skills programs. We developed a method for evaluating each study for the quality of the research (internal validity). We then looked at each research area and, based on the direction and significance of the results and the research methods score, we drew conclusions about whether the program was (1) effective ("Worked"), (2) promising, (3) not effective, or, at this point, there was not enough research to tell. This work led me to an interest in meta-analysis as a statistical technique for evaluating the effectiveness of a body of research (e.g., on drug courts, drug treatment). With colleagues, I have completed a series of articles using meta-analyses (e.g., sex offender treatment, correctional boot camps, drug treatment, drug courts).

ADVICE TO STUDENTS

If you are interested in the type of work I do, then I suggest that you make sure to get a good academic background in criminology and criminal justice including both the sociological and psychological views of offenders and the causes of crime. The viewpoints, perspectives, and theories of the two disciplines differ dramatically and it helps to know both perspectives. Additionally, it is helpful to take as many statistical and methods courses as possible while you are in graduate school. It is difficult to get these courses at a later time. Find a good mentor while you are in graduate school. And, very important to consider in an academic career is that there are many advantages if you really love what you are doing. If you don't love such things as learning, research, and students, don't go into an academic profession.

stages. Some of these organizations have moved to adopt codes of ethics in the 1990s. In 1996, the American Society of Criminology established a committee charged with the responsibility to draft a code of ethics acceptable to its membership. In 1998, an Ethics Committee was formed by the Academy of Criminal Justice Sciences (ACJS) at its annual meeting in Albuquerque, New Mexico. Both of these organizations tended to emulate the Code of Ethics established years earlier by the American Sociological Association.

A good example of a Code of Ethics is the one evolved by the ACJS. Ethics Committee members originally crafted a detailed document, outlining a code of ethics and other standards. Subsequently a finalized version of the ACJS Code of Ethics was approved and is shown in Box 12.4 (Academy of Criminal Justice Sciences, 2004).

Notice in the Code of Ethics in Box 12.4 that certain elements of the Nuremberg Code have been incorporated into items #13, #14, and #16. Reassurances of respondent anonymity are also pervasive throughout the document. Most of the other provisions of this Code of Ethics address matters relating to researcher conduct. Essentially, investigators are admonished by this Code to be honest, objective, and sensitive to proper research procedure that characterizes the discipline.

BOX 12.4   ACADEMY OF CRIMINAL JUSTICE SCIENCES CODE OF ETHICS

PREAMBLE

Criminal justice is a scientific discipline and those who teach, research, study, administer or practice this discipline subscribe to the general tenets of science and scholarship. They also recognize that the discovery, creation, transmission, and accumulation of knowledge in any scientific discipline involves ethical considerations at every level.

The Code of Ethics of the Academy of Criminal Justice Sciences (ACJS) sets forth (1) the General Principles and (2) Ethical Standards that underlie members of the Academy's professional responsibilities and conduct, along with (3) Policies and Procedures for enforcing those principles and standards. Membership in the ACJS commits individual members to adhere to the ACJS Code of Ethics in determining ethical behavior in the context of their everyday professional activities. Activities that are purely personal and not related to criminal justice as a scientific discipline are not subject to this Code of Ethics.

The Ethical Standards set forth enforceable rules for the behavior of individual members of the Academy in specific situations. Most of the ethical standards are written broadly, to provide applications in varied roles and varied contexts. The Ethical Standards are not exhaustive—conduct that is not included in the Ethical Standards is not necessarily ethical or unethical. The Ethical Standards should always be interpreted in the context of the General Principles. Violations of the Code of Ethics may lead to sanctions associated with individual membership in the ACJS, including restrictions on or termination of that membership.

GENERAL PRINCIPLES

In their professional activities, members of the Academy are committed to enhancing the general well-being of society and of the individuals and groups within it. Members of the Academy are especially careful to avoid incompetent, unethical or unscrupulous use of criminal justice knowledge. They recognize the great potential for harm that is associated with the study

BOX 12.4   CONTINUED

of criminal justice, and they do not knowingly place the well-being of themselves or other people in jeopardy in their professional work.

Members of the Academy respect the rights, dignity and worth of all people. The worth of people gives them the right to demand that information about them remain confidential. In their work, members of the Academy are particularly careful to respect the rights, dignity and worth of criminal justice personnel, crime victims and those accused or convicted of committing crimes, as well as of students and research subjects. They do not discriminate on the basis of age, gender, race, ethnicity, national origin, religion, sexual orientation, health condition, or domestic status. They are sensitive to individual, cultural and role differences among peoples. They acknowledge the rights of other people and groups to hold values, attitudes and opinions that are different from their own.

Members of the Academy are honest and open in their professional dealings with others. They are committed to the free and open access to knowledge, to public discourse of findings, and to the sharing of the sources of those findings whenever possible. They do not knowingly make false, misleading or deceptive statements in their professional roles. In particular, they do not knowingly present false, misleading, or deceptive accounts of their own or other people's professional work for any reason.

Members of the Academy strive to maintain high levels of competence in their work. They recognize the limits of their expertise and undertake only those tasks for which they are qualified by education, training, and experience.

In some situations, the above general principles may seem to come into conflict with each other, in the sense that different principles may seem to call for different courses of action. In addition, members of the Academy might be members of other organizations with their own code of ethics, which at times might dictate different courses of action. The following Ethical Standards attempt to clarify the present thinking of the Academy of Criminal Justice Sciences regarding ethical courses of actions in some of those situations. However, to some extent, each individual member of the Academy should evaluate the ethical requirements of a specific situation, decide on an ethical course of action for that situation, and take responsibility for those actions.

MEMBERS OF THE ACADEMY AS TEACHERS, SUPERVISORS, AND ADMINISTRATORS

1. When acting as teachers, members of the Academy should provide students with an honest statement of the scope and perspective of their courses, clear expectations for student performance, clear description of criteria used in grading, and fair, timely, and easily accessible evaluations of their work.

2. When acting as teachers and/or administrators, members of the Academy should refrain from disclosure of personal information concerning students where such information is not directly relevant to issues of professional competence.

3. When acting as teachers and/or administrators, members of the Academy should make all decisions concerning textbooks, course content, course requirements, and grading solely on the basis of professional criteria without regard for financial or other incentives or disincentives that may directly affect them.

BOX 12.4 CONTINUED

4. When serving as supervisors/administrators, members of the Academy should ensure that instructors are qualified to teach the courses for which they are assigned.

5. When acting as supervisors/administrators, members of the Academy should provide students with explicit policies and criteria about conditions for admission to the program, program requirements, financial assistance, retention, employment, funding, and evaluation process.

6. Members of the Academy should not coerce or deceive students or others into serving as research subjects.

7. Members of the Academy have an explicit responsibility to acknowledge the contributions of students and to act on their behalf in setting forth agreements regarding authorship and other recognition.

8. Members of the Academy should not coerce or obtain through manipulation personal or sexual favors or economic or professional advantages from any person, including students, respondents, clients, patients, research assistants, clerical staff or colleagues. In addition, members of the Academy should recognize that romantic or intimate relationships with individuals vulnerable to manipulation, such as current students in their programs or employees under their supervision, may create the appearance of, or opportunities for, favoritism and/or exploitation, and thus such relationships should be avoided.

9. Members of the Academy should not let their personal animosities or intellectual differences deter students from contact with other professionals.

OBJECTIVITY AND INTEGRITY IN THE CONDUCT OF CRIMINAL JUSTICE RESEARCH

1. Members of the Academy should adhere to the highest possible technical standards in their research.

2. Since individual members of the Academy vary in their research modes, skills, and experience, they should acknowledge the limitations that may affect the validity of their findings.

3. In presenting their work, members of the Academy are obliged to fully report their findings. They should not misrepresent the findings of their research or omit significant data. Details of their theories, methods, and research designs that might bear upon interpretations of research findings should be reported.

4. Members of the Academy should fully report all sources of financial support and other sponsorship of their research.

5. Members of the Academy should not make any commitments to respondents, individuals, groups or organizations unless there is full intention and ability to honor them.

6. Consistent with the spirit of full disclosure of method and analysis, members of the Academy, after they have completed their own analyses, should cooperate in efforts to make raw data and pertinent documentation available to other social scientists, at reasonable costs, except in cases where confidentiality, the client's rights to proprietary information and privacy, or the claims of a field worker to the privacy of personal notes necessary would be violated.

7. Members of the Academy should provide adequate information, documentation, and citations concerning scales and other measures used in their research.

BOX 12.4   CONTINUED

8. Members of the Academy should not accept grants, contracts or research assignments that appear likely to violate the principles enunciated in this Code, and should disassociate themselves from research when they discover a violation and are unable to correct it.

9. When financial support for a project has been accepted, members of the Academy should make every effort to complete the proposed work on schedule.

10. When a member of the Academy is involved in a project with others, including students, there should be mutually accepted explicit agreements at the outset with respect to division of work, compensation, access to data, rights of authorship, and other rights and responsibilities. These agreements should not be exploitative or arrived at through any form of coercion or intimidation. Such agreements may need to be modified as the project evolves and such modifications should be clearly stated among all participants.

11. Members of the Academy have the right to disseminate research findings, except those likely to cause harm to clients, collaborators and participants, those which violate formal or implied promises of confidentiality, or those which are proprietary under a formal or informal agreement.

DISCLOSURE AND RESPECT OF THE RIGHTS OF RESEARCH POPULATIONS BY MEMBERS OF THE ACADEMY

12. Members of the Academy should not misuse their positions as professionals for fraudulent purposes or as a pretext for gathering intelligence for any individual, group, organization, or government.

13. Human subjects have the right of full disclosure as early as it is appropriate to the research process, and they have the right to an opportunity to have their questions answered about the purpose and usage of the research.

14. Subjects of research are entitled to rights of personal confidentiality unless they are waived.

15. Information about subjects obtained from records that are open to public scrutiny cannot be protected by guarantees of privacy or confidentiality.

16. The process of conducting criminal justice research should not expose respondents to more than minimal risk of personal harm, and members of the Academy should make every effort to ensure the safety and security of respondents and project staff.

17. Members of the Academy should take culturally appropriate steps to secure informed consent and to avoid invasions of privacy. In addition, special actions will be necessary where the individuals studied are illiterate, under correctional supervision, minors, have low social status, are under judicial supervision, have diminished capacity, are unfamiliar with social research or otherwise occupy a position of unequal power with the researcher.

18. Members of the Academy should seek to anticipate potential threats to confidentiality. Techniques such as the removal of direct identifiers, the use of randomized responses, and other statistical solutions to problems of privacy should be used where appropriate. Care should be taken to ensure secure storage, maintenance, and/or destruction of sensitive records.

19. Confidential information provided by research participants should be treated as such by members of the Academy, even when this information enjoys no legal protection or privilege and legal force is applied. The obligation to respect confidentiality also applies to members of research organizations (in-

BOX 12.4   CONTINUED

terviewers, coders, clerical staff, etc.) who have access to the information. It is the responsibility of administrators and chief investigators to instruct staff members on this point and to make every effort to insure that access to confidential information is restricted.

20. While generally adhering to the norm of acknowledging the contributions of all collaborators, members of the Academy should be sensitive to harm that may arise from disclosure and respect a collaborator's need for anonymity.

21. All research should meet the human subjects requirements imposed by educational institutions and funding sources. Study design and information gathering techniques should conform to regulations protecting the rights of human subjects, regardless of funding.

22. Members of the Academy should comply with appropriate federal and institutional requirements pertaining to the conduct of their research. These requirements might include, but are not necessarily limited to, obtaining proper review and approval for research that involves human subjects and accommodating recommendations made by responsible committees concerning research subjects, materials, and procedures (*ACJS Today,* 1998:15–16).

QUESTIONS OF AUTHORSHIP AND ACKNOWLEDGEMENT FOR MEMBERS OF THE ACADEMY

1. Members of the Academy should acknowledge persons who contribute to their research and their copyrighted publications. Claims and ordering of authorship and acknowledgements should accurately reflect the contributions of all participants in the research and writing process, including students, except in those cases where such ordering or acknowledgement is determined by an official protocol.

2. Data and material taken verbatim from another person's published or unpublished written work should be explicitly identified and referenced to its author. Citations to original ideas and data developed in the work of others, even if not quoted verbatim, should be acknowledged.

3. Editors should continually ensure the fair application of standards without personal or ideological malice or favoritism.

4. Journal editors should provide prompt decisions to authors of submitted manuscripts. They should monitor the work of associate editors and other referees so that delays are minimal and reviews are conscientious.

5. An editor's commitment to publish an essay should be binding on the journal. Once accepted for publication, a manuscript should be published expeditiously.

6. Unless journal policies explicitly allow multiple submissions, a paper submitted to one journal may not be submitted to another journal until after an official decision has been received from the first journal. An exception can be made for journals in two substantially different languages, where readers of one journal would not typically be able to read the other.

7. Members who commit to participate in the annual conference (i.e., present a paper, act as a chair or discussant, etc.) are expected to do so.

8. Members of the Academy should decline requests for reviews of the work of others where strong conflicts of interest are involved. Such conflicts may occur when a person is asked to review work

BOX 12.4   CONTINUED

by teachers, friends, or colleagues for whom he or she feels an overriding sense of personal obligation, competition, or enmity. Members of the Academy should also decline requests for reviews when such requests cannot be fulfilled on time, or when they feel unqualified to review the work.

9. Materials sent for review should be read conscientiously, carefully, and confidentially. Evaluations should be justified and explained clearly. Reviews of manuscripts should avoid personal attacks on the author(s).

10. Members of the Academy who are asked to review manuscripts and books they have previously reviewed should inform the editor requesting review of this situation.

Source: Abridged from the Academy of Criminal Justice Sciences (2004). *Code of Ethics.* Greenbelt, MD.

University Guidelines for Research Projects: The Use of Human Subjects

Colleges and universities, especially the latter, are known for conducting extensive research on virtually every academic subject. Botany and other sciences, such as chemistry and physics, seldom rely on the participation of human subjects for experiments. However, the social sciences, including sociology, psychology, anthropology, criminology, and criminal justice, conduct numerous studies and experiments where human subjects are involved. An example of university policy relating to unethical research practices is shown in Box 12.5.

Most of the time, social scientific research consists of soliciting information from human subjects in different contexts. Probation or parole officers are interviewed or surveyed in order to determine their work interests and motivation. Inmates of prisons and jails may be studied for various reasons. Corrections officers and administrators might be studied. Judicial decision making or plea bargaining between defense counsels and prosecutors might be investigated. Patterns of behavior are described. The decision-making process in law enforcement might be portrayed.

University professors and both undergraduate and graduate students carry out ongoing research to answer various questions relating to their discipline. Most of the time, conventional data collection techniques are used, including questionnaires or surveys, interviews, and/or observation. Seldom are research subjects exposed to chemical substances or drugs, or to other physical stimuli that might expose these subjects to some type of biological harm or injury.

Despite the fact that much criminological research seems harmless to humans in terms of the potential for adverse physical or biological effects, it is possible for them to suffer certain psychological effects. In fact, exposure to certain types of questions, either in interviews or on questionnaires, is an educational experience in a sense. Interviewers and investigators may actually trigger certain thoughts and ideas among their respondents. Some respondents may feel, "Whatever these interviewers are asking me must be important. Perhaps I ought to be concerned about it." Furthermore, merely asking respondents questions in their work settings or habitats may set off chain reactions that substantially change these work settings or habitats.

BOX 12.5   UNIVERSITY OF CONNECTICUT POLICY AND PROCEDURES FOR REVIEW OF ALLEGED UNETHICAL RESEARCH PRACTICES

The University of Connecticut is committed to maintaining the integrity of scholarship and investigative research and to fostering a climate conducive to such scientific integrity. The University believes that its research activities are conducted in a responsible and ethical fashion. Therefore, unethical research practices are a major breach of contract between the faculty or staff member involved and the University. Consequently, formal procedures have been established to investigate alleged unethical practices. These procedures incorporate the requirements of the relevant collective bargaining units; they do not supersede nor set up alternatives to established procedures for resolving other kinds of misconduct, such as, but not limited to, fiscal improprieties, issues concerning the ethical treatment of human or animal subjects, or criminal matters.

DEFINITION OF UNETHICAL PRACTICES

Though the concept "integrity in research" embraces a wide range of issues and practices, this policy defines research misconduct as fraudulent or markedly irregular practices in research conduct and in the collection, analysis and reporting of data; including fabrication, falsification, plagiarism, or other practices that seriously deviate from those that are commonly accepted within the scientific community for proposing, conducting, or reporting research.

Primary responsibility for inhibiting misconduct and safeguarding the integrity of research should be exercised by the research community. This responsibility includes: examination of allegations of misconduct, investigation of substantiated allegations, and the imposition of sanctions when appropriate.

ALLEGATIONS

An allegation of unethical research practices involving any faculty or staff member can be communicated, preferably in writing, by any person to the Vice Provost. Alternatively such allegations may be brought first to the attention of the faculty member responsible for the individual whose actions are being questioned, such as the research supervisor, the Principal Investigator, the department head.

BOX 12.5 CONTINUED

NOTIFICATION REQUIREMENTS

Upon initiation of the inquiry, the Vice Provost will notify the respondent within a reasonable time of the charges and the process that will follow. The identity of the complainant will be kept confidential during the inquiry phase to the extent permissible by law.

MAINTENANCE OF CONFIDENTIALITY

Strict confidentiality should be diligently maintained throughout the initial inquiry (fact-finding) process, and only those persons with a need to be informed shall be told of the allegation(s) and the process underway.

PROCEDURES OF THE PRELIMINARY INQUIRY COMMITTEE

The purpose of the Committee in conducting the initial inquiry (fact-finding) is solely to determine whether reasonable grounds exist for conducting a more detailed investigation of the allegation(s). The Committee shall review the allegation(s), and the known facts, and may interview any persons having relevant information, including the person making the allegation(s), the researchers in question, their supervisors, and those assisting in the research. The faculty or staff member against whom the allegation is made shall be informed of the allegation(s) and the fact that it has been referred to a Committee. The faculty or staff member against whom the allegation(s) were made shall be permitted union representation.

FINDINGS OF THE PRELIMINARY INQUIRY COMMITTEE

The Committee shall complete its inquiry within 60 days from the date of its formation and report one of three possible recommendations to the Vice Provost:

1. The complaint should be dismissed as the allegation is without grounds or insignificance.
2. The alleged misconduct is not significant and can be dealt with by procedures outlined in the collective bargaining contracts.
3. A more detailed investigation is warranted.

The Committee shall prepare a report summarizing its findings and conclusions and submit the report and its recommendations to the Vice Provost. The report will state what evidence was reviewed, summarize relevant interviews, and include the conclusions of the Committee. The individual(s) against whom the allegation(s) were made shall be given a copy of the inquiry report. If they comment on that report, their comments may be made part of the record at the individual's discretion.

Source: Abridged from *Policies and Procedures for Review of Alleged Unethical Research Practices.* Storrs: University of Connecticut, 2004.

For instance, as a graduate student, I studied a sample of bank employees near my university. This was an integral part of my doctoral dissertation and research. I thought my questions were harmless. Among other things, I wanted to know about employee job satisfaction and work motivation. When I gave questionnaires to these bank employees and interviewed them, I sensed that they were very uncomfortable with the questions I asked. Later, I confided my feelings about their reactions to a bank officer who had earlier granted me permission to study these employees. She nodded knowingly and said, "You don't know this, but we had a large amount of money missing a few months ago. We decided that all of our employees must submit to a lie detector test or lose their jobs. We had to find out who embezzled the money. Needless to say, the morale of these employees went through the floor. They have been unhappy campers ever since!" Suddenly, I understood the significance of their reactions to me. I was the "enemy" in a sense, since my study of them coincided with the embezzlement. How were they to know I was acting independently of the bank and doing my research for my own self-interest?

Later as a professor at a large university, I had the occasion to prepare a simple questionnaire and send it home with students in my research methods class. The questionnaire was a survey of parents' opinions about different topics. None of the questions contained anything offensive, at least in my view. About a week later, I was called into the office of my department head. He handed me a large envelope containing one of my questionnaires. It had been torn into many pieces. He advised that one of the parents had visited him earlier that day and told him that he didn't want "any damn professor at the university giving his daughter some sex questionnaire. He didn't want that filth in his home." I was flabbergasted. The only reference to sex in my questionnaire was an item indicating whether the respondent was male or female. The other questions were items about the United States space program and how moon space might be utilized if somehow we were eventually able to cultivate it. Other items were of a sociodemographic nature, such as urban–rural background, age, years of education, religious and political affiliation, and other factors. I showed another copy of my questionnaire to the department head and he immediately recognized the innocence of the matter.

Subsequently, I was approached by the co-ed whose father had torn up my questionnaire. She apologized for his behavior and explained that a few weeks earlier, a psychology graduate student had given her psychology class a questionnaire inquiring about the sexual habits and behavior patterns of college students. Her father happened to see the questionnaire as she was completing it at home. Some of the items asked about sexually explicit details of one's behaviors. Her father threw a fit and spent several hours cursing the university and its professors. He hadn't even read my questionnaire. He assumed that if another professor at that "damned university" sent a questionnaire home with his daughter, it must be like the other one. Thus, because of the thoughtlessness of one graduate student, the reputation of the university was irreparably damaged for at least one parent.

Today, most universities and colleges have policies and provisions relating to research conducted under their sponsorship. Any research project conducted by any university employee must first be reviewed by a **human subjects committee** or **institutional review board.** This committee ascertains whether there are any aspects of one's research that might potentially be harmful to human subjects. The committee determines which safeguards, if any, have been implemented to ensure that human subjects are protected. Such screening of research projects is imperative to the extent that any drugs or experimental substances are used and where human subjects might be exposed to biological or physical harm.

Where human subjects are going to be interviewed, exposed to questionnaires, or observed, the research instrumentation and methodology are scrupulously examined to determine if there are any potentially offensive or psychologically harmful effects. Provisions are made for human subjects to be made fully aware of the research goals or purposes. Human subjects must be in a position to give their informed consent, and they may decline to participate if they choose to do so.

These and other safeguards are incorporated into human subjects committee policies. One purpose is to protect the university from subsequent lawsuits if any physical or psychological harm to any human subject occurs. Another purpose is to ensure that all researchers conform to the codes of ethics of their professions. The point is that everything that can be done is done to protect human subjects in every way. At least that is how any university-sponsored research should proceed ideally. There are few sanctioning mechanisms in place in most schools to prevent professors from conducting various types of social research on their own. Anyone can create a questionnaire, xerox it, and mail it to numerous respondents. It is quite difficult to police such independent research efforts. Despite university and professional ethical standards, there are always some persons who depart from them from time to time.

Ethical Issues

Several ethical issues include (1) whether the research is sponsored by an outside agency or the individual investigator; (2) the rights of human subjects; and (3) informed consent and how personal information is used.

Sponsored Research and Investigator Interests: Choice or Chance?

Money is available from external sources to fund research projects. A substantial number of consumers who accept external research funds are university faculty. Most universities and colleges have **seed money** available, or small monetary sums to assist individual faculty in modest research projects. Usually seed money is furnished to professors in order to help defray their paper and postage costs as they prepare questionnaires and distribute them to a chosen set of respondents. If a professor wants to study the local police department or survey its officers, for instance, there will be some expense incurred as the research progresses. Duplication and mailing of questionnaires may be expensive. If the investigator wishes to use interviewers to gather some of the data, then these interviewers will have to be paid. Students are sometimes used as part-time interviewers. Small amounts of up to $1,500 or $2,000 may be available for faculty to use for these limited research purposes to help defray investigation costs.

The National Institute of Justice and Office of Juvenile Justice and Delinquency Prevention are two agencies that fund criminal justice and criminological research. These organizations issue requests for research proposals, or RFPs, on an annual basis. They provide guidelines for the preparation and submission of proposals, where prospective investigators describe their research ideas and how they intend to implement them. Committees within these different agencies review submitted proposals and select those for funding that appear to fit agency guidelines and needs.

One example of RFPs is a National Institute of Justice Solicitation for Fiscal Year 1997. A 12-page booklet was mailed to thousands of persons throughout the United States in June 1997. It was entitled *Policing Research and Evaluation: Fiscal Year 1997*. The booklet contained hundreds of suggestions and requests for research proposals on a variety of topics. The NIJ solicitation contained the following:

> In this solicitation, NIJ seeks local evaluations that will contribute to our understanding of police agencies' efforts to move toward community-oriented policing. NIJ is particularly interested in the learning of efforts to implement community-oriented policing across a variety of community settings including cities, rural communities, small towns, and sheriff's departments. In addition to understanding the process of implementing community-oriented policing, NIJ seeks evaluations that advance our understanding of the consequences of specific community-oriented policing strategies, practices, and styles, including: recruitment and training strategies; use of performance and reward structures; the re-alignment or redefining of supervisory roles; and strategies that promote collaboration or resource-sharing with other public and private agencies and institutions . . . NIJ anticipates supporting up to 7 awards of varying sizes totaling up to $1.5 million. (pp. 2–3)

In the same publication, the NIJ "is interested in the application of problem-solving strategies across a range of topics, including firearms violence, especially among youth; illegal gun markets; gangs and gang violence; the changing nature of drug markets; family and intimate violence; prostitution, panhandling, and other illegal street solicitations; and other predatory crimes, such as auto theft, auto robbery, and ATM-related robbery . . . grants will be made for up to 24 months. Multi-site research is encouraged. NIJ anticipates supporting up to 12 awards totaling up to $2 million under this section of the solicitation" (1997, pp. 3–4). For NIJ purposes, small grants are considered $1,000–$50,000. Large grants are in excess of $50,000.

This is **sponsored research.** When anyone applies for this and other grant money, they must tailor their research proposal to fit the interests of the funding agency, such as NIJ. Thus, if a professor applies for NIJ funding, the proposal must be directly relevant for a specific NIJ interest. Otherwise, the professor's research proposal will not be funded, at least by NIJ. The NIJ says, "While NIJ encourages potential applicants to identify the specific area under which their research application should be considered, promising research applications that *do not fit precisely within a given section of this research agenda* or that may cross over areas may still be considered" (1997, p. 2). The unwritten implication here is that if your proposal doesn't fit the needs of NIJ, it "may still be considered" but probably won't.

Being the Director or Being Directed?   There is a clear difference between doing one's own research and doing research for others. In the former case, a research project is envisioned, planned, and implemented. The research goals and aims are outlined by the investigator. The investigator determines how data will be collected. The investigator determines how the data will be presented and interpreted. The summary and implications of the study will be totally within the control of the researcher. However, in the latter case, where the researcher receives grant money from an external agency such as the NIJ, the interests of the agency are of primary importance. In the case of the NIJ, this organization chooses the research topic, not the researcher. The research objectives for any specific project within NIJ guidelines are also chosen by the NIJ.

For many researchers, the difference between choosing specific research topics and engaging in studies involving predetermined research topics is irrelevant. Rather, the most important consideration is receiving funding. This is because universities and colleges evaluate professors in part on their ability to secure external research funds. Promotions and tenure are granted in part on the basis of one's success in securing research grants from virtually any source.

Some researchers consider doing work under the sponsorship of a federal agency or a private corporation as a form of intellectual prostitution. Investigators are paid for performing a service, not necessarily of their own choosing.

The ethical issue arises as the result of doing sponsored research generally. Using the NIJ example above, it is clear from the solicitation that the NIJ is favorable toward and supportive of community-oriented policing. One method of implementing community-oriented policing is to involve different community elements (e.g., neighborhoods and neighborhood leaders, different ethnic groups and races, business persons, labor organizations). Any integrative theme that explores ways to facilitate acceptance of community-oriented policing is encouraged as a research objective. This is one important vested interest of the NIJ as a major source of research funds. Similarly, the focus of the NIJ on firearms violence, illegal gun markets, and gangs and gang violence mildly suggest gun control, a policy opposed by organizations such as the National Rifle Association.

When an investigator accepts federal money from the NIJ for a specific research purpose, this does not mean that the researcher will deliberately slant findings from the study to fit the goals of the agency agenda. Rather, the entire research project is couched in a particular context that may or may not be consonant with the researcher's own interests and agenda. Presumably, researchers who apply for external funds from any agency or organization have some interest in the topics proposed for study. Thus, the issue of the ethics of doing sponsored research may be a relatively unimportant one.

Rights of Human Subjects

The rights of human subjects involved in any criminological investigation are addressed in the codes of ethics relevant for national organizations, such as the American Society of Criminology and the Academy of Criminal Justice Sciences. Regional organizations, such as the Midwestern Criminal Justice Association, Southern Criminal Justice Association, and Western Society of Criminology, have evolved or are developing their own codes of ethics to apply to their respective memberships.

Any federally sponsored research today automatically includes regulations promulgated by the Department of Health and Human Services and the National Research Act of 1974. Some of the regulations pertain to the informed consent of research subjects who are or may become involved in any study supported by federal funds. One consequence of the National Research Act was the establishment of institutional review boards on university campuses. Institutional review boards are internal committees that screen research proposals where federal funds are solicited. The screenings are designed to protect the right of human subjects who may become involved in one's proposed research. These screenings are especially important for biomedical experiments and studies, where the potential for physical harm is heightened. For social science proposals, the potential for human subject harm is minimized. Nevertheless, these screening committees scrutinize all research proposals to

BOX 12.6   PERSONALITY HIGHLIGHT

MARGARET A. ZAHN
North Carolina State University, Director, Crime Justice
Policy Program, RTI International

Statistics: B.S. (social welfare), M. A. (sociology), Ph.D.
(sociology), Ohio State University

BACKGROUND

I grew up in Lorain, Ohio, and became interested in crime and the criminal justice system when
a 14-year-old friend of mine was unfairly sent to reform school. As an undergraduate at Ohio
State University, I studied social welfare and was an intern at a school for delinquent girls. Social work didn't seem to help these girls since so much that affected their lives—poverty,
parental abuse, and neglect—were beyond their control. It seemed to me at the time that social
policy had to be changed and that switching to the study of sociology would be more useful in
accomplishing such changes. With encouragement from my professors, and with the aid of a
federal fellowship, I went on at Ohio State to receive an M.A. and a Ph.D. in sociology. My first
post-graduate academic position was at Temple University, where I began studying homicide.
Over time, my career led to a series of administrative positions, including serving as department chair at both Northern Arizona University and the University of North Carolina at Char-
lotte, as Dean of Humanities and Social Sciences at North Carolina State University, as Director
of the Violence and Victimization Division of the National Institute of Justice, and most recently
as Director of the Crime and Justice Policy Program at RTI International. I also served as President of the American Society of Criminology. In concert with these many administrative responsibilities, I have always pursued an active research agenda.

RESEARCH INTERESTS AND EXPERIENCES

My central research interest has been understanding violence, why it occurs, and what can be
done to effectively prevent it. I began by studying violence among illegal drug users. This led
to studies of homicide, with a focus on different types of homicide, including stranger and family. Much of this work involved gathering information directly from police and medical examiner records. Such data collection is very time-consuming but allows a much more detailed
understanding of events than what can be gleaned through administrative data such as Vital Statistics and *Uniform Crime Reports (UCR)* data. My later work involved studying determinates

BOX 12.6 · CONTINUED

of changing rates of homicide in urban neighborhoods. The development of Geographic Information System capabilities has made analysis of neighborhoods easier and more productive than was possible using prior mapping procedures.

In addition to many years of research on homicide, I have also studied the impact of gender on some aspects of crime. Recently, my RTI colleagues and I secured a federal grant to complete a comprehensive study of female delinquency. Integrating current knowledge to fully understand the differences in pathways to delinquency for boys and girls will allow us to gender-appropriate delinquency prevention programs in the future. Some of the greatest advances in our understanding of violence in recent years involve domestic violence. I can recall the days when police said, "It's a crime of passion and can't be stopped." Today, we know that domestic violence can be prevented through more effective policing policies and encouraging potential victims to turn to safehouses. Passion, indeed, can be controlled.

While my past work has focused on interpersonal violence, current world events have shifted my interest to collective violence and terrorism. This has led me to explore new bodies of literature in political science and international relations. My ultimate goal in the study of both violence and gender is to advance knowledge that ultimately can improve the human condition.

Through much of my career I have combined my research interests with teaching. I created and taught a course on violence at Temple University, where I began my academic career over 20 years ago, and have continued to update and teach violence courses throughout the years. Consistent with changing events and the latest knowledge, my most recent course, "Violence, Terrorism, and Public Policy," includes material on interpersonal violence and collective violence as well as an analysis of policies and programs intended to prevent and reduce violent behavior.

ADVICE TO STUDENTS

Research can be done in a variety of forums. While I have spent most of my career in academic settings, I have also worked in the federal government, and I have recently joined a nonprofit research organization that does crime and justice research. There is more than one place to do research, and students who have an interest in a research career should remain open to exploring multiple opportunities. In terms of actually doing research, it is most important to conceptualize the research problem well. A well-formulated research question creates a strong foundation upon which the rest of the research rests. My observation is that students and many professionals often fail in this regard. A good background in the philosophy of social sciences and in theory construction is useful in developing the ability to conceptualize research problems. Asking the right questions leads to a better understanding of the big picture.

How you answer the question is also important. Answering a well-formed research question should involve, wherever possible, collecting data from multiple sources. Gathering information from more than one source allows for validation and a richer examination of factors

BOX 12.6   CONTINUED

involved in the topic of interest. For example, much of my work on the study of homicide involved gathering information directly from police and medical examiner records. Such data collection is very time-consuming but allows a much more detailed understanding of events than what can be gleaned through administrative data such as vital statistics and *UCR* data. Researchers involved in data collection must also pay careful attention to detail, however tedious that may be at times, and should take the time to develop a thorough understanding of whatever data sources they may choose. The established data sources such as *UCR* are not always what they appear. What is easiest isn't always best. A successful research career begins with an inquisitive mind and a desire to build knowledge for a purpose. The thrill of learning something that was previously unknown makes a research career a rewarding and invigorating endeavor.

determine if all ethical standards are properly observed. Institutional review boards may also screen projects where federal funds are not sought. These boards may evolve their own standards apart from those mandated under the National Research Act.

Informed Consent and How Personal Information Will Be Used

Informing research subjects about their participation in one's research may include specific types of respondents involved in the criminal justice system in different ways. These types of respondents include (1) victims, (2) arrestees and defendants, (3) prisoners, and (4) persons involved in illegal behaviors.

Victims.   Criminal justicians are interested in crime victims and how they respond or react to being victimized. Perhaps a researcher wants to study police investigation and report writing where one or more victims are involved. It has been found that in at least some jurisdictions, police officers do not always file reports from victims who have been robbed or assaulted (Barker & Carter, 1990). Police lie for various reasons. One of the most frequent reasons given for lying is to avoid the extensive paperwork involved in writing up a street crime incident, which some police officers tend to trivialize. The incidents are certainly not trivial to the victims, however, where personal injuries may have been inflicted by perpetrators. Thus, interviews with various crime victims may disclose certain police officer improprieties. Researchers may learn the names of police officers who investigated the complaints of several victims. Seeking out these officers or examining their paperwork, or lack of it, may create further problems for crime victims. Officers involved in these incidents may retaliate in different ways. They may harass some of these crime victims. Therefore, attention must be given to the preservation of victim anonymity in such investigations. Their confidentiality must be respected (Esbensen, 1991).

Frequently, victims testify at parole hearings or provide written reports about how they have been affected by a perpetrator's crime. These reports are victim-impact statements, and they are often appended to presentence investigation reports prepared by probation officers. Some convicted offenders are very vindictive toward those testifying or giving negative information against them. In the state of Washington, for instance, a female rape victim testified against the rapist who was sentenced to 10 years in prison. When the rapist was released, he tracked the woman down to where she had moved to Oregon and killed her. He had obtained information about her relocation through documents filed by the probation officer who prepared his presentence investigation report. While this information was not generated by a research investigation, it was collected in a way that did not protect the woman's anonymity and whereabouts from public scrutiny, including a request for information from the rapist himself.

Over time a victim's bill of rights has been established. This victim's bill of rights has been designed to protect crime victims from further victimization. In the late 1970s, the New York State Compensation Board established a bill of rights for victims of serious crimes. Among its other provisions, the victim's bill of rights includes the victim's protection from criminal violence. Furthermore, victims must be kept informed by law enforcement agencies of the status of the defendant(s) in custody and if and when the defendant(s) are released. They should be notified of a plea bargain arrangement or any other discretionary disposition of their case. They should also know the release date of the defendants if they were incarcerated.

Any studies of crime victims should include provisions for their informed consent and protection. The information they provide investigators should be treated as confidential. Any victim surveys should be sensitive to the ethics of survey research (Garofalo, 1977).

Arrestees and Defendants.   Arrested persons and criminal defendants are sometimes selected for research investigations. Since these persons have not yet been convicted of a crime, information they might disclose to interviewers could be regarded as potentially incriminating. Sometimes arrestees are eventually released without formal charges being filed against them. Many persons arrested for spousal assault fit this scenario (Williams & Hawkins, 1992). Researchers might contact potential subjects when their names have been reported in local newspapers. Follow-up interviews with these persons might be conducted in an effort to determine the factors that contribute to spousal violence.

Prisoners.   Inmates in jails and prisons are literally captive audiences. Historically, prisoners have been subjected largely to biomedical experimentation, involving tests of prescription drugs and other substances (Schroeder, 1983). Involuntary treatment of mentally ill prisoners with antipsychotic drugs and other types of social or medical interventions has sometimes resulted in inmate deaths or serious personality and physical disorders (Burlington, 1991; Schroeder, 1983; Todd, 1975). Inmates are often in the position of failing to comprehend the full nature and scope of their involvement in social or medical experiments (Schroeder, 1983). There is the very serious question of whether mentally ill inmates can give their informed consent for full research participation (Burlington, 1991). Indeed, the very nature of prisons may be so inherently coercive that it would be virtually impossible for any inmate to give an informed consent to being a subject in research (Smodish, 1974).

For criminologists and others who conduct social research, investigating inmate populations is largely a matter of distributing self-administered questionnaires and/or direct interviewing. But researching inmate populations is not as simple as it seems. For instance, some researchers have conducted extensive interviews with death row inmates and their families (Goldhammer, 1994). Some of this research has involved the families of death row inmate victims and/or the inmate's family (Dicks, 1991; Smykla, 1987). Interviewing any death row inmate is an emotional experience. Interviewers know or have good reason to suspect that the persons they interview will be eventually executed for their crimes. It is difficult to retain objectivity under such circumstances.

Some studies of death row inmates and the conditions under which they are supervised and maintained are designed to advance political agendas. For instance, Amnesty International is an organization that opposes the death penalty for any reason and under any circumstance. Amnesty International has conducted studies of death rows in several prisons, including death-row inmates in Oklahoma (Amnesty International, 1994). Predictably, Amnesty International proclaimed the Oklahoma State Penitentiary maximum-security unit where death-row inmates are housed as a good example of what is meant by cruel and unusual punishment. Amnesty International noted the physical conditions, such as windowless cells, inadequate exercise yards, the length of confinement (23 1/2 hours per day), and isolation and lack of education or other ameliorative programs.

Presently inmates are afforded certain rights by prison administrators. Thus, they may refuse to become involved as research participants where investigators wish to study them. Most prisons have informed consent provisions to guard against involuntary participation in social research projects. The concern for inmate rights is almost universal, with provisions to protect inmates implemented in Australia, England, and Japan (Bowery, 1997; Dixon, 1997; Yokoyama, 1994).

Persons Involved in Illegal Behaviors.   Harold Grasmick, Robert Bursik, and John Cochran (1991) studied 330 adult respondents who disclosed religious and tax-related information about themselves. These researchers wanted to know what factors might be influential on deterring persons from cheating on their income taxes. Respondents disclosed in **self-reports** certain factual information about their religiosity or religious commitment. Also, they furnished information about the likelihood that they might violate the law and not pay their full taxes. It was found that persons who were deeply religious were more inclined to pay their full share of taxes in order to avoid potential social embarrassment and shame. While this study is interesting, it depicts a situation where the respondents were asked to admit to illegal behavior, whether or not they paid their full taxes due. As information about these respondents was collected, the investigators were in the position of identifying tax cheaters.

Kevin Minor (1988) studied 45 delinquent youths who had been adjudicated by the juvenile court and placed on probation. Minor was able to obtain self-reports from these youths about their illegal activities. He was particularly interested in the effectiveness of an intervention program for reducing their illegal activity. The intervention program involved job preparation workshops, outdoor adventure experiences, and family relationship counseling. While Minor's findings were inconclusive, the fact is that Minor obtained a substantial amount of incriminating information from these delinquents about illegal acts they had committed.

Were Grasmick, Bursik, and Cochran under any special duty to report their tax cheaters to the Internal Revenue Service? Should Kevin Minor have reported to police the fact that certain delinquent youths had admitted to various illegal acts? In these instances, the illegal behaviors were not reported to any law enforcement agency or the IRS. The information solicited by these researchers was generated in a research context, regardless of the illegality of it.

Sometimes investigators discover information about research participants that may not be illegal but is otherwise potentially dangerous to others. For instance, an investigation of prison inmates in a Canadian federal correctional institution conducted by Ralf Jurgens and Norbert Gilmore led to the identification of several HIV-infected prisoners (Jurgens & Gilmore, 1994). In the context of examining the state of correctional health care, were these researchers under any obligation to report that certain prisoners had the HIV virus? In another similar study of HIV among prison inmates, Hammett and Dubler (1990) found that when HIV-infected inmates were identified in different U.S. prisons, they were administratively segregated from the rest of the inmate population and treated differently. This time, their confidentiality was not respected and they considered themselves discriminated against because of their illness. The fact that certain inmates were discriminated against because they were HIV infected raises a serious ethical question. For some investigators, the ethical question is difficult. The rights and interests of HIV-infected inmates must be recognized. However, the direct, hazardous risk of HIV to uninfected inmates must be considered as well. Thus, the dilemma exists over which rights are more important. Prison institutions have already resolved this matter by segregating infected inmates from uninfected ones. But investigators should recognize that depending on the details of their investigations in such settings, ethical considerations will emerge that are not easily resolvable.

SUMMARY

Ethics are standards of professional groups or organizations, as well as their normative codes or behaviors of right or wrong. Ethics bind group or organizational members to standards of conduct and practices that would not be considered illegal, immoral, or improper. Ethical codes have evolved over time because of different kinds of harm that have involved the clients of organizational members, the reputations of organizations and groups, and other persons who have come into contact with investigators conducting social and/or psychological research. Almost every professional organization has promulgated an ethical code or set of standards to govern member conduct. Whenever violations of ethical codes occur, specific sanctioning mechanisms are implemented that may result in one's expulsion from the group or organization.

Apart from the codes of ethics of organizations but closely related to the actions of group members are ethical dilemmas that often arise in the course of social research. Because social research involves the study of human subjects, either directly or indirectly, the effects of social research upon these subjects are potentially extensive and may or may not have adverse consequences for them. Different ways of gathering information from persons may include questionnaire administration, observation, interviewing, and/or the collection of other written information or documents. Sometimes the subject matter of one's investigation may involve sensitive topics or inquiries into subjects that are potentially harmful to participants in various ways. Research subjects possess information desired by criminological investigators. Therefore, how criminologists acquire this information and what they eventually do with it have several important implications for those providing such information. Although a high degree of social responsibility is encouraged among persons conducting research, it is not always the case that this responsibility is taken seriously.

Several types of ethical problems arise in the course of social research. Plagiarism is sometimes found, where someone uses the work of someone else and passes such work off as one's own. Although plagiarism is most frequently associated with student papers, it also involves dubious behaviors of professors and others who misuse or misrepresent the work of others as their own. Plagiarism exists in various forms. Although not technically plagiarism, sometimes the publication of works in multiple outlets, such as dual-article submissions and acceptances by several journals, are considered improper, where someone allows his or her work to be published in two or more sources at once. This dual-publication question does not pertain to works known as readers, where articles are reprinted later by editors who compile interesting materials on selected topics. In these instances, monies are paid as reprinting fees and proper credit is given to article contributors.

Another ethical problem arises as the result of fraudulent research and/or statistical manipulation of research results. Sometimes, research findings are reported where that research was never done. It is difficult to detect instances where such fraudulent findings have been reported, largely because in the general research presentation, anonymity both protects those studied from having potentially embarrassing information disclosed about them and assures the investigator that other researchers will have no way of knowing where the research was conducted or if it was actually conducted.

Any research that is potentially harmful to human subjects raises ethical questions. The most harmful types of research usually involve substances consumed by research subjects or experimental drugs or medical procedures. But social scientific research may raise similar questions about the harm done to experimental subjects. Under certain experimental conditions, research subjects may be exposed to different types of stress or to material that they consider offensive, sensitive, and/or harmful in various ways. Psychological harm may be just as serious to experimental subjects as physical harm through the introduction of experimental drugs.

Some amount of deception may be practiced as researchers gather important information about events from research subjects. Deception may occur where anonymity is assured but where researchers know who the respondents are and are in positions to use this information against respondents in harmful ways. Even if deception is only practiced so as to improve a respondent's likelihood to respond or to give truthful responses, this fact may be considered unethical.

Much information sought by social researchers is confidential, such as juvenile records, inmate records, or probationer or parolee files. Some of this information is protected by various shield laws. Information not generally available to the public may be accessed by persons with some degree of authority and for official purposes. However, sometimes researchers may seek this information and use devious means to retrieve it. There is not a lot of consistency about the types of information made available to the public, however. Records of sex offenders or drunk drivers may be released to entire communities so that they may know more about those who live among them. Under some conditions, the Freedom of Information Act (FOIA) may permit investigators to gain access to otherwise confidential information that was subject to governmental protections and shield laws from previous years.

Sometimes, information sought by researchers can only be obtained from groups or organizations by joining those groups and participating in their activities. This conduct, which many researchers justify by the new knowledge about groups it generates, may be regarded as unethical if the groups or organizations are not advised as to the true purposes of the investigators who infiltrate them. And in some instances, persons in authority of others may grant investigators permission to study their subordinates. Prison wardens may permit investigators to interview and/or observe inmates for varying periods. Probation departments may permit interviewers to seek out and interview probationers and parolees at their homes or workplaces.

In recent decades, universities and other organizations have evolved codes governing the conduct of persons who do work under their auspices and where it is anticipated that human subjects will be studied. Influencing these ethical policies is the Nuremberg Code, which relates to a set of principles under which human subjects can be used in social and medical experiments. Formulated in the aftermath of World War II, the Nuremberg Code set forth the principles of informed consent and voluntariness, where prospective research subjects must be given both a warning about the potentially harmful effects of experiments involving them as well as the option to decline to participate in such research. In universities and research organizations, human subjects committees are often formed to review research proposals that involve human beings and to evaluate the potential harm the research of their members may cause.

Several ethical issues that arise in the course of learning more about persons and events involve sponsorship, basic rights of human subjects, and informed consent. When an organization sponsors research and solicits proposals, there are often implicit expectations that the research will be conducted in certain ways with particular research goals to be pursued. These goals may not be consistent with the research objectives of those eventually doing the research. Human subjects also have the right to refuse to participate. They also have the right to be informed as to the nature of an investigator's intentions and whether any harmful effects may arise resulting from the planned research activity. Human subjects also have the right to know how the information about them will be used and if such uses will be harmful to them.

QUESTIONS FOR REVIEW

1. What is meant by ethics? What are the purposes of codes of ethics for professional organizations?

2. How can we distinguish between ethics in the research process and ethics involved in the performance of law enforcement or corrections work?

3. Why is it difficult to detect fraudulent research conduct whenever it occurs?

4. What is plagiarism? What are some forms of plagiarism?

5. Why is the dual-submission policy of professional journals important?

6. What was the significance of Stanley Milgram's obedience research?

7. What ethical problems were obvious in the study of the "Tearoom Trade" by Laud Humphreys?

8. What is the Nuremberg Code and why was it established? Is it applicable today? What elements of the Nuremberg Code have been preserved in contemporary codes of ethics?

9. How is deception harmful to human subjects? What are several forms of deception?

10. Whenever juveniles are studied, what safeguards are taken to preserve their confidentiality? Why are these safeguards in place?

11. What is an institutional review board? What are its functions?

12. What ethical problems are associated with sponsored research?

13. What is meant by informed consent? Under what conditions should informed consent be extended to research participants?

Writing Papers and Research Reports

Introduction

Criminology and criminal justice involve a great deal of writing. Professors expect students to write term papers and undertake other projects for various courses. At important points in their pursuit of graduate degrees, many students will become involved in more elaborate research projects. These projects result in master's theses and/or doctoral dissertations. This chapter examines the nature and types of writing undertaken by persons who take classes or complete work toward graduate degrees. Several types of writing are examined, including term papers, literature reviews, position papers, theses, and dissertations.

An important part of any writing project is to cite or footnote properly. There are several standard footnoting styles. It is beyond the scope of this book to examine all of these styles, but a few styles will be illustrated. Each professor, academic department, and university or college has differing expectations about the citation style students should use in their written work. Some generic citation styles will be described.

Because some of the work done by criminologists and criminal justicians involves legal research and writing, some examples of legal citations will be provided. Sources of legal cases for both the state and federal systems will be listed and described.

Types of Papers and Research Reports

Term Papers

The most common form of writing in university settings is the term paper. Term papers are more or less lengthy documents. Usually students who write term papers will focus on a particular topic, such as community policing, the use of K-9s in law enforcement, deadly force, probation officer turnover, or correctional officer burnout and stress. Instructors' expectations of students vary from class to class. Some professors demand that students follow specific footnoting styles, including observance of rigid formatting (e.g., number of lines per page; left, right, top, and bottom margins; type style; letter spacing; type of justification). Other professors merely ask students to be consistent in their citations. Students are free to choose any citation style.

The topics for term papers are unlimited. Usually professors attempt to guide students in particular directions for their papers by suggesting different topics. These topics are usually narrowed to the class subject matter, such as policing, courts and judges, or corrections. During the 1998 school year, I kept track of all topics selected by my students for term papers. These are the topics I compiled from students in no particular order: juvenile waivers; jury selection; hot pursuit; deadly force; domestic violence; judicial bias; police stress/burnout; jury selection; drug enforcement; terrorism; police discrimination; probation and parole; female police officers; deinstitutionalization of status offenders; probation and parole officer training; personality and crime; juvenile rehabilitation; suicide; Indian tribal law; prison gangs; electronic monitoring; home confinement; jail and prison suicides; death penalty; prison industries; K-9s in law enforcement; serial killers; Royal Canadian Mounted Police; police history; boot camps; British female inmates; Mexican prisons; police brutality; probation officers and firearms; child sexual abusers; police misconduct; women and stress in law enforcement; court watchers; female prison inmates; spousal abuse; aging offenders; asset forfeiture; hate crimes; missing children; private counsel; police personality; victim and witness participation in sentencing; sentencing hearings; juvenile rights; juvenile death penalty; ineffective assistance of counsel; police patrol styles and effectiveness; prison violence; delinquency; FBI training; juvenile risk assessment; police professionalism; police cautioning; selective incapacitation; jury size and deliberations; habitual offenders; war on drugs.

The length and detail required in term papers also varies greatly. Term papers can be short, from 5–10 pages, or quite lengthy, 25 pages or more. There is no reliable average paper length to be given. Different class requirements dictate that a certain paper organization should be followed.

Term papers usually involve library research, where books and periodicals are examined for background information about the topic. Professors may specify certain numbers of sources. Thus, an acceptable term paper might include 10 sources or more. These sources may be specified as well, such as "only research articles from professional journals." This specification means that students cannot rely exclusively on textbooks for their term paper information.

Term papers are largely descriptive. Except under unusual circumstances, it is unrealistic for professors to expect that their students will generate original data and analyze it in a research report. Sometimes this is done for certain types of classes, such as research methods. A research methods class may carry out a limited research project, where questionnaires are constructed and administered. Later during the semester, data are tabulated and analyzed. These analyses are often superficial. Each student might be expected to write his or her version of what is found and its significance. Each student is also responsible for finding selected references relevant to the problem examined.

Generally, term papers are not particularly elaborate. Ten or fifteen sources are consulted and pulled together. If the topic is deadly force, it might be appropriate to describe different kinds of deadly force and the circumstances under which deadly force is applied. Some leading cases about deadly force may be mentioned and discussed. Different authorities raise several interesting issues about deadly force and its use by law enforcement officers. A term paper might be written that highlights several important issues about the use of deadly force. The student preparing the paper might consider summarizing these issues and expressing an opinion about deadly force. Some substance is usually expected whenever personal opinions are expressed. Thus, it is insufficient to say, "Deadly force shouldn't be used." Rather, some compelling argument should be presented in defense of one's position taken on the subject. This exposition of one's opinion about a given topic makes the paper interesting.

Reviews of the Literature

Some papers are called literature reviews or reviews of the literature. If a paper is written on sentencing disparities and the factors that influence such disparities, then the relevant literature pertaining to sentencing disparities will be reviewed. This means that students must hunt down articles and papers written about sentencing disparities and find out what others have written about it. Reviews of literature are very important, since they can disclose convergences of opinion and/or differences of opinion about the incidence of sentencing disparities and which factors seem most influential in triggering disparities.

It is common to discover certain inconsistencies in the literature. For instance, we might find that one study reports considerable sentencing disparity attributable to race and socioeconomic status. Another study may report that sentencing disparity occurs because of gender and is not related to socioeconomic status. Yet another study may report that sentencing disparities are attributable to the type of attorney used. Thus, in sentencing decision making, judges may impose harsher sentences on convicted offenders if they are represented by public defenders instead of private counsel. What should be made of these inconsistencies?

Some studies are outright contradictory. Whenever contradictions or inconsistencies occur in the research literature, these inconsistencies provide the foundation for some interesting writing. Students may attempt to explain these contradictions or inconsistencies in some way. Sometimes experimentation helps. Articles expressing one view or finding may be grouped together, while those expressing a contrary or inconsistent view may be grouped together. Perhaps the definitions of sentencing disparity are different. Different definitions of the same terms may help to explain why there are inconsistencies or contradictions in the literature.

Basically, literature reviews examine what is known about a particular topic. Some topics are more popular than others and therefore, larger numbers of articles may exist. Some topics are less popular, and therefore there is less research literature generated. If a popular topic is selected, such as electronic monitoring, 100 articles or more may be written about it. Some limitations may be necessary, such as limiting the literature review to the most recent 5- or 10-year interval. It is important for the literature review to be current or up-to-date. This means that only the most recent journals and written work should be consulted. By "recent" we might refer to articles, books, and other materials written within the last 10 years.

Critical Essays and Position Papers

A critical essay or position paper is essentially the same as a term paper, where the writer wishes to assess or evaluate some issue. Perhaps someone wishes to write a critical essay about some criminological theory or explanation of delinquency. Suppose a researcher wanted to write a critical essay about differential association theory or strain theory. The essay itself would vary in length, depending on the amount of detail expended by the writer and/or the length and format requirements of the professor. If the article is prepared for a journal or some other publication outlet, then certain requirements must be observed.

The critical essay would examine the contents of the theory and an objective evaluation of the theory's efficacy for explaining crime or delinquency. Criticisms may include both positive and negative statements. Examples from the literature may be used to support one position or another.

Perhaps the critical essay or position paper is about capital punishment. Suppose the writer opposes capital punishment and decides to write a position paper about it. If the position taken is opposition to the death penalty, then objective thoroughness would require an examination of all possible issues surrounding the death penalty and its application. An argument could be made against the death penalty, and supporting information for this position could be gleaned from the research literature.

Research Papers

A research paper differs from term papers and position papers or critical essays in that some original data collection is involved. A project is outlined with specific research goals. In more than a few research methods classes, professors engage the students in collecting data from a sample of students or community residents. These are easy research targets, largely because they are accessible. Once information has been collected, usually by questionnaires, the data are coded and tabulated. Students are then expected to write up their version of an analysis of the data and what it means.

Research papers involve brief literature reviews and an exposition of what the literature says about the research problem under investigation. Research papers for classes may vary from 10 to 30 pages or more, again depending on the course requirements and professor's expectations. Usually a certain format is required. Often the intent is to enable students to acquire research report writing skills. The professor may follow up these research papers with a discussion of the significance of the project and what different students said about it in their own writing.

Master's Theses and Doctoral Dissertations

A master's thesis or doctoral dissertation in criminal justice or criminology is a comprehensive study, an elaborate research project, a creative enterprise, a significant undertaking, designed to investigate a researchable problem in any substantive area (e.g., criminal justice, sociology, psychology) for the purpose of testing a theory and hypotheses derived from that theory.

What a thesis/dissertation is *not:*

1. A term paper.
2. A general literature review of some topic (e.g., delinquency and poverty, racism in the United States, the death penalty).
3. Throwing together some hastily prepared questions, distributing them to the first 100 students you can find, and summarizing the results of your findings.
4. A purely descriptive piece about your thoughts on some issue.
5. A lengthy conjecture about your personal beliefs about unfairness in our city, county, state, or nation.
6. Some document intended to prove some obscure point you happen to think about and that is of concern to you.

What is the proper length for thesis proposals?   Theses and/or dissertation proposals range in length from 10 to 100 pages. There is no optimum length for a thesis proposal. This decision depends on your research problem, how much literature exists about the problem, how sophisticated the theory is that you are testing, how many hypotheses you are deriving for testing, how sophisticated your methodology is, and so on. It is probably the case that a good thesis proposal is going to range in length from 20 to 30 pages (double-spaced, typed), including all of the relevant components described below.

What does a thesis or dissertation proposal do?   A thesis proposal is a blueprint for your research work. It shows, in great detail, what you plan to do; why it is significant, both theoretically and substantively; what your major (and minor) objectives are; where you will get your sample; how you will collect data; how you will analyze your data; what tabular presentations you will make; what statistics you will choose for your analyses; what sorts of things you will be able to say as the result of conducting your study; and what the study's shortcomings are.

What is the role of the thesis/dissertation advisor?   Thesis advisors assist students in the selection of manageable and important research problems; give them feedback on their thinking; guide them to articles or books where relevant materials about their problem can be found; and criticize their work and offer constructive criticisms about data collection, data analysis, and theoretical scheme development and hypothesis formulation.

What level of statistical sophistication is appropriate for theses/dissertations?   All appropriate statistical procedures cannot be learned in a few statistics courses. Those who teach statistics attempt to convey selected procedures that students might find useful for their own research. Often a foundation is provided for doing some elementary independent study. But statistical learning does not end in the classroom. Graduate work of any kind, whether it is a doctoral dissertation or master's thesis, must show initiative and originality.

Where can students find good examples of statistical analyses of data?   Examining articles in leading criminal justice or criminology journals, such as *Criminology, Justice Quarterly, Journal of Crime and Justice, Journal of Crime and Delinquency, Journal of Criminal Justice, Law and Society Review, Criminal Justice Review, Journal of Contemporary Criminal Justice, Judicature, Journal of Criminal Law and Criminology, Journal of Quantitative*

Criminology, and *Journal of Criminal Justice Education* are some of the leading journals containing sophisticated statistical techniques applied to criminological data. The university library contains an index of all periodicals available.

What if these articles contain methodological and statistical techniques beyond what students have learned?   Sometimes, students will need to familiarize themselves with new methodological techniques and statistical strategies in order to make meaningful interpretations of studies they examine.

A Thesis/Dissertation Proposal Outline

Ideally, all research is preceded by a research proposal. A research proposal is a relatively brief statement of the problem to be investigated. It also includes specific study objectives, a representative review of literature pertinent to the problem, a theoretical and/or substantive justification for the study, and some methodological guidelines to follow.

The research proposal is referred to by different names according to the type of research it precedes. For instance, a doctoral student preparing for a doctoral dissertation may refer to the research proposal as a dissertation proposal. A master's candidate may prepare a thesis prospectus. Others may simply refer to the proposal as a research plan, although as indicated, the notion of a research plan is frequently used synonymously with research design. In order to avoid semantic problems, research plans may be viewed as integral components of the proposal or prospectus. Research plans constitute the methodological portion of the proposal.

Research proposals vary in length, complexity, and/or sophistication according to the particular standards of the investigator in charge of the research activity. The format of a research proposal presented below is by no means considered the only way of outlining the project for social investigation. The various components included (as well as the order in which each is presented) are merely suggested as constituting a possible compilation and arrangement of the bare essentials. Many departures from the scheme below are to be expected, especially when we consider the vast array of topics of social interest as well as the diversity of researcher preferences that exists. One way of outlining a research proposal is as follows:

1. Introduction
2. Statement of objectives
3. Review of the literature
4. Theoretical structure and/or conceptual scheme
5. Hypotheses
6. Methodology
7. Statement of theoretical and substantive implications

Short discussions of each of these components are provided below. The discussions are general in nature. They are included to indicate the importance and/or significance of each section, and they are designed to be broadly applicable to projects reflecting diverse interests.

Introduction.   The introduction of a research proposal should place the problem to be studied in some kind of historical perspective. The researcher should briefly illustrate the historical development of the current problem under investigation. Researchers should also locate their particular interests in the problem fairly precisely. In short, researchers reveal the problem to be studied and what dimension or dimensions of it will be given extensive analysis or treatment. For example, if researchers were to be interested in studying the social and psychological effects of automation in a business setting, they might begin by describing the early origins and applications of automation in various work environments. They could follow up this historical description by discussing present uses of automation in specific settings. At this point, they could reveal their precise interests in learning about the potential social and psychological impacts of automation in contemporary businesses. Another way of looking at the introduction is as a way of moving from very general to very specific subject matter you intend to study. When we say, "Put the problem you study in a historical context," this means to provide a historical foundation for the problem. For instance, "Labor turnover among probation departments throughout the United States has increased during the last four decades. From 1950 to 1990, the proportion of probation officers leaving probation work annually to seek alternative employment has increased from 4 percent to over 30 percent. In California by 1990, labor turnover among probation officers had reached 40 percent. According to Jackson (1991, p. 3), the costs of training new probation officers to replace those who quit are prohibitive. This study examines the problem of labor turnover among California probation officers . . ."[and from here, you specify **and introduce** what specific aspect of probation officer labor turnover you plan to describe].

Statement of Research Objectives.   The objectives of research projects detail what researchers wish to accomplish as the result of their investigative activity. What are the specific goals to be achieved? Sometimes this section is broken down into subparts to include major and minor objectives. There are primary concerns of investigators as well as secondary concerns. In this event, researchers possibly arrange their objectives into a hierarchical fashion, listing them from most important to least important. Some proposals make explicit the distinction between major and minor (primary and secondary) objectives (goals).

There is no limit to the number of research objectives. Decisions about how many objectives will be identified are based on the breadth of the research, the interests of the investigator, time, cost, and person-power considerations. Some studies may have a single objective, whereas other projects may have 20 or 30 of them. Although there are no limitations concerning the number of research objectives a project may have, it is possible for investigators to bite off too much of a given problem. There is little wisdom spreading oneself too thin, however. If researchers have too many research objectives, they may encounter great difficulty in trying to tie together a lot of loose ends. Too many research objectives also necessitates a more complex theoretical scheme. Therefore, it is recommended that investigators limit their objectives to a reasonable number. What is "reasonable" again depends on the time limitations, budgetary considerations, and person-power restrictions under which researchers must often work. It is possible, for example, for a single objective to involve more time and effort to achieve than 10 objectives in a related study. Researchers must assess subjectively the objectives of their research in determining whether they have the capability to deal effectively with the problem they have chosen. It is wise to pick objectives that are challenging but not impossible to achieve.

Fairly precise statements of objectives are functional guidelines for research activity. Using the automation example cited above, vague or nebulous objectives might be "to see if the introduction of automation into an employee work setting will bring about attitudinal change" or "to see if the introduction of automation will bring about significant role changes among employees." These statements are considered vague because they fail to specify which attitudes and which employee work roles are involved or are possibly affected by automation. Of course, it can be argued that an exploratory study may be loosely constructed so as to identify more specific research targets to be investigated with greater precision at a later date. But it would be more meaningful to state which attitudes of employees are considered most relevant for examination. A more specific statement of an objective might be "to investigate the impact of the introduction of electronic data processing (a form of automation) on employee depersonalization (an attitudinal variable)." This statement clearly indicates that the independent variable, *automation,* may be followed by a change of a specific dependent variable, *depersonalization,* in this case. One interest of researchers, therefore, is to examine the relationship between these variables as a means of more accurately depicting some of the potential social and psychological implications of technological change on people in work environments.

Review of the Literature.   The literature review is designed to familiarize the investigator with any relevant information pertaining to the topic being studied. Opinions vary concerning the extent to which a literature review should be conducted. Some researchers may be concerned with identifying all available literature on a given subject, whereas others are content to review literature in major professional journals for the most recent 10-year period. In research proposals, it is usually not necessary to discuss all relevant and available literature uncovered by the researcher. A positive feature of a proposal literature review is to highlight representative ideas from current articles and books on the subject investigated. For instance, if there are 1,000 articles on a particular topic that reflect varying and opposing points of view, investigators may select 20 or 30 of them that seem to represent the major viewpoints and conflicting opinions and/or findings. Of course, when a dissertation or thesis is involved, the expectation may be that researchers review a much larger portion of the literature to be included and used in the final research report, the thesis or dissertation.

The question of how many articles should be included in a research proposal is difficult to answer in quantitative terms. If the research topic is relatively new, it is likely that little or no information exists in the available literature that bears directly on the subject. Researchers may be forced to cite available literature that is only remotely connected to the topic under investigation. For example, in the 1950s, little, if anything, was known about the impact of electronic data processing systems on school structure and administration. However, there were articles in existence that examined the impact of electronic data processing systems in petroleum refineries and airlines reservations offices. If researchers elected to study this automation form and its impact on school systems, they would include in their literature review only information that was indirectly relevant to this chosen topic. Any pioneering effort (a research project delving into previously unexplored social/psychological/criminal justice/criminology areas) is subject to this significant limitation. On the other hand, if there is an abundance of material on a given topic, it is up to the researcher to determine how many articles will be selected for a representative review. There are no clear-cut standards to dictate how many articles should be reviewed. Again, we return to the matter of how many are considered reasonable. Reviewing too many articles may be regarded by some researchers as superfluous activity. Other researchers may consider a particular literature review to be too scanty and inadequate. When researchers themselves feel comfortable with the articles they have reviewed, this subjective criterion will usually suffice.

Footnoting and referencing in literature reviews in proposals and in research reports can be handled quickly and easily by following certain conventional procedures established by such professional associations as the American Psychological Association. Although several footnoting and referencing styles exist, some are much more simple to follow than the others. For instance, "Smith (2004:222–224) indicates that . . ." is considerably less awkward than "James R. Smith, *Problems of the Inner City,* Holt, Rinehart, and Winston, New York, NY, 2004, pps. 222–224, indicates that . . .". Another style of footnoting is "Smith (15) says that . . .". In the first footnoting case [Smith (2004:222–224)], a list of references is compiled and placed at the end of the proposal. The entire reference to Smith's work is included there. The second instance [Smith (15)] is indicative of a referencing system that numbers the authors alphabetically. Smith (15) means that this work is the 15th in the list of references included at the end of the proposal. This is not an especially desirable footnoting style, however. What if researchers want to add one or two more references to their list of references? Then they will have to renumber all references and make those renumbering changes throughout the entire proposal. The first footnoting style is preferred because of its simplicity. Multiple articles or writings by a single author in the same year are also handled easily. What if Smith has written three articles from which you have quoted? These can be cited as Smith (2004a), Smith (2004b), and Smith (2004c).

The literature review should have an effective summary, highlighting the important findings that bear directly upon the problem to be studied. This helps the reader to understand the relationships between the various articles presented. Of course, it is assumed that the researcher has presented the articles reviewed in a coherent fashion and has woven them together meaningfully in the main presentation. A summary following their presentation will be of great assistance and value to readers as well as to the researcher.

In the quest for scientific objectivity, researchers should make every effort to present articles (particularly in controversial areas) that represent a balanced position. Discussing articles favorable to one viewpoint while ignoring those favoring the opposing view reflects researcher bias. We don't need this in social research. This practice should be avoided because it is misleading and contrary to the canons of science and scientific inquiry.

Theoretical Structure and/or Conceptual Scheme.   In a sense, this section of the research proposal is the heart of it. This is where researchers formulate and develop an explanation for the relationships between variables investigated. How does it come to be so that variables X and Y are associated with one another? Not only are the variables X and Y defined here, but their logical connection is delineated. Included here are the assumptions, propositions, and definitions of variables researchers use to develop the explanatory framework upon which the entire research project rests. Subsequent research will either support or fail to support the existing theoretical framework presented here.

Hypotheses.   Hypotheses are logically deduced from the theoretical framework above. Within the context of the research proposal, hypotheses may be viewed as specific statements of theory in testable form. There is no limit to the number of hypotheses that can be derived from the theoretical scheme and subjected to empirical testing. However, it should be noted that usually the number of hypotheses (as well as their nature) coincides closely with the numbers of objectives of the project stated earlier. In other words, by subjecting the various hypotheses to empirical testing, some or all of the objectives of the research project are achieved partially or fully.

Methodology.   The methodology section makes explicit the study design and constitutes the "how to do it" phase. This section includes:

1. The population to be studied.
2. The type of sampling plan to be followed (e.g., simple random sampling, stratified proportionate random sampling, quota sampling).
3. The size of sample to be drawn and the rationale for this sample size in relation to the population size.
4. The type of instrumentation and/or data collection procedures (e.g., questionnaires, interviews, participant observation, analysis of secondary sources such as statistical records, letters, autobiographies, and so forth).
5. The statistics to be used (e.g., gamma, lambda, the t test, the F test for analysis of variance, multivariate analysis, path analysis, the Pearson r, etc.) and the rationale for selecting these procedures.
6. The type of tabular presentation (e.g., graphs, tables, charts, figures, etc.).
7. Some **dummy tables** illustrating how you plan to graphically portray your data to be analyzed.

The methodology section is the blueprint for researcher activity and specifies how the investigator intends to test the hypotheses, study the people or research subjects, or describe the social settings. Researchers are at liberty to choose from among a variety of data collection techniques and study designs as well as alternative approaches to the problem. Because so many options are available to the investigator in order to study the same problem, this fact has led some persons to label social research as an "art" as opposed to a body of strategies that have specific and limited applications.

Statement of Theoretical and Substantive Implications.   Although some researchers seldom give a lot of thought to the relevance of their research activity theoretically and substantively, others feel more comfortable investigating topics where several *raisons d'être* exist. If someone were to ask us the question, "So what?" at the end of our research proposal or project, what kinds of answers could we provide to demonstrate the theoretical and practical utility or relevance and significance of the investigation? Although there are some researchers who pursue knowledge for the sake of knowledge and give little attention to the meaningfulness of their research activity from the standpoint of practical application to problems in the real world, there are many other investigators who sense an obligation to themselves and to others to defend the studies they have undertaken or proposed to undertake.

Research can be assessed from several dimensions. Some people react favorably to social research if they can see some immediate and direct benefits, such as reducing crime, divorce rates, and the psychological stresses associated with urban renewal programs. Can the research help people to overcome some of their social adjustment problems? Can the results of research be of value in the solution of ecological crises? A different kind of assessment is made of social research in terms of the time dimension. Will the results of my research today be applicable 20 or even 50 years from now even though no practical value of it is apparent presently? The work of Sigmund Freud is a case in point. In his day, people were quick to discard his notions of the significance of dreams, to label the id, ego, superego, and libido as nonsensical. Present-day psychologists and psychiatrists and other social researchers find his work fascinating and insightful for assisting people with various sorts of mental problems.

Research can also be assessed in terms of its theoretical value. Does the research contribute to (support or help to substantiate) existing theories of social behavior? Or does the research refute existing theoretical schemes and orientations? Couched in the context of a relation to existing social theories, research in given areas can eventually prove to have profound significance for the nature and growth of the academic discipline.

However, it must be acknowledged that some people prefer to study a topic simply for the pleasure and interest of understanding it more fully. They are unconcerned about the opinions of others relating to the theoretical and/or practical (substantive) significance of what they do. There must be tolerance and room for all positions taken and motives reflected in the process of social inquiry.

Sources for References

There are many sources for references. The most common sources are (1) research articles in professional journals, (2) books and monographs, and (3) papers presented at professional conferences.

Research Articles in Professional Journals.   Professional journals contain both research articles and essays about a myriad of criminological subjects. Most university and college libraries have modest collections of sources for students to consult when they are preparing papers. In recent years, *Criminal Justice Abstracts* has been made available on CD-ROM in many libraries. Thus, students can search these CD databases for key words involved in their research topics.

Abstracts of articles are brief synopses of what the articles contain. Most of these abstracts summarize the major article findings or article contents. Students can make a fairly easy determination of which articles they might wish to examine more closely. If the library doesn't have the journal with the article desired, then the article may be acquired often through an interlibrary loan service. There may or may not be a nominal charge for this service.

Often, however, article abstracts usually have sufficient information about the study conducted that students can determine what was found as well as its significance. A review of a sample of abstracts shows that much rich information is included in them. Several sample article and book abstracts from a 2004 *Criminal Justice Abstracts* CD are shown below on the subject of "Electronic Monitoring" as examples.

EIGHT SAMPLE ARTICLE ABSTRACTS ON ELECTRONIC MONITORING

RECORD 1 OF 8—CRIMINAL JUSTICE ABS. 1968–2004/06

TI: House arrest with electronic monitoring: An incarceration model for the future?
OT: Elektronisch nberwachter hausarrest: Ein zukunftsmodell fnr den anstaltsvollzug?
AU: Haverkamp-Rita
PY: 2002
ST: Kriminologische Forschungsberichte, Vol. 107
PB: Freiburg, Germany: edition iuscrim
PD: 621pp., Appendix.
AB: This comparative study examines the legal framework and the attitudes of practitioners regarding electronically monitored house arrest in Germany and Sweden. Questionnaire data were obtained in 1998 from 541 experts from criminal courts, public prosecutors offices, parole offices, and penitentiaries in the state of Lower Saxony, Germany, and from 440 experts from the lower criminal courts and agencies dealing with intensive surveillance of convicted offenders in Sweden. In Sweden electronic monitoring was introduced during the 1990s within a generally favorable climate, but Germany has seen a heated debate over the effectiveness of this measure on the one hand, and human rights issues on the other. A majority of experts in both countries view house arrest with electronic monitoring as a positive alternative to imprisonment. More than one third of the German respondents also favor the application of electronic monitoring for a harsher form of probation. Experts in both countries agree that first time offenders with residence and employment are best suited. This emphasis can be interpreted as a reflection of the security focused criminal policy debate in Germany and Sweden during the 1990s.
DT: Book
AN: 89920

RECORD 2 OF 8—CRIMINAL JUSTICE ABS. 1968–2004/06

TI: Toward a woman-centered approach to community-based corrections: A gendered analysis of electronic monitoring in eastern Canada
AU: Maidment-MaDonna-R
JN: Women-and-Criminal-Justice, 13, (4), pp. 47–68.
PY: 2002
AB: This study provides a gendered evaluation of a community-based electronic monitoring (EM) program in Newfoundland, Canada. Data are from semi-structured interviews with 16 females and 16 males. At the time of the research (fall 1997), 25 women had participated in the program since its implementation in November 1994. Findings illustrate the contradictions of a woman-centered philosophy built on a male-dominated model. Correctional

CONTINUED

administrators fail to account for the gendered differences of offenders in the design and administration of the EM program. It appears that, for women, EM may actually be a more onerous and draconian form of punishment than incarceration. Based on women's structural location in society, their primary responsibilities for child care and domestic labor, the nature and extent of their criminal convictions, and the level of state intrusion into their lives (e.g., welfare officers, child protection agencies), EM serves to further marginalize women due, in part, to the lack of feminist guiding principles being extended to the community setting.
DE: CORRECTIONS-; Community-Corrections; ELECTRONIC-MONITORING; WOMEN; Female-Offenders
CL: Adult-Corrections (CR)
DT: Journal-Article
AN: 86916

RECORD 3 OF 8—CRIMINAL JUSTICE ABS. 1968–2004/06

TI: Is home detention in New Zealand disadvantaging women and children?
AU: King-Denise; Gibbs-Anita
JN: Probation-Journal, 50, (2), pp. 115–126.
PY: 2003
AB: This article examines the use of home detention with electronic monitoring in New Zealand, specifically considering the effect of home detention on women who are subject to this disposal, as well as the impact on the women and children who support those on home detention. The discussion draws largely on research conducted in 2001 that examines the development, operation, and impact of home detention in New Zealand within the first 18 months following its inception in October 1999. As part of that research, case records and statistical materials are gathered, and more than 70 interviews with detainees, their sponsors and key stake-holders are conducted. Most women are positive about the home detention/electronic monitoring option; however, increased tensions in the home and deprivation of liberty for some families are found to be clear disadvantages of the scheme. The impact of home detention on relationships between detainees and sponsors depends largely upon the quality and status of the relationship prior to home detention, as well as whether the relationship is family or partner focused. Detainees also tend to struggle with boredom and being under-occupied, both of which add tension to relationships already affected by the confinement of home detention. However, it is women who are burdened most by home detention. Even when women choose to sponsor detainees, the criminal justice system and its stakeholders are still exploiting womens' caring talents; and little extra support is given for their efforts, whether financial, emotional or practical. Women also experience greater tension in the home when their male partners are residing there on home detention or when they are subject to home detention themselves; and the children, on occasions,

CONTINUED

may also be affected negatively by home detention, something which women detainees felt particularly guilty about. These significant structural and systems issues need to be addressed by future research in order to more accurately determine the impact of home detention on women and children, and on the ways of addressing the exploitation of women by the criminal justice system. The challenge for New Zealand policy makers, practitioners, and other researchers, therefore, is to consider gender as an important issue There is a need to recognize that women are expected to look after bad men and they unequivocally bear the burdens or pains of home detention as much—if not more so—than the men they look after.

DE: FAMILY-; GENDER-; Women-; HOME-CONFINEMENT; NEW-ZEALAND
CL: Adult-Corrections (CR)
DT: Journal-Article
AN: 89393

RECORD 4 OF 8—CRIMINAL JUSTICE ABS. 1968–2004/06

TI: Home detention with electronic monitoring: The New Zealand experience
AU: Gibbs-Anita; King-Denise
JN: Criminal-Justice, 3, (2), pp. 199–211.
PY: 2003
AB: This article outlines the development and research of home detention in New Zealand. Home detention with electronic monitoring was introduced in New Zealand in October 1999 as an early release option for people sentenced to varying lengths of imprisonment. Detainees are released to their homes, monitored by means of an electronic bracelet attached to their ankle, and supported and supervised by the probation service, as well as by their families and sponsors. To assess the overall effectiveness of home detention, 80 home detention reports are reviewed; interviews were conducted with 21 detainees, 21 sponsors including family members, 6 probation officers and 2 security staff; and observations are made of over 20 Prison Board members in their discussions of home detention cases. The stories of detainees and their families lead to two initial conclusions: that home detention works well for families by keeping them together, but it also places extra burdens on women and children especially. Whereas home detention has been viewed positively, the negative impacts on families and children, and the broader acceptance of electronic monitoring in New Zealand, reveal a worrying level of tolerance for the coercive surveillance of families. The public, and those in power—politicians, judges, and Prison Board members—do not know the real impact of home detention. It is within the control of criminal justice stakeholders, however, to review their practices towards detained families, or to reduce the more punitive aspects of home detention. It is also within the control of policy makers to listen to both consumers and advocates of home detention and to reassess the effectiveness of the option in light of the families' actual experiences.

CONTINUED

DE: CRIMINAL-LAW; ELECTRONIC-MONITORING; Home-Confinement; NEW-ZEALAND
CL: Adult-Corrections (CR)
DT: Journal-Article
AN: 88762

RECORD 5 OF 8—CRIMINAL JUSTICE ABS. 1968–2004/06

TI: Thinking about the demand for probation services
AU: Morgan-Rod
JN: Probation-Journal, 50, (1), pp. 7–19.
PY: 2003
AB: This essay explores three questions regarding probation services in England and Wales. It considers who does and should determine the demand for probation services; why the current pattern for the demand and supply of probation services exists; and how the future demand and supply of probation services might be altered. In the past decade, an increasing array of community penalties have been introduced: the combination order, the curfew order with electronic monitoring, the drug treatment and testing order, the exclusion order, and the drug abstinence order. A separate set of new orders has also been introduced for juveniles. Custody, however, has not yet been replaced. On the contrary, these changes have fuelled an increasingly interventionist and punitive sentencing trend resulting in a record prison population and a probation service overburdened with low-risk offenders to supervise. The National Probation Service, both nationally and at area level, must develop more effective means to inform the judiciary about the day-to-day reality of community penalties. Second, there is an urgent need to resuscitate the use of financial penalties, considering that a high proportion of the offenders currently being made subject to community penalties, particularly community punishment orders, would have been fined 10 years ago. Third, the scope for making restorative justice an option both presentence and post-sentence should be actively explored. Fourth, community service must be moved up-tariff, where it used to be. Finally, if these low-risk offenders cannot, on whatever grounds, be fined or given discharges, then consideration might be given to introducing less intensive, or less professional, supervision or surveillance for some categories of offenders. If crime reduction is to be achieved and the public better protected, the probation service must proactively, with government and sentencers, better determine the use to which its scarce resources are put.
DE: COMMUNITY-CORRECTIONS; PROBATION-; Community-Corrections; UNITED-KINGDOM
CL: Adult-Corrections (CR)
DT: Journal-Article
AN: 88596

CONTINUED

RECORD 6 OF 8—CRIMINAL JUSTICE ABS. 1968–2004/06

TI: Changing attitudes toward house arrest with electronic monitoring: The impact of a single presentation?
AU: Gainey-Randy-R; Payne-Brian-K
JN: International-Journal-of-Offender-Therapy-and-Comparative-Criminology, 47, (2), pp. 196–209.
PY: 2003
AB: The notion that community support is critical to program success is a consistent theme in the literature on community-based corrections. Unfortunately, most people know little about alternative sanctions, are misinformed about then, or view them unfavorably. At issue is whether information about these sanctions affects attitudes toward them. To address this question, this study collected survey data from 61 college students enrolled in an upper-division criminal justice course before and after a presentation on house arrest with electronic monitoring. Most respondents indicated that they did not know much about the sanction before attending the guest lectures. However, prior to the stimuli, participants viewed the sanction as a weak punishment but one that might be cost-effective and useful because work and family ties were less likely to be harmed compared to traditional punishments. Following the presentation, students were more likely to agree that electronic monitoring is punitive and that it meets several goals of the justice system. Implications for policy makers and educators are considered.
DE: COMMUNITY-CORRECTIONS; HOME-CONFINEMENT; Electronic-Monitoring; PUBLIC-ATTITUDES; Public-Opinion
CL: Adult-Corrections (CR)
DT: Journal-Article
AN: 88546

RECORD 7 OF 8—CRIMINAL JUSTICE ABS. 1968–2004/06

TI: The influence of demographic factors on the experience of house arrest
AU: Payne-Brian-K; Gainey-Randy-R
JN: Federal-Probation, 66, (3), pp. 64–70.
PY: 2002
AB: This study examines whether various aspects of house arrest with electronic monitoring are experienced differently among different groups of offenders. Recent research suggests that offenders' preferences for sanctions vary based on important demographic characteristics such as race, gender, and age. A survey is administered to 49 electronically monitored offenders. Overall, with the exception of a few subtle differences based on offender demographics and sentence length, house arrest with electronic monitoring appears to be experienced relatively equally among various groups. Female offenders may experience more

CONTINUED

shame from wearing the bracelet than male offenders, and Black offenders may see the sanction as more restrictive than do White offenders. With regard to age, older offenders are more likely to have problems with the visibility of the monitor as well as the inability to leave when they want. Finally, with regard to length of sentence, the sanction may become unbearable over time. These subtle differences cannot be ignored because they may be very telling insofar as appropriate supervision strategies are concerned.
DT: Journal-Article
AN: 88298

RECORD 8 OF 8—CRIMINAL JUSTICE ABS. 1968–2004/06

TI: Prisoner reentry and the role of parole officers
AU: Seiter-Richard-P
JN: Federal-Probation, 66, (3), pp. 50–54.
PY: 2002
AB: This study examines the perceptions of what parole officers consider most important to successful prisoner reentry, as well as their own job contributions to this success. Data are obtained from 114 surveys, completed by parole officers of six district offices within the Eastern Region of Missouri, and interviews with 11 officers. Parole officers identify steady employment, staying drug free, receiving support from family and friends, and developing stable patterns of behavior as the most critical aspects of success. Officers further believe that the job aspects related to offender success include close monitoring of behavior, assessing and referring parolees to community agencies based on their needs, helping parolees maintain employment, and holding offenders accountable for their behaviors. In a time when parole officers are increasingly charged with close surveillance of parolees through the use of intensive supervision, electronic monitoring, urine testing, and specialized supervision programs for offenders with histories of violence, officers continue to believe that the most effective functions they perform are those that help and assist those under supervision. Parole administrators and correctional policy makers, therefore, may need to reconsider such surveillance policies to prevent them from overriding the importance of traditional casework activities in improving the success rates of offenders returning to the community from prison.
DT: Journal-Article
AN: 88295

Scanning the database of the 2004 *Criminal Justice Abstracts* in CD-ROM format, there were 239 article abstracts included between the years 1968–2004 on the subject of electronic monitoring (EM). Eight of these articles have been downloaded and printed for inclusion here. An examination of these abstracts reveals the following abbreviations:

TI = Title of work/article/book
AU = Author(s)
JN = Journal (may be publisher if a book), volume, and page numbers
PY = Publication year of work
AB = Abstract material
DE = Alternative search terms one might use besides "Police Misconduct"
CL = Article/book classification
DT = Type of document (book, journal article, paper)
AN = Reference number

Thus, just about all of the relevant information for a citation for prospective authors is presented in these abstracts. Most libraries have copies of these documents, either on hard copy (the journals themselves) or in CD-ROM format. Accessing this information is most often a free library service. Reviewing these eight article/book abstracts briefly, let's see what we can learn about EM from them.

The first abstract is of German origin and is a book by Rita Haverkamp published in 2002. The abstract says that questionnaires were obtained in 1998 from 541 experts from criminal courts, public prosecutors' offices, parole offices, and penitentiaries from Lower Saxony, Germany, and from 440 experts in similar agencies in Sweden. Haverkamp says that Sweden has accepted EM favorably while Germany has had heated debate over its use. Sweden emphasizes the effectiveness of EM as an offender monitoring tool, while German officials emphasize human rights issues. Both countries are in agreement that EM works best with first-offenders who have a residence and are employed. The article is a reflection of the criminal policy debate between the two countries during the 1990s.

The second abstract is from a journal article by MaDonna Maidment published in 2002 and describes a study of an EM program in Newfoundland. Semi-structured interviews with 16 males and 16 females were conducted during the fall of 1997. At the time of Maidment's study, 25 women had participated in the EM program since it was commenced in 1994. Maidment discloses contradictions between a women-centered philosophy built on a male-dominated model and indicates that correctional officials have failed to take into account gender differences in EM programming. Maidment further indicates that women have a more difficult time with EM than men, and she provides several explanations for this difference.

The third abstract is a journal article by Denise King and Anita Gibbs published in 2003. It describes a home detention program in New Zealand where EM was used during the first 18 months of its inception in October 1999. These writers note that more than 70 interviews with clients and their sponsors were obtained, and that many of the women involved in the EM program felt comfortable with it. Some of the problems described by King and Gibbs focus on family conflicts and the social relationships established between clients and their families prior to EM and home confinement. One challenge for those operating EM programs and where female clients are involved is that women experience greater tension when their male partners are residing there under home confinement and EM supervision. These writers emphasize the importance of examining the issue of gender in future EM programming in New Zealand.

The fourth abstract is also by Gibbs and King, published in 2003, and outlines the development of home detention with EM in New Zealand. It is different from their earlier study because it describes 80 home detention reports; interviews with 21 detainees, 6 probation officers, and 2 security staff; and observations of over 20 Prison Board members. Using stories disclosed by EM/home confinement clients, Gibbs and King conclude that home detention works well by keeping families together, but that it also places extra burdens on women and their children. These writers observe that the coercive surveillance of clients is worrisome to Prison Board members, and that generally, most people in New Zealand don't know a great deal about EM and its supervisory consequences or effectiveness. They suggest that those in power should consider minimizing the punitive aspects of EM to reduce the strain on families so that greater rehabilitation will occur.

The fifth abstract is a journal article by Rod Morgan published in 2003. It explores three general EM questions regarding the probation services of England and Wales. Who determines the demand for probation services? Why does the current demand for these services exist? And how might future demand and supply of probation services be affected? They observe that during the 1990s, many community penalties have been introduced as a part of an offender's supervision. Furthermore, juveniles have been subjected to many new rules and program requirements. These writers argue for the reimplementation of financial penalties for offenders, such as fines, and that restorative justice should be used as an option for increasing numbers of low-risk clients. They encourage the probation services of these jurisdictions to become more proactive politically to provide better supervisory services for offenders and improve public protection. This article is essentially an essay and commentary on EM and other types of supervision used by the probation services of these jurisdictions. It probably contains valuable arguments for different programs that are promoted or encouraged. It does not present any information about a sample of clients that has been studied. Nevertheless, its policy statements are important.

The sixth abstract describes a journal article written by Randy Gainey and Brian Payne and published in 2003. It argues that community support is critical for EM program success. These writers contend that the general public still knows relatively little about EM, and there is considerable misinformation about its use and capabilities. Survey data are presented that were gathered from 61 upper-division university criminal justice majors both before and after a lecture on EM. Most respondents disclosed that they had known little about EM before the lecture and had regarded it as a weak punishment. After the lecture, most students agreed that EM is punitive and a cost-effective way of supervising low-risk offenders in their communities. The writers also discussed several implications of EM for policymakers and educators.

The seventh abstract, also a journal article published by Brian Payne and Randy Gainey in 2002, is an actual investigation of the use of EM on a sample of 49 offenders. Based on survey information from these offenders, the writers learned that female offenders tend to experience greater shame than their male counterparts because of the EM anklets and wristlets they must wear during their EM programs. Black offenders tend to see EM as more punitive than white offenders. Older offenders have more problems with EM than younger offenders, particularly relating to the visibility of the EM devices that must be worn and one's inability to leave one's home while in the EM program. Furthermore, the longer clients are on EM, the more unbearable EM becomes as a punishment. The writers argue that community corrections officials should consider sociodemographic characteristics as important considerations in determining the circumstances under which EM should be used.

Finally, the eighth abstract is a 2002 journal article summary published by Richard Seiter. Seiter focuses on parolee reentry into the community and the relationship between parolees and their supervising parole officers. Six district parole offices in the Eastern Region of Missouri were surveyed and 114 responses were obtained from parole officers. Also, interviews with 11 officers were conducted. Parole officers disclosed that offender reentry into their communities is facilitated by parole officer assistance in various forms, such as employment assistance, counseling, EM supervision, urine testing, and holding clients accountable for their conduct. They believe that EM assists them in closely supervising offenders, which tends to ensure closer compliance with parole program requirements. Seiter admonishes parole administrators to reconsider their surveillance policies so that they will not overshadow the importance of traditional casework activities performed by parole officers.

It is clear from these few abstracts selected from an original listing of 239 that much information can be gleaned about EM, and from different countries besides the United States. Often it is important to understand how other countries are coping with and implementing EM and other supervisory methods for their offender populations. Certain problems encountered in other countries and issues raised will tend to direct the attention of U.S. community corrections officials toward similar issues relating to their own offender-clients.

Whenever anyone accesses the *Criminal Justice Abstracts* database to research particular subjects, therefore, it is anticipated that much information can be gleaned from whatever article or book abstracts are yielded as a result of these literature searches. Of course, students and others can review the actual sources for more detailed information. Although abstract information is very important in literature reviews of various topics, abstracts cannot possibly contain all of the relevant information that would be found in articles or books themselves. Thus, it may be unwise for anyone to rely exclusively on abstract information for their literature reviews.

Books and Monographs.   Besides research articles and theoretical pieces published in professional journals and magazines, books may be consulted. Some books are readers, where editors compile numerous articles written by others. These articles are usually focused around an integrating theme, such as community policing or probation and parole. Many books are called monographs because they are specialty books or trade publications written for fairly narrow audiences. Someone may write a book about juvenile transfer hearings or the pros and cons of the death penalty. The topics of such books are well defined. It is unlikely that specific courses in criminology and criminal justice might use such specialized books. More often than not, these books might be used as supplemental reading because of their limited scope.

Textbooks are another source of information. However, while textbooks are useful at providing factual information about a broad array of events and topics, they are often dated. It usually takes about one year for a textbook to be published once the author has submitted the final manuscript to the publisher. Much time is spent copy editing the work and proofreading several more refined versions at different publication stages. Thus, source materials may be as much as 2 or 3 years old by the time the textbook is in print. This is not the fault of the author. Rather, the pace of publishing causes this dating to occur. Thus, textbooks may not contain up-to-date information that might be found in the latest research articles. It is recommended that the most recent journals should be consulted over textbook sources.

Papers Presented at Professional Conferences.   Annually, different regional and national organizations hold conferences. These organizations include the Midwestern Criminal Justice Association, the American Sociological Association, the American Society of Criminology, the Academy of Criminal Justice Sciences, the Western Society of Criminology, the Southern Sociological Society, the Southern Criminal Justice Association, the Western and Pacific Criminal Justice Association, the American Correctional Association, and the American Probation and Parole Association. The proceedings of these associations are often published and can be acquired by those attending the conferences. The American Society of Criminology, for instance, publishes abstracts of papers presented. These abstracts are the same as article abstracts published by *Criminal Justice Abstracts.*

Using abstracts from recent criminological and criminal justice conferences is one way of obtaining the most recent, up-to-date information about various subjects, since paper presenters are often in the midst of writing up their research for journal article submissions and other publication outlets. Many researchers scan these conference proceedings and write letters to presenters with requests for copies of their papers if available. It is often the case that these papers presented at professional conferences will eventually be published in research journals 1–2 years later. Therefore, it is obvious that obtaining the freshest research from presenters gives the student an edge over those who rely on textbooks for paper information or even recently published journals.

Legal Research in Criminal Justice

When students examine legal cases from different sources, they may wish to quote from them or cite them in their papers. The material below provides some conventional practices relating to legal citations.

The U.S. Supreme Court cases cited in this section, as well as cases cited from U.S. District Courts or Circuit Courts of Appeal and state courts, are cited by the *names* of persons involved in the cases as well as the *volume numbers* and *page numbers* where the cases can be found. A *hypothetical* citation might appear as follows:

Smith v. Jones, 358 U.S. 437, 122 S.Ct. 229 (2004)

Or a citation might appear as:

Smith v. Jones, 226 F.Supp. 1 (2004)

or

Smith v. Jones, 442 P.2d 433 (2004)

These cites are important to anyone interested in legal research or learning about what the law says and how it should be interpreted or applied. They specify particular sources or *reporters* where these cases can be found. A *reporter* is a collection of books containing published opinions of different courts. In the list of cases discussed in this book, *most* are U.S. Supreme Court cases, while several are from state supreme courts. The first numbers in each citation above specify a *volume number,* while the second number is a *page number* in the volume. In the hypothetical example above, *Smith v. Jones* is found in the 358th volume of the *United States Reports* on page 437. Also, the same case can be found in volume 122 of the *Supreme Court Reporter* on page 229. Below are several rules or guidelines governing citations and information about what is contained in them.

U.S. Supreme Court Decisions

All U.S. Supreme Court opinions and decisions are printed in various sources. The *official source* for all U.S. Supreme Court opinions is the *United States Reports,* abbreviated as *U.S.,* and it is published by the U.S. Government Printing Office. The U.S. Supreme Court convenes annually for a *term,* where numerous cases are heard and decided. All U.S. Supreme Court actions are recorded in the *United States Reports.* There is a substantial time lag between the time the U.S. Supreme Court delivers its opinions and when they are published in the *United States Reports,* however. Other sources exist, therefore, that distribute these opinions in a more timely fashion to interested lawyers and researchers.

Unofficial sources also print U.S. Supreme Court opinions in bound volumes on an annual basis. These unofficial sources include West Publishing Company's *Supreme Court Reporter* and the Lawyer's Cooperative *United States Supreme Court Reports, Lawyer's Edition.* The *Supreme Court Reporter* published by West is abbreviated as *S.Ct.,* while the *United States Supreme Court Reports, Lawyer's Edition* is abbreviated as *L.Ed.* Within days following a particular ruling by the U.S. Supreme Court, unofficial versions of the entire text of U.S. Supreme Court opinions are published by West Publishing Company and the Lawyer's Cooperative. For instance, West Publishing Company distributes **advance sheets** to its subscribers. Advance sheets are booklets published about once every 2 or 3 weeks that contain recent U.S. Supreme Court actions. During any given U.S. Supreme Court term, as many as 22–24 booklets or advance sheets will be sent to subscribers.

Another source is *United States Law Week,* which is published by the Bureau of National Affairs, Inc., and the *United States Supreme Court Bulletin,* published by Commerce Clearing House, Inc. The *United States Law Week* is abbreviated as *U.S.L.W.* A major strength of the unofficial *United States Law Week* is the most recent U.S. Supreme Court opinions are made available to interested legal researchers and lawyers within days following particular decisions.

Whenever a U.S. Supreme Court opinion is cited, more than a few scholars use **parallel citations** to indicate where any given case can be found. For instance, a case with its *typical* parallel citations might be *Brewer v. Williams,* 430 U.S. 387, 97 S.Ct. 1232, 51 L.Ed.2d 424 (1977). According to the Harvard Law Review Association in Cambridge, Massachusetts, as well as *The Process of Legal Research* (Kunz et al., 1992), it is proper to rely exclusively upon the official reporter, which would be the *United States Reports* in U.S. Supreme Court cases. Thus, we would only need to cite *Brewer v. Williams,* 430 U.S. 387 (1977), and this cite would be sufficient to comply with legal protocol. However, because of the time lag between U.S. Supreme Court opinions and the publication of the *United States Reports,* it is proper to cite the next most recently available *unofficial* source. This would involve a citation from the *Supreme Court Reporter* published by West. Thus, if we didn't know the *United States Reports* cite yet *but* we knew the *Supreme Court*

Reporter cite, we could cite it as follows: *Brewer v. Williams,* _____U.S._____, 97 S.Ct. 1232 (1977). The blank spaces indicate that we do not know yet which volume or page number *Brewer v. Williams* will be found in the *United States Reports.* Later, when the *United States Reports* is published as the official version of U.S. Supreme Court opinions, we can supply the appropriate page numbers.

There are several hundred volumes of each of these reporters. Obviously, it would be very expensive for any college or university library to acquire each of these compendiums of U.S. Supreme Court opinions. Many libraries subscribe to the *United States Reports,* while other libraries might subscribe to the *Supreme Court Reporter.* Other libraries might subscribe to the *United States Supreme Court Reports, Lawyer's Edition.* Several large law school libraries have all of these volumes and more. However, since many colleges and universities cannot afford to maintain all three versions, and since these are parallel citations and are virtually identical opinions, it makes little sense for an average library to have three different compendiums of opinions that say the same thing. Therefore, many libraries will have either one source or another. Scholars sometimes give three standard parallel citations whenever cases are cited. Thus, researchers can look up the same U.S. Supreme Court opinion in any one of these sources, depending on which version is maintained by their library.

When students read introductory textbooks in criminology or criminal justice, therefore, it should not be considered unusual or confusing to see the same case in different books with different citations. For example, one criminology book may cite *Brewer v. Williams,* 97 S.Ct. 1232 (1977), while another criminology book may refer to *Brewer v. Williams,* 430 U.S. 387 (1977). Yet another criminology book may use the Lawyer's Cooperative version and cite *Brewer v. Williams,* 51 L.Ed.2d 424 (1977). All of these citations are considered proper. When an author of a textbook provides *all three* parallel citations, it may not be necessary, but it may be helpful for persons more or less restricted to particular sets of U.S. Supreme Court volumes.

When "2d" or "3d" follow a reporter, this doesn't mean that a new edition of the source has been published. Rather, it means that the publishing company has started over with a fresh numbering system. For instance, *Brewer v. Williams,* 51 L.Ed.2d (1977) means that the case can be found in volume 51 of the *United States Supreme Court Reports, Lawyer's Edition, Second Series.* There are no fixed rules governing when publishing companies will commence new series for their volume renumbering.

Lower Federal Court Opinions

There are no official sources for reporting the opinions of lower federal courts, such as the different Circuit Courts of Appeal or U.S. District Courts. However, West Publishing Company publishes the *Federal Reporter,* abbreviated as *F,* or *F.2d,* to indicate where various opinions can be found for the U.S. Circuit Courts of Appeal. Not all of these opinions are published each year. Whatever opinions are published are at the discretion of the publisher, and often, decisions to include or not include particular Circuit Court of Appeals opinions is influenced by their constitutional relevance. Another source, also published by West, is the *Federal Supplement,* abbreviated as *F. Supp.* This source publishes selected opinions from U.S. District Courts, U.S. Customs Courts, and the U.S. Court of International Trade.

State Supreme Court Decisions

Separate state supreme court reporters are published. Several publishing companies, including West Publishing Company, publish these state supreme court opinions. A chart provided below shows which outlets publish which state supreme court opinions and which abbreviations are used for such compilations.

Reporter	States Included
Atlantic Reporter (A or A.2d)	Connecticut, Delaware, Maine, Maryland, New Hampshire, New Jersey, Pennsylvania, Rhode Island, Vermont, and the District of Columbia
Northeastern Reporter (N.E. or N.E.2d)	Illinois, Indiana, Massachusetts, New York, and Ohio
Northwestern Reporter (N.W. or N.W.2d)	Iowa, Michigan, Minnesota, Nebraska, North Dakota, South Dakota, and Wisconsin
Pacific Reporter (P or P.2d)	Alaska, Arizona, California, Colorado, Hawaii, Idaho, Kansas, Montana, Nevada, New Mexico, Oklahoma, Oregon, Utah, Washington, and Wyoming
Southeastern Reporter (S.E. or S.E.2d)	Georgia, North Carolina, South Carolina, Virginia, and West Virginia
Southwestern Reporter (S.W. or S.W.2d)	Arkansas, Kentucky, Missouri, Tennessee, Texas, and Indian Territories
Southern Reporter (So. or So.2d)	Alabama, Florida, Louisiana, and Mississippi

Individual states publish their supreme court opinions in separate publications. For example, the Alabama Supreme Court has its opinions published in the *Alabama Reports.* The Colorado Supreme Court's opinions are published in the *Colorado Reports.* Other reporting outlets include the *North Dakota Reports, Ohio State Reports, Tennessee Reports, Virginia Reports,* and *Wisconsin Reports.* These and other *Report* sources can be consulted to find specific state supreme court opinions for different years.

Federal and State Statute Compilations.   Criminal and civil statutes for the federal system are contained in the *U.S. Code.* Connecticut has the *The General Statutes of Connecticut.* Tennessee has the *Tennessee Code Annotated.* Texas has *Vernon's Texas Codes Annotated.* Virginia has the *Virginia Reports.* Washington has the *Revised Code of Washington Annotated,* and so on. These statutory compilations are being rewritten annually as new laws are passed and old or existing laws are modified or eliminated.

Glossary

Accidental sampling   Selecting elements for one's sample based on immediate accessibility and cooperativeness of respondents; questionnaires distributed to students in the classroom are distributed to "accidental samples" as an example; the roving reporter on the street interviews "accidental sample" elements.

Advance sheets   Booklets distributed by various publishing companies who publish U.S. Supreme Court opinions within weeks after they have been rendered; these documents are unofficial versions of what eventually become permanent volumes in a legal library of published court opinions.

After-only design   Method seeking to compare an experimental group with a control group *after* an experimental variable has been introduced to one group but not the other.

Alternative hypothesis   Same as the research hypothesis in relation to a null hypothesis.

Altruistic appeals   Cover-letter appeals to respondents where they are requested to complete and return their questionnaires as a favor to others.

Analysis of secondary sources   Data collection strategy that utilizes materials collected by other investigators for purposes other than those of the present investigator; includes studies of public documents, letters, diaries, and private reports.

Anonymity   Assurances given to respondents in one's research that their answers will be confidential and disclosed to no one.

Applied research   Investigations undertaken primarily for practical reasons; policy-relevant form of research.

Arbitrary scales   Indices developed and based on face validity and individual discretion.

Archival analysis   Use of historical records, such as court documents, in order to discover patterns.

Area sampling, area probability sample   *See* Multistage sampling.

Association   Preferred term to describe relationships or correlations between two or more variables, regardless of level of measurement of test variables.

Assumptions   Similar to empirical generalizations, these are statements that have a high degree of certainty; they require little, if any, confirmation in the real world; examples of assumptions might be, "All societies have laws," or "The greater the deviant conduct, the greater the group pressure on the deviant to conform to group norms."

Atheoretical evaluations   Descriptive research that is not directly connected to a theoretical scheme; a study of some event simply to know what causes the event; not grounded in any particular theory.

Attitudes   Tendencies to think or act in given ways; intangible dispositions of persons, measured by scales, intended to differentiate persons according to their dispositions and inclinations; inferred dispositions from paper-and-pencil questionnaires containing scales.

Attributes   Characteristics of people or things.

Autobiographical information   Method of studying persons by paying attention to their own accounts of their lives and social events.

Axiomatic theory   Use of truisms or axioms in a logical fashion to derive testable statements about events; ordering of propositions and assumptions in ways that yield other statements capable of being tested.

Axioms   Truisms; statements about reality that are largely unquestioned; assumptions.

Bar graphs   Either vertical or horizontal bars that represent frequencies of occurrence of different values.

Basic research   Investigations conducted to test theoretical issues; contributes to knowledge base of criminal justice or criminology.

Before–after method, before–after design   Improvement over the after-only design, the before–after design consists of obtaining measures on some dependent variable for two groups that are presumed equivalent for experimental purposes, introducing an experimental variable to one group and withholding it from the other, and comparing the two groups after the experiment has been completed.

Bias   A misrepresentation of reality as the result of inappropriate or inaccurate measures; any question encouraging a particular response.

Biographical information   Method of acquiring information about persons by studying accounts written about them by others.

Birth cohort   Aggregate of persons born in the same year and studied at different intervals over time.

Bogardus social distance scale   Measurement technique for determining willingness of persons to associate with others who are different ethnically or racially; disclosing varying degrees of closeness with such persons.

Branching technique   Method of asking questions that narrows the focus of the topic; used in situations where sensitive topics such as rape or incest are discussed.

Canned data sets   Readily available databases of information compiled by private and public sources made available to researchers for diverse purposes.

Case study   A qualitative study where the researcher collects large amounts of information from individual cases; reliance upon interview or observational information.

Case study design   Thorough examination of specific social settings or particular aspects of social settings, including detailed psychological and behavioral descriptions of persons in those settings.

Categorical variable   Any factor measured according to a nominal scale.

Causal variable Any treatment variable or stimulus, usually introduced during an experiment, and intended to bring about a change on some dependent variable or a particular desired or expected result.

Causal relation One variable, designated as independent, functioning to create changes in another variable, designated as dependent; relation where one variable follows another variable's occurrence.

Causality Relationship between two or more variables, where values for one variable are determined or strongly influenced by another variable; study of factors that elicit other factors; process of linking one condition with another, such that one condition elicits changes in another in predicted or anticipated directions.

Cause–effect relation *See* Causal relation.

Cell frequencies Number of observations in a particular cell of any $r \times c$ table.

Census Study of entire population; U.S. Census Bureau collects information periodically from population.

Classic experimental design If there are two or more cases and in one of them observation Z can be made, while in the other it cannot be made; and if factor C occurs when observation Z is made, and does not occur when observation Z is not made; then it can be asserted that there is a causal relationship between C and Z.

Cluster sampling *See* Multistage sampling.

Code of conduct Outline of expected moral and ethical behaviors for members of an organization or profession.

Code of ethics Prescription for moral behaviors and standards expected of members of an organization or profession.

Coding Assignment of numbers to information collected by investigator; questionnaires are coded when questions and responses are classified numerically, and numbers are transmitted to software programs designed to facilitate data analysis.

Coding manual, codebook Document compiled by researchers to identify meanings of numbers assigned to different variables and variable subclasses.

Coefficient of association Numerical expression of the degree of relationship or correlation between two or more variables; ranges in magnitude from $\pm$ 1.00, respectively meaning either perfect negative or perfect positive association; 0 = no association.

Coefficient of reproducibility Measure used in conjunction with Guttman scaling that determines whether one's responses to individual items may be predicted solely on the basis of knowing one's total test score; .90 means that the scale is reproducible, hence unidimensional; .80 is a quasi-reproducible scale.

Cohort Any aggregate of persons studied at different points in time; birth cohorts are persons born in the same year and subsequently studied periodically.

Collapsing tables Reducing a table size with more rows and columns to a smaller table size with fewer rows and columns; refers to combining certain row and column cells into fewer of them to create a smaller table; intent of collapsing is to increase numbers of cell frequencies in remaining cells.

Comparative research　Investigations seeking to contrast persons of different cultures; sometimes called cross-cultural research; generally any comparison research highlighting characteristics and differences between two or more groups.

Computer-Assisted Telephone Interviewing (CATI)　Method of contacting respondents by dialing telephone numbers at random; objective is to circumvent problems in contacting respondents with unlisted telephone numbers.

Computer-determined draw　Software program designed to generate random digits; method of generating random samples of elements by a random-numbers program on a computer.

Concepts　Terms used in language that have direct empirical referents.

Conclusions　Final observations and deductions about collected and analyzed data; final tentative interpretations of the significance about what one has found.

Concurrent validity　Form of test validation where scores of predicted behavior are obtained simultaneously with the exhibited behavior.

Confidentiality　The privilege requirement that any information disclosed by participants in a study will not be made public or available to outsiders; provision that information collected will not be used to harm research subjects in any way.

Constant　Any variable that doesn't change in value during the course of a study.

Construct validity　Both a logical and a statistical validating method; also known as *factorial validity,* construct validity is useful for measuring traits for which external criteria are not available, such as latent aggressiveness; this type of validity is determined through the application of *factor analysis.*

Constructs　Terms used in language that have indirect empirical referents.

Contamination of data　Experiences or events that might adversely affect the experimental or control group and thus disrupt the experiment and undermine experimental integrity.

Content analysis　Systematic qualitative and quantitative description of some form of communication.

Content validity　Face validity based on the logical inclusion of a sampling of items taken from the universe of items that measure the trait in question; the only way content validity can be demonstrated is by examining the test or instrument items and comparing them with the universe of items that could theoretically be included, if known.

Contingency questions　Survey items designed to be answered only by some respondents who have previously been screened by other questions.

Continuous variables　Any factors that have an infinite number of subclasses.

Control　Holding constant one or more factors while others are free to vary; manipulation of variables to elicit predictable effects; also a reference to groups or individuals, control groups, who are not exposed to experimental variables, whatever they might be.

Control group　Persons not receiving experimental stimulus; if we were to administer a particular drug to persons in one group and withhold the drug from persons in another group, the group receiving the drug would be called the *experimental group,* while the group not receiving the drug would be called the *control group;* ordinarily, the reactions of the experimental group and the control group are observed and compared; differences between the two groups are attributed largely to the effects of the experimental stimulus, or in this case, the drug.

Control of variables   Manipulating variables so as to determine their experimental impact on other variables; distributing variable subclasses in tables to determine their influence on other variables with which they have been cross-tabulated.

Control variable   Any factor that is held constant in an attempt to further clarify the relation between two other variables.

Convenience sampling   Method of selecting elements because of their availability to the researcher; same as accidental samples; researchers sometimes study those with whom they work, or they may take advantage of their teaching situation and use large classes of students that happen to be conveniently available.

Convention   Practice of following whatever is customary; applied to criminology and criminal justice, certain actions of professionals are guided by convention, including setting particular significance levels such as .05 or .01 in statistical tests; convention also applies to tabular formats and certain kinds of data presentation consistent with the customary usage within the academic discipline.

Cornell technique   *See* Guttman scaling.

Correlation   *See* Association.

Cost–benefit analysis (CBA)   Comparison of the useful and practical results of an intervention or experimental variable and the costs of these results compared with alternative interventions.

Crime clocks   Circular portrayals of the frequency of occurrence of particular crimes; *see* Pie charts.

Crime rate   Number of crimes during a given period, such as one year, divided by the population and then multiplied by 100,000.

Criterion validity   *See* Predictive validity.

Criterion variable   The dependent variable.

Cross-sectional study   Survey designed to elicit opinions or attitudes about one or more issues from designated persons at one point in time.

Cross-tabulations   Tabular arrangements where two or more variables and their subclasses are arranged so that "interactions" between variables may be observed.

Cross-tabulations of variables   Tabular representations of data, where two or more variables have been placed in tables with several rows and several columns to determine their interaction and influence upon one another.

Data   Collected information.

Data analysis   Evaluation of the significance of collected information by means of statistical assessment or the significance of the contents.

Data cleaning   Close inspection of responses to questionnaire and coding procedures to detect any errors in recording information.

Data collection   Process of acquiring information about research subjects, usually through interviews or questionnaires.

Data collection methods   Any way of obtaining information about events; includes questionnaires, surveys, interviews, observation, analysis of secondary sources.

Data entry   Process of creating machine-readable data sets from collected data; process of entering values into a statistical software program, such as *SPSS.*

Data set   Collection of variables for a group of research subjects to be studied.

Deception   Deliberately deceiving research subjects about the nature of the experiment, study, or research being conducted and the role played by these subjects in the research.

Deduction   Process of deriving conclusions logically from several related theoretical statements.

Deductive theory   Based on reasoning from the work of the early Greek philosopher, Aristotle (384–322 B.C.); logical statements are deduced or derived from other statements; typically, assumptions are made and conclusions are drawn that appear to be logically connected with these assumptions; a common example is, "All men are mortal. Aristotle is a man. Therefore, Aristotle is mortal." Symbolically, "All A's are B's; C is a B, therefore, C is also an A:" Using deduction, we abstract by generalizing.

Definitions   Indicators we consider significant in influencing various events that assist us in constructing a logical explanatory framework or theory.

Dense sampling   Selection of elements where approximately 50 percent of the population is obtained; method of obtaining sample is irrelevant, since it is assumed that the overwhelming numbers of such a sample, even obtained accidentally, would be sufficient to warrant some amount of generalizing to and inferences about populations.

Dependent variable   Any factor whose value is determined by other variables.

Description   One of several functions of statistical procedures to depict sample and population values and characteristics.

Descriptive design   Considerably more structured than casual descriptions of social settings; involves depictions of social patterns that persist over time; the most common design objective in criminology and criminal justice.

Descriptive research   Any investigation that depicts patterns of behavior or elaborates relationships between variables.

Diagonal distributions of frequencies   In 2×2 tables or larger, distributions of frequencies that are considered desirable, in that cell frequencies accumulate in cells a and d or b and c.

Dichotomy   Division of three or more subclasses on any variable, measured according to any level of measurement, into two subclasses only.

Diffusion of treatment   Control groups learn about and imitate the experimental group, thus contaminating and confounding study results.

Dimension   A specific facet or aspect of a concept.

Directional hypothesis test   Any statistical verification of a statement where a specific direction of difference has been indicated.

Discrete variables   Any factors that have a finite number of subclasses.

Disproportionate stratified random sampling   Probability sampling plan where one or more variables are controlled; elements obtained are chosen such that these characteristics are not distributed throughout the sample in the same way that they are distributed within the population.

Distribution   Array of collected scores and their arrangement.

Double-barreled questions   Two questions contained in a single statement; cannot be answered with a single response.

Dual-submission policy   Regulation adopted by most professional journals that prohibits authors from submitting their original scholarly articles to more than one journal at a time; in past years, some authors would send their articles to several different journals at once, whereupon two or more journals might subsequently publish the same article; currently an unacceptable practice.

Dummy tables   Blank tables that are constructed prior to conducting research; intent of tables is to suggest the type of data to be collected to answer research questions.

Egoistic appeals   Cover-letter appeals to respondents that are designed to solicit their opinions as a way of increasing response.

Elements   Persons or objects; in social research, one of several persons selected for inclusion in a sample from a larger population of them.

Empirical   Amenable to the senses; measurable.

Empirical generalizations   Facts; observable regularities of human or social behavior.

Empirical referent   Any object or idea referred to by a single word.

Empiricism   Belief that measurable data can lead to understanding problems and issues.

Environmental factors   Field conditions under which questionnaires are administered or studies are conducted.

Epistemic correlates   Parallel phenomena that indicate the existence of a variable; behaviors that are concomitants of the term describing the behaviors.

Equal-appearing intervals   *See* Thurstone scaling.

Equality of draw   Provision in probability sampling that each element has the same chance of being drawn each time elements are included.

Equivalent groups   Persons in two or more samples that are considered similar in a sufficient number of respects.

Ethics   Normative standards of professional groups or organizations, articulations of what is right and wrong; morally binding normative code upon members of a group.

Evaluation research   Investigations that attempt to answer practical and applied questions; any investigation geared to test the efficacy of a strategy or intervention in relation to some event, such as delinquency or criminality.

Experiment   Study attempting to approximate laboratory conditions for identifying causal relations between variables.

Experimental designs   A method of experimentation with the objective of implicitly or explicitly including the control of variables; researchers experiment by observing the effects of one or more variables on others under controlled conditions.

Experimental group   Persons receiving experimental stimulus during an experiment.

Experimental mortality   The loss of subjects in an experiment over time.

Experimental research, experimental social research   Any investigation where variables are controlled or manipulated by researchers, in order to determine cause–effect relationships between variables; any study conducted where hypotheses are tested; generally refers to controls exerted over different variables to determine their effects on other variables; characterized by high degree of control over extraneous variables.

Experimental stimulus   *See* Experimental variable.

Experimental variables   Factors manipulated during an experiment; stimulus given to an experimental group; also known as treatment variable.

Explanations   Rationales for why an event occurs; theorizing about the nature of phenomena and their occurrence.

Exploratory design   Characterized by several features, including assumption that investigators have little or no knowledge about the research problem under study; potentially significant factors may be discovered and may be subsequently assessed and described in greater detail with a more sophisticated type of research design.

Exploratory research   Investigations undertaken when little is known about the phenomena studied; purpose of exploratory research is to discover subject matter that might be studied in greater detail later.

Ex post facto study   Investigation that looks at experimental outcomes and works backward to determine cause of outcomes.

External reliability checks   Any method used to assess the dependability of a measuring instrument through either parallel forms of the same test or test–retest.

External validity   Generalizability of study to other social situations.

Face validity   *See* Content validity.

Face-to-face questionnaire administration   Conducting a questionnaire administration directly with respondents rather than by mail.

Factor analysis   A statistical technique designed to determine the basic components of a measure.

Factorial validity   Statistical means of determining the contents of a measuring instrument that purportedly measures two or more separate variables; application of factor analysis to numerous items; measure is said to possess factorial validity if it "factors" into predictable parts associated with measured variables.

Field notes   Written observations of social interactions and events recorded by observers and researchers.

Fishbowl draw   Method of obtaining a sample by drawing numbered pieces of paper or other items from a fishbowl.

Fixed-response items   Individual instrument questions with limited choices as alternative answers.

Fixed-response questionnaires   Measuring instruments comprised of different scales consisting of items (questions or statements) that have a finite list of alternative responses.

Focus groups   Persons brought together for a specific experimental purpose, such as to evaluate their reaction to witnessing an execution.

Focused interview   Interviews with respondents who have shared some common experience that has, in turn, been carefully scrutinized by investigators to generate hypotheses about the effects of the experience on participants; the interview context focuses on the actual effects of the experience as viewed by the participants.

Follow-up questions   Any query designed to elicit more detailed information after a respondent has answered a certain way to a previous question.

Foot-in-the-door technique   Method of interviewing where the researcher asks respondents for a few minutes of their time, overtly implying the interview will be short; but as the interview progresses, it is more time-consuming; this more lengthy interviewing process is known in advance by the interviewer, and he or she anticipates that a respondent who will give a few minutes for an interview will probably allow for a more extensive interview as it develops.

Frame of reference   The way chosen by a researcher for looking at or approaching a problem for scientific study.

Freedom of Information Act (FOIA)   Legislation passed to permit private citizens access to government documents collected about them.

Frequency   Number of times an observation occurs.

Frequency distribution control matching   Group matching method relying on group characteristics as matching criteria; equating groups according to group properties rather than individual ones.

Generalizability   Degree to which study findings can apply to other social settings or situations.

Graphic presentation   Any visual or pictorial portrayal of data, either through charts, stick figures, bars, pie charts, maps, or other illustrative data.

Graphs   Charts or figures depicting fluctuations of events or occurrences.

Grounded theory   The view that researchers enter research settings without preconceived theories about what they will find; explanations for events are generated by the nature of observations and occurrences; theorizing is modified as new information emerges from observation and experience.

Group distribution matching   *See* Frequency distribution control matching.

Guttman scaling   Method of attitude measurement professing to measuring a single dimension of an attitudinal phenomenon; devised by Louis Guttman.

H_0 The null hypothesis.

H_1 The research hypothesis.

Halo effect   Assigning higher scores or giving great weight to persons who have scored well or performed well on other test conditions; false credit assigned to persons who are believed to be special in relation to some other characteristic they exhibit; observer bias through prejudging those observed and deciding which ones are better than others.

Hands-on research   Actual and direct collection of one's data for the purpose of conducting a scientific investigation; not relying on data collected by others, such as governmental agencies or private sources.

Hawthorne effect   Effect of being observed, where observed persons who know they are being observed will act differently than under conditions when they don't know they are being observed.

Hawthorne experiment   Experiment at the Hawthorne plant of the Western Electric Company in the 1920s, involving bank wiring for telephones; workers were given special attention by observers and behaved differently compared with their behavior when not being observed.

Historical method   Use of case histories and archival data to discover social patterns; *see also* Archival analysis.

History   Factor influencing the internal validity of a study and involving events that occur between time 1 and time 2 that may influence subsequent comparisons on some dependent variable in an experiment.

Human subjects   Any participants in one's research; research subjects; study elements.

Human subjects committee   Any university or organizational body designed to oversee the physical and psychological effects of anticipated research projects by faculty or organization members.

Hypotheses   Statements or assertions derived from theory; statements to be tested by scientific inquiry, capable of being refuted; tests of hypotheses result in support or nonsupport for theory from which they were derived.

Hypothesis sets   Pair of hypotheses, including a research hypothesis and a null hypothesis; conventional presentation of hypotheses in statistical analyses.

Hypothesis testing   Process of determining truthfulness or falsity of any speculative statement, usually derived from a theory; most frequently involves statistical tests.

Independence of draw   In probability sampling plans, provision that the draw or selection of one element will not affect the chances of inclusion of remaining elements.

Independent samples   Samples that are mutually exclusive of one another and are not related through any type of matching.

Independent variable   Quantity that determines values, value fluctuations, or subclass distributions on other quantities or variables.

In-depth interviews   Any questioning of respondents designed to uncover detailed information about their behaviors or characteristics.

Index   Type of composite measure that summarizes several specific observations and represents some more general dimension.

Indicator   An observation that is considered a reflection of the variable studied.

Individual matching   Used for experimentation, method for equating groups by matching persons in groups to be compared according to individual properties.

Inductive logic, induction   Use of specific cases to form generalizations or theories.

Inductive theory   A process whereby a specific event is examined and described, and where generalizations are made to a larger class of similar events; using induction, we generalize by abstracting.

Informant   Someone who is knowledgeable about the social setting studied who will provide inside information about what is going on and why.

Informed consent   Agreement given by research subjects that they are aware of what will occur in an experiment and they are knowledgeable of the facts and potential harm that may accrue.

Institutional review boards   Organizational screening committees that examine research projects and attempt to discover anything that might be harmful to human subjects; quality-control board that oversees ethical procedures used in conducting research.

Instrument   Questionnaire or interview guide containing questions or items intended to measure variables.

Instrumentation   Any effect on the internal validity of a study having to do with the measures used to assess attitudes or any other variable, including the scoring procedures used, differences between evaluators, and certain mechanical factors.

Intensity continuum   Continuum of attitudinal expression, representing extremes of low to high, with moderate points near the center.

Interaction effects   Combined effects of two variables as they impact on a third variable; investigated as a part of the two-way analysis of variance test.

Internal consistency   Amount of correlation between items on a scale intended to measure a variable.

Internal reliability checks   Any method designed to determine the dependability of a measuring instrument through either item discrimination analysis or the split-half procedure.

Internal validity   Soundness of actual study conducted; evaluated according to accuracy of instruments used to measure variables, soundness of theory, adequacy of sample selected, appropriateness of statistics chosen for data analysis; study integrity.

Interpretation   Explanation of an event based on data analysis; the research outcome in which a control variable is discovered to be a mediating factor through which an independent variable has an effect on the dependent variable.

Interrater reliability   Degree of consensus among observers or recorders of information who observe the same social setting, or social and/or individual behaviors.

Interrupted time series design   Multiple measures at different points in time before and after an experiment.

Interval level of measurement   Scale where distance between values is equal; such information can be averaged arithmetically.

Intervening variable   A third variable that may affect the relation between two other variables.

Interventions   Stimuli administered to an experimental group during an experiment intended to bring about a desired result; in evaluation research, a controlled independent variable intended to act on one or more dependent variables to effect changes in predictable ways or produce desired effects.

Interview   A verbal communication with one or more research subjects for the purpose of acquiring information.

Interview guide   A loosely structured set of open-ended questions that interviewers may use as a general guide for conducting interviews with respondents.

Interview schedule   A questionnaire consisting of a predetermined set of questions and fixed-response replies that interviewers can fill in themselves when they conduct interviews.

Item analysis   *See* Item discrimination analysis.

Item discrimination analysis   An internal consistency method for improving instrument reliability; objective is to eliminate items that poorly differentiate between subjects who possess some attitudinal property to varying degrees; eliminating poorly discriminating items creates greater internal consistency.

Item weights   Numerical values assigned alternative responses to items in an attitudinal measure; summated weights enable researchers to determine one's attitudinal position relative to others.

John Henry effect   Phenomenon occurring when persons know they are being observed and compared; they may seek to outperform or produce in order to justify their value to the organization; named after a worker, John Henry, who matched his human strength with that of a machine and outperformed the machine to demonstrate his value; may cause distorted results in an experiment since true assessment of individual behaviors cannot be determined.

Judgmental sampling   Hand-picked samples from designated populations; believed in some cases to be superior to randomness, especially if those selecting the sample are quite familiar with the population; used in community research.

Key informants   Persons who have access to a restricted group or organization; able to provide information to researchers about behaviors of organizational participants or group subjects.

***K*-variable hypotheses**   Any statement containing two or more variables or factors.

Labeling theory   Explanation for deviant and criminal conduct that focuses on social definitions of acts of crime and deviance rather than on the acts themselves; some of the assumptions underlying labeling theory are that (1) no act is inherently criminal, (2) persons become criminals through social definition of their conduct, (3) all persons at one time or another conform to or deviate from the law, (4) "getting caught" begins the labeling process, (5) persons defined as criminals will, in turn, cultivate criminal self-definitions, and (6) they will eventually seek out and associate with others who are similarly defined and develop a criminal subculture.

Levels of measurement   Four levels of measurement identified by S.S. Stevens, including the nominal, ordinal, interval, and ratio levels; each of these levels of measurement are equated with certain permissible arithmetic procedures; statistical tests and measures require satisfaction of a certain measurement level before they may be applied properly.

Lie detector tests   Polygraphs designed to measure one's heart rate and other physical factors to determine whether one's responses to questions are truthful; not reliable for criminal court use. *See also* Polygraph.

Lie factors, lie scales   Questions or items included in questionnaires that measure respondent truthfulness.

Likert scale   Named after Rensis Likert, the method of summated ratings is based on the idea that variable numbers of items with alternative responses may be weighted to yield ordinal-level attitudinal positions; most popular attitudinal scaling device.

Literature review   Examination of existing sources focusing on a particular topic of study; a preliminary examination of materials available as resources to bolster one's ideas about and explanations for events.

Longitudinal research   Investigation conducted over time; designed to examine trends or changes; time interval may be measured in months or years.

Mailed questionnaires   Surveys distributed through the U.S. Post Office to respondents; considered an inexpensive way of obtaining large amounts of data from large numbers of respondents separated from one another geographically; enhances respondent anonymity.

Masking effects   Experimental treatments may have opposite effects on different kinds of participants.

Matching   Method of equating two or more groups according to individual or group properties shared by persons in each group.

Maturation   Biological or psychological changes occurring within research subjects over time that are not attributable to the experimental variable.

Mean   Arithmetic average, obtained by summing scores and dividing by the number of scores.

Measurement   Assignment of numbers to characteristics and the degree to which they are possessed by individuals or groups.

Mechanical factor   Any factor influencing the internal validity of a study that pertains to the measures administered, including misspelled words, missing pages or items, and anything else related to instrument defects.

Meta-analysis   Literally analysis of analysis; statistical analysis of numerous studies of the same phenomena in order to determine general findings.

Method of equal-appearing intervals   *See* Thurstone scaling.

Method of summated ratings   *See* Likert scaling.

Methodology   Study of research methods.

Model   Any logical collection of concepts and statements designed to explain a phenomenon.

Multidimensional scales   Any attitudinal measure containing two or more dimensions of an attitudinal phenomenon; Likert scales and Thurstone scales are multidimensional scales.

Multiple time-series design   Similar to conventional time series design except an additional comparison group is included.

Multistage sampling   Also cluster or areal sampling; successive selections of squares from horizontal and vertical grids of geographical areas; smaller areas representing square miles or city blocks within which reside those who are designated for inclusion.

Mutually exclusive   Occurrence when an observation cannot fall into two different categories; a male cannot be included in both "male" and "female" subclasses of the gender variable.

N   Population size; N is often used to apply to samples of elements and for formula terms; distinction between N and n is made only to illustrate sampling techniques.

n   Sample size; N is commonly used in formulas to represent sample size rather than entire population size.

National Crime Victimization Survey (NCVS)   Victim survey conducted annually by the U.S. Census Bureau; investigates 60,000 households.

National Incident-Based Reporting System   Unit-record reporting system used by the redesigned *Uniform Crime Reports* where each law enforcement agency reports each individual arrest and crime occurrence.

National Youth Survey (NYS)   An ongoing longitudinal study of delinquent behavior and alcohol and drug use among the American youth population; uses a fairly typical sample of youth ranging in age from 11 to 17; self-report questionnaires are administered, where youths disclose whether they have committed any status or criminal offenses and whether they have been apprehended for any of these offenses; utilizes this sample of youth over successive time periods as a panel.

Nominal definition   Dictionary definition of various phenomena, where inherent properties of concepts are described; definition is far-removed from numerical expression; nominal definitions are useful for theory-building; eventually, nominal definitions are operationalized to yield operational definitions.

Nominal level of measurement   Lowest of four measurement levels described by S.S. Stevens; nominal-level measurement consists of describing variable subclasses of attributes; numerical quantities assigned nominal-level measurement differentiate subclasses from one another, without any implication that values serve any other purpose.

Nondirectional hypothesis tests   Any statistical verification of a statement's truthfulness where the direction of difference has not been specified.

Nonparametric procedures, nonparametric statistical tests   Class of statistical tests and measures considered less restrictive compared with parametric procedures; for the most part, these procedures are designed for variables measured according to nominal or ordinal scales; the assumption of a normal distribution is relaxed; smaller samples may be handled easily; these procedures are less powerful compared with parametric procedures.

Nonparticipant observation   Nonparticipant observation is structured observation of others with or without their knowledge, and without actually participating in the behaviors and activities being observed.

Nonprobability samples, nonprobability sampling plans   Elements for sample are selected in a way that will not permit generalizations to larger populations in a probability theory context.

Nonresponse   The proportion of the sample that does not return questionnaires sent to them by researchers or who refuse to answer interviewer questions.

Nonresponse rate   Proportion of persons selected for one's original sample from a designated population but who do not respond to questionnaires, interviews, or to any other type of contact.

Null hypothesis   Any hypothesis that has been created from a research hypothesis; purpose of null hypotheses is to permit indirect tests of research hypotheses; such hypotheses are usually, though not always, statements of no difference.

Nuremberg Code   Set of principles specifying conditions under which human subjects can be used in medical and/or social experimentation.

Obedience research   Questionable investigation of the propensity of research subjects to follow orders from research directors, even though such orders are potentially harmful to experimental subjects.

Objectivity   Detached approach to research from an unbiased perspective; nonjudgmental.

Observation   Method of data collection involving visual inspection of research subjects.

Observational research study   Method of data collection seeking to preserve the natural context within which observed behaviors occur.

One-shot case study   Intensive examination of a single element or group or social setting at a single point in time; no provisions are made for follow-ups or subsequent observation or testing; a study of a group at one point in time only.

One-tailed test   Directional hypothesis test, where direction of difference is expected and predicted; refers to statistical test of significance where only one "tail" or extreme region of the sampling distribution is used as the critical region.

Open-ended items   Questions asked in interviews or on questionnaires that require respondents to respond at length to questions; written replies are requested.

Open-ended questionnaires   Consisting of questions that require short or lengthy written replies by respondents.

Operational definitions   Product of operationalization; numerical indicator of attitudinal phenomenon; being able to point at phenomenon measured while enunciating the term, according to George Lundberg.

Operationalization   Process of converting constructs into concepts; creating numerical expressions of nominal definitions; bringing less tangible phenomena into the empirical world.

Ordinal level of measurement   Scale where scores may be ranked or ordered in relation to one another, but where the distances between scores are unknown.

Oversample   Selecting more elements for a sample than are actually desired, anticipating that some nonresponse will occur; a means of obtaining a desired number of elements taking into account some nonresponse or unusable questionnaires.

Panel, panel study   Designated sample that is studied repeatedly over time, and comparisons are made between "panels" or the responses given by these youths within each time frame.

Parallel cititations   Legal references to the same case in different reporter volumes of published court opinions.

Parallel forms of the same test   Major reliability check is the use of parallel forms of the same test; researchers use parallel forms of the same test by devising two separate measures of the same phenomenon.

Parameter   Characteristic of the population of elements about which we seek information.

Participant observation   Structured observation of social settings of which the observer is a part; this is a popular form of observation, since researchers may find it convenient to describe the settings wherein they work or the groups in which they have membership.

Persons used as their own controls   Method for creating equated groups for experimental purposes; method uses persons over time, through various experimental periods, where different stimuli are introduced; individual reactions of persons are charted over time to determine experimental effects.

Pie charts   Type of graphic presentation, such as crime clocks, shaped like pies to portray proportions of a whole.

Pilot studies   Pretests that are designated as trial runs of questionnaires before audiences similar to those where the final form of the questionnaire is to be administered; pilot studies are small-scale implementations of the actual studies researchers are prepared to conduct; they enable investigators to detect faults associated with their research instruments and obtain ideas about how best to carry out the final project.

Placebo, placebo effect   Tendency of control groups to react to believed treatment in a positive manner; often in biochemical research, introduction of bland substance with no known properties to affect human behavior induces changes in behavior anyway, since research subjects believe substance is mind-altering or affects their behavior in some way; placebo is a "sugar-coated" pill designed to trigger a placebo effect.

Plagiarism   Using someone else's work as your own; taking credit for work done by another.

Point estimate, point estimation   A designated value believed to be the true population value of whatever characteristic we are measuring; statistical procedure of predicting in advance some value that is believed to be the true population value on some measured characteristic.

Point estimation hypothesis   Statement specifying that the population characteristic is a specific value.

Policy analysis   Study of the causes and consequences of governmental mandates and behaviors.

Polygraph tests   Designed to measure physical responses while answering questions; calculated to discriminate between truthful and untruthful responses to questions; not reliable for criminal court use.

Population   Aggregate of elements about which we seek information; the target number of elements from which we will obtain our sample.

Postcard questionnaires   Abbreviated versions of survey instruments confined to a single postcard, which is mailed to designated respondents.

Posttest   A reexamination of study subjects once an experimental treatment has been administered.

Potentates   Very powerful people or those protected by law from researchers, such as children.

Pragmatic validity   Either concurrent or predictive validity; a form of validity based on the successfulness of any particular attitudinal measure as a predictor.

Prediction   Attempts by researchers to forecast social and psychological events with a knowledge of certain variables; specifying patterns of behavior in advance of their occurrence on the basis of criteria.

Predictive validity   Also known as criterion validity; is based on the measured association between what an instrument predicts behavior will be and the subsequent behavior exhibited by an individual or group.

Pretest   Testing study subjects prior to the introduction of an experimental variable; *see also* Pilot study.

Pretest effects, pretest bias   Possible familiarity of experimental subjects with questionnaire administered to them; possible familiarity with research goals and interests of investigators may elicit untrue responses from subjects; may result from repeated testing.

Probability   Likelihood that an event will occur.

Probability sample   Random sample selected in such a way so that each element has an equal and an independent chance of being included.

Probability sampling, probability sampling plans   Drawing a sample in such a way that each element has an equal and independent chance of being included.

Probability theory   Explanatory context in which scientific observations are made when statistical tests are applied; some uncertainty always exists, which is attributable to studying only samples from populations rather than total populations of elements; over time, our certainty about events and their explanations increases through replication research and additional study.

Probes, probing   Follow-up questions in an interview or questionnaire.

Problem formulation   Selection, identification, and specification of the research topic to be investigated.

Proportion   Quantity obtained by dividing a part of the sum by the sum.

Proportionate stratified random sampling   Method of including elements where one or more variables are controlled, such that the sample element characteristics are distributed proportionately similar to the way those same characteristics are distributed in the population.

Propositions   Statements about the real world that lack the high degree of certainty associated with assumptions; examples of propositions are, "Burnout among probation officers may be mitigated or lessened through job enlargement and giving officers greater input in organizational decision making," or "Two-officer patrol units are less susceptible to misconduct and corruption than one-officer patrol units."

Pure research   Investigations undertaken simply for the sake of knowing.

Purposive sampling   *See* Judgmental samples.

Q-sort   Attitudinal scaling procedure in which respondents sort questions on cards into predetermined categories; a way of determining item intensity.

Qualitative research   Investigations that do not rely heavily on statistical analyses; participant observation, historical method, and content analysis are examples of qualitative research.

Quantitative analysis   Numerical representation and interpretation of observations for the purpose of discovering underlying meanings and patterns of relationships.

Quantitative research   Investigations that involve heavy use of statistical procedures; statistical manipulations of data considered primary in an effort to discover patterns of behavior.

Quasi-experiments   Experiments where random assignment has not been used to establish equivalent experimental and control groups; such experiments utilize matching, frequency distribution control matching, or persons used as their own control in before–after experiments.

Questionnaire length   Actual number of pages or numbers of items contained on a survey instrument.

Questionnaires   Self-administered inventories that seek descriptive information about people and their opinions about things.

Quota sampling   Persons selected to ensure inclusion of elements with particular characteristics.

Rand Seven-Factor Index   Measure of an offender's potential for dangerousness and recidivism.

Random assignment   Method for equating two or more groups by using randomness to assign persons from a larger group to two or more smaller groups; the basis for true experiments or true experimental designs.

Random digit dialing   Programmed telephonic contact with potential respondents who are randomly called by computer; no attempt is made to control who is called; results are considered random and representative of those who have telephones.

Random numbers   Digits generated by computer that occur in no particular order and with no consistent frequency; digits are not dependent upon the occurrence of other digits.

Random sample   Persons drawn in accordance with probability sampling principles; sample drawn in such a way so that each element has an equal and an independent chance of being included.

Randomness   The primary control in probability sampling plans; elements are selected so that each has an equal and independent chance of being included; no attempt is made to deliberately include or exclude certain elements.

Ratio level of measurement   Highest scale of measurement where proportional statements can be made about numerical information; 1 is to 2 as 4 is to 8; an absolute zero point exists for ratio scales.

Ratios   Proportions of elements in relation to a common standard, such as 4 to 1 or 2 to 1.

Raw scores   Uncoded actual scores persons receive on a questionnaire or scale.

Reactive effect   Phenomenon that occurs when persons are exposed to a prettest and learn enough to influence their behaviors when subsequent posttests are conducted; individual or group reactions to experimental variables may become less sensitive because of greater familiarity with the testing procedure or protocol.

Reactivity   Atypical or artificial behavior produced by respondent's awareness of being studied.

Regression   Statistical technique designed to predict scores on a dependent variable from a knowledge of scores on one or more independent variables.

Related samples   Two or more different samples that share several common characteristics; cannot be considered independent samples; persons may act as their own controls in before–after experiments.

Relationship   *See* Association.

Reliability   Property of a measuring instrument that enables researchers to say that whatever is being measured is being measured consistently; the reliability of a measuring instrument is the ability of that instrument to measure consistently the phenomenon it is designed to measure.

Replication, replication research   Conducting a subsequent study based on the general guidelines of a previous study; an attempt to obtain the same results from a different sample by conducting fresh research at a later point in time; repetition of experiments or studies that utilize the same methodology.

Representativeness   The degree to which sample characteristics are similar to the population characteristics and the population from which the sample was drawn.

Reproducible scales   According to Louis Guttman, Guttman scales that may disclose individual item responses based on one's total test score, with at least 80 percent accuracy.

Research   Investigations, studies, or any systematic investigative efforts designed to increase our knowledge about events and their occurrence.

Research design   Detailed plans that specify how data should be collected and analyzed.

Research hypotheses   Testable tentative statements directly deduced from theory.

Research problem   Any event in need of an explanation; may be criminal activity, recidivism, correctional officer stress and burnout, employee turnover, or any other phenomenon in need of an answer.

Research process   All activities that pertain to problem formulation and definition; includes developing a theoretical explanation for why problems exist; collecting information that will verify or refute the explanation of problems; analyzing, presenting, and interpreting this information; and drawing tentative conclusions that will either support or refute the theoretical explanation provided.

Research questions   Any queries for which no immediate answer is apparent; investigations are guided by queries seeking solutions to research problems.

Respondents   Persons who provide data for analysis by answering questions in an interview or completing a questionnaire.

Response rate   The number of persons participating in a survey divided by the original number selected for the sample.

Response set   Answering all questionnaire items by selecting the first answer, regardless of whether it is descriptive or not descriptive of one's attitudes or characteristics; usually indicative of respondent carelessness in taking the study seriously or answering questions truthfully.

Rows and columns   Number of subclasses on two variables in a cross-tabulated table, represented by $r \times c$.

Salient Factor Score (SFS 81)   Parole prediction scheme used to forecast parole success and potential for recidivism.

Sample   Smaller proportion of elements taken from a larger population of them.

Sample representativeness   *See* Representativeness.

Sample size   Number of persons in one's sample.

Sampling   Method for obtaining a smaller proportion of elements from a larger population.

Sampling error   The amount of difference between the characteristics of a sample and the population from which it was drawn; some error is always present when the full population is not available; sampling error usually declines as sample size increases.

Sampling fraction   Designated proportion of sample elements considered ideal in relation to a population; sample size is usually considered one-tenth of a population as a conventional sampling fraction; not an absolute standard, however.

Sampling frame   The actual list of persons in the population from which the sample is derived.

Sampling with replacement   Method of obtaining elements from a population and replacing them in the population before drawing other elements; possibility exists that some elements may be drawn two or more times under such a sampling condition; assumption underlying all tests of statistical inference.

Sampling without replacement   Method of obtaining elements from a population where elements once drawn cannot be drawn again.

Saturation sampling   Selection method of elements from populations, regardless of the sampling method used, where over 90 percent of the population elements are obtained.

Scale   Index designed to measure a variable and how much each person possesses it; a collection of questions or items focused on a single variable, such as police professionalism.

Scalogram analysis   *See* Guttman scaling.

Science, scientific inquiry   Method of acquiring information about events by relying on empirical observations; pursuing questions about events by adhering to objectivity, ethical neutrality, and limitations to empirical phenomena.

Secondary source analysis   Any type of analysis of secondary sources or any information originally collected for purposes other than their present scientific one.

Seed money   Small sums allocated for pilot studies or small-scale research projects in order to determine the feasibility of undertaking a more elaborate research enterprise later.

Selection bias   Including elements in a sample who have already been screened according to other criteria; affects generalizability and representativeness.

Selection–maturation interaction   Occurs when members of experimental and control groups mingle together and compare their experiences, thus distorting the final experimental results.

Self-administered questionnaire   Survey instrument requiring respondents to write their responses or to indicate answers that best fit them; respondents complete their own questionnaires.

Self-reports   A data collection method relying on disclosures by respondents of personal behaviors including deviant or criminal conduct.

Sellin–Wolfgang Crime Severity Index   Procedure for assigning weights to crime seriousness.

Semantic differential   Consists of a series of bipolar characteristics, such as hot–cold, popular–unpopular, witty–dull, cold–warm, sociable–unsociable; the semantic differential is a useful measure of psychological, social, and physical objects to various respondents.

Serendipity   Unusual, surprising, and unanticipated findings or outcomes.

Set response   Respondent tendency to mark first responses to individual items in a questionnaire with fixed responses; indicative of carelessness or failure to read items; set responses may be detected by a high rate of inconsistency of responses that purportedly measure the same thing.

SFS 81   *See* Salient Factor Score (SFS 81).

Shield laws   Statutes that protect researchers from being compelled to reveal their sources of information in court.

Simple random samples   Most basic probability sampling plans, where elements are selected from a larger population without controlling for inclusion of specific characteristics; elements have an equal and an independent chance of being included.

Simulation   Game that attempts to emulate key features of reality.

Single samples   One-sample scenario where researchers obtain no more than one sample from the population for subsequent study; also known as one-shot studies, since only one sample is investigated; one set of elements which is a proportion of a larger set of a population of elements and are studied in their entirety without being subdivided into smaller sets of elements.

Single-variable hypotheses   Any statement containing one variable only, such as "The mean of group 1 is 50."

Snowball sampling   Type of relational analysis using a sampling technique where those interviewed disclose friendship relations with others who are subsequently interviewed; process continues until social patterns can be identified or charted.

Social desirability   Propensity of respondents to place themselves in a favorable light when being interviewed or questioned.

Social responsibility   Moral integrity and obligation to uphold code of conduct of one's organization or profession.

Somers' *d*   Measure of association between two variables, where each has been measured according to an ordinal scale; has *PRE* interpretation.

Spearman's rho, r_s   Measure of association for two variables measured according to the interval level of measurement; conventionally applied to two ordinal-level variable situations; has *PRE* interpretation.

Split-half technique, split-half reliability method   Designed to correlate one half of the test items with the other half of them; an internal reliability test.

Sponsored research   Any investigation underwritten by an external agency; funded investigations where the funding source is other than the researcher undertaking the research.

SPSS   Statistical Package for the Social Sciences; a multipurpose software program designed for sophisticated analyses of data; includes numerous tests and procedures for significance and correlation.

Spuriousness   An apparent relation between two variables that is subsequently explained by the presence of a third, unknown variable; false relationship that can be explained away by other variables.

Statistical analysis   Application of significance tests to collected data; determining the significance of one's findings through quantitative methods.

Statistical hypothesis   Symbolic expression of research and null hypotheses.

Statistical regression   Problem arising and influencing a study's internal validity when the lowest or highest performers are selected for either the experimental or control group; the lowest performers are bound to show improvement over time simply due to repeated testing and the learning that occurs.

Statistical significance   Probability associated with conducting a test of the relation between two variables or difference between two or more groups on some measured characteristic; arises from magnitude of observed values, which are in part a function of sample size and standard error.

Statistics   Field of study; refers to numerical evidence that has been compiled, such as the "Vital Statistics" compiled by the U.S. Bureau of the Census; a collection of tests and techniques used to describe and make decisions and inferences about collected research data; characteristics of a sample of elements; a procedure or measure for analyzing sample characteristics and making a decision about them.

Stimulus   Either a treatment variable or a causal variable; introduced during an experiment to bring about or cause a predictable or desired result on some dependent variable.

Stratification   Grouping of persons into homogenous aggregates before sampling from the population.

Stratified random sampling plans   Any means of drawing elements where control is exercised over the inclusion of persons with specific characteristics, such as year in school, type of prior offense, and where elements are selected in a way that each element has an equal and an independent chance of being included.

Stratified sample   Elements distributed either proportionately or disproportionately according to one or more traits or characteristics.

Stratifying   *See* Stratification.

Structured interviews   Consist of a predetermined list of fixed-response questions or items.

Subclass   Any subdivision of a variable.

Subjects   Persons included in an experiment or study.

Subpopulations   Smaller numbers of elements within a larger population.

Subsamples   Different samples of elements that may be created from a single, larger sample.

Substantive implications   Research results that have practical applications.

Survey design   Specifications of procedures for gathering information about a large number of people by collecting information from a smaller proportion of them.

Survey research   Method of gathering information about a large number of people by interviewing a few of them.

Systematic sampling   Technique for including elements where elements are selected according to their location in an ordered list; researchers select every nth person from a list; considered a random sampling plan by some investigators.

Table of random numbers   Method of drawing elements from numbers that have been randomly generated by computer; digits in table occur in no particular order, and no digit occurs any more frequently than any other digit; the systematic derivation of a sample from a table of random numbers is, by definition, a random sample.

Tabular presentation   Any portrayal of information in a cross-tabulated fashion, with one or more rows and one or more columns.

Target population   Aggregate of persons about which one seeks information.

Telephone interview   Any questioning of respondents by telephone; dialing respondents and asking them questions by telephone instead of face-to-face.

Testing effect   Pretest effect or bias introduced and resulting from having been pretested.

Test–retest   External reliability check based on comparison of attitudinal measure's results over two separate time periods; if persons receive same or similar scores on the same attitudinal measure over two different time periods, without the intervention of an experimental stimulus of any kind, then the measure possesses reliability on the basis of test–retest.

Tests of significance   A broad class of tests designed to reveal statistical differences between observed statistics and predicted parameters; any procedure yielding a probability that significance exists or does not exist between two or more groups according to some measured characteristic.

Tests of significance of difference   Any procedure designed to determine the statistical differentiation between two or more samples according to some measured characteristic.

Theoretical implications   Research results where there may or may not be immediate application; contribution is largely designed to explain a theory and how it enhances our understanding of events.

Theory   Integrated body of propositions, assumptions, and definitions that are related in ways that explain and predict relationships between two or more variables.

Thurstone scaling   Method of attitudinal scaling, devised by L.L. Thurstone, based on judges' ratings and averages of item weights; items are sorted into 7, 9, or 11 categories by judges; choices of responses by respondents are weighted in advance; average of items selected purportedly discloses respondent position on attitudinal intensity continuum.

Time 1, time 2   Designated points during an experiment when measures are taken for different variables from the experimental and control groups; usually scores from measures administered to two or more groups during the experiment are compared to see whether or not changes occur on some dependent variable.

Time-series design   Measurement of a single variable at successive points in time.

Treatment variable   Known as an experimental variable; variable introduced to elicit predictable effects in experiments.

Trend study, trend information   Type of longitudinal research where a given characteristic of some population is monitored over time.

Triangulation   Use of two or more data-gathering strategies when investigating the same sample of elements or a common research problem; intent of triangulation is to verify accuracy of reported information disclosed by different data collection techniques.

True experiment   Procedure in which randomization, pretests and posttests, and experimental and control groups are used.

Tuskegee Syphilis Study   Notorious medical experiment conducted by U.S. Public Health Service at Tuskegee Institute between 1932–1970 and involving 1,000 black research volunteers who were diagnosed with syphilis; some volunteers received treatment while others did not receive treatment in order to study the progressiveness of syphilis; considered unethical research and widely condemned for insensitivity to human subjects.

Two- and k-sample situations   Research scenarios where investigators study two or more samples simultaneously; samples may be related or independent.

2×2 tables   Most common tabular form, where table is constructed with two rows and two columns.

Two-tailed tests   Hypothesis tests involving two extreme areas of a sampling distribution of some statistic; a nondirectional hypothesis test, where simple differences between values are tested without any expectation of directional differences.

Two-variable hypotheses   Any statements containing two factors or variables.

Typology   Classification of observations in terms of their attributes on two or more variables.

Unethical conduct   Any behavioral departure from expected and articulated codes of a profession or association that would raise moral issues.

Unidimensional scale   In the case of attitude statements, this means that a person with a more favorable attitude score than another person must also be just as favorable or more favorable in his response to every statement in the set than the other person; when responses to a set of attitude statements meet this requirement, the set of statements is said to constitute a unidimensional scale.

Unidimensionality   Property of an attitudinal measuring instrument that means the instrument measures only one dimension of the phenomenon; *see also* Guttman scaling.

Uniform Crime Reports (UCR)   Annual FBI publication of official statistics of reported crime by law enforcement agencies.

Universe of items   Abstract and theoretical population of items from which attitudinal items are selected and used for test purposes by researchers; an infinite population of items.

Unstructured interviews   Loosely constructed interview guides with open-ended questions; most flexible interview tool, where researchers may probe extensively in different directions, depending on responses given from subjects interviewed.

Validity   The property of a measuring instrument that enables researchers to say that they are measuring whatever it is they say they are measuring.

Values   Standards of acceptability we acquire from our peers or from society in general; cause us to prioritize, or to allocate greater importance to some things and less importance to others.

Variable subclasses   Any number of subdivisions on a variable.

Variables   Any phenomena, quantities, factors, or attributes that can assume more than one value or subclass.

Variation   Amount of dispersion among scores; how much scores differ from one another.

Verification   Confirmation of the accuracy of one's findings.

Weighting   Multiplying individual sample means by their respective sample sizes, if sample sizes differ; also refers to assigning different values to item responses that can be gradated from high to low (Strongly Agree = 1, Agree = 2, Strongly Disagree = 6).

Working hypotheses   Testable statements derived from theory that are subsequently operationalized.

List of References

Abbott, Jack Henry. (1981). *In the Belly of the Beast.* New York: Random House.

Academy of Criminal Justice Sciences. (2004). *Code of Ethics.* Greenbelt, MD: Author.

Accordino, Michael P., and Bernard Guerney, Jr. (1998). "An Evaluation of the Relationship Enhancement Program with Prisoners and Their Wives." *International Journal of Offender Therapy and Comparative Criminology* **42:**5–15.

American Correctional Association. (1993). *The State of Corrections.* Laurel, MD: Author.

Amnesty International. (1994). *Conditions for Death Row Prisoners in H-Unit Oklahoma State Penitentiary.* New York: Amnesty International.

Anderson, Patrick R., and L. Thomas Winfree, Jr. (1987). *Expert Witnesses: Criminologists in the Courtroom.* Albany: State University of New York Press.

Archer, John. (2002). "Sex Differences in Physically Aggressive Acts between Heterosexual Partners: A Meta-Analysis Review." *Aggression and Violent Behavior: A Review Journal* **7:**313–351.

Austin, Thomas L., and Don Hummer. (1999). "What Do College Students Think of Policewomen? An Attitudinal Assessment of Future Law Enforcement Personnel." *Women and Criminal Justice* **10:**1–24.

Ayres, Ian, and John J. Donahue. (2002). "Shooting Down the More Guns, Less Crime Hypothesis." Working Paper. Cambridge, MA: National Bureau of Economic Research.

Backstrom, Charles H., and Gerald D. Hursh. (1963). *Survey Research.* Evanston, IL: Northwestern University Press.

Bahn, Charles, and James R. Davis. (1991). "Social Psychological Effects of the Status of Probationers." *Federal Probation* **55:**17–25.

Bailey, Kenneth D. (1987). *Methods of Social Research (3e).* New York: Macmillan.

Barker, Tom, and David Carter. (1990). " 'Fluffing Up the Evidence and Covering Your Ass:' Some Conceptual Notes on Police Lying." *Deviant Behavior* **11:**61–73.

Baron, Stephen W. (2004). "General Strain, Street Youth, and Crime: A Test of Agnew's Revised Theory." *Criminology* **42:**457–484.

Bazemore, Gordon, Jeanne B. Stinchcomb, and Leslie A. Leip. (2004). "Scared Smart or Bored Straight? Testing Deterrence Logic in an Evaluation of Police-Led Truancy Intervention." *Justice Quarterly* **21:**269–299.

Beck, Robert J. (1997). "Communications in a Teen Court: Implications for Probation." *Federal Probation* **61:**40–48.

Bednar, Susan G. (2003). "Substance Abuse and Woman Abuse—A Proposal for Integrated Treatment." *Federal Probation* **67:**52–57.

Berkowitz, Marvin. (1975). *Evaluation of Merchant Security Program.* New York: New York Police Department.

Bersani, Carl, Huey-Tsyh Chen, and Robert Denton. (1988). "Spouse Abusers and Court Mandated Treatment." *Journal of Crime and Justice* **11:**43–60.

Binder, Charles J. (2003). "Organizational Change and Staff Empowerment." *Corrections Today* **65**:67–69.

Black, James A., and Dean J. Champion. (1976). *Methods and Issues of Social Research.* New York: Wiley.

Black, Shannon. (2001). "Correctional Employee Stress and Strain." *Corrections Today* **63**:83–118.

Blalock, Hubert M., Jr. (1972). *Social Statistics.* New York: McGraw-Hill.

Boatwright-Horowitz, Su L., Kristen Olick, and Robert Amaral. (2004). "Calling 911 During Episodes of Domestic Abuse: What Justifies a Call for Help?" *Journal of Criminal Justice* **32**:89–92.

Bonanno, George A., et al. (2003). "Predicting the Willingness to Disclose Childhood Sexual Abuse from Measures of Repressive Coping and Dissociative Techniques." *Child Maltreatment* **8**:302–318.

Bouffard, Leana Allen. (2003). "Examining the Relationship between Military Service and Criminal Behavior During the Vietnam Era." *Criminology* **41**:491–510.

Bowery, Margaret. (1997). *Private Prisons in New South Wales.* Sydney, AUS: New South Wales Department of Corrective Services.

Brame, Robert, Shawn D. Bushway, and Raymond Paternoster. (2003). "Examining the Prevalence of Criminal Desistance." *Criminology* **41**:423–448.

Brandt, A.M. (1978). "Racism, Research, and the Tuskegee Syphilis Study." *Hastings Center Report* **7**:15–21.

Brannigan, Augustine, J.C. Levy, and James C. Wilkins. (1985). *The Preparation of Witnesses and Pretrial Construction of Testimony.* Calgary, ON. Canada: Research Unit for Socio-Legal Studies.

Brooks, Alexander D. (1996). "Megan's Law: Constitutionality and Policy." *Criminal Justice Ethics* **15**:56–66.

Brown, Alison P. (2003). "From Individual to Social Defences in Psychological Criminology." *Theoretical Criminology* **7**:421–437.

Burlington, Bill. (1991). "Involuntary Treatment: When Can Mentally Ill Inmates Be Medicated Against Their Will?" *Federal Prisons Journal* **2**:25–29.

Campbell, D., and J. Stanley (1963). *Experimental and Quasi-Experimental Designs for Research.* Chicago: Rand-McNally.

Campbell, Robin, and Robert Victor Wolf. (2002). "Problem Solving Probation: An Overview of Four Community-Based Experiments." *APPA Perspectives* **26**:26–34.

Carey, Shannon M., and Michael W. Finnegan. (2004). "A Detailed Cost Analysis in a Mature Drug Court Setting." *Journal of Contemporary Criminal Justice* **20**:315–338.

Carvalho, Irene, and Dan A. Lewis. (2003). "Beyond Community: Reactions to Crime and Disorder among Inner-City Residents." *Criminology* **41**:779–812.

Cashel, Mary Louise. (2003). "Validity of Self-Reports of Delinquency and Socio-Emotional Functioning among Youth on Probation." *Journal of Offender Rehabilitation* **37**:11–23.

Chamlin, Mitchell B., and Steven G. Brandl. (1996). "A Quantitative Analysis of Vagrancy Arrests in Milwaukee, 1930–1972." *Journal of Crime and Justice* **19**:23–40.

Champion, Dean J. (1981). *Basic Statistics for Social Research (2e).* New York: Macmillan.

Champion, Dean J. (1988). "Private Counsels and Public Defenders: A Look at Weak Cases, Prior Records, and Leniency in Plea Bargaining." *Journal of Criminal Justice* **17**:253–263.

Champion, Dean J. (1996). *Probation, Parole, and Community Corrections (2e).* Upper Saddle River, NJ: Prentice-Hall.

Champion, Dean J. (2000). *Research Methods for Criminal Justice and Criminology (2e).* Upper Saddle River, NJ: Prentice-Hall.

Charles, Michael T. (1989). "Research Note: Juveniles on Electronic Monitoring." *Journal of Contemporary Criminal Justice* **5**:165–172.

Chiricos, Ted, Kelly Welch, and Marc Gertz. (2004). "Racial Typification of Crime and Support for Punitive Measures." *Criminology* **42**:359–389.

Clemmer, D.C. (1940). *The Prison Community.* New York: Holt, Rinehart, and Winston.

Cohen, Morris R., and Ernest Nagel. (1934). *An Introduction to Logic and the Scientific Method.* New York: Harcourt, Brace.

Cole, Danny. (2003). "The Effect of a Curfew Law on Juvenile Crime in Washington, DC." *American Journal of Criminal Justice* **27:**217–232.

Coleman, James S. (1959). "Relational Analysis: The Study of Social Organizations with Survey Methods." *Human Organization* **17:**28–36.

Coleman, James S., E. Katz, and H.M. Menzel. (1957). "Diffusion of Innovation among Physicians." *Sociometry* **20:**253–270.

Collins, Mark F. (1988). "Some Cautionary Notes on the Use of the Sellin–Wolfgang Index of Crime Seriousness." *Journal of Quantitative Criminology* **4:**61–70.

Cook, T.D., and D.T. Campbell. (1979). *Quasi-Experimentation: Design and Analysis Issues for Field Settings.* Boston: Houghton Mifflin.

Cook, William J., Jr. (1990). *The Effect of Terrorism on Executives' Willingness to Travel Internationally.* Ann Arbor, MI: University Microfilms International.

Coston, Charisse T.M., and Lee E. Ross. (1996). "Criminal Victimization of Prostitutes: Empirical Support for the Lifestyle/Exposure Model." *Journal of Crime and Justice* **19:**53–70.

Cowell, Alexander J., Nahama Broner, and Randolph Dupont. (2004). "The Cost-Effectiveness of Criminal Justice Diversion Programs for People with Serious Mental Illness Co-Occurring with Substance Abuse." *Journal of Contemporary Criminal Justice* **20:**292–315.

Crank, John P., et al. (1986). "Cynicism among Police Chiefs." *Justice Quarterly* **3:**343–352.

Cross, Theodore P., et al. (2003). "Prosecution of Child Abuse: A Meta-Analysis of Rates of Criminal Justice Decisions." *Trauma, Violence, and Abuse: A Review Journal* **4:**323–340.

Crouch, Ben M., and James W. Marquart. (1990). "Resolving the Paradox of Reform: Litigation, Prisoner Violence, and Perception of Risk." *Justice Quarterly* **7:**104–123.

Curry, G. David. (2000). "Self-Reported Gang Involvement and Officially Recorded Delinquency." *Criminology* **38:**1253–1274.

Decker, Scott H., and Barbara Salert. (1987). "Selective Incapacitation: A Note on Its Impact on Minorities." *Journal of Criminal Justice* **15:**287–299.

del Carmen, Alejandro, and Elmer O. Polk. (2001). "Faculty Employment in Criminology and Criminal Justice: Trends and Patterns." *Journal of Criminal Justice Education* **12:**1–17.

Denzin, Norman K. (1989). *The Research Act: A Theoretical Introduction to Sociological Methodologies (3e).* Upper Saddle River, NJ: Prentice-Hall.

Dicks, Shirley. (1991). *Victims of Crime and Punishment: Interviews with Victims, Convicts, Their Families, and Support Groups.* Jefferson, NC: McFarland & Company.

Dingwall, R., and P. Lewis (eds.). (1983). *The Sociology of the Professions.* New York: St. Martin's Press.

DiRenzo, Gordon J. (ed.). (1966). *Concepts, Theory, and Explanation in the Behavioral Sciences.* New York: Random House.

Dixon, David. (1997). "Ethics, Law, and Criminological Research." *Australian and New Zealand Journal of Criminology* **30:**211–216.

Doerner, William G., et al. (1976). "An Analysis of Victim Compensation Programs as a Time-Series Experiment." *Victimology* **1:**295–313.

Dow, Steven B. (2004). "Redrawing the Line: A Commentary on *Overton v. Bazzetta.*" *Corrections Compendium* **29:**1–5.

Dowden, Craig, and D.A. Andrews. (2003). "Does Family Intervention Work for Delinquents? Results of a Meta-Analysis." *Canadian Journal of Criminology and Criminal Justice* **45:**327–342.

Dowden, Craig, and S.L. Brown. (2002). "The Role of Substance Abuse Factors in Predicting Recidivism: A Meta-Analysis." *Psychology, Crime, and Law* **8:**243–264.

Dowden, Craig, and Claude Teller. (2004). "Predicting Work-Related Stress in Correctional Officers: A Meta-Analysis." *Journal of Criminal Justice* **32:**31–47.

Dozois, David J.A., and Brad R.C. Kelln. (1999). "Factor Analysis of the MCMI-III on an Offender Population." *Journal of Offender Rehabilitation* **29:**77–87.

Dreznick, Michael T. (2003). "Heterosexual Competence of Rapists and Child Molestors: A Meta-Analysis." *Journal of Sex Research* **40:**170–178.

Eck, John E. (2002). "Learning from Experience in Problem-Oriented Policing and Situational Prevention: The Positive Functions of Weak Evaluations and the Negative Functions of Strong Ones." In *Evaluation for Crime Prevention,* Nick Tilley (ed.). Monsey, NY: Criminal Justice Press.

Edwards, A.L. (1957). *The Social Desirability Variable in Personality Assessment.* New York: Dryden.

Elliott, Delbert S., Franklyn W. Dunford, and David Huizinga. (1987). "The Identification and Prediction of Career Offenders Utilizing Self-Reported and Official Data." In *Prediction of Criminal Behavior,* John D. Burchard and Sara Burchard (eds.). Newbury Park, CA: Sage.

Elliston, Frederick A., and Jane van Schaick. (1984). *Legal Ethics: An Annotated Bibliography and Resource Guide.* Littleton, CO: Fred B. Rothman.

Empey, Lamar T., and Maynard Erickson. (1972). *The Provo Experiment: Evaluation of Community Control of Delinquency.* Lexington, MA: Lexington Press.

Engel, Robin Shepard, and Robert E. Worden. (2003). "Police Officers' Attitudes, Behavior, and Supervisory Influences: An Analysis of Problem Solving." *Criminology* **41:**131–166.

Esbensen, Finn-Aage. (1991). "Ethical Considerations in Criminal Justice Research." *American Journal of Police* **10:**87–104.

Esbensen, Finn-Aage. (1999). "Gang Resistance Education and Training (GREAT): Results from the National Evaluation." *Journal of Research in Crime and Delinquency* **36:**194–225.

Esbensen, Finn-Aage, and L. Thomas Winfree. (1998). "Race and Gender Differences between Gang and Nongang Youths: Results from a Multisite Survey." *Justice Quarterly* **15:**505–526.

"Failure to Report Ethical Approval in Child Health Research: Review of Published Papers." (2001). *British Medical Journal* **323:**318–329.

Farkas, Mary Ann. (1997). "The Normative Code among Correctional Officers: An Exploration of Components and Functions." *Journal of Crime and Justice* **20:**25–40.

Farrington, David P. (2003). "Methodological Quality Standards for Evaluation Research." *The Annals of the American Academy of Political and Social Science* **587:**49–68.

Faulkner, Paula L., and William R. Faulkner. (1997). "Effects of Organizational Change on Inmate Status and the Inmate Code of Conduct." *Journal of Crime and Justice* **20:**25–38.

Faulkner, Robert R., et al. (2003). "Crime By Committee: Conspirators and Company Men in the Illegal Electric Industrial Cartel, 1954–1959." *Criminology* **41:**511–554.

Feierman, Jay R. (ed.). (1990). *Pedophilia: Biosocial Dimensions.* New York: Springer-Verlag.

Feminist Press. (2002). *Wall Tappings: An International Anthology of Women's Prison Writings 200 to the Present.* New York: Feminist Press at the City University of New York.

Finkelhor, David, and Melissa Wells. (2003). "Improving Data Systems about Juvenile Victimization in the United States." *Child Abuse and Neglect: The International Journal* **27:**77–102.

Fishman, Joseph F. (1934). *Sex in Prison.* New York: National Liberty Press.

Fitzgerald, Jack D., and Steven M. Cox. (1987). *Research Methods in Criminal Justice.* Chicago: Nelson-Hall.

Fox, James W., Kevin W. Minor, and William L. Pelkey. (1995). "The Relationship between Law-Related Education Diversion and Juvenile Offenders' Social and Self-Perceptions." *American Journal of Criminal Justice* **19:**61–77.

Frank, Mark G., et al. (1995). "Individual Perspectives on Police Ethics." *Ethics and Policing* **125:**1–27.

Frazier, Charles E., and Donna M. Bishop. (1990). "Obstacles to Reform in Juvenile Corrections: A Case Study." *Journal of Contemporary Criminal Justice* **6:**157–166.

Garcia, Luis, Dale K. Nesbary, and Joanne Gu. (2004). "Perceptual Variations of Stressors among Police Officers During an Era of Decreasing Crime." *Journal of Contemporary Criminal Justice* **20:**33–50.

Garofalo, James. (1977). *Local Victim Surveys: A Review of the Issues.* Washington, DC: U.S. National Criminal Justice Information and Statistics Service.

Gaskins, Donald "Pee-Wee," and Wilton Earle. (1992). *Final Truth: The Autobiography of Mass Murderer/Serial Killer.* Atlanta, GA: ADEPT.

Geiger, Brenda, and Michael Fischer. (2003). "Female Repeat Offenders Negotiating Identify." *International Journal of Offender Therapy and Comparative Criminology* **47:**496–515.

Gerstenfeld, Phyllis B., Diana R. Grant, and Chau Pu Chiang. (2003). "Hate Online: A Content Analysis of Extremist Internet Sites." *Analysis of Social Issues and Public Policy* **3:**29–44.

Giordano, Peggy C., Stephen A. Cernkovich, and Donna D. Holland. (2003). "Changes in Friendship Relations Over the Life Course: Implications for Desistance from Crime." *Criminology* **41:**293–328.

Glaser, Barney, and Anselm Strauss. (1967). *The Discovery of Grounded Theory: Strategies for Qualitative Research.* Chicago: Aldine.

Goldhammer, Gary E. (1994). *Dead End.* Bunswick, ME: Biddle Publishing Company.

Goode, William J., and Paul K. Hatt. (1952). *Methods in Social Research.* New York: McGraw-Hill.

Gordon, Rachel A., et al. (2004). "Antisocial Behavior and Youth Gang Membership: Selection and Socialization." *Criminology* **42:**55–87.

Gottfredson, Denise C., Stacy S. Najaka, and Brook Kearley. (2003). "Effectiveness of Drug Treatment Courts: Evidence from a Randomized Trial." *Criminology and Public Policy* **2:**171–196.

Grasmick, Harold G., Robert J. Bursik Jr., and John K. Cochran. (1991). "'Render Unto Caesar What Is Caesar's': Religiosity and Taxpayer's Inclinations to Cheat." *Sociological Quarterly* **32:**251–266.

Green, Helen Taylor, Shaun L. Gabbidon, and Myisha Ebersole. (2001). "A Multi-Faceted Analysis of the African American Presence in Juvenile Delinquency Textbooks Published Between 1997 and 2000." *Journal of Crime and Justice* **24:**87–101.

Greenfield, Patricia. (1977). "CIA's Behavior Caper." *APA Monitor,* **1:**1–20.

Greenwood, Peter W., and Allan Abrahamse. (1982). *Selective Incapacitation.* Santa Monica, CA: Rand Corporation.

Grkinich, David. (2001). "The Evolution of Pretrial Services in Los Angeles County." *American Jails* **15:**71–73.

Gura, Philip F., et al. (eds.). (2001). *Buried from the World: Inside the Massachusetts State Prison, 1829–1831.* New York: Praeger.

Guralnik, David B. (1972). *Webster's New World Dictionary of the American Language.* New York: World.

Gurley, John D., and Jamie F. Satcher. (2003). "Drug Use or Abstinence as a Function of Perceived Stressors among Federally Supervised Offenders." *Federal Probation* **67:**49–53.

Guttman, Louis. (1944). "A Basis for Scaling Qualitative Data." *American Sociological Review* **9:**139–150.

Haapanen, Rudy, and Lee Britton. (2002). "Drug Testing for Youthful Offenders on Parole: An Experimental Evaluation." *Criminology and Public Policy* **1:**217–244.

Hafley, Sandra Riggs, and Richard Tewksbury. (1996). "Reefer Madness in Bluegrass County: Community Structure and Roles in the Rural Kentucky Marijuana Industry." *Journal of Crime and Justice* **19:**75–94.

Hagan, Michael, and Robert P. King. (1992). "Recidivism Rates of Youth Completing an Intensive Treatment Program in a Juvenile Correctional Facility." *International Journal of Offender Therapy and Comparative Criminology* **36:**349–358.

Hammett, Theodore M., and Nancy Neveloff Dubler. (1990). "Clinical and Epidemiologic Research on HIV Infection and AIDS Among Correctional Inmates: Regulations, Ethics, and Procedures." *Evaluation Review* **14:**482–501.

Hashimoto, Henichi, et al. (1968). "A Study of the Treatment Effect on Juveniles in Reform and Training Schools." *Bulletin of the Criminological Research Department* **6:**21–23.

Heinze, Michaela C., and Arnold D. Purisch. (2001). "Beneath the Mask: Use of Psychological Tests to Detect and Subtype Malingering in Criminal Defendants." *Journal of Forensic Psychology Practice* **1:**23–52.

Helfgott, Jacqueline. (1997). "Ex-Offender Needs versus Community Opportunity in Seattle, Washington." *Federal Probation* **61:**12–24.

Hemple, William E., William H. Webb, and Stephen W. Reynolds. (1976). "Researching Prediction Scales for Probation." *Federal Probation* **40:**33–37.

Henderson, Joel H., and Ronald L. Boostrom. (1989). "Criminal Justice Theory: Anarchy Reigns." *Journal of Contemporary Criminal Justice* **5:**29–39.

Higgins, Michael F. (2002). "The Modern Detention Center: Progress Through Programs." *American Jails* **16:**28–31.

Hoffman, Peter B., and James L. Beck. (1985). "Recidivism among Released Federal Prisoners: Salient Factor Score and Five-Year Follow-Up." *Criminal Justice and Behavior* **12:**501–507.

Humphreys, Laud. (1970). *The Tearoom Trade.* Chicago: Aldine.

Hyman, Herbert. (1955). *Survey Design and Analysis.* Glencoe, IL: Free Press.

Iannuzzi, Joseph "Joe-Dogs." (1993). *Joe Dogs: The Life and Crimes of a Mobster.* New York: Simon and Schuster.

Jenuwine, Michael J., Ronald Simmons, and Edward Swies. (2003). "Community Supervision of Sex Offenders: Integrating Probation and Clinical Treatment." *Federal Probation* **67:**20–27.

Johnson, Byron R. (2004). "Religious Programs and Recidivism among Former Inmates in Prison Fellowship Programs: A Long-Term Follow-Up Study." *Justice Quarterly* **21:**329–354.

Johnson, Richard E. (1986). "Family Structure and Delinquency: General Patterns and Gender Differences." *Criminology* **24:**65–84.

Johnson, Richard R. (2001). "Intensive Probation for Domestic Violence Offenders." *Federal Probation* **65:**36–39.

Jones, Mark. (1996). "Do Boot Camp Graduates Make Better Probationers?" *Journal of Crime and Justice* **19:**1–14.

Josephson, Trevor K., and Wally R. Unruh. (1994). "A Q-Sort Assessment of Personality and Implications for Treatment in Child Welfare and Young Offender Settings." *Residential Treatment for Children and Youth* **12:**73–84.

Jurgens, Ralf, and Norbert Gilmore. (1994). "Divulging of Prison Medical Records: Judicial and Legal Analysis." *Criminologie* **27:**127–163.

Kaci, Judy, and Shira Tarrant. (1988). "Attitudes of Prosecutors and Probation Departments Toward Diversion in Domestic Violence Cases in California." *Journal of Contemporary Criminal Justice* **4:**187–200.

Kakar, Suman. (1998). "Youth Gangs and Their Families: Effect of Gang Membership on Family's Subjective Well-Being." *Journal of Crime and Justice* **21:**157–172.

Karp, David R. (2003). "Does Community Justice Work?" *APPA Perspectives* **27:**32–37.

Keen, Mike Forrest. (2004). *Stalking Sociologists: J. Edgar Hoover: FBI Surveillance of American Sociology.* New Brunswick, NJ: Transaction.

Kelling, George L., et al. (1974). *The Kansas City Preventive Patrol Experiment: A Summar Report and a Technical Report.* Washington, DC: The Police Foundation.

Kenney, Dennis J. (1986). "Crime on the Subways: Measuring the Effectiveness of the Guardian Angels." *Justice Quarterly* **3:**481–496.

Kerlinger, Fred. (1965). *Foundations of Behavioral Research.* New York: Holt, Rinehart, and Winston.

Kingsnorth, Rodney F., and Randall C. Macintosh. (2004). "Domestic Violence: Predictors of Victim Support for Official Action." *Justice Quarterly* **21:**301–328.

Kleck, Gary. (2004). "Measures of Gun Ownership Levels for Macro-Level Crime and Violence Research." *Journal of Research in Crime and Delinquency* **41:**3–36.

Klinger, David A. (1995). "The Micro-Structure of Nonlethal Force: Baseline Data from an Observational Study." *Criminal Justice Review* **20:**169–186.

Knight, Kevin, and Matthew L. Hiller. (1997). "Community-Based Substance Abuse Treatment: A 1-Year Outcome Evaluation of the Dallas County Judicial Treatment Center." *Federal Probation* **61:**61–68.

Komorosky, Dawna. (2004). "The Impact of Jail Visitation on the Parent–Child Bond." *American Jails* **18:**13–16.

Kowalski, Gregory S., Alan J. Shields, and Deborah C. Wilson. (1985). "The Female Murderer: Alabama 1929–1971." *American Journal of Criminal Justice* **10:**75–104.

Krisberg, Barry, et al. (1987). "The Incarceration of Minority Youth." *Crime and Delinquency* **33:**173–205.

Kunz, G., et al. (1992). *The Process of Legal Research.* Cambridge, MA: Harvard Law Review Association.

Kurlychek, Megan C., and Brian D. Johnson. (2004). "The Juvenile Penalty: A Comparison of Juvenile and Young Adult Sentencing Outcomes in Criminal Court." *Criminology* **42:**485–517.

Lambert, Eric, Nancy Lynne Hogan, and Shannon M. Barton. (2002). "Building Commitment among Correctional Staff." *Corrections Compendium* **27:**1–5, 24–28.

LaPiere, Richard T. (1934). "Attitudes vs. Actions." *Social Forces* **14:**230–237.

Larzelere, Robert E., and Gerald R. Patterson. (1990). "Parental Management: Mediator of the Effect of Socioeconomic Status on Early Delinquency." *Criminology* **28:**301–324.

Launay, Gilles. (1994). "The Phallometric Assessment of Sex Offenders: Some Professional and Research Issues." *Criminal Behavior and Mental Health* **4:**48–70.

Lemert, Edwin M. (1951). *Social Pathology.* New York: McGraw-Hill.

Lewis, Peter. (1994). *Report of the Advisory Comittee on Human Radiation Experiments.* Washington, DC: Advisory Committee on Human Radiation Experiments.

Lewis, Ricki. (2000). "Reevaluating Sex Reassignment." *The Scientist* **14:**6–14.

Liberman, Akiva M., et al. (2002). "Routine Occupational Stress and Psychological Distress in Police." *Policing: An International Journal of Police Strategies and Management* **25:**421–439.

Likert, Rensis. (1932). "A Technique to Measure Attitudes." *Archives of Psychology* **21,** No. 40.

Loader, Ian, and Aogan Mulcahy. (2001). "The Power of Legitimate Naming: Part I: Chief Constables as Social Commentators in Post-War England." *British Journal of Sociology* **41:**41–55.

Lucente, Stephen W., et al. (2001). "Factor Structure and Reliability of the Revised Conflict Tactics Scales for Incarcerated Female Substance Abusers." *Journal of Family Violence* **16:**437–450.

Lundman, Richard J. (2003). "The Newsworthiness and Selection Bias in News About Murder: Comparative and Relative Effects of Novelty and Race and Gender." *Sociological Forces* **18:**357–386.

MacKenzie, Doris Layton, and James E. Shaw. (1990). "Inmate Adjustment and Change During Shock Incarceration: The Impact of Correctional Boot Camp Programs." *Justice Quarterly* **3:**15–32.

Magers, Jeffrey S. (2004). "Compstat." *Journal of Contemporary Criminal Justice* **20:**70–79.

Magnusson, David. (1967). *Test Theory.* Reading, MA: Addison-Wesley.

Maguire, Edward R., and Stephen D. Mastrofski. (2000). "Patterns of Community Policing in the United States." *Police Quarterly* **3:**4–45.

Maguire, Kathleen, and Ann L. Pastore. (2004). *The Sourcebook of Criminal Justice Statistics.* Albany, NY: The Hindelang Criminal Justice Research Center.

Markey, Vicki K., Sunny Ariessohn, and Margaret Mudd. (1997). "Outcome-Based Supervision for Pregnant, Substance-Abusing Offenders." *APPA Perspectives* **21:**21–23.

Marquart, James (1986). "Doing Research in Prison: The Strengths and Weaknesses of Full Participation as a Guard." *Justice Quarterly* **3:**15–32.

Marshall, W.L., Pam Kennedy, and Pamela Yates. (2002). "Issues Concerning the Reliability and Validity of the Diagnosis of Sexual Sadism Applied in Prison Settings." *Sexual Abuse: A Journal of Research and Treatment* **14:**301–311.

Marston, Jimmie L. (2003). "Peer Support Programs: Looking Out for Our Own." *American Jails* **16:**73–76.

Martin, Christine, et al. (2003). "An Examination of Rearrests and Reincarcerations among Discharged Day Reporting Center Clients." *Federal Probation* **67:**24–30.

Maruna, Shadd. (2004). "Desistance from Crime and Explanatory Style." *Journal of Contemporary Criminal Justice* **20:**184–200.

McCamey, William P., and Gayle Tronvig Carper. (1998). "Social Skills and Police: An Initial Study." *Journal of Crime and Justice* **21:**95–102.

McCollister, Kathryn E., et al. (2003). "Post-Release Substance Abuse Treatment for Criminal Offenders: A Cost-Effectiveness Analysis." *Journal of Quantitative Analysis* **19:**389–407.

McIntyre, Thomas J. (1986). "The Freedom of Information Act." *International Criminal Police Review* **39:**58–64.

McShane, Marilyn D. (1987). "Immigration Processing and the Alien Inmate: Constructing a Conflict Perspective." *Journal of Crime and Justice* **10:**171–194.

Meadows, Robert J., and Lawrence C. Trostle. (1988). "A Study of Police Misconduct and Litigation: Findings and Implications." *Journal of Contemporary Criminal Justice* **4:**77–92.

Medlicott, Diana. (2001). *Surviving the Prison Place: Narratives of Suicidal Prisoners.* Aldershot, UK: Ashgate.

Mednick, S.A., and J. Volavka. (1980). "Biology and Crime." In *Crime and Justice: An Annual Review of Research,* N. Morris and M. Tonry (eds.). Chicago: University of Chicago Press.

Melvin, Kenneth B., et al. (1985). "A Scale to Measure Attitudes Toward Prisoners." *Criminal Justice and Behavior* **12:**241–253.

Mercer, Ron, Murray Brooks, and Paula Tully Bryant. (2000). "Global Positioning Satellite System: Tracking Offenders in Real Time." *Corrections Today* **62:**76–80.

Merton, Robert K. (1957). *Social Theory and Social Structure.* New York: Free Press.

Merton, Robert K., M. Fiske, and Patricia L. Kendall. (1956). *The Focused Interview.* New York: Free Press.

Metraux, Stephen, and Dennis P. Culhane. (2004). "Homeless Shelter Use and Reincarceration Following Prison Release." *Crime and Public Policy* **3:**139–160.

Milgram, Stanley. (1974). *Obedience to Authority: An Experimental View.* New York: Harper.

Miller, Delbert C., and Neil J. Salkind. (2002). *Handbook of Research Design and Social Measurement.* Los Angeles: Sage.

Miller, J.L., and Glenna Simons. (1997). "A Case of Everyday Justice: Free Press v. Fair Trial in A Burglary Case." *Journal of Crime and Justice* **20:**1–22.

Minor, Kevin. (1988). *An Evaluation of An Intervention Program for Juvenile Probationers.* Ann Arbor, MI: University Microfilms, Inc.

Minor, Kevin I., David J. Hatmann, and Stephen F. Davis. (1990). "Preserving Internal Validity in Correctional Evaluation Research: The Biased Assignment Design as an Alternative to Randomized Design." *Journal of Contemporary Criminal Justice* **6:**216–225.

Moran, Nathan Ryan. (2002). *The Globalization of Russian, Columbian, and Chinese Organized Crime from 1991–2001: A Time-Series Analysis.* Ann Arbor, MI: University Microfilms International.

Muschert, Glenn W. (2002). *Media and Massacre: The Social Construction of the Columbine Story.* Ann Arbor, MI: University Microfilms.

National Archive of Criminal Justice Data. (1990). *Data Available from the National Archive of Criminal Justice Data.* Ann Arbor, MI: The Inter-University Consortium for Political and Social Research.

National Association of Attorneys General Committee on the Office of Attorney General. (1976). *Privacy: Personal Data and the Law.* Raleigh, NC: National Association of Attorneys General.

National Council on Crime and Delinquency. (1979). *Information Needs in Juvenile Justice.* Hackensack, NJ: National Council on Crime and Delinquency.

Nunn, Samuel. (2001). "Cities, Space, and the New World of Urban Law Enforcement." *Journal of Urban Affairs* **22:**259–278.

Osgood, Charles. (1965). "Cross Cultural Comparability in Attitude Measurement via Multilingual Semantic Differentials." In *Current Studies in Psychology,* I.D. Steiner and M. Fishbein (eds.). New York: Holt, Rinehart, and Winston.

Paschall, Mallie J., et al. (2001). "African American Male Adolescents' Involvement in the Criminal Justice System: The Criterion Validity of Self-Report Measures in Perspective." *Journal of Research in Crime and Delinquency* **38:**174–187.

Payne, Brian K., and Charles Gray. (2001). "Fraud By Home Health Care Workers and the Criminal Justice Response." *Criminal Justice Review* **26:**209–232.

Peatman, John G. (1963). *Introduction to Applied Statistics.* New York: Harper and Row.

Pepper, John V., and Carol V. Petrie. (2003). *Measurement Problems in Criminal Justice Research: Workshop Summary.* Washington, DC: National Academies Press.

Pettus, Ann Burnett. (1986). "An Investigation of Jury Decision Making Based on Posttrial Interviews." Ann Arbor, MI: University Microfilms International.

Piquero, Nicole Leeper, and Michael L. Benson. (2004). "White-Collar Crime and Criminal Careers." *Journal of Contemporary Criminal Justice* **20:**148–165.

Porterfield, Austin L. (1943). "Delinquency and Its Outcome in Court and College." *American Journal of Sociology* **49:**199–208.

Powell, Thomas, Jack Bush, and Brian Bilodeau. (2001). "Vermont's Self-Change Program." *Corrections Today* **63:**116–119.

Prenzler, Tim. (1994). *Attitudes to Police Gratuities.* Brisbane, Australia: Griffith University.

Quillen, Jim. (1991). *Alcatraz from Inside: The Hard Years, 1942–1952.* San Francisco: Golden Gate National Park Association.

Rebellon, Cesar J., and Michelle Manasse. (2004). "Do 'Bad Boys' Really Get the Girls? Delinquency as a Cause and Consequence of Dating Behavior among Adolescents." *Justice Quarterly* **21:**355–389.

Reddington, Frances P., and Betsy Wright Kreisel. (2003). "Basic Fundamental Skills Training for Juvenile Probation Officers: Results of Nationwide Survey of Curriculum Content." *Federal Probation* **67:**41–45.

Regoli, Robert M., et al. (1987). "Police Professionalism and Cynicism Reconsidered: An Assessment of Measurement Issues." *Justice Quarterly* **4:**257–286.

Riedel, Marc. (2000). *Research Strategies for Secondary Data: A Perspective for Criminology and Criminal Justice.* Thousand Oaks, CA: Sage.

Riedel, Marc, and Tammy A. Rinehart. (1996). "Murder Clearances and Missing Data." *Journal of Crime and Justice* **19:**83–102.

Rojek, Dean G., James E. Coverdill, and Stuart W. Fors. (2003). "The Effect of Victim Impact Panels on DUI Rearrest Rates: A Five-Year Follow-Up." *Criminology* **41:**1319–1340.

Rose, Arnold M. (1965). *Sociology: The Study of Human Relations.* New York: Alfred A. Knopf.

Rosen, Karen Hanula. (1992). "The Process of Coping with Dating Violence: A Qualitative Study." Ann Arbor, MI: University Microfilms International.

Rotton, James, and Ellen G. Cohn. (2003). "Global Warming and U.S. Crime Rates: An Application of Routine Activities Theory." *Environment and Behavior* **35:**802–825.

Rucker, Walter. (2001). "Conjure, Magic, and Power: The Influence of Afro-Atlantic Religious Practices on Slave Resistance and Rebellion." *Journal of Black Studies* **32:**84–103.

Sanchez, Reymundo. (2000). *My Bloody Life: The Making of Latin King.* Chicago: Chicago Review Press.

Santiago, Anna, George Galster, and Kathryn Pettit. (2003). "Neighborhood Crime and Scattered-Site Public Housing." *Urban Studies* **40:**2147–2163.

Saylor, W., and K. Wright. (1992). "A Comparative Study of the Relationship of Status and Longevity in Determining Perceptions of Work Environment among Federal Employees." *Journal of Offender Rehabilitation* **17:**133–160.

Schauer, Edward James. (1990). *A Validation of the Case Classification System in Texas Probation: A Replication Study.* Ann Arbor, MI: University Microfilms International.

Schoenthaler, Stephen, et al. (1997). "The Effect of Randomized Vitamin-Mineral Supplementation on Violent and Non-Violent Antisocial Behavior among Incarcerated Juveniles." *Journal of Nutritional and Environmental Medicine* **7:**343–352.

Schreck, Christopher, Bonnie S. Fisher, and J. Mitchell Miller. (2004). "The Social Context of Violent Victimization: A Study of the Delinquent Peer Effect." *Justice Quarterly* **21:**23–47.

Schroeder, Kathleen. (1983). "A Recommendation to the FDA Concerning Drug Research on Prisoners." *Southern California Law Review* **56:**969–1000.

Seiter, Richard P. (2002). "Prisoner Reentry and the Role of Parole Officers." *Federal Probation* **64:**50–54.

Sellin, Thorsten, and Marvin Wolfgang. (1966). *The Measurement of Delinquency.* New York: Wiley.

Selltiz, Claire, et al. (1959). *Research Methods in Social Relations.* New York: Holt, Rinehart, and Winston.

Sells, David J., et al. (2003). "Violent Victimization of Persons with Co-Occurring Psychiatric and Substance Use Disorders." *Psychiatric Services* **54:**1253–1257.

Selltiz, Claire, S.W. Cook, and L.S. Wrightsman. (1976). *Research Methods in Social Relations (3e).* New York: Holt, Rinehart, and Winston.

Seng, Mangus J. (1996). "Theft on Campus: An Analysis of Larceny-Theft at an Urban University." *Journal of Crime and Justice* **19:**33–44.

Seng, Magnus J., Loretta J. Stalans, and Michelle Repp. (2004). "Violent and Non-Violent Probationers: Do They Really Differ?" *APPA Perspectives* **28:**30–41.

Sev'er, Aysan. (2002). *Fleeing the House of Horrors: Women Who Have Left Abusive Partners.* Toronto: University of Toronto Press.

Shah, Saleem A., and Loren Roth. (1974). "Biological and Psychophysiological Factors in Criminology." In *Handbook of Criminology,* Daniel Glaser (ed.). Chicago: Rand McNally.

Shearer, Robert A. (2003). "Identifying the Special Needs of Female Offenders." *Federal Probation* **67:**46–51.

Shockley, Carol. (1988). "The Federal Presentence Investigation Report: Postsentence Disclosure Under the Freedom of Information Act." *Administrative Law Review* **40:**79–119.

Short, James F., Jr., and F. Ivan Nye. (1958). "Extent of Unrecorded Juvenile Delinquency: Tentative Conclusions." *Journal of Criminal Law and Police Science* **49:**296–302.

Siegel, Judith. (1985). "The Measurement of Anger as a Multidimensional Construct." In *Anger and Hostility in Cardiovascular and Behavior Disorders,* M. Chesney and R. Rosenman (eds.). New York: Hemisphere.

Siegel, Sidney M. (1956). *Nonparametric Statistics for the Behavioral Sciences.* New York: McGraw-Hill.

Simon, Leonore M.J. (1996). "The Effect of the Victim–Offender Relationship on the Sentence Length of Violent Offenders." *Journal of Crime and Justice* **19:**129–148.

Smith, Carolyn A., and Marvin D. Krohn. (1991). *Delinquency and Family Life: The Role of Ethnicity.* Hindelang Criminal Justice Research Center. Albany, NY

Smith, Cindy J., and Kimberly S. Craig. (2004). "Profiles of Judicially Waived Youths." *Corrections Today* **66:**28–31, 63.

Smith, R.L., and R.W. Taylor. (1985). "A Return to Neighborhood Policing: The Tampa, Florida Experience." *Police Chief* **52:**39–44.

Smodish, Susan D. (1974). "Recent Legislation Prohibiting the Use of Prison Inmates as Subjects in Medical Research." *New England Journal on Prison Law* **1:**220–243.

Smykla, John Ortiz. (1987). "The Human Impact of Capital Punishment: Interviews with Families of Persons on Death Row." *Journal of Criminal Justice* **15:**331–347.

Spitzberg, Brian H. (2002). "The Tactical Topography of Stalking Victimization and Management." *Trauma, Violence, and Abuse: A Review Journal* **3:**261–288.

Stapinski, Helen. (2001). *Five-Finger Discount: A Crooked Family History.* New York: Random House.

Stevens, S.S. (1951). "Mathematics, Measurement, and Psychophysics." In *Handbook of Experimental Psychology,* S.S. Stevens (ed.). New York: Wiley.

Suris, Alina, et al. (2001). "Validation of the Inventory of Depressive Symptomatology (IDS) in Cocaine Dependent Inmates." *Journal of Offender Rehabilitation* **32:**15–30.

Sykes, Gresham. (1958). *The Society of Captives.* Princeton, NJ: Princeton University Press.

Taylor, Janet. (1953). "A Personality Scale of Manifest Anxiety." *Journal of Abnormal Social Psychology* **48:**285–290.

Theoharis, Athan (ed.). (1991). *From the Secret Files of J. Edgar Hoover.* Chicago: Ivan R. Dee.

Thompson, Kevin M. (1990). "Refacing Inmates: A Critical Appraisal of Plastic Surgery Programs in Prison." *Criminal Justice and Behavior* **17:**448–466.

Thompson, Wendy M., James M. Dabbs, and Robert L. Frady. (1990). "Changes in Saliva Testosterone Levels During a 90-Day Shock Incarceration Program." *Criminal Justice and Behavior* **17:**246–252.

Thurstone, L.L., and E.J. Chave. (1929). *The Measurement of Attitudes.* Chicago: University of Chicago Press.

Todd, W.G. (1975). "Non-Therapeutic Prison Research: An Analysis of Potential Legal Remedies." *Albany Law Review* **39:**799–825.

Touhy, John W. (2001). *When Capone's Mob Murdered Roger Touhy: The Strange Case of Touhy, Jake the Barber, and the Kidnapping That Never Happened.* Fort Lee, NJ: Barricade.

Tripodi, Tom, and Joseph P. DeSario. (1993). *Crusade: Undercover Against the Mafia and KGB.* Washington, DC: Brassey's.

Turner, Michael G., and Alex R. Piquero. (2002). "The Stability of Self Control." *Journal of Criminal Justice* **30:**457–471.

Tyler, Tom R., and Cheryl J. Wakslak. (2004). "Profiling and Police Legitimacy: Procedural Justice, Attributions of Motive, and Acceptance of Police Authority." *Criminology* **42:**253–281.

Umbreit, Mark, Robert B. Coates, and Betty Vos. (2002). "Restorative Justice Circles: The Impact of Community Involvement." *APPA Perspectives* **26:**36–40.

U.S. Department of Energy Advisory Committee on Human Radiation Experiments. (1996). *Final Report.* Washington, DC: Author.

Vaishnav, Abhilash R. (1994). *Task Force Reports on Fernald Studies.* Cambridge, MA: The Tech.

Vohryzek-Bolden, Miki. (1997). "Ethical Dilemmas Confronting Criminological Researchers." *Journal of Crime and Justice* **20:**121–138.

von Lampe, Klaus. (2001). "Not a Process of Enlightenment: The Conceptual History of Organized Crime in Germany and the United States of America." *Forum on Crime and Society* **1:**99–116.

Walters, Glenn D. (2003). "Development of a Self-Report Measure of Outcome Expectancies for Crime." *Journal of Offender Rehabilitation* **37:**1–10.

Walters, Stephen. (1988). "Correctional Officers' Perceptions of Powerlessness." *Journal of Crime and Justice* **11:**47–59.

Wang, Zheng. (1996). "Is the Pattern of Asian Gang Affiliation Different? A Multiple Regression Analysis." *Journal of Crime and Justice* **19:**113–128.

Ward, Tony, et al. (1995). "A Descriptive Model of the Offense Chain for Child Molesters." *Journal of Interpersonal Violence* **10:**452–472.

Wardlaw, Grant R. (1979). "Aversion Therapy: Technical, Ethical and Safety Issues." *Australian and New Zealand Journal of Criminology* **12:**43–54.

Webster, Stephen D. (2002). "Assessing Victim Empathy in Sexual Offenders Using the Victim Letter Task." *Sexual Abuse: A Journal of Research and Treatment* **14:**281–300.

Wei, Evelyn H., Rolf Loeber, and Helene Raskin White. (2004). "Teasing Apart the Developmental Associations between Alcohol and Marijuana Use and Violence." *Journal of Contemporary Criminal Justice* **20:**166–183.

Weiss, Alexander, and Steven M. Chermak. (1998). "The News Value of African-American Victims: An Examination of the Media's Presentation of Homicide." *Journal of Crime and Justice* **21:**71–89.

Weitekamp, Elmar G.M., and Hans Jurgen Kerner. (1995). "On the 'Dangerousness' of Chronic/Habitual Offenders: A Re-Analysis of the 1945 Philadelphia Birth Cohort Data." *Studies on Crime and Crime Prevention* **4:**159–175.

Weitzer, Ronald, and Steven A. Tuch. (2004). "Reforming the Police: Racial Differences in Public Support for Change." *Criminology* **42:**391–416.

Wexler, Laura. (2003). *Fire in a Canebrake: The Last Mass Lynching in America.* New York: Scribner.

Whetstone, Thomas S. (2001). "Copping Out: Why Police Officers Decline to Participate in the Sergeant's Promotional Process." *American Journal of Criminal Justice* **25:**147–159.

Whitbeck, Les B., Danny R. Hoyt, and Kevin A. Ackley. (1997). "Families of Homeless and Runaway Adolescents: A Comparison of Parent/Caretaker and Adolescent Perspectives on Parenting, Family Violence and Adolescent Conduct." *Child Abuse and Neglect* **21:**517–18.

Williams, Kirk R., and Richard Hawkins. (1992). "Wife Assault, Costs of Arrest, and the Deterrence Process." *Journal of Research in Crime and Delinquency* **29:**292–310.

Willis, C.L. (1983). "Criminal Justice Theory: A Case of Trained Incapacity?" *Journal of Criminal Justice* **11:**447–458.

Winer, Ben J. (1962). *Statistical Principles in Experimental Design.* New York: McGraw-Hill.

Wiseman, Jacqueline P. (1970). *Stations of the Lost: The Treatment of Skid Row Alcoholics.* Englewood Cliffs, NJ: Prentice-Hall.

Wolfgang, Marvin. (1983). "Delinquency in Two Birth Cohorts." In *Perspective Studies of Crime and Delinquency* Katherine Teilmann Van Dusen and Sarnoff A. Mednick (eds.). Chicago: University of Chicago Press.

Wolfgang, Marvin, Robert M. Figlio, and Thorsten Sellin. (1972). *Delinquency in a Birth Cohort.* Chicago: University of Chicago Press.

Woodiwiss, Mike, et al. (2003). *Transnational Organized Crime: Perspectives on Global Security.* New York: Routledge.

Wooldredge, John, and Amy Thistlewaite. (2004). "Bilevel Disparities in Court Dispositions for Intimate Assault." *Criminology* **42:**417–456.

Yacoubian, George S., Meghan K. Green, and Ronald J. Peters. (2003). "Identifying the Prevalence and Correlates of Ectasy and Other Club Drug (EOCD) Use among High School Seniors." *Journal of Ethnicity in Substance Abuse* **2:**53–66.

Yeager, Matthew G. (2002). "Rehabilitating the Criminality of Immigrants Under Section 19 of the Canadian Immigration Act." *Immigration Migration Review* **36:**178–192.

Yokoyama, Minoru. (1994). "Treatment of Prisoners Under Rehabilitation Model in Japan." *Kokugakuin Journal of Law and Politics* **32:**1–24.

Zimbardo, Philip G. (1972). "Pathology of Imprisonment." *Society* **9:**4–6.

Legal Citations

Furman v. Georgia, 408 U.S. 238 (1972)
Gregg v. Georgia, 428 U.S. 13 (1976)
Skinner v. Oklahoma, 115 P.2d 123 (1942)

NAME INDEX

CASES CITED

SUBJECT INDEX